| DATE | | | |
|---|---|---|---|
| | | | |
| | | | |
| | | | |
| | | | |
| | | | |
| | | | |
| | | | |
| | | | |
| | | | |
| | | | |
| | | | |
| | | | |

# Law of the Real Estate Business

# Law of the Real Estate Business

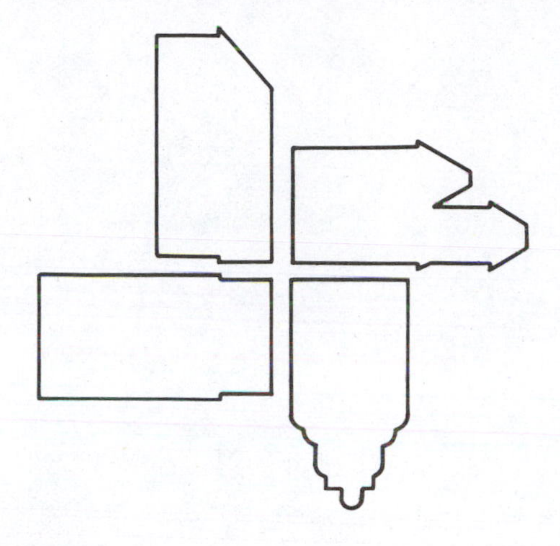

**William B. French**
*St. Mary's College*

**Harold F. Lusk**
*Late Professor Emeritus*
*Indiana University*

Fifth Edition

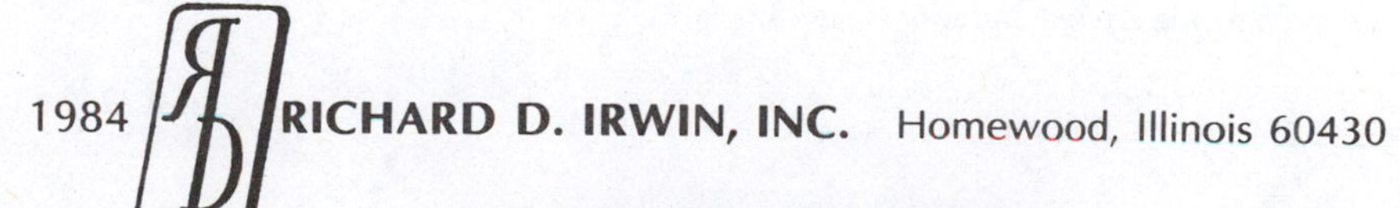

1984 RICHARD D. IRWIN, INC. Homewood, Illinois 60430

ISBN 0-256-02853-2
Library of Congress Catalog Card No. 83–83151

*Printed in the United States of America*

1 2 3 4 5 6 7 8 9 0 K 1 0 9 8 7 6 5 4

# Preface

This fifth edition has been restructured to approach its broad subject in a way that is logical and organized so as to be useful for reference purposes. At the outset certain fundamental legal concepts are examined because of their general application in the real estate business. It is essential to any study of business law to consider the basic rules of contracts, their negotiation, and enforcement. The widespread use of the professional agent in the real estate business requires consideration of the law of principal and agent. Certain general statutory rules, such as statutes of frauds and limitations, are important in determining the enforceability of real estate contracts as well as in proving ownership of real estate.

The exact nature of the ownership of real estate is the next topic considered. It is important to grasp the symbolism that has developed to express the concept of ownership, which does not always include complete physical control of the property owned. This concept includes and depends upon the written document. The many documents generated over the years must be preserved by a permanent system of records to protect the property owner. This system embodies the evidence of ownership upon which all real estate transactions depend.

Title to real estate may be held in many ways. Each has its advantages and disadvantages, which must be understood before an intelligent selection can be made. Whether real estate is acquired for personal use or as an investment also makes a difference in the selection of the ownership vehicle. The technical rules that govern the ways in which real estate may be acquired also must be understood because each of these ways affects the quality or extent of ownership that is purchased, inherited, or simply taken.

In recent years the financing of the purchase of real estate has become a most important consideration. The magnitude of most real estate transactions nearly always requires the use of borrowed money. The long-term nature of such loans has always required some security as assurance of repayment. The currently high cost of borrowed funds and the unpredictability of the financial future have led to a great deal of innovation in real estate finance. In this edition a substantial effort has been expended to classify the new financing devices in terms of their legal consequences.

Sales of real estate have, to a great extent, become the work of the professional agent, the real estate broker. Continued development of consumerism and warranty concepts has increased the complexity of this person's function and made it more demanding. At the same time the nature of the real estate sale has become even more complicated by virtue of the use of more sophisticated financing schemes and the expansion of governmental regulation. Specialists now are required to assist the buyer, seller, and broker to "close" or complete the sale. Yet another professional sales agent has appeared, the auctioneer. This ancient method of marketing has found new vitality in today's real estate market. All of these subjects are considered in some detail.

The use of real estate, whether for personal satisfaction or to earn a return on investment, is subject to many limitations, imposed either by government or by private parties. The effect of these limitations upon both enjoyment and profitability must be considered. Conversion of real estate ownership into a stream of income is accomplished through the lease. The relationship of landlord and tenant is one of the most important areas of real estate law to understand. The extent to which ownership of real estate can be transferred by a lease is limited only by the ingenuity of the parties. Liabilities as well as benefits can be transferred: the range of possibilities is endless because of the flexibility of the lease concept. Its importance in making real estate ownership profitable would be difficult to overstate.

Real estate education has changed over the years, but even this fifth edition owes a great deal to the author of the first edition, which appeared in 1958, the late Dr. Harold F. Lusk of Indiana University. He had a uniquely clear vision of real estate law. The typical property owner today is better informed than ever before. At the same time, however, real estate transactions have become legally and financially far more complex. The need for professional guidance in real estate transactions was never greater than it is today. The obligation of the real estate professional to become even better educated has increased accordingly. It is hoped that this edition will assist in meeting that need.

**William B. French**

# Contents

# Law of the Real Estate Business

# Section 1

# Introductory Concepts

This initial section provides a certain amount of orientation for the detailed areas discussed later. Certain fundamental legal rules have particular significance in real estate law. For this reason the first chapter is not about real estate at all: it discusses instead some fundamental general legal rules, particularly in the area of contracts.

One of these concepts is that real estate is a unique form of property requiring unusual treatment. Under our law there are no two identical pieces of real estate. No matter that there are two lots in a subdivision with exactly equal road frontage, identical dimensions, the same terrain and slope, facing the same direction; no matter that they appear to be identical; the law says that they are *not* identical. Each is unique unto itself. When a bargain is struck for one of them the purchaser cannot be compelled to accept the other in its place. The buyer is entitled to that precise piece of real estate contracted for and may compel the seller to deliver that piece of real estate. Our law says that a wronged buyer cannot be made whole by being paid money damages for the difference in value because each piece of real estate is unique and there is no way to assess his damages in terms of mere money. The purchaser of real estate is entitled to the advantage of the extraordinary remedy of specific performance, not generally available in breach-of-contract actions.

No matter how significant or unique the law considers real estate, there are limits to the protection afforded the owner. When there is a possible dispute over the question of ownership, our legal system requires that the issue be settled within a reasonable period of time. An unusually long delay in bringing a lawsuit to protect a claim of ownership against others makes the question of ownership more difficult to resolve. Important documents are lost. Witnesses die or disappear. Worse yet, witnesses forget. To avoid such problems the law requires that any legal action be brought within a time limitation or the claim may be lost by failure to act. This result can come from the application of statutes of limitation or the doctrine of *laches.*

Next considered in this section is the broad range of interests in real estate that are recognized and protected by our legal system. These are broken down into two separate chapters, more for convenience than as the result of logic. In Chapter 2, those interests that constitute ownership in the ordinary sense of that term are discussed. It will be seen that varying degrees of ownership can exist in a parcel of real estate. Just what it is that we own when we own a piece of the earth's surface is also an important issue. Therefore, the benefits and limitations of ownership of air rights and subterranean rights are discussed in some detail.

The general degree of protection of the owner's right to the undisturbed use of his real estate is also considered. The doctrines of trespass and nuisance are explored because they are the major civil remedies available for the protection of ownership. It will be found that trespass is easy to define and that the presumption that a trespass causes some damage benefits the owner suing to protect his interests. It is also possible, however, for the property owner to suffer very serious loss in value even when no one has intruded onto the property. There is a remedy available called a suit for nuisance, but there are no meaningful presumptions of damage to help the owner. The existence of the nuisance must first be proved and then the fact of damages. The inherent advantage in the nuisance action is the availability of relief by way of injunction. The court has the power to order the nuisance abated and also has sufficient power to compel obedience by the wrongdoer.

In this section also we will draw an important distinction between interests in land that qualify as estates and those that are of lesser scope. The estate concept is fundamental to an understanding of real estate ownership. If the interest qualifies as an estate in land it will be recognizable by the fact that it includes the right of *exclusive possession.* Such an interest need not be shared with anyone, and the full protection of our legal system will be available to protect it. This estate concept is therefore of great importance. It is easy to see that the absolute owner of real estate has the right to exclusive possession. It may not be quite so easy to accept the notion that a tenant under a valid lease has the same right, even as against his landlord. Nevertheless, under the estate concept and in view of the fact that a lease creates an estate in land, this is precisely the rule.

Lesser interests in real estate also exist—interests that do not include the right of exclusive possession. Typically, these interests give the owners of them some limited right to use property owned by someone else for a limited purpose and for no other purposes. By far the most important of these interests is the easement. Its value lies in the fact that one can own the right to use another's property for a purpose that benefits one's own property and increases its value. Most important is the fact that one can do so without the expense of purchasing the adjoining property. This concept is then broadened to include certain easements needed for general commercial use rather than to increase the utility of an adjoining property. It would be prohibitively expensive for public utility companies to purchase absolute ownership of all the land over or through which their lines and pipes must cross in order to serve their customers. They can make do with the very limited right to construct and maintain their utility delivery systems. For the most part this is just what they do. It must not be overlooked, however, that the property that is subjected to an easement is burdened or limited by it and may be less valuable than it would be without the easement. That is, easements are attended by both benefits and burdens and each has a financial consequence.

Finally considered in this section is a distinctly negative aspect of real estate ownership: the power of government literally to take it under the doctrine of eminent domain. At a later point we will consider the limitations of zoning and private restrictions. We will see that they limit the use to which we may put our property even if we own it. Eminent domain is another matter. It goes to the heart of the issue: What is private ownership of real estate if it can be taken away? It can hardly be denied that the possibility that our property can be taken from us by our government constitutes a limitation upon the extent of our ownership. This important subject is mentioned at this point to illustrate the fact that even today the right to own real estate is not absolute. The exercise of the power of eminent domain is conditioned upon the existence of some benefit to the general public that outweighs the rights of the individual property owner. Fortunately, in our legal system not only must that public benefit exist but we are also entitled to be paid if our private property is taken to serve it.

# Chapter 1

# General Legal Concepts

Before considering the detailed legal aspects of the real estate business it may be beneficial to review certain fundamental concepts of business law in general. In this chapter are included a variety of concepts that will be of value for an easy understanding of the material in later chapters. The *rule of reasonableness,* the *bona fide purchaser,* the *reasonable man* are all introduced. The *fair* man, under the doctrine of *estoppel,* is also identified. Fundamental contract law is reviewed in depth because any business is based upon agreements that involve value and that are expected to be enforceable. The real estate business, as a general rule, requires that these agreements be written and the statute of frauds is of great importance. In addition, unreasonable delays in protecting one's rights to ownership are frequently a factor when dealing with real estate; therefore, statutes of limitations and the doctrine of *laches* are important in the establishment or loss of rights of ownership of real estate.

## The Rule of Reasonableness

It may be reassuring before embarking upon the study of the law of the real estate business to become familiar with the notion that the law is ultimately reasonable. Too often, emphasis is placed upon the highly technical nature of the specific rules that are at play, many of which are of ancient origin. Even though it is true that many of the rules with which we must acquaint ourselves are based upon very old concepts of property law, it is also true that some of these concepts are unchanging because they are and have always been *reasonable.* Still others have proven to be very elastic and quite capable of being adapted by our courts to serve the needs of today's world. A couple of examples may serve to illustrate this point:

1. We recognize today that even though an individual owner of real estate has broad rights to the free use of that property there are certain limitations that must be imposed on that individual so that his neighbors may also enjoy *their* property rights. We will not therefore permit one individual to maintain a serious antisocial use of his property, a nuisance. He may not, for example, so landscape his property that all casual water will run off onto a neighbor's property. We might at first conclude that this is a relatively new concept that has had to be developed to suit 20th century living with its high density of population. It is only reasonable under today's circumstances that this rule should come into being. In point of fact, however, we find this precise rule of law ably presented to a court in the year 65 B.C. by a well-known lawyer of the time named Demosthenes. His argument, to the effect that the diversion of casual water by one owner onto another's property was a civil wrong, is as cogent and compelling as one we would expect to hear today. Here is an excellent example of the reasonableness of a rule that has remained timeless.

2. The elasticity of the law as it relates to real estate is perhaps well illustrated in the law of fixtures, under which personal property undergoes a transformation and becomes real property by virtue of attachment. At one time this phenomenon was felt to depend upon the degree of permanency of the attachment: if the personal property were not more or less permanently attached, so that it could not be removed without damaging the real estate, then it was not a fixture. Today the physical test of attachment has largely given way to the test of the intent of the parties as it would be perceived by a reasonable man having full knowledge of the circumstances surrounding the association of the two types of property. So it is that today a modern court may conclude that when a refrigerator is furnished along with an apartment unit by a landlord he intended that refrigerator to become a part of the apartment (and therefore included with the building when it is sold) even though it could have been removed with no damage to the building whatsoever.

Throughout the material covered in the succeeding chapters will run this common thread of reasonableness. Nevertheless, it will be found that in one area an unbending rule is reasonable because we have come to rely upon its unchanging character when we spend money to buy an interest in real estate. In another area the rule is flexible and subject to change as circumstances change because it is reasonable to anticipate that it will change: e.g., that a restriction on the use of land will become unenforceable when it has outlived its usefulness or has served its purpose.

Apparently technical rules and doctrines that are at play in many transactions and under differing fact situations are based upon their inherent reasonableness. Even though the materials that follow have been organized so as to be broken down into digestible portions, some common concepts need to be kept in mind. While these are discussed as they arise it would unnecessarily interrupt the text to discuss them at the first point at which they occur. Therefore, the material in this chapter has been inserted by way of background without attempting to relate it to any specific topic. The concepts discussed below follow no particular logical order, and they are not presented in order of descending importance. They are presented here because they are fundamental to the clear understanding of later chapters.

## The Reasonable Man

Throughout our system of law we encounter the reasonable man, the mythical objective standard by which we measure the prudence of everyone else's conduct. There is of course no reasonable man. He is a fiction created by our courts, and in decision after decision we are taught the subtle definitions of reasonableness as perceived by our judges and juries. Sometimes the results are a little startling because we find (to our secret shame) that no reasonable man signs a legal document without reading it. Or we find that the reasonable man is a busybody who knocks on doors and asks people why they are living in a particular house or apartment. Or we find that the reasonable man is one who carefully measures a lot he is about to purchase to determine whether or not the eaves of the building on the property next door overhang or encroach upon the property about to be purchased. Such behavior may not appear to be reasonable at first blush; however, when we take into account the significance of a typical real estate transaction in terms of money, and also recall the significance with which our legal system thinks of real estate, *then* such behavior is reasonable. More important, anything less than this standard of prudence will be judged to be less than reasonable and may result in the loss of protection that would otherwise be provided by our legal system. There is a corollary to the rule that the law will protect the reasonable man: The law will not permit a person to be unreasonable in seeking to protect his position. We see this aspect of the rule in connection with sales of real estate. The reasonable man is expected to inspect the property being purchased and to determine the rights of parties in possession of it at the time of purchase and is expected to read and understand a contract of sale that he signs. We will find, however, that when the parties have agreed upon the sale, on the basis of a *merchantable* or marketable title to the real estate, that the buyer is not entitled to insist upon a *perfect* title. He will be compelled to accept that quality of title that is freely bought and sold by others in the community, even though that title may have some imperfections in it. Closely associated with the reasonable man is the *bona fide purchaser,* introduced below.

## Bona Fide Purchaser for Value

This discussion of the concept of the bona fide purchaser for value also includes lenders and tenants. The terms *bona fide* and *for value* are meant to be taken literally. That is, to qualify as bona fide an individual must be able to demonstrate that he was acting in good faith and was unaware either in fact or constructively of any facts that would disqualify him from being bona fide. The term *for value* means something more than just a nominal sum of money. It does not have to be equal to *full value* or *fair market value* of the interest or property under consideration, but it may not be so low a value that it is contradictory to the notion of good faith. When we say, for example, that a good faith purchaser for value is entitled to rely upon the facts as shown by the public records regardless of what the *actual* facts are, we necessarily imply that he has no actual knowledge of unrecorded documents *and* that he has no knowledge of any other facts that would make a resonable man suspicious and put him *on inquiry* (under an obligation to investigate further). The extent of the duty to inquire will depend upon the fact situation in which the question is raised.

In order for a bona fide purchaser, or BFP, for value to qualify in the purchase of real estate from the apparent owner, our law requires him to meet three basic tests:

1. He must be without actual knowledge of any prior sale of the property that has not been made a matter of public record.
2. He must have inspected the public records since he is charged with knowledge he would have thus obtained, and a failure to perform this inspection will not relieve him of the burden of the knowledge he would have obtained.
3. He must inspect the property he is purchasing in order to determine that no third person claims ownership or other interest in the property, and he is bound to make further inquiry if the results of that inspection would have motivated a reasonable man to do so; and he is charged with the knowledge that such an inquiry would have produced even if he made none.

If the BFP has met these tests then, upon purchase of the property, he will acquire it free of any unperfected and unrecorded interest of any previous buyer who has failed to take the necessary action to obtain the protection offered by the recording system.

For example, suppose Arnett, as seller, deeds real estate to Bennett, but the deed does not comply with statutory requirements, although it does state clearly that Arnett thereby conveys the real estate to Bennett. As between Arnett and Bennett, Bennett becomes the owner of the real estate. However, if Arnett thereafter deeds the real estate by a valid deed to Clark, who has no knowledge or notice of the prior conveyance to Bennett, and who purchases the property in good faith, paying value therefor, Clark will acquire good title to the real estate.

In the foregoing example it appears that Arnett is a wrongdoer and that either Bennett or Clark must suffer as a result. Our law in this regard is somewhat arbitrary, *provided* that Clark is able to qualify as a BFP. The law, by implication, is imposing upon Bennett certain duties to look out for his own interests or run the risk of consequent loss. Here he clearly had the obligation of seeing to it that Arnett's deed to him did meet the statutory requirements. Bennett is not, of course, without a remedy for the injury he has suffered: he may maintain a suit against Arnett for the return of his purchase money and any consequential damages he may be able to prove. The important point here is that he will be unable to obtain title to the property for which he bargained. Such an arbitrary rule, which may appear harsh when applied, is essential to the orderly maintenance of reliable records relating to legal title to real estate. In our discussion of requirements of a valid deed, we shall set out those elements that must be contained in a deed if it is to convey legal title to real estate and if it is to be eligible for record under the laws of the state in which the real estate is located. In Chapter 5, we will study the recording system in detail, and the necessity for this rule will be apparent. In subsequent chapters the application of this concept to lenders and tenants will be considered in context.

## Estoppel

The concept or doctrine of estoppel is, of course, not restricted to real estate; however, it is so frequently encountered in real estate transactions that its review here is appropriate. Simply stated, the doctrine of estoppel provides that, when one who has taken a position—whether by written document or representation, action or inaction—upon which another has relied, then he will be prohibited from thereafter adopting a contrary position or one inconsistent with that originally taken. We frequently encounter the doctrine in situations that range from fraudulent misrepresentation to the mere acceptance of a free benefit and in which it would be unjust or unfair to permit the party charged to retain that benefit without paying for it in some way. In the area of mechanics' liens, for example, even though technically the owner of property may not be held liable to pay for improvements made to his property without his authorization, he may be found to be responsible for payment if the improvements were ordered by his tenant and he knew they were being made and failed to tell the contractor that he would not pay for them. That is, he will be *estopped* or prohibited from denying that he authorized the improvements even though the fact is that he did not authorize them. The rule is subjective and must be applied in light of the surrounding circumstances to determine whether or not the acceptance of the benefit is so inequitable or unjust that the owner will not be permitted to prove the fact that he did not authorize the improvements.

The doctrine will be seen applied to sales of real estate in connection with the question of necessary rights of way. For example, a seller of property that is effectively landlocked may not deny to his purchaser the right to cross land he has retained, because to do so would be obviously unjust since he has accepted payment for the property sold. This result will follow even though there is no mention of such a right of way in any of the documents surrounding the transaction.

Estoppel was developed by courts of equity to strike down an unfair or unjust result that would otherwise follow from a strict application of legal rules. That is, even though one may have the law on his side, he will not be permitted to prove the facts that make it applicable if the result would be inequitable. Once again it is important to note that the strictly legal rule and right created by it are not affected except to the extent that no proof of the essential facts will be permitted because to do so would effect an unjust result.

## Basic Contract Rules

Throughout the materials that follow it is also helpful to bear in mind that to a great extent the law of the real estate business is a specialized area of the law of contracts. Whether an agreement is made to purchase real estate, rent it, hire someone to act as agent, or anything of the kind, a contract is involved. For this reason a discussion of basic contract law, utilizing the sale of real estate as the sample transaction, is included at this point.

## Enforceability of Contracts

To be enforceable by court action a contract must fulfill certain technical requirements. The parties to the agreement must have capacity to contract, and they must reach a mutual agreement; that is, one party must make an offer that is accepted by the other party. The agreement must be entered into voluntarily and must be supported by consideration, and the objective of the agreement must be legal; that is, the performance of the agreement must not require the performance of a crime, a civil wrong, or an act that would be a violation of public morals or detrimental to the public welfare.

## Capacity of Parties

In general, infants (minors), insane persons, or drunken persons have limited capacity (legal ability) to enter into binding contracts. Their contracts are said to be *voidable,* as opposed to *void.* A void contract is one that, in the eyes of the law, does not exist and cannot be enforced. A voidable contract is, legally, a true contract that cannot be enforced against one of the protected classes listed above. At common law, married women had no legal capacity to enter into binding contracts, but under the modern-day married women's statutes, this incapacity has been partially or totally removed. The powers of a corporation will be set out in its articles of incorporation, and it will have only such capacity to enter into contracts involving rights in real estate as is granted to it by the state. This capacity to deal with real estate is generally freely given to corporations. With some exceptions, aliens have full power to enter into contracts.

## Infant's (Minor's) Capacity to Contract

If an infant enters into a contract with an adult, the infant has the right to disaffirm the contract, to have it set aside. The adult, however, has no such right. The age of majority traditionally was 21 years; however, modern statutes have changed this for purposes of entering contracts (as well as other purposes) to 18 years. An infant may disaffirm his general contracts either during infancy or within a reasonable time after reaching the age of majority. Under this rule an infant would have the right to disaffirm a contract to sel! real estate or to list it for sale with a broker within any reasonable time after reaching the age of majority. The courts have held, however, that an infant cannot disaffirm an already completed sale of his real estate until he or she comes of age.

An infant's right to disaffirm a contract is absolute. The infant does, however, owe a duty, if he disaffirms a contract, to return to the other party to the contract any payment that he has received and that he still has at the time he disaffirms, and he has the right to recover all of the payment that he gave.[1] (There are some exceptions to this latter rule.)

The courts have held infants liable for the *reasonable value* of necessaries *furnished* to them. Necessaries are those things personal to the infant, such as food, clothing, shelter, medical care, elemental education, training for a trade, and the tools of a trade, suitable to the infant's station in life. A house has been held to be a necessary for the married infant who is not furnished housing by his or her parents or guardian.[2] An infant cannot be held liable for damages for breach of a lease, but he can be held liable for the reasonable rental value of the premises during the time he or she occupied them, provided they would be classed as a necessary and would have been suitable to his station in life.

### Insane and Drunken Persons

If a person is insane or drunk at the time he enters into a contract, the contract is voidable, provided the insanity or drunkenness was such that he lacked the mental capacity to comprehend the nature of the transaction. If and when such a person regains his sanity or becomes sober, he may disaffirm the contract and recover the consideration given, but he must put the other party back into the same position as he was prior to the contract.[3]

The situation is much different when a person has been legally *adjudged* to be insane and a guardian or conservator of the estate has been appointed. Any contract entered into by the adjudged incompetent person is void. Since the proceedings by which guardians or conservators are appointed are a matter of public record, all those dealing with the incompetent are presumed to know of that person's inability to enter into contracts. This is true even though the party dealing with the incompetent does not *in fact* know of the proceedings.

### Married Women

At common law a married woman had no legal capacity, and her contracts were null and void. Every state has enacted statutes conferring some legal capacity on married women, but these statutes are not uniform in their scope. The statutes of some states give married women full capacity to contract, whereas others are so drafted that married women have no capacity to enter into certain classes of contracts.

---

[1] *Fletcher* v. *A. W. Koch Co.,* Tex. Civ. App. 189 S.W. 501.

[2] *Johnson* v. *Newberry,* Tex., 267 S.W. 476.

[3] *Brooklyn Trust Co.* v. *Podvin et al.,* 14 N.J. Super. 470, 82 A.2d 485.

Under the laws of some states the contracts of a married woman, if they affect an interest in her real estate, are void unless her husband joins her in the execution of the contract. The laws of the state with jurisdiction over the contract control and should be checked to determine the capacity of a married woman to contract.

### Unincorporated Associations

As a general rule, an unincorporated association cannot contract in the name of the association. However, a contract entered into in the name of an unincorporated association will bind the members who authorized the contract or ratified it after it was negotiated.

## The Proposition or Offer

In the real estate business the most commonly encountered contract is that for the sale of real estate. In the industry the offer to purchase real estate has come to be known as the proposition. A well-drafted proposition will comply with the technical requirements for a valid offer. It will state (1) what the offeror (buyer) is willing to do and (2) what he or she demands from the offeree (seller) in return.

In order to be a valid offer, the terms of the proposition must be reasonably certain and complete. If any material term is left to be determined by the future agreement of the parties, the proposition is not a valid offer and cannot be the basis for a binding contract.[4] Likewise, if the terms of the proposition are stated in vague general language, such as "what is fair" or "an amount which I deem reasonable," the proposition is not an offer, since the terms are uncertain. The courts generally follow the rule that the terms of the contract must be sufficiently definite to enable the court to determine the meaning of the contract and to fix the rights and liabilities of the parties.[5] The courts will not make a contract for the parties. If a printed form is used, care should be exercised in filling in the blanks and also striking out any provisions that do not apply. If the transaction involves much detail, one should have an attorney draft a purchase agreement that would include terms suitable to the particular transaction.

### Acceptance of the Offer

To accept the buyer's proposition, all the seller need do is indicate her willingness to be bound by its terms. If she adds to or changes any of the terms stated in

---

[4] *Bonk* v. *Boyajian,* 128 Cal. App. 2d 153, 274 P.2d 948.

[5] *Corthell* v. *Summit Thread Co.,* 132 Me. 94, 167 A. 79.

the proposition, she will have rejected the buyer's offer, thereby terminating it; and in turn, she will then become the offeror, offering to sell the property on the terms stated in the buyer's proposition as added to or changed by the seller. The buyer can then either reject or assent to the seller's proposition.

After a proposition has been accepted, a contract results; thereafter, neither party has the right to alter the terms of the contract in any respect unless such alteration is made by mutual agreement.

***Custom and Usage.*** An offer may contain terms not expressly stated by the offeror but written into the offer by custom and usage or by operation of law. For example, suppose that Albert offers to sell a house and lot to Bert, and the offer is silent as to whether or not the electric light fixtures go with the house. Bert accepts the offer, and in his acceptance states that the lighting fixtures go with the house. If it is an established custom in that community for lighting fixtures to go with the house, such a provision will be implied in the offer, and Bert's acceptance will not have added a term.

Hudson and Buehring entered into a written contract whereby Hudson agreed to sell and convey, and Buehring agreed to purchase, Hudson's home. The contract was complete in every detail except that it stated no time for the completion of the transaction. Hudson sold the property to other parties, and Buehring sued to recover damages for breach of the contract. Hudson set up that since no time was specified for the performance of the contract, it was void for uncertainty of terms. The court held for Hudson, and Buehring appealed. The judgment was reversed, and judgment entered for Buehring.

Justice Cody said: "The fact that the contract of sale fixed no time for its performance did not evidence that the minds of the parties had not met with respect to an essential element of the contract. 'When a contract of sale fixes no time for performance, the law allows a reasonable time. In other words, if the parties do not agree upon the time, an agreement for performance within a reasonable time will be implied.' " *Buehring* v. *Hudson,* Tex. Civ. App., 219 S.W. 2d 810 (1949).

Routzahn owned a tract of land consisting of 30 acres. Routzahn and his wife signed a counter offer to sell the property to Lucille Binus. The real estate broker who had induced the Routzahns to sign the counter offer returned on the day following the signing with an acceptance of the counter offer signed by Anna Cromer. Routzahn refused to sell, and Cromer brought suit for a decree of specific performance of the contract. The court granted the decree, and Routzahn appealed. The decree was reversed.

Judge Prescott said: "On the above statement of facts, the appellants raise several questions, but, in the view that we take of the case, it will be necessary to consider but one. It is apparent, when the Routzahns, after adding new terms and conditions thereto, signed the paper writing that had been previously signed by Lucille Binus, that this constituted a counter offer to Lucille Binus by the Routzahns. It is also clear that one of the necessary terms of any proposed contract is the person with whom the contract is to be made; consequently, an offer made to one person cannot be accepted by another. And, as a party has a right to contract with whom he pleases, and another cannot be thrust upon him without his consent, it makes no difference whether it was important for the offeror to contract with one person rather than another. Therefore, when the signature of Lucille Binus was stricken from the instrument and Anna Cromer's substituted therefor, no contract between the Routzahns and Anna Cromer resulted; this instrument, after such substitution merely constituted a new offer by Anna Cromer to the Routzahns to create a contract, which, in order to ripen and culminate into one had to be accepted by the Routzahns." *Routzahn* v. *Cromer,* 220 Md. 65, A.2d 912 (1959).

## Effect of Misrepresentation and Fraud

If one of the parties to a contract is induced to enter into the contract by misrepresentation of a material fact or by fraud, duress, or undue influence, he is not bound by the contract and may, at his election, disaffirm the contract, tender back whatever he has received, and recover a judgment for any payment that he has given. If a seller, in negotiating a sale of real estate, misrepresents, either positively or by omission, the condition of the property, the rental received from the property, or any other material fact concerning the property, and the buyer purchases the property in justifiable reliance on the seller's misrepresentations, the buyer, on discovering the misrepresentations, may rescind the contract or revoke and recover any payments he has made. If the buyer wishes to rescind, he must act within a reasonable time after he discovers the misrepresentations.[6]

Schlemeyer owned an apartment house which he sold to Obde. At the time of the sale the apartment house was infested with termites, and this condition was known to Schlemeyer. Schlemeyer had had some repairs made to the apartment house and had engaged a specialist in termite control to treat the building, but the specialist had informed Schlemeyer that the treatment was not a complete remedy of the condition. Schlemeyer did not disclose the presence of termites to Obde. Schlemeyer contended that since Obde did not raise the question of the presence of termites in the apartment house, he (Schlemeyer) owed no duty to disclose such condition to Obde. Obde brought suit in tort to recover damages for the fraudulent representation of the condition of the apartment house. Judgment for Obde, and Schlemeyer appealed. The judgment was affirmed.

Judge Finley said: "The Schlemeyers urge that, in any event, as sellers, they had no duty to inform the Obdes of the termite condition. They emphasize that it is undisputed that the purchasers asked no questions respecting the possibility of termites.

"Without doubt, the parties in the instant case were dealing at arm's length. Nevertheless,

---

[6] *Halla* v. *Chicago Title & Trust Co. et al.,* 412 Ill. 39, 104 N.E.2d 790.

we are convinced that the defendants had a duty to inform the plaintiffs of the termite condition. In *Perkins* v. *Marsh,* a case involving parties dealing at arm's length as landlord and tenant, we held that,

" 'Where there are concealed defects in demised premises, dangerous to the property, health, or life of the tenant, which defects are known to the landlord when the lease is made, but unknown to the tenant, and which a careful examination on his part would not disclose, it is the landlord's duty to disclose them to the tenant before leasing, and his failure to do so amounts to a fraud.'

"We deem this rule to be equally applicable to the vendor-purchaser relationship." *Obde* v. *Schlemeyer,* 52 Wash.2d 449, 353 P.2d 672 (1960).

### Consideration

Consideration is the surrender of some right or privilege or payment of the price bargained for and given in exchange for a promise. It is an essential element of a valid contract. If Albert promises to deed real estate to Bert as a birthday present and then refuses to fulfill the promise, Bert cannot recover a judgment in an action against Albert for breach of promise. Albert's promise is not supported by consideration and is therefore not enforceable. Bert has given up no right or privilege (has made no payment or promise) in exchange for Albert's promise.

### Illegality

Any agreement is illegal and void if the performance of such agreement would require the violation of a statute or the commission of a criminal or immoral act, or an act that would be detrimental to the general public welfare.

## Statutes of Frauds

All jurisdictions today have some form of the ancient statute of frauds. Because of its profound effect upon the real estate business it is important that at the outset we analyze the policy that it serves so that we can understand its application to real estate transactions. Quite simply, the statute of frauds was designed to protect the illiterate and uneducated individual from entering into important legally binding contracts without knowing or understanding either that they were legally binding or that they were significant and important. To understand the need for this protection we must note that during the Middle Ages, when the original statute of frauds became effective, by far the vast majority of people could neither read nor write. When a written document was presented to such a person for his consideration (let alone his signature) he had no choice but to seek out a learned person who could read and explain the document or contract to him.

The statute of frauds presumed that he would do so and the statute therefore required that significant contracts must be in writing and signed in order to be legally enforceable.

It is easy to jump to the conclusion that the statute of frauds required that in order to be a contract there had to be a written agreement by the parties and that in the absence of that written agreement there could be no contract. This is not true today, nor was it true even at the inception of the statute of frauds. The purpose of the statute was to impress upon the uneducated that a contract was presented in writing meant that the contract was important, so important that he should seek advice before entering into it. That is, the writing was *symbolic* rather than substantive. The basic protection afforded by the statute was that certain contracts, because of their importance, could not be *enforced* in a court of law unless they were in writing and signed by the party against whom the lawsuit was brought. It should be carefully noted that the statute of frauds does not today nor did it ever say that there could be no contract if it were not in writing. What it *does* say is that no legal action can be brought to compel its performance unless there is written *evidence* of the agreement.

In short, the statute of frauds is not a condition precedent to the existence of a contract. Parties may (and do) enter into contracts of great consequence and value without a written agreement. The statute of frauds is an affirmative defense that may be raised by either of the parties who fails to perform his side of the contract. If strict compliance with the statute of frauds were insisted upon by all business people today, commerce would suddenly stop. There would be no trading on the major stock exchanges because the vast majority of transactions in the exchanges are, technically, governed by a statute of frauds, which requires almost all trades to be in writing to be enforceable. Obviously, the statute of frauds is not the compelling force that makes so many thousands of important transactions enforceable. What makes them enforceable is the rigid code of ethics and the importance of individual business reputations. In the real estate business, however, all contracts are as a matter of course put into writing and signed because the statute of frauds has always applied to contracts that have as their subject matter real estate or an interest in real estate and because of the relative complexity of the transaction itself.

In the eyes of our law, real estate has always been considered unique and therefore of great value. The earliest statute of frauds and the most modern and liberal statute of frauds have one thing in common: all contracts relating to real estate must be in writing and signed by the parties in order to be enforceable in court. Throughout the materials that follow, the fact of an underlying written agreement or document reflecting an agreement is an inherent consideration.

We will not consider, for example, a verbal deed of real estate because our law cannot, after centuries of the statute of frauds, conceive of such a thing. Verbal contracts of sale will not be considered because, as a practical matter, they do not exist. Some exceptions, to be sure, have grown up over the years, such as the short-term lease, which need not be in writing. Verbal permission may be given by a landowner to another to make some limited use of his land. For the most part, however, the significance of the written document remains a paramount consideration in the real estate field.

## Parol Evidence Rule

If the parties to a contract have reduced the contract to writing, the writing is the best evidence of the terms of their agreement; and neither party, in the event of a suit, will be permitted to offer parol (oral) evidence to alter or vary the terms of the writing. If it is obvious that the writing is incomplete, parol evidence would be admissible to prove the omitted terms. However, if the contract is a contract to sell real estate and it is incomplete, it would not be enforced if the lack of a sufficient note or memorandum were set up as a defense.

Parol evidence is admissible to prove that a contract is illegal; or that it was induced by misrepresentation, fraud, duress, or undue influence; or that, at the time the writing was signed, the parties agreed that it was not to become binding until the occurrence of some future event and that the event had not happened. Parol evidence is also admissible to prove that the parties, subsequent to the signing of the writing, entered into a mutual agreement whereby they changed some of the terms of the existing contract.

## Options

An option is a combination of an offer and a binding contract to hold the offer open for a stated period of time. To be valid, the option must fulfill the technical requirements for a valid offer and for an enforceable contract. The offer part of the option must state with reasonable certainty the terms of the offer, and the promise to hold the offer open must state the time limit of the offer and must be supported by consideration. If the person to whom the offer is given wishes to exercise the option (accept the offer), he must do so before the expiration date of the offer. For example, suppose that Albert offers to sell a piece of real estate to Bert, the offer setting out a description of the real estate, the price, and all of the other terms of the proposed sale, and, in consideration of $10 paid to him by Bert, Albert promises to hold the offer open for 30 days.

Albert has given Bert an option on the real estate and cannot revoke his offer during the 30-day period. Bert can convert the option into a valid contract of purchase and sale of the real estate at any time during the 30 days by giving Albert notice that he elects to exercise the option and by complying with the terms of the offer.

Since consideration was paid for the option, Bert may exercise the option on the last day even if he had indicated during the period of the option that he did not intend to do so.[7] Nor will any changes proposed by Bert during the term of the option relieve Albert from his obligation to perform when Bert exercises the option in accordance with its original terms.[8] The exercise must, however, be accomplished precisely in accordance with its terms in order to be effective. At least one court has concluded, for example, that the tender of payment by personal check was ineffective because the agreement specified that payment was to be in ''cash.''[9]

If, after the expiration of the 30-day period, Bert attempts to exercise the option, he will, in legal effect, have made an offer to Albert, which Albert may accept, thus, contracting to sell the real estate to Bert on the terms of the offer; or he may refuse to sell, thus rejecting Bert's offer. The courts have generally held the payment of $1 to be sufficient consideration to make an option binding.

The Carmodys (husband and wife) and Miller, on October 10, 1959, entered into an option agreement that provided that for a consideration of $5,000 the Carmodys ''do hereby grant unto Miller the option to purchase [from the Carmodys] on or before October 10, 1960,'' certain described land in Jefferson County, the property being approximately 235 acres. The agreement went on to provide that ''if, on or before September 10, 1960, the said purchaser [Miller] shall notify sellers [Carmodys] in writing of his intention to exercise said option, and shall on or before October 10, 1960, make a further payment of a sum equal to 20 percent of the total purchase price, sellers do hereby agree to execute a warranty deed to said land.''

Prior to September 10, 1960, Miller had the tract surveyed and a part thereof platted, and a plat thereof prepared and presented to the Carmodys. A dispute arose as to some of the terms of the option.

Miller gave notice of his election to exercise the option; but at no time before October 10, 1960, did he tender to the Carmodys 20 percent of the purchase price of the land. The Carmodys refused to convey the land to Miller, and Miller brought action for specific performance of the contract. At the trial, he alleged that at all times he had been ready, willing, and financially able to comply with the terms of the option. He did not, however,

---

[7] *Ryder* v. *Wescoat,* 535 S.W.2d 269 (Mo. app. 1976).

[8] *Humble Oil & Refining Co.* v. *Westside Investment Corp.,* 428 S.W.2d 92 (Tex. 1968).

[9] *Nance* v. *Schooner,* 521 P.2d 896 (Utah 1974).

allege that he had at any time tendered 20 percent of the contract price of the land. The court refused to grant to Miller a decree of specific performance.

Justice McWilliams said: "After extended arguments the trial court granted Carmodys' motion for summary judgment, concluding that Miller did not comply with the provisions of the option contract which required him to make payment of a sum equal to the total purchase price on or before October 10, 1960, and further that from the affidavits it was quite evident that Miller was in no wise prevented from making such payment by any act of the Carmodys. In so holding we conclude that the trial court was correct and its action in this regard should be upheld.

" The general rule as stated in 91 C.J.S. Vendor and Purchaser § 10 pp. 856–857 is that payment or tender is not essential to acceptance unless the option instrument makes it a condition precedent to, or a part of the option . . .' but that 'where an option contract provides for payment of all or a portion of the purchase price in order to exercise the option, to entitle the optionee to a conveyance he must, as a rule, not only accept the offer but pay or tender the agreed amount within the prescribed time.' " *Miller* v. *Carmody*, Colo., 384 P.2d 77 (1963).

## Doctrine of Specific Performance

Under the doctrine of specific performance, contracts relating to real estate are generally enforceable in strict accordance with their terms. To appreciate the significance of this doctrine it is necessary to understand two factors:

1. The English common law, from which the law of this country generally developed, was deeply impressed by the unique character of real estate. That is, it was always held that there are no two pieces of real estate on the face of the earth that are identical. As a result, one who bargained for a particular piece of real estate and entered into a contract to buy it did not have to accept an equivalent piece of land in its place simply because, by definition, there was no other piece of land that was equivalent. Nor could money ever replace that piece of land because no other could be purchased that was identical. This notion continues to the present day. It is still the conclusion of our legal system that money alone cannot make the wronged purchaser of real estate whole. He is entitled to have that specific piece of land for which he contracted. Thus, he is entitled to specific performance of the contract to purchase real estate.

2. At early English common law the only courts were *law* courts who equated every civil wrong, including the breach of a contract to sell real estate, to some amount of money that would make the injured party whole. Furthermore, the law courts had no authority to order the defendant to do anything; their power was limited to determining the rights of the parties, not to enforcing those rights. At an early time it was recognized that the law courts could not effectively dispense

true justice in all cases: the only power able to do so was the king himself. Therefore, petitions for relief from a law court judgment or for something more than money damages were brought directly to the monarch. The power to dispense the king's justice, which included the power to order a defendant to do something and to provide meaningful punishment for disobedience, became called upon more and more frequently. Ultimately this power was delegated to the chancellor, who literally created his own body of law based not upon what the letter of the law provided, but rather upon what was just or *equitable.* Thus began the court of equity, which was not restricted to the remedy of an award of money damages but could order a defendant to "do equity" or suffer the consequences—traditionally imprisonment—until there was compliance.

The notion that real estate was unique and that money damages as a substitute were inadequate and the vast power of the court of equity to literally compel the defendant seller to perform his contract joined together to provide real meaning to the extraordinary remedy of specific performance. The seller could be effectively compelled to transfer that very piece of ground for which the purchaser had bargained. Even though today most courts have both law and equity powers, the two are exercised separately and under different concepts and rules. The remedy of specific performance remains viable and of great significance. The doctrine is not limited to sales of real estate. It includes the enforcement of a wide variety of promises, both affirmative and negative, relating to the use of real estate. For example, in the surface water case argued by Demosthenes in 65 B.C., were it brought today, the correct remedy would not be an award of money damages; it would be an order from a court of equity to cease and desist or suffer the consequences because there is continuing damage to the injured property owner that cannot be established in terms of mere money. (Unfortunately, we do not have the argument of Demosthenes' opponent nor the decision of the court, and we must console ourselves with the thought that the rhetoric of losers is seldom preserved for future study.) Throughout the materials that follow, the enforcement provisions of the doctrine of specific performance and the broad powers of a court of equity should be kept in mind because of their significance to the real estate business and the rights and duties of owners and users of real estate.

While the doctrine of specific performance may be made available to the purchaser of real estate, it may not be available to the seller. The reason for this unequal treatment of the parties lies in the unique character of real estate as opposed to mere money. That is, should the purchaser default the seller has an adequate legal remedy: a suit for money damages. There is nothing unique, in the eyes of the law, about money. Since specific performance has always been considered an extraordinary remedy, its application has been restricted to those situations in which the payment of money would not be an adequate remedy.

## Statutes of Limitations

From time to time there will appear references to several statutes of limitations in connection with the establishment or loss of some right to real estate. The typical statute of limitations is similar, at least in concept, to the statute of frauds. That is, the statutes of limitations do not provide that after the lapse of a stated number of years some right to real estate has either been acquired, lost, or modified. What statutes of limitations do provide is a negative method of acquiring or losing a right. The theory behind statutes of limitations is that there must be a predictable end to the possibility of litigation over an issue. They therefore typically provide that: "After _____years no action shall be brought . . . ," or words of similar import. In the real estate area such statutes are usually encountered in situations where the rights of parties to an interest in land have been established in *fact* rather than in law over a long period of time. We will encounter them in studying the acquisition of ownership of real estate by adverse possession. In this act, one moves into the property of another and holds it for a long period of time with no legal action by the true owner to remove him. When the owner waits many years without doing anything to protect his rights, the statute of limitations cuts off his right to bring such legal action. The theory of such legislation appears to be that if the true owner is uninterested in protecting his interests, so are the courts. It should be noted that statutes of limitations, like the statutes of frauds, are not substantive. They do not transfer ownership of land to the adverse possessor from the true owner. They simply provide that no legal action may be maintained by the true owner to enforce his rights after the lapse of the statutory period of time. At early common law such statutes ran for very lengthy periods; however, today they have been substantially reduced on the theory that with modern methods of transportation and communication those who have interests in real estate do not need a period of many years in which to become aware of what is happening to their property and to take effective legal action to protect their property rights.

### Laches

Statutes of limitations provide for a definite cutoff point for the bringing of certain legal actions; however, under certain conditions the courts will find that it would be inequitable to permit even this period of time. In such a case they will apply the equitable doctrine of laches, which means simply that there has been an unreasonable delay on the part of the plaintiff in bringing his action and he will not be permitted to enforce his legal rights. This equitable defense of laches does not take away the plaintiff's legal rights, but they are effectively negated by the fact that they may not be enforced by legal action. Usually this doctrine is reserved for aggravated situations. For example, may the owner stand idly by while another builds a house on his property and take no action until it is essentially completed? Even though those building on the property are wrong-doers (whether they know it or not) it would be inequitable to permit the property owner to have the value of the improvements without paying for them. Assuming that the applicable statute of limitations has not run, the owner would be entitled to remove the offenders from his property and keep the improvements; however, a court of equity may conclude that he has been guilty of laches and prohibit him from maintaining his legal action even though he is clearly legally entitled to do so. This will not end the matter, of course, because such action leaves the dispute in limbo. Generally, some compromise will be forced, such as a purchase of the property by the offending builder or a payment for the value of the improvement by the owner of the property. Because our courts feel that it is not their function to force such agreements upon the parties, this remedy is sparingly applied.

## Conclusion

The foregoing discussion has been limited to a few of the most significant ideas that are encountered frequently in transactions involving real estate. Others of lesser importance or narrower application are discussed at that point in the text where they logically raise themselves. The concepts discussed in this chapter should, however, be kept in mind throughout because they are of more or less general application. One warning is in order, however, and that is that the application of fundamental rules is apt to be distorted when some branch of government or the exercise of some governmental power is involved. In the areas of taxation, eminent domain, regulation of business practices, and the like, there is an overriding governmental purpose to be served and the rule of reasonableness must be refocused from What would reasonable business people conclude? to What would a reasonable governmental agency (a contradiction in terms, perhaps) conclude under the same circumstances? The question is not as specious as one might first suppose as will be seen in the materials that follow.

# Chapter 2

## Ownership Interests in Real Estate

This chapter considers the extent of ownership of real estate that is recognized by our modern legal system. The historical development of the modern notion of ownership has represented a dramatic reversal from the feudal concepts from which it all began. In feudal times owners had only such rights as were specifically granted to them by their government. Today we like to think we have all the powers of ownership that we have not specifically surrendered to our government. The true status of ownership today lies somewhere between these two extremes.

Property ownership as a concept and, especially, the estate theory of ownership are important fundamental ideas. The fact that one who owns the *fee simple absolute* owns the property in perpetuity may seem to be of academic interest only. Yet it is this degree of ownership that permits a person who is 50 years old to grant a 100-year lease of his property to another. He must clearly have the power and extent of ownership to control the property long after his normal life expectancy. In everyday transactions, such as the purchase of a residence, it is this extent of ownership for which we bargain and that we expect to acquire. More than this, it is the extent of ownership to which we are legally entitled in every purchase of real estate unless we deliberately agree to accept something less. Something less than complete ownership should cost less. In negotiating the price for ownership we need, therefore, to know the extent of ownership we are buying.

Unbridled ownership of real estate is seldom seen today. We will find that some sacrifice of ownership rights must be made by each property owner so that we can have a legal system that protects the bulk of those rights. Some sacrifice must be made in order to make our property useful to us. This is the reason that we can not effectively prohibit the flight of aircraft through the airspace above our property: the air transportation industry benefits us and our property in some way. To the extent that we have a legitimate use for such airspace, however, it can be protected by civil remedies, which are discussed in this chapter. The extent of our ownership rights below the surface of the earth has yet to be tested except for the rights to minerals that lie only a short distance below the surface.

Regardless of the extent of our property rights when we are an owner of real estate, we may not exercise them in such a way that would unreasonably interfere with our neighbor's use and enjoyment of his property. We, of course, are entitled to the same consideration from him, and the law provides enforcement vehicles for each of us. While we may own real estate absolutely today, there are limitations upon our exercise of the rights of ownership.

## Historical Background

### Origin of Real Estate Law

Land and rights in land play an important part in the social, economic, and political development of all peoples. The earth's surface was here when we arrived, and no matter how we may alter its exterior, it will be here to be used by generations that follow us. This self-evident fact has been and is basic in the development of laws relating to rights in land. Another fundamental fact is that laws do not exist except as a part of some social organization; that is, some form of government, no matter how primitive. Since land has always been of prime importance in the lives of people, it was only natural that as soon as men began to band together in some form of social organization, they developed laws defining rights in land.

### Real Estate Law and Social Development

The development of land law tended to parallel general social evolution. When a people changed from a social structure of nomadic tribes into an agricultural society with established farms and accompanying villages and cities, land law was developed to define the rights of the people in the land that they were cultivating and the houses in which they lived. Many of our present-day concepts in regard to rights in land were known to and practiced by the Egyptians long before the birth of Christ. The Egyptians had laws regulating the conveyance of land, the recording of titles to land, rights to dispose of land by will, and other land laws that were similar in many respects to our present ones.

### Feudal System

Although the land law of any country might be traced back to primitive times, there is, as a general rule, some particular event of outstanding importance that scholars select as the beginning point in discussing the historical development in a particular area. The Norman Conquest in 1066 is universally accepted as marking the beginning of our land law. After the conquest the Normans established in England the feudal system of land tenure, the underlying theory of which was that title to all land was vested in the king, and that all land was held either directly or indirectly from the king. The feudal system involved more than mere rights in land. In its entirety, it incorporated a system of government, a military organization, and the economic structure of the people. We are primarily interested in the rights in land under feudalism.

The king was the source of all rights in land; in theory, he was title owner of all land. The king, as lord, granted land in large tracts to the great lords, who held as tenants of the king. The great lords, in turn, granted their land in smaller tracts to lesser nobles, who held as tenants of the great lords. These lesser lords might, in turn, grant to still lesser noblemen and on down to the villeins, who lived on and cultivated the land. Under this system, with the exception of the highest lord and the lowest villein, each person occupied a double relation: He was tenant as to his overlord and lord as to his tenant. Under the feudal system as originally established, the highest estate that anyone, other than the king, could hold in land was a life estate, the use of land for his lifetime. The tenant owed duties of fealty, faith, and feudal service to his lord; in return, he was entitled to receive protection from his lord.

### Development of Real Estate Law in England

Although land law is—and, under the English law, has been—conservative, it has nevertheless been in a state of growth from its beginning. The feudal system of land tenure was established at a time when mutual protection was of paramount importance and when the feudal obligations that were imposed on the tenancies were not unduly oppressive. The more onerous duties were connected, either directly or indirectly, with military service; at this early period the performance of these services was necessary for the defense of the realm. As the country developed, the need for protection diminished, and the old feudal services became burdensome. The tenants attempted to devise ways to avoid these duties and were successful to a degree. As early as 1290, legislation was adopted that protected the rights of the lord to feudal services.

Another important feature of the feudal land law was the tenants' right to convey his interest in the land. One of the rights acquired by the lords from the king through the Magna Carta was the right to pass their interest in the land they held to their heirs. Little reliable information is available regarding the right of alienation of land during the first 200 years of the existence of the feudal system in England. It is known that in the latter part of the 13th century, tenants did alienate their interest in the lands they held. The statute *Quia Emptores* (1290) recognized the tenant's right to convey his interest in the land and also protected the lord's rights by providing, in effect, that he would have the same rights against the transferee that he had against the original tenant.

In the year 1660, substantially all the old feudal services were abolished by a statute of Charles II, but this legislation did not do away with the idea that land was held from an overlord, either the king or someone lower in the hierarchy of noblemen.

### Feudal Rights versus Individual Rights

Under the feudal system of land tenure the government, which at that time was synonymous with the king, held the majority of the rights in the land; the individual had relatively few rights. The individual was, in most respects, a tenant having only the right of occupation and use. Under the real estate law as it exists in the United States today, the individual has many rights in the land he owns. The powers of the government—federal, state, and local—are limited to the right to tax; the right, under its police power, to control the use made of the land in order to protect the health, safety, and general welfare of the people; and the right, under the power of eminent domain, to take the land for a public use.

All land privately owned in the United States is alodial land—that is, land held in absolute independence, without being subject to any rent, service, or acknowledgment to a superior. Such an estate in land is the opposite of a feudal estate.

### Real Estate Law in the United States

Land in America that was discovered and settled by English subjects or that was acquired by military conquest was claimed in the name of the king and was granted by the crown to the colonies. These grants were made under terms that recognized many of the features of the feudal system. However, the recipient of such a grant paid only a nominal rental; he was not subject to the payment of feudal dues and the performance of feudal services, and his relation to the king was no different from that of any other subject—that is, he did not have to swear fealty or do homage.

After the Revolution the states succeeded to the rights of the crown. All unoccupied land was recognized as the property of the federal government. Since that time, the states have passed statutes that have abolished substantially all of the burdens incident to feudal tenure. In general, the individual does not hold his land from the state as overlord. The state does have jurisdiction over the land within its borders: it has the right to tax, it has the right of eminent domain, and if an owner of land dies intestate and without heirs, his land escheats to the state.

## Ownership

### Nature of Ownership

The concept of ownership of property is not difficult to grasp when we are considering the ownership of a small item of personal property, such as a watch or a book, because the facts of possession and control are easy to demonstrate. These facts of possession and control are clear evidence of the possessor's claim of ownership. The fact of possession plus the claim of ownership breed the *right* of ownership. When we speak of ownership of real estate, however, such as an 80-acre farm or a house and lot, it is not quite so easy to demonstrate the complete dominion characteristic of the ownership of personal property. It is obviously impossible for one who claims to own a house and lot to demonstrate this claim by carrying them about with him; one must demonstrate his claim by occupying the property and preventing others from doing so. In the case of the 80-acre farm it is even more difficult to demonstrate the claim of right to ownership because it is impractical to physically occupy such a large tract of ground and it is difficult to prevent others from entering upon it. We must therefore resort to some symbolic claim of the right to possession that flows from the right of ownership, and we do so by erecting fences or other artificial boundaries and by using the land while consistently maintaining our *exclusive* right to do so. In developing the concept of ownership of real estate we have come to rely upon the "bundle of rights" as a way of defining or limiting the extent to which we own real estate. That is, we accumulate the rights to use real estate, the right to control it, the right to possess or occupy it, the right to prevent others from using it, the right to oust those who enter upon it, and the like, and this accumulated bundle of rights constitutes ownership of real estate as we recognize it today. Once we have established our right of ownership and the extent of it in a particular parcel of real estate, our legal system will recognize and protect it. This bundle-of-rights concept is made necessary because varying degrees of ownership of real estate can exist, ranging from complete and absolute ownership to the mere right of temporary possession or use of property belonging to another.

### Extent of Ownership Recognized

Today we recognize the ownership of one who has the fee simple interest in real estate as being alodial as opposed to feudal. It is absolute as opposed to depending upon the pleasure of another. To understand this concept fully, we need first to state it in its broadest terms and then illustrate its limitations. Theoretically today, ownership of a parcel of ground upon the surface of the earth carries with it full rights to the exclusive possession and use of that area of ground down to the very center of the earth and upwards "to the heavens." The concept is relatively easy to diagram and grasp:

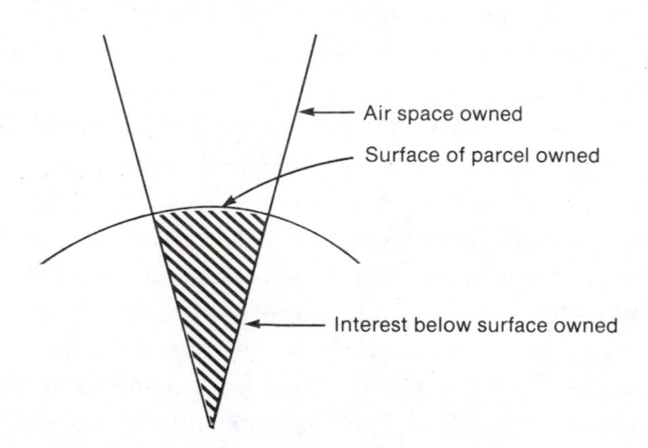


While this concept is fairly straightforward in theory, its practical application can become a thorny matter, and the apparent rights of the owner of the earth's surface are subject to some severe limitations. This concept of ownership of land developed, of course, at a time when the rights to the air space over land were of little consequence or value because there was then no known use for them. At the same time, neither was much more serious consideration given to other below-ground rights than the right of lateral support and the right to compel a neighbor to refrain from weakening the base of a structure built upon the land.

## Ownership Below the Earth's Surface

Today, of course, since the advent of deep mining for oil, gas, and other important minerals, the value of the surface owner's rights to what lies beneath the surface is of very substantial importance, and these rights have become quite valuable. It is now of some practical significance to be able to establish and control the ground beneath the surface, and a well-developed body of law defining and limiting these rights has emerged. The precise angle at which, for example, a well or mine shaft is driven on a neighboring piece of property may well determine whether the minerals taken from it belong to one property owner or another. The development of this branch of property law has become exceedingly complex and is far beyond the scope of this work. However, it is important to recognize here that ownership of real estate is not limited to the earth's surface nor to any arbitrary depth into the earth. Our modern legal system both recognizes and protects the rights of property owners below the earth's surface. Up until the present time there has been little reason for this area of private property rights to be invaded by the needs of the general public, but such invasion is not inconceivable.

## Ownership of Air Space

The rights of the property owner to the air space over the surface of his property have become much more significant today than they were at early common law, and the development of the law to protect and limit those rights has been much more obvious. The value of the air rights over certain land, particularly in major metropolitan areas, has received considerable notoriety. Major office buildings have been built over real estate whose existing uses did not require them. The Prudential Insurance Building in downtown Chicago is frequently pointed out as an outstanding instance of the efficient use of air space over the Illinois Central Railroad Company's tracks, space not needed for the use of the ground itself but of very considerable value for office building purposes because of its choice location. In connection with that particular building it might be noted that, while all the notoriety was given to the use of the air space, the building does not float upon air. It is built upon an elaborate system of caissons extending deep into the ground below the surface and requiring quite substantial lateral support directly *beneath* the surface. The project therefore is as much an example of the value of ownership rights below the surface as it is an example of the value of the air rights above. The full legal description of the property actually purchased is reported to have been so complex that it was as long as this entire textbook.

In another area, the air rights of real estate owners have also been subjected to substantial limitation in the name of the public interest. In our diagram and definition of property rights of landowners, it is only logical to assume that the landowner should have the exclusive possession of a vast body of air space with the accompanying right to deny possession or use that space to all others. That this is not true today is obvious from the fact that commercial and private aircraft fly across private property constantly without any thought of reimbursing the owners of the property below for the use of their air space. This does not mean that the concept of ownership "to the heavens" is an empty phrase. What it does mean, of course, is that the national policy to encourage and foster air transportation is more important than the protection of private property rights of real estate owners at altitudes for which they have no need or use. To the extent that the landowner does make some use of the air space, or to the extent that his surface use requires protection of his air space, our system still protects his property rights. The way it does so is discussed below and, to some extent, in the chapter on eminent domain.

## Protection of Ownership Rights

The protection granted to private rights of ownership in this country today stems from two sources: public controls on the use of real property and the private remedies of trespass and nuisance. Public controls and limitations are discussed at a later point; however, the doctrines of trespass and nuisance have developed as part of our common law as the bases of the fundamental private methods of protecting one's own property rights and limiting interference with them by others.

*Common law* is a term that distinguishes judge-made law from statutes passed by our legislatures. The common law is composed of an immense number of court decisions in which basic personal rights and property rights have developed. Given the notion that our law will protect private property rights, even though there is no statute doing so, it remains to determine how this protection is to be provided. It is accomplished, in the real estate area, by characterizing any interference with property rights as a *tort.* A tort is simply a civil wrong as opposed to a crime. Certain acts have come to be recognized under the common law as wrongful because they interfere with the recognized and protected rights of others. When there has been a civil wrong or tort committed, the remedy of the injured party is to seek relief through a civil lawsuit against the person who committed the tort. In most cases the relief provided will take the form of an award for money damages that are shown to have resulted from the tort. When the wrong complained of is an isolated act, the remedy is usually restricted to the award of money damages to the injured party. In many cases, however, the wrong complained of will be of a continuing nature rather than an isolated occurrence. The injured party might logically be required simply to bring additional lawsuits each time the wrong was repeated; however, as a practical matter our legal system will not require him to do so. The reasons are that bringing several lawsuits for the same repeated injury would burden our court system and, more importantly, several awards for damages may be an ineffective remedy. The injured party is entitled to more than money; he is entitled to have the repeated injury halted. In such a case the remedy provided is an *injunction,* which is a court order restraining the one committing the tort from doing so again. This is an important concept and a strong remedy because the subsequent violation of the court's order would constitute a contempt of court with possibly harsh results, even including imprisonment. In the protection of rights of ownership of real estate, the most significant concepts are those of trespass and nuisance, which are discussed below.

**Trespass**

Trespass took several technical forms at common law, but the various distinctions are of little practical significance today. The essence of the tort of trespass is some physical entry onto the property of another without permission. This stands in contrast to the tort of nuisance, which requires no physical entry but consists rather of an unwarranted interference with the use and enjoyment of the property of another. In either case, the action complained of is a *civil* as opposed to a criminal wrong and is therefore a matter between the two parties and the courts. The distinction between trespass and nuisance is more than just a technicality. When there has been a physical entry onto the property of another without permission, the proof of this fact alone will necessarily result in an award of damages because there is a *presumption* that at least some damage was sustained. Our courts are fond of platitudes, such as "the crushing of but one blade of grass" results in damage; however, true understanding of the significance of the tort of trespass requires full comprehension of the term *entry.* This is the key element of the tort. Courts always presume some damage because there is a physical entry without permission, with the consequent possible breach of the peace. More than just property rights are at issue. There is the possibility of an attempt physically to *remove* the trespassor, by violence if necessary, and it is this confrontation that the law seeks to discourage by automatically finding some damage. It is at least partially a punitive remedy to discourage the entry upon the land of another. Once the fact of unauthorized entry has been established, of course, it is up to the defendant to show that the *actual* damage suffered was only nominal as opposed to being substantial.

**Nuisance**

The tort of nuisance does not require that there have been a physical entry upon the land of another. It is enough to show that the defendant interfered with the plaintiff's use and enjoyment of his property. But a little more must be shown by the plaintiff than the mere fact that he was made uncomfortable by the defendant's action; he must also show that the interference was *unreasonable*. While it might at first appear that nuisance is the easier remedy for the injured property owner to pursue (because there is no need to prove a physical entry upon his property), there is a major disadvantage to the use of this remedy: there is no presumption of damages, even if it is shown that the defendant's actions interfered with the plaintiff's enjoyment of his property. The burden of showing that there was any compensable damage at all is solely that of the plaintiff. Typically, the tort of nuisance is claimed when one property owner makes some use of his property that unreasonably interferes with the rights of his neighbors to the peaceful use and enjoyment of their properties. A classic case is the maintenance of an open dump on a lot in a residential neighborhood. Even if local zoning and health ordinances did not prohibit such activity, the neighboring property owners could bring an action on a nuisance theory to obtain an injunction against such use. Whether and to what extent they could also establish damages in terms of money is problematical, and they are not favored with a presumption of damages (as they would be in a trespass action) because there has been no physical entry upon their properties by the defendant.

The distinction between trespass and nuisance is significant in terms of the plaintiff's technical approach to the protection of his property rights. However, the distinction also represents a form of compromise on the part of our legal system. When there is a physical entry upon the property of another, with the consequent potential breach of the peace, there is a public as well as a private interest to be protected, and the added element of a presumption of damage is designed to *deter* such actions. When a mere nuisance is claimed, in the absence of aggravating circumstances, there is usually no such imminent possibility of breach of the peace, and the requirement of actual proof of damages (as opposed to a presumption) is justifiable. The attempt on the part of the aggrieved party to bring his case within the framework of a trespass action results, of course, in some strained definitions in the decided cases. Both remedies are viable forms of protection of the rights of owners of real estate, though, and they add to the strength of the concept of alodial, unqualified ownership as we understand it today.

## The Estate Concept

To the English common-law system of categorizing degrees of ownership one element was of crucial importance: the right to *exclusive* possession of real estate. Any interest in real estate that included this right was classified as an *estate in land* and connoted ownership to a greater or lesser degree. All other interests in land, such as the temporary limited right to go upon the land of another for a specific purpose only, were classed simply as "less than estates." This distinction is preserved even today, and the rights, benefits, and duties that flow from each interest recognized by our law today largely depend upon whether or not the interest owned is an estate in land.

Those interests in land that are significant enough to be classified as estates in land are further divided into two distinct categories: (1) freehold estates and (2) leasehold (less than freehold) estates. The distinction between the two is based more upon historical development than logic, the freehold estate being based upon its quantity or duration. A freehold estate continues for an indefinite period. It may be perpetual or potentially perpetual and therefore may be inherited. It may, on the other hand, be an estate for life only and therefore, by definition, incapable of being inherited.

The freehold estates that may be recognized today are the (1) fee simple, (2) fee tail, (3) determinable fee, and (4) life estate. The first three, since they will or may survive the death of the owner, are estates of inheritance. The life estate, however, terminates upon the death of the person or persons by whose life or lives it is measured. Each of these estates is discussed below.

Leasehold estates fall into four categories: (1) estates for years, (2) estates from year to year (or period to period), (3) estates at will, and (4) estates at sufferance. These are discussed in detail in Chapter 19.

## Freehold Estates

### Fee Simple

An estate in fee simple is the highest form of ownership of real estate recognized by our law. The owner of the fee simple holds the entire bundle of rights that we have discussed, and he holds them, at least theoretically, in perpetuity. As a practical matter, of course, there is no way that the owner of the fee simple can enjoy these rights in perpetuity. However, it is from this basic concept that we conclude that he has the unconditional power to deal with the entire ownership of the property. He may sell the real estate, dispose of it by gift, create lesser interests in the property in others, or encumber it to secure borrowings and, upon his death intestate (leaving no valid will), it will pass to his legal heirs. The terms used to denote this interest include *fee, fee simple,* and *fee simple absolute.* At one time the term *fee simple* was used to distinguish this estate from lesser estates in land.[1] In modern practice, however, the term *fee* alone would be enough to describe the estate, since it is presumed that the entire fee simple absolute is intended unless some qualifications or restrictions are included.

The power of the holder of the fee simple estate in land to grant more limited interests to others while retaining control of the fee is quite broad. The creation of lesser interests in others may be made upon whatever reasonable conditions the owner of the fee chooses to impose. Upon the termination of these lesser interests, they return to the balance of the rights held by the fee owner and are *merged* into the fee simple. Under the doctrine of merger, whenever two interests in the same real estate are owned by one person the lesser is merged into the greater, and thereafter only the greater interest is recognized. For instance, should the owner of the fee simple give a short-term lease of the property to another, upon termination of that lease, the right of the tenant to possession returns to the holder of the fee simple, and, since the right of possession for a short period of time is the lesser interest, it is merged into the fee simple and only the fee simple survives.

The owner of the fee simple may create several well-recognized lesser interests in the land to different parties at the same time. For example, Allen, who owns real estate in fee simple, may give Beech a mortgage on the land, may grant Call an easement of right of way over the land, may lease the land to Faris for a period of years, and may grant Gale a license to hunt upon the land. Although a wide variety of rights have been granted to others, Allen still owns the land in fee simple. Upon the termination of these rights they are merged back into Allen's fee simple, and similar interests may then be granted to still others.

## Creation of the Fee Simple

In order to create the fee simple it is important that the intent to do so be clear. It is enough, under modern practice, that there be no limitation expressed

---

[1] *Hay's Estate et al.* v. *Commissioner of Internal Revenue,* 181 F.2d 169.

in the deed to create or transfer the fee simple interest. If there are limitations expressed in the instrument, something less than the fee simple will be transferred.

Etheridge conveyed to the United States 10 acres of seashore property under a statute authorizing the Treasury of the United States to acquire ". . . the right to use and occupy sites for life saving or life boat stations." The consideration was $100, and the deed included the following: ". . . the said Secretary . . . deems it advisable to acquire . . . the right to use and occupy the hereinafter described land as a site for a Life Saving Station." The land was used as a lifesaving station from 1912 until July 16, 1956, when the United States began to use it for other purposes. Etheridge claimed the right to the land and demanded rent for the period from July 16, 1956, to the time the United States surrendered possession of the land to him. The United States claimed that it owned the land in fee simple. The court held that the deed conveyed limited rights in the land and did not convey a fee simple.

District Judge Larkins said: "A good title in fee simple is indefeasible, marketable and unencumbered. By definition a fee simple title cannot be qualified or limited, but carries with it full legal rights with respect to the property." *Etheridge* v. *United States,* 218 F. Supp. 809 (1963).

The above case also illustrates an important rule of interpreting deeds: that each word will be construed to have some meaning or it would not be included. If the deed in this case had not included the statement expressing the limited use to which the land was to be put, a different result would have occurred.

**Limitations on the Fee Simple**

Even though the owner of the fee simple has the maximum rights of ownership recognized under the law, this does not mean that those rights are absolutely unrestricted nor that he or she may do whatever he or she wishes with the property. The same body of law that recognizes and protects the rights of the owner of the fee simple estate also limits the extent to which the owner may exercise those rights. Individual rights that result from private ownership of property are always subject to the superior rights of society, which are in turn based upon protection of the general public. Therefore, the owner of the fee simple must be said to have the right to use his or her property for any *lawful* purpose.

He has the right to sell it, dispose of it on his death by will (with limitations), encumber it, or lease it. He has the right to open mines, drill for gas and oil, remove sand or gravel or other aggregate that may be on the land, cut the timber, burn the buildings if he does not endanger the property of his neighbors in the process, flood the land, and so forth, so long as his acts do not jeopardize the health, safety, or welfare of others.

A fee simple owner will not be permitted to maintain a nuisance on his property. The property of any owner, including the fee simple owner, may be taken for the benefit of the public under the power of eminent domain, and the use of all property may be restricted under the police power of the state.

**Determinable Fee**

A determinable, qualified, or base fee is an estate of inheritance, and the holder of the fee has all the rights that the holder of a fee simple has. However, the estate of the holder of the determinable fee will be extinguished on the occurrence of a designated event, the time of the happening of which must be uncertain. The event on the happening of which the determinable fee is to be extinguished may be an event that is certain to happen, although the time of its happening is uncertain, or it may be an event that may never happen.

Whether a conveyance creates a determinable fee, places a limitation on the use of the real property conveyed, or creates a fee simple conditional will depend on the wording of the conveyance. There is a lack of harmony in the decisions of the courts as to the interpretation of language used. In addition, this branch of real estate law (future interests in real estate) is exceedingly technical. If a person engaged in the real estate business should encounter a transaction involving the rights of parties to such conveyance, the wise course of action would be to refer the entire matter to a competent attorney and follow his advice in the matter.

In the above case of *Etheridge* v. *United States,* the court held that the deed conveyed a fee simple determinable. Judge Larkins, quoting from Tiffany, *Law of Real Property,* 3d ed., Section 220, said, ". . . So, when land is granted for certain purposes, as for a schoolhouse, a church, a public building, or the like, and it is evidently the grantor's intention that it shall be used for such purpose only, and on the cessation of such use, the estate shall end, without any re-entry by the grantor, an estate of the kind now under consideration is created. It is necessary, it has been said, that the event named as terminating the estate be such that it may by possibility never happen at all, since it is an essential characteristic of a fee that it may possibly endure forever."

The court said: "The conveyance in question falls squarely within the preceding definition. The language employed by the grantors in the deed clearly manifests their intention that the land be used and occupied as a site for a lifesaving station and for that purpose only. It is sufficiently evident that the grantors intended that, on the cessation of such use, the estate would terminate without a re-entry by them. When the defendant ceased using the land for a lifesaving station the land automatically reverted to the plaintiffs by operation of law."

The determinable fee is frequently created with something less than precision. This is frequently the case when there is a grant of private property to some public or charitable user. Very often such a transfer is made as a gift, and there is little reason to examine the wording of the conveyance with great care because no payment is being made for the property. As a result the conveyance might read: ". . . to the ABC Church for so long as the property is used for church purposes." Since there is no expressed limitation on the extent of ownership being conveyed, the modern rule would treat this as a transfer of the fee simple. Nevertheless, the clause sets up a condition that must be taken into account in order to accurately define the extent of the rights being conveyed. Clearly, so long as the ABC Church uses the property for its own purposes, the condition will not be broken and the fee simple will not be terminated. If, however, at any time the ABC Church goes out of existence or moves to another location, a serious question is raised as to the disposition of the fee simple estate. The land may not be sold to a commercial user, since this would clearly terminate the estate held by the ABC Church. The property would then return to the previous owner or his heirs. A closer question is presented, however, where the ABC Church sells or otherwise transfers the property to the XYZ Church, which continues using the property for "church purposes." The previous owner or his or her heirs may attack such a transfer on the grounds that the intent of the grant was to benefit the ABC Church only and no other. If the land has appreciated substantially in value, costly litigation may be required to settle the matter.

Even though no exact language is required to create the determinable fee, any failure to clearly express the condition upon which it will terminate will result in the transfer of the fee simple. In a recent case a developer made a dedication of land for a public park. This was accomplished by the filing of a subdivision plat and its acceptance by the city. The city never used the property and later sold it to another developer, who subdivided it, built houses upon it, and sold them to private buyers. The court held that the plat merely recited the purpose for which the property was to be used and did not clearly create a determinable fee, and the city therefore took the land in fee simple.[2]

In another recent case, property was deeded to a city for use as a golf course and upon failure to so use it the property was to revert to the grantor (or his heirs). After 34 years the city changed the usage of the property; however, instead of finding that a conditional fee had been intended, the court defined the clause as a restrictive covenant and ruled that the city had complied with the restriction long enough. The city therefore held the fee simple and had the power to use the property for another purpose.[3] In still another case, a parcel of ground was conveyed to the city of Portland to be used as a public park named "Winslow

---

[2] *Wheeler* v. *Monroe,* 68 N. Mex. 296, 523 p.2d 540 (1974).

[3] *Barnett* v. *County of Washoe,* 86 Nev. 730, 476, P.2d 8 (1970).

Park." The city complied with this condition for many years until the ground was taken by the state in eminent domain proceedings for use in constructing an interstate highway. In the dispute over ownership of the payment received, the city prevailed and took the full award for the purpose of constructing a new "Winslow Park" nearby. The reasoning of the court was that such a result accomplished the charitable motive of the grantor.[4] It seems clear that in cases like those digested above, the courts will tend to interpret the determinable fee to be something other than a condition, particularly where a municipality is involved.

## Fee Tail

An estate tail or fee tail is an estate given to a person and the heirs of his body. At common law, such property was, in effect, owned by the bloodline and could not be alienated. If the bloodline terminated, as it would in the event there were no heirs of the body of the grantee, the title to the land would revert to the original grantor. At an early date, methods were devised whereby the inalienability of an estate tail could be defeated. In the United States today the estate tail has been abolished by statute in all but a few states.[5] In those states that recognize it, the duration of an estate tail is usually limited to life or lives in being.

The deeds in litigation conveyed certain farm land to Carl M. Thompson and wife and to Raymond T. Thompson and wife. The granting clause in each of the deeds conveyed the land to the above-named grantees and "the heirs of their bodies." In other portions of the deeds the grant was to "their heirs and assigns." The question presented to the court was whether a fee simple or a fee tail was conveyed. The court held that a fee tail was granted.

Judge Fisher said: "It is universally conceded in English and American jurisprudence that an absolute fee simple estate is the entire interest in the land, with infinite duration, and inheritable by the collateral as well as the lineal heirs of the person having such estate; whereas an estate in fee tail is one restricted in its course of descent at law to certain heirs, namely, those of the body. The first matter for consideration is, therefore, whether the 1949 deed conveyed a fee simple or a fee tail estate.

"The word 'heirs' was necessary to create a fee simple estate by deed at common law, but in 1925 a statute was enacted in Ohio, declaring that words of inheritance or succession are not necessary to create an estate in fee simple and that every grant or conveyance shall be construed to pass the whole estate or interest unless it clearly appears by the deed that the grantor intended to convey a lesser estate. The usual form of conveyance in fee simple is a grant 'to A and his heirs and assigns forever,' and one of the

---

[4] *State of Maine* v. *Rand,* 366 A.2d 183 (Me. 1976).

[5] Paul E. Bayse, *Patton on Titles,* 2d ed. (St. Paul: West Publishing Co., 1957), sec. 205.

incidents of such an estate is the power of unlimited alienation. However, in a fee tail estate the course of descent is usually restricted to the heirs of the donee's body. The form most generally used is 'to A and the heirs of his body.' These latter estates are of common law origin, having derived their existence from the statute de donis which had the effect of making them inalienable where the limitation was to some particular heir or class of issue of the grantee instead of the general heirs. If there were no heirs of the class to whom the estate was limited, the property reverted to the donor. If the donee in tail died leaving heirs of the class to whom the estate was limited by the grant, as heirs of the body, it passed to them in fee simple by operation of law. Thus, where lands were conveyed by deed 'to A, the heirs of his body and assigns, forever,' A took an estate tail." *Guida* v. *Thompson,* 80 Ohio Abs. 148, 160 N.E.2d 153 (1957).

# Chapter 3

# Lesser Interests in Real Estate

In the previous chapter the estate concept was introduced. It was emphasized that the right to exclusive possession was the distinguishing characteristic of an estate in land. Absolute ownership, to the extent that it really exists, was considered. In this chapter are considered those interests that do not constitute full ownership. They are methods by which some of the characteristics and rights of ownership can be transferred to others. Two of these methods, the life estate and the leasehold estate, are so significant that they qualify as estates in land. In the life estate we can have, for all practical purposes, all of the benefits of ownership, limited only by our lifetime. In the lease we can transfer as much of these benefits as we choose for as long as we choose. The lease is so important in the real estate business that we will only introduce it at this point. Extensive discussion of it is reserved for Chapter 19, where its uses will be explored in depth.

Interests in land that are less than estates are very valuable to us. They can be used to enhance the value of property that we own without requiring us to buy more property. The most familiar interest of this kind is the easement of right of way. It is not uncommon to see and use such interests in our daily lives. The right to have easy access to our real estate is one that we take for granted, but that access clearly involves the use of property that belongs to others. The existence of such rights is very basic to our enjoyment of property that we own. Without easements and other limited interests discussed in this chapter, real estate development, as we know it today, would not be possible. The extent of these interests in terms of benefits and burdens for each of the parties involved is therefore an important matter.

## Life Estates

### Nature and Creation of Life Estate

A life estate is a freehold estate in land and is limited in duration to the life of the owner, or to the life or lives of some other person or persons. It is not an estate of inheritance.[1] A life estate may be terminated on the happening of a future, uncertain event. For example, a devise to "my wife Ann for her natural life or so long as she shall remain my widow" creates a life estate in Ann which would terminate on her remarriage.[2]

There are two classes of life estates: (1) conventional and (2) legal. The conventional life estate is created by the acts of the parties; a legal life estate is created by operation of the law. The life estate created by the acts of the parties may be for the life of the life tenant, or for the life of some other person or persons. The latter is known technically as an estate *pur autre vie*. Legal life estates are dower, curtesy, and, in some states, homesteads.

### Nature of Life Tenant's Ownership

The life tenant possesses legal title to the real estate, since the life estate is a freehold; but his rights in the property are limited both as to their scope and as to their duration. Since a life estate is real estate, it must be created by a grant, that is, by a deed or will. No formal wording need be used to create such an estate. If the grantor or testator uses in the deed or will language that indicates, with reasonable certainty, his intention to grant a life estate, such phraseology will be sufficient.

Under the statute of frauds, any contract for the sale of land or any interest in or concerning land must, if it is to be enforceable, be evidenced by a note or memorandum in writing signed by the party to be bound or by his duly authorized agent. A life estate is an interest in land; consequently, any contract affecting a life estate, if it is to be enforceable, would have to comply with the statute of frauds.

Since the life tenant's estate in real property terminates on his death, or on

---

[1] *Weekly* v. *Weekly et al.*, 126 W.Va. 90, 27 S.E.2d 591.

[2] *Greenleaf et al.* v. *Greenleaf et al.*, 332 Mo. 277, 58 S.W.2d 448.

the death of the person or persons upon whose life the duration of the estate is limited, the life tenant does not own the entire property in the real estate. That portion of the entire property not owned by the life tenant is owned either by the original grantor of the life estate, by his heirs or assigns, or by the remainderman. When the life estate terminates, the rights of the life tenant merge into the fee. If the grantor has retained the fee, the interest of the life tenant will revert to him or her, in which case that person's interest in the property during the existence of the life estate is known as a *reversion*.

If the grantor has granted a life estate to one person and the fee to another person, the interest of the fee owner is known as a *remainder*. For example, if Ames, who owns real estate in fee simple, grants it to Bell for life, Bell's interests, on the termination of the life estate, merge into the fee retained by Ames. During the period of the life estate, Ames has a reversionary interest in the real estates. If Ames grants the real estate to Bell for life and the remainder to Call in fee simple, Call will have the fee in the land subject to Bell's outstanding life estate. Bell is life tenant, and Call is remainderman.

William D. Robinson left a will in which he devised all of his real estate as follows: "Third: I give all my Real Estate to my wife, Lelia S. Robinson, and at her death it goes to F. M. Robinson (Frank M. Robinson), and at his death to his two boys, David Robinson and Richard Robinson." Caldwell and other heirs of Lelia Robinson claimed that a fee simple title vested in Lelia and that Frank M. Robinson and his two sons would take nothing. The trial court decided in favor of Caldwell et al., and Robinson appealed. The judgment was reversed.

Justice Miller said: "The devises in the wills to the first takers are general devises and use no words indicative of intent to give more than a life estate. At common law such a general devise to the first taker created only a life estate.

"But unless the intent appears upon the face of the devise to give more than a life estate, the common law rule applies to devises as to conveyances, and nothing but an estate for life passes. . . .

"Section 55–11, Code 1950, has, however, changed this common law rule, and such a general devise now conveys the fee simple unless a contrary intention shall appear by the will, conveyance or grant.

"Though neither will devises an express life estate, yet the respective wills clearly disclose that the testator and testatrix intended to and did, by the limiting phrases that they employed, create mere life estates in the first takers with vested remainders in David and Richard Robinson." *Robinson* v. *Caldwell,* 200 Va. 353, 105 S.E.2d 852 (1958).

### Extent of Life Tenant's Rights

The life tenant's interest in the real property is an ownership interest; she is not answerable to a superior owner. However, since she is not absolute owner, her rights are limited; and in the enjoyment of her rights, she must not encroach upon those of the remainderman or the reversioner, as the case may be.

The life tenant is entitled to all the income and profits arising from the property during the term of her tenancy.[3] She may sell her interest, or she may lease or mortgage the property. If she leases the property, the lease will end on the termination of the life estate. If she mortgages the property, the mortgagee acquires a lien only on the life tenant's interest; consequently, on the termination of the life estate the mortgagee would have no lien on the real property. The life tenant cannot create a lien on the interest of the remainderman or reversioner.

If mines, quarries, or oil or gas wells are open at the time of or before the creation of the life estate, the life tenant, unless expressly precluded, has a right to work such mines, quarries, or wells to exhaustion. She may sell the production thereof without having to account to the remainderman or reversioner for depletion.[4] If there are no mines, quarries, or wells open at the time of the creation of the life estate, the life tenant has no right, unless such right is provided for, to open new mines, quarries, or wells. However, if the owner, prior to the creation of the life estate, has granted the right to mine or to drill for gas and oil, the life tenant will be entitled to the royalties from the mines opened or to the income and profits from the gas and oil wells drilled under the grant or lease for the duration of the life estate.[5]

### Duties and Liabilities of Life Tenant

The life tenant owes a duty to refrain from conduct that does permanent injury to the remainder or reversion. An act that does permanent injury to the real estate subject to the life estate is known as *waste*. No exact statement can be made as to what acts on the part of the life tenant will be held to be waste. For example, the cutting, selling, and removal of timber would, as a general rule, be considered waste; but if the cutting of the timber enhances the value of the property (clearing land for cultivation or other beneficial purposes), the cutting and removal of the timber would not be considered waste.[6]

As a general rule, the removal or destruction of buildings that are a permanent part of the real estate is waste, even though the life tenant is tearing down a building to make room for a better one. If a life tenant tears down a structure

[3] *Croasdale* v. *Butell,* 177 Kan. 487, 280 P.2d 593.

[4] *In re Crozer's Estate,* 336 Pa. 266, 9 A.2d 535.

[5] *Benson* v. *Nyman,* 136 Kan. 455, 16 P.2d 963.

[6] *Sallee et al.* v. *Daneri et al.,* 49 Cal. App.2d 324, 121 P.2d 781.

and sells the material to a third person, the third person is liable to the remainderman or reversioner for the value of the material.[7]

Failure on the part of the life tenant to make ordinary repairs is waste; but he owes no duty to make permanent improvements. There is no clear-cut line of distinction between ordinary repairs and permanent improvements. In borderline situations, each case must be decided on the basis of its particular facts.

If the life tenant fails to make ordinary repairs and, after due notice and request, refuses or fails to make them within a reasonable time, the remainderman or reversioner may bring an appropriate action to require him or her to make such repairs or may have them made and recover the cost from the life tenant.[8]

If the life tenant makes permanent improvements for his own benefit and convenience, he must pay the entire cost of the improvement. If the life tenant completes improvements begun by the donor, makes permanent improvements required by municipal authority, or makes permanent improvements necessary to assure a reasonable return on the property, the courts have generally held that the entire cost of the improvement need not be borne by him. No basic standard for the distribution of the cost of permanent improvements between the life tenant and the remainderman or reversioner has been developed by the courts. They have attempted to make an equitable adjustment based on the facts of each individual case.

If the life tenant and remainderman or reversioner enter into an agreement for the making of the improvement and the apportionment of the cost, the courts will, in the absence of fraud, duress, or undue influence, enforce the agreement. A contract in writing, setting out the agreement for apportionment of the cost of the improvement, will, as a general rule, prevent expensive litigation.

The life tenant in possession sold the standing timber on the land. The remainderman brought suit against the purchaser of the timber, who had cut and removed it, to recover a judgment for the value of such timber. The court granted a judgment to the remainderman.

Judge Franklin said: "Under the theory on which the case was tried, the only question on which the defendant's liability depended was whether the tenant had authority in the exercise of her rights under her life estate tenancy to sell the timber in question. She could rightfully cut only such timber as she needed for firewood or for making repairs to the premises or such as was necessary to clear up the land for cultivation, or such as was necessary to be cut in the exercise of good husbandry or forestry. In this case there was not one shred of evidence that the cutting of timber here involved was for the purpose

---

[7] *Hayden* v. *Boetler,* 263 Ky. 722, 93 S.W.2d 831.

[8] *In re Stout's Estate,* 151 Ore. 411, 50 P.2d 768.

of providing the life tenant with firewood or for the purpose of clearing up and for cultivation or the exercise of good husbandry or forestry. *Ola B. Campion* v. *McLeod,* 108 Ga. App. 261, 132 S.E.2d 848 (1963).

Property was conveyed by will to Toler. The will provided: "I give, devise and bequeath to my brother, Benjamin Edward Toler, for and during his natural life, with the right to full use and benefit of all the rents, issues and profits therefrom with the remainder over in fee to the following persons. . . ."

Ponder, the remainderman, contended that the court improperly determined income allocable to the life tenant, and that it should have charged operational expenses to income. The court held that the life tenant was liable for operational expenses.

Justice Shepard said: "Ordinarily where the will is silent on the subject of expenses, the owner of the life estate will be held responsible for the upkeep of the improvements, against waste and for taxes, and a just proportion of extraordinary assessments benefiting the whole inheritance. . . . The charging of taxes to corpus in any year in which a loss occurred is amply supported by precedent." *In re Toler's Estate,* 18 Cal. Rptr. 684, 345 P.2d 152 (1959).

### Insuring the Property

Both the life tenant and the remainderman or reversioner have an insurable interest in the property. Neither owes to the other a duty to insure the property. If either insures it for his individual benefit, the other party does not share in the insurance. The life tenant and the remainderman or reversioner may join in insuring the property.

Under some circumstances, the life tenant may owe a duty to keep the property insured. For example, when there is a mortgage on the property executed by the donor, which mortgage requires the mortgagor to keep the premises insured, there have been instances in which the life tenant has been required to insure the premises.[9]

A life estate in a 400-acre farm was devised to Bertha Adams subject to a power in William Adams to operate the farm during Bertha's tenancy. William was directed to pay Bertha the reasonable rental value of the farm. A controversy arose as to the life tenant's obligation to pay taxes, insurance, repairs, and improvements. The court held that these items were chargeable to the life tenant, not to the remainderman.

Judge Montgomery said: "In such cases the rules are plain and of long standing. It is the duty of the life tenant to keep up the property and preserve the estate for the remainderman. To that end the life tenant is bound to pay taxes, insurance, repairs and improvements and cannot charge them against the remainderman. Under this rule it is obligatory that

---

[9] *Livesay* v. *Boyd et al.,* 164 Va. 528, 180 S.E. 158.

appellant [Bertha Adams] pay the items mentioned." *Adams* v. *Adams,* Ky. App., 371 S.W.2d 637 (1963).

**Payment of Taxes and Assessments**

The life tenant in possession owes a duty to pay all ordinary taxes. Failure on his or her part to do so is the commission of waste. However, the courts have generally held that the duty to pay taxes is limited to the amount of the income of the property and that, if the taxes exceed the income, the life tenant is not obligated to pay the excess out of the life tenant's own fund.[10]

In the majority of the states, taxes assessed against real estate are a lien on the property; if they are not paid, the property may be sold at tax sale. If the life tenant fails to pay the taxes, the remainderman or reversioner may pay them and recover from the life tenant the amount disbursed.

In the event of the death of the person on whose life the tenancy is based, thus terminating the tenancy, the courts have in most instances apportioned the taxes, charging the life tenant for the portion of the tax year during which he or she was in possession and charging the remainderman or reversioner for the remaining portion of the year. If taxes have not been paid, they are a charge against the life tenant's estate.

**Mortgages, Liens, and Other Charges**

If, at the time of the creation of a life estate, the property is encumbered by a mortgage, lien, or other charge, the life tenant owes a duty to pay the interest on the encumbrance, but not the principal.[11] Some authorities have held that the life tenant's duty to pay interest on an encumbrance is limited to the amount of income received from the property or to the rental value thereof. If the life tenant mortgages the property or permits a lien to be obtained on the property for his debt, he must pay both interest and principal. Only the interest of the life tenant, on default, is subject to foreclosure or sale. If the remainderman or the reversioner mortgages the property or permits a lien to be obtained on the property for his debt, the life tenant is not obligated to pay either the interest or the principal; and any foreclosure or sale, on default, must be made subject to the outstanding life estate.

If the life tenant and the remainderman or reversioner join in mortgaging the property, and enter into an agreement defining the obligation of each to the other, each is obligated to pay his agreed share of both interest and principal. In the absence of an agreement, expressed or implied, both the interest and

---

[10] *Schofield et al.* v. *Green,* 115 Ind. App. 160, 56 N.E.2d 506.

[11] *Oldham et al.* v. *Noble et al.,* 117 Ind. App. 68, 66 N.E.2d 614.

the principal will be apportioned between them. In the event of default, the entire property is subject to foreclosure and sale.

The life tenant may, in order to preserve the estate, pay off an encumbrance. If the life tenant pays off an encumbrance that the remainderman or reversioner is obligated to pay, he acquires a lien on the share of the property belonging to the remainderman or reversioner; he is, prima facie, a creditor. The remainderman or reversioner may, if he acts within a reasonable time, reimburse the life tenant for the amount paid and thus discharge the lien of the life tenant.

The rule frequently applied in determining the amount due the life tenant, in the event he has redeemed from a mortgage or other lien or charge, is to subtract from the amount paid by the life tenant the amount of an annuity equal to the annual interest for the life expectancy of the life tenant. In the event the remainderman or reversioner redeems the property, the life tenant may protect his interest by contributing his share of the indebtedness. The life tenant's contribution is the equivalent of the interest on the encumbrance during the continuance of the life estate.

Neither the life tenant nor the remainderman or reversioner can cut off the rights of the other by permitting a default, foreclosure, or sale and then purchasing the property at the sale, either in his own name or through a third person. If either party buys the property, he will be deemed to have purchased it for the benefit of all interested parties; the purchaser will, by operation of law, be converted into an involuntary trustee holding for the benefit of all; and he will be required to convey to the other interested party or parties on terms that are equitable. Other interested parties may lose their right to claim an interest in the property by delaying an unreasonable length of time before offering to make contribution.

In June 1919, a life estate in 120 acres of land was granted to Bethea, Sr., and the remainder to his issue. In 1925, Bethea, Sr., gave Bank of Lotta a mortgage on the land to secure a $5,543.38 loan. The loan was not paid. Bank of Lotta assigned the claim and mortgage to Bass, who foreclosed the mortgage and purchased the property at foreclosure sale. The master's deed purported to convey a fee in the property. Bass took possession on March 1931, and remained in possession until his death in May 1954, when his interest in the property passed to his wife and children, who continued in possession. Bethea, Sr., died on November 29, 1959, leaving Bethea, Jr., his sole surviving issue. Bethea, Jr., brought this action to recover possession of the property. The court held that the mortgage encumbered only the interest of the life tenant and that Bethea, Jr., was entitled to possession of the property.

Acting Justice Legge said: "The grant in the case at bar not being within the rule in Shelly's case, Thomas M. Bethea, Sr., took a life estate only, and the respondent, Thomas

M. Bethea, Jr., a contingent remainder, which became vested upon his father's death in 1959. The mortgage from Thomas M. Bethea, Sr., in 1925, though purporting to include the fee, covered only his life estate, for that was all he had; and the master's deed in the foreclosure could convey no more. Nor did the length of possession under the deed bar respondent's claim, for his cause of action did not accrue until his father's death." *Bethea* v. *Bass,* 240 S.C. 398, 126 S.E.2d 354 (1962).

## Termination and Rights on Termination

A life estate terminates on the death of the person on whose life it is limited. If it is based on the life of two or more persons, it terminates on the death of the last survivor. The instrument creating the life estate may provide that it shall terminate on the happening of some stipulated, future, uncertain event, as, for instance, a conveyance so worded that it would create a life estate in the widow that would terminate on her remarriage.

Whenever a greater and a lesser estate in real property vest in the same person, the lesser estate is merged into the greater and is terminated. If the interest of a life tenant is conveyed to the remainderman or reversioner, or the fee of the remainderman or reversioner is conveyed to the life tenant, the life estate is terminated by merger, since the interest of both the life tenant and the remainderman or reversioner vests in the same person. If the remainder or reversion is vested in two or more persons, a conveyance of the life estate to one of the remaindermen or reversioner will not terminate the life estate, since both the greater and the lesser estates, in such situation, are not vested in one and the same person.

A life estate may be terminated by forfeiture. Under the statutes of some states a life tenant forfeits his estate by the willful commission of waste.[12] Also, under the statutes of some states the life tenant forfeits his estate if he fails to pay taxes and permits the property to be sold on tax sale, and then fails to redeem the property within the permitted period.

On the termination of the life estate, all the rights of the life tenant and those claiming under him are cut off. One exception to this general rule is the right of the life tenant or a lessee of the life tenant to harvest annual crops planted before the termination of the tenancy.[13]

## Life Estates and Estate Planning

The conventional life estate has long been used as a vehicle for estate planning by owners of substantial real estate holdings, particularly farms. This plan of disposi-

---

[12] *McCartney et al.* v. *Titsworth et al.,* 104 N.Y.S. 45, 119 App. Div. 547.

[13] *In re Mischke's Estate,* 136 Neb. 875, 287 N.W. 760.

tion typically has taken the form of a life estate to the surviving spouse with the remainder going to the children at the subsequent death of the surviving spouse. One clear advantage to its use is that of certainty of protection of the surviving spouse for life. That is, the children cannot sell the real estate except *subject to* the right of the surviving parent to the income or use of it for life. By the same token, of course, the surviving spouse cannot sell the fee simple since he or she does not own the fee simple but only a life estate. In addition to the severe restriction upon the marketability of such property during the lifetime of the life tenant, the interests of the remaindermen must be carefully and clearly specified. As noted in connection with the conditional fee, the creation of future interests is the province of the attorney. When such dispositions are not clearly drafted, disputes may arise that can result in costly litigation. For example, in the typical use of the life estate outlined above, what happens when one of three children dies before the surviving spouse (the life tenant) dies? Does the interest of the deceased child go to the surviving brothers or sisters, or does it go to the children of the deceased child (the grandchildren of the creator of the life estate)? The answer will depend upon whether the remainder was *vested* or *contingent*.

Vested remainders create an absolute right in the remainderman that comes into being at the time the life estate comes into being. As a result, if the remainder were vested in our example above, then the interest of the deceased child would go to the grandchildren.[14] If however, the remainder were contingent or conditioned upon the fact of surviving the life tenant, then the children of the deceased child would get nothing and the two children who did survive would each get one half of the property instead of one third each. Clearly, the use of the life estate-remainder combination as an estate planning device must be carefully structured.

## Legal Life Estates

### Nature of Legal Life Estates

Legal life estates are distinguished from conventional life estates by the fact that they arise by implication of law from the marriage relationship. They were intended at common law to make some provision for the surviving spouse in the lands acquired by the other spouse during the marriage. The legal life estates were designed to take effect at the time of the death of the land-owning spouse

---

[14] *Witcher* v. *Witcher*, 231 Ga. 49 (1973).

for the benefit of the surviving spouse, who had no ownership interest in such property. These interests are *dower* (the right of the surviving wife in real estate purchased by her deceased husband during the marriage) and *curtesy* (the right of the surviving husband in his deceased wife's real estate purchased during the marriage). The nature of the interest under both dower and curtesy under the common law was a life estate in a fractional portion of each parcel of land purchased during the marriage by the deceased spouse.

In order to protect each spouse from the defeat of the survivor's interest by a transfer of ownership made during lifetime, the common law rules recognized that the interests arose during lifetime and attached to all real estate purchased by either spouse individually during the marriage. That is, dower or curtesy came into existence at the time the property was acquired; however, it did not become a freehold estate in the land until the death of the purchasing spouse with the other surviving. During the interim the interest of dower or curtesy was said to be *inchoate,* or unperfected, and did not become a true estate in land until the acquiring spouse died, leaving the holder of the inchoate interest surviving, at which time the interest became *consummate.*

Until the spouse who purchased the property died, the dower or curtesy interest of the other spouse did not ripen into a freehold estate; but it was throughout the marriage potentially a freehold estate, until the death of the spouse holding the inchoate interest. If, of course, the spouse holding the dower or curtesy interest in the other's real estate predeceased him or her, the interest never ripened into a present possessory interest. On the other hand, unless and until the holder of the inchoate interest died, the ownership interest of the purchasing spouse was rendered unmarketable without some formal release of the inchoate dower or curtesy interest.

Largely as a result of these highly technical rules, modern probate and property laws have substantially modified the interests of dower and curtesy. In some states the interest has been converted to a fee simple interest and, in others, the interests are limited to real estate actually owned at the time of death. In the majority of states, however, neither interest is recognized at all, and the surviving spouse is protected by being given a mandatory minimum share of *all* of the deceased spouse's estate, personal property and money as well as real estate. As a result, the problems generated by the inchoate interest during lifetime and the consummate interest after death in property that was sold by the purchasing spouse are avoided and the property made marketable.

It must be noted, however, that in a minority of states some form of dower and curtesy is still recognized and must be dealt with. In these states reference must be made to local law to determine the extent of the interest recognized. In most states where dower and curtesy are still recognized, the inchoate interest can be transferred by the signature of the spouse holding the interest on the deed of the purchasing spouse when the property is sold. Such an execution will be effective to transfer the interest, even though the public records will not reveal that he or she has any present interest in the property.

## Leasehold Estates

While leasehold estates or leases are of such significance that they are discussed in great detail in a separate chapter, it is important to note at this point the fact that a leasehold estate is an *estate in land* that is created by a contract between the landlord and the tenant known as a lease. As our common law has developed the concept of the leasehold estate, it has given recognition to certain very important rights held by the tenant. As we shall later see, the tenant is theoretically the "owner" of the real estate for many purposes, even though his interest will last only as long as the term of his lease. In many ways the rights of the tenant under a lease are quite similar to those of the holder of a life estate. In the development of the bundle-of-rights concept, it is therefore important that this significant interest be noted at this point, even though the detailed discussion is reserved for a later time.

## Nature of the Relationship

The relationship of landlord and tenant comes into being as the result of an agreement between the owner of the real estate (the landlord or lessor) and one to whom the possession and use of the property is transferred for some period of time (the tenant or lessee); this agreement is referred to as a *lease*. In view of the widespread use of this relationship, today it is somewhat surprising to find that the legal rules that govern this relationship have been so slow to develop. What we are witnessing today in this area of real estate law is a truly dramatic change, not just in the application and interpretation of time-honored legal rules, but indeed a sudden change in or abandonment of these rules. Throughout this chapter it is important to bear in mind that, in residential leases particularly, the rules and their application are in a state of flux. We are considering here, from the tenant's standpoint, an essential service: housing. Regardless of the fact that from the landlord's standpoint the ownership of leased residential property is a strictly business matter, the same is not true for the lessee, the consumer.

While the legal principles discussed in this chapter represent the law today, they are subject to substantial change on short notice. Technical rules that have always governed the landlord and tenant relationship are giving way to rules of essential fairness as seen by our courts and legislatures in the light of consumerism.

### Leases, Easements, and Licenses

Leases, easements, and licenses have common characteristics, and in some transactions, elements of each may be present. For example, if a fence or side of a building is leased for the purpose of placing signs thereon, the elements of an easement or license predominate. On the other hand, if land is leased for the purpose of erecting billboards thereon, the characteristics of a lease predominate. Other transactions that present similar problems are, for instance, "leases" of a department in a department store, crop leases, and lodging arrangements. In such mixed transactions the courts, in determining the rights of the parties, usually give the terms of the agreement major weight but, at the same time, give some consideration to the fairness and justice of the result of applying the rules of law of leases, easements, or licenses.[15]

### Essential Elements of Relation

Although the relation of landlord and tenant arises from contract, the reservation of rent is not essential to the creation of the relation.[16] However, it is essential to the relation that the occupancy by the tenant occur by permission of the landlord and, in addition, be in subordination to the rights of the landlord. That is, the landlord must retain such an interest in the leased property that the tenant's rights will revert to the landlord on the termination of the tenant's right of occupancy. For example, if a tenant assigns all his interest in the lease to another, the relation is that of assignor and assignee, since the tenant (assignor) has retained no rights in the leased property. But if a tenant contracts with another to permit that person to occupy a portion of the leased property or to occupy the leased property for a period of time less than the term of the tenant's lease, the relation of landlord and tenant will arise, since the person to whom the right of occupancy is granted holds in subordination to the original tenant, and on the termination of the occupancy the rights granted revert to the original tenant.[17]

---

[15] *Thiokol Chemical Corporation* v. *Morris County Board of Taxation,* 41 N.J. 405, 197 A.2d 176.

[16] *Peerless Sugar Co., Inc.* v. *35 Steuben St. Realty Corp.,* 66 N.Y.S.2d 839.

[17] *Fairmont Park Raceway, Inc.* v. *Commissioner of International Revenue,* 327 F.2d 780, 784.

### Importance of Leases

The law of landlord and tenant is complex and, in many areas, archaic. Nevertheless, the lease transaction is extremely important in the real estate business because it permits one party to have the use of property that belongs to another. The interest in real estate that the tenant acquires under the lease can be substantial, approaching complete ownership, and can be used as security for financing in some cases. The fact that the law in this area is cumbersome and outdated is a matter of great concern in many quarters. While change has been slow to come in the past and may be slow to come in the future, the matter is receiving attention. The reader's attention is directed to the "Model Residential Landlord-Tenant Code" prepared by the American Bar Foundation with financial support for the project from the Office of Economic Opportunity. This work represents an effort to codify the law surrounding the landlord-tenant relationship and to clarify the rights and duties of the parties. Some form of codification appears likely in many states within the relatively near future.

## Leasehold Estates

There are four types of leasehold estates: (1) estates for years, (2) estates from year to year (or period to period), (3) estates at will, and (4) estates at sufferance.

### Estates for Years

An estate for years includes all leaseholds that are to continue for a definite or ascertained period of time. The estate for years may be a leasehold for one year, for less than one year, or for more than one year. A lease for six months is a lease for years; likewise, a 99-year lease is a lease for years. A lease for years gives the lessee the right to possess and use the leased property to the exclusion of all other persons, including the landlord, and on the termination of such a lease the lessee owes a duty to vacate the premises. The rights of the lessor (landlord) and lessee (tenant) may, however, be altered by agreements in the lease.

### Estates from Year to Year

An estate from year to year—or from period to period, as it is sometimes termed—may be created by agreement or by operation of law. The distinguishing characteristic of this estate is that it continues for successive periods until one of the parties ends it by giving notice of termination. The landlord and tenant may enter into an agreement whereby real estate is let by the month or by the year, the relationship to continue for an indefinite number of months or years.

The estate is also created when a tenant for years holds over and the landlord acquiesces in the holding-over. Usually, the acceptance of rent is conclusive proof of the landlord's acquiescence. Other acts on the part of the landlord may be sufficient proof of his acquiescence.

If the estate from year to year is created by the tenant's holding over, the courts have held that the successive periods of the lease will be for the term of the original lease, provided the period is less than one year; but in no event will the successive periods be more than one year. For example, if the original tenancy was for one year, six months, one month, or one week, the successive periods of the estate from year to year would be one year, six months, one month, or one week, respectively; but if the original lease was for five years, the resulting estate from year to year would be for successive periods of one year.

In order to terminate an estate from year to year, either the landlord or the tenant must give proper notice. The time at which notice must be given is generally set out in the statutes of the state; in some states the form of notice and the service of the notice are stipulated in the same statutes. As a general rule, in order to terminate an estate from week to week, one week's notice is required; in order to terminate an estate from month to month, one month's notice is necessary. There is little uniformity in the statutory time for giving notice to terminate an estate from year to year. The time ranges from six months to three months.

On June 15, 1959, Flynn entered into a written agreement with Dworkin to rent described premises and took possession on the same date. Flynn continued in possession of the premises and paid the required rental therefor until September 14, 1961, at which time he vacated the property after having advised the landlord by letter of his intention so to do.

The agreement, Section 5, reads as follows: "5. The within premises are hereby rented for a period of 12 months, commencing June 15, 1959, and this agreement shall automatically renew itself thereafter, meaning continuously for like periods, unless tenant shall give to landlord not less than thirty days' written notice, prior to the expiration of the term then running, of tenant's intention to terminate said tenancy at the expiration of the then existing time. . . ."

The agreement was not executed as provided by the statutes of the state, and the court held that the lease was void. Suit was brought to recover rent for the unexpired portion of the 12-month period (September 14, 1961 to June 14, 1962). The trial court held for Flynn; but on appeal, the judgment was reversed, and judgment was entered for rent as claimed.

Presiding Judge Kovachy said: "However, it is also the law that while a lease in excess of three years that is not attested and acknowledged is void, the lessee in possession thereunder is, nevertheless, a tenant from year to year at the will of the lessor and subject to all the provisions of the lease excepting duration.

"The defendant tenant here started a 'third period of 12 months' on June 15, 1961, when he continued in possession of the premises without giving the landlords written notice thirty days prior to the expiration of the term, then running, of an intention to terminate his tenancy at the expiration of the then existing term as provided in the lease and by reason thereof made himself liable for the payment of rental until the end of the 'period of 12 months' namely: June 14, 1962.

"The Supreme Court in *Baltimore & Ohio Railroad Co.* v. *West,* stated the law in the syllabus as follows:

'1. An entry under a lease for a term of years at an annual rent, void for any cause, and payment of rent under it, creates a tenancy from year to year upon the terms of the lease, except as to its duration.

'2. Where, after the expiration of the term, the tenant holds over and pays rent for a part of another year, without any new agreement with the landlord, he becomes a tenant for that year at the same rent, and cannot terminate the tenancy before the end of the year without the landlord's consent.

'3. The obligation of the tenant to pay the rent for the year, in such case, is not within the statute of frauds; the holding over being equivalent to a new entry.' " *Frank* v. *Flynn,* Ohio App., 197 N.E.2d 657 (1964).

## Tenancy at Will

A tenancy at will is an estate that gives the tenant the right to possession with the consent of the landlord. It may be created by express agreement or by implication of law,[18] and during its existence the tenant has all the rights incident to the relation of landlord and tenant. The term of the estate at will is indefinite, and either party may terminate it by the giving of proper notice. At common law an estate at will was terminable without notice; but today, notice is generally required, frequently because of statutory requirements. The statutes of some states set out the time for the giving of notice, and some statutes provide the form of notice that shall be used and the method of service of notice. In those states that require notice but have no statutory requirements, reasonable notice must be given. The estate at will is terminated by the death of either the landlord or the tenant.

## Tenancy at Sufferance

A tenancy at sufferance arises when the tenant comes into possession of the real property lawfully and then, after his rights have expired, holds possession of the premises without the consent of the person entitled to possession. The

---

[18] *In re Wilson's Estate,* 349 Pa. 646, 37 A.2d 709.

estate at sufferance is not a true estate in land at all. The reason for characterizing the interest of the tenant who wrongfully holds over at the expiration of valid lease is to distinguish that "tenant" from a mere trespassor. A trespassor has no right to possession and, indeed the taking of possession is wrongful at the outset. The same is not true of the tenant who holds over: his initial possession was not unlawful and he must therefore be treated with more care than a trespassor.

An estate at sufferance may be converted into an estate at will or an estate from year to year by the acquiescence of the owner of the real estate. If a mortgagor holds over after default, foreclosure, sale, and expiration of the redemption period, and the other interested person consents, either expressly or impliedly, to the holding-over, an estate at will generally results; but if a tenant for years holds over with the consent of the landlord, an estate from year to year generally results. No notice is required to terminate an estate at sufferance. The tenant is in possession without any right of possession and is therefore not entitled to notice.

## Homestead

In its popular sense the term *homestead* signifies the dwelling house in which the family resides. Homestead laws provide that the homestead shall be immune from seizure to satisfy creditors. Homestead rights were unknown at common law. They are peculiar to the United States and are created either by the constitutions or by the statutes of the several states. The objective of homestead laws is the protection of the family against eviction from its home by creditors. The homestead laws, in general, protect the wife and family from the improvidence of the husband and, in some states, give the widow protection against the creditors of the husband in addition to the protection afforded her by her dower rights.

The homestead laws of the states having such laws are not uniform in their wording or in their scope; consequently, our discussion of homestead rights must be very general.

In order to create a homestead, (1) there must be a family, (2) the family must occupy the premises as a home, and (3) the head of the family or household must have an ownership interest in the property. In some states the homestead interest attaches by operation of law; in others the homestead interest must be perfected by a filing, as required by the state statutes.

Although there is considerable diversity in the wording of the homestead statutes as to what constitutes a family, there must be, as a general rule, two or more persons living together as a unit under one head, who owns a property interest in the premises, and who owes some duty of support to the other members of the unit. Usually, the husband is the head of the family; but if the husband is dead or has abandoned the family, or if the husband and wife are divorced and the wife has custody of the children, the widow or wife could qualify as the head of the family. In fact, anyone supporting the other members of the unit, if he is under a legal or moral obligation to do so, could qualify, under the homestead laws of most states, as the head of a family.

To constitute a homestead, the premises must be occupied by the family as a home. The householder, in order to claim homestead rights in the premises, need not own the property in fee but must have some property rights in it. He may, for instance, have a determinable fee or life estate; he may be purchasing the property on contract, thereby acquiring an equitable interest; he may have a lease on the premises; or he may own as joint tenant or as a tenant in common with others. His homestead rights cannot exceed his property interest in the premises.

The courts of some states have held that the homestead laws of the state create an estate in the homestead property, whereas the courts of other states have held that their homestead laws do not create an estate in the property but exempt it from sale for the obligations of the householder.

There are some differences as to the protection provided by the homestead laws of the several states. Under the laws of some states the homestead is not protected against debts in existence at the time of the declaration of the homestead; whereas under the homestead laws of other states the homestead is protected against all debts, regardless of when created. The homestead laws do not protect against liens and encumbrances on the property at the time the homestead claimant acquired it nor against mechanics' liens acquired for reason of improvement of the homestead property, nor against taxes and assessments.

The homestead may be mortgaged or conveyed; but as a general rule, if the householder is married, his or her spouse must join in the execution of the mortgage or deed. Under the laws of some states the mortgage or deed must contain a clause expressly waiving homestead rights.

### Extent of Homestead

The extent of the property that may be claimed as a homestead varies widely. It will depend somewhat on whether the property in which the homestead is claimed is an urban home or a farm home. In the case of an urban home the property may be limited, for instance, to a single-family dwelling and the lot on which it stands; whereas in the case of a farm home the property may be limited to the home and the outbuildings and not to exceed 40 acres of land on which they stand. In some instances a dollar value may be placed on the homestead, such as, for instance, "not exceeding $8,000 in value."

Under the laws of the states the homestead, on the death of the householder, passes to the surviving spouse and minor children, and is not subject to the debts of the deceased householder. As a general rule, under such statutes the widow has no homestead right in property that was not occupied as a homestead at her husband's death. However, under the laws of some states the widow and minor children are entitled to homestead rights in the property of the deceased husband, even though he had made no declaration of homestead during his lifetime. Such homesteads are known as *probate homesteads.*

### Termination of Homestead

The homestead rights in property may be lost by abandonment. Whether or not a householder has abandoned the homestead is primarily a question of intention to be determined from all the surrounding circumstances. A temporary cessation of occupancy is not an abandonment. The declaration of a homestead in other property or the use of the property for purposes not permitted for a homestead is an abandonment.

## Easements

### Nature of Easement

An easement is a nonpossessory interest in the real estate of another. It is an interest in land and is classed as real estate but is not an estate in land. It is intangible and does not carry with it any rights or interest in the corpus of the land. An easement may be appurtenant or in gross, and may be affirmative or negative.

To have an easement appurtenant, there must be two tracts of land owned by different parties. The one tract having the benefit of the easement is known as the *dominant tenement,* and the tract subject to the easement is known as the *servient tenement.* The dominant and servient tenements do not have to be adjoining tracts of land, but one of the termini of the easement must be on the dominant tenement. For example, dominant tenement lot A, which is at the north end of a block of lots, could have an easement of right of way over servient tenement lot E, which is at the south end of the block and lots, even though lot A is separated from lot E by lots B, C, and D, and each is owned by a different owner, provided one of the termini of the easement is located on lot A. If it were necessary for the right of way to begin on lot B, C, or D, then lot A could not have an easement of right of way over lot E.

An easement appurtenant is considered as part of the dominant tenement, and on the conveyance of the dominant tenement the easement passes with the title. In assessing the dominant tenement for taxation, the value of the easement is included. The easement is an encumbrance on the servient tenement, and any conveyance of the servient tenement is subject to the encumbrance of the easement. An illustration is set out below:

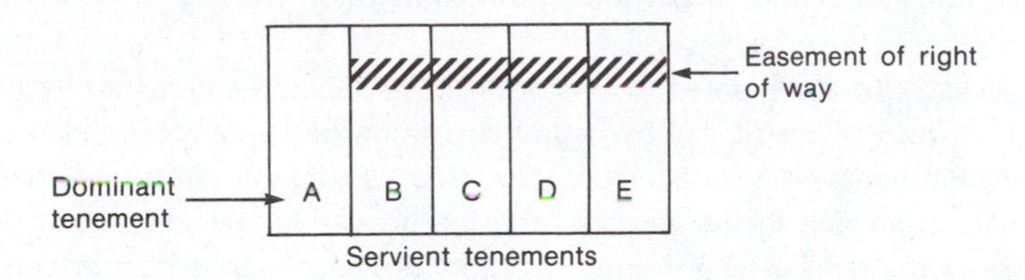


Lots B, C, D, and E in the above illustration are all, of course, servient tenements to lot A. Such an easement of right of way is affirmative because it creates a positive right on the part of whoever owns lot A to make use of the other lots.

### Affirmative and Negative Easements

An easement may be affirmative or negative. An affirmative easement is the right to make some use of the property of another, such as an easement of right of way over the land of another. A negative easement is the right to have another refrain from making certain lawful use of his land. For example, an easement of light and air is the right to have an adjoining landowner refrain from erecting on his land a structure that will cut off light and air from the property of the owner of the easement.

In the illustration used above, if the right in favor of lot A were the right to have the owners of lots B, C, D, and E "refrain from erecting any structures thereon to a heighth in excess of 20 feet," the diagram would then illustrate a negative easement because the owners of the servient tenements are restricted from making some use of their properties that they would otherwise have the right to exercise.

If, on the other hand, the deeds of all five of the owners contained such a limitation this would be an illustration of *reciprocal* negative easements.[19]

### Easements in Gross

An easement in gross is a mere personal interest in, or right to use, the land of another. It is not appurtenant to any estate in land. At common law an easement in gross was purely a personal right; it could not be assigned, conveyed, or inher-

---

[19] *Land Developers, Inc.* v. *Maxwell,* 537 S.W.2d 904 (Tenn. 1976).

ited. This is still true if the easement in gross is held by an individual and the benefits to be derived from the easement are personal in their nature. However, it is not true if the easement is one that is sometimes referred to as a *commercial easement in gross,* such as a railroad right of way, or the right of way for a pipeline or high-tension lines, for examples. Such an easement in gross may be assigned or conveyed and, if owned by an individual, may be inherited.

Smith owned lot M and granted to Didion Brothers, Inc., an easement of right of way over lot M "for use as a walkway by pedestrians from the Hultz Manor Plan of Lots to and from the Pittsburgh Railways Company car stop." Didion Brothers, Inc., had divided a tract of land adjoining lot M and sold the lots to various persons. Smith interfered with the use of the right of way by the residents of Hultz Manor Plan of Lots, and an action was brought to enjoin Smith from further interference. Smith contended that the easement granted to Didion Brothers, Inc., was an easement in gross and could not be assigned. The court held that the easement was an easement appurtenant and enjoined further interference with its use.

Judge Montgomery said: "An easement will never be presumed to be a mere personal right when it can fairly be construed to be appurtenant to some other estate. Whether an easement is in gross or appurtenant must be determined by the fair interpretation of the grant or reservation creating the easement, aided if necessary by the situation of the parties and the surrounding circumstances.

"We have no trouble in finding that the easement in this case was appurtenant to the land owned by Didion Brothers, Inc., in the Hultz Manor Plan. Clearly, it was intended to benefit the Didions in the use of their land, and not personally." *Rusciolelli* v. *Smith,* 195 Pa. Super. 562, 171 A.2d 802 (1961).

From the discussion in the above case it should be apparent that the personal easement in gross will be seldom encountered in practice. In modern real estate practice, when something less than an easement appurtenant is intended the parties are more likely to cover the matter by a carefully worded description of rights being created. The *license,* discussed later, is more likely to be the result than is a personal easement in gross.

## Acquisition of Easement

An easement may be acquired by express grant, by a reservation in a grant, by implication, by estoppel, by necessity, or by prescription. Under the statutes of most states a grant of an easement must be executed with the same formality as is the grant of a fee in real estate. There is some controversy as to the creation of an easement by an exception or a reservation in a deed. For example, suppose that Anthony is the owner in fee of 80 acres of land. Anthony deeds 40 acres of the land to Bates and includes in the deed a clause excepting and reserving, for the benefit of the 40 acres retained, an easement of right of way over the 40 acres sold. Some courts have held that since no easement could exist at the time of the conveyance (a person cannot have an easement in his own property), an easement cannot be created by exception. An easement could probably be reserved in such a case.

Under the modern rule followed in most states, the courts would hold that an easement can be created by either an exception or a reservation. Some conveyancers recommend that instead of attempting to create an easement by exception or reservation in a deed, the grantee named in the deed execute a separate grant giving to the grantor of the property the desired easement right. If this practice is followed, the uncertainty surrounding the effectiveness of an exception or reservation in a deed is avoided.

An easement by implication may be created when the circumstances surrounding the transfer indicate with reasonable certainty that the parties had intended to create the easement. An easement by implication is an exception to the rule that an easement can be created only by a grant in writing. In order to have an easement created by implication, there must be in existence a quasi easement that must be apparent, reasonably permanent, and reasonably necessary to the enjoyment of the dominant tenement. For example, if the grantor,[20] at the time the grantee acquired title, was using one portion of her land for the benefit of the portion sold, it would indicate that the parties intended the benefits to continue.

An easement by estoppel arises when the grantor conveys a part of her land, knowing that the grantee intends to make a certain use of the part granted that will interfere with the enjoyment of the part retained. The grantee will have an easement that will enable her to make the intended specific use of her land.

An easement by necessity arises when it is necessary for the enjoyment of the part of the land granted. For example, if Adams grants land to Bates, and this land is so located that Bates cannot reach it unless he travels over the land retained by Adams or over the land of others, Bates would have an easement of right of way by necessity over the land of Adams.

An easement is acquired by prescription when the claimant has made use of the land, for the prescriptive period, openly, notoriously, continuously, and exclusively, with claim of right and adversely to the owner. It is analogous to the acquisition of possessory rights in land by adverse possession.[21] (Adverse possession is discussed in detail in Chapter 11.)

---

[20] *Lane* v. *Flautt,* 176 Md. 620, 6 A.2d 228.

[21] *Mumrow* v. *Riddle,* 67 Mich. App. 693 (1976).

Richardson owned adjoining lots 5 and 6. A building had been constructed on lot 6, the eaves of which overhung lot 5 by about sixteen inches. In 1949, Richardson constructed a building on lot 5, and the rainwater from the roof of the building on lot 6 was discharged on the roof of the building of lot 5. Lot 5 and the building thereon were sold by Richardson, Brannin's predecessor in title, in the year 1954. Lot 6 and the building thereon were conveyed by Richardson to Tangner in the year 1954. The deeds to the lots conveyed to each grantee rights in a party wall. Brannin sued Tangner to recover a judgment for damage to his building caused by water dripping from the eaves of Tangner's building onto his building. Tangner claimed that he had an easement right to discharge the water onto Brannin's building. The court held that Tangner had an implied easement as claimed.

Justice Welch said: "A deed may, of course, grant or reserve an easement and the instrument should be construed to carry out the intention of the parties. But an easement may be implied also and the intention of the parties is determined by all the facts and circumstances in order that effect may be given to the apparent intent. An implied easement is based upon the theory that whenever one conveys property he includes in the conveyance whatever is necessary for the use and enjoyment of the land retained. . . .

"There is ample evidence in the case at bar indicative of knowledge by the plaintiffs of the servitude of the property they purchased. The existence of the party-wall clause in the deed by which plaintiffs acquired title to Lot 5 directed attention to the probability of the overhanging of the roof-eave. Ordinary observation would have confirmed it as a fact." *Tangner* v. *Brannin,* Okla., 381 p.2d 321 (1963).

## Rights and Duties of Parties to Easements

The scope and extent of an easement depend on the wording of the grant or, if acquired by prescription, on the use made by the dominant tenement at the time of acquisition. The owner of the servient tenement may use the entire premises for any purpose he or she desires so long as such use does not interfere with the enjoyment of the easement.

The owner of the servient tenement may erect gates or put up bars across a right of way if they do not unreasonably interfere with its use. An easement that gives the owner exclusive possession of a portion of the premises, such as a railroad right of way, does not give the owner of the easement the right to drill oil or gas wells thereon. Such use would be in excess of the scope of the easement; however, some limited additional use of such an easement may be permitted where the added use does not increase the burden on the land. For example, a power company having a commercial easement in gross to construct and maintain power lines may "sublet" its right to a cable television company to use the same easement for the purpose of transmitting television signals.[22]

---

[22] *Jolliff* v. *Hardin Cable Television Co.,* 26 Ohio St. 2d 103, 269 N.E.2d 588 (1971).

The owner of the easement must keep the affected part of the servient tenement in repair and has the right to enter upon the servient tenement for the purpose of making repairs or improvements reasonably necessary to the enjoyment of the easement. If the easement is acquired for the general benefit of the dominant tenement, a change in the use of the dominant tenement will not affect the easement. However, if the easement is limited in its scope, its use will be confined to the designated scope.

Also, if the owner of the dominant tenement acquires additional property adjoining the dominant tenement, the easement cannot be enlarged to include use for the benefit of the additional property. For example, suppose that Albert owns a factory and the land upon which it stands, and has an easement of right of way over the land of Bates. Albert purchases an additional tract of land adjacent to his factory and enlarges his factory so that it is partly on the additional tract of land. Albert cannot use the right of way over the land of Bates for the benefit of the enlarged factory.[23] The scope of an easement may be enlarged by prescription.

### Description of Easement

If an easement is imperfectly described in a grant, or in an exclusion or reservation clause in a grant, a court will interpret the instrument and resolve the uncertainties and, if necessary, establish the location of the easement.

### Extinguishment of Easement

An easement is extinguished if the ownership of the fee of both the dominant and the servient tenement is in the same person; but this rule does not apply if one of the tenements is held in a representative capacity. For example, Albert may own the dominant tenement in his own right and have title to the servient tenement as trustee for Bates.

An easement granted for a specific purpose or for a limited time, or an easement by necessity, is extinguished by the fulfillment of the purpose, the expiration of the time, or the ceasing of the necessity. Also, an easement is extinguished by abandonment. A mere nonuse of an easement without an accompanying intent to relinquish the right to it is not an abandonment of the easement.

An easement may be extinguished by prescription. If the owner of the servient tenement uses his land in a manner inconsistent with the rights of the owner of

---

[23] *D. M. Goodwillie Co.* v. *Commonwealth Electric Co.,* 241 Ill. 42, 89 N.E. 272.

the easement and continues such use for the statutory period, the easement will be extinguished. The sale of the servient tenement for nonpayment of taxes does not extinguish the easement.

### Unrecorded Easement

An unrecorded easement created by a grant will be extinguished by a conveyance of the servient tenement to a bona fide purchaser for value who has no notice or knowledge of the existence of the easement.[24]

## Profits

A profit in land, technically known as a *profit a pendre,* is the right to take part of the soil or produce of land owned by someone else. The term includes the right to take soil, gravel, minerals, oil, gas, and the like from the land of another. A profit is like an easement in almost all respects. It may be appurtenant—that is, the profits may be taken only for the benefit of the dominant tenement—or it may be in gross.

Frequently, it is difficult to determine whether a grant conveys a fee in the minerals underlying the surface or conveys a profit in the land. The wording of the grant, interpreted in the light of the surrounding circumstances, will determine the nature of the interest conveyed.

Because of the highly technical nature of the rights created by a true *profit a pendre* they are seldom seen, and when they do occur they can prove to be quite troublesome.

A deed executed in 1868 by Eldred to Miller conveyed certain real estate and granted the "privilege of . . . obtaining sand outside of said boundaries for building roads and sanding . . ." a cranberry bog located on the conveyed land; through a series of conveyances the land was acquired in 1930 by Hardy, who opened a sandpit operation on the adjoining property. In a petition to register title to the land free of any claim by Hardy, it was decided that a true *profit a pendre* had been intended that gave the successor owner the right to continue to remove sand from the adjoining property. *Gray* v. *Hardy,* Supr. Jud Ct. Mass., 208 N.E. Vol. 829 (1965).

Because it is an interest in land a *profit a pendre* must be created with the degree of formality required of other interests; a written conveyance.[25]

---

[24] Recording of instruments and the effects of recording on the rights of parties will be discussed in a subsequent chapter.

[25] *Van Camp* v. *Menominee Enterprises, Inc.,* 68 Wis Vol. 332, 228 NW Vol. 664 (1975).

## Licenses

A license is a privilege to go upon the land of another. It is not an estate in land and is personal to the one to whom it is given; and it has been held with some exceptions, that a license cannot be assigned or inherited. Since a license is not an interest in land, it can be created orally.

Permission to hunt or fish on the land of another is an example of a typical license, as is also the right of a person to attend a theatrical performance or ball game after purchasing a ticket.

As a general rule, a license is revocable at the will of the licensor. If the license is created by contract, written or oral, and is to continue for a specified time, the licensor, under the general rule, may revoke the license at any time. However, if his revocation would be a breach of the contract granting the license, he would be liable to the licensee for damages for breach of the contract.

Under some circumstances, a license has been held to be irrevocable. For example, if a license that contemplates expenditures on the part of the licensee in the improvement of the premises is granted, it has been held by some courts that after substantial expenditures have been made, the power of revocation is suspended until the term of the license expires or the purpose of the license is accomplished.[26] The effect of such a holding is to convert a license into an easement. Some courts have refused to hold such cases to be exceptions to the general rule.

An oral grant of an easement that is unenforceable under the statute of frauds creates a license that is revocable before it is acted upon. Some courts have held that when the oral grant has been acted upon and the grantee has expended substantial sums in the improvement of the premises, he has an easement; but other courts do not so hold.[27]

Du Bose contracted to sell to Bishop timber to be cut by Bishop from a tract of land owned by Du Bose. The contract was in writing and, in addition to stating the price per thousand feet to be paid for logs cut, provided that the seller had the right to direct the portions of the tract from which the trees were to be cut. It did not state the quantity of timber to be cut, nor did it state that all merchantable timber on the tract should be cut.

After Bishop had cut between 30,000 and 40,000 feet of timber, Du Bose ordered him to cease cutting timber and denied him the right to come onto the land. Bishop sued Du Bose to recover damages for breach of contract. Bishop claimed that he had acquired title to the timber on the tract. Du Bose claimed that the contract was unenforce-

[26] *Binder* v. *Weinberg,* 94 Miss. 817, 48 So. 1013.

[27] *Baird* v. *Westberg,* 341 Ill. 616, 173 N.E. 820.

able for uncertainty of terms and that Bishop had only a license to cut timber. The court gave judgment to Bishop, and Du Bose appealed. The judgment was reversed.

Justice Moore said: "The contract in the case at bar is not a conveyance of standing timber. Defendant 'agrees to sell' and plaintiff 'agrees to pay for . . . logs on the stump' from defendant's Avery Creek farm at a specified price per thousand feet to be paid before removal of the logs from the land. This is an executory contract for sale of 'logs,' title to pass after logs are severed, measured, and paid for, with license to enter the land, sever and remove the logs.

"A contract to remove timber, providing for measurement of logs before removal from the premises and for payment at the time the logs are measured and containing no direct promise on the part of the buyer to sever or pay for the timber in any event, lacks mutuality to pass present title and is a mere license revocable at any time by the landowner without liability. 'A license to enter on land and cut timber, while it remains executory, is revocable at any time. It is revocable at the will of the licensor, and terminates when he gives notice not to cut the timber further or refuses permission of the licensee to perform.' However, there are exceptions to this rule: (1) a license coupled with an interest may not be revoked; (2) 'a license cannot be revoked as to acts done under it; the revocation is prospective not retrospective'; (3) . . . Where the licensee has made expenditures upon the faith of the license, . . . it cannot be revoked at the will of the licensor unless the license is placed in statu quo.

"Plaintiff's evidence fails to bring him within either of the enumerated exceptions." *Bishop* v. *Du Bose,* 252 N.C. 158, 113 S.E.2d 309 (1960).

To contrast the license with the easement that runs with the land and can therefore be effectively transferred to successive owners of the benefitted property, a recent case may be illustrative:

Present property owner's predecessor in title had the right to the use of the swimming pool on the adjoining property by virtue of its creation in a contract of purchase. This right was not, however, included in the deed by which the predecessor took title. In a suit to enforce an easement that ran with the land, the court determined that the earlier agreement created merely a license and that it could not be transferred to the present owner as an interest that ran with the land. *Bunn* v. *Offutt,* 22 S.E.2d 522 (Va. 1976).

## Interests in Land

### Estates in Land

***Fee Simple Absolute.*** Includes all rights of ownership recognized by our law today; includes the power to create lesser interests in the real estate; because potentially perpetual in nature, it is an inheritable interest; may be freely bought and sold.

***Fee Simple Determinable.*** Includes all rights of ownership as the fee simple absolute, but is *conditional* and either will or may terminate by the occurrence of the condition that defeats it; limited saleability because of the condition.

***Life Estates.*** Include *most* of the rights of ownership; a true estate in land because it includes ownership rights for an *indefinite* period of time; lasts for a life (or lives) and, by definition, is therefore not inheritable; estate terminates at end of measuring life; rights of holder are significant but may not encroach upon the interests of the remainderman's succeeding fee interest.

***Leasehold Estates.*** Include many rights of ownership, such as exclusive possession and use, but for a specific period of time; this period may be lengthy but does have specific termination point at which landlord resumes full ownership. Covered in detail in Chapter 19.

### Limited Interests in Land

***Easements.*** Include only limited rights to use land belonging to another, but may be quite significant; even though extent of use is limited, the length of time may be quite extensive, even perpetual.

***Profits.*** Permit the actual taking of some product from the land of another and therefore significant; may last indefinitely even though of limited scope; seldom seen today because rules are archaic.

***License.*** Purely personal right to go on land of another for specific purpose; not an interest in land as such and can be terminated at will.

# Chapter 4
# Eminent Domain

## Nature and Scope of Power

Eminent domain has been defined as the right of the nation or state, or those to whom the power has been lawfully delegated, to condemn private property for public use, and to appropriate the ownership or possession of such property for such use, upon paying the owner just compensation, to be ascertained according to law.[1] This right extends to every kind of property. The power of eminent domain is an attribute of sovereignty. It is an inherent power of the state, not derived from, but limited by the fundamental principles of the constitution.[2]

The ability of the federal government to exercise the power of eminent domain is limited by the Fifth Amendment to the Constitution of the United States, which provides that (1) no person shall be deprived of life, liberty, or property without due process of law; and (2) private property shall not be taken for public use without just compensation. Like limitations are imposed on the states by the 14th Amendment, which provides, among other things, that no state shall deprive any person of life, liberty, or property without due process of law. Consequently, under the constitutional limitations imposed on the exercise of the power of eminent domain, private property can be lawfully taken only for public use, and it cannot be taken without just compensation.

---

[1] *Leonard* v. *Autocar Sales & Service Company,* 392 Ill. 182, 64 N.E.2d 477.

[2] *Public Utility District No. 1 of Pend Oreille County* v. *Inland Power & Light Company,* Wash.2d, 390 P.2d 690.

## Eminent Domain Distinguished from Other Powers

A government has, in addition to its power of eminent domain, police power and the power to tax. In relation to individual ownership of real estate, these powers have certain common characteristics. Under each, the power of the sovereign is superior to that of the individual, and it is exercised for the general welfare of the people.

Eminent domain differs from police power in the following respects:

1. Under the power of eminent domain, compensation is required, whereas under police power, the restrictions may be imposed without compensation.
2. Under the power of eminent domain, the condemned right in the property is taken from the owner and transferred to the public agency to be enjoyed by it; whereas under the police power, there is no transfer of the ownership of the property effected.
3. Under the power of eminent domain, the property is taken for public use; whereas under the police power, the use of the property is restricted for the protection of the health, safety, or general welfare of the public.

The exercise of police power and that of eminent domain have much in common, and there is no clear line of distinction between them. If an attempted restriction under the police power deprives the owner of all the profitable use of his property and leaves him with only the burden of paying taxes and other such charges, the courts have held that such restriction is in fact a taking of property without just compensation, and they will hold the restriction to be void.[3]

There is a clear distinction between the power of eminent domain and the power to tax.[4] The tax paid by a citizen is the payment of his just share of the support of the government. If a property owner fails to pay a justly assessed tax, his property may be sold at a tax sale. Property sold at a tax sale is not taken for a public use.

Under the power of eminent domain, only the property of the individual is affected, and it can be taken only for public use on payment of just compensation; whereas a tax is laid on the whole community or a class of persons in the community, and the tax constitutes the property owner's contribution to the expense of the government. A special assessment is a special tax imposed on property for the purpose of raising money to pay for an improvement that is beneficial to the property on which the tax is imposed.

---

[3] *Granger* v. *Board of Adjustment of City of Des Moines,* 241 Iowa 1356, 44 N.W.2d 399.

[4] *State of Texas ex rel. Pan American Production Co. et al.* v. *Texas City,* 157 Tex. 450, 303 S.W.2d 780.

In 1951, Eller owned approximately 13 acres of land, on which were located a house, a barn, a chicken house, and a double mushroom house. In 1952 the township enacted a zoning ordinance that classified the entire township "District A," a residential and farming district. Permitted use included a "mushroom house provided it is located at least 500 feet from the nearest official roadside line and 1,000 feet from all lot boundaries." Eller's mushroom house was 400 feet from the nearest roadside line and 180 feet from the nearest property line. His mushroom house was therefore a nonconforming use. In 1956, he was granted permission to expand his nonconforming use 100 percent. In 1959, he was denied a permit for further expansion. Eller brought action to obtain permission for the requested expansion. The trial court held that the zoning ordinance was unconstitutional; and on appeal, the order was affirmed.

Justice Roberts said: "In the words of the court below: 'Mathematical calculation of the effect of the limitations of Sec. 24 *(e)* of the Ordinance demonstrates the absurd effect of the limitations upon a permitted use in an area which is part of the acknowledged mushroom growing center of the world. A set-back of 500 feet from any roadside line and a distance of 1,000 feet from any property boundary (without considering the dimensions of the mushroom house itself) requires that a property be 1,500 feet deep from the roadside line to the rear boundary and 2,000 feet in width, containing an area of 3,000,000 square feet, or 68.86 acres. Under those requirements no property containing less than about 69 acres may have even a single mushroom house. When the dimensions of a single mushroom house are necessarily calculated in addition thereto the absurdity is more apparent, and when it is considered that not less than three double mushroom houses, each 40 × 60 feet in dimensions, will support a growing operation without economic loss the confiscatory nature of the regulation is clear, amounting to a taking of property without compensation and a violation of due process of law.'

"Appellant urges that the constitutional issue was decided in a vacuum, that the real issue is whether it is unreasonable to prohibit the location of appellee's new mushroom house 100 feet from one property line and 200 feet from another. However, the authority on which the board necessarily based its decision is the ordinance itself. Therefore, its constitutionality was a proper issue for determination." *Eller* v. *Board of Adjustment of London Britain Township,* 414 Pa. 1, 198 A.2d 863 (1964).

## Who May Exercise Power

Since the power of eminent domain is an attribute of sovereignty, it can be exercised by the federal government or by a state government. The federal government may condemn property within a state, a territory, or the District of Columbia. A state has the right to exercise its power of eminent domain only within its borders, and such right is subject to the limitations placed on it by its constitution.

The power of eminent domain may be delegated either by Congress or by a state legislature, and such power is subject only to the limitations imposed by the federal or state constitution. It must be delegated by statute, either expressly or by implications.[5]

The right to exercise the power of eminent domain may be delegated to public corporations, agencies or boards, drainage districts, road districts, park districts, school districts or other public institutions, officers, or boards. It may also be delegated to private corporations, partnerships, or individuals. The validity of the delegation of the right to exercise the power of eminent domain does not depend on the status of the party to whom the power is delegated.[6] But the power must be limited to the taking of property for a public use, and just compensation must be paid.

If the state delegates the right to exercise the power of eminent domain, such delegated rights cannot be assigned. If a corporation transfers its property and franchises to another corporation, such transfer will not vest in the transferee the transferor's right to exercise the power of eminent domain. Although the courts are not in complete accord in their decisions, they have generally held that if a corporation leases its property, it is not deprived of its right to exercise the power of eminent domain delegated to it by the legislature.[7]

A statute delegating the right to take private property from one person and transfer it to another, the property to be used for private purposes, is void. However, property may be taken from a private owner under the power of eminent domain and then leased to private operators, provided the taking is for a public use, even though the private operators may make a profit from the operation of the leased property.[8]

Exeter & Hampton Electric Co. (hereinafter referred to as Electric Co.) condemned a right of way for a high-tension line across Harding's land. The line was intended to serve Sylvania Electric Co., but Electric Co. planned to extend the line in 1967 to serve the easterly part of Exeter and Stratham. The right to condemn the property was granted to Electric Co. by the Public Utility Commission, and its power was granted by a statute that provided: "Whenever it is necessary, in order to meet the reasonable requirements of service to the public, that any public utility should construct a line . . . across the land of another . . . such public utility may petition the public utility commission for such rights and easements and for permission to take such lands or rights, as may be needed for said purpose." Harding questioned the right of Electric Co. to condemn and

[5] *Heppe et al.* v. *State of Nebraska,* 162 Neb. 403, 76 N.W.2d 255.

[6] *Central Louisiana Electric Company, Inc.* v. *Pugh et al.,* La. App. 96 So.2d 523.

[7] *Reuter et al.* v. *Milan Water Company, Inc.,* 209 Ind. 240, 198 N.E. 422.

[8] *Court Street Parking Company* v. *City of Boston et al.,* 336 Mass. 224, 143 N.E.2d 683.

contended the taking was for wholly private use. The court upheld the decision of the Commission; and on appeal, its holding was affirmed.

Justice Wheeler said: "It is elemental law that the property of an individual can not be taken for a wholly private use. The question to be determined is whether the proposed taking is for a public use, even though it will presently serve but a single customer. It will however fit into a proposed master plan to loop the town of Exeter with high voltage transmission lines and more adequately serve anticipated demands in the future. No claim is made here that such proposed service will not be open to the public generally and of service to more than one customer. The law is clear that property may be taken not only for present demands but for uses which may be fairly anticipated in the future. The evidence did not require a finding that the proposed line will benefit merely a single customer or that the condemnation is for private use for that reason." *Exeter & Electric Co.* v. *Harding,* N.H., 199 A.2d 298 (1964).

## Public Use

Under the provisions of the Constitution of the United States and the constitutions of the several states, the right to take property by the exercise of the power of eminent domain is either expressly or impliedly limited to a taking for a public use. Whether or not a particular use is a public one is a question to be determined ultimately by the courts.[9] However, if the legislature, by statute, has declared a particular use to be a public use, the courts will uphold the declaration, unless the declared use is clearly and manifestly of a private character.

If the property is condemned for a public use, the necessity and expediency of taking the property for such public use is a legislative—not a judicial—question; and as long as private property is taken only for public use, and damage caused is compensated, the legislature has power to determine, either directly or through agencies chosen by it, when convenience or necessity requires that the property be taken and what particular property shall be taken.[10] The decision of an agency chosen by the legislature that the taking of private property is necessary will not be set aside by a court except for fraud, capriciousness, or illegality.

From an early date the courts have recognized that the taking of private property for the establishment of public transportation systems is a taking for public use. The taking of land for highways is not limited only to land necessary for actual travel. It may include land for widening a highway or street for ornamental purposes, or land for parking space, or land for other similar purposes where common

---

[9] *McAuliffe & Burke Co.* v. *Boston Housing Authority,* 334 Mass. 28, 133 N.E.2d 493.

[10] *Arco Pipeline Co.* v. *3.60 Acres, More or Less,* 539 P.2d 64 (Alaska, 1975).

convenience and necessity justify the taking. The taking by eminent domain of land to be used for offstreet parking has been held to be a taking for a public use.[11]

The fact that property that has been taken for a public use is leased to an individual or a corporation for the purpose of operation or that a concession to operate is granted to an individual or corporation does not prevent the condemnation of such property if it is operated for the public benefit. Turnpikes, toll roads, and toll bridges, open to public travel, whether operated by a governmental unit or by a private concern, have been recognized as public uses for which private property may be taken under the power of eminent domain. Likewise, railroads; street railways; railroad, bus, and truck terminals; and similar transportation facilities that are used by public carriers to fulfill their obligation to serve the public are devoted to a public use and are granted the power of eminent domain. However, private property cannot be taken under the power of eminent domain by a common carrier if the property taken is not essential to the construction, maintenance, or operation of its transportation facility. For example, a railroad cannot condemn land to be used as building sites for houses for its employees, or for factories for manufacturing cars or locomotives, or for warehouses not used in connection with its freight service, or for the purpose of parks or flower gardens at a station or terminal.[12]

The furnishing of water to a community is a public use for which private property may be taken under the power of eminent domain. Also, the courts have held that irrigation, the erecting of dams, and the flowage of land for the creation of water power, the building of canals, the widening or deepening of streams for the improvement of navigation, the building of piers and docks, and so forth, are public uses for which private property may be taken under the power of eminent domain.

The taking of private property for public buildings, public schools, public institutions of higher learning, parks, and recreation facilities and for the preservation of places of historical interest, has been upheld by the courts as the taking of property for a public use.[13]

The right to take private property under the power of eminent domain in the furtherance of a slum clearance project has been held to be a taking for a public use. The taking is justified on the ground that conditions of slum areas in large cities are matters of state concern, since they affect the health, safety, and general

---

[11] *Poole et al.* v. *City of Kankakee,* 406 Ill. 521, 94 N.E.2d 416.

[12] *Potter* v. *Board of Public Utility Commissioners et al.,* 89 N.J.L. 157, 98 A. 30.

[13] *Craddock* v. *University of Louisville et al.,* Ky., 303 S.W.2d 548.

welfare of the city.[14] However, the courts have held that private property cannot be taken under the power of eminent domain for the purpose of selling lots to working people at low cost.[15]

The City of Johnson City condemned 10.63 acres of land adjacent to a city park, the land to be used as an extension of an existing golf course. The land was being condemned for "public park purposes." Cloninger brought action asking that the condemnation proceedings be dismissed on the ground that the use of the land for a golf course was not a "public use." The trial court dismissed the original condemnation; and on appeal, the judgment was reversed.

Justice White said: "The word 'park' is certainly broad enough, in the every day sense of the word, to include a golf course as well as a swimming pool, croquet court, baseball diamond, band shell, zoo, and a host of other recreational facilities to which the public normally turn for relaxation and recreation. It is stated that as long as the use is by the public through its officers or agents, or by its enjoyment of greater safety, health and comfort, eminent domain may unquestionably be employed and that this is true even though the public is to be rigorously excluded from the land taken.

"Where the question of 'public use' is a close one, the tendency of the courts is to be more liberal in favor of permitting a taking where the condemnor is the government or one of its subdivisions or agencies.

"In the instant case the public is not to be excluded; in fact, since it is a public park and municipal golf course every citizen will have the right to play on this golf course if he so chooses. It is true that there are those in the community who do not choose to play golf or are physically unable to do so, but this is true of almost any activity that is carried on in a park. To cite a few: swimming, tennis, and nature walks." *Johnson City* v. *Cloninger,* Tenn., 372 S.W.2d 281 (1963).

## Necessity

In addition to the requirement that private property taken under the power of eminent domain must be taken for a public use, the property taken must be necessary for that public use. This does not mean that the property taken must be absolutely necessary and that the objective could not be attained without the taking of the property. It means only that the taking is reasonably necessary for the accomplishment of the objective in view under the particular circumstances.[16]

---

[14] *Berman et al.* v. *Perker et al.,* 348 U.S. 26, 75 S. Ct. 98.

[15] *In re Opinion of the Justices,* 211 Mass. 624, 98 N.E. 611.

[16] *Latchis et al.* v. *State Highway Board,* 120 Vt. 120, 134 A.2d 191.

## Property Subject to Condemnation

Property of every kind and nature may be taken under the power of eminent domain. Although the taking of property under the power of eminent domain is not limited, the right to take property in a particular situation will depend on the provisions of the authorizing statute, and only such property may be taken as is expressly or impliedly authorized by the statute conferring the power.[17] The authority to condemn real estate may include not only the surface soil but everything attached thereto, and all rights and interests therein, including buildings, timber, gravel, stone, oil, gas, and minerals.

The right of the government or a governmental unit to take property already devoted to a public use presents some special problems. The courts have generally held that property devoted to a public use cannot be taken under a general authorization to take property under the power of eminent domain. However, since the legislature has the power to determine necessity, it may under some circumstances authorize the taking of property already devoted to a public use and provide that such property shall be appropriated to another public use.

Also, as a general rule, the federal government or a state may, under its sovereign power, take property that is held by an individual or private corporation, even though such property is already devoted to a public use.

Property held by the United States and by it devoted to a particular purpose cannot be taken by a state under its power of eminent domain. The authorities are not in accord as to the right of a state to condemn public lands under its power of eminent domain.

Property held by a state or municipality and devoted to a public use cannot be taken under a general authorization to condemn property; but it may be taken if the authority to take is conferred, expressly or by necessary implication, by the legislature. As a general rule, property owned by a state or municipality and not devoted to a public use may be condemned in the same manner and to the same extent as privately owned property. Property owned by one state and situated in another state occupies the position of private property.

The United States filed a complaint in condemnation against the Internal Improvement Fund of the State of Florida to acquire tidal lands held in trust for the citizens of Florida. Linning and others, as citizens and taxpayers of Florida, intervened and objected on the ground that the property was held for a public use and the United States had no power to condemn it. The district court held that the United States had the right to take the property; and on appeal, the holding was affirmed.

The court said: "Ownership by or in trust for the public does not create an ownership

---

[17] *Ellis* v. *Ohio Turnpike Commission,* 162 Ohio St. 86, 120 N.E.2d 719.

interest in individual citizens and taxpayers such as requires or permits them to be parties to a condemnation action by the United States. It is well settled that the United States may acquire for its use lands held by a State even though the land be already dedicated to a public use." *Linning* v. *United States,* 328 F.2d 603 (1964).

## Extent of Interest Acquired

The extent of the interest acquired by a taking under the power of eminent domain will depend on the authority granted by the legislature, the purpose for which the property is taken, and the interests requested in the pleadings of the party condemning the property. The state has the right to take, or to delegate the right to take, under the power of eminent domain, the fee in real estate, free from all liens and encumbrances; or it may take any lesser interest, such as a determinable fee, an easement, or a leasehold interest. If the state or an agency of the state wishes to take the fee free from all liens and encumbrances, it must join as defendant in the condemnation proceedings all parties having an interest in the condemned property.

As a general rule, under the statute authorizing condemnation, the party condemning can take no greater interest than is reasonably necessary for the public use for which the property is condemned. In no event can a greater interest be taken than that authorized by the legislature; however, if the condemnor wishes, he may take a lesser interest than he is authorized to take.

In the event the estate or interest to be taken is not definitely set out, no greater estate or interest may be taken than is reasonably necessary to accomplish the purpose of the public use for which the property is to be taken.[18]

When less than the fee of the property condemned is taken, the landowner may, as a general rule, enter upon and use the property for any purpose that is not inconsistent with the purpose for which the interest in the property was taken or that does not interfere with the accomplishment of that purpose. For example, when a railroad acquires a right of way by condemnation, it acquires only an easement; and to the extent the right of way is not presently needed for railroad purposes, it may be used by the original owner.[19]

If property has been condemned for a public use and the fee is acquired on condemnation, the property may be transferred without regard to the use to which the transferee intends to put the property. However, if the fee is acquired subject to a trust to use the property for a particular purpose, it cannot be trans-

---

[18] *City of Waukegan* v. *Stanczak et al.,* 6 Ill.2d 594, 129 N.E.2d 751.

[19] *Carolina & Northwestern Ky. Co.* v. *Piedmont Wagon & Manufacturing Co.,* 229 N.C. 695, 51 S.E.2d 301.

ferred, unless the transfer is authorized by the legislature. If less than the fee is condemned for a particular public use, the transferee, in the absence of special statutory authorization, can acquire only a right to use the property for that particular use or for a use which is incidental to the main purpose.[20]

## Compensation and Damages

The Constitution of the United States and the constitutions of the several states expressly provide that private property shall not be taken without just compensation. The constitutions of some states, in addition, provide for the payment of damages. Although it is impossible to say precisely what is meant by just compensation, the term, as it is used in law, means full indemnity or remuneration for the loss sustained as the direct result of the taking of property. Generally, no distinction is made between *compensation* and *damages,* although it has been held that *compensation* is the sum paid for the property taken and *damages* signifies the allowance made for injury to the residue of the owner's property that is not taken.[21]

The statute authorizing the taking of private property for public use is invalid if it does not make some provision for reasonable and certain compensation to the owner of the property taken and for the payment of damages to the owner of property injured, if payment of damages is required by the constitution.[22] Unless a person has an interest in the property taken, he is not entitled to compensation, even though the value of his adjoining property may be affected by the taking.[23]

### Determination of Just Compensation

The constitutional provision for the payment of just compensation for condemned property does not set up standards for its determination. That task is left to the courts, as well as the task of determining damages, if the condemnee is entitled to such.[24] All of the elements that contribute to the value of a property must be considered, weighed, and determined; and the sum total is the amount to be awarded. Such elements as loss of access to the highway, loss of business, loss of profits, the effect of restrictions on the use of the real estate, the effect of the possibility of rezoning on the value of the real estate, and loss of the value of personal property on the condemned real estate have all been considered

[20] *Rose et al.* v. *Bryant et al.,* Ky., 251 S.W.2d 860.

[21] *American Louisiana Pipe Line Company* v. *Kennerk,* 103 Ohio App. 133, 144 N.E.2d 660.

[22] *In re Opinion of the Justices,* 300 Mass. 607, 14 N.E.2d 468.

[23] *McBride et ux.* v. *Arkansas County et al.,* Tex. Civ. App., 304 S.W.2d 450.

[24] *Chick Springs Water Co., Inc.* v. *State Highway Department,* 159 S.C. 481, 157 S.E. 842.

in determining the amount of compensation or damages to be awarded a condemnee. Each case must be considered in light of its own fact situation; no rigid rules can be laid down whereby the compensation and damages to be paid for condemned property may be determined.

The courts, however, have developed standards that aid in determining compensation and damages and help give a degree of uniformity to the results. The standard generally applied is the market value of the real estate at the time it is taken. Although the term *market value* defies specific definition, it has attained a reasonably definite meaning in the business world and is frequently defined as "the price which would be agreed upon at a voluntary sale between an owner willing to sell and a buyer willing to buy."[25] The courts have held that testimony as to the price at which similar property located in the community had been recently sold is admissible evidence of market value.[26] If the property is of such a nature that it has no market value, such as a church or a cemetery, the true or intrinsic value must be sought by a consideration of other factors and circumstances. Such other factors may not include the intended use to which the condemning agency will put the property. For example, the value of land to be taken for use as a missile testing range may not be arrived at by reference to that intended use.[27]

If an entire tract is taken, the ordinary measure of compensation is the market value of the property at the time it is taken. In determining the market value, all the elements on the land—such as deposits of gravel, stone, and coal—that would affect its value must be taken into consideration.[28] Also, the possible uses that might be made of the property in the near future should be considered. For example, the fact that land taken is suitable for real estate development purposes, although the land has not been developed, should be considered in determining its value.[29] In general, the best use that may be made of the property condemned is considered in determining just compensation.

The courts are not in complete accord as to the standard to be applied in determining the compensation to be paid when only a part of the condemnee's property is taken. This problem arises when a strip of land through or along the side of a farm is taken for a highway right of way. Under the provisions of the

---

[25] *Housing Authority of New Orleans* v. *Waters et al.,* 233 La. 259, 96 So.2d 560.

[26] *State* v. *Powell,* Tex. Civ. App., 376 S.W.2d 929.

[27] *United States* v. *46,672.96 Acres of Land,* 521 Fed.2d 13 (10th Cir. 1975).

[28] *United States of America* v. *69.67 Acres of Land in the Town of Oyster Bay,* 152 F.Supp. 441.

[29] *Latchis et al.* v. *State Highway Board,* 120 Vt. 120, 134 A.2d 191.

constitutions of some states, damages resulting from the taking of property by condemnation must be included in computing the compensation to which the condemnee is entitled. If only part of his property is taken and the taking results in the diminution of the value of the remainder, such diminution in value of the remainder would be damages resulting from the taking. If, as the result of the taking, the remainder is enhanced in value, the question then arises as to whether this benefit should be set off against any damages suffered.

The courts have distinguished between special benefits and general benefits. Special benefits are those resulting from public works that enhance the value of property not taken when its enhanced value is the result of its advantageous relation to the improvement of the property condemned. General benefits are those that adjoining property owners share with the public generally.[30]

If less than a fee simple interest in property is condemned, the compensation paid will be the fair market value of the interest taken. In determining the compensation to be paid for an easement, the standard generally applied is the difference between the fair market value of the whole premises before the taking of the easement and its fair market value immediately afterward.[31] This formula takes into consideration any element of damage resulting to the remaining property.

Where an existing easement is taken, the value of the easement is generally based on the diminished value of the servient tenement. If a leasehold estate is condemned, the value of the leasehold taken is the market value of the use and occupancy of the premises for the remainder of the tenant's term, less the agreed rent that the tenant is required to pay for such use and occupancy under the terms of the lease.[32]

Union Electric Company sought to condemn 127.24 acres of land constituting a part of 134 acres owned by Saale. The county was zoned, and the land in question was zoned "agricultural." It was located six miles from the city of West Alton and 15 miles from the city of St. Charles. On the trial of the case, evidence of the value of the land as "industrial" was admitted. No proof of an intent to rezone the land as industrial was offered, nor was there proof of an application for such rezoning by Saale. A new trial was granted on the ground of the inadmissibility of this evidence. On appeal, the order of a new trial was affirmed.

Commissioner Stockard said: " 'Just compensation' for the taking by condemnation of a part of a tract of land, generally speaking, is the fair market value of the land actually

---

[30] *Board of Commissioners of Dona Ana County* v. *Gardner,* 57 N.M. 478, 260 P.2d 682.

[31] *Northeastern Gas Transmission Company* v. *Tersana Acres, Inc.,* 144 Conn. 509, 134 A.2d 253.

[32] *City of Columbus, Ohio* v. *Huntington National Bank,* Ohio App., 143 N.E.2d 874.

taken, and the consequential damages, if any, to the remainder of the land caused by the taking. The fair market value of the land taken is what a reasonable buyer would give who was willing but did not have to purchase, and what a seller would take who was willing but did not have to sell. In the determination of what constitutes the fair market value the jury may consider uses of the land for which it is reasonably adapted or suited and for which it is *available,* having regard to the existing business wants of the community, or such as may be reasonably expected in the future. When the land is *not available* for a certain use by reason of a zoning restriction, its suitability or adaptability for such use may be shown as affecting its value as of the time of the taking if, but only if, the evidence indicates a reasonable probability of a change in the zoning restriction in the reasonably near future. The rule is well stated in Orgel on *Valuation Under Eminent Domain* (2d ed.), p. 34, p. 167, as follows: 'It is generally held that although an ordinance may prohibit the use of the property for certain purposes at the time of condemnation, yet if there is a reasonable probability that the ordinance may be changed or an exception made, the value for that purpose *as affected by the existing ordinance* may be considered.' Whether such probability of a change exists is a question of fact, and whether there exists an exception as to some use either by the terms of the zoning ordinance or by statute is a question of law. However, if there is a showing of a reasonable probability of a change or the creation of an exception, 'an important *caveat* to remember in applying the rule is that the property must not be evaluated as though the rezoning were already an accomplished fact. It must be evaluated under the restrictions of the existing zoning and consideration given to the impact upon market value of the likelihood of a change in zoning.' " *Union Electric Company* v. *Saale,* Mo., 377 S.W.2d 427 (1964).

### Compensation for Trade or Business

As a general rule, injury to a trade or business is not an element to be considered in determining just compensation for property taken under the power of eminent domain. The profits from a trade or business are generally considered as arising from the investment of capital by the owner and from the industry of the owner of the trade or business, and not from the property.[33] However, the owner of a trade or business is entitled to compensation if the trade or business is condemned along with the property on which it is located.[34]

Generally, the owner of condemned property has been held not to be entitled to compensation for loss of business caused by temporary obstruction of highway or lands not belonging to the claimant, although, in some cases, compensation has been allowed. Likewise, compensation has been denied for loss of business

---

[33] *State of New Jersey by State Highway Commissioner* v. *Hudson Circle Service Center,* 46 N.J. Super. 125, 134 A.2d 113.

[34] *State of Alaska* v. *Hammer,* 550 P.2d 820 (Alaska 1976).

as the result of the diversion of traffic caused by improvement of streets or highways.[35]

Christian claimed damages resulting from loss of trade to his business due to the construction of a new highway. The new highway was built some 400 feet north of U.S. Highway 90 and behind the truck stop and residence building of Christian. After the new highway was opened to traffic, Highway 90 was still open, and the access therefrom to the remaining southern portion of Christian's property had not been impaired, but traffic preferred to travel on the new highway. As a result of the loss of traffic on the old highway, Christian's business suffered. The court denied Christian compensation for loss of business, and he appealed. The judgment was affirmed.

Chief Justice Hightower said: "Essentially, appellees are in the position of seeking to recover damages for loss of trade to their business occasioned by the limited and inconvenient ingress and egress to their place of business due to the construction of the new highway. An individual whose property abuts a public way does not have a vested interest in the travel thereon. . . . There is no question but what appellees' business suffered severely by reason of said construction and the public's preference to use the same, but. . . . there was actually no evidence to support the damage award." *State* v. *Christian,* Tex. Civ. App., 376 S.W.2d 803 (1964).

The position of the court in the foregoing case has been consistently taken by other courts considering the flow of traffic past a particular property where, for example, a median strip is placed in the middle of a busy artery, making it impossible for the traffic in one direction to turn directly into the property.[36]

### Inverse Condemnation

During recent years, primarily as the result of major highway construction programs, there has been a great deal of litigation seeking compensation for lack of direct access to highways. While some courts have taken the position that there can be no compensation for loss of direct access unless there has also been an actual taking of part of the affected property,[37] others have reached the conclusion that the loss of direct access is the loss of a property right and have found such "takings" compensable.[38] The doctrine of inverse condemnation has also been applied in connection with the noise generated by modern jet aircraft during takeoff and landing. Property owners adjoining airports have successfully shown that there is substantial interference with their property rights

---

[35] *Rudolph Ramelli, Inc.* v. *City of New Orleans et al.,* 233 La. 291, 96 So.2d 572.

[36] *Doyle* v. *State,* 194 Neb. 36, 229 N.W.2d 656 (1975).

[37] *State* v. *Wineberg,* 74 Wash.2d 378, 444 P.2d 787 (1968); *Elias* v. *Pennsylvania Department of Transportation,* 362 A.2d 459 (Pa. Commonwealth Court 1976).

[38] See 45 Notre Dame Lawyer 3 (1970) at pp. 421 & ff.

and that they are entitled to compensation for the taking that has resulted.[39] It seems clear that the doctrine of inverse condemnation has added a new dimension to the definition of "taking" that will permit recovery in certain situations where there has been no actual loss of ground itself.

### Payment of Compensation

The person, corporation, or political subdivision taking private property under the power of eminent domain is primarily liable for the compensation payable to the owner. Whether or not the compensation must be paid or secured before or at the time the property is taken will depend on the constitution and statutes of the state in which the land is located. Generally, if private property is taken under the power of eminent domain, by a private corporation or an individual, the compensation must be paid or secured before or at the time the property is taken.

The compensation must be paid to the person who owns the property or who has some interest in the property at the time it was taken or damaged, or to one who has taken a voluntary assignment of the rights from the owner. As a general rule, the amount of compensation to be paid for the condemned property is based on the market value of the property as a whole, and the amount awarded is then apportioned among the several owners according to their respective interests.

If the several claimants to the award cannot agree on the basis for apportionment of the award, the money may be paid into court, and the court can then determine the respective rights of the claimants. The procedure followed in determining the rights of claimants, in the event there are conflicting claims and the parties resort to court action, will depend on the statutes of the state in which the action is brought.

## Proceedings to Condemn Property and Assess Compensation

Condemnation proceedings are statutory and are distinct in character from other types of procedure. There is no uniformity in the procedure followed in the several states. Since the proceedings are statutory, and since there is no uniformity in the proceedings, any adequate consideration of this subject would

---

[39] *Karen* v. *City of Los Angeles,* 40 Cal. App. 3d 471, 115 Cal. Rptr. 162 (1974).

entail a study of the condemnation proceedings statutes of each state; such a discussion is beyond the scope of this book. Efforts to introduce uniformity in the condemnation process have not been successful. A proposed Uniform Eminent Domain Code has been in existence since 1975; however, it has not been enthusiastically received by the states and prospects for uniformity are dim.

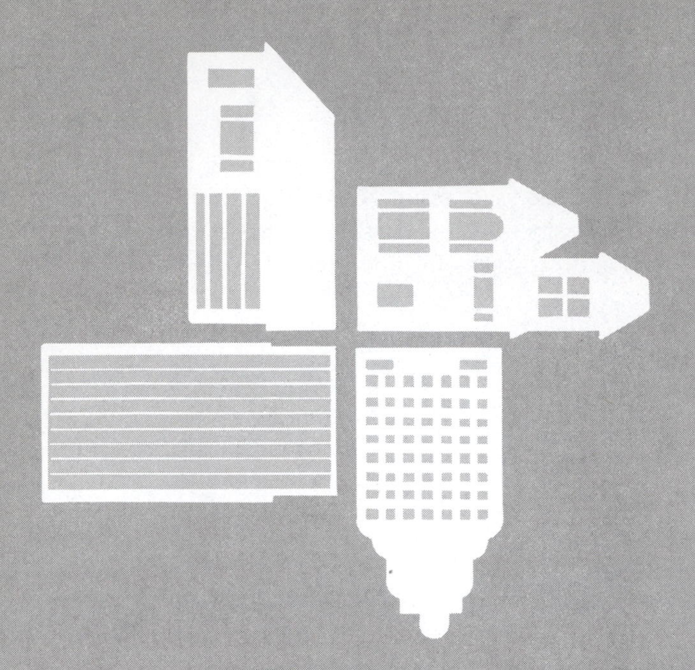

# Section 2

# Ownership of Real Estate

Ownership of personal property is usually quite easy to demonstrate. We do so by simply possessing the property, subjecting it to our physical dominion and control. Our claim of ownership is obvious to others because of our actual possession of the property. With real estate it is not quite so simple to show our claim of ownership by physical control. We cannot transport real estate or carry it with us. We must therefore resort to some other means of demonstrating our ownership. We do this by symbolic evidence: fences, for example, that show the limits of our claim of ownership even though we are not in constant possession and physical control of every square foot of our real estate. In addition, we have established an elaborate system of documents that evidence our ownership. The mere existence of documentary claim of ownership is, however, not enough. We must have some way of showing this documentary evidence to others in a way that they cannot ignore. We do this with our public recording system. It permits us to make our documentary evidence a matter of public record. When this is accomplished all others are legally bound to know what the documents reveal about the quality and extent of our ownership.

In order to make the public recording system work we must have a way to organize the countless thousands of documents that relate to real estate ownership. Without some index or key to the system it would be impossible to locate all the documents that relate to a specific piece of real estate. If they could not be found we could hardly insist that all others be aware of their contents. We index our recording systems, basically, by reference to the legal description of the property. Once this description is established all documents that relate to the property must be made part of it. It is both a means of identification and indexing. As documents accumulate that evidence changes in ownership, we are able to establish a chain by which we can trace the history of ownership. We will use this *chain of title* as the evidence that we presently own the property.

The quality and extent of our ownership will be determined by a careful examination of the documents by the abstractor who accumulates the history of our title and by the attorney who determines the legal meaning of the documents. Thus we assure ourselves of the quality of our ownership. We may use an alternative approach, title insurance, which relies upon these same two steps and then adds an insurance fund. These matters are considered initially in Chapter 5 to provide a foundation for later subjects that depend upon them.

The legal difference between personal property and real property is explored in Chapter 6. It is most important that we grasp the concept that personal property can be changed to real property and thereafter is governed by a completely different set of rules. When personal property is attached to real estate in a more or less permanent fashion and with the *intent* that the marriage of the two be permanent, it becomes a *fixture* and is thereafter real estate. The law of fixtures is most fundamental and important because it is through the use of fixtures that we make real estate more productive, make it produce income or amenities. The most common example of this transformation from personalty to realty is the construction of a home upon a vacant lot. The lumber, nails, bricks, and mortar are all quite obviously personal property when they are brought to the construction site. At that point they belong to the contractor; the contractor's creditors may have at least a partial interest in them as well. When they are incorporated into the house they become the property of the owner of the real estate because they have *become* real estate. This is true even if the property owner has not yet paid the contractor; the property owner's creditors now have a potential interest in them.

Obviously some protective device must be employed to protect the contractor or supplier of materials that will become fixtures. They must have assurance of payment or they will not provide materials or services except for cash in advance. This would greatly impede progress in all construction or repair activity. As a result, our legal system has devised the mechanic's lien, which is discussed in detail in this chapter. The lien permits the contractor to compel payment by the property owner under threat of foreclosure of the lien and sale of the property. The subject can be complex, but it is very important to construction activity. We must weigh the equities of the two parties. The contractor is clearly entitled to be paid for improving the owner's property. The owner is just as clearly entitled to resist paying for faulty work. The rights of the creditors of each of them cannot be ignored. Much of the law in this area is statutory and often in conflict with common law principles. In such a situation courts employ the rule of strict construction of the law. The parties will get no more or no less than their statutory rights.

The law of fixtures is also important in the areas of transfer of ownership by sale or transfer of the right to use by a lease. Disputes are apt to arise between buyer and seller: Is the wall-to-wall carpeting a part of the house so that it now belongs to the new homeowner or is it removable personal property that the seller is entitled to take when he moves out? What about the television antenna, the built-in oven and refrigerator, the fireplace screen, the window air conditioners, and so on, *ad infinitum.* The rule seems to be that if it can be moved it can become the subject of argument. This is also the case when the departing tenant takes with him improvements that he has made either for his own comfort and enjoyment or for the conduct of his trade or business. A different rule will apply, depending upon the purpose of the lease. "Trade fixtures" may be rather permanently attached and still remain the property of the tenant. Consider the walk-in cooler or bar in a tavern, the heat-treating furnace in a factory. No matter how permanently attached, the test will be the *intent* of the parties. Did the tenant intend to improve the landlord's property as part of the rent? These and related questions will be considered in Chapter 6.

Closely related to the matter of basic ownership of real property is the subject of co-ownership. For several reasons it may be desirable for more than one person to share in the ownership of a piece of real estate. Often the motivation is the desire to invest in real estate. Because of its relatively high cost it may be impossible for one individual alone to accumulate the funds necessary for a meaningful investment. On the other hand, where investment is of little or no matter, we may be motivated by a desire to control what will happen to the ownership of real estate at our death. A form of co-ownership that *directs* the transfer of title to our surviving co-owner is desirable so that we can be sure our goal will be achieved even after our death. We might simply desire to make a gift of a valuable piece of real estate to our children in shares so that the property needn't be divided up. It might, for example, be an apartment building, which cannot be divided up without severely limiting its income-producing capability. This is also frequently the case with productive farmland: it is easily divided but not as profitable when farmed in small parcels.

All of these goals can be achieved through the use of well established common law forms of co-ownership, which are discussed in depth in Chapter 7. The concept of co-ownership, as it has developed over centuries, is not without its problems. Fairly inflexible rules have evolved with which we must be familiar because they may limit our ability to achieve a desired result. Certain protective rules have become established to avoid the forced co-ownership of real estate. In the tenancy in common, for example, we will see that any one of the co-owners has an absolute right to compel a division of the property at any time by an action called a suit for partition. Such a step may have disastrous consequences for our indivisible apartment building. No matter. We can force a sale of it instead; we can always divide money. The same approach with the family farm can have equally serious financial consequences. If we can, for example, set off part of it to one co-owner, what are the consequences on the value of the portion left undivided? We must be familiar with the limitations as well as the advantages of co-ownership.

If we use the joint tenancy with right of survivorship we can be sure that the entire property must go to our surviving co-owner at our death and nowhere else. But this is true even if we leave a valid will that gives our share to someone else. The cause of this dilemma is the fact that our share of ownership ceases to exist as a separate property interest at the moment of our death. Our will has no effect because we no longer own any interest that we have the power to dispose of by will. In close family situations this may be our primary motive in using the joint tenancy. In an investment entered into with nonfamily fellow investors it is almost certainly *not* our desire to enhance their fortunes at the expense of our estate. Because this unhappy result will necessarily occur if we use the joint tenancy, modern statutes attempt to protect us by discriminating against the joint tenancy. They require as an essential element the clearly expressed *intent* to create this tenancy. Proof of intent can be difficult. Proof of *lack of intent* to do what we appeared to have intended may be impossible. In addition, the best witness as to our intent will be dead when the issue is to be decided. Knowledge of the consequences and care in the selection of the joint tenancy are our best weapons to avoid an undesired result.

Co-ownership between spouses is, in some states, singled out for further benefits. These may be obtained by using the tenancy by the entireties. It is based upon the unique concept that neither the husband nor the wife has any separate interest in the real estate; the marriage itself is the owner. Unusual benefits flow from this tenancy where it is recognized. Some limited protection from the creditors of only one of the spouses (as opposed to creditors of both of them) is available. There may even be the opportunity to avoid local inheritance taxes at the death of one spouse. On the other hand, since the concept of ownership is that the marriage owns the property, what happens in the event of a divorce? The answer is, of course, that rather difficult problems of co-ownership arise unless care is taken in the divorce proceeding to clearly establish new ownership rights for the two parties as individuals. This subject also is explored in Chapter 7.

As suggested above, a common reason for co-ownership is the desire to invest in valuable real estate. While the common law forms can be adapted to this use, practice has shown that they have severe limitations. As a result a variety of other forms of *shared* ownership have been developed or adapted for real estate investment. Some of these are familiar: the corporation and the general partnership. Others are less familiar: the real estate investment trust, the limited partnership, the cooperative. Still others are becoming more significant: the private land trust, time-sharing through interval ownership. Some of these are, to be sure, of questionable value as investment vehicles. History has shown us, however, that most unlikely forms of shared ownership have hidden potential that will ultimately be found by resourceful investors and their inventive attorneys. Chapter 8 is devoted to a discussion of various forms of shared ownership, including common law forms of co-ownership, as they have developed as investment vehicles.

Real estate, like other forms of investment, has periods when it is most attractive. Sometimes, the advantages seen are income tax avoidance through sheltering of taxable income. Sometimes the potential for capital appreciation, taxed at favorable capital gains rates of taxation, is very great in real estate investments. In still other times, the pure rate of return in terms of earned income can be attractive, regardless of income tax considerations. Like other investments, real estate does not provide all of these advantages at all times. It is even possible to lose money in real estate investing just as it is in the traditional stock and bond markets. *Unlike* many other investments, real estate is nonliquid. The marketing process may hinder aggressive trading, and favorable markets may be lost because of the length of time required to find the buyer and complete the sale. With this inherent limitation, the real estate investor is well advised not to compound his problems by selecting an investment vehicle that is cumbersome in administration because this will further delay the marketing process. Real estate markets are fleeting things. There is competition between properties for the most desirable (financially) use, and vehicles that hinder the marketing process can become quite expensive in terms of lost opportunities.

While investment vehicles are the subject of Chapter 8, it is helpful to remember that real estate investing in this country has become quite dependent upon leverage, the use of borrowed money to maximize the return on money actually invested. For this reason a good investment vehicle must also be a good *borrowing* vehicle as well. Real estate finance is considered later; at this point, however, it is well to be aware that the concept of real estate investment, as it has developed in this country, is not unlike the concept of commercial banking. It depends upon the extensive use of other people's money. Just as a bank must attract funds, so must it seek out profitable investment of those funds. It profits on the difference. So do real estate investors when they employ leverage.

Frequently, the ideal investment vehicle (the corporation, for example, which limits personal liability) is the very worst borrowing vehicle. If the corporation has little substance or capitalization, it also has little borrowing power. The shareholders may find themselves involved in a cumbersome and time-consuming personal guaranty process for each borrowing. Protection from personal liability will be waived in the process. Perhaps the partnership would have been a better choice if liability for debt was the major risk foreseen. The important point is that different kinds of real estate investments will demand different vehicles. Trade-offs frequently have to be made, depending upon the single most important element in a particular investment. The benefits and shortcomings of each investment vehicle must be known so that an intelligent and profitable choice can be made.

# Chapter 5

# Recording, Evidence of Title, and Legal Descriptions

Several related topics concerning proof of ownership are considered in this chapter. The recording system devised to prove ownership by virtue of documents is explored in depth. The limitations on the quality of this ownership and the protections available to demonstrate it are also covered. These are the abstract and opinion and title insurance methods of assuring the extent of ownership rights held by the record owner. Because of the dependency upon an accurate system of records and precise identification of real estate that are essential to establishing rights of ownership, the subject of legal descriptions is considered in detail. Various methods of describing real estate, the governmental survey, the metes and bounds description, the recorded plat of a subdivision, and informal descriptions are each covered in this chapter.

## Recording

### Purpose of Recording

The purpose of recording real estate transactions is to provide a systematic and efficient way of transferring title to real estate. The general rule that a person can acquire no better title to property than that held by his grantor applies to real property. However, the equally well-established rule that an innocent purchaser for value takes free from outstanding equities also applies.

At common law, no public records of titles or rights in land were kept. When land was sold, the grantor delivered to the grantee all the deeds, mortgages, discharges of mortgages, and so forth, that affected the title to the real estate. A lost or destroyed instrument presented a serious problem, since its absence resulted in a break in the chain of title. Under this system, if an owner of real estate had deeded or mortgaged the property to one person and then, later, deeded or mortgaged the same property to another, who took as an innocent purchaser for value, the subsequent purchaser or mortgagee acquired no greater rights than those held by the grantor or mortgagor.

The rule that a person takes subject to notice of the rights of the person in possession provides some protection to a grantee if he takes possession of the property purchased, but it provides no protection to a mortgagee or to a person who purchases land that is unoccupied.

All of the states have enacted recording statutes, which provide for the maintaining of a permanent public record of land titles and all interests in land. An unrecorded instrument is void as to an innocent purchaser or mortgagee for value, or as to other persons who have, for value and without notice or knowledge of the outstanding interest, acquired rights in the land. The recording of an instrument, as provided by the statutes, is notice to all persons of the contents of the instrument and rights created thereby.

Recording of an instrument conveying an interest in real estate has no effect on the validity of that instrument. The sole purpose of recording such an instrument is to give public notice of the right conveyed by it. If Arthur deeds or mortgages real estate to Bert, Bert acquires, on the execution and delivery of the deed or mortgage, a title to or a lien on the real estate. Recording is not required to perfect Bert's rights in the real estate and, as between Arthur and Bert, has no effect on the interest acquired by Bert. As to third parties, however, a failure to record the document means that they have no notice of the transaction and are not obligated to know of Bert's interest in the property.

### Recording Statutes

Although the recording statutes of the states are not uniform, they are alike in their major provisions. In general, they provide for the recording of instruments that affect the title to real estate. All titles to land within a county are recorded in an office located within the county, indexes of recorded instruments are kept, prerequisites for the recording of instruments are set up, the types of instruments eligible to record are defined, and the parties whose rights are affected by recording are designated.

Under the provisions of the recording statutes, a person buying real estate, or lending money and taking a mortgage on real estate, takes with notice of all outstanding interests affecting the title if the existence of such interests would be disclosed by a careful examination of the records. The recording of an instrument properly executed, eligible for recording, and, in most states, filed for record is notice to the public of all matters contained therein. As was stated previously, the purpose of recording is to give notice. If a person has notice or knowledge of an existing interest in real estate, he is bound thereby, and recording becomes immaterial.

M. G. Austin, on August 27, 1953, had two deeds prepared, granting certain land to his son Butler and other land to his son Oliver. Oliver was present at the time the deeds were prepared and executed, and knew their contents. On October 29, 1953, M. G. Austin had a third deed prepared, which granted to Oliver part of the land granted to Butler in the deed of August 27, 1953. The deed of October 29, 1953, was recorded immediately after its execution, but the deed of August 27, 1953, was not recorded until December 28, 1953. The court held that the fact that the deed of October 29, 1953, was recorded before the deed of August 27, 1953, in no way affected Butler's rights acquired under such deed.

Justice Holt said: "It is undisputed in this case that Oliver had actual notice and knowledge of his father's deed, dated August 27, 1953, to Butler when Oliver, as grantee, took the later deed, dated October 29, 1953. Butler was unaware of the execution of the deeds on August 27 and October 29 until after they were made. Since Oliver had notice of a prior unrecorded deed to his brother at the time the October deed to him was executed and recorded, Oliver was in the same legal position as if Butler's deed were actually recorded." *Austin* v. *Austin,* Ark. 372 S.W.2d 231 (1963).

***Prerequisites for Recording.*** An instrument, in order to be eligible for recording, must be drawn and executed in conformity with the provisions of the recording statutes of the state in which the real estate is located. The prerequisites for recording are not uniform. In nearly all states the instrument must be acknowledged before a notary public or another officer with authority to take acknowledgments. Some states provide that the instrument must be attested; and some states, in addition to the acknowledgment, require that the instrument be witnessed by one or more witnesses. In some states a local transfer tax must be paid on deeds and mortgages before they are eligible for recording.

The courts are not in accord as to the effect of the recording of an instrument that does not comply with all the statutory prerequisites. The majority of the courts hold that the recording of an instrument that does not comply with the statutory requirements is notice to no one.[1]

Some states have enacted curative statutes validating defective acknowledg-

---

[1] *Haverell Distributors* v. *Haverell Mfg. Corp.,* 115 Ind. App. 501, 58 N.E.2d 372.

ments; under them, the instrument is to be regarded as being properly acknowledged if third-party rights have not intervened.

## Instruments Entitled to Recording

Instruments that are eligible for recording will be set out in the statutes of the state in which the real estate is located. In all the states the statutes provide for the recording of deeds, mortgages, assignments of mortgages, discharges of mortgages, and release of liens. Usually, provision is also made for the recording of land contracts, long-term (three years or over) leases on real estate, and notice of mechanics' liens on real estate; and in some states a miscellaneous record is kept, in which are recorded unclassified instruments that affect the title to real estate. Under the Uniform Commercial Code, provision is made for the recording or filing of security interests in goods that are, or are to become, fixtures.

As a general rule, only original instruments are entitled to be recorded, not copies or abstracts of instruments; and if an instrument is recorded when it is not entitled to recordation under the statutes of the state, the recording is of no effect. It is notice to no one.[2]

Six persons owned, as tenants in common, a tract of timberland. McLeod, one of the six owners, executed a contract whereby he convenanted to convey the timber on the tract to Cameron. This contract was recorded. Later, the remaining owners deeded the timber to Chandler. Cameron contended that since his agreement with McLeod was recorded, Chandler took with notice of his (Cameron's) rights. The court held that the McLeod-Cameron instrument was not eligible to record and was notice to no one.

Justice Ervin said: "We conclude, therefore, that the registration of the agreement did not give Chandler constructive notice of the existence or terms of the purely personal contract on the part of McLeod to convey to Cameron the interest in the timber which McLeod did not originally own. This is true because the record of an instrument 'does not constitute constructive notice, if it is not of a class which is authorized or required by law to be recorded.' Our conclusion is not affected in any way by the fact that the contract to convey and the personal contract were both embodied in the same instrument because the registration of an instrument 'operates as constructive notice only when the statute authorizes its registration; and then only to the extent of those provisions which are within the registration statute.' " *Chandler* v. *Cameron,* 229 N.C. 62, 47 S.E.2d 528 (1948).

## Liens That Need Not Be Recorded

Real estate tax liens, inheritance tax liens, franchise tax liens, and similar liens held by a governmental unit need not be recorded and are valid liens on the real estate, although not recorded.

---

[2] *Dreifus* v. *Marx,* 40 Cal. App.2d 461, 104 P.2d 1080.

## Where and When the Instrument Is Recorded

Any instrument that has an effect upon the title to real estate must be recorded in the county in which the real estate is located. The reason for this is that anyone investigating the status of title to real estate is, generally, not obligated to look beyond that county's records to find documents that affect the title. Normally, a county officer, such as the county recorder, is charged with the responsibility of making a public record of all such documents. Any document that is eligible for recordation is generally held to be recorded when it has been deposited with and accepted by the authorized county official and when the statutory fee for recording it has been paid.[3] It is usually the obligation of the recording officer, when he receives the document, to endorse upon it the date, hour, and minute it was received for filing or recording. In many areas, of course, the hour and minute are not significant, but in a large metropolitan area such detail is essential.

## How the Instrument Is Recorded

The statutes usually require that the instrument be recorded at length and in *haec verba* (exact words). No particular method of recording is necessary. Any method that carries out the purpose of the statutes, that is, gives the instrument publicity and perpetuity and meets the requirements of accuracy and durability, is sufficient.[4] The early records consisted of handwritten copies of recorded instruments. Today, in some counties, the records consist of typewritten copies of instruments. In other counties, form pages are used, and the blanks are filled in. In the more populous counties the records consist of photostatic or xerographic copies of instruments.

In addition to the recording of instruments, the statutes generally require the indexing of recorded instruments. The purpose of the index is to enable a person to find any recorded instrument he may wish to examine. The statutes may define in detail what indexes must be kept, or they may merely provide that adequate indexes shall be kept.

Two types of indexes are in use: the cross index and the tract index. In the cross index of names, the type of index in general use, the names of the parties to the instrument are listed in alphabetical order. The names of grantors, mortgagors, and so forth, will be indexed in one column; and the names of grantees,

---

[3] *Bank of Marlinton* v. *McLaughlin,* 123 W. Va. 608, 17 S.E.2d 213; and *Maddox* v. *Astro Investments,* 45 Ohio App. 2d 203, 343 N.E.2d 133 (1975).

[4] *People* v. *Haas,* 311 Ill. 164, 142 N.E. 549.

mortgagees, and so on, will be indexed in another column. In the tract index a page is kept for each tract of land in the county, and all instruments affecting the title to the tract are indexed under the tract heading. The book and page where the instrument is recorded are given.

Under the statutes of some states the index is made a part of the record, and the recording is not completed until the instrument is indexed.[5]

### Errors in Recorded Instrument

A slight error in a recorded instrument will not affect its validity and will not prevent the recording from being notice. If the error is of such a nature that a prudent person would not be put on inquiry, the recording of the instrument will be ineffective as notice. An error in the description of the real estate, if it is of such a nature as to cause improper indexing of the instrument, will prevent recording of the instrument from being notice.

For example, if a deed to land in Section 18 is erroneously drafted and it reads Section 8, such deed, when recorded, would not be notice, since one examining the records would not be expected to examine deeds, mortgages, and so forth in Section 8 when he was interested in land in Section 18. A deed, mortgage, or other instrument that is recorded and that, when read in its entirety, discloses the interest conveyed, is sufficient to give notice of its contents, even though it may be defective in some respects.[6]

The party filing the instrument for record is responsible for its accuracy and validity; the recording officer does not pass on the validity of instruments offered for recordation.

H. Saxon and wife executed a deed to certain lands, and the section number—Section 13—was omitted from the description. On March 11, 1935, the grantees named in this deed conveyed the property by warranty deed, using the same description as that used in the deed to them. Both deeds were recorded. The court held that the deeds were void and that the recording did not constitute notice to subsequent purchasers.

Justice McElroy said: ". . . Constructive notice arising from the record of a muniment is imputed to purchasers and creditors from a mere presumption of law, and it imputes only such knowledge as the instrument there recorded discloses, and not what a diligent inquiry into its meaning might disclose. The registration of an instrument is constructive notice to the world of the contents of the paper there recorded or intended to be recorded, and of its particular contents only, and it will have no operation or effect unless the original instrument correctly and sufficiently describes the premises which are to be affected.

---

[5] *Tocci* v. *Nowfall,* 220 N.C. 550, 18 S.E.2d 225.

[6] *Phoenix Mutual Life Insurance Co.* v. *Kingston Bank & Trust Co.,* 172 Tenn. 335, 112 S.W.2d 381.

The effect of the registration law is to give a purchaser notice of what the instrument recorded or intended to be recorded actually conveys, and has no operation in the way of putting him on inquiry as to what premises were intended to be conveyed, unless they be substantially described therein." *Saxon* v. *Saxon,* 242 Miss. 491, 136 So.2d 210 (1962).

### Errors in Recording the Instrument

The majority of the courts have held that when a person has filed an instrument with the proper officer for recording, he has fulfilled his duty, and the filing is constructive notice of the content of the instrument. If the recording officer makes an error in the indexing or in the recording of the instrument, the person who purchases, leases, or takes a mortgage on the property after the recording of the instrument takes subject to the erroneously recorded instrument, even though, as a result of the error, he would not have discovered the instrument by a customary examination of the records.[7] If the officer has made an error in recording an instrument, the courts have held that he has the right to correct the error in the record.

### Duty of Party Offering Instrument for Recording

Some courts have held that the party offering an instrument for recordation owes a duty to check the records to see that the instrument is recorded and to see that no errors have been made in its recording. In these jurisdictions the person offering the instrument for recording must bear any loss resulting from errors made in its recording.

### Parties Protected by Recording

Persons who have purchased or mortgaged property for value and in good faith are protected by the recording statutes. Some statutes extend protection to judgment creditors, and a few afford protection to both judgment creditors and general creditors.

In determining whether or not a person is a purchaser or mortgagee for value, the courts do not inquire into the adequacy of the consideration given. However, if it is established that property has been sold for a wholly inadequate consideration and conveyed for the purpose of defeating the rights of creditors or for the purpose of defeating rights acquired in the property, such deed will be set aside in a proper action. A mortgagee is entitled to payment of the debt secured by the mortgage, and no more.

---

[7] *Willie* v. *Hines-Yelton Lumber Co.,* 167 Ga. 833, 146 S.E. 901.

A person who acquires real estate as a gift, by descent, or as beneficiary under a will is not a purchaser for value.

## Knowledge and Notice

To qualify as a good-faith purchaser, a person must acquire the property without knowledge or notice of outstanding interests. Since recording of an instrument is constructive notice to the public, a person takes with notice of all recorded instruments. He also takes with notice of all matters set out in recorded instruments. For example, suppose a recorded deed states that certain real estate is sold subject to a mortgage, and the mortgage is described in the deed. The recording of the deed is notice of the existence of the mortgage, even though the mortgage has not been recorded; and a subsequent purchaser or mortgagee of the property would take with notice of the mortgage.

The courts follow the general rule that a purchaser or mortgagee takes with notice of the rights of persons in possession of the property.[8] The fact that the purchaser or mortgagee does not have actual knowledge that the real estate is in the possession of some third person is immaterial. The purchaser or mortgagee has a duty to inspect the real estate and is bound by the facts that would be disclosed by a reasonable inspection. If a third person is found in possession, the purchaser or mortgagee is obligated to interview the party in possession to learn what rights he claims in the property.[9]

Although a person does not have to investigate every rumor he hears relating to title to property, he is bound by any reliable information that he obtains relating to the property.

Henderson owned a 28-acre tract of land with a house thereon, in which she lived. Through fradulent representations, she was induced to execute a deed to the premises, conveying them to Lila Lloyd. The deed to Lloyd was duly recorded. Lloyd conveyed the property, by warranty deed, to Lawrence. Henderson brought this action to have the deeds canceled and title decreed to be in her. She contended that Lawrence had notice or knowledge that the execution of the deed granting the property to Lloyd was obtained by fraud. The action of the trial court dismissing the bill was reversed on appeal and trial ordered.

Justice White said: "A bona fide purchaser is one who buys for a valuable consideration without knowledge or notice of facts material to the title.

"It is well established in this State that there can be no innocent purchaser of land from a vendor who is out of possession at the date of conveyance.

---

[8] *Willard* v. *Bringoff,* 103 Ind. App. 16, 5 N.E.2d 315.

[9] *Sarafin* v. *Wolff et ux.,* 5 N.J. Super, 386, 69 A.2d 347.

"The appellant, Eurydice Henderson, was in actual possession of the property in question and this alone is sufficient notice to the purchaser to put him on inquiry as to her rights in and to the property in question." *Henderson* v. *Lawrence,* Tenn., 369 S.W.2d 553 (1963).

***Grantee under Quitclaim Deed.*** There is a division of authority as to whether or not a grantee under a quitclaim deed can qualify as a good-faith purchaser. Some courts have held that a quitclaim deed conveys only the title that the grantor has; and consequently, the grantee takes subject to all outstanding claims against the real estate. A majority of the courts hold that a quitclaim deed is a conveyance, not merely a release, and that the grantee can take as a good-faith purchaser. No notice of outstanding interests can be implied from the giving of a quitclaim deed.[10]

## Recordation and the Chain of Title

As a general rule, the recording of an instrument is not constructive notice unless the recorded document is in the chain of title. The examiner, in examining the records, proceeds to check all instruments in chronological order; any instrument not in this chain of title would, in the normal course of the examination, be missed.

For example, suppose that a tract of land was patented by the government to Albert on May 6, 1820. This transfer would be indexed under the name of Albert. Suppose that Albert then deeded the tract to Bates on October 25, 1825. The examiner would look for instruments executed by Bates in the indexes after that date. Suppose that Bates, on April 13, 1825, executed a mortgage on the tract to Clark and Clark recorded the mortgage on that date. This mortgage would not be in the chain of title, and the recording of the mortgage would not be constructive notice to good-faith purchasers for value.

Again, suppose that Albert deeded the tract to Bates and Bates did not record the deed. Then Bates deeds or mortgages the tract to Clark, and Clark records the deed or mortgage. The deed or mortgage to Clark is not in the chain of title. Since the deed to Bates is not recorded, the examiner would not look in the index under "Bates" and would not discover the deed or mortgage to Clark.

A person examining the records will check the indexes under the name of a person who, according to the records, has acquired an interest in the real estate, and he will check only from the time the interest was acquired. He will not

---

[10] *Williams* v. *McCann,* Okla., 385 P.2d 788.

check for instruments recorded prior to the date a person acquired his interest in the real estate.

There are two exceptions to this general rule, and these exceptions are followed by a few, but not a majority, of the courts.

1. If a person executes a warranty deed to real estate that he does not own at that time, and later acquires title to the real estate and the deed by which such title is acquired is recorded, the recording of this deed is constructive notice to all persons dealing with the real estate subsequent to the recording of the deed.
2. The other exception arises under the following circumstances: Suppose that Albert owns two or more lots in a block. He deeds one of the lots to Bates, and the deed contains a covenant imposing building restrictions mutually enforceable on the owners of all the lots. Later, Albert sells another of the lots to Clark but does not insert the restrictive covenant in the deed to Clark. However, Clark purchases with constructive notice of the restriction. Some courts hold that the restrictive covenant in the deed to Bates is constructive notice of the restriction to all subsequent purchasers of the other lots.[11]

Lone Star Gas Company sold to Sheaner a gas heater and installed it in a house owned by Funk. The heater was installed in the house without Funk's knowledge or consent and as a replacement for a gas heater that was in the house. Gas Company sold the gas heater to Sheaner on a contract mortgage, which was duly recorded as a lien on the premises. Funk sold and conveyed the house to Tomlin. At the time of the sale, Funk was in possession of the house, and Tomlin had no notice or knowledge of Gas Company's claim to a lien. Gas Company contended that its lien, since it was duly recorded, was valid against Tomlin. The court held that Gas Company's lien was not valid against Tomlin.

Chief Justice McDonald said: "It is the law of this state that the record of a deed or mortgage by a stranger to the title to real estate, although duly recorded, is not constructive notice to a subsequent purchaser of the property, because the instrument is not in the chain of title to such property." *Lone Star Gas Company* v. *Sheaner,* Tex. Civ. App., 297 S.W.2d 855 (1956).

### Priorities

The courts are in accord in holding that if Albert deeds or mortgages real estate to Bell and Bell does not record his deed or mortgage, and, at a later date, Albert deeds or mortgages the same real estate to Clark, who takes as a good-faith purchaser or mortgagee for value and without notice, Clark's rights in the real estate are prior (superior) to the rights of Bell.

---

[11] *Hawley* v. *McCabe,* 117 Conn. 558, 169 A. 192.

However, the courts are not in accord as to which party has prior rights in the above situation if Bell has not recorded his deed or mortgage at the time of the sale or mortgage to Clark, but does record his deed or mortgage before Clark records his. Some courts hold that the person who first records his deed or mortgage has priority. Other courts hold that if the deed or mortgage was not recorded at the time the second deed or mortgage was executed and delivered, the second purchaser or mortgagee has priority.

## Torrens System

### Title Registration

The Torrens system of land title registration is a relatively recent development. Under the older and established system of recording title to real estate, the grantee acquires title to real estate when a properly executed deed is delivered to the grantee—recording is not essential to the validity of the transfer. Under the Torrens system, the deed or mortgage has more of the characteristics of a contract than of a conveyance, and does not directly affect the title to the real estate. The deed or mortgage constitutes authority to the registrar. The title to the real estate does not pass to the grantee or mortgagee until the completion of the registration by the registrar in accordance with the statutes.[12] In those states that have adopted the Torrens system of land title registration, the older and established recording system is still in use. The owner of real estate may record his title, or he may, if he wishes, register his title under the Torrens system; registration of land titles is not compulsory.[13]

The provisions of the Torrens system statutes are not uniform. However, the procedure to be followed in registering land titles is substantially the same under all of the statutes. An application in writing for the registration of the title to the real estate is made to the county court in the county in which the real estate is located. The application sets out all material information relative to the title to the real estate. The court will then inquire into the title. All persons known to have an interest in the real estate are given personal notice if they can be located. All other persons are given notice by publication. Any interested party may appear and state his claim. If no appearance is made, proof of the title in the applicant is taken, and an order is entered for the registration of the real estate.[14]

---

[12] *People* v. *Mortenson,* 404 Ill. 107, 88 N.E.2d 35.

[13] Colorado, Massachusetts, Minnesota, New York, North Carolina, Ohio, Oregon, Virginia, and Washington have statutes adopting the Torrens system.

[14] *State* v. *Westfall,* 85 Minn. 437, 89 N.W. 175.

### Transfer of Title

When real estate is registered under the Torrens system, a certificate of registration is prepared and filed in the registrar's office; and at the same time, signature cards are signed by the owners of the property. A duplicate certificate is prepared and delivered to the owners. When the property is conveyed or mortgaged, or encumbered in any way, the owner delivers the deed, mortgage, or other instrument, as the case may be, to the grantee or mortgagee, together with the owner's registration certificate. All of these documents are presented to the registrar, who owes a duty to check the signatures. If everything is in order, he then registers the transfer and issues to the party the proper duplicate certificate. For example, if the owner has conveyed the property, the registrar will issue to the grantee a duplicate owner's certificate showing all encumbrances on the property. If the property is mortgaged, a "mortgagee's duplicate certificate" will be issued to the mortgagee. If the registrar accepts forged instruments and issues a certificate to the forger, it does not create rights in the registered property. Anyone, however, who suffers damage as the result of a mistake on the part of the registrar will be reimbursed from the fund accumulated from registration fees.[15] To this extent the Torrens system provides more protection to the user of the system than does the traditional recording system. The recorder maintains no funds from which damages can be paid for losses resulting from his mistakes.

## Assurance of Title

There are in use today (apart from the Torrens system) two basic methods by which the quality of title to real estate is assured. The older of the two is the abstract and opinion method, under which a digest of the history of the title to a particular parcel, called the *abstract,* is prepared by a specialist in this field of work, the abstractor. When the abstract, the abbreviated history of the title, has been completed it is furnished to the attorney for the buyer or the lender (or both), who examines the abstract and renders an opinion on the quality of the present owner's title. By this method the purchaser is alerted to any defects that exist, their significance, and what corrective action should be taken before paying value for the property. The other method of assurance of quality of title is to provide for title insurance. Under this method no abstract is prepared; however, the same investigation of the history of the title is made and the defects are evaluated by the insurance company by their own attorney. Then the decision is made either to insure the title or not and, if so, with what exceptions. Each

---

[15] *Hoffman* v. *Schroeder,* 38 Ill. App.2d 20, 186 N.E.2d 381.

of these two methods is examined below, but it should be kept in mind that when substantial amounts of money are involved, it is not unusual to utilize *both* methods in the same transaction, since each has its advantages and disadvantages.

### Abstract and Opinion Method

As noted above, there are two steps in the abstract and opinion method of assuring the quality of title, each of them performed by a different professional. The first of these is the abstractor, who undertakes, for a fee, to search the relevant records relating to the ownership of the land in question. The abstractor is one who is trained and skilled in the workings of the recording system and is knowledgeable as to the significance of the documents in the public records. He does not merely copy every significant document found in the system but, rather, he *digests* those documents to show only the essential elements. (In a recent case involving the purchase of a square mile of land, thought to be oil bearing, the client insisted that each and every document of any significance be *copied* rather than digested. The result was a collection of 10,000 pages of legal documents. In contrast, the abstract for such a property might consist of only 200 to 300 pages of digested material.)

The function of the abstractor is critical to the ultimate goal because a great deal of reliance is placed upon the abstract in determining the quality of the title. Nevertheless, it is important to bear in mind that his investigation or "title search" is limited to the public records. He does not inspect the property to determine who is in possession nor does he survey it to see that the improvements are actually located upon the real estate. Finally, his search and the evidence of title that he finds are necessarily limited by the accuracy of the recording system itself. Documents that would not be found by a diligent search of the records will not be included in the abstract.

### The Abstractor's Duty and Liability

The abstractor's duty is to examine the indexes and discover all the entries of record that are in the chain of title, and to prepare a short statement that will enable a person examining the abstract to determine the nature of the instrument and whether or not it was properly executed.

The abstract is merely a history of the title to the real estate. It is in no respect a guarantee of the validity of the title. The abstractor does not express an opinion as to the validity of any recorded instrument or the validity of the title.

The abstractor may be engaged to check the title from the original patent granted by the U.S. government; or he may be engaged to examine the records only back to the last entry on a previously prepared abstract and to bring the abstract down to date; that is, add to the abstract all instruments recorded after the last entry on the old abstract.

The abstractor will attach to the abstract a certificate that will state what records have been examined and the dates covered by the abstract.

The abstractor does not guarantee the title to the real estate and is not liable if the title is defective. He is liable for losses resulting from his negligence in the preparation of the abstract. If the abstractor negligently omits an entry and, as the result of the omission, the person who has employed him suffers a loss, the abstractor is liable for the resulting loss. If the abstractor merely brings an abstract down to date, he is liable only for omissions of entries made during the period his examination was to cover.

Some courts have held that the abstractor is liable only to the party who employs him. The better view is that the abstractor is liable to anyone who relies on the abstract. The guarantee in the certificate of some abstractors runs to all persons, both present and future, who rely on the abstract. In effect, the guarantee runs with the land.

### The Attorney's Duty and Liability

When the completed abstract is delivered to the client (usually the purchaser or lender) it is his responsibility to satisfy himself that it shows title in satisfactory condition. Few people are able to analyze the abstract and make an intelligent evaluation of the quality of the title. This is the function of the real estate attorney. The abstract is therefore delivered to him for review and for the rendering of an *opinion* on the title held by the seller or borrower. On the basis of his review of the abstract the attorney will render a written opinion, in letter form, to his client, advising the client, whether the title is marketable or, if not, what defects need to be cured and what action is necessary to cure them to the attorney's satisfaction. Today it is a rare title indeed that does not have some defects. Some of these may be of a minor nature or may have become insignificant by the passage of time, but the opinion letter will point them out.

It is important to note that the letter furnished by the attorney is limited in the same way in which the abstract is limited. That is, no responsibility is assumed for matters that would be revealed by a physical inspection or survey of the property. More importantly, the opinion furnished is limited to the evidence presented to the attorney for review: the abstract itself. Finally, it is, when all is said and done, an *opinion.* Whether reached by a highly skilled and exceptionally well qualified attorney or one with lesser qualifications, it is still an opinion. Liability for error in reaching an erroneous opinion may be difficult to prove by one who has relied upon that opinion.

## Insurance of Title

### Introduction

The title insurance industry is an outgrowth of the abstracting business motivated by the inherent shortcomings of the abstract and opinion method of assuring title. No matter how careful the abstractor may be or how competent the attorney may be, losses still may result from errors in the recording system itself or errors in judgment by the abstractor or the attorney. When a loss does occur, it may be difficult or impossible to obtain financial satisfaction. As a result of these factors a demand existed for some form of insurance that would provide economic protection to the property owner. Still more important, mortgage lenders, who are primarily interested in recovering the funds advanced, strongly support the title insurance industry. The abstract companies, because of their familiarity with the recording system, found the title insurance business a natural area in which to expand. Attorneys have also formed title insurance companies to provide financial protection to their clients.

### How Title Insurance Works

Title insurance works much like any other form of casualty insurance in that it speads the risk of loss of title over many insured parties. Rates are established on the basis of experience in a given area. When title insurance is ordered, the title insurance company searches the records in much the same way that the abstractor does, but an abstract is not prepared. Instead, any defects that are found are noted and this information then is reviewed by the title insurance company's attorney to determine how serious the defects may be and whether or not the title is insurable. The company then decides whether or not it will insure the title and what exceptions it may take in the policy when it is finally issued. Usually the amount of coverage will be the purchase price (in an owner's policy) or the amount of the mortgage debt (in a mortgagee's policy), although additional coverage may be purchased. The purchaser of the real estate, the insured party under the policy, does not receive an abstract or an opinion; he receives instead an insurance policy, which simply describes the interest being insured, the real estate, the amount of coverage, and any exceptions other than the standard exceptions discussed below. In the event that there is a defect in the title, the title insurance company will be called upon to pay the loss or defend the title much the same as other casualty insurers.

### Limitations on Title Insurance Coverage

Title insurance is based upon an examination of the quality of the title as of a particular date and time. The policy provides insurance that—as of a specified moment—insurable title is vested in the name of the seller of the property and that upon conveyance to the buyer, the latter will have an insured title. As a result, title insurance does *not* protect the owner against defects that come into existence after he takes title to the property. There are also standard exceptions in the typical title insurance policy against mechanics' liens that may not have been recorded at the time the title was examined; defects that a survey would have revealed, unless a survey was performed and made available to the title insurer; rights of parties in possession under unrecorded leases or conditional sales contracts. Another important limitation on the insurance coverage is that it is limited to the named insured, and subsequent purchasers may not rely upon the previous owner's policy. New title insurance must be purchased by each new owner of the property. The cost of such subsequent policies, however, will likely be reduced because the insurer needs only to update his earlier examination of the title.

Nor can an owner of real estate rely upon his mortgagee's title insurance policy, since it provides limited coverage to the lender only for the balance of his loan. Reliance upon the fact that there is mortgagee's title insurance can result in a substantial loss to the owner who does not obtain separate coverage. While it is true that the balance of the debt would be paid, the owner would lose all the investment previously made in purchasing the property. Depending upon when the title loss occurs this can be a quite significant loss. As a practical matter the purchase of just mortgagee's title insurance without owner's coverage represents only a modest saving in premium expense. Typically, both policies are issued at the time the property is purchased. All of the expense of the title investigation is usually charged to the owner's policy, and the mortgagee's policy is issued for a nominal additional premium. If only the mortgagee's policy were issued, all of the investigation costs would be charged to it, so that purchasing only the mortgagee's coverage is false economy.

### Subrogation

The complexities of the law of subrogation will not be covered here; however, it is important to note that when there has been a loss, the title insurer succeeds to the rights that his insured may have against other parties, including, most importantly, the seller of the property. If the seller gave a general warranty deed he can be sued on his warranties by the buyer, and the title insurer succeeds to this remedy. The lesson here is that the seller who provides title insurance to his buyer remains liable for defects in his title, and he does not escape liability by providing title insurance. This is particularly true where the defect is created by the seller himself.

### Conclusion

Title insurance is becoming more and more widely used, particularly in older metropolitan areas. Most title insurers welcome inquiries about their business from the general public, considering it a form of public relations. In addition, many of them will provide informative booklets and films for the asking.

## Legal Descriptions

Because of the heavy reliance placed by recording systems upon accurate identification of real estate, it is important to understand how real estate is legally described. Several types of legal descriptions are in use today, but all of them have one common source: the original governmental survey. There are, of course, some exceptions to this general rule in certain parts of the country, where descriptions are based upon grants made by other countries prior to acquisition by the United States, as well as some grants made by the United States itself. In these areas a different original survey may be relied upon. In either case, however, the original survey is the cornerstone of all legal descriptions because it pinpoints the exact location of the property on the surface of the earth. All descriptions must have a *point of beginning* before they can be meaningful and useful in accurately identifying a specific property. This point is established from the governmental survey, and the legal description proceeds from there.

### Governmental Survey

After the United States gained its independence, Congress decided to raise money to pay the war debt by selling unoccupied land that the federal government had acquired. This land was a wilderness, and there were few landmarks by which it could be described. A survey of the land was ordered, and a system of rectangular surveys was adopted.

An easily identified landmark, such as the mouth of a river, was selected as the beginning point, and a base line running east and west was drawn through this point. Then a principal or prime meridian was established by drawing a line perpendicular to the base line, intersecting it at the selected point and running north and south.

Since the earth is round, it was necessary to compensate for its narrowing as the survey moved from south to north and from north to south from the base line. To accomplish this, correction lines were drawn every 24 miles. These correction lines—or *guide meridians,* as they are called—run due north and south, but run for only 24 miles until a new series of guide meridians is established. These squares are called *tracts.* Each tract is divided into townships six miles square, and each township is divided into sections one mile square.

Each township is identified by its position in relation to the intersection of the principal meridian and the base line. The position either east or west of the principal meridian is designated as the *range,* and the position either north or south of the base line is indicated by stating whether it is north or south.

Each township is divided into 36 sections, which are numbered from 1 to

Divisions into Townships

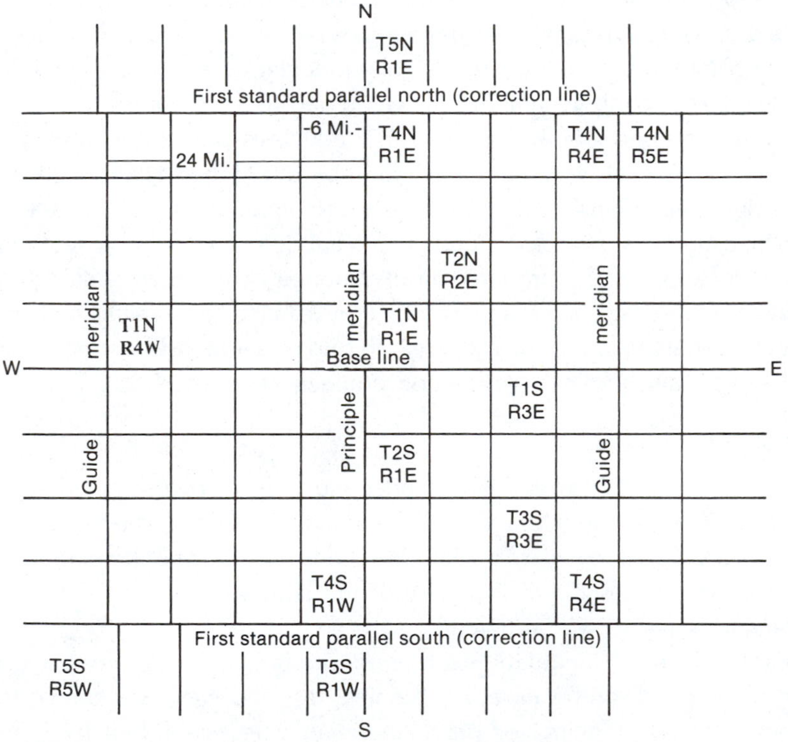

Township Section Numbering

| 6 | 5 | 4 | 3 | 2 | 1 |
|---|---|---|---|---|---|
| 7 | 8 | 9 | 10 | 11 | 12 |
| 18 | 17 | 16 | 15 | 14 | 13 |
| 19 | 20 | 21 | 22 | 23 | 24 |
| 30 | 29 | 28 | 27 | 26 | 25 |
| 31 | 32 | 33 | 34 | 35 | 36 |

36. Starting with Section 1, which is in the northeast corner of the township, the sections are numbered west across the north side of the township to the west side, then down one tier south and back east to the east line of the township. This back-and-forth pattern of numbering is followed until all the sections are numbered.

If less than an entire section (640 acres) is being conveyed, it is possible to describe a parcel by reference to the section itself, *provided* that the parcel is a fraction of the section that can be succinctly described. An example of such a description would be: 40 acres of land being the northeast quarter of the southeast quarter of Section 12, Township 4 north, Range 4 east of the First Principal Meridian. If the diagram below is the Section 12 referred to, then the foregoing description accurately describes the shaded portion of the diagram.

Such descriptions are far less confusing if they are read in reverse order. That is, begin with the section first; then find the southeast quarter (which eliminates the other three quarters) and then locate the northeast quarter of this smaller

Division of a Section

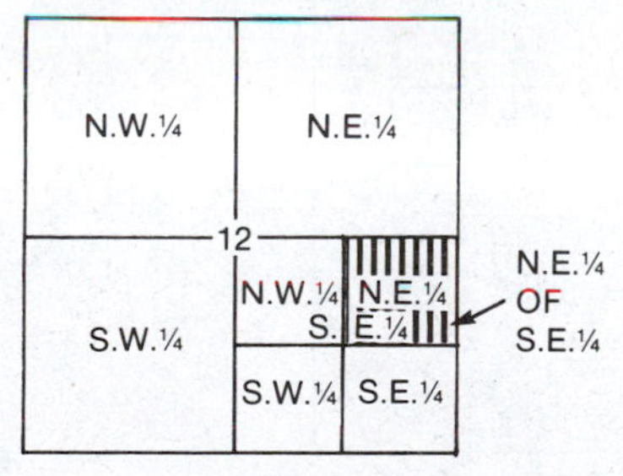

portion of the section. The above example is a rather simple one; however, the system can be used to describe smaller tracts that are not necessarily quarters or fractions of quarters. Consider the following description: 5 acres, by parallel lines, off the north end of the north one-half of the West one-half of the northwest one-quarter of the southwest one-quarter of Section 12, Township 4 north, Range 4 east of the First Principal Meridian. The property thus described is graphically shown in the accompanying illustration, and the complexity of the description illustrates the value of working backwards through the description to accurately locate the property.

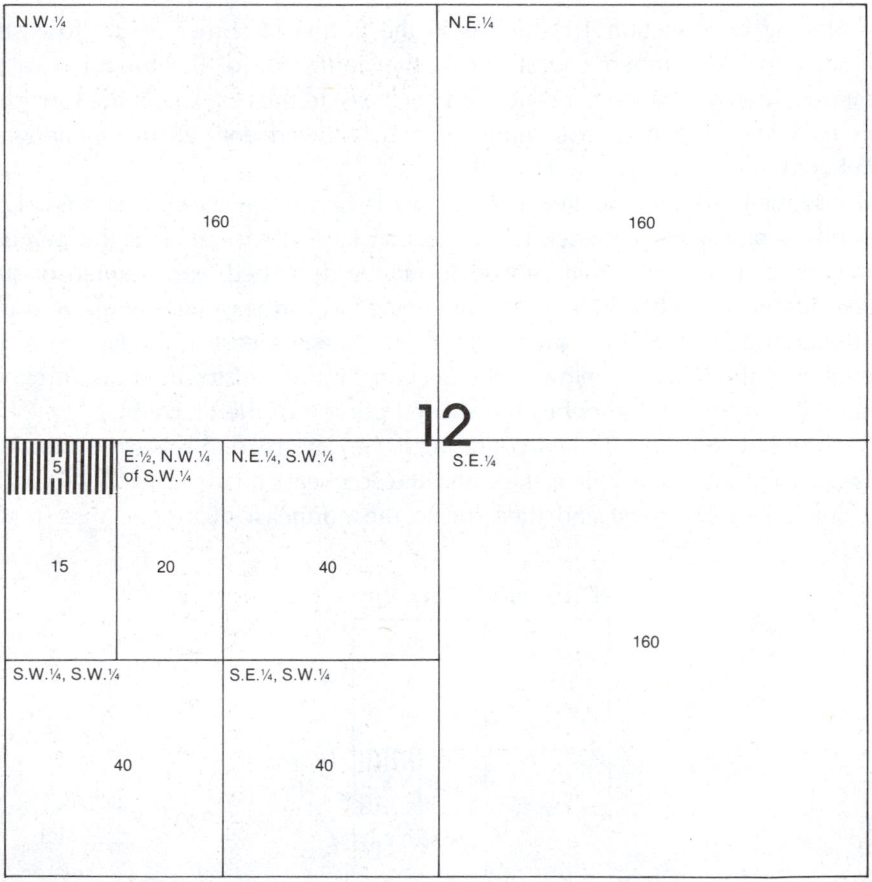

Disregarding the curvature of the earth and assuming that Section 12, above, has the full 640 acres it should have, we can, from the above description, accurately spell out the dimensions of the property described. Each section of land is one mile (5,280 ft) square. Therefore, the north line of the described property will be 660 feet in length, determined as follows:

1. The north boundary of the southwest one-quarter is 2,640 feet (one-half of the total distance across the section of 5,280 feet).
2. The west one-half of this distance will be 1,320 ft (one-half of 2,640 feet).
3. The west one-half of the above will be 660 feet.

The south boundary will have the same length because the callout in the description was "by parallel lines." Now we must determine the length of the eastern and western boundaries. Since we know the western boundary of the southwest quarter to be 2,640 feet, and that of its northwest quarter to be 1,320 feet, we can also reason that 5 acres is exactly one-quarter of the 20 acres located in the west half of that one-quarter of one-quarter. The west (as well as the east) boundary will therefore be 330 feet. To check the accuracy of this conclusion, we might multiply the two dimensions to determine the total square footage:

$$660 \text{ ft.} \times 330 \text{ ft.} = 217{,}800 \text{ sq. ft.}$$

and divide the result by 43,560 (the number of square feet in an acre) to arrive at acreage described:

$$217{,}800 \text{ sq. ft.} \div 43{,}560 \text{ sq. ft.} = 5 \text{ acres}$$

While the dimensions of the property are theoretically accurate, they are based upon the assumption that Section 12 is perfectly proportioned. This is seldom true in practice because of the inaccuracies of the early surveys. A new survey of the section might show that the northern boundary is actually only 654 feet. In that case we would have to establish the western and eastern boundaries at *333.03* feet in order to come up with the specified acreage. It must be clearly understood that the callout in the deed's legal description will prevail. Here, by definition, the conveyance was of "5 acres, by parallel lines. . . ." It did not mean a "nominal" 5 acres. Because of the inaccuracies of the original governmental survey, such a description can prove to be troublesome because it may not describe correctly the parcel the parties bargained for. For this reason today it would be better practice to use the metes-and-bounds description, discussed next.

### Metes and Bounds

A metes-and-bounds description of a tract of land starts at a designated point and proceeds to bound the tract by reference to lineal units of measurement and directions. It is also frequently called a description by courses and distances.

As noted above, in connection with descriptions utilizing the governmental survey, it is preferrable today to rely upon a new survey and a metes-and-bounds description. The same parcel of land described in Section 12 could also be described by the following metes-and-bounds description: "a portion of Section 12, Township 4 north, Range 3 east of the First Principal Meridian, beginning at a point 2,640 feet directly south of the northwest corner of said section, thence due east a distance of 660 feet to a point, thence due south a distance of 330 feet to a point, thence west 660 feet to a point, thence north 330 feet to the place of beginning, containing 5 acres." In such a description we have much more precision and accuracy. If the parcel of land involved has an odd shape, the metes-and-bounds description may be the only way in which it can be accurately described.

Portions of lots in a city are frequently described by metes and bounds. The point of beginning may be the intersection of two streets. If the point of beginning is to be the intersection of Dodds Street and Main Street, for instance, the description should read: "At the intersection of the center line of Dodds Street and Main Street" or "the intersection of the north side of Dodds Street with the west side of Main Street."

## Monuments

Monuments are visible marks or physical features, either natural or artificial, that are used to bound the property. A monument may be a stake or a stone set up as a marker of the boundary. It may also be a natural object, such as a tree, a stream, or the crest of a hill. While courses and distances are frequently included in such a description, the following description, even though prepared in 1935, was still considered accurate enough in 1966 to permit title insurance to issue:

The Southeast quarter of the Northeast quarter of Section 17, Township 13 North, Range 1, East, excepting a tract of Four (4) acres, more or less, situate in the Northeast corner of the tract above described and further described by metes and bounds as follows, viz: Commencing at a Beech at a point 707 feet East of the Northwest corner of the above described Southeast quarter of the Northeast quarter of said Section 17, Township 13 North, Range 1 East, thence running a Southeasterly direction 342 feet to a sugar tree 9 inches in diameter standing on the South side of ravine at the edge of the hill, thence in a more Easterly direction along the edge of the hill to a sugar tree 7 inches in diameter the distance of 104 feet, thence continuing Easterly down and along the edge of the hill on the South side of the channel of the ravine the distance of 450 feet to an elm tree a short distance from East line of said Southeast quarter of the Northeast quarter, thence East to said line, thence North following said East line to the Northeast corner of said Southeast quarter of the Northeast quarter, thence West to the place of beginning, containing 36 acres, more or less, in Morgan County, Indiana.

Such a description would, in many instances, be inadequate because the monuments are not permanent, particularly elm trees. The above description was selected, however, to illustrate an additional point: It is a description by *exception* as well as being a description by monuments. Note that the subject parcel of 36 acres is basically described in terms of the governmental survey: it consists of a quarter of a quarter section of ground, *excepting* the portion so elaborately described.

### Reference to Recorded Plat or Map

When a tract of land is subdivided, a plat or map of the subdivision will be recorded. This plat will, as a general rule, be given a distinguishing name or a number, so that it can be identified, and it will be entered into the plat book. On this plat the size and shape of each lot will be shown, and each block and lot will be numbered. Streets, alleys, easements for utilities, and so forth, will also be indicated on the plat.

The preparation of a plat of a subdivision is a very complex and time-consuming surveying task, particularly with the popularity of meandering streets and cul de sacs. The legal description of a lot in a modern subdivision by use of the governmental survey or of metes and bounds, or a combination of them, would be unintelligible to the property owner and would be prohibitively expensive. Both of these methods are used in laying out the plat of the subdivision, however, and from them the plat or map is prepared, showing the boundaries of each lot in the subdivision and assigning to each lot an identifying number. From that point on, the legal description used in conveyances is deceptively simple: "Lot 45 in Colonial Acres, an addition to the City of Miami, as per plat thereof, recorded in Plat Book 54, page 62, in the office of the Recorder of Dade County, Florida." These few words accurately describe property that might not otherwise be describable is less than five pages of detailed surveying data.

### Descriptions to Be Avoided

Although an informal description may be sufficient to convey title to real estate, such descriptions should not be used in deeds, leases, or contracts relating to interests in real estate. The courts have held descriptions by popular name—such as "my farm, Hoosier Acres"—to be adequate. The courts have also held to be sufficient such descriptions as "all my land in Monroe County, Indiana," or "all my real property in the city of Indianapolis, Indiana"; but a deed describing the property conveyed as "all my real estate" is void because of the inadequacy of the description.

Description by street number is sometimes used, especially in leases and contracts to sell improved urban property, but this practice is dangerous. Such a description gives no indication of actual boundaries, and a controversy may arise as to the amount of land included with the building at the street number.[16] Moreover, street names and street numbers may be changed.

Descriptions by areas, such as "two acres in the southeast corner of the S.E. ¼ of the S.W. ¼ of section 17, etc.," should be avoided. A description of this sort does not indicate whether the area is to be rectangular or square. In one such case the court held that the description was sufficient and that the area should be square in shape.

"The East one-half of Lot 6, etc.," is sufficient to pass title but is inadequate as a description, especially if the lot is irregular in its boundaries. The courts have held that such a description would be interpreted as an intent to convey one-half of the lot in area, without reference to the frontage or other considerations. A metes-and-bounds description should be used; or if the lot lines are parallel and run due east and west, and north and south, a description such as "the west 30 feet (if it is a 60-foot lot) of Lot 6, etc.," should be used. When the remaining portion of the lot is conveyed, the description used should read: "Lot 6, etc., except the west 30 feet of said lot." By such a conveyance, the entire remaining portion of Lot 6 will be conveyed. If the description reads "the east 30 feet of Lot 6" and, on resurvey, it is found that the lot is more than 60 feet wide, title to a narrow strip lying between the two portions conveyed will remain in the grantor. If the lot were found to be less than 60 feet wide, the second grantee would get less than the 30 feet he bargained for.

## Incomplete, Erroneous, and Conflicting Descriptions

The general rule—that a description is sufficient if, by reference thereto, the real estate intended to be conveyed by the deed can be identified—is applied in determining whether or not an omission in the description in a deed invalidates the deed. Under the parol evidence rule, oral evidence is not admissible to alter or vary the terms of a written instrument; and under the provisions of the statute of frauds, the deed (writing), in order to be sufficient, must contain all the material

---

[16] *Killian* v. *Welfare Engineering Co.,* 328 Ill. App. 375, 66 N.E.2d 305.

terms of the transaction. Consequently, if the omission is such that the real estate cannot be identified from the description in the deed, the conveyance will fail.

In a description of a lot by reference to a recorded plat, the omission of the block number, if the subdivision is divided into blocks and lots, will render the description inoperative, since the lot cannot be located from the description. In a description by governmental survey, the omission of the prime meridian in a description, if the name of the city, county, and state are included, will not be fatal, since the real estate can be located without reference to the prime meridian.[17]

In describing real estate, errors may be made, such as indicating the "N.E. ½" when the true description should be "S.E. ¼," or stating "thence south to place of beginning" when the description should be "thence north." When such errors, obviously clerical or typographical, are made, the court will reject the false and impossible part of the description, if the real estate can be identified from the remaining part of the description, and will hold the description to be sufficient.[18]

The courts have adopted some general rules of construction that are usually applied in interpreting descriptions in deeds when there are conflicting elements. If the description is ambiguous, parol evidence is admissible to clear up the ambiguity, but not to add to or alter the terms of the deed.

If the description is stated in general terms followed by specific terms and there is a conflict between the general and the specific terms, the specific terms will control.

If there is a conflict in a description between courses and distances and monuments, the monuments control. Also, if, in addition to a description of land, there is a statement of area, and there is a variation between the area described and the area stated, the description of the area will control.[19]

### Streets, Highways, and Waters as Boundaries

As a general rule, if a description gives a public street or highway as a boundary, the land generally runs to the center of the street or highway. This presumption may be overcome by using language in the description that will clearly indicate a contrary intent. In drafting a description of real estate that is bounded by a street, a highway, an alley, or a stream, controversies can be avoided by stating that the boundary is the center line of the street, highway, alley, or stream. If

---

[17] *Harrington* v. *Goldsmith,* 136 Cal. 168, 68 P. 594.

[18] *Moore et al.* v. *Whitley,* 234 N.C. 150, 66 S.E.2d 785.

[19] *Frank Towers Corporation* v. *Laviana et al.,* 140 Conn. 45, 97 A.2d 567.

land is bounded by a private road or alley, the rule followed in the majority of states is the same as that applied to public streets, highways, and alleys, but a few states hold otherwise. If land is bounded by a stream, the general rule is that the center of the stream is the boundary line.

Three deeds described the land conveyed as follows:

1. "Thirty acres in the northern part of Spanish Grant No. 2425 and West and adjoining the ten acre tract known as the Will Lemon's Tract."
2. "Forty (40) acres in the Northern part of Spanish Grant No. 2425, adjoining the ten (10) acre tract known as the Will Lemon's tract."
3. "Northwestern part of Spanish Grant No. 2425 containing twenty acres, (20) more or less, same being all the land owned by us in said Grant No. 2425 having previous sold (by the two other deeds) balance owned by A. N. Best."

In an action of ejectment and for rents against the Miller brothers, who claimed the title through a grant from Tom Miller, a prior owner, the Miller brothers claimed that deed No. 3 was insufficient to convey title to the land. The court held that the description of the land in the three deeds was insufficient.

Justice George Rose Smith said: "It is settled that 'part' descriptions such as these are void for indefiniteness. Although a surveyor testified that he was able to locate the tracts from the descriptions we have quoted, he must have relied upon physical evidence such as fences, for the language of the deed supplies no clue that could lead to an identification of the property. The rule is that the conveyance itself must furnish that clue." *Miller* v. *Best,* Ark., 361 S.W.2d 737 (1962).

A deed described the land conveyed as "Tract 87, Zimmerman's Map, 1904." Zimmerman's Map, 1904, was a map prepared by a surveyor employed by the county to prepare a map to be used as the basis for assessment of taxes. Although the map did not show points of beginning and was not certified to by the surveyor and was never officially made a matter of record, it did bear on its face the following endorsement: "Filed this 31st day of December, A.D. 1904, at 5 o'clock P.M. Celso Lopez, Recorder, by Deputy." From the map, directions could be determined, and aided by arroyos, natural boundaries, road crossings, and curves in arroyos shown on the map, the boundaries of the various tracts of the city could be determined. The trial court held that the description was insufficient. On appeal, this holding was reversed, and the Supreme Court held the deed valid.

Chief Justice Compton said: ". . . it is not necessary that the description of the land be contained in the body of the deed. It is sufficient if it refers for identification to some other instrument or document, but the description must be contained in the instrument or its reference, expressed or implied with such certainty that the locality of the land can be ascertained. . . . The rule has also been held to apply to maps and plats, including surveys, and to an assessor's plan. The deed is not void because the instrument referred to is incomplete, not official, unacknowledged, unrecorded or unattached or misdescribed in some particular or even invalid." *Hughes* v. Meem, 70 N.M. 122, 371 P.2d 235 (1962).

# Chapter 6

# Personal Property, Fixtures, and Mechanics' Liens

In the following discussion several distinct topics have been joined because of the common thread of legal theory that is involved when personal property and real property are joined. While different bodies of law apply to each type of property, one of them must prevail when the two types are joined in such a way that they cannot be physically separated without damage or that they may not be *legally* separated without doing violence to the clear intent of the parties. The different tests that the law has developed to determine when property changes its character and is governed by different rules of law are considered, with the emphasis being placed on the most important test: What did the parties intend or what would have been the intent of *reasonable* men? The basic law of fixtures has not changed, but the flexibility of the common law is dramatized by the application of the law of fixtures.

Also introduced in this chapter is the concept of *security* interests in real estate. This important subject will be expanded upon in later chapters, but the essential notion—that one who has increased the value of another's real estate by adding something to it that increases its value is entitled to be assured of payment—is easier to grasp when the addition is obvious. The concept of a *lien* or charge upon real estate is an important one because without it all improvements would have to be paid for in cash (as a practical matter) so that the supplier would be assured of payment. The high cost of improvements to real estate today makes cash payment much less likely; but the extension of credit for improvements to real estate is made easier by granting the supplier the right to hold a lien upon the real estate that he has improved.

## Distinction between Personal Property and Real Estate

The distinction between personal property and real estate is both practical and logical. It was recognized at an early period in the development of society and is now a part of the law of all civilized nations. Simply stated, the earth's crust and all things attached thereto are real estate; all other property is personal property. However, this elementary rule is inadequate as the basis for the solution of problems arising in our complex society. We change the character of property from real estate to personal property by severance, and we change personal property to real estate by attachment. Stone, in its natural condition in the earth's crust, is real estate; but when it is severed from the earth's crust—quarried—it becomes personal property, and is bought and sold as such. When the quarried stone is fashioned into a building, it becomes real estate, and is bought and sold as such, along with the land on which the structure has been erected.

In dealing with real estate, many situations arise in which it is necessary to determine whether or not a particular item of property passes as real estate to the purchaser of land or remains the personal property of the seller. This area of the law is known as the *law of fixtures.*

## Fixtures

The term *fixture,* as used in real estate law, has an important and legally significant meaning. It is used to describe an item of personal property that would normally be governed by the body of law relating to personality. In connection with real estate, however, the significance of the term is that a fixture is an item of personal property which has, by being attached to or associated with a parcel of real estate, changed its character and has become *real property* and thus governed by a different body of law. The two bodies of law have developed, of course, along different lines because personal property is usually portable, while real estate is fixed in location and cannot be moved. The resulting conflict becomes troublesome when personal property, governed by one set of legal principles, becomes real property and thereafter governed by a different set of legal concepts and rules. The major difficulty one encounters in the law of fixtures is recognition of the point at which the property changes character. In this area the rule of reasonableness is put to a difficult test. At the same time, however, the elasticity of the common law is clearly evident.

Original common-law notions in the law of fixtures demanded some form of attachment of the personal property to the real estate that was obvious, permanent in nature, and suitable for the use to which the real estate was being put. This idea is easy to grasp when one considers the construction of a house upon a lot in a subdivision. Clearly, the lumber, bricks, windows, doors, heating system, and the like are personal property when they are brought upon the real estate. When they are assembled into a completed residence that is permanently attached to the ground, it is not difficult to accept the conclusion that the two types of property have become one: real property, because the unit that results is not easily transportable. It is far more difficult to accept this consequence when the personal property is not so attached that its removal would damage the structure, as in the case of an electric range that is merely plugged into the proper outlet. Yet, there are situations in which the conclusion that the electric range is part of the real estate is perfectly reasonable.

In attempting to provide meaningful guidelines in determining just when personal property has become real property, our courts have developed several specific tests, which are discussed below. In applying these tests the courts have also recognized that the relationship between the parties disputing the issue must also be taken into account. What is a reasonable rule, for example, between a buyer and seller of a residence has no bearing on the relationship between a landlord and tenant of commercial space. It is suggested at this point that, even though the various tests discussed below are quite valid, and are taken directly from the decisions written by our courts, the true test being applied is the intent of the parties. When the tenant of an apartment laid down carpeting that can be removed without damage to the flooring, did he *intend* to make that carpeting a part of the building and to leave it behind when he vacates the apartment? Did the oil company, when it built a gas station upon a choice commercial location under a 25-year lease, *intend* to leave the building when the lease expired? Does the homeowner who installs central air conditioning *intend* to take it with him when he sells the house to another?

The above questions could, conceivably, be answered by one of the standard tests that have evolved: Is the method of attachment of such a nature that structural damage would result from its removal? Even this test, which has the advantage of more or less easy proof, is not satisfactory for all situations. It is for this reason that the suggestion has been made that our courts are, in reality, looking to the intent of the parties even when they decide a case on the basis of the mode of attachment. Caution is required at this point, as it is with any generalization about real estate law. The courts are not attempting to determine the *actual* intent of the parties, unless, of course, some express agreement between them is at issue.

What the courts *are* attempting to determine is: What would the intent be, under a given set of circumstances, of a *reasonable* person? The intent of the fool is of no consequence. In addition to the concept of imposing the "reasonable person" test, we must always keep in mind that reasonableness is colored by the judgment of the court: what the court thinks a reasonable person would conclude is what the court thinks is reasonable. Finally, the courts are obligated to look only at those facts that are properly placed into evidence, and the failure of one party to be able to prove a key fact cannot be cured by the court. It is for this last reason that occasionally a court will decide a case under the rule of reasonableness that outside observers cannot comprehend or accept as being correct. In the vast majority of such cases, a careful analysis will show that the facts required to reach a different conclusion were not proven and could not, therefore, be considered by the court.

## Standard Tests

### Express Agreement

If parties agree that personal property attached to or used with real estate shall remain personal property and may be detached and removed, the courts will enforce the agreement. However, if personal property is built into a structure and the severance of such property would destroy or seriously injure the structure, the courts will refuse to enforce the agreement. An agreement was enforced whereby a landlord permitted a tenant to install an oil burner in the furnace on the leased premises with the right to remove it on the termination of the lease, provided the tenant restored the furnace to its original condition.[1]

If the owner of real estate purchases, under a conditional sales contract, supporting I-beams that are to be used in the construction of a building on the premises, and the contract expressly provides that the I-beams shall remain personal property and may be repossessed if not paid for, the courts, in case there is a default, will not permit the removal of the I-beams, since such removal would destroy or seriously damage the structure. The courts have held that a person purchasing real estate from an owner not in possession takes it subject to the right of the person in possession to remove attached personal property.[2]

Haverfield Company leased from Siegel certain designated space in a building which, at the time the lease was executed, was under construction. Eight wall cases were specially

---

[1] *Brandt* v. *Koppelman et al.,* 169 Pa. Super. 236, 82 A.2d 666.

[2] *Sarafin* v. *Wolff et ux.,* 5 N.J. Super. 386, 69 A.2d 347.

constructed for the building. The cases served as a partition wall between the sales area and the fitting rooms. The lease provided that the lessee would pay for the cases and their installation; that they would be depreciated at the rate of 10 percent per year; and that if the lease were terminated, the lessor would pay the lessee the cost of the cases less the depreciated value. The lease further provided that "the fixtures, except trade fixtures, shall become the property of the lessor." The lessee had possession of the premises for twelve years; consequently, under the terms of the lease the price of the cases was completely depreciated. Haverfield Company claimed the cases as trade fixtures. The court held that by the terms of the lease the cases were fixtures and the property of the lessor, Siegel.

Justice Pope said: "The intention of the parties is expressed and governed by the lease agreement. . . . The parties contemplated that those items which were part of the permanent construction, . . . were the items termed (fixtures) in the lease." *Haverfield Company* v. *Siegel,* Tex. Civ. App., 366 S.W.2d 790 (1963).

### Mode of Attachment

At one period in the development of the law of fixtures, the only test applied by the courts was that of attachment. Today, attachment or—more specifically—the mode of attachment is of outstanding importance but is not controlling. If personal property has been firmly attached to the real estate, it is strong evidence that the party so attaching the property intended it to become a part of the real estate; but if the property is so affixed that it can be easily removed without injury to it or to the real estate to which it is attached, then there is strong evidence that the parties intended it to retain its own character as personal property.

At one time, lighting fixtures were owned by the tenant and were generally held to be the personal property of the tenant. Today, lighting fixtures, furnaces, and similar equipment installed in a building are generally held to be fixtures, even though they are so attached that they can be removed without injury to either the equipment or the real estate to which they are attached. Such items are usually considered as part of the completed structure.[3]

Whether appliances such as gas and electric stoves, refrigerators, freezers, washers, and dryers are held to be fixtures or personal property will depend more on the surrounding circumstances than on the mode of attachment. The courts may come to opposite conclusions in cases in which the mode of attachment is substantially the same. A careful analysis of the facts of the cases, however, will usually reveal differences in the surrounding circumstances that justify the

---

[3] *Batcheler* v. *Lally,* Pa. Com. Pl., 40 Luz. L. Reg. Rep. 166.

variance in the decisions of the courts.[4] In the absence of an agreement to the contrary, the courts have been consistent in holding that "built-in" appliances are fixtures.

At one stage in the development of the law of fixtures, the courts held that if a structure was set up on blocks or stones that were not embedded in the earth, there was no attachment, and the structure was personal property. However, under present-day law a building, in the absence of an express agreement to the contrary, will be held to be a fixture, even though its foundation is not embedded in the earth.[5] In one case the court held that a statue and sundial set on a cement foundation, not fastened by bolts or clamps but held in place by gravity, was a fixture.[6]

If a building is set on a foundation, or is joined with the land by being set over a basement and is connected with the sewer and water mains, it will be held to be real estate, unless there is an agreement to the contrary.[7]

## Adaptation to Use with Real Estate

Another important consideration is the adaptation or appropriation of the personal property to the use or purpose of the real estate to which it is attached. If personal property has been attached to the real estate to promote the purpose for which the realty is held, the courts will presume that the party affixing it to the realty intended it to become a part of the real estate, regardless of the mode of attachment.[8] In the more recent cases the courts have, as a general rule, given more weight to the adaptation of the article to the use of the real estate than they have to the method of attachment. If the personal property is attached to the real estate for the purpose of improving it and making it more valuable, it will generally be held to be a fixture; but if it is brought onto the realty for temporary use that does not enhance the value of the realty and may be removed at the pleasure of the person making the attachment without injury to the realty, it will usually be held to retain its character as personal property, even though it is attached to the realty.

---

[4] *Leisle* v. *Welfare Building and Loan Association,* 232 Wis. 440, 287 N.W. 739.

[5] *Cornell College* v. *Crain et al.,* 211 Iowa 1343, 235 N.W. 731.

[6] *Snedeker* v. *Warring,* 12 N.Y. 170.

[7] *Standard Oil Company* v. *Braun,* 53 N.D. 104, 204 N.W. 972; *Crawford-Fayram Lumber Co.* v. *Mann,* 203 Iowa 748, 211 N.W. 225.

[8] *Citizens Bank of Greenfield* v. *Mergenthaler Linotype Co.,* 216 Ind. 573, 25 N.E.2d 444.

### Intention of Parties

The courts, in determining whether or not an item of property is a fixture, attempt to ascertain the intention of the parties. It is obvious that in many cases the parties did not consider the question and could not have entertained an intention regarding it. Consequently, the courts have set up and applied the following standard: What would a man of ordinary prudence, familiar with the business at hand, with the customs of the community, and with all the facts and circumstances of the transaction, be justified in believing the parties intended? In applying this standard, certain factual elements are important, but none is conclusive.

The lessee drilled a well on the leased premises and installed pumping equipment costing between $20,000 and $25,000. The well was a failure, and at the time of the expiration of the lease the pumping equipment was standing on wooden blocks, unattached to the land. The lessee claimed the pumping equipment as his personal property, and the lessor claimed it was a fixture. The court held that it was personal property.

Presiding Justice Conley said: "The authorities apply a threefold test in determining whether or not an article is a fixture: '(1) the manner of its annexation; (2) its adaptability to the use and purpose for which the realty is used; and (3) the intention of the parties making the annexation.'. . . It was reasonable for the trial court to consider that there was no intention to make a gift of equipment costing $20,000 or $25,000 to the owner of the premises. *Banks* v. *Clintworth,* 20 Cal. Rptr. 431 (1963).

Aegen, Inc., obtained a construction loan from Union Savings, which was secured by a mortgage on a new apartment building to be built by Aegen. Some 6,500 yards of carpeting were installed in the apartments by stapling it to thin layers of plywood covering the fireproof concrete floors. After the installation Aegen sold the carpeting to Exchange Leasing Corp., and then leased it back over a three-year period. In a suit by Exchange to recover possession of the carpeting, Union Savings intervened and asserted its mortgage on the theory that the carpeting was a fixture and subject to the mortgage on the land and building. In finding that the carpet became part of the building and therefore subject to the mortgage, the court said in part: "The law of fixtures has not changed materially since the development of the rule, that a chattel closely associated with and dedicated to the use of land when so intended was to be treated as a part of the land, was determined, at a very early date. . . . However, the kind of property subject to the rule has developed materially as new methods in the use of materials in construction or manufacturing enterprises, decorative desires and personal requirements have advanced to meet the needs of a changing industrial civilization. . . . The carpet cases which hold that carpet when tacked to the floor does not without more become a part of the realty are cases where the owner of the property seeks to and claims a tenant's carpet where the tenant installed such carpeting for his own use and enjoyment. This is quite different from the facts in the case at bar, where the owner of an apartment building installed carpeting as a permanent facility for the use of the tenants of each suite." *Exchange Leasing Corp.* v. *Finster N. Aegen, Inc.,* 7 Ohio App. 2d. 11,218 NE2d 633 (1966).

***Unattached Property.*** The courts have held, with a few exceptions, that an article of personal property particularly adapted for use with certain real estate, but useful elsewhere and not attached to the real estate, is not a fixture.[9] However, in a few cases the courts have held that such articles are fixtures if it was reasonably clear that the owner intended them to be used permanently with the real estate. In one case the court held that rollaway beds were fixtures, since closets had been constructed for the sole purpose of receiving the beds when not in use.[10] The courts have held machinery and other articles brought into and fastened to a building to be fixtures if they were essential to the carrying-on of the business to which the building was devoted.[11] And in some instances the courts have held such machinery to be a fixture even though it was not physically attached to the building.[12]

In an unusual situation, drapes and their hardware, having been installed, were treated as fixtures, while the matching bedspreads remained personal property.[13]

### New Housing Concepts

The notion expressed by the court in the *Aegen* case, noted above, is indicative of the fact that, while the basic rules of law regarding fixtures have not changed, courts will give effect to new developments in the application of those rules. An important and relatively new concept to which the law of fixtures must be applied is that of the mobile home. In the early days of the industry the term house trailer was in vogue, and it was quite appropriate because such living units were essentially *trailers* and quite correctly categorized as personal property. Today, however, many mobile homes are true *homes,* and they are mobile only in the sense that it is *possible* to move them. Special hauling equipment is usually required to do so, adding support to the argument that they are homes that are intended to be more or less permanently attached to real estate, even though the real estate normally utilized is characterized as a mobile home park, as opposed to a subdivision consisting of residences that are usually not capable of being moved. To further confuse the issue there has been the advent of the so-called "modular" home, which is assembled for the most part in factories and delivered to the pre-prepared site on trailers, at which point the modules are, literally, set

---

[9] *Fry et al.* v. *Lost Key Mine, Inc. et al.,* 108 Col. App. 568, 239 P.2d 69.

[10] *Leisle* v. *Welfare Building and Loan Association,* 232 Wis. 440, 287 N.W. 739.

[11] *Atlantic Die Casting Co.* v. *Whiting Tubular Products, Inc.,* 337 Mich. 414, 60 N.W.2d 174.

[12] *Pennsylvania Chocolate Co.* v. *Hershey Bros.,* 316 Pa. 292, 175 A. 694.

[13] *Sears, Roebuck & Co.* v. *Seven Palms Motor Inn,* 530 S.W.2d 695 (Mo. 1975).

into place and bolted together to form a complete residential unit or units. It would appear that there is little difference between the mobile home and the modular home; in fact, some modular units are hinged so that, quite conceivably, they could be knocked down, moved, and reset at a different location.

While surprisingly few cases have appeared that consider the characterization of this form of housing as a fixture that becomes a part of the real estate when put into place in a more or less permanent fashion, this may result from the awareness of suppliers of cases like the *Aegen* decision. As a practical matter these suppliers treat their products as personal property, but at the same time insist upon full payment before the units are set into place. This maneuver avoids the question of whether or not their products become fixtures and therefore subject to the primary lien of the mortgage lender. On the other hand, there have been a great many cases in the areas of zoning and enforcement of restrictive covenants against "temporary" housing, which have consistently held that at least the mobile home is not a permanent building, while modular houses have not been attacked on these same grounds. Largely by default of cases, it appears that the modular home will be treated as a permanent dwelling while a mobile home may not. This is a dangerous generalization to make, however, since it is based upon the theory that courts will apply the same thinking in determining questions raised under the law of fixtures as they apply in the areas of zoning and restrictive covenants. (Further discussion of this matter is included in Chapter 20.)

## Relation of Parties

### Owner

Since the owner of property is free, within limits, to use his property as he wishes, he is at liberty to attach personal property to his real estate and detach it at will, and no question arises as to whether the property attached remains personal property or becomes a fixture. The ownership of both the attached property and the real estate is vested in the same person, and the character of such attached property is immaterial. It is only when the real estate is sold, mortgaged, or leased that a question may arise as to the character of personal property that is attached to or used with the real estate.

### Vendee versus Vendor

When the owner of real estate attaches to it personal property that is appropriate for the purpose for which the real estate is used, there is a strong presumption that he intends the article to be a fixture. If the property is sold and there is no reservation in the contract of sale or deed, the courts will resolve all doubt in favor of the purchaser.

Frequently, articles have been held to be fixtures as between vendor and vendee that would not have been held to be fixtures if the relation of the parties had been different—landlord and tenant, for example.[14]

The same rules apply to a mortgage transaction. The mortgagee of real estate acquires all the rights of a vendee; that is, the mortgage is a lien on all fixtures that were a part of the realty at the time the mortgage was executed, unless they are excluded by an agreement in writing or by a provision in the mortgage.[15]

Peed owned a duplex, which he sold to Bennett. At the time of the sale, Peed was living in the lower apartment, and the upper apartment was rented. Peed had installed in the upper apartment a refrigerator and stove for the use of tenants occupying the apartment. At the time of the sale, Peed told Bennett that the apartment rented for $60 per month by reason of the fact that the refrigerator and stove were furnished to the apartment. There was no reference to the refrigerator and stove in the purchase agreement or deed. Peed claimed the refrigerator and stove as personal property, and Bennett claimed them as fixtures. The court held that the refrigerator and stove were fixtures.

Judge Dowell said: "The instant case is one between vendor and purchaser of real estate and of this much there can be little doubt, that as between such parties the modern doctrine is that the rule for determining what is a fixture is strongly construed against the vendor and in favor of the purchaser. . . .

"Many chattels have been held to be fixtures as between vendor and purchaser of lands or as between mortgagor and mortgagee thereof which do not lose their character of personal chattels when the question is between landlord and tenant or others." *Peed* v. *Bennett,* 114 Ind. App. 412, 52 N.E.2d 629 (1944).

***Exceptions and Reservations.*** In handling a transaction, if there is any question as to the character of items, one should clearly state in the contract of sale the items that are to become the property of the vendee, and those that are excepted from the sale and reserved by the vendor. As a general rule, an oral exception or reservation is ineffective, although under some circumstances, such an exception or reservation might be enforced.

Under the statute of frauds, any contract affecting an interest in real estate is unenforceable unless it is evidenced by a note or memorandum in writing. Since a fixture is real estate, a reservation, in order to be enforceable, must be in writing.[16] In addition, under the parol evidence rule, oral evidence is inadmissible

---

[14] *Peed* v. *Bennett,* 114 Ind. App. 412, 52 N.E.2d 629.

[15] *Fusor* v. *Whittaker et al.,* 28 Tenn. App. 338, 190 S.W.2d 305.

[16] *Bricker* v. *Whisler,* 65 Ind. App. 492, 117 N.E. 550.

to add to, alter, or vary the terms of a written instrument; consequently, if there is no exception or reservation in the contract or deed, oral evidence offered to prove an oral exception or reservation would be inadmissible.[17]

### Holders of Security Interest in Attached Personalty versus Owner

If the owner of real estate purchases personal property and gives a security interest in it under the provisions of the Uniform Commercial Code; or if the owner gives a chattel mortgage or buys on a conditional sales contract in a non-Code state; or if a security interest either under the Code or under a chattel mortgage, in a non-Code state, is given on attached personal property to secure an obligation, the court will hold that the security transaction is, in effect, an agreement that the attached property shall be personal property, and the secured party, in the event there is a default, will have the right to detach the property from the real estate and proceed to foreclose his lien.[18]

As a general rule, if the owner of real estate permits another, as a licensee, to affix to the real estate personal property owned by the licensee, the attached article remains personal property and may be removed by the licensee.[19]

### Vendee versus Holder of Security Interest

If, at the time a person purchases real estate, there is attached to it personal property on which there is a perfected security interest under the Uniform Commercial Code, or under a chattel mortgage or conditional sales contract if the property is in a non-Code state, the rights of the vendee will depend on whether or not he had notice or knowledge of the outstanding interest in such attached personal property. The vendee will have notice if the purchase agreement or deed contains provisions excepting or reserving the personal property or if the purchase agreement states that the real estate is sold subject to the outstanding security interest in the specific attached personal property.

Under the Uniform Commercial Code, provision is made for perfecting a security interest in fixtures; if the secured party complies with the requirements of the Code, his security interest in the fixture will have priority over all persons subsequently acquiring an interest in the real estate, subject to certain stated exceptions.[20]

The Uniform Conditional Sales Act, Section 7, provides for the recording in

---

[17] *Wellman* v. *Tomblin,* W.Va., 84 S.E.2d 617.

[18] *Swift Lumber and Fuel Company* v. *Elwanger et al.,* 127 Neb. 740, 256 N.W. 875.

[19] *Wilson* v. *Modica,* Tex. Civ. App., 80 S.W.2d 411.

[20] *Uniform Commercial Code,* Sec. 9–313.

the real estate records of conditional sales contracts of personal property that is to be attached to real estate; and if a conditional sales contract is properly recorded under the provisions of the act, a subsequent purchaser or mortgagee of the real estate takes subject to the rights of the conditional vendor. An improperly recorded or an unrecorded chattel mortgage or conditional sales contract is void against a bona fide purchaser or an innocent mortgagee of the real estate to which the article is attached.[21]

### Landlord and Tenant

***Domestic Fixtures.*** Domestic or ornamental fixtures are fixtures attached to a dwelling for the purpose of making it a more comfortable and attractive place in which to live. The early English courts held that any personal property attached to leased real estate by the tenant became the property of the landlord, but the modern courts favor the tenant and have held that he may remove such fixtures, provided they can be detached without material injury to the real estate. If the article attached is a substitute for one that was there at the time of the lease, it may not be removed unless the old fixture has been preserved and can be reinstalled without material injury to the real estate.

In those cases in which the landlord and tenant have entered into an agreement that gives the tenant the right to remove personal property that the tenant has attached to the leased premises, the court will enforce such agreement. In the event the agreement does not state a time within which such property shall be removed, the courts have generally held that the tenant will have a reasonable time after the termination of the lease in which to remove attached property.[22] Some courts have held, however, that if the lease is for a specific term, the tenant must remove the property before the expiration of the lease.

***Trade Fixtures.*** A trade fixture is an article attached to the leased real estate by the tenant to aid him in carrying on the business or profession he is operating on the leased premises. In determining whether or not an article is a trade fixture, the mode of annexation and the size of the article are of secondary importance. However, if a tenant incorporates an article into the building in such a manner that its removal would weaken the structure, the courts have held that the article is not a trade fixture, even though it was attached to the building by the tenant for the purpose of making the structure more suitable for carrying on the business

---

[21] The rights of a real estate mortgagee against the holder of a security interest in fixtures is discussed in Chapter 12.

[22] *Hubert* v. *Collard,* Tex. Civ. App., 141 S.W.2d 677.

conducted on the premises.[23] A provision in a lease stating that certain items attached to the real estate shall or shall not become a part of the realty will be enforced.

Under the common-law rule, if the tenant did not remove trade fixtures before the expiration of a lease for a specific term, the fixtures became the property of the landlord. Some courts based the rule on the ground that if the fixtures were not removed before the end of the term, the tenant must have intended them to be permanent additions to the realty. Other courts held that if the tenant entered the premises after the expiration of the term, he would be a trespassor and that therefore he forfeited his right to remove the fixtures. A majority of the courts have held that if the tenant is left in possession of the premises, with the consent of the landlord, after the expiration of the lease, the tenant has the right to remove trade fixtures during the period of possession.[24] If the lease is for an indefinite period, the tenant has a reasonable time after the termination of the lease within which to remove his trade fixtures.

Kelm owned a building, which he leased as a tavern to Timper. Without the consent of Kelm, Timper removed a bar that was built against one of the walls and replaced it with a circular bar built in the center of the room. In installing this bar, approximately twelve holes, varying in diameter from one to six inches, were drilled in the floor. These holes were made so that the bar could have the necessary electrical and water connections, and so that beer could be piped from the basement of the building. A bottle chute was also installed. The cost of restoring the floor to its original condition would be about $350. In order to make the change in the bar, Timper borrowed money and gave Loan Corporation a chattel mortgage on the bar as security. Timper abandoned the lease, and Loan Corporation claimed the bar. Kelm claimed that the bar was a fixture, not a trade fixture, and that it was his property. The court held that the bar was a fixture and was the property of Kelm.

Justice Wilkie said: "The most important single fact in this case is that when defendant [Kelm] leased the premises to the tenant as a 'tavern' it contained a 'bar.' From this it is easy to conclude that there was an intention on the part of the tenant and landlord to make the new bar part of the premises. When the tenant, who had been utilizing the premises for four years, substituted a new fixture and discarded the old fixture, which he did not initially own, it is reasonable to conclude that he intended that the new fixture was to be substituted for the old fixture and to become the property of the owner of the old fixture." *Auto Acceptance and Loan Corporation* v. *Kelm,* Wis.2d 178, 118 N.W.2d 175 (1962).

---

[23] *Stockton* v. *Tester,* Mo. App., 273 S.W.2d 783.

[24] *Anderson-Tully Company* v. *United States,* 189 F.2d 192.

### Rights under Renewal Lease

The courts are in conflict as to whether or not a tenant's right to remove trade fixtures is lost if he takes a renewal lease or a new lease that does not, by its terms, specifically reserve his right to remove the trade fixtures attached to the premises during the prior terms. The early view, which is still adhered to by some courts, is that if, on the expiration of the first term, the tenant did not remove the fixtures and, on renewal or on the making of a new lease, he did not reserve his right to the fixtures, he thereby abandoned such right.[25]

Some courts have repudiated the rule; some have held that it does not apply to trade fixtures; and some have inferred an understanding, from the circumstances of the case, that the fixtures are removable.

In some states the tenants' rights are protected by statute.[26] If the right to remove fixtures is expressly reserved in the renewal lease or new lease, the courts will enforce the provision.

***Agreement that Tenant Shall Not Remove Property.*** As a general rule, the courts have held that a provision in a lease to the effect that all "alterations, additions, or improvements" to the premises shall, on the expiration of the lease, become the property of the landlord does not include trade fixtures. What would be included as alterations, additions, and improvements is a question of fact to be determined according to all the surrounding circumstances.

### Agricultural Fixtures

Today, we consider the operation of a farm as a business and apply to agriculture fixtures the rules of law relating to trade fixtures.[27]

## Crops, Trees, and Shrubs

### Rights in Crops, Trees, and Shrubs

Technically, crops, trees, and shrubs are not fixtures; but in real estate transactions the problems relating to crops, trees, and shrubs are, from a practical standpoint, similar in many respects to the problems relating to fixtures. Vegetation

---

[25] *Niestadt* v. *Joseph,* 81 Ind. App. 355, 139 N.E. 336.

[26] *Handler* v. *Horns,* 2 N.J. 18, 65 A.2d 523; Maryland, *Flock Annotated Code, 1951,* Art. 53, Sec. 38.

[27] *Old Line Life Insurance Company of America* v. *Hawn et al.,* 225 Wis. 627, 275 N.W. 542.

growing on land is divided into two categories: (1) vegetation that is produced annually by human labor, and (2) vegetation that is the natural product of the soil and is perennial in nature. The former is classed as personal property and the latter as real estate.

As in all classifications, there is no natural, clear line of demarcation between the classes, and disputes often arise as to the classification in which a particular article belongs.

In general, crops that are planted and cultivated annually and fruits, berries, and so forth, that are harvested annually are personal property, and may be bought and sold as such. However, if the land on which such crops are growing is transferred and there is no reservation or exception of the growing crops, the crops pass with the land and become the property of the transferee.

Some courts have enforced oral reservations of crops; at the same time, other courts have held that evidence of an oral reservation of crops is inadmissible under the parol evidence rule or that the reservation must be in writing to satisfy the statute of frauds.[28]

The courts have distinguished between growing crops, matured crops, and severed crops. Growing crops, if not excepted or reserved, pass with the land; severed crops do not. Matured crops—that is, crops that are ripe and ready for harvest but have not been severed from the land—do not, as a general rule, pass with the land.

In all real estate transactions, controversies regarding the rights to crops, trees, and shrubs may be avoided, or at least minimized, by including in the purchase agreement or deed a provision defining the rights of the parties.

The courts are in substantial accord in holding that trees and shrubs are a part of the land and that any exception or reservation relating to them must be in writing.

### Standing Timber

The sale of standing timber, to be left on the land for an appreciable period of time, is the sale of real estate and must be treated as such. A sale of trees to be cut, either by the seller or by the buyer, within a short period of time has been held to be a sale of personal property. The courts so holding have based their decisions on a theory of constructive severance. They hold that the sale is a sale of the severed logs, not of the standing trees.[29]

---

[28] *Dick* v. *Horn,* 97 Okla. 258, 223 P. 393.
[29] *Edwards* v. *Glaske,* 165 Pa. Super. 108, 67 A.2d 798.

### Nursery Stock

Nursery stock is personal property. The operation of a nursery is considered to be the operation of a business, and the nursery stock is considered to be the stock in trade of the business. Plants, trees, and shrubs in the nursery are all held to be personal property.[30]

The city of Los Angeles condemned a tract of land owned by Pedersen and leased to Hoover Nursery Company. The lease gave Hoover Nursery Company the right to remove the nursery stock. A controversy arose as to the right of Hoover Nursery Company to compensation for condemned nursery stock. The court held that the nursery stock was part of the real estate and that under the terms of the lease, Hoover Nursery Company had an interest in the real estate and was entitled to compensation for it.

The court said: "Respondent [City of Los Angeles] contends, however, that, because the lease between the parties provided that nursery stock might be planted and grown by the nursery company for resale by it, such trees and plants acquired the character of personal property exclusively. . . . Growing trees, shrubs and other plants were generally considered a part of the realty to which they are attached by their roots, and continued to be such until they were severed, when they became personal property. The occasion to declare trees, plants, crops, etc., to be personal property while they were attached to the land by their roots, was merely to apply a fiction in law in order to arrive at a just determination in particular cases." *City of Los Angeles* v. *Hughes,* 202 Col. 731, 262 P. 737 (1927).

## Mechanics' Liens

### Introduction

The subject of mechanics' liens is inserted at this point because of its similarity, in terms of subject matter at least, to the law of fixtures. That is, in most instances the right to hold a mechanic's lien against real estate arises from the addition to that real estate of some form of personal property (and the necessary labor to do so) that then clearly becomes real estate under the law of fixtures. At common law one who improved the real estate of another by either the addition of materials or the performance of the necessary labor could acquire no lien against the real estate that would secure payment for the resulting improvement. Neither could such a person acquire a lien on the real estate by operation of law, and the early chancery courts did not grant equitable liens on real estate.

---

[30] *Story* v. *Christin et al.,* 14 Cal.2d 592, 95 P.2d 925.

Under modern law, liens for such improvements to real estate to secure payment for them are granted by statute. All states have enacted statutes providing for mechanics' liens on real estate. The scope of such liens and the liabilities of the parties involved will depend on the provisions of the lien statute of the state in which the real estate is located and the interpretation of the statute by the courts of that state.

### Nature of Mechanic's Lien Statutes

The mechanic's lien on real estate is based on the principles of the common-law artisan's lien. The objective of each is the same: the protection of anyone who by his labor or by the addition of his material improves the property of another. The artisan's lien is a possessory lien on personal property, and the artisan must have the possession of the property improved before such a lien can be granted him; whereas the mechanic's lien on real estate is not a possessory lien, since the property improved remains in the possession of the owner. Under the mechanic's lien statutes the owner must have contracted, either expressly or impliedly, for the improvement of his real estate, and the lien claimant must have improved the real estate by his labor or by the addition of his materials. A lien can then be granted for the reasonable value of the labor or materials furnished, which normally is the contract price.

Although the mechanic's lien statutes are based on the same fundamental principle, they vary widely in their provisions as to who is entitled to a lien; the property subject to the lien; the procedure followed in perfecting the lien; the rights of materialmen, laborers, and subcontractors; priorities; waivers; and similar details. In addition, the statutes are, in many respects, general in their terminology, and the right to a lien depends, in particular situations, on the court's interpretation of the statute. The mechanic's lien statutes of the various states differ in so many particulars that it is impossible to discuss them in detail in a work of this nature. Nevertheless, some important general rules are discernible.

### Necessity for Compliance with Statute

Since the mechanic's lien on real estate is created by constitutional provision or statutory enactment, the lien claimant, in order to obtain a lien, must comply strictly with the provisions of the law. A person engaging in any phase of the real estate business should familiarize himself with the general provisions of the mechanic's lien law. However, if he should have occasion to avail himself of the benefits of the law, he would be wise to consult a competent local attorney at the inception of his transaction. Failure to comply with some detail of the lien law could result in the loss of lien rights, since they are very technical and are strictly construed by our courts.

## Necessity of Contract for Improvements

Under a basic principle of law, universally followed, an obligation cannot be imposed on a person without his knowledge or consent, either expressed or implied, or unless the person has so acted that he is estopped from denying liability. Under this principle, if a person who has no right or interest in a piece of real estate contracts for the erection of a building on the real estate, and the building is erected without the knowledge or consent of the owner of the real estate, and without the owner's being negligent in failing to discover that a building is being erected on his real estate, the persons furnishing labor and material for the erection of the building are not entitled to a lien on the real estate.

## Co-Owned Property

Several different persons may have ownership interests in the same piece of real estate. If one of the owners contracts, authorizes, or consents to an improvement, the right of the person making the improvement to a mechanic's lien affecting the ownership interests of the other owners who are not parties to the contract or have not authorized or consented to the improvement will depend on the relationship of the several owners and the circumstances of the particular case. As a general rule, a person furnishing labor or materials for the improvement of real estate must ascertain the ownership interest in the real estate of the person engaging him.

## Improvements by Lessee

The mere existence of the landlord-tenant relationship does not empower the tenant to subject the leased premises to a mechanic's lien. He may subject his interest, however, since he does have a property interest in such premises. Whether or not he may subject the landlord's title to a mechanic's lien will depend on the provisions of the mechanic's lien statutes of the state, on the terms of the lease, on the knowledge and the conduct of the landlord relative to the making of the improvements, and on all other circumstances of the case. In many cases the court must determine whether or not the landlord has consented to the improvement. In general, if the lease expressly provides that the lessee shall make improvements to the leased real estate, or if he has made any improvements under a contract with the lessor, the lessor's title to the real estate will be subject to a mechanic's lien.[31]

---

[31] *Denniston & Partridge Company* v. *Romp et al.,* 244 Iowa 204, 56 N.W.2d 601.

In the absence of some evidence of authorization by the landlord, however, the lien will be limited to the leasehold estate.[32]

### Property Sold on Land Contract

As a general rule, when real estate has been sold on a land contract, the buyer of the real estate cannot subject the seller's interest to a mechanic's lien, and the seller cannot subject the buyer's interest to such a lien. Each can subject his own interest to a mechanic's lien. In most respects, the situation of the buyer and seller is like that of lessee and lessor. Under the mechanic's lien laws of some states, if a lessee or buyer under a land contract has improved the property, the contractor is entitled to a mechanic's lien on the improvement.[33]

### Infant's Contract

As a general rule, an infant cannot subject his real estate to a mechanic's lien, since he is under a disability and his contracts are voidable.

### Persons Entitled to a Mechanic's Lien

There is no uniformity in the provisions of the mechanic's lien statutes as to the persons who are entitled to a mechanic's lien on real estate. Some statutes state in general terms who will be entitled to such a lien—for instance, contractors, subcontractors, and materialmen—and leave it to the courts to interpret the statute. The statute of the state of Washington specifies "any person who, at the request of the owner, his agent, contractor or subcontractor. . . ."[34] Other statutes, in addition to a general statement, list specifically the persons who are entitled to a lien. For example, the statute of the state of New York provides: ". . . contractor, subcontractor, laborer, materialman, landscape gardener, nurseryman, person or corporation selling fruit or ornamental trees, roses, shrubbery, vines and small fruit, persons who perform labor or furnish materials for the improvement of real property. . . ."[35] In general, the courts have held that lien rights extend to a person who performs work for or furnishes materials to a general contractor who has a contract with the owner, provided such work or materials enhance the value of the owner's real estate.[36]

---

[32] *Wilmington Trust Co.* v. *Branmer Inc.,* 353 A.2d 212 (Del. Super 1976).

[33] *Strand Lumber Company* v. *Dostie et al.,* 260 Mich. 422, 245 U.W. 777.

[34] Revised Code of Washington (May 1, 1952), Title 60, "Liens," p. 60–04–040.

[35] *McKinney's Consolidated Laws of New York Annotated,* Book 32, "Lien Law" (1940), Art. 2, § 3.

[36] *Morin Lumber Company* v. *Person et al.,* 110 Mont. 114, 99 P.2d 206.

## Nature of Improvements

If a laborer or materialman is to be entitled to a lien on real estate, the labor expended or materials furnished must become a part of the real estate.[37] The nature and scope of the building or improvement for which a lien may be claimed will be set out in the statute of the state in which the real estate is located. Some states have statutes that are very general in their terms, whereas other states have statutes that set out in detail the nature and scope of the improvement for which a lien may be claimed.

As a general rule, the improvement must be permanent in nature.[38] Under the statutes of some states a person furnishing fixtures, such as lighting fixtures, heating equipment, and other types of built-in fixtures, is entitled to a mechanic's lien on the real estate if such fixtures are intended as permanent additions to the building; but if the fixtures are such as would be classed as trade fixtures, the person furnishing them is not entitled to a lien.[39]

Under special provisions of some state statutes, improvements such as repairs, alterations, additions, excavations, the moving or wrecking of a building, the laying of foundations, the addition of machinery that is firmly attached to the building, landscaping, the drilling of wells, the building of roads or sidewalks, and so forth, are specifically included in the improvements that will entitle the person making the improvement to a lien on the real estate.

Liberto owned a building that was leased to Landers for the operation of a grocery. Landers, with the knowledge and consent of Liberto, contracted for the installation of shelving in the store. The shelving was constructed at Landers' home in eight-foot sections and then brought to the store and placed against the wall. The sections were screwed together and attached to the wall by first nailing a 1 × 8-inch plywood strip along the wall at the height of the cabinets and attaching the cabinets to this strip. The only purpose of attaching the cabinets to the strip was to keep the shelves from toppling over when filled with groceries. The parties admitted that the shelves could be removed without material injury to the shelves or to the building. Broadmoor Lumber Co., Inc., sold the plywood and lumber for the shelves to Landers, who did not pay for it. Broadmoor Lumber Co., Inc., filed a lien on the building, and Liberto contended that the shelves were not an improvement to the building and that Broadmoor Lumber Co., Inc., was not entitled to a lien. The trial court held for Broadmoor Lumber Co., Inc., and Liberto appealed. The judgment was reversed.

Judge Hall said: "It is immaterial where the shelves were constructed. The fact that they were prefabricated and brought to the building does not of itself prevent application

---

[37] *Stone* v. *Rosenfield et al.,* 141 Conn. 188, 104 A.2d 545.

[38] *Alexander Lumber Co.* v. *Swindlehurst et al.,* 309 Ill. App. 433, 32 N.E.2d 637.

[39] *Silverman* v. *Mazer Lumber & Supply Co.,* 252 Ala. 627, 42 So.2d 542.

of the lien law. What is material is whether they were attached to the building in such manner that they became immovables by destination. We conclude that the cabinets are movables and have not become immovables by destination.

"Since the lien statute is restricted to immovables and since plaintiff has no recourse against the owner except by virtue of the lien statute, we conclude that plaintiff cannot recover for the materials amounting to $303.68 which were used in the construction of the cabinets." *Broadmoor Lumber Co., Inc.,* v. *Liberto,* La. App., 162 So.2d 800 (1964).

## Labor for Which Lien May Be Claimed

Labor, manual or physical, expended in the making of an improvement for which a daily wage is paid is clearly the basis for a lien under the mechanic's lien statutes. The statute may, in addition, extend the scope of the lien right to include personnel in a supervisory capacity or those performing professional services directly connected with the improvement. Generally, an architect would not, under such a statutory provision, be entitled to a lien for his charges for preparing preliminary sketches or plans and specifications, if he performed no further services; but if, in addition, he supervised the work, he would be entitled to a lien.

The courts of some states have held that the work need not, in all instances, be done on the premises. A person preparing, in the shop of the contractor, materials for inclusion in a building may, under the terms of some mechanic's lien statutes, have a lien on the real estate for the value of such services.[40]

## Materials for Which Liens May Be Claimed

As a general rule, the laws pertaining to mechanics' liens do not define specifically the nature of the materials for which a lien may be claimed. If the materials used are such as are usual and reasonably necessary for the job that is the subject matter of the contract, the person or persons who furnish the materials will be entitled to a mechanic's lien on the real estate. The materials must be actually furnished for the particular job. Under the statutes of some states the materials must be furnished for a particular building and on the credit of the building, not on the general credit of the purchaser of the materials.[41]

Under the mechanic's lien laws of some states the materialman, in order to be entitled to a lien, must prove that the materials were used in the building. Generally, if the materialman proves that the materials were delivered to the site of the building for inclusion in the building, he has established his case; the

---

[40] *Wells* v. *Christian et al.,* 165 Ind. 622, 76 N.E. 518.

[41] *Rosebud Lumber & Coal Co.* v. *Homes et al.,* 155 Neb. 459, 52 N.W.2d 313; *Schuman* v. *Teague et al.,* 195 Okla. 328, 156 P.2d 1010.

owner, if he is to defeat the materialmen's right to a lien, would have to prove that the materials were not used in the building. The owner cannot defeat the materialmen's right to a lien by diverting to some other use, without the materialmen's knowledge or consent, materials delivered for incorporation into a building.[42]

## Waiver of Lien Rights

Whether or not an express provision in a contract to improve real estate waiving all rights of the contractor, subcontractors, laborers, and materialmen to claim a lien on the real estate under the mechanic's lien laws of the state will be effective will depend on the wording of the waiver provision, the provisions of the mechanic's lien statutes of the state in which the property is located, and the court decisions of the state. A clearly worded waiver provision in the contract may, in some states, preclude the contractor from claiming a lien, but not preclude subcontractors, laborers, and materialmen from so doing.[43] In other states the courts have held that such a waiver provision will preclude subcontractors, laborers, and materialmen from claiming a lien.[44] A few states have held that such a waiver-of-lien provision in the contract will not preclude the principal contractor from claiming a lien,[45] whereas a few other states have held that it will.[46]

## Perfecting the Lien

Since the right to a mechanic's lien on real estate is created by statute, which is in derogation of the common law, the lien claimant must comply with all the material provisions of the lien statute to obtain a lien. There is an almost complete

---

[42] *Ohio Oil Company* v. *Fidelity & Deposit Company of Maryland,* 112 Ind. App. 452, 42 N.E.2d 406.

[43] Apparently, a waiver in the principal contract does not affect the rights of subcontractors, laborers, and materials handlers to a lien, especially if they do not have notice of the waiver provision, in the following states: Alabama, Arizona, Arkansas, Colorado, Indiana, Maine, Massachusetts, Michigan, Montana, Nebraska, New York, Ohio, Oregon, Washington, and Wisconsin.

[44] Apparently, the following states have adhered to this rule: California, Illinois, Missouri, and New Jersey. In Indiana the mechanic's lien statute provides that the contract containing the waiver provision must be in writing, must be acknowledged before a notary public, and must be filed in the recorder's office in the county wherein the real estate is situated within five days after execution; the owner must post, and keep posted, on the premises a sign, no smaller than three feet by three feet, giving notice that the work is being done under a no-lien contract.

[45] Arkansas, Idaho, Massachusetts, Texas, and Washington.

[46] Arizona, Connecticut, Indiana (if statute is complied with), Iowa, Maryland, Minnesota, Missouri, Nebraska, Oregon, Pennsylvania, and Wisconsin. Illinois and New York have cases holding that under some circumstances, the contractor is not precluded from claiming a lien; whereas under other circumstances, he is precluded from doing so.

lack of uniformity in the requirements that the lien claimant must satisfy in order to perfect his lien. In all of the states, some type of notice of the claim of a lien must be given to the owner of the property interest to which the lien is to attach.

Generally, the lien claimant or his authorized agent must file, in the office of a designated county officer, a verified statement of claim. Everything required by the statute should be stated in reasonably clear and concise language. The statement should be compared with the statute to make certain that all the information required by the statute is included, since all such information is material and its omission would defeat the right to the lien.

### Time for Filing

The lien claim and notice of the lien must be filed or served within the time designated in the statute. Failure to do so is fatal to the claim, since the courts cannot excuse a late filing or extend, by judicial order, the time for service of notice or filing. Usually, the time for filing the lien claim or serving the notice is computed from the time the last labor was performed or the last materials were furnished, the determination of which is primarily a question of fact to be determined by the court. In general, the test applied is whether all the labor has been performed or all the materials necessary to the fulfillment of the contract have been furnished. The courts have not permitted a contractor, subcontractor, laborer, or materials handler to extend the time for filing by returning to the job to correct trivial imperfections in the work.

### Estate Subject to Lien

Under a basic principle of property law a person cannot convey a greater interest in property than he has. This principle applies in determining the scope of a lien claimant's rights in the property he has improved. Only the property interest of the person who has contracted for or consented to the improvement is subject to a lien.

In some of the states the extent of the property that may be subjected to the lien is set out in the statute. For example, in California the statute provides that the lien shall be on the improvement and so much of the ground around the same as is required for its use and occupation; in Delaware, the building and the land on which it is situated; and in Minnesota, not exceeding 40 acres, if the improvement is outside the limits of an incorporated city or village, and 1 acre, if it is within such limits. Provisions such as those in the California and Delaware statutes predominate.

## Sale of Real Estate Subject to Lien

Real estate that is subject to a mechanic's lien may be sold, but the purchaser takes subject to existing lien rights. Since, in most states, notice of a lien does not have to be filed or recorded, or does not have to be given until some designated period of time after the last labor is performed or the last materials furnished, a purchaser cannot rely entirely on the records to determine whether or not there are outstanding mechanic's lien rights. The purchaser should inspect the property to determine whether or not work is being done on the property or has been done recently. For additional protection, he may retain a percentage of the agreed price until the time for filing liens expires. In some instances, it may be good business to obtain from the seller an affidavit stating that no work has been performed on the premises and that the premises are not subject to mechanics' liens.

## Priorities of Mechanics' Liens

The mechanic's lien statutes of the several states define the priority rights of the various classes of persons who may claim security rights in the real estate; however, they are not uniform in their priority provisions. In some states the priority provisions of the statutes are elaborate and set up several classes of security claimants, whereas in other states the priority provisions of the statutes are relatively simple.

The general rule of "first in time is first in right" governs mechanics' liens. The concept of first in time, however, when determining the priority rights of mechanics' liens, is not based on recording, as is generally the case with mortgages and similar liens. The time for computing priority rights of mechanics' liens is, in most states, from the time the first labor is performed or the first materials are furnished, although filing of the lien is postponed by statute, and subsequent purchasers or lienees take subject to the mechanics' liens. In a few states the mechanic's lien dates from the execution of the contract for the improvement, thus in effect creating a potential secret lien for one who acquires rights in the property between the time of the execution of the contract and the commencement of the work.

There is no priority between mechanics' liens claimants. Since all laborers and materialmen have contributed to the improvement of the property, it is only fair that all should share ratably in the finished result; and those who, by the nature of their contribution, performed their labor or furnished their materials first should not be given priority over later contributors.

In a majority of situations, mechanics' liens have priority over mortgages that have not been recorded until after the performance of the work on the improvement has commenced, even though the money was loaned and the mortgage executed before the beginning of the work. A mortgage must be recorded before the work is started on the improvement if such mortgage is to have priority over mechanics' liens. In a few states, mechanics' liens are given priority, at least in part, over their liens. This rule is justified on the ground that the property has been enhanced in value by the expenditure of labor by the lien claimants and by the addition of their materials, and they should therefore share in the total property in proportion to their contribution to its value.

A mortgage given to secure future advances, if made in good faith, and if recorded before the commencement of work on the improvement, is entitled, as a general rule, to priority over liens for labor or materials, although the advancements are not made until after the commencement of the work, provided the lender is *obligated* by contract to make the advances.[47] If, however, the mortgagee is not obligated to make the advancements he is not entitled to priority.[48]

### Duration of Mechanics' Liens

The mechanic's lien statutes of all states provide that unless action is brought to foreclose the mechanic's lien within a stated time after the perfecting of the lien, the lien will be lost. The time for starting foreclosure proceedings varies from six months to six years, with the periods of six months and one year predominating.

In some states, if the owner gives the lien claimant notice, as required by the provisions of the statute, the lienholder's right to foreclose his lien will be barred, unless he brings his action within the time stated in the statute—usually 30 or 60 days.

### Discharge of Mechanics' Liens

Under the mechanic's lien statutes of some states a mechanic's lien may be discharged by the owner's posting a bond or depositing in court a sum sufficient to pay the claim. A mechanic's lien is discharged by merger—that is, the lienholder acquires the owner's interest in the real estate that is subject to the lien. A mechanic's lien is also discharged by a release given for a sufficient consideration.

---

[47] *Kemp* v. *Thruman,* 521 S.W.2d. 806 (Tenn. 1975).

[48] *National Bank of Washington* v. *Equity Investors,* 83 Wash.2d 435 (1974); *Akron Savings and Loan Co.* v. *Ronson Homes,* 15 Ohio St.2d 6 (1968).

If a mechanic's lien is discharged but the lienholder refuses to release the lien of record and thereby remove the lien as an encumbrance on the owner's title to the property, the court, in a proper action, will force the lienholder to discharge the lien of record.[49]

## Foreclosure of Mechanics' Liens

A perfected mechanic's lien on real estate is comparable in most respects to a real estate mortgage, and the procedure followed in the foreclosure of the lien is similar to that followed in the foreclosure of a real estate mortgage by action and sale. The action will be brought in the court having jurisdiction over the real estate involved, and the laws of the state in which the land is located will apply. All parties having an interest in the real estate that will be affected by the foreclosure of the lien, including all mechanics' lienholders, are made parties to the suit. Any party in interest may appear and defend. The court will determine the validity of the claimant's lien and will find the amount due the lienholder if the claim is held to be valid.

This foreclosure of a mechanic's lien has some of the characteristics of a receivership. Consequently, if there is more than one mechanic's lien on the property, the court will, as a general rule, determine the validity and the amount of the claims of all such holders. In addition, the court may, if the circumstances require, determine the priority right of lien claimants other than mechanic's lien claimants. The court will then order the real estate sold and the proceeds distributed according to the priority rights of the various lien claimants as set out in the mechanic's lien statutes of the state in which the real estate is located.

## Public Improvements

Public improvements and, as a general rule, improvements to public utilities are not subject to mechanics' liens. Each state has regulated, by special statutes, the rights of laborers and materialmen furnishing labor and materials for public improvements; but a discussion of these statutes is outside the scope of this work.

---

[49] *Gibson et al.* v. *Koutsky-Brennan-Vana Company,* 143 Neb. 326, 9 N.W.2d. 298.

# Chapter 7

# Co-Ownership

In this chapter are considered the various methods by which ownership of real estate is divided by two or more persons or entities. First discussed are the common forms of joint tenancy with right of survivorship, the tenancy in common, tenancy by the entirety, and community property. The partnership is also considered in this chapter. In addition, the more recent developments of the cooperative and condominium forms of ownership are discussed. Also included are the concepts of time sharing through interval ownership. The rights of the holders of these interests, as well as the rights of their creditors, are included in this discussion. The widespread use of some form of shared ownership of real estate today makes an understanding of its consequences quite important.

## Introduction

The common law concepts of co-ownership of real estate and the terminology used to describe them frequently result in confusion. This is usually because it is difficult to grasp the notion that two or more individuals can each have an "individual" interest in the whole property along with the right to possession of the whole property. Problems with terminology are aggravated by the term "estate in severalty," with its connotation that there are several owners, when in fact this term describes ownership by only one individual. That is, when title to real estate is vested in one person or entity (such as a corporation) that person or organization owns the property in severalty. When two or more persons or entities hold title to the same real estate, they are co-owners. In the classic forms of co-ownership (the joint tenancy, the tenancy in common, and the tenancy by the entirety) the interests of each of the participants is said to be *undivided.* This means simply that the share of each co-owner has not been physically set off or segregated from that of the other co-owners. The result is that, while each co-owner may have a clearly established fractional interest in the property (such as ½, ⅓, ¼, or the like), each has the right to the possession of the *entire* property unless and until that fractional interest has been divided and set off either by the agreement of the parties or an appropriate legal proceeding brought for that purpose.

In the discussion that follows, the joint tenancy with right of survivorship is considered first, solely because of the familiarity of most people with the joint bank account. In the typical joint checking account, for example, we are familiar with the concepts that each owner may deposit to the account or draw against it, even to the exhaustion of funds, without any joinder or concurrence of the other owner of the account. The feature of survivorship under which one joint tenant succeeds to the ownership of the entire balance in the account has been widely publicized and is generally well understood. The joint tenancy of real estate operates in a similar fashion for the most part, the most difficult idea to accept being the fact that one piece of real estate is involved as opposed to a number of dollars that are easily divisible.

The tenancy in common may exist in personal property as well as real estate. However, it is not as common in personal property as is the joint tenancy, and its use is frequently avoided because of the mechanical problems it creates. In the real estate area, however, the tenancy in common occurs quite frequently for the opposite reason: a desire to *avoid* the consequences of the joint tenancy. Under the tenancy in common of real estate, there is no feature of survivorship and the interest of one of the tenants descends to his heirs at his death rather than going to his surviving co-owners. This result is generally favored under our legal system and the joint tenancy with right of survivorship is discriminated against.

The tenancy by the entirety is a unique form of co-ownership that can exist only between a husband and wife. It was developed to protect each spouse from the irresponsible acts of the other in dealing with the family home. While it is perhaps most easily understood, at least initially, as a joint tenancy with right of survivorship between a husband and wife, this is not entirely accurate. In fact it is ownership by the marriage itself with neither spouse having any individual interest, divided or undivided. It is not universally recognized in this country, but a substantial number of states do permit its creation, and in those states it frequently includes important advantages to the owners.

Community-property states recognize another unique form of ownership by the marriage or the "community," which also may have substantial benefits to the parties. Community property as a concept did not, however, exist under the English common law but instead is adopted from Spanish law. As a result it is considered separately from the common law forms of co-ownership.

Relatively recent forms of co-ownership that have evolved, but that were not recognized at common law, include the co-operative apartment and the condominium. Each of these forms of co-ownership is discussed apart from the common-law forms since each of them is based upon contract and statutory bases not shared by the common-law forms of co-ownership. Timesharing arrangements are also included.

Partnership ownership of real estate is included in this chapter as well because of the transformation that has occurred from the common-law rule—that only the individual partners could own real estate and the partnership itself could not—to the newer concepts adopted by the Uniform Partnership Act, under which the partnership itself can own real estate in its own name. The variations that result under the limited partnership are also discussed.

## The Joint Tenancy

### Characteristics of the Joint Tenancy

It should be recognized at the outset that the term *joint tenancy,* commonly used in practice and in this discussion, is more correctly referred to as the "joint tenancy with right of survivorship" since the feature of survivorship is its key element. The joint tenancy is a single estate in land owned by two or more persons, the fundamental concept of which is unity of ownership; that is, there is only one title, and it is vested in the unit, which is made up of two or more persons. The death of one of the joint tenants does not destroy the unit; it simply reduces by one the number of persons who comprise the unit. The remaining joint tenants take the rights of the deceased joint tenant by virtue of survivorship. This result happens by operation of law, and no affirmative action by the deceased tenant is necessary to accomplish it. By the same token, however, neither does a valid will of the deceased tenant defeat this result. It is this automatic transfer of the deceased joint tenant's interest to the surviving joint tenants by right of survivorship that is the distinguishing feature of the joint tenancy. The last surviving tenant takes the entire estate in severalty, and on his death the property will go to his heirs or devisees.

The reason that even a valid will executed by the deceased joint tenant has no effect upon the transfer of his interest to the surviving joint tenants is the fact that none of his interest in the land survives him. Therefore, there is nothing in existence upon which the will can operate. It is this result, which has the effect of removing valuable property rights from the deceased tenant's estate and effectively taking it from his surviving spouse and heirs, that has led to the adoption in many states of legislation that discriminates against the joint tenancy. In those states that have adopted such legislation, there is created a presumption that a conveyance to two or more persons does not create a joint tenancy with right of survivorship unless there is a clearly expressed intention in the deed itself to do so. This requirement is in addition to the technical requirements for its creation, which developed at common law and are discussed below.

Our courts have been called upon to decide some unusual cases that have illustrated the problems that can result from the use of the joint tenancy when it clashes with other fundamental policies. For example, in an extreme case to be sure, decided by the Supreme Court of Wisconsin, a husband and wife owned real estate as joint tenants with right of survivorship. The husband murdered his wife and then committed suicide. In the ensuing dispute between the heirs of each of them, the court concluded that even though the husband had survived his wife he would not be permitted to profit from his wrongful act and at the moment of his death he remained only a joint tenant. The problem presented by this conclusion of course is: With whom was he a joint tenant? The court's answer was that the deceased wife's executor replaced her at the moment of her death as joint tenant, and when the husband died his interest passed by operation of law to the wife's executor and the entire estate then passed to her heirs, with the husband's heirs taking nothing.[1] Other courts considering similar situations have reached another conclusion: in a recent Oklahoma case it was decided that the wife's murder of her husband converted the joint tenancy between the two of them into a tenancy in common, with the result that the husband's heirs become entitled to one-half of the property and the wife's entitled to the other one-half.[2]

While the above cases are extreme, they illustrate the potential difficulties inherent in the joint tenancy when there are unusual circumstances. The possibility of accidental death of both joint tenants in the same accident has led to widespread

---

[1] *In Re King's Estate,* 261 Wisc. 266, 52 N.W.2d 885.

[2] *Duncan* v. *Vassaur,* 550 P.2d 929 (Okla. 1976).

adoption of the Uniform Simultaneous Death Act, which provides in essence that their interests are to be treated as though each had survived the other. The practical effect of this statute, where it applies, is to split the joint tenancy and permit it to descend in equal shares to the descendants of each tenant, much as though it had been converted to a tenancy in common. The Uniform Act will apply only if there is no clear-cut evidence of the order of death, however; if there is evidence available as to the order of death the statute does not apply. Some rather grisly cases have resulted from the disputes that may arise in such instances.

### Creation of Joint Tenancy

A joint tenancy cannot be created by operation of law but must be created by grant, purchase, or devise.[3] Four unities are required to create a joint tenancy: unity of title, unity of time, unity of interest, and unity of possession. Unless all four of the unities are present, a joint tenancy is not created. Consequently, the joint tenancy must be created by one and the same instrument, executed and delivered at one and the same time, and convey equal interests to the grantees, who must hold undivided possession.

Today, joint tenancies are not favored; in order to create a joint tenancy, the instrument must show clearly that such was the intention of the parties. A grant to "Amos and Bert" or to "Amos and Bert jointly" will not create a joint tenancy. A grant to "Amos and Bert as joint tenants" will be sufficient to create a joint tenancy in some states but not in others.[4] A careful conveyancer prefers using "to Amos and Bert as joint tenants, with right of survivorship and not as tenants in common." When such language is used, there is no room for doubt as to the grantor's intention to create a joint tenancy.

At common law, if the owner in severalty of real estate wished to create a joint tenancy between himself and another or others, he would have to convey the property to an intermediary and have the intermediary convey it back to the parties as joint tenants. The reason for this holding was that if the owner in severalty attempted to convey directly to another a joint interest in the property, a joint tenancy could not result, since the four unities essential to its creation would not be present. The title would not be created by one and the same instrument at one and the same time. Moreover, under the early common law the courts held that a person could not make a grant of his own property to himself.

---

[3] *Porter et al.* v. *Porter et al.,* 381 Ill. 322, 45 N.E.2d 635.

[4] *Howell* v. *Kline et al.,* 156 Pa. Super. 628, 41 A.2d 580.

In some states the necessity of using an intermediary has been abolished by statutory enactment; in other states the courts, holding that the clear intention of a party should not be defeated by a technicality, have refused to follow the common-law rule.[5] However, in case of doubt, the use of an intermediary is recommended.

### Rights of Joint Tenants

One of the unities of a joint tenancy is the right of possession. Each tenant has equal right to the enjoyment of the joint property, and the possession of one is considered the possession of all. If the joint tenants occupy the premises as a house, or if the joint property is a farm and the joint tenants work the farm as a cooperative venture, each is, in contemplation of law, exercising his or her right of possession of the entire property. The idea of unity of possession would be carried out even though each tenant, by mutual agreement, occupied a portion of the house or worked certain fields.

If the joint property is rental property and is not occupied by any of the tenants, no problem is presented. In such a case the rent received, after deductions for taxes, insurance, and necessary repairs, is distributed equally.

If one or more, but not all, of the joint tenants occupy the joint property, the tenant who does not occupy the property is not entitled to rent from the occupying tenants, unless there has been an agreement to the contrary, or unless the occupying tenants have excluded him from living on the premises.

If one of two or more joint tenants is in sole possession of the joint property, he is considered as possessing not only for himself, but also for his cotenants; and he is not liable to his cotenants for rent, unless there has been an agreement to the contrary, or unless he has excluded his cotenants.[6]

John Black, who was contemplating a second marriage, conveyed, through a dummy, an orange grove to himself and his three sons as joint tenants. John Black remarried, and he and his wife operated the orange grove, retaining for themselves all of the income therefrom. On the death of John Black the sons brought an action against the widow, asking an accounting for the profits realized from the operation of the orange grove. The request was denied.

Presiding Justice Moore said: "A joint tenant in the sole and exclusive occupancy of the land is not required to account to his cotenant for any portion of the revenues derived therefrom so long as they are the fruitage of his own capital, labor and skill. The risks incurred by the occupier of the land (held jointly) in the cultivation of crops are his as are also the profits he may enjoy or the losses he may sustain in producing crops by his

---

[5] *Lipps* v. *Crowe,* 28 N.J. Super. 131, 100 A.2d 361.

[6] *Swartzbaugh* v. *Sampson et al.,* 11 Cal. App.2d 451, 54 P.2d 73.

industry. In taking all the fruits grown upon the land, decedent herein received no more than his just share inasmuch as it is no more than the reward for his own labor and capital to no part of which is his cotenant entitled. It is thus seen that there is no equity in the claim that the mere fact of being named as joint tenant entitled one to share in the revenue produced on the land as the result of the labor, management and money of him who is in sole possession when the claiming cotenant has neither demanded possession, contributed to the expense of production nor previously made himself liable for possible losses." *Black* v. *Black,* 91 Cal. App.2d 328, 204 P.2d 950 (1949).

## Termination of Joint Tenancy

A joint tenancy is destroyed when any of the essential unities is destroyed. A joint tenant has the right to convey his interest in the joint property, but such a conveyance destroys the unity of interest and consequently destroys the jointure as to the interest conveyed. If the unity holding title is composed of three or more persons and one of the joint tenants conveys his interest, the grantee would hold his interest as a tenant in common with the remaining joint tenants, but the remaining joint tenants would hold in jointure as to each other. For example, suppose that Amos, Bert, Charles, and David own real property as joint tenants and Amos deeds his interest to Earl. Earl will hold his interest with Bert, Charles, and David as tenant in common; but Bert, Charles, and David will continue to hold as joint tenants as to each other. Since the interest of a joint tenant goes, on his death, to the surviving tenant or tenants, an attempt by a joint tenant to devise by will his interest in the joint property is inoperative; consequently, a joint tenancy cannot be destroyed by a devise.

If a joint tenant or all the joint tenants enter into a conditional land contract whereby the joint tenant or tenants contract to sell his or their interest in the joint property to another and give the vendee possession, and contract to execute a deed to the property on the payment of the purchase price, the joint tenancy is destroyed. The conditional vendee becomes the equitable owner of the property, and the conditional vendor or vendors hold the legal title as security for the payment of the purchase price. The unity of possession is destroyed.[7]

## Mortgaging Joint Estate

A joint tenant or all the joint tenants may mortgage his or their interest in the joint property without destroying the joint tenancy. However, if there is default, foreclosure, and sale of the property, and one of the joint tenants does not redeem the property from the foreclosure sale, the joint tenancy is destroyed. If a joint tenant redeems from the foreclosure sale, he will be deemed to have done so

---

[7] *Buford* v. *Dablke et al.,* 158 Neb. 39. 62 N.W.2d 252.

for the benefit of the defaulting tenant or tenants. However, if the defaulting tenant or tenants do not reimburse the redeeming tenant within a reasonable time, the court will, after appropriate action is brought, enter a decree cutting off the right of the defaulting tenant or tenants and vesting title in the redeeming tenant.

One joint tenant may lease his or her interest in the jointly owned property without destroying the tenancy. However, upon his or her death the lease is automatically terminated regardless of the time it has to run.[8]

A judgment creditor of one of the joint tenants may levy an execution on the judgment debtor's interest in the joint property. Such a levy does not destroy the jointure; and if the judgment debtor tenant dies before the execution sale, the judgment debtor tenant's interest in the joint property passes to his or her cotenant or cotenants by right of survivorship, and the judgment creditor takes nothing.

When the joint property is sold at an execution sale, if the interest of the debtor tenant's creditor is purchased by a person other than one of the joint tenants, the joint tenancy is destroyed in the same manner and to the same extent as though the debtor tenant had deeded his interest in the property to the purchaser at the execution sale. If one of the joint tenants purchases at the execution sale, the situation is the same as that arising when one of the joint tenants purchases at a mortgage foreclosure sale.

### Sale of Joint Estate for Taxes

If the joint property is sold for taxes and one of the joint tenants purchases the property at the tax sale, the joint tenancy is not destroyed, since the purchasing tenant will be deemed to have acted for the benefit of his cotenants. The situation is the same as when one of the joint tenants buys the joint property on a mortgage foreclosure sale or on an execution sale.

If one of the joint tenants arranges to have a third person purchase the property at the tax sale and the property is then deeded to the joint tenant, the rights of his cotenants will not be cut off. However, if the third-party buyer is a bona fide purchaser and the later sale to one of the joint tenants is a bona fide sale, the joint tenancy will have been destroyed, and the purchasing joint tenant will hold the property free from any rights of his former joint tenants.

On November 1, 1944, Juanita I. Ellis and W. O. Ellis purchased a two-story duplex and took title as joint tenants with right of survivorship and not as tenants in common.

---

[8] *Tenket* v. *Boswell,* 18 Cal.3d. 150, 554 P.2d. 330, 33 Cal. Rptr. 10 (1976).

In 1951, Juanita I. Ellis was granted a divorce from W. O. Ellis, and the decree of divorce provided that the property be sold and the proceeds be divided equally, W. O. Ellis to pay certain expenses and costs out of his one half of the proceeds. Juanita I. Ellis was given a 60-day option to purchase W. O. Ellis' one-half interest at its appraised value. On the expiration of the 60 days the parties, by written contract, agreed to sell the property for $20,000, each to live in and maintain one of the apartments until the property was sold. Before the sale of the property, W. O. Ellis died, leaving a will whereby he devised his one half of the premises to his daughter, Mrs. Carson. Juanita I. Ellis claimed the entire property by right of survivorship. The court held that Mrs. Carson took a one-half interest in the property, and Juanita I. Ellis appealed. The judgment was affirmed.

Justice Wertz said: "The four essential elements of a joint tenancy are of interest, title, time and possession. To meet these requirements, the several tenants must have one and the same conveyance commencing at the same time and held by one and the same undivided possession. A joint tenancy will be severed by the destruction of any one or more of its necessary units.

"It has also been held that a joint tenancy may be terminated by a mutual agreement between the parties, or by any conduct or course of dealing sufficient to indicate that all parties have mutually treated their interests as belonging to them in common.

"An analysis of the two contracts entered into between the parties clearly reveals it was their intent to sever the joint tenancy. The contracts and the actions of the parties obviously destroyed the unity of possession. These contracts and the acts and conduct of the parties were clearly inconsistent with the existence of a joint tenancy and indicated an intention and agreement that such relationship should no longer exist." *Carson* v. *Ellis,* 186 Kan. 112, 348 P.2d 807 (1960).

## Tenancy in Common

### Characteristics of Tenancy in Common

A tenancy in common is a holding by two or more persons of separate titles in the same real estate. The estate of each tenant in common is an estate of inheritance. Since each tenant holds separate title, his interest in the common property descends on his death to his heirs or goes to his devisees. If a contenant of a tenancy in common leaves a wife surviving, she takes the same widow's rights in his interest in the common property as she takes in his property that he held in severalty. A tenant in common acquires no rights in the common property by right of survivorship.

The only unity in a tenancy in common is the unity of possession. The interests of the tenants in common need not be acquired at the same time—they may be acquired by separate deed—and the interests need not be equal, but they do have equal rights of possession. These rights of possession held by a tenant in common are substantially the same as the rights of possession of a joint tenant in the joint property.

### Creation of Tenancy in Common

A tenancy in common can be created by grant, by purchase, by devise, or by operation of law. If a person dies intestate and leaves real estate, his heirs will take the real estate as tenants in common. Also, if two or more persons take real estate by operation of law, they generally take as tenants in common. A grant of real estate to two or more persons, not husband and wife, will create a tenancy in common, unless appropriate language clearly indicating a contrary intent is used in the grant. For example, a grant to "Amos and Bert" or to "Amos and Bert jointly" will create a tenancy in common.

The owner of real estate in severalty can create a tenancy in common between himself and another or others by a direct grant. For example, if Amos owns real estate, he can create a tenancy in common in the real estate between himself and Bert by granting to Bert a designated interest in the real estate, such as, for instance, a one-fourth interest.

### Termination of Tenancy in Common

A tenancy in common may be destroyed by partition of the real estate held by the tenants in common. The tenants may enter into an agreement for the partition of the property, in which event each tenant would grant to his cotenant his interest in the portion of the real estate set aside to him. For example, suppose that Amos and Bert own 80 acres of land as tenants in common, each owning an undivided one-half interest, and they agree to partition the land—Amos to take the north 40 acres and Bert the south 40 acres. Amos would grant Bert his (Amos') one-half interest in the north 40 acres. As a result, Amos would own the north 40 acres in severalty, and Bert would own the south 40 acres in severalty. If the property is such that it cannot be partitioned, it may be sold, each tenant in common executing the deed of conveyance, and each tenant taking his share of the proceeds of the sale in proportion to his interest in the property.

If the parties cannot agree as to the division of the property, any of the tenants may bring court action asking for partition of the real estate held by them as tenants in common. The court may decree a partition in kind if the nature of the property is such that an equitable division can be made. If an equitable division cannot be made, the court will order the property sold and the proceeds of the sale distributed among the tenants in proportion to their interest in the property.

A tenancy in common is also destroyed by merger—that is, by vesting in one person the interests of all the tenants in common.

A tenant in common may sell, mortgage, devise, or dispose in any way of his interest in the property held with his cotenants without destroying the tenancy in common.

If real property held by tenants in common is sold for taxes and one of the tenants in common bids the property in at the tax sale, the purchasing tenant will be deemed to have acted for the benefit of all the tenants in common, and the tenancy will not be destroyed. However, the tenant paying the taxes is entitled to contribution from his cotenants; if they refuse to contribute, he will have a lien on their interest for their share of the tax paid.

Pennie Shull and Morris Shepherd, while living together as husband and wife although they were not married, purchased in July 1949 the real property in issue. They lived together in the house until 1953, when they separated; and Shepherd then continued to live there alone. Both subsequently married other persons. Following their separation, Shepherd offered Shull $800 for her interest in the property, but she refused to sell. On March 31, 1961, Shull brought this action to recover her interest in the property. Shepherd claimed that he had acquired her interest in the property by adverse possession. The court held that Shepherd had not acquired Shull's interest and that Shull owned a 45.2 percent interest in the property and Shepherd owned a 54.8 percent interest.

Judge Hamilton said: "In the absence of additional facts or circumstances sufficient to show an ouster, exclusive possession by one tenant is not adverse as against his cotenant, but is ordinarily the possession of both. Mere possession by one cotenant alone will not ripen into title by adverse possession, even though it be continued without interruption for the period of the statute of limitations. There must be an ouster followed by adverse possession for the statutory period to determine the estate of the tenant not in possession.

"Property acquired with contributions from both parties is held as tenants in common, and the courts will presume they intended to share the property, in proportion to the amount contributed, where it can be traced, otherwise they share it equally." *Shull* v. *Shepherd,* Wash.2d, 387 P.2d 767 (1963).

## Tenancy by the Entirety

### Characteristics of Tenancy by the Entirety

At early common law a husband and wife were held to be one legal person. The woman, on marriage, lost her identity as a legal person; her legal personality merged with that of her husband, and the husband was the sole legal representative of the unity. This legal concept is the basis for the law relating to tenancies by the entirety. Property so owned is considered as being held by one indivisible legal unity.[9]

There are two distinguishing characteristics of a tenancy by the entirety: (1) the tenants must be husband and wife, and (2) there must be right of survivorship. The four unities of a joint tenancy are essential to the existence of a tenancy by the entirety. However, the tenants by the entirety, since husband and wife are considered as a legal unit, do not own equal shares in the property.

At common law the husband, during the continuance of the marriage, had the exclusive right of control over the property, and was entitled to all the rents and profits from the property. This rule is still in effect in some of the states that recognize tenancy by the entirety.[10]

Some states have held that under their statutes relating to the separate property of married women, the husband and wife each have an interest in the rents and profits derived from the real estate held by them as tenants by the entirety; a few states have held that during the continuance of the marriage, each spouse holds one half of the estate in common with the other.[11]

## Creation of Tenancy by the Entirety

A tenancy by the entirety, like a joint tenancy, cannot be created by operation of law, but must be created by grant, purchase, or devise. It is not an estate of inheritance. Tenancies by the entirety are recognized in less than one half of the states. In those states that recognize tenancy by the entirety, the holdings of the courts are not in harmony as to the language that will be interpreted as creating such a tenancy.

In most of the states, if land is granted to persons who, at the time of the grant, are husband and wife, and the grant contains no language indicating a contrary intent, the court will interpret the grant as creating a tenancy by the entirety. For example, a deed naming John Jones and Mary Jones as grantees would create a tenancy by the entirety; likewise, a grant to John Jones and Mary Jones, husband and wife, would create a tenancy by the entirety in most of the states recognizing such tenancy. However, in some states the grant would have to state clearly the intent to create a tenancy by the entirety. A grant to "John Jones and Mary Jones, husband and wife, as tenants by the entirety with right of survivorship," would be sufficient under the laws of any state recognizing tenancies by the entirety.

---

[9] *Wilson et al.* v. *Florida National Bank & Trust Co. at Miami et al.,* Fla., 64 So.2d 309.

[10] *Hale* v. *Hale,* 332 Mass. 329, 125 N.E.2d 142.

[11] *Ross* v. *Ross,* 35 N.J. Super. 242, 113 A.2d 700.

The states are not in accord as to whether or not a tenancy by the entirety can be created by a direct grant. The same rules are applied to the creation of a tenancy by the entirety as are applied to the creation of a joint tenancy in this same situation, with like results. These rules were discussed earlier in this chapter under the heading "Creation of Joint Tenancy."

### Termination of Tenancy by the Entirety

Neither the husband nor the wife, without the consent of the other, can dispose of or encumber any part of the real estate held by them as tenants by the entirety. As a general rule, any real estate that is held by a husband and wife as tenants by the entirety is not subject to levy of execution and sale for the individual obligations of either spouse, but is subject to levy and sale in satisfaction of a judgment against both.[12] In those states that hold that the husband has the exclusive right to control the real estate owned with his wife as tenants by the entirety, and the exclusive right to the rents and profits from such real estate, the courts have held that the husband can convey or encumber the rents and profits; but such conveyance or encumbrances will not be valid after the death of the husband, the wife surviving.

If a mortgage, contract to sell, or deed to real estate that is held by a husband and wife as tenants by the entirety is signed by the husband alone, such signing will not defeat the right of the wife, on the death of the husband, to take the property free of any claim of the mortgagee, contractee, or grantee. If the husband lists such property for sale with a broker and the broker finds a customer ready, able, and willing to buy, the wife is under no obligation to convey the property. However, the husband will be individually liable to the broker for his commission. Neither the husband nor the wife has any power to convey, by will, any interest in property that is held by husband and wife as tenants by the entirety.

In the event of divorce, the rights of the husband and wife in property held as tenants by the entirety will be determined by the courts according to the statutes of the state. As a general rule, after an absolute divorce, property formerly held by the husband and wife as tenants by the entirety will be held as tenants in common.[13]

In a minority of states, however, divorce converts the tenancy by the entirety to a joint tenancy with right of survivorship.[14]

If either spouse redeems property held as tenants by the entirety from foreclo-

---

[12] *Lake* v. *Callis et al.,* 202 Md. 581, 97 A.2d 316.

[13] *In re Cochran's Real Estate,* 31 Del Ch. 545, 66 A.2d 497.

[14] *Shepherd* v. *Shepherd,* 336 So.2d 497 (Miss. 1976)..

sure, judgment, or tax sale, or purchases the property at such sale, he will be deemed to have redeemed or to have bought the property for the benefit of both, and the property will be held by them as tenants by the entirety.

On February 15, 1954, Andrew Bradish contracted to purchase a tract of land. On July 14, 1956, Bradish applied to Western Pennsylvania National Bank for a loan of $3,500, the money to be used to pay the unpaid balance of the contract price of the tract of land. The Bank made the loan to Bradish, and he executed his promissory note, signed only by Bradish, to the Bank for the amount of the loan. The money was used as agreed to pay the balance of the purchase price of the land. The title to the land was taken in the name of Andrew Bradish and Virginia Bradish, husband and wife, as tenants by the entirety.

Andrew Bradish was killed in an automobile accident on July 17, 1956. There were insufficient assets in his estate to pay his debts in full. Western Pennsylvania National Bank claimed that since the $3,500 loaned to Andrew Bradish was loaned for the purpose of paying the unpaid balance of the purchase price of the land deeded to Andrew and Virginia and was used for that purpose, the Bank should be granted a lien on the land for the unpaid balance of the $3,500 loan. Virginia Bradish claimed that she took the land by right of survivorship free from the claims of the individual creditors of Andrew Bradish and that since the Bank was an individual creditor of Andrew Bradish, it had no right to a lien on the land. The court held that the Bank was not entitled to a lien on the land.

Judge Gunther said: "In order to seek the enforcement of an equitable lien under the circumstances here present, the evidence must be clear, precise and indubitable as to the intention of the parties. We agree with the court below that the evidence offered lacks the clearness and sincerity upon which the equitable doctrine of a lien may be applied. These proceedings were commenced only after a claim for the sum in question had been made upon the estate and when it was discovered that payment in full might not be realized on the note. In connection with this claim against the estate, the evidence discloses that the estate, without the claim, is not insolvent but becomes so if the full amount of the note be paid off.

"Appellant [bank] knew how to obtain a valid lien against the real estate here involved. It has done so in the past and its negligent practice cannot be made the basis of an equitable lien." *Western Pennsylvania National Bank* v. *Bradish,* 194 Pa. Supp. 126, 166 A.2d 104 (1960).

## Community Property

### Characteristics of Community Property

Community property is property that is owned in common by a husband and wife as a kind of marital partnership. It had its origin in the Spanish law and was adopted by Mexico, and it has been adopted by eight of the western and southwestern states.[15] Under the early Spanish law the husband was the owner of the community property and could dispose of it during his lifetime without the wife joining in the conveyance. The interest of the wife in the community property was an expectancy; that is, the wife took a one-half interest in it on the death of the husband, and this right could not be defeated by a testamentary disposition by the husband.

In the United States the community property laws of the states are statutory, and they are not uniform in their provisions as to the nature of ownership of community property. They are alike, however, in their basic provisions.

### Acquisition of Community Property

Regarding the acquisition of community property, the statutes make no distinction between real and personal property. The statutes likewise make no distinction in the character of community property based upon its sources as between the spouses. Each has an equal, present, and existing interest therein, whether it originates entirely from the earnings of the husband, entirely from the earnings of the wife, or partly from each.

The statutes do, however, define separate property, and the courts have held that all property that does not come within the definition of separate property is community property. For example, the California Code (Civil Code, §162) defines the separate property of the wife as follows: "All property of the wife owned by her before marriage, and that acquired afterwards by gift, bequest, devise, or descent with the rents, issues, and profits thereof, is her separate property. The wife may, without the consent of her husband, convey her separate property." The definition of the separate property of the husband is stated in almost identical language (Civil Code, §163).

### Management of Community Property

In general, the husband has the right to manage the community property. Under the early community property statutes the husband's power of disposal of community property was absolute and unrestricted; whereas under the existing community property statutes, the husband is given the right to manage the community property, but his right of disposal of it is restricted. Generally, the wife must join the husband in any conveyance or mortgage of community real estate. The statutes of the community-property states and the holdings of their courts are not in accord as to the rights of creditors to have their claims satisfied out of community

[15] Arizona, California, Idaho, Louisiana, Nevada, New Mexico, Texas, and Washington.

real estate. No general statement can be made in this regard, since a creditor's rights depend primarily on whether the claim is for a prenuptial debt of the wife or husband, a postnuptial separate debt of the husband or wife, or a community debt. As to the husband's right to dispose of community property, the California Code (Civil Code, §172) provides that the husband may not dispose of community property by gift, nor may he sell or encumber furniture, furnishings, or fittings of the home, or clothing or wearing apparel of the wife or minor children, without the written consent of the wife.

### Effect of Mutual Agreement

In community property states, a husband and wife may hold real estate as joint tenants or as tenants in common. They may also, by mutual agreement, declare property that would otherwise be community property to be the separate property of either the husband or the wife. Under the statutes of some of the states, such an agreement, if it is to be enforceable, would have to be entered into before the marriage.

The statutes of some states permit married persons moving into the state to enter into such an agreement, provided the agreement is made within a designated period of time after they move into the state.

### Rights on Divorce or Death

In the event of divorce between a man and wife who are holding property as community property, each spouse is generally granted a one-half interest. However, the statutes of some states provide that if the grounds for the divorce are adultery, extreme cruelty, or other such reasons, the judge may, in his discretion, grant a greater portion of the community property to the innocent spouse.

There is a lack of uniformity as to the disposition of the community property in the event of the death of the husband or wife. As a general rule, on the death of the husband the wife is entitled to one half of the community property. The husband may make a testamentary disposal of one half of the community property; but under the statutes of some of the states, if he dies intestate, the wife takes all of the community property. Under the laws of some states the wife may make a testamentary disposal of one half of the community property; whereas under the statutes of other states the husband, on the death of the wife, takes all the community property.

Earl Wiggins sold to Fairchild the timber on a tract of land that was community property. Alice M. Wiggins, Earl's wife, did not join him in the execution of the bill of sale of the timber. Fairchild brought an action asking that he be adjudged the owner of the timber. The court held that the timber was community real estate and that since Alice M. Wiggins did not join her husband in the execution of the bill of sale, it was void, and Fairchild acquired no title to the timber.

Justice McFadden said: "I.C. § 32–912 provides: 'The husband has the management and control of the community property, except the earnings of the wife for her personal services and the rents and profits of her separate estate. But he cannot sell, convey or encumber the community real estate unless the wife joins him in executing and acknowledging the deed or other instrument of conveyance, by which the real estate is sold, conveyed or encumbered. . . .'

"That the bill of sale to the timber created an encumbrance upon community real estate is not disputed, and hence the attempted conveyance of such an interest in the community real estate, without the wife's signature and acknowledgement, is void." *Fairchild* v. *Wiggins,* 85 Idaho 402, 380 P.2d 6 (1963).

## Partnership Property

### Nature of Partnership Property

At common law the ownership of real estate by a partnership was not recognized. A partnership is not a legal entity; and from a technical, common-law standpoint, a partnership cannot own real property. The title must vest in the partners, not in the firm.

At common law, if a partnership was named in a deed as grantee and the partnership name did not include the name of any of the partners, no title to the real estate would pass by the deed. The Uniform Partnership Act provides that any real estate may be acquired in the partnership name and that title so acquired can be conveyed only in the partnership name. In those states that have adopted the Uniform Partnership Act or have enacted statues of similar import, the common-law rule is not followed.

Partnership ownership of real estate is a type of quasi-entity ownership. No partner has a particular interest in partnership property; he holds as a tenant in partnership with his partners. The incidents of a tenancy in partnership are set out in Section 25 of the Uniform Partnership Act.

Only real estate intended by the partners to be partnership property is partnership property. Although the form of a conveyance is not conclusive of the nature of the rights conveyed, it is of great weight in determining whether or not property is partnership property. The grantee, if a partnership, should be named in the deed in such a way that the intent of the parties is clearly indicated. For example, if John Jones and Henry Smith, who are partners doing business as "The Big Busy Bee," purchase real estate as partnership property, the deed should clearly indicate this intent. If the grantee is named as "John Jones and Henry Smith, partners, doing business as 'The Big Busy Bee,' " the deed will clearly indicate that the real estate is acquired as partnership property. If the grantee is named as "John Jones and Henry Smith," title technically vests in John Jones and Henry Smith as tenants in common. However, in an equitable proceeding for an accounting or for a dissolution and winding-up of the partnership business, parol (oral) evidence would be admitted to prove that the property was partnership property. Under the Uniform Partnership Act a deed naming "The Big Busy Bee" as grantee would vest title to the property in the partnership.

### Conveyance of Partnership Real Estate

Under the general law of partnership, every partner is a general agent of the firm, with authority to execute in the name of the partnership any instrument for apparently carrying on in the usual way the business of the partnership. Under this rule, any partner has the power to execute a deed in the name of the partnership conveying partnership real estate, provided such conveyance is for the apparent purpose of carrying on in the usual way the business of the partnership.

If a partnership is organized for the purpose of buying and selling real estate, any partner (unless his authority is limited by the agreement of the partners and such limitation is known to the purchaser) may execute in the partnership name a deed conveying partnership real estate sold in the regular course of the partnership business.[16]

If a partnership is dissolved by the bankruptcy or death of a partner, the partners not bankrupt, or the surviving partner or partners, have the right to wind up the partnership business. In the event the partnership is dissolved by the death of a partner, the title to real estate held by the partnership in the partnership name vests in the surviving partner or partners—subject, however, to a duty to wind up the partnership business and pay over to the estate of the deceased the deceased partner's interest in the partnership. The surviving partner or partners have the power to transfer to a bona fide purchaser for value good title to partnership real estate. If there are no partnership creditors, the estate of the deceased partner and the surviving partner or partners may, by mutual agreement, distribute partnership real estate in kind or hold it as tenants in common.

O. L. Littleton loaned $10,000 to L. T. Littleton; and as security, L. T. Littleton deeded a dairy farm to O. L. Littleton. During the years 1953 and 1954 the Littletons operated the dairy farm as partners. O. L. Littleton claimed the farm. L. T. Littleton claimed that the farm became partnership property and that he (L. T. Littleton) owned a one-half interest

---

[16] *Robinson* v. *Daughtry,* 171 N.C. 200, 88 S.E. 252.

in it. The court held that the farm was not partnership property and that even if it were, L. T. Littleton, as a partner, would not have a one-half interest in it.

Chief Justice Bell said: "If the partnership continued to exist, appellant [L. T. Littleton] would not own title to any specific property belonging to the partnership. If the property under the evidence was shown to be partnership property, the court could not legally award a judgment decreeing title to one half of specific property. The court could merely declare ownership in the partnership with a particular interest in such partnership being owned by appellant." *Littleton* v. *Littleton,* Tex. Civ. App., 341 S.M.2d 484 (1960).

## Modern Types of Common Ownership

### Social and Economic Needs

As society developed and the population began to concentrate in urban areas, there arose a need for some type of multiunit housing, and the apartment building seemed to fulfill this need. The apartment dweller was, however, a tenant and as such was not free, as a general rule, to make any changes and improvements he might desire to make to the apartment that he was occupying. Those who wished to own their own apartments and thereby acquire some, if not all, of the freedom of individual ownership found it difficult to work out such an arrangement under the types of co-ownership recognized by the common law. In order to overcome this difficulty, two different plans were devised that gave the multiunit housing resident ownership rights in the apartment that he occupied. Under these plans, he obtained some, but not all, of those freedoms enjoyed by an owner of a single-family residence.

In the United States the first plan used for this type of living was the cooperative. Recent legislation, usually termed the Horizontal Property Act, lays the foundation for a second type of ownership of apartments—the condominium. This is a plan whereby a party is the owner of his own apartment and, in addition, is co-owner of the common elements of the apartment building and grounds.

### The Cooperative

The cooperative plan of ownership of real estate was, in its origin, applied almost exclusively to apartment buildings. In recent years, it has been expanded to include developments involving ownership of city lots and the single-family homes erected thereon. From the standpoint of types of ownership of land the cooperative property is owned in severalty.

Ordinarily, the title to the cooperative property is vested in either a stock or a membership corporation. If a stock corporation is the vehicle, stock of a total par value equal to the purchase price of the cooperative property will be authorized. If a membership corporation is used, the total value of the memberships issued will be equal to the purchase price of the cooperative property. If a stock corporation is used, the authorized stock will be allocated between the individual units according to their estimated relative value. The value of a membership in a membership corporation is determined on the same basis.

A party wishing to "buy" an apartment or house and lot pays the agreed price (subscription) equal to the money value of the unit involved. The "buyer" is then issued stock or a membership of a value equal to the price of the unit "purchased" and is granted a proprietary lease to a particular unit for the life of the corporation. The operating expenses of the cooperative are divided among the individual units in the form of monthly assessments. These and the payment on the subscription, comprise the monthly outlay of the owner.

In this manner the residents of the cooperative property control the corporation that owns and manages the entire property. Each cooperative member has one vote, regardless of the number of shares or the value of his membership, and the majority can determine the proper management and expenditure policies in the light of their own best interests as they see them. It is the right of the "unit owners" to have a voice in choosing those who will be their neighbors. Most cooperatives provide that the lease and stock or membership cannot be transferred without the approval of the buyer by the elected representatives of the members.

### Restraint on Alienation

Our courts have been consistent in holding that a direct restraint on the alienation of property is against public policy and is void. Yet, if a cooperative is to function successfully, it is necessary that extensive restraints be placed on the alienation of the cooperative units. This restraint has been accomplished by several devices that accomplish the desired objective without placing a direct restraint on the alienation of the cooperative unit. A common plan used is one that provides that the proprietary lease cannot be assigned or the unit sublet without the written consent of a committee of unit owners or of a stated portion of the unit owners, or without the consent of the board of directors. Another plan provides that the corporation would have the first right to purchase the stock or membership and lease of the unit owner. The courts have recognized the desirability of permitting extensive restraints in cooperative cases.[17]

---

[17] *Penthouse Properties. Inc.* v. *1158 Fifth Avenue, Inc.,* N.Y. App. 685, 11 N.Y.S.2d 417; *Gale* v. *York Center Community Center, Inc.,* 21 Ill.2d 86, 171 N.E.2d 30.

### Restrictions on Use

A cooperative has been called a municipality within a municipality. Our courts have recognized the right of corporations, fraternal organizations, churches, and similar associations to adopt rules and regulations for the guidance and control of their members, and have enforced such rules and regulations provided they were reasonable and not against public policy or illegal. The broad rule has been applied to the rules and regulations adopted by cooperatives. The community type of living, which is part of the cooperative plan, necessitates the adoption of extensive rules setting out the rights of the unit owners to use and alter their units and their rights in the common property, such as halls, elevators, grounds, and so on, and also the duties they owe to other unit owners. The penalty for violation of such rules and regulations is, as a general rule, cancellation of the unit owner's lease. However, other penalties may be available, depending on the circumstances of the individual case.

Carolyn Green, a member of Greenbelt Homes, Inc., a cooperative, was found to be guilty of violation of the rules and regulations of the corporation. The procedure set out in the contract of membership and in the bylaws of the corporation was followed, and the required number of members voted to terminate Mrs. Green's membership. Mrs. Green contended that she owned the house she occupied and that she could not be deprived of her ownership by the action of the corporation. The court upheld the termination of Mrs. Green's membership in the corporation and held that she had forfeited her right to the continued possession and occupation of the unit she had acquired.

Judge Horney said: "We think it is clear from the mutual ownership contract that the restrictions on the use of the cooperative dwelling unit were covenants between the member and the corporation, the breach of which gave the corporation the right to terminate the contract. We see no practical difference between this contract and a lease which provides that it can be terminated by the lessor when its provisions as to the use to be made of the premises by the lessee are breached. . . . It is apparent, we think, that the objectionable conduct of the member was a sufficient breach of covenant to warrant the corporation exercising its right to terminate the interest of the member in the dwelling unit." *Green* v. *Greenbelt Homes, Inc.,* 232 Md. 666, 194 A.2d 273 (1963).

### Condominium

The condominium has many of the features of a cooperative, but it has one major distinguishing characteristic: The units of the condominium are owned in fee by the members. The common areas, that is, the walls, roof, footings, halls, elevators, heating system, plumbing, and so forth, and the land on which the building stands are held by the owners as tenants in common. Under the usual arrangement the transfer of a unit in the condominium includes a transfer of the unit owner's interest in the common areas. Several states have enacted enabling statutes, generally titled Horizontal Property Acts, that set out the procedure to be followed in the organization of a condominium. At the same time the National Housing Act has been amended,[18] authorizing the Federal Housing Administration to insure a first mortgage given to secure the unpaid purchase price of a fee interest in a one-family unit or in an apartment in a multifamily structure together with the purchaser's undivided interest in the common area and facilities that serve the structure.

## Condominium Statutes

Condominium statutes usually provide that each apartment, together with its undivided interest in common areas and facilities, shall for all purposes constitute real property. The rights in the common areas are defined in detail, and the statutes provide that the common areas are not subject to partition. Provision is made for the filing in the office in which records of the title to real estate are filed or recorded of a declaration that includes a description of the land on which the building and improvements are to be located, a description of the building to be erected, a description of the common areas, a statement of the value of the property and of each apartment, a statement of the purpose for which the building and each apartment are to be used, the voting rights, the restrictions on use of the apartment and common areas, and other details necessary for the effective organization of the condominium. The floor plan of the building must be recorded and each unit described. The requirements for the conveyance of the individual units and for the recording of the title to the units must be set out.

The owner of a unit may mortgage his unit or subject it to a lien; but he cannot, by his individual act, impose a lien on the property as a whole. By authorized acts of the managers the property as a whole may be subjected to a lien for repairs or improvements of the common area. The owner of a unit may discharge his unit and his interest in the common area by paying his proportionate share of the indebtedness secured by the lien.

Under the statutes of some states, taxes and assessments are assessed against and collected on each individual apartment. Each unit owner may insure his holding, and the manager may insure the whole property; and the rights of the unit owners in the event of damage to or destruction of the building are set out.

---

[18] National Housing Act, Sec. 234.

## Management

The Horizontal Property Acts usually set out general guidelines for the management of the condominium, but the details of the management plan are left for the unit owners to work out. A person may be appointed as manager; a board of trustees elected by the unit owners may be authorized to manage the property; a nonprofit corporation may be organized, and its board of directors act as managers, or some other plan may be adopted. In general, the management of a condominium follows the general pattern of the management of a corporation. For instance, monthly assessments are made to cover the costs of maintaining the common areas and facilities, rules are adopted for the conduct of the occupants of the units, and provision is made for the enforcement of these rules; and such other matters as are necessary for the efficient operation of the whole property are delegated to the management.

Although there is some diversity of opinion as to the procedure to be followed in the enforcement of the rules and regulations, the general expectation is that the courts will hold that the rules and regulations are covenants between the unit owners and are enforceable as such by the managers. The remedies that are available to a landlord against a defaulting tenant in the operation of a cooperative will not be available to the managers of the condominium.

## Commercial Uses of the Condominium

All that has been said above regarding individual ownership of condominium units or apartments has been aimed at the widespread use of the condominium for residential purposes. It should be noted, however, that the use of the condominium has been expanded in recent years to include business properties as well. That is, the basic idea of individual ownership of a specified area in a building applies to office buildings as well as apartment buildings. The use of this device permits individual business entities (or the principal owners of the businesses) to own office spaces when this is advantageous to them. Typically, the greatest appeal for this use has been to minimize income tax consequences. While the subject of taxation is considered in detail at a later point, the fact that an individual conducting business in a corporate form may own property in his own name and lease it to his corporation provides him an additional way in which to extract income from the business and still obtain favorable income tax treatment. At the same time, because the owner of a condominium unit (whether office or residential) is the true owner and may rent his space to others, the condominium unit has become quite popular as a personal investment.

### Conclusions

The condominium provides for individual ownership of the units involved in communal property. This individual ownership permits the owner to finance his unit as he wishes within the scope of the general plan, and it gives him some tax advantages. To some extent, it relieves him from the burden imposed on a unit owner in a cooperative in the event a co-owner defaults, since liens on the condominium are on the individual units, whereas liens on a cooperative are on the whole property. Which form of community ownership will be the better will depend on the objectives of the parties, the laws of the state, and many intangible elements.

## Timesharing

The concept of sharing the use or ownership of real estate has been adapted from industry's practice of sharing computer facilities. The basic idea is that more than one user can have the exclusive use of a property for a limited period of time on a recurring basis. This is in contrast to the common-law forms of undivided ownership. Under the common-law tenancies we have just considered, the basic concept is that all of the co-owners have the right to the use of the entire property all of the time. For this reason their ownership interests were said to be "undivided" or not set off into divisions of time or space. Under the timesharing concept as it has evolved in real estate, co-ownership is *divided* not only as to the particular portion of space but also as to a specified fraction of the time. In a time shared project each co-owner obtains the exclusive possession and use of a specific part of the real estate, usually an apartment, with shared use of the common areas. Also, this exclusive use is limited in terms of time, usually a specified week or weeks each year for a definite period of years or into perpetuity.

This concept of shared ownership has thus far found application primarily in resort or vacation properties. It has been based upon the condominium concept of exclusive possession of a specified apartment plus shared possession of common areas needed to make the apartment useful, convenient, and desirable. This will usually include recreational facilities that are a part of the project. Timesharing can proceed on two different bases: a long-term lease or outright ownership. Under the lease concept the holder of the timeshare has a recognized legal estate in land that is limited to the specified apartment. He may very well have only a license to use certain of the facilities that are made available to the tenants in the project. This will be determined by the documentation and how the project has been structured. For purposes of control and ease of administration many projects are structured as leases or licenses. When this is the case the limitations that are imposed by the landlord are a matter of negotiation at the time the agreement is entered into.

The ownership approach to timesharing is known as "interval ownership" because the purchaser is buying an estate that is limited to a period of weeks each year. Furthermore, this right of ownership may be limited to a specified period of years, making it more in the nature of a determinable fee. It may just as well, of course, be an interest in perpetuity and be a fee simple absolute interest. Where interval ownership is the basis of timesharing, the owner is exposed to the same liabilities and responsibilities as any other property owner. Such interests may be mortgaged, sold, traded or exchanged, foreclosed against for nonpayment of debts or taxes, and so on. There are practical problems of maintenance and insurance on an ongoing basis. There is the ultimate problem of disposition when the property is worn out and ready for demolition, sale, or rebuilding. In short, there are all of the problems that exist with condominium ownership. They are aggravated by the far greater number of owners who must somehow agree on all significant actions.

A simple illustration, based upon the marketing techniques that have been employed in timesharing schemes, will illustrate the magnitude of the management problem. The concept has been sold to the public as a form of "annual vacation at guaranteed cost" as opposed to ownership. In fact, one of the major attractions has been the modest cost when compared with condominium ownership. Marketing has been geared to time periods of one week intervals with two such intervals normally being sold to the typical buyer. If, for example, the year is divided into 52 weeks with 2 of those weeks reserved for major maintenance, there are left to sell 50 one-week intervals. If we assume that buyers will buy two one-week intervals apiece, we will have 25 owners, each owning a two-week period each year *for each apartment.* If the project has 100 apartments there will be *2,500* separate owners, each of whom has some limited fee interest and each having the right to participate in the decision-making process. Clearly the governing of such a project over a period of many years requires a carefully drafted agreement.

The development of the timesharing concept for real estate has created several satellite industries. One of these is that of financing timeshare purchases. Where true interval ownership is the basis for the project, the buyer obtains a property interest of value that can be financed by use of traditional mortgage concepts. As a practical matter the ultimate security for the loan is the apartment itself. Its continued marketability into the future will determine its value as security for a loan. Typically, lenders view vacation properties as less stable than primary residential properties. Therefore, financing of timeshared ownership is seen as a specialized area of finance. Companies have appeared that concentrate on this kind of financing to service the growing market. When the timeshare is based upon a lease or license concept, its financing becomes more risky in terms of the salability of the collateral, and it tends to be accomplished upon a basis similar to that for consumer durables rather than traditional mortgage financing. Generally, this higher risk commands a higher rate of interest. This is particularly true when there are limitations upon the transferability of the interest that make it difficult or impossible for the lender to compel a sale as the ultimate source of repayment. While it is possible to purchase timeshare interests that "float," and so may be used within a time range rather than the same precise period each year, these are not common. As a result, the vacation period for the owner of the typical timeshared interest is fixed at the same time each year. This inflexibilty has led to the creation of a separate industry to exchange these interests between owners. Since the concept has spread to vacation areas as diverse as Colorado and Florida the need or desire for this flexibility has increased. It is possible to exchange such interests not only for different time periods but also for different locations. The free transferability of the timeshare interest has come to be recognized as an important and valuable element of ownership because of the flexibility that it creates.

The industry has not developed without problems. Complaints have arisen over the high-pressure sales techniques sometimes employed. Communities in which such projects have been developed have sometimes found municipal facilities overtaxed because of more constant pressure of population density. Some projects have been ill-conceived and unsuccessful, leaving buyers who purchased before construction with sizable losses. Disputes among the owners of the interests, as suggested earlier, are magnified by the sheer number of the participants. Some areas of the country have been led to forbid the sale of timesharing interests because of the notoriety given to the industry's problems. Therefore, local law must be looked to in order to determine limitations on the use of the concept. It remains an innovative technique that, upon further development and refinement, may well find much broader application to other types of real estate.

# Chapter 8

# Real Estate Investment Vehicles

Investing in real estate is different from other forms of investment. Many popular investments, such as stocks, bonds, precious metals, and even art objects, are essentially *passive* investments. No day-to-day effort is required. Real estate investments are frequently *active* investments, requiring day-to-day decision making and activity, either by the investor or one to whom the investor has delegated the work: the property manager. Real estate investments differ from other investment forms in other ways as well. For example, the dollar value of most real estate investments requires the use of borrowed funds. This fact exposes the investor to continuing liability in the event the investment is unsuccessful. Very often the investor will find it necessary to pledge his personal assets as well as the real estate in order to secure financing. At the same time real estate must be used by someone who will pay rent in order to make the investment income-producing. This introduces a whole area of risk for the investor: that of liability for personal injury and property loss by the user.

Not only the risks but also the rewards make the selection of the investment vehicle an important decision. Some risks may be avoided by the use of the corporation as the investment vehicle. That is, the investment may be made in the form of corporate stock so that the risk is limited to the amount invested. By the same token, however, the use of the safer vehicle may also limit the reward that is hoped for: corporations are taxed first on earnings and those earnings are taxed again when they are paid to the investors as dividends. The selection of the investment vehicle therefore must often be a compromise.

Decisions must be made that involve extent of control versus exposure to liability. Estate planning is frequently an additional consideration because of the long-term nature of many real estate investments. The economic goals of the investor (current income versus capital appreciation, for example) may change from time to time, requiring different strategies and, perhaps, different investment vehicles.

The nature of each type of real estate investment that is available will be a factor in selecting the investment vehicle. Development and building of a condominium project, for example, proceeds upon market assumptions that indicate profitability. Changes in economic conditions may wipe out the profit and replace it with a significant capital loss. To what extent can the investment vehicle insulate the investor against this possible loss? Purchasing a factory for the sole purpose of leasing it back to the seller may suggest that profits may be maximized by abandoning the protective features of the corporation in favor of some simpler form of co-ownership that saves income taxes.

The standard common-law forms of co-ownership suggest themselves because of their apparent simplicity when we consider our residence as an investment. There is little need for a complex arrangement in this situation. There is, for example, no current income to be divided. Therefore, the tax brackets of the owners are not really a factor. Management of such an asset is a family affair. The income is in the form of amenities rather than rent receipts. Why would we even think of our residence as an investment? In recent years we have witnessed almost continuous increase in the market value of our residences. At times the increase has been both rapid and substantial in terms of current dollars. This has been true in spite of the fact that economically the residence is wearing out, depreciating, and actually becoming less valuable all the time. The reason for the increase in value has come from some cause outside the property itself: inflation, which has been continuous for many years. Recognition of this fact makes our treatment of our residence as an investment of doubtful validity. Nevertheless, the more or less continuous increase in the value of our residence should not be ignored. Even if we view it as a hedge against inflation rather than an aggressive investment for profit, this too is a matter of significance to us in our financial planning. As a result of this potential for capital appreciation or preservation it should be viewed as an investment. We should therefore give some consideration to the ownership vehicle we will use.

It appears that the type of real estate investment, the investor's goals (both short- and long-term), and many other factors must be taken into account in selecting the investment vehicle. In this chapter a variety of devices, ranging from simple co-ownership to the limited partnership, are considered. The legal characteristics of each are explored in order to illustrate which is most useful for a particular investment. An overriding consideration will be the personal goals of the investor.

## The Tenancy in Common

Frequently a real estate investment requires no more than a very few investors, either because of its relatively low cost or because of the financial capacity of the investors themselves. When this is true the investment vehicle can be kept relatively simple. For example, the real estate syndicate which conjures up visions of a very complex arrangement, is very often nothing more or less than a tenancy in common. Obviously, there must be something more than this simple tenancy to delineate the aims and goals of the investors and to provide some element of control of the venture. This is true because, without some overriding agreement, each tenant owns an undivided interest in the real estate with which he can deal as he pleases without consulting with his co-owners. To permit this situation to exist is to permit potential chaos in the event of disagreement between the cotenants. Granted this fact, consider the confusion and loss of control that would result upon the death of one of the cotenants or his financial death through insolvency or bankruptcy.

It is apparent that the utilization of the tenancy in common as an investment vehicle requires considerable care in the selection of the cotenants and that there should also be a written, enforceable contract between them so that basic investment decisions can be made, such as: selling or continuing to hold; the sales price to be sought and/or accepted; conditions under which the cotenancy will be continued; options and option prices at which one cotenant can be removed; restrictions upon the right of one cotenant to sell or otherwise dispose of his interest with or without the consent of his cotenants. All of these are matters that must be considered in the agreement between the investors.

It should be recalled at this point that in the tenancy in common there is no requirement that the interests of the tenants be equal, and frequently the agreement will reflect a greater degree of control by the investors who contribute the greater proportion of the investment. Then at least some degree of flexibility is possible through the use of the simple tenancy in common. There are, of course, mechanical problems in dealing with the title to the property, and these multiply with the number of investors or tenants. For example, in those states that still recognize some form of dower or other interest in an owner's spouse, the wives of all the tenants may be necessary parties to any sale, mortgage, lease, or other formal dealings with the property. As a result of these factors the tenancy in common has inherent limitations when more than a few investors are involved. Nevertheless, it should not be overlooked as a possibility because of the advantages of its simplicity and one more very important tax advantage: each investor or tenant preserves his independence as a separate tax-paying entity. That is, the tax consequences of dealing with the investment for each investor are unaffected by the tax consequences that may befall his cotenant. It is conceivable, for example, that one investor in the venture may qualify for capital gains treatment on a profit from subsequent sale of the investment, even if his cotenant is classified as a dealer and taxable on his profit at ordinary income tax rates. Clearly the use of the tenancy in common, even with a well-drafted agreement between the parties, should not be undertaken without the benefit of qualified legal and tax counseling. Even more obvious, it should never be undertaken without an agreement between the parties, but it sometimes is, and the results can be disastrous and costly when close business associates disagree on policy or even tactics.

When the tenancy in common is used between husband and wife as the ownership vehicle for their residence, the choice is often the result of some estate planning goal. If, for example, each of the spouses independently owns a significant estate, which will be taxable at death, it may be beneficial to own the residence in common. In this way we avoid "dumping" the value of the deceased spouse's share of value into the estate of the survivor, where it then will be exposed to a second round of estate taxes. When this approach is taken, however, we must be aware of the results dictated by the tenancy in common. Records of any capital improvements, for example, must reflect the contribution of each party. In the event of disputes over the management of the property, there is the unhappy possibility of a partition proceeding and forced sale of the property. In view of marital ups and downs, it may be quite impossible to provide for every unfavorable contingency. Nevertheless, the husband and wife must attempt to think like investors if capital appreciation is one of their goals.

## The Joint Tenancy

The joint tenancy of real estate suffers from all the shortcomings of the tenancy in common with the additional complication of survivorship itself. It would require unique circumstances indeed for an investor to desire that his interest in the venture be transferred at death to his fellow investors rather than to his estate or to his heirs. This is not to say that the joint tenancy is never useful as an investment vehicle. In certain situations, such as an investment by co-investors who are close family members, it may have desirable results such as assurance of control of the title by the surviving investor and the avoidance of the delays and expenses of probate proceedings in the deceased co-owner's estate. On the other hand, it may have serious adverse economic consequences in the deceased tenant's estate, not the least of which may be the lack of liquidity for payment of death taxes. There is loss of control of a valuable asset, which might be mortgaged to raise the necessary cash, because it is now owned by the surviving tenant. There are serious problems to be faced in the use of the joint tenancy as an investment vehicle, and it should be used only under unusual circumstances. The need for competent legal and tax advice is obvious.

The use of the joint tenancy between spouses for residential property is too common to be ignored. The most obvious advantage is the feature of survivorship and the certainty that title will go to the surviving spouse. From an investment standpoint this may well be its most desirable feature because of the marital relationship. There will be no interruption in the investment program being followed because there are no new owners entering the picture. It places control over the property precisely where most married investors want it: in the sole control of the surviving spouse. Perhaps the major danger in the use of the joint tenancy for this purpose is the failure of the parties to review their circumstances periodically. With advancing age some uncomfortable changes may take place that make the joint tenancy a liability rather than an asset. One of these is the specter of incompetency that haunts us all. There may well come a time when the ability of the either spouse may become impaired. The avoidance of a loss that might result from a faulty decision requires that alternatives be considered. One of these is the trust, which is discussed later in this chapter.

## The Tenancy by the Entireties

Other forms of co-ownership that include the feature of survivorship, such as the tenancy by the entireties or the community, which are unique to the marital relationship, have the obvious advantages of continuity of control and the dispensation with formal probate proceedings to transfer title to the surviving spouse; on the surface these forms appear quite advantageous in what is the classic example of a "close family relationship." Nevertheless, the estate tax consequences may be quite undesirable, and the selection of another available form of co-ownership may have distinct advantages. Local law will determine whether the tenancy by the entireties has any advantage over the joint tenancy for purposes of investment, which includes estate planning to preserve wealth. There may be, for example, significant inheritance tax advantages. Estate tax advantages under federal law do not exceed those available in the joint tenancy. In this area the qualified estate planner should be consulted, and the need for his advice becomes more important with the advancing age of the parties.

## The Partnership

The partnership is far from a new device. It has been a recognized vehicle for the conduct of a wide variety of businesses for many years. Under the common-law partnership a great degree of flexibility in the conduct of business was possible. At the same time there were several drawbacks, not the least of which was the fact that each partner was exposed to unlimited liability for the acts of any other partner. That is, not just the assets of the partners that were devoted to the business were subject to the losses of the business, but the personal assets of each partner could be reached as well. This unlimited exposure to liability was, and still is, an inhibiting factor in the use of the partnership as an investment vehicle.

The advent of the Uniform Partnership Act and its widespread adoption throughout the United States has eliminated many of the technical difficulties that previously existed at common law. For example, under the Uniform Partnership Act the partnership itself can hold title to real estate; the partners themselves are not required to hold title as individuals. The result of the UPA has, however, been one of merely streamlining the mechanics of doing business rather than working any basic changes in the underlying concepts of partnership law. This is particularly true of the feature of unlimited personal liability of each partner for the acts of his copartners, which remains as a deterrent to the use of the partnership, even under the Uniform Partnership Act.

Even with its limitations, however, the partnership remains a viable and useful device and an attractive vehicle for investment in real estate ventures. The element of ease of control remains, and this is supplemented by attractive income tax treatment of the partnership as opposed to corporations other than Subchapter S corporations, discussed later in this chapter. That is, the income earned by the partnership is passed off to the partners and is taxed directly to them rather than being taxed once to the business entity and then again to the participants, as is true with the typical corporation. These factors continue to make the partnership attractive as an investment vehicle. Even so, the most important element in the use of the partnership is, just as with the syndicate, a well-drafted partnership agreement. The same considerations discussed above in connection with the tenancy in common need to be considered in structuring the partnership: control, division of profits, buyout of a dissenting partner, settlement of accounts at death, and so on. All of these matters demand the services of an attorney in the preparation of the agreement as well as continuing advice in the management of the enterprise.

Real estate investors are eternal optimists. Their aggressive approach to maximizing profits by minimizing income taxes is frequently best served by the partnership. This is true in spite of the risks that may be involved. Periodic upheavals in financial markets underscore the degree of risk involved in the use of the partnership. When a highly leveraged investment fares badly the personal liability for borrowings can be quite disastrous to the investor who does not maintain sufficient liquidity. The current practice of periodic renegotiation of commercial mortgages introduces a whole new area of personal risk that should not be ignored in structuring the investment program. The subject of finance is discussed in Section IV of this book.

## The Limited Partnership

The limited partnership represents an attempt to combine the flexibility and the tax treatment of the partnership with the insulation from liability of the investors that is available in the corporation. In the limited partnership one or more general partners exercise control of the enterprise and assume a greater degree of risk. The limited partners contribute money to the enterprise and share in the profits proportionately. Up to this time the attraction of the limited partnership has been its ability to pass off to the limited partners all or substantially all of the income tax deductions generated by the enterprise, such as depreciation, interest, and local taxes. Frequently the motive for investment is almost solely the acquisition of those deductions that the limited partner may apply against ordinary income from other sources (such as salaries for highly paid executives and fees for successful professionals), and the attractiveness of the investment is directly related to the investor's income tax bracket. The term "tax shelter" is particularly appropriate in this context because the deductions generated by the limited partnership's activity can be used to "shelter" income from other sources. The marketing of limited partnership interests has been aimed therefore at the sophisticated investor, and the number of limited partners has generally been rather small (although some limited partnerships are quite large because of the size of the venture itself and the need for large amounts of capital).

In addition to the normal risks of any real estate enterprise (such as the construction and management of an apartment complex) there are very real risks from an income tax standpoint. That is, in addition to the possible loss of the investment itself if the project fails, there is risk of exposure to serious income tax "recapture" penalties. For this reason the investment opportunities in limited partnerships have so far been restricted to the truly sophisticated investor who can demonstrate both the sophistication and that he can afford the investment. The reader is invited to obtain a copy of the prospectus or proposal on such a limited partnership venture and to study the qualifications imposed upon the investor himself as well as the disclaimers of responsibility on behalf of the general partner and the promoter.

## The Corporation

The corporation as a vehicle for real estate investment has the classic advantage of the corporation for other business ventures: limited liability for the shareholder. He is exposed to loss only up to the amount he has paid for his stock in the absence of unusual circumstances. By the same token the individual shareholder's voice in the management of the corporation depend upon his percentage of ownership. This determines his power to elect directors, who appoint the officers of the corporation, who conduct its business. Since the goal of the corporation investing in real estate is profit, the income tax treatment of the corporation is an important consideration. While it is true that recognition of income can be sheltered to some extent by the corporation by retention for reserves, and so forth, the income that is paid out to the shareholders is exposed to liability for income taxes twice rather than once. That is, the corporation itself is a taxpaying entity that must pay its own taxes on net income it has earned. From the residue, after taxes, is paid to the shareholders their distribution of earned income: the dividend. In the individual shareholder's hands the dividend is taxable as ordinary income. Clearly, the earned income from the enterprise is taxed twice before the investor can measure his net, spendable return on his investment. This appears to be a severe penalty to pay in return for limited liability, but this depends upon the character of the investment. For example, for the investment in raw ground with a goal of subsequent sale at a profit the penalty appears too severe because the exposure to liability is slight. Investment in an apartment complex, on the other hand, may expose the investor to substantial liability for personal injuries on the premises and a variety of other sources. Another consideration that favors the selection of the corporation is the need for large amounts of money. That is, when vast sums are required because of the cost of the investment, its development, and marketing, the corporation may be an attractive vehicle simply because the unit cost of investment may be kept very low and the funds obtained from many investors.

## Subchapter S Corporations

For many investors the low unit cost of investment and freedom from personal liability are enough to make the corporation an attractive vehicle, in spite of the limited amount of control exercisable by each shareholder. With the additional feature of double taxation upon the income, however, the corporation as a vehicle for real estate investments is far less attractive. One possible alternative exists: the so-called Subchapter S corporation, which is a creation of the federal income tax laws. A detailed discussion of the Subchapter S corporation and all of its ramifications is beyond the scope of this book, but certain fundamental points should be noted for further investigation. Essentially, the Subchapter S corporation is a corporation in the true sense of the legal term, although it may elect to be treated as though it were a partnership for purposes of federal income taxes and, in some states, for state income tax purposes. In order to qualify for this treatment, which eliminates the tax on the corporation and taxes all net income directly to the shareholders, certain rigid requirements must be met. Perhaps the most significant are these two: the number of shareholders is limited to 25, and *all* of the earned income, with few exceptions, must be actually charged to the shareholders for tax purposes. The obvious advantage is that the net income is taxed directly to the shareholders only, and not to the corporation and then the shareholders; limited liability. The disadvantages include: (1) the limitation upon the number of shareholders, which inhibits the accumulation of large sums; (2) the fact that substantially all of the net income must be charged to shareholders when earned, even though this may fluctuate widely from year to year, thereby "bunching" income in some years and sending individual tax rates soaring; and (3) the fact that the degree of control exercisable by an individual shareholder is limited by the percentage of his ownership, as previously explained. There are other, highly technical aspects to the use of the Subchapter S corporation that need to be considered with competent legal and accounting advice, such as: the effect on the corporate structure of the death of one of the shareholders; the fact that certain entities, such as many trusts, cannot qualify as shareholders under the tax laws; and the requirements of the Internal Revenue Code, which must be met on a continuing basis in order to avoid disqualification from Subchapter S status. In those situations that justify its use the Subchapter S corporation can be invaluable, but it is surrounded with many technical rules of income tax law and should be the result of only a carefully considered decision.

## Simple Trusts

The use of the trust in the real estate field is hardly a novel idea. It goes back to before the time this country was organized. The development of the trust for use as a real estate investment vehicle has, however, in recent years been the subject of a great deal of sophisticated development, from both a legal standpoint and a tax standpoint. In an oversimplified way the trust results in a split of the rights of ownership between the holder of the legal title, the *trustee,* and the holder of the equitable title, the *beneficiary.* Under basic trust rules the trustee, even though he has the legal title, is obligated to deal with the trust property for the profit of the beneficiaries only and not for himself. The creator of this arrangement is called the *settlor* or *grantor* of the trust estate. Almost universally the trust must be created in writing to comply with either the statute of frauds or applicable state trust law.

The settlor of the trust may become the beneficiary of the trust when it is established, and there is no limit on the number of either settlors or beneficiaries. Neither is there any limit on the number of trustees, but because of the general rule that trustees must act unanimously in making certain decisions, it is seldom that more than one trustee is appointed. While the creation of the trust can be relatively simple, the relationship is governed by many complex rules and its operation is governed by applicable state laws. A thorough discussion of these matters is beyond the scope of this book, but the trust is such a useful device that a limited discussion of its working is in order.

In its simplest terms the real estate trust is an arrangement under which the settlor transfers title to real estate to the trustee, subject to the terms of the trust agreement, which spell out in detail the duties, powers, obligations, and liabilities of the trustee, as well as specifying his compensation. The trust agreement will charge the trustee with the responsibility of managing or dealing with the property solely for the benefit of the named beneficiaries, who may also be given the right to direct the trustee in his conduct with respect to the trust property. In a real estate trust the realty will be conveyed to the trustee *as trustee* and not outright. This will be a formal legal conveyance of the title to the realty but subject to the obligations and limitations spelled out in the trust agreement.

The trust has several significant advantages over many other forms of co-ownership. Among these are the ease with which the transfer of title can be accomplished; no matter how many beneficiaries there may be, a deed from the trustee will pass the legal title since the trustee is the sole *legal* titleholder. This eliminates the need for a conveyance from many individuals who may be beneficiaries of the trust and, as such, the true parties in interest. The fact of participation in the benefits from the trust can remain a private matter in most cases; that is, the names of the beneficiaries, the true owners of the property, are not a matter of public record. (In some states today the trustee can be forced to reveal their identities under certain circumstance, such as the violation of health and fire regulations.) A certain amount of notoriety has resulted from this secrecy aspect because it has been used at times to conceal the identity of the true owners of real estate that has been involved in public scandals; however, the device is nevertheless very valuable and useful for the smooth accomplishment of many perfectly legitimate business transactions.

A trust is a separate taxpaying entity, just as is a corporation; however, for tax purposes it can be structured in such a way that it is treated as is a partnership. That is, if all the earnings are paid out to the beneficiaries of the trust, the trust files an information return only, disclosing the amounts and the distributees, and the tax liability is passed off to the beneficiaries.

Because of the nature of the relationship between the trustee and the beneficiaries and the fact that the trustee has the legal title to the trust property and could easily convert it for his own use and benefit, the law surrounds the relationship with substantial safeguards. It is characterized as a fiduciary relationship, requiring a much higher standard of good faith on the part of the trustee than is required of either party in any normal business transaction. The penalties for breach of this relationship are harsh and will usually not be limited to the actual monetary loss suffered by the wronged beneficiary. As a result, trustees generally do not serve without compensation related to the degree of risk assumed. On the other hand, the selection of the trustee is a serious decision that must be based upon matters such as his integrity and financial responsibility. Performing this function has become an important business of banks acting through their trust departments. There is, however, no reason that an individual may not act as a trustee. Generally, corporations other than banks are prohibited from the trust business by applicable state law.

As with the common-law forms of co-ownership, some safeguards are required in structuring the simple trust when it is being used by a group of investors. Usually an elaborate agreement between the parties will be needed, much in the nature of a partnership agreement. This agreement will detail the circumstances under which the trustee will be directed to deal with the property. It will also establish who is authorized to provide this direction to the trustee. For its part the trustee will usually demand that it be held harmless (free from liability) if it follows the directions of the elected representative of the group. This freedom from liability will be structured to continue until the trustee is notified formally of the appointment of a successor with authority to give such directions.

### Documenting the Trust

The preparation of the documents required in order to use the private trust as an investment vehicle is not a simple task. As noted above, there must first be prepared a detailed agreement between the parties who will be the investors. This agreement should specify the manner in which decisions will be reached by the group and the fact that they will be binding upon all the participants, whether unanimous or not. Some mechanism for settling disputes, the sale or other transfer of the shares of the parties, and succession of their interests in the event of death should be provided. Valuation procedures for the purpose of a buyout of a dissenting participant and for estate and inheritance tax purposes are also important. For ease of administration one of the group should be granted the authority to provide directions to the trustee in dealing with the real estate. Some orderly process for appointment or election of a successor should also be included.

The trust agreement itself will detail the duties and obligations of the trustee. Typically these will be limited to normal administration; significant actions such as sales or leases remain subject to the direction of the settlors, who are usually also the beneficiaries. Frequency of accountings, income distributions, and the like will also be specified. It is not necessary, of course, that the settlors retain control of the trust. The entire management of the investment may be turned over to the trustee with as much discretionary power over sales, leasing, borrowing, and so on as the settlors choose to vest in the trustee. Quite often it is the skill of the trustee in real estate investing that prompts the use of the trust in the first place. Ultimate control can still be retained by the investor group by simply reserving the right to revoke the trust at any time. The extent of powers given to the trustee will depend upon the purpose for the selection of the trust as an investment vehicle: management or pure administration. The trust agreement will specify the fractional share of ownership of each investor and will spell out how these interests can be transferred. The trustee will typically require insulation from liability if it follows the directions of the settlors in dealing with the property. Of course, the greater the extent of responsibility and expertise demanded of the trustee, the more significant will be the management fee for its services.

The deed used in this arrangement will usually include a very elaborate listing of the powers of the trustee to deal with the property. The goal of the attorney preparing the deed by which title passes to the trustee will be to omitt nothing in the way of powers that could conceivably be required in dealing with real estate. The purpose of this wealth of detail in the deed is to insure that the record will disclose that the trustee has all necessary power. This makes it unnecessary to record the trust agreement itself, which is usually intended to be a private and confidential document. The trust agreement may very well absolutely prohibit the trustee from using any of these powers without a specific order or direction from the settlors, but so far as others are concerned, the trustee has all the necessary power to bind the trust and its assets to any legal agreement executed by the trustee.

**Financing through the Trust**

The trust can be structured in a way that facilitates financing. When the trustee is the trust department of the bank that is financing the investment it is a relatively simple matter to include in the trust agreement a clause that effectively makes the bank a beneficiary of the trust. This provision would include the power to veto any proposed action directed by the investors that would adversely affect the bank's security interest in the property. It can go further and transfer the power of direction to the bank's loan department at any time the loan is in default, so that the loan department could direct the trust department to sell the property and apply the proceeds to the loan balance. There is no need in such a transaction to have a mortgage on the property, although this might be found to be prudent by the lender in some jurisdictions. It must be recognized that this arrangement represents a clear conflict of interest for the trust department acting as trustee. It is unlikely that a trust department would enter into such an arrangement unless the parties are sophisticated investors (in the legal sense of that term) and are also represented by legal counsel.

The foregoing illustration of the flexibility of the trust as a financing vehicle and, therefore, as an investment vehicle is not intended to suggest that the loan is likely to be made without more traditional safeguards. It may still be necessary for the investors to personally guarantee the borrowings, even though the loans are made directly to the trust. As noted, in some jurisdictions a formal mortgage may still be required in order to protect the lender. These matters will depend upon the quality of the investment and the bargaining power of the investors. Where it can be successfully used, it provides considerable privacy as to the terms of financing, which may be advantageous to both the investors and the lender.

## The Real Estate Investment Trust

The real estate investment trust (REIT) is a creature of the income tax laws. It was authorized by the Real Estate Investment Trust Act in 1960.[1] The effect of this legislation is to permit the organization of an unincorporated trust or association for the purpose of investing in real estate, real estate mortgages, and other interests in real estate. Such trusts and associations are relieved from the payment of corporate income taxes, provided they are organized and operated in compliance with the act. The more important provisions that must be met are: (1) there must be 100 or more certificateholders (or beneficiaries) during each year and five or fewer of those holders must not own more than 50 percent of the certificates outstanding; (2) the purchase and sale of real estate may not be a substantial part of the trust's business; and (3) the major portion of its income must be derived from dividends, interest, rents from real property, or gains from the sale of real property. In addition, in order to avoid being taxed as a corporation it must pay out at least 90 percent of its earned taxable income each year. Failure to meet all of the requirements of the act during any given year will result in the taxation of the trust as though it were a corporation. Such failure to qualify would, of course, seriously limit the advantages of the REIT to its certificateholders. It should be noted that there are other rules that must be met in order to qualify under the act and that the above information is greatly oversimplified.

The REIT has become tremendously popular as an investment vehicle because certificates of beneficial ownership can be issued in small denominations and prices just as can stock in a corporation. Markets for these certificates have been organized so that they can be traded in much the same way corporate stock is traded. Rates of return on investment have been attractive to many investors, and many REITs have been quite successful. There have, however, been many failures of such trusts with disastrous consequences for the certificate holders. As with any other business the ability and integrity of its management are key ingredients to success. The development of capable management (both real estate and financial) has not occurred as quickly as the explosive growth in popularity of the REIT itself. Great care must be taken by the investor to assure himself of the quality of management of the REIT. On the other hand, qualified management of such trusts commands a premium for its services, and this field therefore represents an attractive career for knowledgeable real estate people.

### Condominiums

The condominium has proven to be a vehicle quite adequate for many persons who desire to participate in an investment of some magnitude. It has become

---

[1] Public Laws 86–779, Sec. 856, United States Code, Annotated, Title 26, §§856, 857.

quite common for an individual to own a condominium apartment in a popular vacation area and to rent it out for all or most of the time. While there is no rule that restricts such investments to resort or vacation property, these have attracted most of the investor attention. A part of the reason for the popularity of such an investment is the favorable treatment of them by the income tax laws: the investor can use the property for his own vacation without losing the benefits of owning it as investment property. Severe limitations exist as to the amount of time that an investor may live in his investment before it is deemed a home rather than an investment for tax purposes.

The structuring and management of such an investment can be quite simple. The apartment owner can act as his own rental agent and property manager, seeing to the renting, collections, maintenance, and janitorial work himself. If this proves impractical the property can be managed by someone specializing in that business. Some projects have been carefully designed to provide these services on a highly professional basis, even including the ultimate sale of the investment apartment. One example frequently pointed to is the Innisbrook Golf and Country Club, located in Tarpon Springs, Florida. Owners of apartments there have the option of putting them into a professionally managed "rental pool" while they are not occupying them. The management company charges a fee for its services, which even include necessary redecorating and furniture replacement to maintain high quality, which enhances the investment and its rewards for the owner. The sheer size of Innisbrook and its reputation for quality combine to provide a very important fringe benefit: an active market in which to sell or buy. It is quite possible to treat these apartment investments as though they were marketable securities: buy and sell orders may be entered at specified prices once financial responsibility is established. This factor creates liquidity, the lack of which generally is a major shortcoming of real estate investments.

Financing the condominium investment is an important issue that must be addressed by the investor. Financing depends upon the ability of the borrower to show how the loan will be repaid. When the prospects for income are uncertain the borrower may have difficulty in qualifying for favorable terms because of the riskiness of the loan. While it is true that the condominium is today a well-established ownership right that can be pledged or mortgaged, favorable terms are not usually based upon the salability of the collateral. The first consideration is always the degree of assurance that the loan will be repaid on schedule from predictable income.

Some form of co-ownership of the condominium itself is quite common. Between close family members, where control is the most important consideration, the common-law forms are adequate. If the condominium apartment will be owned by more than one investor, however, the already stated shortcomings of these devices still apply. The limited personal use permitted by the income tax laws without loss of investment status may provoke very costly disputes between the co-owners. There are, therefore, practical limitations on the extent to which such an investment can be successfully divided.

While the resort applications of the condominium have received most of the notoriety, the concept is just as valuable for commercial applications, such as office complexes or residential apartments that the owner has no intention of using for his own personal purposes. The difficulty inherent in this approach to real estate investing is primarily one of management. That is, disagreements often arise between apartment owner-residents and owner-investors as to the quality of maintenance, esthetics, and density of use. One class views the apartment as a home and may demand amenities that do nothing to increase the return on investment for the other class. Such disputes may be unavoidable because of the different motivation of each class of owners. One solution, of course, is to limit the type of ownership permitted in a project to one class or the other. Even then, however, some clear-cut method of settling such disputes is needed in order to avoid costly lawsuits. The bitterness with which such disputes can be contested is well documented. From an investment standpoint, such disputes tend to limit profitability and should be avoided.

## Timesharing

Neither the right-to-use nor the interval-ownership approaches to timesharing have been designed or marketed as investment vehicles. At the outset, however, neither were condominiums. The purchase of a timeshare interest represents an investment in a property right that has some value. How marketable such interests are depends upon the precise terms of the grant of the interest, particularly any limitation on transferability. The right-to-use timeshare would seem to have almost no attraction as a possible vehicle for serious real estate investment other than the value of the share itself in the open market. Interval ownership, however, would appear to offer some potential since it is an *ownership* interest. It is not unlike the complete ownership of the condominium apartment itself. To the extent that the interval-ownership interest in an apartment represents a share of the ownership of the underlying condominium apartment itself, it can function in much the same way. From a practical standpoint, however, it would seem that the administrative problem of dealing with such a great number of interests would inhibit its development as an investment vehicle. Nevertheless, to say that these problems cannot be overcome if profit and tax motivation will be served seems rash in light of the historical development of the condominium.

## Conclusions

Undoubtedly, additional investment vehicles will be designed in order to attract the small as well as the large investor into the real estate field. In addition there are frequent combinations of existing vehicles. A few observations about real estate investment are in order. First, it must be borne in mind that the promoter or salesman may no longer be selling real estate; he may have entered into the securities business, which has its own legal framework and its own system of regulation. The regulations, imposed by both state and federal governments, are designed to protect the investor from fraud. The penalties for failing to comply with these regulations can be quite severe. Anyone intending to pursue this field as a career should therefore seek additional education and training in the securities business. This is true even with the relatively simple vehicles, such as the private trust or even the tenancy in common. Many states, for example, restrict the number of investors who may be *solicited* for such an investment, even if the number of actual investors still stays below the statutory number of participants. This is the difference between a private offering, which can be quite simple, and a public offering, which may require registration and control by a state agency.

Second, it should be unnecessary to point out that the basic reason for a higher rate of return on investment almost universally is a higher degree of risk. Even in those investments in which the income tax advantages increase the net return, there is always the risk of change in the income tax law, which can seriously impair marketability and result in partial loss of the investment. This is in addition to the normal risks encountered in any real estate investment. An important fact to consider is that real estate investment properties are high unit-value investments, and their marketability is therefore impaired. Quick reactions to changes in economic conditions are not always possible. The liquidation of a real estate investment may be quite costly in terms of economic loss and may be a disaster from an income tax standpoint. It is not intended to imply that losses are not possible in the stock and bond markets, but the character of the real estate investment is unique and this must be kept in mind by the investor as well as his counselor.

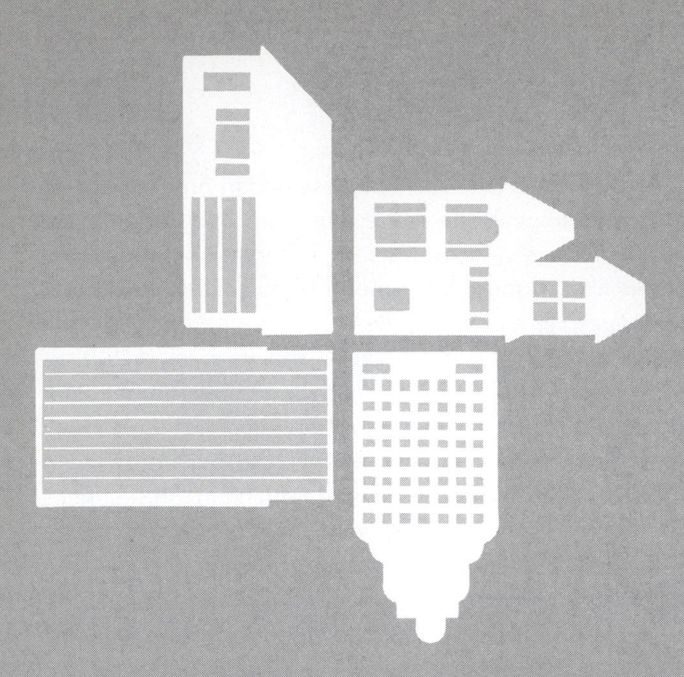

# Section 3

# Acquiring Ownership of Real Estate

In descending order of frequency of occurrence, we acquire ownership of real estate in three ways: purchasing it, inheriting it, or taking it. The quality of the title we obtain will vary depending upon the way in which we acquire it. When we purchase real estate we are entitled to negotiate on the question of the quality of title and to pay more or less for it, depending upon what we are willing to accept. When we inherit real estate we must be aware of the legal rule that a man must be just before he may be generous. As a result of this rule, we can inherit no better title than our ancestor or benefactor had. If the property is encumbered by a mortgage to secure a debt, for example, we may inherit the debt and the mortgage along with the title. When we simply take real estate belonging to another we must expect no assurances whatever as to the quality of the title of the owner from whom we took it. Indeed, we can logically expect that proving we own it at all will be difficult. The legal rules will not surprise or disappoint us. We will get what we pay for, what is given to us, or what we take—nothing more.

In this section we will explore the mechanics of various ways of acquiring title to real estate. Emphasis will be placed upon the most common method:

the deliberate transfer of ownership by use of a deed. This is the garden variety of real estate transaction: we pay an agreed-upon price; we receive a deed making us the new owner. What needs to be investigated is the extent of ownership transferred by the deed. Related to this matter is the question. To what extent, if any, does the seller guarantee the quality and extent of ownership being sold? We will find that our legal system has devised several levels of guarantee, or lack of it, of title. We must know what level it is that we are bargaining for so that we can place the correct value upon it.

In most transactions we are seeking absolute and perfect title. We want complete ownership without any flaws or defects. In the bargaining process we will insist that the seller provide us a guarantee to this effect. He does this by delivering to us a *general warranty* deed. This is a formal document stating that he is the true and only owner of the property and that he is transferring that ownership to us with no exceptions or limitations. He is said to convey and generally warrant the property to us. This is his personal undertaking to protect us against any and all defects that may later appear, no matter when they arose or whether he even knew of their existence. We can take as much comfort from this guarantee as we can find in the seller's financial responsibility or ability to pay us if he is mistaken. If all sellers were able to respond in money damages for any defect in title, there would be no need for the abstract and opinion nor for title insurance. Nevertheless, such a deed does legally obligate the seller to deliver what he has promised or to pay our damages if he fails to do so.

Often the seller will be unable or unwilling to make such a broad guarantee as is included in the general warranty deed. For one reason or another he may be willing only to guarantee that the quality of the title did not deteriorate during his ownership. In such a case he will be willing to give a deed of only *limited* warranty for that period of time. This leaves open the question of just how good the title was when he acquired it and exposes the new owner to the risk of any such defects.

Still lower on the scale is the quitclaim deed, in which the seller or whoever gives such a deed makes *no* warranties of any kind. The grantor in such a deed not only does not guarantee us against any defects; he does not even guarantee that he owns the property at all. Such deeds are highly suspect, of course, when we are parting with value in return. We shall see that they nevertheless perform a valuable function in the real estate business by foreclosing technical claims that have no merit. Their primary use today is to cure defects in the quality of title, and they can be quite useful in this function.

Next considered is the possibility that we may acquire title to real estate as the result of the death of the previous owner. This can happen in one of two ways. We might inherit the property under the statutes of descent and distribution because of our relationship to the deceased owner. This will happen automatically if the decedent leaves no will disposing of his property at his death. We might, however, receive the real estate as a gift made by a valid will of the decedent. In such a case the gift does not depend upon our relationship to him. In fact we may be unrelated. The crucial test is: Did he leave a valid will that directed that the property pass to us? Recalling that he must be just before he may be generous, the decedent's immediate family may have a claim that will defeat the gift in whole or in part. So may his creditors.

Regardless of the method by which we may succeed to the ownership of the decedent's real estate, the quality of the title we will get will necessarily depend upon how good his title was at the time of death. We will find that the death of the owner does not improve the quality of title to his real estate. Quite the contrary. New defects may attach as the result of his death: claims for debts and inheritance taxes, for example. We may find that the property must be sold to satisfy these claims rather than become a gift. When such a sale takes place we must recognize what limitations on quality of title may exist and what limitations exist in terms of warranties made by the personal representative charged with the responsibility of settling the estate.

Finally, we will consider the possibility that we may acquire title to real estate by simply taking it from the rightful owner. We may take the entire fee interest under the doctrine of adverse possession. Or we might take some limited right, such as an easement of right of way, under the doctrine of prescription. Each of these concepts presumes that the rightful owner did not invite us to use his property for such a long time that we are entitled to treat it as though we owned it. On the contrary, our claim to ownership must be *adverse* to that of the true owner. If we consistently maintain possession or use for a very long time *without* his permission the courts will decline to help him to recover the title. His failure to act in a timely fashion to protect his ownership creates in us a title by default.

The validity of the title that we take from another is very questionable. Initially, we can safely conclude that our title cannot be better than that of the owner from whom we took it. Certainly, we can hardly expect any warranty from him since we did not, by definition, pay him for the property. Assuming we overcome these hurdles, we then face the acid test: How marketable is the title we have acquired? We will see that perfecting our claim to ownership may be a lengthy, difficult, and expensive task.

Since we presume that few people today will permit others to take valuable property from them, we might conclude that these doctrines have no modern application, but this is incorrect. Adverse possession frequently serves as the only practical method of settling boundary disputes based upon historical claims of ownership. The value of the property may have become very great, but the doctrine still applies. Fences on open rangeland that have been accepted as boundaries for generations may turn out to be the legal boundaries when oil is discovered beneath the range. Very significant property ownership questions are even today resolved by resort to the doctrine of adverse possession.

# Chapter 9

# Acquisition of Title by Conveyance

Ownership of real estate may be acquired in a variety of ways; the most common method is to purchase it. When this is the case, title to the real estate is transferred by means of a formal written document, the deed. In this chapter the technical, formal requirements for an effective deed are considered in detail. Over the years a variety of deeds has developed, with each type having certain limitations as to the quality of the title being transferred. They range from the *general warranty* deed, which purports to transfer complete ownership with no defects in the title, to the *quitclaim* deed, which simply transfers to the new owner whatever degree or quality of title was held by the preceding owner without any guarantees of quality. Recognition of the differences in various types of deeds is of obvious importance to the purchaser who is paying value for the rights of ownership.

## Introduction

### Original Title to Land

Title to land is based on a conveyance from a government that has acquired sovereignty over it. When the original 13 states gained their independence, much of the land within their boundaries had been granted to individuals who held either directly or indirectly from crown grants made by the country that had acquired sovereignty over the land through discovery and settlement, or by conquest or treaty. Each state had sovereignty over the vacant and unappropriated land within its borders. The Northwest Territory was granted to the United States by the states having claims thereto, and the vacant and unappropriated lands in this area came under federal jurisdiction.

Most of the land within the borders of the United States other than that of the 13 original states and the Northwest Territory was acquired by purchase or treaty from France, Spain, and Mexico. The land obtained from Spain and Mexico was partially settled. The owners of such land traced their titles to grants from the crown of the government that had colonized and settled the areas, and the rights of these owners were preserved under the terms of the treaties whereby these lands were acquired. There were no established settlements in the area acquired from France—the Louisiana Purchase. Most of the unowned land acquired by the United States has since been granted to individuals under laws enacted by Congress. The basis for private ownership of this land is a direct transfer of ownership from the U.S. government to an individual by a document known as a *patent*.

## Conveyance of Real Estate by Deed

The right of alienation, the right to transfer ownership or to *convey* real estate to another, is of great significance. As noted earlier, at one stage in the development of real estate law an individual could not freely transfer his rights in real estate and he certainly could not convey ownership because all he held was the right to possess and use real estate. In the United States both alodial ownership and the right to freely convey that ownership to another were early recognized as being in the public interest. The free alienability of real estate was felt to be essential to social and economic development. We do recognize that certain reasonable restraints upon alienability are both necessary and desirable, but a *total* restraint on alienability is against public policy and is void.

The method by which we convey title to real estate involves a written instrument evidencing the transfer of ownership. The document used to accomplish this is the *deed*. Technically, a deed is an instrument in writing by which the owner of land (the grantor) transfers to another (the grantee) some right, title, or interest in or to real estate. Throughout the years there have developed several more or less standard types of deeds, each designed to suit a particular purpose. While there are minor variations in form from state to state, the deeds commonly used today generally fall into three categories: warranty deeds (both general and special), quitclaim deeds, and deeds of bargain and sale.

***Warranty Deeds.*** A warranty deed purports to convey title or ownership to real estate and also makes certain warranties or guarantees as to the quality of title and extent of ownership being conveyed:

1. That the grantor has title to the real estate being conveyed.
2. That the title being transferred to the grantee is good as against third persons; that is, no one else has any interest in the property.
3. That there are no liens or encumbrances against the property.
4. That, upon failure of the title either in whole or in part, the grantor will compensate the grantee in money for any loss sustained.

When there are no limitations expressed in the deed, and even if the above warranties are not spelled out in detail, the deed is a *general* warranty deed and the grantor is liable for any loss suffered by the grantee, no matter how old the defect may be and in spite of the fact that the grantor neither created the defect nor knew of it. As a result the grantor is effectively guaranteeing the quality of title all the way back to its original private ownership stemming from the patent or other original grant.

The mere fact that the grantor is willing to make such a broad warranty or guarantee of his title does not mean that he or she in fact owns the property or that the title to it is free of defects. It simply means that he or she is willing to assume this financial risk in return for the agreed-upon payment for the property. As we will see in subsequent chapters, it is this quality of title for which the purchaser is usually bargaining; but because of the complex history of titles to real estate today, some additional assurance is usually demanded, rather than the naked reliance upon the seller's willingness to generally warrant the title.

A *special* warranty deed also purports to convey the title to the property. It also makes the same warranties or guarantees that are made in the general warranty deed; however, it *limits* those warranties to those defects that rose after the time he acquired the property. Therefore, while the term "special" would seem to imply that such a deed carries with it broader guarantees than the general warranty deed, this is not the case. Rather than warranting the quality of title without reservation, the grantor under the special warranty deed is warranting against only his own acts or other facts that arose after he purchased or otherwise acquired the property. It is more correct, therefore, to refer to the special warranty deed as a deed of limited warranty. Such deeds are frequently used by trustees or others who did not actually purchase the real estate and therefore were not motivated to investigate the quality of the title.

***Quitclaim Deeds.*** A quitclaim deed does not purport to convey title, nor does it contain any warranties of quality whatsoever. It simply transfers such right, title, and interest as the grantor has in the real estate, *if any.* It is effective to transfer all of the interest owned by the grantor in the property at the time of the execution and delivery of the deed to the grantee. If, at that time, the grantor owns the entire fee simple interest in the property, then the grantee under the quitclaim deed will acquire that interest. If, on the other hand, the grantor had no right, title, or interest of any kind in the property at the time of the execution and delivery of the deed, then the grantee will acquire nothing. At the same time the grantee will have no cause of action to bring against the grantor for any failure of or defect in the title, because no warranties were made.

While it is true that in the typical purchase of real estate the parties contemplate the transfer of title along with the warranties included in the general warranty deed, there are frequent instances in which the quitclaim deed is quite valuable. Typically, the quitclaim deed is used today to clear up technical defects in the title; quite often the grantor does not even claim to have any estate or interest in the property.

George W. Hudson owned 160 acres of land. After his death, this land was sold for delinquent taxes. Under the laws of descent and distribution, his widow, Myrtle Hudson, took a one-third interest in the land in fee, and each of his four children took one quarter of the remaining two thirds in fee. Jackson, the husband of a daughter, redeemed the land from the tax sale; and a deed naming George W. Hudson as grantee was executed by the county and delivered to Myrtle Hudson. She executed and delivered a deed which read as follows: "Said party of the first part [Myrtle Hudson] do hereby convey and quit to the said party of the second part, [Hans Frandson] his heirs and assigns forever, all right, title and interest in and to a certain tract of land in the county of Mountrail, State of North Dakota, described as follows" [there followed a description of the 160 acres of land].

Frandson died, and his heirs claimed the land. The four children of George W. Hudson claimed a two-thirds interest in the land. The court held that the deed executed by Myrtle Hudson conveyed only her one-third interest in the land and that the heirs of Frandson acquired only such one-third interest.

Judge Johnson said: "We must next determine whether the quitclaim deed issued by Myrtle Hudson purporting to convey all of the property to Hans Frandson did in fact convey anything more than a one-third interest in the property. . . . The deed is labeled as a quitclaim deed and is on a printed form. It did not operate to convey the entire fee in the land. . . . Nowhere does the word 'grant' appear in the instrument. Where such word is used in a conveyance by which an estate of inheritance or fee is to be passed, certain convenants are implied. The quitclaim deed contains no covenants of warranty. A quitclaim deed is one which purports to convey, and is understood to convey, nothing more than the interest or estate in the property described of which the grantor is seised or possessed, if any, at the time, rather than the property itself. A quitclaim deed does not purport to convey the property, but only the grantor's right, title and interest therein." *Frandson* v. *Casey,* N.D., 73 N.W.2d 436 (1955).

***Deed of Bargain and Sale.*** A deed that recites the fact of payment of consideration and that purports to convey the real estate is a deed of bargain and sale. Under this definition it is clear that such a deed may be either a quitclaim deed (if it includes no warranties of any kind) or it may be a warranty deed (either general or special, depending upon the extent of the warranties *actually* made.) It is important to note that no warranties will be "read into" or implied in such a deed, so that any assurance of the *quality* of the title must be expressed in the deed itself. Other than the personal undertaking by the grantor that his deed is passing legal title, there are no other guarantees. To this extent then, the deed of bargain and sale is quite similar to the special or limited warranty deed.

***Fiduciary's Deeds.*** There is a wide variety of deed forms that have developed for special applications, including: executor's and administrator's deeds, trustees' deeds, guardian's deeds, sheriff's deeds, receivers' deeds, and so on. In all of these it is important to note that the grantor is actually conveying real estate that belongs to someone else, and that the grantor is acting in a representative capacity only. Such deeds are almost always quitclaim deeds, although a trustee will frequently be willing to execute a special warranty deed. The limitations upon the authority of fiduciaries to execute even a valid quitclaim deed are discussed in the next section, in which the legal requirements of a valid deed are explored in detail.

## Equitable Rights and Legal Title

An instrument that does not fulfill the legal requirements for a valid deed may convey to the grantee an equitable interest in the property. That is, although the instrument is not sufficient to convey to the grantee the legal title to the property, it will transfer to him the equitable ownership of the property. Such ownership is valid as between the parties, but it is not good against a bona fide purchaser for value.[1]

For example, suppose Arnett, as grantor, deeds real estate to Bennett, but the deed does not comply with statutory requirements, although it does state clearly that Arnett thereby conveys the real estate to Bennett. As between Arnett and Bennett, Bennett becomes the owner of the real estate. However, if Arnett

[1] *Mertzger* v. *Miller,* 291 F. 780.

thereafter deeds the real estate by a valid deed to Clark, who has no knowledge or notice of the prior conveyance to Bennett, and who purchases the property in good faith, paying value therefor, Clark will acquire good title to the real estate.

## Formal Requirements

### Importance of Form

The preparation of deeds requires both skill and careful attention to details. The legal profession refers to this activity as the "art of conveyancing." Reference to the simplified form deeds in common use today may appear to make the preparation of the deed a simple function and to require no particular skill, but countless decisions by our courts in interpreting the poorly prepared deed are clear evidence that the task is simple only to one who is legally trained and skilled enough to make his art appear simple to others. Because the deed is of crucial importance in accomplishing the legally effective transfer of ownership of real estate, it is discussed in substantial detail below. Even so, the preparation of deeds is the province of the attorney and not the layman, no matter how well informed.

### Basic Requirements

While the formal requirements for a valid deed are not uniform in all states, certain considerations are fundamental to the effectiveness of all deeds:

1. A grantor with legal capacity to execute a deed.
2. A grantee, named with reasonable certainty, so that he can be identified.
3. A recital of consideration.
4. Words of conveyance.
5. An adequate description of the land conveyed.
6. Signing or execution of the deed by the grantor.
7. Delivery of the deed to the grantee.
8. Acceptance of the deed by the grantee.

To these fundamental requirements must be added at least one technical addition that is a practical requirement, if not a legal one: the *acknowledgment* of the deed by the grantor. Some form of acknowledgment is generally required in order to qualify the deed to be recorded. Since the lack of recording may make the deed ineffective, as against subsequent good-faith purchasers for value (discussed earlier), it is of obvious importance. The statutes of many states require the acknowledgment of the deed, at least by implication, as the ninth requirement for a valid deed. Other requirements of modern origin include the necessity of identification of the preparer of the deed on its face before it may be recorded; however, such requirements do not generally go to the validity of the deed itself.

There may also be in deeds a wide variety of restrictions, conditions, exceptions, and limitations; however, these will be dictated by the circumstances surrounding the particular transaction and the agreement of the parties. These subjects are considered at various points in later chapters. Here we are considering only those elements that are essential to every deed as opposed to additional terms that are merely desirable or necessary to serve a particular purpose.

## Grantor

### General Requirements

To have a valid conveyance of real estate, the grantor must have legal existence and legal capacity to contract. In general, an unincorporated association, club, or society, except a partnership, does not have legal existence and cannot own or convey real estate in its name.[2] Under the statutes of some states, certain special types of unincorporated associations have been granted legal capacity to own and convey real estate conferred on them.

### Natural Person as Grantor

A deed is in many respects a contract, and the rules relative to a natural person's capacity to contract apply in determining his capacity to convey his real estate. To make a valid conveyance, he must be of lawful age and of sound mind. At common law a person reached his majority at the age of 21 years. The age of infancy has been modified in most states today for many purposes. Unfortunately, no uniform rule has been established, and the statutes of each state must be consulted. Even in those states that have reduced the age of majority to 18 this has frequently been done on a selective basis so that age 18 is not the age of majority for all purposes.

A deed executed by an infant is voidable, not void. The rule generally followed is that an infant cannot disaffirm a conveyance of real estate until he reaches his majority. After reaching his majority, he has a reasonable time in which to disaffirm. What constitutes a reasonable time is a question to be determined by

---

[2] *Popovich et al.* v. *Yugoslav National Home Society, Inc. et al.,* 106 Ind. App. 195, 18 N.E.2d 948.

the court. Each case must be decided according to its particular facts and circumstances.

A grantor is generally held to have sufficient mental capacity to execute a deed if he is capable of understanding the nature and effect of his act. A deed executed by a person of unsound mind is voidable, not void, and may be set aside by proper court action, usually an action in equity to set aside the deed, brought by the grantor on regaining his sanity, or by a guardian or conservator of his estate. If such action is brought, the person of unsound mind must restore the grantee to his original position. Under the statutes of many states a deed is void if it is executed by a person who has been officially adjudged insane and is under guardianship at the time he executes the deed.

At common law a married woman had no capacity to contract, and any deed executed by a married woman was a nullity. In the United States today the married women's property acts enacted by many of the states permit a married woman to convey her separate estate as though she were a *femme sole* (unmarried woman). However, the married women's property acts are not uniform in their provisions; in several states, unless the husband of a married woman joins in the execution of a deed, it is a nullity.

### Artificial Person as Grantor

A duly incorporated corporation may hold real estate in the corporate name and has the power to convey its real estate in the corporate name. However, if a corporation is the grantor in a deed, the corporate name must be signed by some duly authorized officer or officers of the corporation. Generally, the officers who sign the deed in the name of the corporation must be authorized to execute the deed by a resolution, duly adopted, at a legally called meeting of the directors or trustees.

If the sale involves a substantial portion of the corporate assets, a favorable vote of a designated portion, frequently two thirds, of the outstanding stock having voting rights is required. Often, a favorable vote of a majority of the members of a nonprofit corporation is required to authorize the sale of real estate.

A New York statute provides that: "A religious corporation shall not sell, mortgage or lease for a term exceeding five years any of its real estate without applying for and obtaining leave of the court therefor pursuant to the provisions of Article five of the general corporation law. . . . "[3]

The requirements for the execution of deeds by municipal corporations and

---

[3] *McKinney's Consolidated Laws of New York,* "Religious Corporations," Book 50, Sec. 12, as amended.

by other governmental agencies and units are set out in the statutes of the state in which the real estate is located. These statutes vary in their provisions; therefore, no general statements regarding the required procedure can be made.

A government official has only those powers that are conferred on him by the statutes of the state. Consequently, in conveying public property, government officials must comply strictly with all the material provisions of the enabling statute. Likewise, the requirements for the execution of deeds by sheriffs, trustees in bankruptcy, receivers, guardians, and so forth, are set out by statute.

The powers of trustees of trust estates and executors of the estates of deceased persons to convey real estate will be set out in the trust instrument or will. These instruments must be examined to determine the extent of the power of the trustee or executor.

### Grantor's Spouse

Whether or not both the husband and the wife must join as grantors in the execution of a deed depends on the laws of the state in which the property is located. The right of a married woman to convey her separate estate without the husband joining is discussed above.

If the real property is held by the husband and wife as co-owners, the rules discussed in Chapter 7, "Co-ownership," apply. Briefly, if they own as joint tenants or tenants in common, either may convey his or her interest in the property subject to the limitations placed by local law on the right of a husband or wife to convey his or her separate real estate. If they hold as tenants by the entirety, both must execute the deed as grantors.

If the wife, under the statutes of the state in which the property is located, is entitled to dower or some substitute for dower in all real estate that her husband has owned during the marriage, she must join in the execution of the deed, or the grantee will take subject to the inchoate dower of the wife. This outstanding interest is a defect in the title to the land until the wife dies, the husband surviving. In some states the deed, in order to convey the inchoate dower interest of the wife, must include appropriate language of conveyance; and under the statutes of some states a separate acknowledgment by the wife is required. In at least one state the wife has a dower interest only in the real estate owned by the husband at the time of his death. Under such a statute the wife would not have to join the husband as grantor.

In states having homestead laws, if the real property is occupied by the husband and wife as a homestead, both, as a general rule, must join as grantors in the execution of the deed. In most of the states with community property laws the husband and wife must join as grantors of community real property.

For practical as well as legal reasons the grantor or grantors should be described in a deed as husband, wife, unmarried, widow, widower, or divorced and not remarried, as the case may be. If the marital status of the grantor or grantors is properly stated in the deed, the deed will show on its face whether or not it has been properly executed. Failure to indicate the marital status of the grantor or grantors creates a technical defect in the record, which may have to be corrected later at no little inconvenience and expense.

### The Grantor's Name

The greatest care should be exercised to be certain that the grantor's name is spelled correctly and that there is no variation in the name or in the spelling of the name wherever it appears in the deed. Moreover, the name should be spelled the same as it was spelled in the deed or will whereby the grantor acquired the property. For example, if the grantor, in the instrument conveying the property to him, was designated as John Edward Doe, and in the deed whereby he conveys the property is designated as J. E. Doe, John E. Doe, or J. Edward Doe, such a change in the name would create a technical defect in the record, since there would be nothing on the record to show that John Edward Doe was the same person as J. E. Doe, John E. Doe, or J. Edward Doe. Some attorneys would insist that this technical defect be corrected before they would approve the title to the real estate.

From a legal standpoint, a mistake in the spelling of the grantor's name, or a variance in the spelling of the name in the body of the deed and the signature, does not affect the validity of the deed.[4]

In all deeds, a grantor must be named. In a properly drafted deed, the grantor will be named in the body of the deed; but if the deed reads, "I hereby sell and convey," or if similar language is used and it is signed by the grantor, this is sufficient to satisfy the legal requirement that the grantor be named in the deed.

## Grantee

### Grantee's Name

From the earliest times the courts have held that the title to real estate must vest in someone; consequently, every valid deed must have a grantee. The grantee

---

[4] *Lyon* v. *Kain,* 36 Ill. 362.

must be named or indicated in the deed in such a way that it will be possible to identify him. The early courts were strict in their interpretation of the language in deeds, whereas the modern trend is to read the deed in its entirety and attempt to determine the intent of the parties. For example, a deed naming the heirs of Amos, a living person, would, under strict rules of interpretation, be held to be void for the lack of a grantee, since a living person cannot have heirs.[5] Under the more liberal approach, however, if the deed in its entirety would so indicate, the court would interpret "heirs" as "children" and hold the deed to be valid. A deed naming the grantees as "Amos and wife" indicates the grantees with reasonable certainty and is valid; nevertheless, a carefully drafted deed would name the grantees as "John Amos and Mary Amos, husband and wife."

A deed naming a fictitious grantee is a nullity.[6] Likewise, a deed naming an unincorporated association, society, or club as grantee is a nullity, since such an organization cannot sue or be sued and has no capacity to own or convey real estate.[7] However, the natural persons who are members of an unincorporated association may take title to the real estate and hold it in trust for the association.

### Grantee's Name Left Blank

A closely related question concerns the validity of a deed in which no grantee is named at the time the grantor executes the deed. The courts have litigated such a question in four different situations, as follows:

1. If the omission of the name of the grantee is a clerical error and the name of the grantee is filled in when the error is discovered, the courts have generally held that the deed is valid.
2. If the name of the grantee is left blank and a grantee's name is filled in without authority, the deed is void.[8] However, if the grantor has been guilty of negligence in the execution of the deed, he may be estopped from setting up the invalidity of the deed against an innocent purchaser or mortgagee for value.
3. If the name of the grantee is left blank and the deed, after execution, is given to the grantors' agent, who is authorized in writing to fill in the grantee's name, and does so before delivery of the deed, the deed is valid.[9]

---

[5] *Hickel* v. *Starcher,* 90 W.Va. 369, 110 S.E. 695.

[6] *Cox* v. *Pearson,* 212 Ga. 294, 92 S.E.2d 25.

[7] *Lael* v. *Crook et al.,* 192 Ark. 1115, 97 S.W.2d 436.

[8] *Trout* v. *Taylor et al.,* 220 Cal. 652, 32 P.2d 968.

[9] *Bryant* v. *Barger,* 112 Ind. App. 17, 42 N.E.2d 429.

4. If the grantee's name is left blank at the time the deed is executed and the agent of the grantor is given oral or implied authority to fill in the name of a grantee, the courts are not in accord as to the validity of such a deed. A majority of the courts have held that oral authority to fill blanks is sufficient,[10] but there are holdings to the contrary.

Mrs. Green acquired title to several parcels of real estate that she wished to sell. At the direction of her attorney, MacAdam, she signed several quitclaim deeds in blank. The deeds, when signed by Mrs. Green, were not dated, did not describe the land, and did not name a grantee. MacAdam found a buyer for one of the tracts of land owned by Mrs. Green. He filled out one of the deeds, naming Carol B. Bryson, his secretary, as grantee, and had her execute a quitclaim deed to Koskie, the purchaser. Koskie paid the purchase price to MacAdam, who appropriated the money to his own use. Mrs. Green brought suit to quiet title to the land, claiming that the deed to the land to Carol B. Bryson was a nullity and that Koskie acquired no title thereto. The court held the deed to be a nullity and held for Mrs. Green.

Justice pro tem Monroe said: "According to the great weight of authority, a deed executed in blank is void and passes no title. "There must be, in every grant, a grantor, a grantee and a thing granted, and a deed wanting in either essential is absolutely void.' In the instant case each of the instruments signed by the respondent [Mrs. Green] was wanting in all three of these essentials of a valid deed. Though the decisions of other jurisdictions are not in entire harmony upon the question, it has been definitely decided in this state that under our statute of frauds the name of the grantor or the grantee or the description of the property cannot be inserted by an agent of the grantor, in the absence of the latter, unless the agent's authority be in writing. If the authority of the agent be not in writing, his insertion of the name of the grantor or grantee or description of the property does not pass title." *Green* v. *MacAdam et al.,* 175 Cal. App.2d 481, 346 P.2d 474 (1959).

## Assumed and Misspelled Names

A person may, if he wishes, use an assumed name in the transaction of business; and a deed in which an assumed name—not the true name of the grantee—is used will be valid. However, when the real estate is again conveyed, the assumed name must be used as the name of the grantor; otherwise, there will be a break in the chain of title on the record.[11]

The misspelling of the grantee's name—whether the grantee be a natural person, a partnership, or a corporation—will not invalidate the deed, although an inconsistency in the spelling of names in a deed does create a technical defect in the record.

---

[10] *Calhoun* v. *Drass,* 319 Pa. 449, 178 A. 568.

[11] *Trout,* v. *Taylor et al.,* 220 Cal. 652, 32 P.2d 968.

### A Partnership as Grantee

In those states that have adopted the Uniform Partnership Act or have statutes of similar import, a deed to a partnership naming the partnership as grantee is valid. In those states in which the common-law rule applies, the names of the partners or the name of one of the partners must be used in indicating the grantee. (See Chapter 7, "Co-ownership.")

### Corporation as Grantee

Prior to the time a proposed corporation receives its charter, it has no existence, and a deed naming such a proposed corporation as grantee would be a nullity. However, in some instances when the deed was not delivered until after the corporation received its charter, the deed was held to be valid. Also, if the grantor has received the agreed consideration for the transfer, he is estopped from setting up the invalidity of the deed.[12]

If a corporation is named as grantee in a deed, the official name of the corporation as it appears in the articles of incorporation should be used. If the name in the articles of incorporation is "Beeler Bros., Inc.," that name—and not "Beeler Brothers, Incorporated"—should be used.

Three questions arise in regard to the conveying of real estate to corporate grantees:

1. What is the result if the named corporation has not been chartered at the time the deed is executed and delivered, but receives its charter at a later date?
2. What is the result if the grantee corporation is a foreign one not licensed to do business in the state?
3. What is the result if the grantee corporation has the power to "own only such land as is needed for its corporate purposes," and the land in question is not needed by the corporation for such purposes?

If a foreign corporation is not licensed to do business in a state and, under the laws of that state, has no power to own land in the state, a deed naming such a corporation as grantee is a nullity. From a legal standpoint the unlicensed corporation has no existence insofar as the state is concerned. However, if the laws of the state in which the land is located do not prohibit an unlicensed foreign corporation from owning land in the state, and the corporation has the power to own real estate, a deed naming such a corporation as grantee is valid.[13]

---

[12] *Harwood* v. *Masquelette et al.,* 95 Ind. App. 338, 181 N.E. 380.

[13] *Spivey* v. *Spivey Building Corporation et al.,* 367 Ill. 25, 10 N.E.2d 385.

If land is granted to a corporation, the deed is valid; the title to the land vests in the corporation even though the corporation, under the powers granted it in its charter, does not have the power to own land in excess of the needs of the corporation and the land granted is clearly in excess of such needs. A deed by the corporation to a bona fide purchaser will vest title to the land in such buyer.

### Recital of Consideration

Accepted standards of conveying dictate that a deed contain a clause reciting a consideration. However, under the laws of most of the states, failure to recite a consideration in a deed does not affect the validity of the deed, except in the case of a deed of bargain and sale, in which event the deed is void unless a valuable consideration is given.

If a person makes a gift of his real estate, lack or failure of consideration will not render the conveyance void. If the gift deed is in the form of a warranty deed, the donee cannot enforce the covenants of warranty, since they are not supported by a consideration.

A gift deed or a deed given for a wholly inadequate consideration is valid between the parties; but if such a deed is given to defraud creditors, the grantor's creditors, in an appropriate action, may have it set aside. Likewise, if a conveyance is induced by misrepresentation, fraud, duress, or undue influence, and no consideration, or an inadequate consideration, has been given, a court, in a proper action, will set the deed aside.

### Words of Conveyance

A deed is an instrument that conveys a present interest in real estate. In order to transfer the title to the property, the deed must contain apt words of grant that manifest the grantor's intent to make a present conveyance. An expression of intention to convey at some future time is inadequate. No technical words are required; however, such words as "convey and warrant," "grant, bargain, and sell," and "convey and quitclaim" are commonly used in deeds.

## Description of Real Estate

### Importance of Accurate Description

One of the essentials of a valid deed is an adequate description of the thing granted. If the description in a deed of the real estate granted is to be sufficient, the real estate must be identifiable from the words in the deed, aided by evidence explaining the terms used in the deed or by references to other instruments. Such accuracy of description is of outstanding importance to a person engaged in the real estate business, for it enables him to avoid inconvenience, delay, and the expense of legal action. There is a great difference between the preciseness of a technically accurate description and a legally sufficient description of real estate. Although the courts have been exceedingly liberal in finding ambiguous descriptions of real estate to be sufficient, the cost of a court action is a high price to pay to correct an error in the record or to clarify a carelessly drafted description when care in drafting the deed would have prevented all such inconvenience and expense.

In a majority of real estate transactions the same tract of land, without alteration in its boundaries, is conveyed a number of times. In describing the land, if the description used in the caption of the abstract of title or in prior deeds is accurately copied, discrepancies in the record will be avoided.

### Methods of Describing Real Estate

The methods of describing real estate in common use are (1) governmental survey, (2) metes and bounds, (3) monuments, (4) recorded plat, and (5) informal descriptions. Because of the importance of legal descriptions to the recording system, each type of legal description is discussed in detail in Chapter 5.

## Estate Conveyed by Deed

### Words of Inheritance

At common law, if a deed did not grant the real estate to the grantee "and his heirs," a fee simple estate was not granted. Today, under the statutes generally in force throughout the United States, words of inheritance are not necessary to create a fee simple estate. The courts interpret a deed as granting a fee simple estate, unless an intent to grant a lesser estate is clearly stated or indicated in the deed.[14]

### Habendum Clause

The habendum clause in a deed usually follows the granting clause and defines the extent of the estate granted. It begins with words such as "to have and to hold." It is not an essential part of the deed and is usually not included in statutory form deeds.

---

[14] *Mechtle* v. *Topp,* 78 N.D. 789, 52 N.W.2d 842.

At common law, if the grant was to the grantee and his heirs, a fee simple vested in the grantee, and a statement in the habendum clause that an estate less than a fee simple was granted was ineffective. If the terms of a deed were ambiguous as to the estate granted, the granting clause controlled.

However, today the courts read the deed in its entirety; and if a clear intention to grant an estate less than that indicated in the granting clause is expressed, the courts will not follow the early technical rule, but instead will give effect to the later clause in the deed.[15] In the drafting of a deed the grant should not be made to the grantee and his heirs unless the grantor intends to grant an estate in fee simple.

### Warranties

A warranty is not an essential element of a valid deed. A warranty deed purports to convey to the grantee title to the land described in the deed. The grantor may, in addition to transferring title, assume responsibility for stated defects in the title and obligate himself to defend against or reimburse the grantee for any loss resulting from the defects covered by the warranty. A warranty may protect only the immediate transferee, or it may be of such a nature that it "runs with the land," that is, the protection of the warranty extends to all subsequent holders who can trace their title back to the deed containing the warranty.

At an earlier date it was, and is today in some states, customary to set out in full warranties against all possible defects in title and to include covenants of seisin, covenants against encumbrances, and covenants of quiet enjoyment. Such deeds are referred to as long-form deeds. The recording of a long-form deed entails much unnecessary work. Many states have enacted statutes under which a short-form warranty deed is provided for. If the deed includes such words as "convey and warrant" or "bargain, sell, and warrant," the deed, by statutory implication, includes the usual covenants of warranty.[16]

### Exceptions and Reservations

In the event there are known defects in the grantor's title or there are known liens against the real estate conveyed and the grantor wishes to exclude these

---

[15] *Pachter et al.* v. *Gray et al.,* 231 Ind. 487, 109 N.E.2d 412.

[16] Form of warranty deed—any conveyance of lands worded in substance as follows: "A B conveys and warrants to C D [here describe the premises] for the sum of [here insert the consideration]" the said conveyance being dated, and duly signed, sealed, and acknowledged by the grantor—shall be deemed and held to be a conveyance in fee simple to the grantee, his heirs and assigns, with covenant from the grantor, for himself and his heirs and personal representatives, that he is lawfully seized of the premises, has good right to convey the same, and guarantees the quiet possession thereof, and that the same is free from all encumbrances, and that he will warrant and defend the title to the same against all lawful claims (Burns's *Annotated Indiana Statutes,* Vol. XI, Part 1, 56–115 I.R.S. 1852, Chap. 23, § 12, 232).

defects from his covenants of warranty, this exclusion can be accomplished by including in the covenants of warranty, if such are written into the deed, a provision expressly excepting from the covenants the known defects or liens.

If a statutory short-form deed is used, it is customary to insert therein provisions expressly excepting from the warranty the known defects or liens. For example, if there is an easement of right of way over a portion of the premises and the premises are subject to a mortgage lien, the warranty deed would contain a provision to the effect that the grantor was granting good title free from liens and encumbrances except an easement of right of way (describing it) and subject to a mortgage (giving name of mortgagee, where mortgage is recorded, original amount of mortgage debt, and unpaid balance of mortgage debt). Usually, this clause will state whether or not the grantee assumes and agrees to pay the mortgage debt.

A reservation in a deed retains or withholds certain rights in the real estate. These reserved rights do not pass to the grantee but remain in the grantor. For example, the grantor might grant a fee simple title to a tract of land and in the deed include a provision reserving to the grantor an easement of right of way over a described portion of the land granted.

### Restrictions

The grantor may, within reasonable limits, place restrictions on the right to use the real estate conveyed. If he wishes to place such restrictions on the property conveyed, he will include an appropriately worded restrictive covenant in the deed. Restrictive covenants will be discussed in more detail in a later chapter.

### Homestead and Dower Rights

Under the laws of some states, unless a deed contains a clause specifically waiving homestead, dower, or curtesy rights, the property conveyed will be subject to such rights.

Randolph executed a deed conveying to Austin 7.51 acres of land. The granting, habendum, and warranty clauses were in the terms of a conveyance in fee simple.

After the description, but before the habendum and warranty clauses, the following provision was set forth: "And this Deed is made subject to the following conditions, reservations, and restrictions which constitute covenants running with the land and binding upon the parties hereto, their heirs and assigns, to wit: . . ." The conditions, reservations, and restrictions were then set forth in eleven separate (numbered) paragraphs. They included, among other things, restrictions that the property should be used only for residential purposes; restrictions on the size of the lots in the event of subdivision; and restrictions on the location, cost, and composition of any residence constructed thereon. Too, they included reservations of rights of way for installation of power and telephone lines.

Austin claimed that the conditions, restrictions, and reservations in the deed limited the estate granted, were in conflict with the granting clause and the habendum and warranties, and therefore were invalid. The court held that the covenants, reservations, and restrictions were valid.

Justice Bobbitt said: "In the interpretation of a deed, the intention of the grantor or grantors must be gathered from the whole instrument and every part given effect, unless it contains conflicting provisions which are irreconcilable or a provision which is contrary to public policy or runs counter to some rule of law.

"The foregoing impels us to express the view . . . that the conditions, reservations and restrictions set forth in the Randolph-Austin deed are not void *ab initio* on the ground they are repugnant to the granting habendum and warranty clauses of the deed." *Barrier* v. *Randolph,* 260 N.C. 741, 133 S.E.2d 655 (1963).

## Execution of Deed

### Date

Although it is customary to date a deed, omission of the date does not invalidate the deed. Statutes setting out a permissive deed form may include the date of execution in the recommended form. However, these statutes are directive and not mandatory; consequently, omission of the date is not a violation of the statute and does not invalidate the deed.

### Signature

The signature of the grantor is essential to the validity of a deed. If there is more than one grantor named in the deed, each must sign, unless the grantors are partners—in which event, one partner, as a general rule, may sign for his copartners. Some states, by statute, require that the deed be subscribed—that is, the signature must be in writing. In such states a typed or stamped signature would not be sufficient.

A person who cannot write may sign by making his mark. In the event the deed is signed by the grantor's making his mark, it is customary for his name to be written close to the mark, together with a statement that the mark is the grantor's. Some states, by statute, require that the mark be witnessed by one or two persons, who must sign as witnesses. For example:

*John Jones*
Witness *Quinn Lloyd* *X*
Witness *Henry Hewitt* (His Mark)

A third person may sign the grantor's name at his direction and in his presence, or with his express or implied authorization.[17]

The misspelling of the grantor's name in the deed, or a variance between the spelling of the grantor's name in the deed and in his signature, does not invalidate the deed; but it does result in a technical defect in the record, and this defect may be ground for objection on the part of an attorney who examines the abstract of title.

**Signature by Agent**

A deed may be signed by the duly authorized agent of the grantor. Under the recording statutes of most states the authority of an agent to sign a deed in the name of his principal must be in writing and executed with the same formality as is required for the execution of the deed. Such an authorization is known as a *power of attorney.*

The deed should be signed in the name of the principal, followed by the name of the agent; and the agent should sign in such a way as to indicate clearly that he is signing as agent. For example:

*John Jones* *(Seal)*
By *Frank Drake*
His Agent (or His
Attorney in Fact)

**Seal**

In its origin the seal was used to indicate that the person sealing the instrument intended to create a legally binding obligation. Today, since most people can read and write, the signature of the obligor has been accepted as the authentication of a written instrument, and the seal is not used as extensively as it was in an earlier era.

In some states, especially in the East, a deed must be sealed to be valid. In some states, deeds executed by natural persons need not be sealed, but deeds executed by persons other than natural persons (corporations and so forth) must be sealed to be valid.

Deeds are generally signed and sealed, although the seal is not essential to the validity of the deed. The seal may be in the form of a wax wafer bearing a

---

[17] *Witt et al.* v. *Panek et al.,* 408 Ill. 328, 97 N.E.2d 283.

distinctive impression, or it may be a distinctive impression in the paper on which the deed is written. It may be merely a pen scroll, and the word *seal,* or the letters *L.S.* (*locus sigilli,* the place of the seal); or the intent to seal may be indicated in some other manner.

### Witnesses

In a few states, if the grantor's signature is not witnessed by one or two persons, the deed will be invalid and will not pass legal title to the real property. In a limited number of states the recording statutes provide that unless the signature of the grantor is witnessed by one or two persons, the deed will not be eligible for record. However, in the majority of states, witnesses to the grantor's signature are not required. As a general rule, the grantor, the grantee, or their spouses are not qualified to act as witnesses.

## Acknowledgment

### Nature of Acknowledgment

An acknowledgment is a formal declaration before an authorized official by a person who has executed an instrument that it is his free act and deed. Although it is customary to acknowledge the execution of a deed to real estate, the acknowledgment is not essential to the validity of the deed unless the statutes of the state in which the real estate is located so provide. However, in the great majority of the states, if a deed, mortgage, or other similar instrument is not acknowledged, it is not entitled to be recorded; and in addition, it is not admissible as evidence in court.

From a practical standpoint an unacknowledged deed is not a satisfactory instrument, since, if such a deed is not eligible to be recorded, the unrecorded deed would not be a valid conveyance against a subsequent innocent purchaser or mortgagee. For the protection of the grantee, all deeds should be acknowledged and recorded.

### Certificate of Acknowledgment

The notary public or officer who takes the acknowledgment fills out a certificate of acknowledgment and attaches it to the instrument, or fills in the form customarily printed on deeds and mortgages. This certifies that the grantor or grantors (naming them) appeared before him (naming his official status) and acknowledged that he (the grantor) executed the instrument as his own act and deed. The certificate will state in the caption the name of the *venue,* that is, the state and the county in which it was executed. It will be signed and sealed by the officer taking the acknowledgment; and as a general rule, if the officer is a notary public, the date of the expiration of his commission will be given (see accompanying sample).

**Sample Certificate of Acknowledgment**

State of Michigan, )
_______________ County ) SS:

On this _________ day of _____________, 19_________, before me personally appeared _________________________________ to me known to be _____________________________ the person _______ described in and who executed the foregoing instrument, and acknowledged that _________ executed the same as _________ free act and deed.

_________________________________
Notary Public
_______________ County, Michigan

My commission expires _________________, 19_________.

## Who May Take an Acknowledgment

Only those persons who are authorized by statute have the power to take acknowledgments. In all states a notary public has such power, and this power is generally granted to judges of courts of record and to justices of the peace.

A person acquiring a beneficial interest under the instrument being executed is disqualified from taking an acknowledgment of the person executing the instrument. This rule has been held in some states to disqualify a stockholder, an officer, or a director of a corporation, or a member of an association, from taking the acknowledgment of the corporation's officer or the association's agent who executes the instrument. As a general rule, relationship by blood or marriage will not disqualify a person from taking an acknowledgment if he acquires no beneficial interest under the instrument.

## Duty of Officer Taking Acknowledgment

An officer, before taking an acknowledgment, should know or satisfy himself that the person presenting the instrument for acknowledgment is the person who executed the instrument. If he does not take reasonable precautions to satisfy himself that the person presenting the instrument is the person who executed it, he may render himself liable for damages.

### Foreign Acknowledgment

A deed to real estate may be executed and acknowledged in any state or county. It does not have to be acknowledged in the state in which the land is located. However, the deed form and the form of the acknowledgment must comply with the statutory requirements of the state in which the land is located.

In some states, if the acknowledgment is taken outside the state in which the land is located, it must have attached to it a certificate of the clerk of the court in the county in which the acknowledgment was taken, certifying that the officer taking the acknowledgment was authorized by law to do so. This is known as a *certificate of authenticity.*

Charles Schroeder, with the connivance of a woman accomplice, mortgaged property which was owned by Charles Schroeder and his wife Marlene Schroeder. Charles Schroeder and a woman impersonating his wife were taken before a notary public, one Alice M. Pocrask, who was an assistant secretary of the mortgagee. She took their acknowledgment, although she had never seen them before. The court held that the signature of Marlene Schroeder was a forgery and that the mortgage was not a lien on her interest in the property.

Justice Schwartz said, in discussing the duties and liabilities of the notary public who took the acknowledgment of Charles Schroeder and the imposter: ". . . We are well aware that in routine procedure, notaries make little or no effort to identify a person whose oath they take or whose signature they attest. But the acknowledgment of a grantor or spouse to a deed or document relating to the transfer of real estate is by statute made an act of more than ordinary significance. Here, any competent person dealing in such matters should understand the requirements and if he does not comply with them must expect to be held responsible. The acknowledgment involved purported to be that of a wife joining a husband in the establishment of a sizable encumbrance on their property.

"The failure of a notary, who is the mortgagee's employee and used by it to take acknowledgment of a document, properly to identify the person whose acknowledgment is taken, is chargeable to the mortgagee. The most that can be said for Avondale [the mortgagee] is that the notary was introduced to the 'Schroeders' by one of their officers who knew Charles Schroeder slightly and Marlene not at all. Such an introduction could not satisfy her duty. A requirement of personal knowledge cannot be met by introduction just prior to the acknowledgment." *Hoffman* v. *Schroeder,* 38 Ill. App.2d 20, 186 N.E.2d 381 (1962).

## Delivery of Deed

### Necessity for Delivery

The act of drafting and executing a deed, although the document is complete in every respect, is not sufficient to convey the property described in the deed to the named grantee. A deed is not legally operative until it is delivered with the intent, on the part of the grantor, that it become legally effective. The physical transfer of the document, the deed, may or may not satisfy the requirement for delivery, depending on the intent of the grantor, determined objectively from all the surrounding circumstances.[18]

**Intent to Deliver**

Delivery of a deed is basically a question of the intent of the grantor—not the subjective intent (what he thinks), but the objective intent (what a reasonable man familiar with all the facts and circumstances is justified in believing the grantor intended).

A grantee may be given possession of the deed for the purpose of reading it, checking the description, and so forth. This would not constitute delivery, since the grantor has in no way indicated his intent that the deed shall become effective as a conveyance of title to the real estate described in the deed.

If the grantee obtains possession of the deed without the knowledge or consent of the grantor, there is no delivery; the deed is inoperative. For example, suppose that after a deed is fully executed, the grantee steals it or obtains it by fraudulent representations or duress. In such a case, there is no delivery, and the deed is inoperative. On the other hand, mere intent to deliver the deed and transfer title, without any act or conduct giving effect to or completing the delivery, passes no title.[19]

A deed may be delivered even though the grantor retains manual custody of it. However, in such cases, there must be clear proof of the grantor's intention to deliver the instrument.[20]

Although certain principles are generally followed in determining whether or not a deed has been delivered, there are no fixed rules that can be applied in all cases. In the final analysis, each case must be determined on its particular facts.

Charlie Overman lived on his 110-acre farm with his daughter Maggie and his grandson Arnold. On March 26, 1947, Charlie Overman went to Silver City and had two deeds prepared—one to Arnold for 45 acres and the other to Maggie for 65 acres, including the home site. Arnold was present at the time Charlie signed both deeds. Both deeds had the following provisions inserted at the end of the description and preceding the

---

[18] *Bryant* v. *Barger,* 112 Ind. App. 17, 42 N.E.2d 429.

[19] *Shuck* v. *Shuck et al.,* 77 N.D. 628, 44 N.W.2d 767.

[20] *In re McKitterick's Estate,* 94 Ohio App. 373, 115 N.E.2d 163.

habendum clause: "I hereby reserve for myself a life estate in the above described land." Upon their return home, Charlie immediately gave Arnold the deed to the 45 acres. Maggie was at work at this time, but when she returned home, Charlie handed her the deed for the 65 acres. She and Charlie went to her bedroom and put the deed in a dresser drawer. She, her father [Charlie], and Arnold regularly used this dresser drawer for their papers. Neither of the deeds was recorded until after Charlie's death in 1957. Maggie's brothers and sisters contended that the deed to Maggie was never delivered and that the 65 acres of land was part of the father's estate. The court held that there was a valid delivery of the deed to Maggie.

Justice Moore said: "The requisites to the valid delivery of a deed are threefold. They are: (1) an intention on the part of the grantor to give the instrument legal effect according to its purport and tenor; (2) the evidencing of such intention by some word or act disclosing that the grantor has put the instrument beyond his legal control; and (3) acquiescence by the grantee in such intention. Presumption of delivery arises from registration, even after the death of the grantor, and in the absence of other evidence is sufficient to support a finding of delivery." *Jones* v. *Saunders,* 254 N.C. 644, 119 S.E.2d 789 (1961).

## Delivery to Third Person

Delivery of a deed may be made to some third person for the benefit of the grantee; the delivery, in order to be effective, must be such that the grantor surrenders all right to control the deed, and the third person must hold the deed as trustee or agent of the grantee. If the grantor reserves the right to recall the deed or to exercise control over its disposal, there is no delivery. The third person, under such circumstances, is the agent of the grantor; and possession by the agent is equivalent to possession by the principal.[21]

If delivery is made to a third person, who is to hold the deed for the grantee and deliver it to him on the happening of some future event, there is no delivery until the occurrence of the event.

The recording of a deed at the grantor's request does not necessarily amount to delivery. It is convincing evidence of intent to deliver, but a contrary intent may be established.[22]

## Delivery after Death

Delivery of a deed, if it is to be effective, must be made during the lifetime of the grantor. If a grantor executes deeds to real estate, and retains possession and control over the deeds, placing them in his strongbox or safe-deposit box,

---

[21] *Hooker* v. *Tucker et al.,* 335 Mich. 429, 56 N.W.2d 246.

[22] *Blachowski et ux.* v. *Blachowski,* 135 N.J. Eq. 425, 39 A.2d 94.

with direction that the deeds shall be delivered after his death, such deeds are ineffectual to pass title.[23]

A delivery to a third person, who is to hold the deed as trustee for the benefit of the named grantee, and who is to deliver it to the grantee on the death of the grantor, is a valid delivery. However, if there is to be a valid delivery, the grantor must intend irrevocably to vest title in the grantee and to surrender all control over the deed.[24]

John Fiore, during his lifetime, executed a deed to his wife Antoinetta conveying his interest in described lands. The deed was prepared by an attorney, and was executed and acknowledged by John Fiore on September 25, 1940. It was not recorded until November 27, 1957, long after the death of John Fiore, who died on September 3, 1942. The deed, after it was executed, was left in the possession of the attorney, who was given no instructions as to its disposition. John Fiore did not tell his wife or any other member of his family that he had executed the deed, and he retained possession and control of the land described in the deed until his death. His son claimed an interest in the land, and his wife claimed the land had been conveyed to her by the deed. The court held that the deed had never been delivered and that the land had not been conveyed to the wife.

Justicee Eagen said: "In order to validate defendant's [Antoinetta Fiore] claim to ownership of the property involved there are two indispensable requisites: (1) a donative intent on the part of the grantor, i.e., an intent to make a gift to the grantee then and there, when the deed was executed; (2) a delivery of the deed to the grantee, either actual or constructive, which divested the donor of all dominion over the property and invested the donee therewith. The recording of the deed was not essential to its validity or the transition of the title. Nor was it essential that the grantee have knowledge of the transaction. By subsequent acceptance, she ratified the original delivery if such had occurred.

"However, there must have been a delivery of the instrument to the grantee and while the execution, sealing, acknowledging and recording of a deed gives rise to a presumption of delivery, this is a factual presumption and as such is rebuttable.

"For a legal delivery to be effected, it is not necessary that the deed be delivered directly to the grantee. It may be placed in the possession of a third party for delivery to the grantee upon the happening of a *specified* contingency. In such cases, the legal delivery date is that when the donor effectuated his intention. However, delivery is not accomplished by the mere handing of the executed deed to a stranger. Likewise, the mere handing of the executed deed, without more, to a third person who is an agent of the grantor is ineffective. In order for the delivery to be effectual and to result in a culmination of the transition of the title, *there must be an express and definite instruction* that the deed is to be given to the grantee then or at some future time." *Fiore* v. *Fiore,* 405 Pa. 303, 173 A.2d 858 (1961).

---

[23] *Dillion et al.* v. *Meister et al.,* 319 Mich. 428, 29 N.W.2d 846.

[24] *Dickason et al.* v. *Dickason,* 219 Ind. 683, 40 N.E.2d 965.

**Sample General Warranty Deed**

This indenture witnesses that ______________________________ of the County of __________, State of __________, for and in consideration of the sum of Ten Dollars ($10.00) and other valuable consideration, the receipt and sufficiency which is hereby acknowledged, [A] does hereby convey and generally warrant [B] to _________________________ of the County of ______________, State of __________, [C] the real estate located in the County of ______________, State of ______________ more particularly described as follows: ____________
____________________________________________________________________
____________________________________________________________________
____________________________________________________________________
____________________________________________________________________
____________________________________________________________________

together with all buildings, improvements and fixtures located thereon, subject to the following limitations, restrictions and conditions: [D] ________________
____________________________________________________________________
____________________________________________________________________
____________________________________________________________________

In witness whereof the said _________________________ has hereunto set _____ hand and seal this _____ day of _______________, 19_____.

_____________________________ (SEAL)
_____________________________ (SEAL)

State of _________________________)
County of _________________________) SS:

Before me this _____ day of _____, 19_____, personally appeared the above named ____________________ to me known to be the person _____, who executed the foregoing deed and acknowledged the same to be his free and willfull act.

__________________________
Notary Public
County, State of
__________________________

My commission expires: __________, 19_____.

## Comments on Sample Warranty Deed

A. The use of only nominal consideration in the body of the deed is common practice. The reason for this is the fact that the deed will become a matter of public record and the parties seldom desire to have the actual price paid to become generally known. At the same time, however, the acknowledgment of the fact of consideration and its sufficiency are needed to support the warranties made in the deed and make them enforceable against the grantor. The inclusion of this statement in the deed also has evidentiary value in the event of a later dispute between the parties. The grantor will have to introduce evidence to overcome the presumption that payment was made and that it was sufficient. A form of estoppel is the result.

B. This deed is in very simple form in that it does not spell out what warranties are included when a grantor "generally warrants" title to the property conveyed. In many states this is sufficient to invoke the warranties that are "read into" the deed by virtue of a statute that imposes them unless the deed clearly negates them. The warranties that are generally interpreted into such a deed are spelled out earlier in this chapter in the section "Conveyance of Real Estate by Deed." In other states it may be necessary to spell out the warranties in order to be sure that they are included. In such cases the deed would go on after the description of the property with language similar to the following:

"Grantor further warrants that:

1. He has good and sufficient title to the above described property in fee simple and has the unlimited right to convey it;
2. There are no liens or encumbrances upon the property other than those specifically set out in this deed;
3. Grantor will warrant and defend the grantee's title against any and all lawful claims against the property."

C. Both the names of the parties and their residence at the time of the deed are generally used in order to provide additional evidence of their identities should it be necessary at a later date. Such careful identification is particularly important if the name of one of the parties is one that is common. In a large metropolitan area the deed might go even further and specify the exact address of that party at the time of the transaction. With the nomadic trend of our population generally, such care in identification may save a great deal of confusion and expense at a future time.

D. Since this is a general warranty deed it is important that *any* limitation upon the rights being conveyed by the grantor be carefully spelled out in the deed itself. Otherwise, the presumption is that the grantor is guaranteeing full and complete rights to the property and any limitation or restriction (even if it in fact benefits the property) is warranted against. In many cases it is the intent of the parties that certain important "defects" remain on the property. For example, an existing mortgage that is being assumed may be the motivating reason for the transaction, not a defect.

## Taxes on Deeds

In many states a tax is imposed on deeds either directly or indirectly. In a few states there is a direct tax on the transfer of title that is represented by the deed. In others the tax in reality is based upon the gross or net receipts from the sale of the property, but the deed is required to show evidence that the tax has been paid before it is eligible for recording; that is, the recordation is simply a convenient way of enforcing the collection of the tax. The federal tax that formerly applied has been allowed to lapse and there are presently no federal taxes on deeds.

# Chapter 10

# Acquisition of Title by Descent or Devise

Quite commonly the ownership of real estate is not purchased but is instead inherited. In this chapter, disposition of real estate at death, whether the owner dies with or without a will, is considered. The function of a will and the quality of title which will pass to the beneficiaries are covered. It will be seen that the transfer of ownership at death is significantly different from a purchase because the post mortem transfer is essentially a gift and there is, therefore, no bargaining for a particular quality of title.

## Acquisition by Descent

### Historical Background

At the time the feudal system of land tenure was established in England by William the Conqueror, the title to all land was vested in the king, and the highest estate an individual could hold in land was a life estate. Since the life estate was granted by the king, the rights of the life tenant, on his death, reverted to the king, who could then, if he wished, grant a life estate in the reverted land to another of his choosing. In A.D. 1215 the nobles, under the Magna Carta, forced the king to permit their rights in the land they held to descend to their heirs and to recognize the privilege of disposing of property by will. Today, in the United States, all real estate is held as alodial land, that is, the owner owes no duties to an overlord or superior; yet some of the features of feudal ownership, such as the *privilege* of taking the land by descent or disposing of it by will, still exist. If the owner of land dies without leaving heirs, his land escheats (reverts) to the state. Also, the right of the state and federal governments to impose inheritance and estate taxes on the transfer of the deceased's property is a recognition of the concept that the taking of property by descent or will is a privilege, not an absolute right.

## Disposition of Decedent's Property

The owner of property may direct the disposition of his property on his death by executing a will. If a person dies leaving a will, he is said to die *testate.* If a person does not make a will, the property will descend on his death according to state statutes; his personal property will descend according to the statute of the state of his domicile, and his real estate will descend according to the statutes of the state in which the real estate is located. If a person dies without leaving a will, he is said to die *intestate.*

## Statutes of Descent and Distribution

If a person dies intestate, the state, in effect, makes a will for him. Each state has enacted statutes that set out who will share in the property of deceased persons and the share each will take. As a supplement to the statutes of descent and distribution, each state has enacted statutes defining the rights of a surviving wife or husband in the estate of the deceased spouse, and these statutes will control in the distribution of the estate of a husband or wife who dies intestate.

## Rights to Real Estate of Intestate

The title to the real estate of a person who dies intestate vests, by operation of law, in his heirs. For the purpose of maintaining an accurate record of real estate titles, there should be recorded a court order identifying the heirs. Who the heirs of the intestate are will be determined by reference to the statutes of descent and distribution of the state in which the real estate is located. Although these statutes are similar in their general provisions, they vary widely in detail.

Under these statutes the title to real estate owned by the intestate at the time of his death passes directly to his heirs. However, the heirs take subject to the prior rights of the creditors of the deceased. If the personal property of the deceased is insufficient when liquidated to pay all the debts of the deceased, his real estate may be sold and his unsatisfied debts paid from the proceeds of such sale.

## Rights of Surviving Spouse

The surviving wife or husband and the children of the deceased are, in all states, given the best claim to the property of the deceased. The widow is generally entitled to a widow's allowance of a stated sum, such as $500 or $1,000, payable out of the personal property; but in many states, if the personal property is insufficient to pay the allowance, the allowance then becomes a charge against the real estate. In all states the widow either has dower rights in the deceased husband's real estate or is given rights in lieu of dower. About one half of the states have abolished common-law dower and instead give the widow one third or some other portion of the deceased husband's real estate in fee simple.

The widow's right in the deceased husband's real estate is generally prior to the claims of heirs and general creditors. It is subject to the right of purchase-money mortgagees and the rights of other mortgagees if the wife has joined the husband in the execution of the mortgage.

In some states, if the wife has predeceased the husband and the husband dies leaving minor children, the minor children are provided for.

A husband is generally given rights in the real estate of the wife if she dies, the husband surviving. In several states the husband takes in fee simple one third of the real estate owned by the wife at the time of her death. Generally, the husband takes subject to the prior rights of the general creditors of the deceased wife.

## Determination of Heirs

In general, the heirs of a deceased person are his close blood relatives. Under the statutes of descent and distribution, such heirs are children, parents, brothers and sisters, uncles and aunts, and, in some states, first cousins of the deceased. They take in order of the closeness of the blood relationship and by representation or, in legal terminology, *per stirpes* (by the stock). More remote relatives each take an equal share or, in legal terminology, *per capita* (by the head).

For example, suppose John E. Doe has four sons—Henry, William, Charles, and Robert. Henry marries and has two children, Mary and Thomas. Henry dies before his father and leaves surviving him his wife and his two children. The father, John, then dies intestate. The estate of John will be divided into four equal shares. William, Charles, and Robert will each take one fourth of the estate. The remaining one fourth (Henry's share if living) will be divided equally between Henry's two children (Henry's representatives). Mary and Thomas will each take one half of one fourth of their grandfather's estate. Henry's wife will take nothing. Since she is an in-law, not a descendant, she is not "of the stock."

If John had had no children, and if, at his death, his closest relatives had been third cousins, each third cousin would have taken an equal share under the laws of descent and distribution of most states. No attempt is made to trace back and determine the rights of remote relatives on the basis of representation. If the owner of real estate dies intestate and leaves no legal heirs, his real estate escheats (goes back) to the state in which it is located.

### Common Plan of Distribution

Although there is no uniformity in the statutes of descent and distribution of the states, they do follow a common plan. They start with the closer relationships and work through all possible combinations of a kinship to the more remote relationships, which are provided for as a class.

If there are close relatives, the remote relatives take nothing. For example, if a husband dies leaving a wife and children surviving, the wife and children, under the statutes of most states, take the entire estate. If a wife and one child survive, each usually takes one half of the estate. If a wife and two or more children survive, a common distribution is for the wife to take one third of the estate and the children to take the remaining two thirds, which will be divided equally among them, the descendants of a deceased child taking his or her share by representation. If a wife and no children or no representatives of a deceased child survive, a customary division is for the wife to take one half and the parents or brothers and sisters of the deceased to take equal shares in one half.

Provisions are made for adopted children. Usually, they take from the adopting parents, but not from the ancestors of adopting parents. Illegitimate children, as a general rule, take from the mother but not from the father, unless he has admitted parentage in writing, or unless parentage has been established by legal procedure. Provisions are also made for relatives of the half blood.

On May 26, 1956, Wilfred B. Sykes died, intestate and unmarried. His father and mother had predeceased him. He was survived by an aunt, Mary E. Connell, who was a sister of his father, on whose petition Elena L. Moore was appointed administratrix of his estate on June 5, 1956. The plaintiffs were cousins of the deceased. Some were children of a deceased brother of his mother, and others were children of a deceased sister of his mother.

On October 21, 1957, the judge of probate decreed that the balance of $14,463.97 in the hands of the administratrix on her final account be distributed to said aunt, Mary E. Connell, as the only heir-at-law of the estate. Coram et al., the cousins, appealed. The order of the probate judge was affirmed.

Justice Lampron said: "It has been settled law in this jurisdiction for many years that under RSA 561:1, 6, an aunt takes to the exclusion of cousins. The decree of distribution made by the probate court is in conformity with this established principle and the denial of plaintiffs' petition by the Superior Court was proper." *Coram* v. *Connell,* 103 N.H. 26, 164 A.2d 251 (1960).

## Wills

### Nature of a Will

In legal effect a will is a gratuitous conveyance of property, to take effect on the death of the testator. The right to so dispose of property is conferred by state statute; and if a will is to be effective, it must conform to statutory requirements as to its form and execution. It differs from a deed in that the latter conveys a present interest in property, whereas a will conveys no interest in the property until the death of the testator. A deed, if it is to be valid, must be delivered in the lifetime of the grantor. A will is not delivered but is left as part of the papers of the deceased.

### Capacity to Make a Will

The age at which a person may make a will varies from state to state, but 18 years is the lawful age in most states. In some states a will disposing of personal property may be made at an earlier age than one disposing of real estate. And in some states a woman may make a will at an earlier age than a man. The statutes of the state in which the real estate is located control as to the disposition of real estate by will.

In all states the testator must be of sound mind at the time he executes the will. There is no arbitrary test of mental capacity to make a will. The standard generally applied takes into consideration the complexity of the testator's estate and his relation to persons who would be the natural recipients of his bounty.

In order to make a valid will, the testator, at the time he executes his will, must have sufficient mental capacity to know the natural objects of his bounty, to comprehend the kind and character of his property, to understand the nature and effect of his act, and to make a disposition of his property according to some plan formed in his mind.[1]

Mrs. Stitt, a woman about 65 years of age, entered the hospital on September 28, 1958, and executed her will on the evening of September 28, 1958. Immediately after signing the will, she underwent an operation from which she never recovered, and she died on October 28, 1958. By her will, she distributed her property among relatives,

---

[1] *Meister et al.* v. *Finley et al.,* 208 Ore. 223, 300 P.2d 778.

devising most of it to relatives of her husband, who had predeceased her. Neighbors and tenants testified that during the last three years of her life she became coarse and profane; that she shrieked and screamed at all hours of the day and night; that she mistreated her brother and cursed him, although he diligently performed his tasks around the house; and that she became utterly careless in her dress, took to wearing very little clothing, rarely combed her hair or bathed, and on occasion was indecently exposed in the presence of neighborhood children. They also testified to numerous other similar idiosyncrasies. The jury found that Mrs. Stitt was mentally incompetent to execute a will, and the judge entered a judgment for the proponents of the will, notwithstanding the verdict. On appeal, the judgment was affirmed.

Chief Justice Bernstein said: "This court has recognized two types of insanity which will vitiate a will. These are (1) insanity of such broad character as to establish mental incompetence generally, and (2) mental delusion which can be shown to have directly affected the dispository provisions of the will at the time of making.

"The rule is that even though a testator does suffer from delusions or hallucinations, unless the will itself was a creature or a product of such delusions or hallucinations it is not invalid.

"While in the instant case the contestants have put on much testimony of what they might consider delusions or hallucinations, they have not put on any testimony that the will was a creature or a product of the supposed delusions or hallucinations." *In re Stitt's Estate,* 93 Ariz. 302, 380 P.2d 601 (1963).

## Kinds of Wills

There are three kinds of wills recognized by the law: (1) formal or conventional will, (2) holographic or olographic will, and (3) nuncupative will.

The formal or conventional will is one drawn and executed in the usual manner. It is drafted and executed in strict compliance with the state statute dealing with the making of wills.

A holographic or olographic will is one written entirely in the handwriting of the testator and signed by him in his own handwriting. Such wills are not witnessed or attested. Under the statutes of several states, holographic wills are valid, provided they comply with the formal requirements of the statutes. The statute may require that the will, in order to be valid, must be dated in the handwriting of the testator and must be signed at the end thereof in his handwriting, or may make other similar requirements. As a general rule, a typewritten will is not a valid holographic will, even though the typing was done by the testator.[2]

A nuncupative will is an oral one. It exists when the testator makes to witnesses an oral declaration of his wishes in regard to the disposition of his estate. In

[2] *In re Towle's Estate,* 14 Cal.2d 261, 93 P.2d 555.

those states that recognize the validity of noncupative wills, the property that may be disposed of by such a will is limited to personal property, the value of which does not exceed a stated amount, usually a comparatively small sum. In addition, the witnesses must reduce the oral statements of the testator to writing within a relatively short period of time, generally not exceeding six months, after the date of the making of the declaration.

### Requirements for Formal Will

As a general rule, a formal will, if it is to be a valid conveyance of real estate, must comply with all the statutory requirements of the state in which the real estate is located; and if the will is to be a valid conveyance of personal property, it must comply with the statutes of the state of domicile (residence) of the testator. However, the Uniform Wills Act, Foreign Execution (adopted by 13 states)[3] provides that a will executed according to the laws of either the state in which it is executed or the state of the domicile of the testator shall be valid in the state in which the property is located, even though it was not executed in accordance with the statutes of that state. Several states that have not adopted the Uniform Wills Act, Foreign Execution, have included similar provisions in their wills statutes.

The statutes of all the states require that the will be in writing and that it be signed by the testator, but differ in most other respects. Usually, witnesses are required; in some states the statutes provide that the testator must sign in the presence of the witnesses, and that the witnesses must sign in the presence of the testator and in the presence of each other.

Some states require the publication of the will; that is, the testator must declare to the witnesses that the instrument is his will. He does not have to disclose the provisions of the will.

The statutes of some states provide that the testator must sign at the end of the will; in other states the place of signing is not material.

Usually, an attestation clause will follow the signature of the testator. This clause states the facts concerning the publication, signing, and witnessing of the will. In most states, it is not required, and its omission does not affect the validity of the will.

Fred E. Palmer executed a will dated September 22, 1960. He died on January 4, 1961. His widow presented for probate a will dated October 14, 1960, and the contestants claimed that this will was not executed as required by statute and was invalid. One of

[3] The Uniform Wills Act, Foreign Execution, has been replaced by the Model Execution of Wills Act, adopted by Tennessee (1957).

the witnesses to the will testified that she did not see Fred E. Palmer sign the will dated October 14, 1960; that she did not see Fred E. Palmer on the evening of October 14, 1960, while in his home; that Fred E. Palmer did not request her to sign his will as a witness; that Fred E. Palmer was not present when she signed as the witness; and that Fred E. Palmer never acknowledged his signature to her. The trial court held that the will was not witnessed as required by the will statute and was invalid. On appeal, the judgment was affirmed.

Justice Snell said: "A will that is eligible for admission to probate must be shown to have been executed in conformity with the provisions of the statute. A testator must sign his will in the presence of the subscribing witnesses or he must acknowledge that the signature exhibited is his own.

"A will must be signed by two competent witnesses at the request of the testator. . . . A request may be implied from the acts of the testator or from the surrounding circumstances. It is not necessary that the testator declare to the subscribing witnesses that the instrument to which they have attached their name as witnesses is his will." *In re Palmer's Estate,* Iowa, 122 N.W.2d 920 (1963).

## Description of Real Estate in Will

In a well-drafted will that disposes of real estate, the devisees are named, and the real estate devised is described with the same degree of precision as is used in drafting a deed to the property. However, the courts, in interpreting wills, have held the designation of the party and of the real estate devised to be sufficient if it is possible from the designation to identify the party and the real estate devised. For example, a provision in a will, "I give to my son my house in Newtown," would be held to be sufficient if the testator had only one son, and if the testator lived in or near a place called Newtown and owned a house there.

## Codicil

The alteration or amendment of an executed will by erasures, striking-out of clauses, interlineations, or other similar means is not permissible. Any such change in a will renders it void. If the testator wishes to change any of the provisions in his will, he may add a codicil (modification) or execute a new will. If the will sets up complex trusts or disposes of an extensive estate and the testator wishes to make substantial changes, the better plan would be to have a new will drafted and executed; but if the desired change is minor, a codicil would serve the testator's purpose.

A codicil, in order to be valid, must be executed with the same formality as is required for the execution of a formal will. The codicil will be attached to and become a part of the original will of the testator. In the interpretation of the will the codicil will be treated as an integral part of the will.

## Revocation of Will

The testator has complete control of his will during his lifetime and may revoke it or make any change in it whenever he so desires. A will may be revoked by the execution of a later will, the provisions of which are in conflict with those of an earlier will, or it may be revoked in part by the addition of a codicil that expressly revokes provisions of the will to which it is attached or that contains provisions in direct conflict with the provisions of the principal will. In drafting a will, a customary practice is to include a provision expressly revoking all prior wills and codicils previously executed by the testator.

The testator may revoke his will by destroying it, by mutilating it, by canceling his signature on it, or by any other overt act that clearly indicates his intention to revoke. The accidental destruction or mutilation of a will does not amount to a revocation, and in the event of an accidental destruction or mutilation, the execution of the will and its provisions may be established by oral evidence or by producing and identifying a copy of the will or notes from which the will was drafted or by other admissible evidence offered to prove a lost or destroyed document. A declaration of intention to revoke a will unaccompanied by the performance of some overt act of revocation is ineffective.

Under the statutes of some states, if the testator is unmarried at the time he executes his will and is married thereafter, the will is revoked, whereas in other states the will is not revoked unless a child is born to the marriage.

A failure to mention a child of the testator in a will does not revoke the will, but a few courts have held that there is a presumption in such a case that the child was forgotten and therefore takes the share of the parent's estate to which he would be entitled under the statutes of descent and distribution. A parent is not obligated to make a devise to a child, and a mention of the child without making a devise to him is sufficient to prevent the operation of the presumption that he was forgotten.

## Limitations on Disposition by Will

In all states a husband cannot dispose of all his property and leave his wife nothing. The wife is given certain statutory rights in the husband's property; the husband cannot, by leaving a will, deprive her of those rights. If the husband makes some provision for his wife in his will and it is clear that he intends these provisions to be in lieu of her statutory rights and not in addition to them, the wife has the right to elect to take either under the statute or under the will.

In some states a testator is limited as to the portion of his estate he may will to charity, particularly if he leaves children surviving him.

### Probating the Will

The probating of a will is the formal proving of the will in a court having jurisdiction over such matters. In most—but not all—states, there is a separate court having jurisdiction over the administration of decedents' estates. These courts are designated by various names in the different states, such as probate court, surrogate's court, and orphans' court.

The procedure to be followed is set out by the state statutes and varies from state to state. In general, the executor or some person interested in the estate presents the will for probate. One or more of the attesting witnesses verify under oath the fact that the will was executed and that the testator was of sound mind, and other facts relative to the validity of the will. Usually, the names and addresses of persons who would inherit if the testator had died intestate are filed with the clerk of the court, and notice of the probating of the will is given to each. If the judge finds that the will has been executed in compliance with the laws of the state, he will order it admitted for probate.

### Contesting the Will

Any person who has an interest in the estate of the testator may contest the will. Interested persons are heirs who would take under the statutes of descent and distribution, and all beneficiaries under the will. A will may be set aside on any of the following grounds: improper execution, minority, lack of mental capacity, duress, fraud, undue influence, or forgery. The statutes of the state will set out the procedure to be followed in contesting a will.

### Administration of Decedent's Estate

The administration of a decedent's estate normally involves collection and management of the assets of the estate; proof and payment of claims; determination of the rights of heirs and next of kin, if there is no will; if there is a will, determination of the rights of beneficiaries under the will; and final distribution of the estate. In addition, estate and inheritance taxes must be determined and paid.

If the deceased has left a will naming an executor who is willing and qualified to serve, he will be appointed by the court to administer the estate. If the deceased dies intestate, or if he does not name an executor in his will, the court will, on proper petition, appoint an administrator. Under the laws of most states a surviving spouse with capacity to act has the right to be appointed administrator.

After the executor or administrator has been duly appointed and has filed the required bond, he takes possession of the assets of the estate, inventories them, and has them appraised. The procedure to be followed and the powers of an administrator will be set out in the statutes of the state. The procedure to be followed by an executor will be set out in the statutes of the state, but his powers will generally be set out in the will. However, a will cannot confer on an executor powers the exercise of which would be a violation of state statutes.

**Effect of Administration on Title to Real Estate**

If a person dies intestate, title to his real estate passes to his heirs. The administration of his estate has no effect on the vesting of title. The heirs own the real estate as tenants in common, and they have all the rights in the property that the deceased ancestor had. The advantage of probation is that the title to real estate can be cleared in a shorter period of time. When the estate is probated, the rights of creditors are determined and cut off within a relatively short period of time—six months to one year; whereas if there is no probating, the statute of limitations on creditors' rights must run, and the time is much longer—usually five to seven years, depending on the statutes of the state. Moreover, unpaid taxes are a lien on the assets of the estate, and the statute of limitations on taxes is 10 years.

The primary purpose for estate administration is to see that the decedent's debts, including taxes generated by the fact of his death, are paid. The residue of the estate is then distributed either to his legal heirs or to those beneficiaries designated in a valid will. It is apparent, therefore, that it may be necessary in some estates to sell the decedent's real estate and other property in order to make cash with which to pay debts, taxes, and the costs of administration. It is quite possible then that the heirs or beneficiaries will not in fact obtain possession of the real estate. Clearly, the quality of title that the heirs and beneficiaries have during the period of administration of the estate is very questionable.

**Sales during Estate Administration**

In the event that it is necessary or desirable to sell real estate belonging to the decedent during the administration of his estate, recourse must be had to the probate law of the state in which the real estate is located. Since, as a general rule, the heirs or beneficiaries have title subject to the possibility of sale to pay debts, it is necessary to follow some degree of formality in order to be sure that the sale carries with it all of the outstanding interests in the land. The safe and sure method of accomplishing this is a formal court proceeding with proper notice to all parties. This may be quite cumbersome and time-consuming, and the quality of title will be no better than the decedent had at his death; in addition, the warranties in an administrator's or executor's deed may be either very limited or nonexistent. Sales or purchases of property from a decedent's estate should therefore never be undertaken without competent legal counsel.

## Conclusion

The probate system in the United States has been under heavy attack in recent years. Its critics insist that the process is costly and time-consuming out of all proportion to its benefits. On the other hand it should be clearly understood what is actually happening: the disposition of one's property to his creditors and heirs when he is not alive to defend himself from claims that may not be valid, taxes that he might feel are unjustified, and gifts to those he might not wish to benefit. To safeguard the decedent and his family, the probate system has created a wealth of formality to ensure proper distribution of the estate. Many of these formalities may no longer be necessary, and the objective of the probate reform movement has been to streamline and shorten the probate process by eliminating those that have outlived their usefulness. New legislation in the form of the Uniform Probate Code has become law in several states and is under serious consideration in several other states. Whether probate law will ever become uniform throughout the United States is very questionable, but some degree of general probate reform to streamline estate administration and minimize its costs seems to be inevitable.

# Chapter 11

# Acquisition of Title by Adverse Possession

A relatively uncommon method of acquiring title to real estate is that of adverse possession—by taking possession and maintaining it against the true owner for so long a time that the law will treat it as a true transfer of title from the original owner to the adverse possessor. The technical requirements to achieve this transfer are discussed in this chapter, as is the modern usefulness of the concept. Proof of the title thus obtained is also considered.

## Doctrine of Adverse Possession

### Historical Background

The doctrine of adverse possession is based on a presumption of a lost grant. The courts, in the application of the presumption of a lost grant, have followed the reasoning of Justice Story and Chancellor Kent, who declared that it is an ancient and settled doctrine that the presumption of a grant of land will be adopted because of the infirmity of human nature, the difficulty of preserving evidence of title, and the public policy of supporting long and uninterrupted possession. The permitting of a person to acquire title to land under the doctrine of presumption of a grant or under the statutes of limitations (adverse possession) is supported by considerations of public policy, such as, for instance, the encouragement of the use of the land, and by the desirability of preventing a claimant from delaying action until documents are lost and witnesses have died.

There is a distinction between establishing title to land under the doctrine of the presumption of a lost grant and under the statutes of limitations, but the results are substantially the same. The courts have held, however, that an adverse claimant may establish title to land against the state under the doctrine or presumption of a lost grant but not under the statutes of limitations.[1]

### Statutes of Limitations

A statute of limitations was first enacted by Parliament in England in A.D. 1275, and similar statutes have been enacted in all of the states in the United States. These statutes are, however, not uniform in their requirements. In general, the statutes of limitations now in force set out various time limits within which a claimant must bring his action if he is to recover the property in controversy. The time limit depends on circumstances defined in the statute. Typical statutes of limitations provide that an action for the recovery of real property sold on execution and bought by the execution debtor, his heirs, or any person claiming under him, must be brought within 10 years after sale. The time limit for recovery of real property sold by executors, administrators, guardians, and so forth is five years; and that on mortgages (with designated exceptions), on deeds of trust, on judgments of courts of record, and for the possession of real estate is 10 years. The statute further provides that the adverse claimant must have paid the taxes and assessments falling due on the land.

### Real Estate That May Be Acquired by Adverse Possession

In general, real estate owned by the United States or a state, or owned by a subdivision of the state or a municipality, if such real estate is used for public purposes, cannot be acquired by adverse possession.[2] Under the statutes of some states, real estate owned by a county, township, school district, municipality, park commission, or similar governmental agency, if such real estate is not used for governmental purposes, can be acquired by adverse possession. Also, in some states in which there are no specific statutory provisions regarding the acquisition of such real estate by adverse possession, the courts have held that it may be acquired by adverse possession. The statutes of a few states provide that real estate owned by a religious organization cannot be acquired by adverse possession.[3]

---

[1] *McCain* v. *Wilson,* 176 Ark. 1205, 5 S.W.2d 338.

[2] *Steele* v. *Fowler, Mayor et al.,* 111 Ind. App. 364, 41 N.E.2d 678.

[3] *Davis,* v. *Union Meeting House Society,* 93 Vt. 520, 108 A. 704.

### Who May Acquire Title by Adverse Possession

As a general rule, any person who has the capacity to own real estate can acquire title to real estate by adverse possession. This includes natural persons (whether infants or adults), corporations, religious societies, states, the United States, and other governmental units.[4]

The holdings of the courts are not in accord as to the right of an alien or of a nonresident or foreign corporation to acquire title to real estate by adverse possession. Some courts hold that they may; other courts hold that they may not.

## Requirements for Acquisition by Adverse Possession

### General Requirements

Before a person can obtain title to real estate by adverse possession, the possession must be (1) actual, (2) open and notorious, (3) exclusive, (4) continuous and uninterrupted, (5) with claim of right, and (6) for the statutory period. In addition to these requirements, the statutes of some states require the payment of taxes by the adverse possessor.

### Actual Possession

Actual possession, in general, consists of the exercise of positive physical acts of dominion or ownership over the land. Actual possession is composed of both act and intention; that is, before a person can acquire actual possession, his intention to hold the land must be indicated by some act.

Casual, isolated, or occasional acts of ownership are not sufficient to establish actual possession. Although the person need not establish his residence on the land, he must occupy the land and use it for the purposes for which it is reasonably suited. Under the statutes of a few states the claimant must fence or enclose the tract that he claims; but mere fencing or enclosing, without use, is generally not sufficient to establish actual possession.

Although the making of improvements or the cultivation of the land is not necessary to establish actual possession, either is generally sufficient. The mere taking of the natural products of the land, such as cutting timber, cutting grass that grows wild, tapping sugar trees, or taking sand, gravel, or stone is not sufficient to establish actual possession.[5]

---

[4] *Trustees of University of South Carolina* v. *City of Columbia,* 108 S.C. 244, 93 S.E. 934.

[5] *West Virginia Pulp & Paper Co.* v. *Cone,* 153 F.2d 576.

Personal occupation by the adverse claimant is not necessary. He may hold possession through his agent, licensee, trustee, or tenant.[6]

Whytock and Green owned adjoining lots. The lot owned by Whytock adjoined the lot owned by Green on the west. In 1920 the predecessors in title to the Green lot had built on the west side of their lot a driveway that led to a garage. A cement curb was built on the west side of the driveway. This driveway was used by Green and his predecessors. In 1951, Whytock had his lot surveyed, and it was disclosed that the driveway and garage encroached on his lot 3 feet 9½ inches at the south end of the lot and 2 feet 6 inches at the north end. The encroachment extended 140 feet in length. Whytock started to erect a fence on the lot line, but Green brought this action, claiming this strip of land by adverse possession. Whytock conceded that Green had acquired the land on which the garage stood but claimed that Green and his predecessors in title had not been in exclusive possession of the driveway strip. The court held that Green had acquired title to the disputed strip by adverse possession.

Justice Berry said: "The construction of this curb and its continued duration can be construed as open, notorious and exclusive exercise of dominion, claim, and ownership of the strip of land in dispute by plaintiffs [Green] as opposed and adverse to that of defendants [Whytock]. . . . The law does not attempt to list all of the acts of dominion which may constitute such possession, so that which constitutes adverse possession, like the question of what constitutes negligence, often depends upon the circumstances of the particular case, as measured by the judgment of reasonable men. It has been said that such determination in a given case must largely depend upon the situation of the parties, the size and extent of the land, and the purpose for which it is adapted." *Whytock* v. *Green,* Okla., 383 P.2d 268 (1963).

## Open and Notorious Possession

No precise statement can be made as to the particular acts that are required to establish open and notorious possession. The question of whether there is open and notorious possession must be determined from the facts of the particular case under consideration. Usually, the acts must be of such a nature that the public in general, and the people in the neighborhood in particular, will know that the land is in the exclusive use and enjoyment of the claimant. The acts required are such as an owner of the land would ordinarily perform in the appropriation of the land and its products to his own use.

The courts consistently hold that a person purchasing land takes subject to the rights of the person in possession of the land. As a general rule, there is nothing on the record of title to the land to put the owner, the purchaser, the mortgagee, or the public on notice that the land is claimed by an adverse possessor. Consequently, the courts have held that the claimant's acts, in order to satisfy

[6] *Howell et al.* v. *Baskins,* 213 ARk, 665, 212 S.W.2d 353.

the requirement of open and notorious possession, must be of such a nature that a person of ordinary prudence inspecting the land would be aware that the land was in the possession of someone claiming rights in it.[7]

In 1943, Rall negotiated with Martin, attorney for Christ Church, for the purchase of the land in controversy. An agreement was reached, and Rall paid the agreed purchase price, but a deed to the land was never executed by the Church and delivered to Rall. There were no buildings on the land, and it was not fenced. Rall arranged with Richterberg to work the land as a tenant on a share-crop basis; and during the period from 1943 to 1961, crops of wheat and milo were raised, trees were set out, bindweed was killed with chemicals, and the land was improved by plowing. At times, cattle were pastured on the land, and an electric fence was installed. No one lived on the farm. Rall paid all taxes assessed on the land from 1943 to 1961. Christ Church tendered the taxes for 1962. In 1961, Rall sold and deeded the farm to Richterberg, and this action was brought by Richterberg against Christ Church to obtain a decree adjudging Richterberg the owner of the land. The court held that Rall acquired title by adverse possession and that this title was conveyed to and vested in Richterberg.

District Judge Daughterty said: "To establish adverse possession of land the claimant need not actually reside upon it or have it inclosed with a fence but it is sufficient if claimant is doing such acts thereon that indicate in an open, public, visible manner that he has exclusive control over the land under a claim of right to such exclusive possession." *Richterberg* v. *Wittich Memorial Church,* 222 F. Supp. 324 (1963).

### Exclusive Possession

To acquire title by adverse possession, the claimant must hold possession for himself to the exclusion of all other claimants. Two or more adverse claimants cannot hold exclusive possession at the same time. A claimant who holds with the title owner or a tenant of the title owner is not in exclusive possession of the property.[8]

### Continuous Possession

The possession of the adverse claimant, if he is to acquire title by adverse possession, must be continuous and uninterrupted for the entire statutory period. This does not mean that the claimant must be on the land every day during the period, but it does mean that he must use the land for the purpose for which it is reasonably adapted, without interruption of such use.

If land is reasonably adapted for a seasonal use, the use of the land each season without skipping a season would be considered as continuous and uninterrupted possession. For example, if the land is reasonably adapted to pasturing

[7] *La Caze* v. *Boycher,* La. App., 80 So.2d 583.

[8] *Oliver* v. *Thomas,* 173 Neb. 36, 112 N.W.2d 525.

and the adverse claimant uses the land each year during the grazing season for the statutory period, he will have been in continuous and uninterrupted possession of the land for the statutory period.[9]

This controversy involves a parcel of land built up as an accretion to upland in the form of a peninsula with its base on the boundary of land owned by Springer and extending past Durette's land but separated therefrom by a slough. Springer's land was managed by his agent Pearmine and was occupied by either Pearmine or a tenant. The peninsula was used as pasture by the occupants of the Springer farm from April to November for a period in excess of twenty years; and during this period, Pearmine, as agent of Springer, had cut and sold timber from the disputed tract. The land was not fenced, but the river and slough formed a natural fence. The court held that Springer had acquired title to the entire tract by adverse possession, and Durette appealed. The judgment was affirmed.

Justice O'Connell said: "The fact that the land was used for grazing only during the period from April to November does not preclude the claim on the ground of lack of continuity. As stated in 3 American Law of Property § 15.3, p. 767, 'possession may exist in a person who uses the land in the way in which an average owner of the particular type of property would use it though he does not reside on it and his use involves considerable intervals in which the land is not actually used at all.'

"We find ample support for our conclusion that by his conduct in grazing cattle on the land in question the claimant has satisfied the requirement of physical possession.

"The intent with which the occupant holds possession is normally determined by what he does upon the land. Where the land is used in the manner that an owner would use it there is a presumption that the possession is adverse.

"It is not necessary for us to decide under what circumstances a tenant's possession is sufficient to establish title by adverse possession in the landlord, because we are of the opinion that the plaintiff proved that the Pearmines were the agents and not the tenants of the Springers. The rule is clear that the possession of the agent is the possession of the principal for the purpose of acquiring title by adverse possession." *Springer* v. *Durette,* 217 Ore. 196, 342 P.2d 132 (1959).

## Tacking

An adverse claimant, as soon as he takes possession of the land, acquires property rights in it that are enforceable against all persons except the true owner. These rights may be conveyed to another in the same manner as other rights in real estate are conveyed. If an adverse claimant, before he has been in possession of the land for the statutory period, passes his rights in the land to another and that person takes immediate possession, he will be required to retain possession only for the balance of the statutory period. This is known as *tacking.*

Tacking will be permitted only if privity of estate exists—that is, if the claimant

[9] *Kellogg* v. *Huffman,* 137 Cal. App. 278,30 P.2d 593.

of the land acquired the rights of the prior adverse claimant by grant, devise, descent, or judicial decree. If an adverse claimant abandons the land and another adverse claimant takes possession immediately, there can be no tacking, since no privity of estate exists.

The courts have held that privity of estate exists even though the land in dispute was not included in the description in the deed, if the parties understood that the disputed tract was included in the conveyance. For example, suppose that Adam claims all of a tract of land up to a cliff, but the description in the deed conveying the land to Adam does not include part of the land claimed. Then, after Adam has been in possession of the land for less than the statutory period, he conveys it to Bell and uses the same description in the deed to Bell as was used in the deed to Adam, both Adam and Bell believing that the description included the land up to the cliff. Bell would acquire Adam's rights as adverse possessor of the land not included in the description in the deed.[10]

Eli Jacobs took possession of the land in controversy in 1900. After the death of Eli Jacobs, Bill Graham, husband of Susanna Jacobs, daughter of Eli Jacobs, took possession of the land. Susanna predeceased Bill Graham, who held possession of the land until his death, when his heirs took possession and held it until they conveyed the land to D. J. Jacobs, who took possession at the time of the conveyance and has held possession since that time. During the time Eli Jacobs and his descendants held the land, they raised tobacco on it, erected a sawmill, cut crossties and timber, and otherwise utilized the land as any owner would. International Paper Company claimed the land by virtue of paper title. Jacobs claimed the land by adverse possession. International Paper Company contended that Jacobs had not held the land for the statutory period of 20 years. The court held that Jacobs was the owner of the land.

Justice Rodman said: "To establish possession for the requisite twenty years, it was, as the court charged, permissible to tie the possession of an ancestor to that of the heir when there was no hiatus or interruption in the possession. As said by Johnson, J., in Newkirk v. Porter '. . . the adverse possession of an ancestor may be cast by descent upon his heirs and tacked to their possession for the purpose of showing title by adverse possession.' " *International Paper Company* v. *Jacobs,* 258 N.C. 439, 128 S.E.2d 818 (1963).

### Claim of Ownership

Possession without claim of ownership will not give the claimant title by adverse possession. The essence of adverse possession is hostile possession—that is, the party claims that he has the absolute right to possession of the property and that he does not hold in subordination to the rights of the true owner or any

---

[10] *Cooper et al.* v. *Tarpley et al.,* 112 Ind. App. 1, 41 N.E.2d 640.

other person. He holds not under, but in opposition to, the title to which his possession is alleged to be adverse.

If the claimant is in possession under a license or permission, his possession cannot ripen into title by adverse possession.[11] The possession of the claimant must be with the intent to appropriate and use the land as his own to the exclusion of all others. The claimant need not have a deed or color of title on which to base his claim of ownership, and he need not notify the title owner of record of his intention to claim ownership of the land. All that is necessary for one to establish hostile possession is that he take possession of the land and use it in the manner in which an owner would use the land, and that he perform those acts that make it apparent that he is claiming ownership of the land.[12]

Where a life tenant is attempting to assert ownership by virtue of adverse possession as against the remaindermen, there must be *actual* notice given to the remainderman, and even a notice placed in the public records will be insufficient to meet this requirement.[13]

### Color of Title

An instrument constitutes color of title if it purports to be a conveyance of title and is defective or void for matters not shown on the record of title. To establish title by adverse possession, the grantee in a defective or void deed must take possession of the real estate and hold it in open and notorious possession continuously for the statutory period. The fact that the adverse claimant took possession under color of title is strong evidence that he claims title and that his possession is hostile. Under the statutes of several states a person who takes possession under color of title and pays the taxes can acquire title in a shorter period of time than one taking without color of title. Color of title, in the absence of a contrary statute, is not an essential element of the acquisition of title by adverse possession.

### Statutory Period

At common law the statutory period within which the owner could bring an action to recover land that was being held adversely was 20 years. In the United States the period for bringing an action to recover land held adversely is controlled by the statutes of the state in which the land is located. The predominant period is 20 years, but a number of states have set a shorter period. In some states,

---

[11] Where an easement was denied because use was permissive, see: *Richmond Ramblers Motorcycle Club* v. *Western Title,* 47 Cal. 3d 747, 121 Cal. Rptr. 308 (1975).

[12] *Guaranty Title & Trust Corporation* v. *United States,* 44 S. Ct. 252, 264 U.S. 200.

[13] *Piel* v. *DeWitt,* 351 N.E.2d 48 (Ind. App. 1976).

one period is set that applies generally, and a shorter period is set that applies if the adverse claimant entered under color of title or has paid the taxes.

### Payment of Taxes

The payment of taxes is not an essential element of the acquisition of title by adverse possession, unless expressly made so by the statute. Several states have enacted statutes that make the payment of each year's taxes by the adverse claimant an essential element for acquisition of title by adverse possession. Whether or not the claimant has fulfilled the requirements of the statute is a matter of statutory construction.

The statutes of some states provide for a shorter period for the acquisition of title by adverse possession if the claimant pays the taxes. Payment of taxes by the claimant is strong evidence that his possession is hostile.

### Constructive Adverse Possession

As a general rule, a claimant acquires title only to the land that he occupies adversely.[14] However, under the concept of constructive adverse possession, a claimant who enters under color of title and takes actual possession of part of the land described in his evidence of title, but claims ownership to the entire description, can acquire title to the entire tract described in his evidence of title.[15]

### Title Acquired by Adverse Claimant

When an adverse claimant has satisfied all of the requirements of the statute of limitations, he not only bars any remedy for the recovery of possession that the holder of the title of record may have, but he acquires a perfect title to the real property that the courts will not permit to be disturbed. The title acquired by the adverse claimant must correspond with that on which his adverse possession operated. If he took possession under color of title, he will, in the absence of special circumstances, acquire title to the lands described in the deed under which he claims ownership; whereas if he does not take under color of title, he acquires a fee in only that land that he has occupied.

A title acquired by adverse possession is a title in fee simple[16] as perfect as though it was acquired by a conveyance. It cannot be divested by legislative enactment after it has been established, but only by written conveyance, by tax sale, or by another adverse claimant. Whether a purchaser from an adverse claim-

---

[14] *Coslin* v. *Crossett Company,* 233 Ark. 13, 342 S.W.2d 303.

[15] *McBeth et al.* v. *Wetnight,* 57 Ind. App. 47, 106 N.E. 407.

[16] *Meyers,* v. *Canutt et al.,* 242 Iowa 692, 46 N.W.2d 72.

ant who has satisfied the statutory requirements for obtaining title but has not yet established his title of record would be required to accept such title as a merchantable title is questionable. If the contract of purchase provided that the title must be good title of record or title satisfactory to the buyer or his attorney, the buyer would not be bound to assume the risk of establishing title by adverse possession.

The same can be said of a contract that required that the title be *insurable* as opposed to marketable. Title insurance companies, as well as attorneys examining the abstract of title, will generally insist that affirmative evidence of the quality of title be presented. In the absence of a conveyance from the record titleholder, this may require formal legal action in the form of a "quiet title" proceeding, discussed below.

### Quiet Title Proceedings

When a serious title defect appears to exist, as in the case of title established by adverse possession, the only solution may be a proceeding to quiet or absolutely establish the title in the purported owner. Such a proceeding takes the form of a lawsuit against all known and unknown persons who may have or may have had an interest of any kind in the property. The formal heading of the complaint will name all persons who ever had any connection with the property as owners, mortgagees, claimants of any and every kind, their spouses, executors, administrators, assigns, or creditors. It is, in law and in fact, a suit against "the whole world," and the heading may indeed say so, that intends to foreclose any right that anyone may have in the property except for that claim of the adverse possessor. Because it may not be possible to identify all of the possible claimants and their exact addresses may be unknown, the controlling statutes usually provide for notice of the action to be given by publication in local newspapers. Since some claimants may not reside in the immediate vicinity of the property, the length of time after the public notice is published before the matter may be heard by the court is usually very lengthy, from 13 to 26 weeks in many states. If, after the statutory period of time and in the absence of any objection to the claim of ownership, the court having jurisdiction of the property will determine the validity of the title claimed by the adverse possessor. In most cases, for all practical purposes, nothing less than this technical, lengthy process will be sufficient to establish either marketable or insurable title to the property.

If an objection is filed to the adverse possessor's claim to title, then there must, of course, be a trial of the issues presented and a judgment as to the status of the title. It is this ultimate judgment of the court having jurisdiction of the real estate that establishes the record title. That is, the judgment takes the place, in the chain of title, of the deed that would have otherwise appeared.

### Acquisition against Co-Owners, Tenants, and the Like

If property is owned by two or more persons as co-owners, possession of one co-owner is deemed the possession of all; and the co-owner in possession cannot acquire title to the property by adverse possession unless he clearly evidences his intention to hold exclusively, which he may do by direct communication or by his acts.

Likewise, a tenant, licensee, or other person who holds permissively cannot acquire title by adverse possession unless he denies the rights of the person under whom he first acquired permissive possession, and either communicates his intention to such person and thereafter holds possession under claim of ownership, or so acts that his intent to hold adversely is brought forcefully to the attention of that person.

### Disabilities

The statutes fixing the period for adverse possession usually contain a clause providing that the statute does not run against persons under stated disabilities. The persons usually protected by such provisions are infants; insane persons; married women who, under the laws of the state, do not have capacity to bring suit; and persons in prison. Under some statutes, the running of the statute is suspended during the period of disability; under others the person under disability is given a stated period after the removal of the disability in which to bring an action to recover the land that is being held adversely.

### Modern Applications

Today, with the relative scarcity of vacant land, the classic case of "taking" another's property by adverse possession seldom occurs. Nevertheless, the doctrine is viable and quite useful as a means for settling boundary disputes and establishing title where there has been a long-standing encroachment. Modern surveying techniques frequently bring to light troublesome encroachments by old buildings, and adverse possession can frequently be used to confirm title in the owner of the building. In the absence of statute, however, the doctrine of adverse possession does not apply against a governmental unit. Therefore, encroachments upon city property (such as an alley) by a building cannot be cured by adverse possession. In such cases available legislation usually can be used to obtain such property from the city or obtain a so-called license to encroach.

The following diagram and facts, taken from actual experience, may be helpful in illustrating the benefits and limitations of the doctrine.

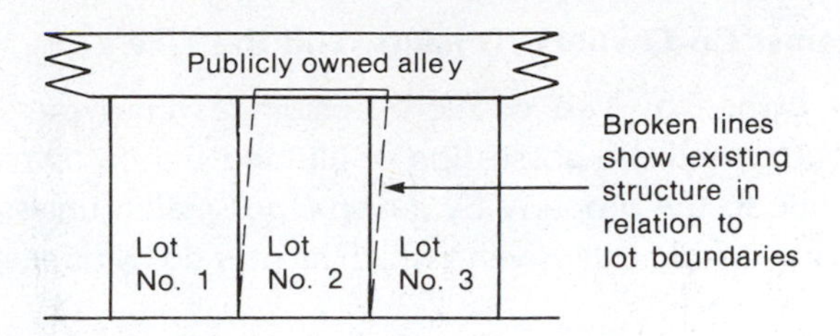


Assuming that the existing building on lot 2 has been in existence for a very lengthy period (long enough to satisfy statutory requirements for adverse possession) three results follow: (1) the owner of lot 2 has acquired title to a strip of lot 3 by virtue of adverse possession; (2) the owner of lot 2 has *lost* title to a strip of ground to the owner of lot 1 (assuming an abutting building on that lot), and (3) the building on lot 2 encroaches upon public land to the extent that it extends into the alley, and no ownership right has been established by this encroachment since the doctrine of adverse possession is not applicable. In this situation, both advantages and limitations of the doctrine are illustrated.

# Section 4

# Financing the Purchase of Real Estate

The high cost of real estate has made the real estate industry sensitive to the cost of funds borrowed on a long-term basis. The very nature of real estate has complicated the process by which security interests may be created to assure the repayment of borrowed funds. The problem thus created is not a new one, and it has historically required ingenuity on the part of buyers and sellers alike. The basic security interest in real estate is the mortgage, which is, in its simplest terms, a pledge of the real estate to assure the repayment of a loan. Certain fundamental variations will also be considered in this section: the deed of trust, which adds the element of a third party stakeholder to protect the security, and the land contract, which creates the security interest by means of an instalment sale in which the seller retains the legal title to the property until final payment has been made. Each of these is different enough from the mortgage to merit separate discussion, but the mortgage concept is discussed first because of its widespread use in real estate transactions.

The importance of understanding the law of mortgages and the creation of security interests in real estate generally can hardly be overstated. Prevailing conditions in credit markets cannot be ignored. In recent years the dramatic increase in long-term interest rate risk has made traditional mortgage lenders respond in one of several ways:

1. By increasing the fixed interest rate charged to such a high level that all foreseeable risks are covered.
2. By transferring the risk of future increases in the cost of borrowed funds to the borrower by the use of variable-rate loans, which adjust the rate being charged to be consistent with the lender's cost of funds.
3. Limiting the exposure of the lender to future interest rate risk by limiting the term of the loan to a relatively small number of years, after which the terms of the loan are renegotiated.

These various approaches tend to obscure the fact that the underlying transaction, the mortgage, is the same in every case. While it is true that the repayment scheme may take many forms, the security or collateral for the loan remains a pledge of the real estate, which may be sold if necessary to pay the debt.

It should also be recognized that very often the buyer and seller themselves will work out the financing for the purchase of real estate without the intervention of a traditional mortgage lender. For example, the seller may agree to become the mortgage lender and accept as partial payment a "purchase money" mortgage for the difference between the selling price and the down payment. The major attraction of this device is the freedom of the parties to negotiate the terms of payment without regard to those forces that dictate rates and terms in traditional financial markets. The seller-lender in such cases is free to establish interest rates and other terms without regard to the legal and financial limitations that apply to professional mortgage lenders or investors. In this case also, however, it should be noted that the fundamental rules of mortgage law still apply and must be fully understood by one who negotiates and structures such a transaction. Much litigation and consternation have resulted in recent years from the use of the purchase money mortgage and similar devices. To a great extent the difficulties appear to stem from the parties' lack of understanding of the legal consequences of such a transaction.

The materials in this section are divided into three general categories:

1. Basic mortgage law, including the rights of the parties during the payment period and the effect of foreclosure after the payment contract has been breached.

2. Recent mortgage practice developments, including discussions of the various types of mortgages in common use today, as well as the marketing of mortgages as investments.
3. Major security devices other than the mortgage: the deed of trust, used in some states instead of the mortgage, and the land contract, in widespread use throughout the country where private financing is being utilized.

# Chapter 12

# The Mortgage Loan Transaction

## The Mortgage Concept

It is helpful at the outset to analyze the transaction from which the mortgage will evolve. There is typically the sale of real estate that will be made conditional upon the availability of borrowed funds. When the transaction is completed it will include the formal borrowing transaction. It is this portion of the overall sale that is considered here.

It must be recognized that there are two separate and distinct steps in the typical mortgage loan transaction. The first step is the borrowing of funds, which is evidenced by two separate facts: the payment of money by the lender to or for the borrower and the execution of a promissory note spelling out the borrower's obligation to repay the loan. A simple diagram is set out below:

Mortgagor ⟵ Loan of money ⟵ Mortgagee
(Borrower) ⟶ Promise to repay ⟶ (Lender)

This simple transaction hardly seems to require an explanation, but it is important to the understanding of what follows to consider briefly what is happening: the mortgagee is advancing a sum of money to the mortgagor. It makes no difference that this money will be immediately paid over to a third party, the seller. Indeed, the money could be paid directly to the seller by the mortgagee, so long as this action was dictated by the mortgagor. This advance of funds creates a duty on the part of the mortgagor to repay them. The conditions under which this repayment must occur are negotiated between the mortgagor and mortgagee and are spelled out in the promissory note. In almost all cases this note will be an unconditional promise by the mortgagor to repay the debt over a period of time along with the rental charge for the use of the money: interest. The note will usually specifically refer to the fact that the loan is for the purpose of purchasing real estate, but this is not essential to the validity of the transaction. It is, in its simplest terms, a loan of money to a borrower who promises to repay it. The key point here is that the mortgage is not essential to the note. The note is a valid and binding obligation to pay the debt, whether or not there is also a mortgage. The borrower cannot escape this duty short of repaying the loan.

Because of the long-term nature of most such loans the lender is both unable and unwilling to predict the borrower's continued ability and willingness to pay the debt far into the future. This introduces uncertainty into the transaction. To illustrate: If the borrower were borrowing $3,000 to be repaid at the end of six months from income to be earned from employment that will generate $25,000 during the same period, the risk that the debt will not be paid is relatively easy to determine. It is quite another matter if the borrower is receiving $75,000 to be repaid with interest at $8,000 per year for a period of 25 years. In the latter case it is impossible to predict with certainty that the funds will continue to be available to the borrower for such a long period of time. This uncertainty of repayment makes it most unlikely that the lender will make such a loan without some added assurance of repayment: security. This is provided by adding to this transaction another element, a mortgage or pledge of the property being purchased. Now the diagram is as follows:

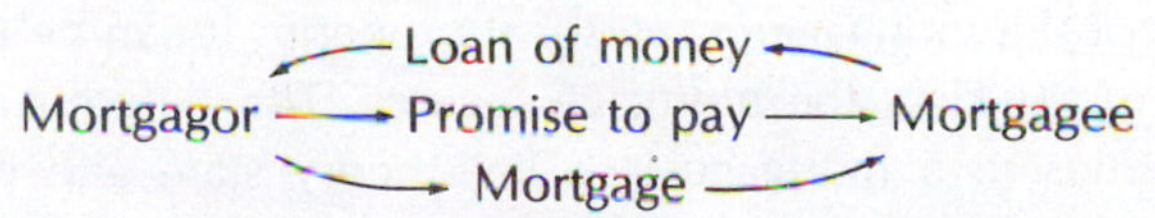


This pledge of the real estate as security for the payment of the debt serves only one purpose: to assure the lender the debt will be paid and that if it is not the property may be sold to generate funds to pay it. Without the existence of the debt the mortgage serves no purpose. For this reason it is frequently said that the debt is the life of the mortgage. The technical effect of this concept will be considered later. At this point it is important only to see how the mortgage fits into the loan transaction. The legal consequences of giving the mortgage are the subject of the material that follows.

**Basic Mortgage Law**

When the United States gained its independence from England, each of the states adopted the laws of England insofar as they were in accord with the social and economic conditions in the state. Almost from the beginning, our courts treated the mortgage as a lien on real estate given to secure the payment of a debt. Some of the states recognize what is known as the *title theory* of mortgages, whereas other states recognize the *lien theory*.

The title theory is a modification of the common-law concept of the mortgage. Under the title theory the mortgage is, in form, a conveyance of the mortgaged real estate to the mortgagee, his title to be defeated on the payment of the debt. As the law developed, however, the mortgagor became the one to be recognized as the true owner of the real estate. His ownership was subject only to the superior rights of the mortgagee. Although, technically, the mortgagee has the right of possession, the mortgagor, either by the terms of the mortgage or by statutory enactment, is given the right of possession until default and foreclosure. If the mortgagee is permitted to take possession, he must account for the rents and profits from the mortgaged real estate.

Under the lien theory of mortgages, title to the mortgaged real estate is not vested in the mortgagee but remains in the mortgagor. Only a security interest is conveyed to the mortgagee. The standard form of mortgage used in many of the lien-theory states reads ''mortgages and warrants'' instead of ''conveys and warrants.'' The mortgagor retains possession of the mortgaged property until default and foreclosure. Since the mortgagee's interest in the mortgaged property is a security interest, it is dependent on the debt secured, and any discharge of this debt automatically terminates the mortgagee's interest in the mortgaged real estate.

Whether the state follows the title theory or the lien theory of mortgages, the security interest of the mortgagee is personal property. It can be transferred only with a transfer of the debt the mortgage secures. The differences between the rights of the parties to a mortgage in a lien-theory state and in a title-theory state are technical rather than real.

## Form of the Mortgage

### Formal Requirements

As a general rule, the formal requirements for a valid mortgage are the same as those for a valid deed[1] and are not uniform for all of the states. Usually, the

[1] The formal requirements for a valid deed are discussed in Chapter 9.

mortgage must name the mortgagor and the mortgagee; must contain words of conveyance; must set out the debt to be secured; must describe the real estate mortgaged; must state, in a title theory state, the condition on which title is to be defeated (the defeasance clause); must be signed by the mortgagor; must, in some states, be sealed; must have, in some states, attesting witnesses; must be delivered and accepted; and must, if it is to be eligible for recording, be acknowledged. Acknowledgment, however, is not essential to the validity of the mortgage between the mortgagor and the mortgagee.

## Deed as Mortgage

From an early date the courts have held that any conveyance of real estate made as security for a debt is a mortgage, regardless of its form. They have held that the mortgagor has the right to pay the debt and redeem the mortgaged property at any time before foreclosure or the running of the statute of limitations. Any agreement entered into at the time the loan is made whereby the debtor-mortgagor is deprived of his right to redeem the mortgaged property is against public policy and is void.

Before the court will declare a deed or similar conveyance to be a mortgage, the grantor must prove by clear and convincing evidence that the true nature of the transaction was a loan and a conveyance as security for a loan. All the facts and circumstances surrounding the transaction are admissible as evidence to establish its true nature. No single fact is conclusive of the rights of the parties. Such facts as the relation between the amount paid and the value of the property at the date of the conveyance, whether the grantor retained possession of the property or surrendered possession to the grantee,[2] who paid the taxes, the relation of the parties, and the conduct of the parties prior to and subsequent to the conveyance in their relation to the property are taken into consideration.

## Sale with Option to Repurchase

Transactions in which property is sold and deeded by absolute deed to the grantee, who then executes to the grantor an option that gives the grantor the right to repurchase the property for the same price, plus interest at a stated rate or plus an amount equivalent to the going rate of interest, have presented some difficult problems for the courts. If the parties intended a sale and a repurchase agreement, the courts will enforce the agreement as drafted. If the seller asks the court to declare the transactions a mortgage and permit him to redeem

---

[2] *Spataro et al.* v. *Domenico et al.,* 96 Cal. App.2d 411, 216 P.2d 32.

the property after the expiration of the option, he will be required to prove by clear and convincing evidence that the transaction was a loan and that the deed was given as security.[3]

Such transactions are not often encountered in practice, but the device can be quite useful in major commercial financing arrangements. Following the recent broadening of the powers of financial institutions to hold title to real estate, its use may become more common in the future. Its use is adaptable, for example, to property that will be developed in stages or phases over a period of years. It may provide an accounting advantage for the lender.

## Rights of Innocent Purchasers

A grantor who has conveyed his real estate by absolute deed as security for a loan will not be permitted to recover the property from a person who has purchased it from the grantee, provided such person can qualify as an innocent purchaser for value.[4] The courts have held that the fact that the grantor is left in possession of the property is not notice that he has retained rights in it.[5] However, if the grantee-mortgagee sells the property, the grantor-mortgagor is not remedyless, even though he does lose his right to redeem the property. He can recover a judgment against the grantee-mortgagee for the difference between the unpaid balance of the debt plus the accrued interest and the fair market value of the property, regardless of the price at which the property was sold.[6]

## Equitable Mortgages

An equitable mortgage arises when a loan is made in reliance upon an agreement that real estate shall be mortgaged as security for the payment of the debt and then the debtor refuses or fails to execute the mortgage. It can also result when the instrument executed is so defective that it does not create an enforceable lien on the property.

For example, suppose that Allen loaned and paid to Bert $1,000 after Bert had agreed to secure the loan by giving Allen a real estate mortgage on a house and lot owned by Bert. Bert, after receiving the money, refused to execute the mortgage. A court would hold that Allen had an equitable mortgage on the house and lot as security for the loan.

An equitable mortgage creates a valid lien on the real estate in favor of the creditor, but it is not valid against an innocent purchaser for value. In the above

---

[3] *Lusher et al.* v. *First National Bank of Fort Worth et al.,* Tex., 260 S.W.2d 621.

[4] *Hoffman et al.* v. *Graaf et al.,* 179 Wash. 431, 38 P.2d 236.

[5] *Roberts* v. *Bass,* Fla., 111 So.2d 455.

[6] *Conley* v. *Henderson et al.,* 158 Ore. 309, 75 P.2d 746.

example, suppose that Bert, after promising to give Allen a mortgage on the real estate as security for the $1,000 loaned, sold the property to Call, who knew nothing about the Allen-Bert transaction, and who paid value for the house and lot. Call would take the house free from Allen's equitable mortgage.[7] Since the mortgage is not in writing it cannot be recorded so as to provide record notice to third parties.

### Property That May Be Mortgaged

As a general rule, any interest in real estate that may be sold may be mortgaged. The basic principle of property law—that one cannot convey greater rights in the property than he has—applies to the right to mortgage with equal force.

Under the common law the mortgage described the land, and it created a lien not only on the land but on all the improvements that, under the law of fixtures, became a part of the land. Under the Horizontal Property acts (Condominium Property Act in some states) a person may own, convey, and mortgage an apartment in a condominium. The apartment is described by reference to a recorded declaration and plat.[8]

A leasehold estate may also be mortgaged because it is an estate in land. While such mortgages have very limited use in connection with residential apartments, they are an important financing vehicle in the commercial field when used with very long-term leases. A mortgage also may, by its terms, include both real estate and personal property. Under the recording statutes of most states, such a mortgage, to be valid against subsequent bona fide purchasers, mortgagees, and lessees for value, would have to be recorded as a real estate mortgage and also recorded or filed as a chattel mortgage.

## The Mortgage Debt

### Nature of Secured Debt

The rule that the debt is the life of a mortgage and that a mortgage cannot exist unless it secures a debt is well established. However, the owner of real estate can make a gift of his real estate; and likewise, he can make a gift of a mortgage on his real estate. If the owner of real estate executes a gift mortgage

---

[7] *McKeighan et al.* v. *Citizens Commercial & Savings Bank of Flint et al.,* 302 Mich. 666, 5 N.W.2d 524.

[8] The Condominium Property Act of Illinois provides (Section 7): "Every deed, lease, mortgage or other instrument may legally describe a unit by its identifying number or symbol as shown on the plat and as set forth in the declaration. . . ."

on the real estate, the mortgage will be valid unless the mortgagor is insolvent and the enforcement of the mortgage would defeat the rights of creditors, or unless the mortgage is part of a scheme to defraud. The fact that the debt secured is unenforceable against the mortgagor for lack of consideration does not make the mortgage void.

A mortgage given to secure a past indebtedness is valid everywhere, even though a promise based on a past indebtedness is not enforceable for lack of consideration.[9] The courts also hold that a mortgage given to secure the indebtedness of a third person is valid.

As a general rule, a mortgage is given to secure the payment of a debt owed by the mortgagor. A mortgage may be given to secure the performance of an obligation of the mortgagor, provided the damages resulting from failure to perform the obligation can be reduced to a duty to pay money. In most mortgage transactions the personal indebtedness of the mortgagor is evidenced by a negotiable note, bond, or other writing; however, a writing or a personal indebtedness of the mortgagor is not essential to the validity of the mortgage.

### Nonrecourse Mortgages

Since the parties are free to negotiate the terms of the debt and the mortgage, they can structure the transaction in any way they can agree upon. It is quite possible that the lender and borrower may agree that the borrower is not to be personally liable for the payment of the debt and that the lender will look solely to the property as the source of repayment in the event of a default. Such waivers of personal liability are rare, but they are occasionally encountered in commercial loans. When such an agreement exists the mortgagee's rights would be limited to the security interest in the property and no lawsuit against the borrower personally could be maintained.

## Rights and Duties of the Parties

### Mortgagor's Right of Possession

In both the title-theory and the lien-theory states, the mortgagor is recognized as the owner of the mortgaged real estate. The mortgagor, as owner, is entitled to the possession of the mortgaged real estate; he has the right to all the rents and profits unless there is an agreement between the parties to the contrary.

---

[9] *Hahn* v. *Hahn et al.,* 123 Cal. App. 97, 266 P.2d 519.

## Duties of Mortgagor

The mortgagor, as owner of the mortgaged real estate, has all the rights of ownership. His duties in relation to the property are limited to refraining from doing any acts in relation to the property that would reduce its value to such an extent that it would no longer be reasonable security for the debt. The owner owes no duty to repair or improve the structures on the mortgaged property, but he has the right to make such repairs or improvements as he wishes. In the event of gross neglect, which would cause serious loss of security, the court would have the power to appoint a receiver to take possession of the mortgaged real estate and to do whatever would be necessary to preserve the property and thereby protect the interest of the mortgagee.

The mortgagor would be enjoined from such acts as the tearing-down and removal of buildings, the cutting of timber in unusual quantities, or the commission of other acts that would impair the value of the property so that it would no longer be adequate security for the debt.[10]

The mortgagor owes a duty to pay all taxes and assessments that would become a lien on the land. The standard mortgage usually includes a clause making the failure to pay taxes and assessments a default, permitting the mortgagee to declare the debt due and payable and to bring foreclosure proceedings. Also, the mortgagee may pay the taxes and assessments, and may add the amount disbursed to the principal of the mortgage debt.

In a mortgage foreclosure case the court allowed, as part of the mortgage debt, $996.81 plus interest in the amount of $121.68, which represented taxes on the real estate paid by the mortgagee. The United States had a tax lien on the property. The parties admitted that the face of the mortgage plus accrued interest and costs had priority over the lien of the United States, but the United States contended that its lien had priority over the mortgagee's claim for real estate taxes paid on the mortgaged property. The court held that the taxes had priority.

Judge Teigen said: "Real estate taxes subsequently levied constitute a prior lien to the mortgage lien. Where the mortgagor fails to pay the real estate taxes, the mortgagee, for his own protection, is entitled by virtue of the statute (Section 35–01–07) to pay such taxes and to enforce payment of the amount so paid by him as a part of the claim for which his mortgage lien exists. The payment of the taxes by the mortgagee extinguishes the original tax lien and the amount paid is secured by mortgage by force of statute and by the covenants of the mortgage. It is a charge upon the mortgaged premises in addition to the original mortgage debt and of the same grade and rank. The mortgage lien attaches

---

[10] *Fountain* v. *Grant,* 210 Ga. 78, 77 S.E.2d 721.

to such payment. This rule is the general rule. It constitutes a single and indivisible demand and claim for taxes paid are collateral and subordinate to the mortgage and may not be separated and collected in an independent action." *Fisher* v. *Hoyer,* N.D., 121 N.W.2d 788 (1963).

## Insurable Interest

In the absence of a provision in the mortgage or in the agreement of the parties, the mortgagor owes no duty to insure the mortgaged premises for the benefit of the mortgagee. The mortgagor and the mortgagee each have a distinct insurable interest in the property. The mortgagor may insure the property for its full value, without deduction because of the mortgage.

The insurable interest of the mortgagee is his security right in the property, and he cannot collect insurance in excess of the value of his security right. If the mortgagee insures in his own right, the mortgagor has no interest in insurance money paid to the mortgagee in the event of damage to or destruction of the insured buildings; and the mortgagee does not owe a duty to apply such money in reduction of the mortgage debt.[11]

## Standard Insurance Clause

As a general rule, the mortgage will contain an insurance clause imposing on the mortgagor a duty to keep the mortgaged property insured for its full value, or for a value stated in the mortgage, for the benefit of the mortgagee, and further providing that on the mortgagor's failure to insure the mortgaged property, the mortgagee may insure and add the cost of the insurance to the amount of the mortgage debt. Usually, insurance policies on mortgaged property provide that the insurance is for the benefit of the mortgagor and the mortgagee as their interests may appear. It is, at the time of loss, the obligation of the parties to prove what their respective interests are.

The insurance clause used in the FNMA standard mortgage provides in part:

"Unless Lender and Borrower otherwise agree in writing, insurance proceeds shall be applied to restoration or repair of the Property damaged, provided such restoration or repair is economically feasible and the security of this mortgage is not thereby impaired. If such restoration or repair is not economically feasible or if the security of this mortgage would be impaired, the insurance proceeds shall be applied to the sums secured by this Mortgage, with the excess, if any, paid to Borrower."

## Rights of Mortgagee

The principal purpose for taking a mortgage is to reduce the risk of loss resulting from the failure of the debtor to pay the debt. Consequently, the primary right

---

[11] *Le Doux et al.* v. *Dettmering et al.,* 316 Ill. App. 98, 43 N.E.2d 862.

of the mortgagee is to have the secured debt paid when due; and the secondary right is, on default in the payment of the debt, to have the mortgaged real estate sold and the proceeds applied in extinction or reduction of the debt. Duties other than the payment of the secured debt may be imposed on the mortgagor by the terms of the mortgage. The mortgagee has the right to have the mortgagor fulfill all such duties.

One of the most important rights of the mortgagee is the right to sell and assign both the note and the mortgage that secures it. Because of its significance in mortgage credit markets this subject is discussed in depth in Chapter 13.

A mortgagor may, at the time the mortgage is executed, make an assignment of rents to the mortgagee, the assignment to become effective on the mortgagor's default. The rent assignment may be included in the mortgage, or it may be made as a separate agreement. In either case the rent assignment should be drafted in language that will make it clear that the parties intended to assign the rents—not merely to pledge them—as security for the loan.

## Recording the Mortgage

### Requirements for Recording

The statutes providing for the recording of conveyances of real estate apply to both deeds and mortgages. The requirements for recording, the necessity of recording, and the effect of recording were discussed in Chapter 5.

### Effect of Recording

Generally, a mortgage creates a lien on the real estate that is mortgaged; it is binding as between the parties to the mortgage and all persons claiming under it, even though it is not recorded. Likewise, statutes that provide that the recording of the mortgage must be renewed or reinscribed within a specified period of time do not affect the validity of the obligation as between the parties to the mortgage or the parties claiming under it.[12]

At common law, prior to the adoption of recording statutes, a valid legal mortgage given to a good-faith mortgagee for value was superior to (cut off) all existing equitable mortgages or equitable claims of which the mortgagee had no notice or knowledge at the time of the execution of the mortgage. As between successive mortgagees, the general rule was: The first in time has the superior rights.

---

[12] *Dr. Joe F. Shuffield* v. *Raney,* 226 Ark. 3, 287 S.W.2d 588.

Under the recording statutes the recording of a mortgage is constructive notice to the public of the existence of the mortgage. It is effective from the date upon which it is recorded rather than the date upon which it was executed. Therefore the common-law rule is modified to place a premium upon prompt recording. Recording by itself, however, will not give a mortgagee priority over claims of which he had actual knowledge whether recorded or not. That is, to have the benefit of the recording system, the mortgagee must be a bona fide mortgagee for value. This concept was discussed earlier, in Chapter 1.

## Discharge of Mortgage

### Discharge by Payment of Debt

In the majority of mortgage transactions the mortgage is discharged by the payment of the mortgage debt. Since the mortgage cannot exist separate and apart from the debt it secures, payment of the debt will, by operation of law, discharge the mortgage. A change in the form of the debt, however, such as reducing the debt to judgment or the giving of a renewal note for the one evidencing the debt secured by the mortgage, will not discharge the mortgage, since the debt secured by the mortgage will not have been discharged. The mortgage debt may be paid by the person primarily liable or by any person at the request of the mortgagor, but a mere volunteer has no right to pay the mortgage debt.[13]

In order to discharge a mortgage, the mortgagor or his successor must pay the mortgage debt to the person entitled to payment, or to his agent who is authorized to accept payment. If the mortgage debt is evidenced by a writing, the person making payment should demand the surrender of the written evidence of the debt along with the mortgage. If a grantee has assumed a mortgage debt and he makes payment to one who is not the holder of the mortgage and the written evidence of the debt, the mortgage is not discharged.[14] Also, if the mortgage debt is evidenced by a negotiable instrument, the person making payment should, in order to protect himself, demand surrender of the negotiable instrument when payment is made.[15]

If payment is made to one who claims to be the agent of the owner of the mortgage and mortgage debt, the person making payment must ascertain, at his peril, whether or not the agent is authorized to accept payment. Payment should

---

[13] *Bourquin* v. *Feland et al.,* 189 Okla. 489, 117 P.2d 789.

[14] *Holvick* v. *Black et al.,* 57 N.D. 270, 221 N.W. 71.

[15] *Henningsen* v. *Title & Trust Co.,* 151 Ore. 318, 49 P.2d 458.

never be made to an agent who does not have possession of the mortgage and the written evidence of the debt. It has become common practice in the mortgage banking business to sell and assign mortgages and notes to investors. Typically, the mortgage lender will act as agent for purposes of loan administration and collection. The physical return of the note and mortgage to the borrower upon final payment is therefore of practical significance.

### Payment by Surety

Under the law of suretyship, if a surety or guarantor pays the debt of the borrower, he is subrogated to all rights of the creditor. Under the concept of subrogation he obtains the same rights the creditor had to enforce the debt against the borrower. If the borrower, in addition to having sureties or guarantors cosign, has secured the payment of the debt by executing a mortgage on real estate and a surety or guarantor pays the mortgage debt, the mortgage will not be discharged, but such surety or guarantor will be subrogated to the mortgagee's rights and may proceed to foreclose the mortgage.

A similar situation arises when co-owners of real estate join in mortgaging the co-owned real estate and one of the co-owners pays the mortgage debt. The mortgage will not be discharged but will be kept alive for the benefit of the person making the payment. Since he is not primarily liable for the entire mortgage debt, he will be subrogated to the rights of the mortgagee against his co-owners.[16]

### Tender of Payment and Prepayment

The courts are not in accord as to the effect on a mortgage of a tender of payment of the mortgage debt. As a general rule, a valid tender of payment of the mortgage debt will discharge the mortgage. In order to make a valid tender, the mortgagor or person primarily liable, or his duly authorized agent, must make an unconditional offer to pay the mortgage debt in money—an offer to give a personal check is not a valid tender. The tender must be made on or after the due date. The mortgagee or owner of the mortgage debt is not obligated to accept payment before the due date. If the mortgagee or owner of the mortgage debt refuses to accept the tender and his refusal is justified, the mortgage will not be discharged.

Modern mortgages will frequently give the mortgagor the privilege of prepaying the debt at any time. The granting of this privilege is not without its price: the prepayment penalty. One reason borrowers desire the prepayment privilege is

---

[16] *Hare* v. *Reddy et al.,* 222 Wis. 508, 269 N.W. 294.

to permit refinancing in the event that prevailing interest rates go down. It is then advantageous to borrow from another source at the lower rate and pay off the existing loan. For the same reason, however, the first lender does not want the loan paid off in advance. The reason is that he will lose the benefit of an above-market interest rate loan because he cannot lend the money out again at the same rate of profit. The compromise usually worked out permits the prepayment but only upon the payment of a penalty that serves to reimburse the lender for his loss of the more favorable rate. (The sample note included in Chapter 14 illustrates such a clause.) Since the inclusion of any clause regarding prepayment is not an essential element of the mortgage loan contract, it is subject to negotiation between the parties. The risk that the borrower might prepay and refinance in periods of low interest rates may be retained by the lender. The price for this concession usually is a higher interest rate on the loan at the outset.

### Discharge by Release

A mortgage may be discharged by a release. The release can be given only by the owner of the mortgage and mortgage debt, or by someone authorized to act for him. No particular form is required for the release of a mortgage. It may be made in any manner that clearly manifests the intent of the mortgagee or owner of the mortgage to release it. However, a formal release of a mortgage that is eligible for record and that would release the mortgage of record must be in writing and executed in compliance with the recording statutes of the state in which the mortgaged real estate is located.

If the mortgage creditor, after receiving payment of the amount due him, refuses or neglects to discharge the mortgage of record or make the assignments to which the person redeeming is entitled, such person may bring an appropriate action, and the court will force the mortgage creditor to execute the release or assignment.

### Discharge by Merger

A mortgage may be discharged by merger, that is, by vesting the interests of the mortgagor and the mortgagee in the same person. If the mortgagor, or a person to whom the mortgagor has conveyed his interest, conveys that interest to the mortgagee, or to the assignee of the mortgagee, the mortgage will in most instances be discharged by merger.

If the merger will result in definite injury and injustice to the person acquiring the interests of both the mortgagor and the mortgagee, the court will hold that no merger resulted. For example, suppose that there are a first mortgage and a second mortgage or other junior liens on the real estate, and the mortgagor conveys his rights in the mortgaged real estate to the first mortgagee. There will be no merger. If the first mortgage were, in such a case, held to be extinguished by merger, the second mortgage or junior liens would become first claims on the real estate; this would result in increasing the value of the subordinate liens at the expense of a senior lienholder.[17]

It is possible for the lender and a defaulting borrower to agree upon a deed of the property to the lender in lieu of foreclosure. The terms of such an agreement will be dictated by the circumstances at the time of default. The lender may release the borrower from personal liability in exchange for a quick transfer of ownership. This will permit the lender to market the property free of the limitations and delays imposed by the foreclosure statutes. The existence of other liens, however, may make this approach impractical because the junior liens will not be cut off. The holders of these liens are not parties to this transaction. In such a case foreclosure may be the only effective solution. Foreclosure is discussed later in this chapter.

## Statute of Limitations

The running of the statute of limitations on the debt does not discharge the mortgage, since it does not discharge the debt—it merely bars any action brought to enforce the debt. Some courts have held that a bar to an action on the debt is also a bar to any action on the mortgage.

## Sample Mortgage and Note

There follow a form of note and mortgage to illustrate the basic contents of each as they have developed in practice. Many forms in use today are far more complex than those that follow; however, the forms used here include all of the essential elements. No form can be devised that will be usable universally, and variations in the law from state to state will require different clauses. At the same time no form should ever be blindly followed, because of the many variables that must be considered in each individual transaction. The forms are footnoted to comments that follow them, rather than being inserted, for ease of study of the forms without interruption.

[17] *Moffet* v. *Farwell,* 222 Ill. 543, 78 N.E. 925.

**Sample Note**[A]

____________________, ________________
(City) (State)

_____________________,19_____________
(Date)

For value received, the undersigned jointly and severally, promise to pay to the order of ______________________________________ the principal sum of _________________________________ Dollars ($__________) with interest on the unpaid principal balance from the date of this Note, until paid, at the rate of __________ percent per annum. Payments of principal and interest shall be paid at ______________________________, or such other place as the holder of this note may from time to time designate in writing, in monthly installments of _________________________ Dollars ($__________), on the __________________ day of each month beginning on __________, 19_____, until the entire amount of principal and interest evidenced by this Note is fully paid, except that the final payment of the entire debt evidenced by this Note, if not sooner paid, shall be due and payable on the _____ day of __________, 19_____.[B]

If any monthly installment payment under this Note is not paid when due and remains unpaid after thirty (30) days after the due date the entire principal amount then outstanding and interest accrued on that amount shall immediately become due and payable at the option of the holder of this note. Failure to exercise this option by the holder shall not constitute a waiver of the right to exercise it at any time the undersigned is in default under the terms of this note. In the event of default in the payment of the debt evidenced by this Note and if the holder shall bring suit on this Note then the holder shall be entitled also to collect all reasonable costs and expenses of such suit, including, but not limited to, reasonable attorney's fees.[C]

The undersigned shall have the right to prepay the principal amount of the debt outstanding at any time.[D]
Presentment, notice of dishonor, and protest are hereby waived by all makers, sureties, guarantors and endorsers of this note and all applicable exemption rights, whether by homestead or otherwise are also waived. This Note shall be the joint and several obligation of all makers, sureties, guarantors and endorsers and shall be binding upon them and their heirs, personal representatives, successors and assigns.[E]

________________________________ (SEAL)
________________________________ (SEAL)

## Comments on Sample Note

A. This note is intended to be negotiable in form so that it can be transferred by assignment to a party other than the original lender. Very often, in practice, such notes and the mortgages that secure them are sold to investors who are not directly involved in the mortgage lending business, such as life insurance companies. Frequently the sale of the notes and mortgages is coupled with a contract, under which the original lender retains the responsibility for making collections and otherwise "servicing" the mortgage for the investor for an agreed-upon fee. This is typically a percentage of gross collections. In order that the investor be able to take the note and mortgage free from any personal defenses that the borrower might have against the original lender, all of the documents are put into negotiable form.

B. This note contemplates equal installment payments until the total debt has been repaid. In many cases the final installment will be an amount that differs from the earlier payments. More important, however, this provision of the sample note permits it to be used if a "balloon" final payment is contemplated. For example, the debt may be so structured that the monthly installment payment is calculated on a 20-year amortization schedule, while the parties intend for the debt to be fully paid off at the end of 5 years. The use of the long-term amortization table results in a relatively low monthly payment for the borrower during the five-year term of the debt. At the end of this period, the entire balance will come due. The device is frequently used when the lender is unwilling to make the loan on a 20-year term at a fixed rate of interest. When the balloon payment approach is used, it has the effect of shifting the risk of increased interest rates to the borrower since he must refinance at the end of the five-year term.

C. The default and acceleration clause in the sample note is one commonly seen in such notes. It makes clear the fact that a default in the payment of any one installment is to be treated as an anticipatory breach of the promise to pay all subsequent payments. It is conceivable that the note could otherwise be interpreted as a series of promises, the breach of each one requiring a separate legal proceeding to enforce it. The acceleration of all subsequent payments gives effect to business reality: there is one debt, the repayment of which is made in installments for the benefit of the borrower.

D. This sample note clearly provides for the privilege of prepayment on the part of the borrower, without the assessment of any penalty for so doing. In periods in which the trend of interest rates is upward, it is in the lender's best interests to encourage prepayment because the money can then be loaned out at the higher rates prevailing at that time. By the same token, of course, should interest rates fall, the borrower is free to refinance at a lower rate. Recent years of generally high interest rates have led some lenders to penalize the borrower for prepayment because it is not certain at the time of the transaction that it will be possible to reloan the money again at equivalent rates. An example of a typical clause penalizing early payment may be found in the sample note in Chapter 14, used with the deed of trust as the security device.

E. The waiver of presentment clause utilized in this note is relatively standard except for the waiver of homestead exemption, which might otherwise prevent full recovery of the debt out of the proceeds of sale of the real estate. The homestead exemption was discussed in Chapter 3. Some states, which do not recognize the homestead exemption as such, nevertheless have some form of exemption of the family home. It is not uncommon to see the term *valuation and appraisement laws* in place of *homestead.* These laws provide for essentially the same type of protection as do the homestead laws. Some careful attorneys will include a reference to both laws.

In the consideration of the sample mortgage that follows it should be kept in mind that the mortgage is an instrument that creates security for the repayment of the debt evidenced by the promissory note discussed above. As such, it creates a *potential* interest in real estate. In view of the well-established rule that each state jealously guards its power to establish real estate law over real estate within its boundaries, it should be noted that no uniformity in terms of the rights of the parties can be anticipated. At the same time, the marketability of mortgages on real estate (which is now more the rule than the exception) demands at least some degree of uniformity. This conflict will ultimately be decided by the investor, the one who purchases mortgages in large dollar volume, and who will require uniformity of terms to limit the expense of administration of such an investment. There is in fact today so much pressure for uniformity that the local mortgage form is rapidly becoming an endangered species. It is with this purely economic consideration in mind that the reader should consider the form that follows. That is, the mortgage form is designed to illustrate fundamental legal rules that must be considered in any mortgage.

**Sample Mortgage**

This mortgage is made and given this _____ day of ___________, 19_____, from the mortgagor(s), ________________________________ (herein "Mortgagor") to the mortgagee, ________________________________ herein "Mortgagee").

In consideration of the indebtedness of Mortgagor to Mortgagee in the principal sum of ________________________________________________

________Dollars, evidence by Mortgagor's promissory note, dated this same date, which provides for monthly installment payments of principal and interest with the balance of the indebtedness due and payable, if not sooner paid, on ______________________; and, in order to secure Mortgagee the repayment of said indebtedness and the performance of the covenants and agreements of Mortgagor set out below, Mortgagor does hereby mortgage to Mortgagee the following described property located in the County of ________________,

**Sample Mortgage** ***(continued)***

State of ____________________________________________:

____________________________________________

____________________________________________

____________________________________________

____________________________________________

____________________________________________

together with all improvements now on or hereafter erected on the above described property as well as all easements, rights, rents, royalties, minerals, oil and gas rights, all of which, including any replacements and additions, shall be taken to be and remain or become a part of the property covered by this mortgage. All of the foregoing are referred to herein as the "Property."

Mortgagor covenants and guarantees that Mortgagor is the lawful owner of the Property and has the right to mortgage it, that the property is not encumbered and that Mortgagor will warrant and defend generally the title of the Property, subject to any exceptions included in Mortgagor's deed to the property and/or any exception to coverage listed in the Mortgagee's title insurance policy on the Property.[A]

Mortgagor and Mortgagee further agree as follows:

1. *Payment of Debt.* Mortgagor agrees to pay when due all payments of principal and interest evidenced by the promissory note secured by this mortgage. All payments shall be applied first to interest and then to principal.

2. *Taxes, Assessment, and Other Charges.* Mortgagor shall promptly pay all taxes, assessments, and other charges which may be levied against the Property during the life of this mortgage which would otherwise have priority over the Mortgagee's lien on the Property. Mortgagor shall, however, have the right to contest the imposition of any such tax, assessment, or charge provided that Mortgagee's lien is protected in a manner satisfactory to Mortgagee.[B]

3. *Insurance.* Mortgagor shall insure the Property and improvements against loss by fire and other causes commonly included within the term "extended coverage." The amount of coverage shall not be less than the amount necessary to pay the indebtedness secured by this mortgage. Such insurance shall be issued by a company or companies selected by Mortgagor subject to the approval of Mortgagee; such approval shall not be unreasonably withheld.[C]

4. *Maintenance of Property and Inspection.* Mortgagor agrees to keep the Property in good repair and shall neither permit nor commit waste of the Property. Mortgagor agrees further that Mortgagee shall have access to the Property for the purpose of inspecting it at reasonable times to assure that the property is being adequately maintained.[D]

**Sample Mortgage *(continued)***

5. *Condemnation.* The proceeds of any award for the condemnation of the Property or any part of it are hereby assigned by the Mortgagor to the Mortgagee and shall be paid to the Mortgagee. Such proceeds shall be applied to the payment of the debt secured by this mortgage with any excess being paid to the Mortgagor.[E]

6. *Forbearance Not a Waiver.* Any forbearance by the Mortgagee in the exercise of any right or remedy created by this mortgage shall not have the effect of releasing the Mortgagor from any obligation or liability created by this mortgage or by law.

7. *Governing Law.* This mortgage is made in and shall be governed by the laws of the state in which the Property is located. All of the provisions of this mortgage and the promissory note which it secures are hereby declared to be severable. That is to say, if any portion of either this mortgage or the note conflict with applicable law, such conflict shall have no effect upon the balance of their provisions.

8. *Sale of Property and Assumption.* If all or any part of the Property is sold or otherwise transferred without the consent of the Mortgagee, then the Mortgagee may, but need not, declare all sums secured by this mortgage to be due and payable immediately. In the event, however, that a written assumption agreement is entered into between the transferee and the mortgagee, then Mortgagee shall release Mortgagor from any and all obligations created by this mortgage and the note which it secures.[F]

9. *Acceleration.* Upon Mortgagor's breach of any promise or agreement either in this mortgage or the note which it secures, Mortgagee at Mortgagee's option and after thirty (30) days' written notice to the Mortgagor addressed to Mortgagor at the address of the property, may declare all sums secured by this mortgage to be immediately due and payable and may foreclose this mortgage by judicial proceedings.

10. *Release of Mortgage.* Upon the payment of all sums secured by this mortgage the Mortgagee shall execute and deliver to the Mortgagor a full and effective relase of this mortgage in recordable form and at no expense to the Mortgagor.

11. *Waiver of Homestead.* Mortgagor hereby waives all right of homestead or of valuation and appriasement laws.[G]

In witness whereof, Mortgagor has executed this mortgage.

______________________________ (SEAL)
BORROWER

______________________________ (SEAL)
BORROWER

**Sample Mortgage *(concluded)***

STATE OF ____________________ SS: ____________________

COUNTY OF ____________________ ____________________

ADDRESS OF PROPERTY

Before me, the undersigned, a Notary Public in and for said County, this _____ day of __________, 19_____, came ______________________________ ______________________________and acknowledged the execution of the foregoing instrument.

Witness my hand and notarial seal

______________________________

NOTARY PUBLIC

My Commission expires: ______________________________

This instrument was prepared by: ______________________________

## Comments on Sample Mortgage

A. The terminology used in this mortgage to create the interest in the mortgagee is practically standard. It should be noted, however, that mortgages almost universally include some form of warranty of title by the mortgagor to the mortgagee. There is little difference between these warranties and those included in the standard general warranty deed. The lender is, of course, as much concerned with the quality of the title to the property as is the mortgagor who is taking title to the property. The lender has the additional concern that the mortgage be a first lien upon the property so as to provide maximum security for the repayment of the loan.

B. The prompt payment of taxes, assessments, and other charges against the property by the mortgagor universally appears in form mortgages. The reason is that these charges either will or may be senior to the lien of the mortgage. This is particularly true of real estate taxes, for example, the failure to pay exposing the property to a tax sale. The obligation to make such payments when due is made a positive duty of the mortgagor so that any failure to pay them is a default permitting the mortgagee to bring foreclosure proceedings. Many mortgages provide the mortgagee the option to make these payments should the mortgagor fail to do so, and then add them to the existing balance of the debt. Still other mortgages provide for the payment of real estate taxes (as well as other recurring expenses, such as insurance) on a monthly basis by the mortgagor to the mortgagee, who holds these additional payments in escrow until the obligation is due. Payment of the mortgagor's obligation is then made by the mortgagee. The use of the escrow approach gives the mortgagee further protection of the security interest created by the mortgage.

C. In the absence of a positive undertaking to insure the mortgaged property, the mortgagor has no duty to do so for the benefit of either party. The imposition of the duty to insure is standard today, and under this form a failure to do so would constitute a default permitting foreclosure action, even though the underlying debt might not be in default.

D. There is no common-law duty on the part of the mortgagor to maintain the mortgaged property in good repair, nor is there any right in the mortgagee to inspect. Therefore, a clause establishing these rights and duties is standard.

E. Upon condemnation, a governmental taking of private property, upon payment of its fair value (discussed in detail in Chapter 4), the award would, in the absence of this clause, be made to the owner. Under this clause the right to the money paid for condemnation is assigned to the mortgagee to the extent of the balance of the indebtedness at that time. While the mortgagee has remedies available to him or her to reach the proceeds, this assignment provides greater assurance of payment without the need to pursue additional remedies.

F. The sale of the real estate by the mortgagor during the existence of the mortgage is discussed in Chapter 13. The fact that the mortgagor may sell the property has prompted the inclusion in modern mortgages of rather severe restrictions upon this right in favor of the supplier of funds. The validity of clauses that accelerate the entire debt upon the sale of the property is well established by court decisions. The practical effect of this clause is, of course, that it gives the mortgagee the opportunity to renegotiate the terms of the loan—particularly important when interest rates have risen dramatically. It also provides the mortgagee time to investigate the credit reputation of the assuming buyer. As provided in this clause, the renegotiation of the debt and mortgage terms with the assuming buyer results in a *novation,* a new contract, and the original mortgagor is entitled to be released.

G. Clauses 9, 10, and 11 closely follow the terms of the note, already discussed. The discussion included there applies to these clauses as well.

H. The acknowledgment of the mortgage is important for the same reasons already discussed in connection with the deed illustrated in Chapter 9: to make it eligible for recordation.

## Foreclosure

### Nature of Foreclosure

Foreclosure of the mortgage is the process by which the creditor secured by the mortgage forces a sale of the mortgaged property and cuts off the rights of the mortgagor to redeem the real estate. At common law, a suit in equity was necessary to accomplish foreclosure. Today foreclosure proceedings are regulated by statute. It is therefore necessary to comply with the foreclosure laws of the state in which the real estate is located. More than one method of foreclosure may be permitted in a given state. In that event the mortgagee may elect the process to utilize, unless there has been a prior agreement as to the method to be followed between the mortgagor and the mortgagee. The foreclosure process may not, of course, be invoked until there has been a default by the mortgagor.

### Default

A default occurs when the mortgagor is guilty of a material breach of the terms of the mortgage. Such breach may, depending on the terms of the mortgage agreement, consist of the failure to pay the mortgage debt or an installment thereof when due, failure to pay interest, failure to pay taxes, or failure to keep the premises insured. A breach may also occur on the commission of waste or on the commission of any other act that might be detrimental to the interests of the mortgagee.

### Who Has Right to Foreclose

If the mortgagee has not assigned the mortgage or the mortgage debt, he is the only person who has a right to foreclose. If there has been an assignment of the mortgage and the mortgage debt, or of the mortgage debt, the laws of the state will determine who shall bring the action to foreclose. Under the statutes of many states only the real party in interest, that is, the party who is entitled to receive the money due, may bring the foreclosure action.[18] The subject of assignment of notes and mortgages is discussed in detail in Chapter 13.

### Foreclosure by Action and Sale

Foreclosure by action and sale is permitted in all states and is the only method of foreclosure permitted in some of the states. Since the proceedings and the sale of the mortgaged property are conducted under orders of the court, the chances of a defective foreclosure are minimized. As a general rule, however, the costs incurred in a foreclosure by action and sale are greater than in a foreclosure by power of sale or entry and possession. The steps to be followed in a foreclosure by action and sale are set out by the statutes of the state in which the mortgaged real estate is located, and they must be substantially complied with.

***Foreclosure Procedure.*** Although the statutes are not uniform, the steps in the procedure are as follows: Suit is brought in the court having jurisdiction. If

[18] *Linahan et al.* v. *Linahan et al.*, 131 Conn. 307, 39 A.2d 895.

the mortgagor or his grantee or other party in interest has a defense to the foreclosure suit, he appears in the case and sets up his defense; the case is tried in accordance with the trial procedure of the state, and a decree is entered. If there are no appearances in the case, a default decree is entered. The court will determine the amount due on the mortgage debt, and an order authorizing the sale of the mortgaged real estate will be entered.

The sale will be conducted in compliance with the statutes of the state and will, as a general rule, be reported to the court for confirmation. Unless there is evidence of fraud or other irregularity in the conduct of the sale, or unless the price bid at the sale is wholly inadequate, the judge will confirm the sale. If the property is sold for less than the amount found due on the mortgage debt, a deficiency judgment may be entered against the mortgagor. In our initial discussion of the mortgage transaction, it was pointed out that the promissory note is an unconditional promise to pay the amount borrowed. The fact that the foreclosure has occurred does not change that original obligation. The mortgagor remains personally liable for the shortage, and his other assets may be pursued if necessary to satisfy the judgment on the note. If there is a surplus, of course, that surplus belongs to the mortgagor, since he was the owner of the property sold.

***Foreclosure Sale.*** In foreclosure by action and sale, the sale is directed by the court and is usually regulated by the statutes of the state in which the mortgaged real estate is located. These statutes vary in their terms from state to state. Also, the court, under its equity jurisdiction, generally has the power to order and direct the sale of mortgaged real estate. As a general rule, the sale is a public one, made under the direction of the sheriff or a court officer appointed for that purpose.

Usually, the statutes require the posting of a certain number of notices of the sale, and give general directions as to where the notices shall be posted. Under the statutes of some states, notice of the sale must be advertised in a newspaper having general distribution in the county in which the mortgaged real estate is located. The notice must give the time, place, manner of conducting the sale, terms of the sale, and such other information as is required by the statutes.

If the mortgage covers two or more distinct parcels of real estate, the statute may provide that the parcels shall be offered for sale separately; and if, upon sale, one or less than all of the parcels will bring a sum sufficient to satisfy the mortgage debt, only such parcels will be sold. If there are several parcels and there are junior liens on some or all of them, the court may order the parcels sold in the order of the priority of the junior lien claimants, so as to give to each lien claimant the maximum benefit to which he is entitled.

A foreclosure sale usually requires confirmation and does not become final until it is confirmed by the court. The court may set a sale aside under some circumstances and order a new sale.[19]

The Production Credit Association of Madison, Wisconsin (hereinafter referred to as PCA), commenced foreclosure proceedings against Chickering and Jacobson. The property consisted of 1,500 acres of muck farm land. PCA held a mortgage in the unpaid amount of $38,511.05. There were other liens against the land; and including the PCA mortgage, the total of the liens, exclusive of interest, was in excess of $110,000. On the foreclosure sale, PCA bid the property in for $87,000. Gumz had bid $86,000, his bid being the next high bid. Chickering and Jacobson petitioned the court to set the sale aside; and Gumz joined in the petition, offering to bid $100,000 and pay $10,000 down. PCA paid $100 down on its $87,000 bid. The petition for resale set out the inadequacy of the advertising, confusion as to the terms of the sale, and lack of authority of the representative of PCA to bid; it was also claimed that the property had special value and that this was not emphasized in the advertising of the property. The trial court granted the petition and ordered a resale. PCA appealed. The order of resale was affirmed.

Justice Wilkie said: "The main question on this appeal is whether or not the trial court abused its discretion in refusing to confirm the sale of the mortgaged premises to the State of Wisconsin and in ordering a resale. This question has been before this court on many occasions and in a very early case of *John Paul Lumber Co.* v. *Neumeister* (1900), the following rule was established which is still the law today: 'The granting or refusing of an application to set aside such sale [foreclosure] and order a resale, as a matter of favor, rests in the sound discretion of the trial court; and its determination will not be disturbed, except for a clear abuse of discretion.'

" 'A further rule is firmly established in Wisconsin that a sale will not be set aside simply because the price obtained by the sale was inadequate. As stated in *A. J. Straus Paving Agency* v. *Jensen,* this rule is confined to cases "where there is absolutely no fact appearing, except that the price is inadequate." The Straus case quotes from *Griswold* v. *Barden* (1911).

" 'Whenever other facts appear, such as mistake, misapprehension, or inadvertence on the part of the interested parties or of intending bidders, as a result of which it seems to the court the failure to obtain a fair and adequate price for the property was due in whole or in part to such mistake, misapprehension, or inadvertence, the court will readily refuse to approve the sale. No fraud is necessary to justify the court in so withholding its approval. The question simply is, is the sale under all the circumstances one of which the court, in justice to all parties, should approve?'

"In other words, a trial court may refuse to confirm a sale if he is satisfied (1) that the price received for the property was inadequate, and (2) that there was a showing of

---

[19] *Bank of America National Trust & Savings Association* v. *Reidy et al.,* 15 Cal.2d 243. 101 P.2d 77.

mistake, misapprehension, or inadvertence on the part of interested parties or prospective bidders." *Gumz* v. *Chickering,* 19 Wis.2d 625, 121 N.W.2d 279 (1963).

***Liability of Bidder.*** The bidder at the foreclosure sale is bound by his bid when the officer in charge of the sale strikes the real estate off to him, even though the sale is not finally binding until confirmation by the court. The court is required to confirm the sale, unless there are valid grounds for refusing to do so. Although some courts hold that the purchaser takes title subject to all existing defects, the better and the majority rule is that the purchaser is entitled to a marketable title, subject only to those defects set out in the notice of sale; and if the court cannot convey to him such marketable title, he may refuse to accept the defective title. The mortgagee or his assignee owning the mortgage debt has the right to bid at a foreclosure sale.

## Other Methods of Foreclosure

In addition to the generally recognized foreclosure by action and sale, several other methods may be used in a minority of states. These include: (1) strict foreclosure; (2) entry and possession, or by writ of entry; (3) writ of *scire facias;* and (4) power of sale. Because of the limitations on their general usage they are discussed in digest form below.

***Strict Foreclosure.*** Under a strict foreclosure, all the rights of the mortgagor are cut off by the strict foreclosure proceedings, and title to the mortgaged property is vested in the mortgagee. There is no actual sale of the property. Where its use is permitted, it is generally limited to cutting off the rights of second mortgagees and others whose claims arose after the date of the first mortgage.

***Entry and Possession, or Writ of Entry.*** Foreclosure by entry and possession is a form of self-help. If the mortgagor refuses to surrender possession peaceably, the mortgagee, after default on the part of the mortgagor, may obtain possession by writ of entry.

When the entry is without process of law, it must be peaceable. In addition to taking possession, the mortgagee must file or record a certificate of entry executed by the mortgagor or witnesses; or he must publish the time, manner, and purpose of the entry, and must execute and file or record an affidavit of such publication.

In the action for a writ of entry, the mortgagee declares on his title to the mortgaged real estate and sets out the default on the part of the mortgagor. An accounting is made to determine the amount due, and a judgment is entered, granting the mortgagee possession of the mortgaged real estate if the mortgagor does not satisfy the judgment within a relatively short period of time. If the mortgagor fails to satisfy the judgment, the mortgagee is put in possession; and if the mortgagor does not redeem the real estate within the statutory period, title to the real estate vests unconditionally in the mortgagee.

In entry by either peaceable possession or writ of entry, the mortgage debt is discharged only to the extent of the reasonable value of the real estate at the time of entry, and the mortgagee is entitled to a judgment for the portion of the mortgage debt not satisfied.[20]

***Writ of Scire Facias.*** Foreclosure by writ of *scire facias sur mortgage* originated in Pennsylvania by colonial legislation. It provides that after default by the mortgagor, a writ of *scire facias* will issue against the mortgagor, his heirs, and personal representatives to show cause why the mortgaged real estate should not be taken in execution to satisfy the mortgage debt. After determination of the amount due, the real estate is sold at a public sale; the proceeds of the sale are applied to the payment of the mortgage debt. Any surplus is paid to the mortgagor. The purchaser gets such title as the mortgagor could convey at the time of the mortgage.

***Power of Sale.*** In the United States the mortgagee does not have the right to sell the mortgaged property on the mortgagor's default unless such right is expressly granted in the mortgage. When granted, it becomes a part of the mortgage and may be exercised by the mortgagee or anyone to whom he assigns the mortgage. In some states, however, the statutes of the state require that all foreclosures take place by action and sale, and in these states a power-of-sale clause in a mortgage is void.[21] Foreclosure by exercise of power of sale is in general use in only 18 states.

The advantage of a foreclosure by exercise of a power of sale is that it enables the party owning the mortgage and mortgage debt to bring about a complete foreclosure of the mortgage without the aid of the court, thereby saving both time and money. Its major disadvantage is that it does not afford the mortgagor reasonable protection from being defrauded by an unscrupulous mortgagee. If the mortgagee, however, has taken an unconscionable advantage of the mortgagor, he (the mortgagor) may bring an action in equity, and the court will set the foreclosure aside.

---

[20] *Louisville Joint Stock Land Bank* v. *Radford,* 295 U.S. 555, 55 S. Ct. 854.

[21] Arizona, Colorado, Idaho, Illinois, Indiana, Iowa, Kansas, Nebraska, Oklahoma, and Oregon.

## Redemption Rights

### Nature of Right

The right of redemption is the right to have the title to the mortgaged real estate restored free and clear of the mortgage lien. The right of redemption may be exercised when the mortgage debt is due; after default, but before any action to foreclose is brought; or under some circumstances, after foreclosure sale.

### Who May Redeem

Under the law in the United States today the mortgagor, his grantee, or any person having in the mortgaged real estate an interest that would be cut off by foreclosure of the mortgage has the right to redeem. This would include all junior mortgagees, junior lien claimants, a wife having a dower interest in the property, a lessee whose leasehold interest would be terminated by the foreclosure, anyone becoming an owner of a fractional portion of the mortgaged real estate subsequent to the execution of the mortgage, or owners of an undivided interest in the mortgaged real estate.[22]

### Payment on Redemption

As a general rule, the person wishing to redeem must pay the entire amount to which the mortgagee is entitled.[23] If the person wishing to redeem has only a fractional interest in the mortgaged real estate or is a junior lien claimant, the mortgage creditor may consent to a partial redemption. Sometimes, a mortgage on a subdivision gives purchasers the right to clear by partial redemption the tracts which they have purchased.

## Federal Regulation of Mortgage Financing

Federal regulation affects many areas of activity in the real estate business. Some of it is very direct, such as regulation of interstate land sales, considered at a later point. The most significant effect, however, has been indirect; it has resulted from the degree of control exerted by the federal government over the lenders of the funds essential to the real estate business. At this point it may be helpful to consider the more important legislation that imposes controls over mortgage lenders.

---

[22] *Anderson* v. *Anderson et al.,* 110 Ind. App. 577, 39 N.E.2d 806.

[23] *Brewster* v. *Terry,* 352 Mo. 967, 180 S.W.2d 600.

## Truth in Lending (Federal Consumer Credit Protection Act)

Truth-in-lending legislation, as its name implies, was originally designed to control the practices of those in the business of granting credit. From the very outset its application was expanded to include the real estate sales industry. While the primary effect of truth in lending on the real estate business has been in the area of advertising to the extent that credit terms are included, it is important that all persons in the real estate sales industry be aware of the fine line that divides the real estate business from the finance business. This requires some knowledge of the fundamental purposes and provisions of the law, which are discussed below.

Contrary to popular opinion truth-in-lending legislation does not purport to *control* interest rates. A lender could charge 200 percent on a credit obligation without violating the truth-in-lending law (although he might very well be violating some form of usury statute) because truth in lending does not control his interest charge. What truth-in-lending laws do require is that the cost of credit be disclosed to the borrower. The logic of the law is simple: not all borrowers are entitled to be treated equally so far as the cost of credit is concerned; this will depend upon the individual borrower's ability to repay and his reputation for willingness to repay any extensions of credit to him. The purpose of truth in lending is to permit the borrower to "shop" for credit, to compare between lenders the expense of borrowing. Many transactions are not covered because they involve loans of such size or such type that the borrower is presumed to be sophisticated enough to be able to discern the cost of credit for himself. For the typical residential sale, however, the legislation is clearly applicable, and this is one reason that brokers and salespersons need to be knowledgeable about it.

The second important reason for considering truth in lending is that there is an important definition to understand: Who is a "creditor" under the act? Clearly, those in the normal business of lending money are governed by the act. Usually, the real estate salesman or broker is not in this category; however, the act also applies to those who *arrange for* credit that is extended by others. It is not at all unusual for a real estate salesman or broker to assist a buyer in finding credit with which to consummate the sale. Indeed, this ability and service frequently represents the difference between completing the sale (and earning a commission) and losing it. In normal real estate brokerage operation, truth in lending will not apply unless two tests are met: the broker has knowledge of the terms of credit *and* he participates in the preparation of the loan documents. Then he is engaged in the business of granting credit and is responsible to see that there is a full disclosure of the terms and that evidence of the borrower's understanding is obtained. Short of this degree of participation the broker (or salesman) need not concern himself with compliance during the lending process.

Perhaps the most important feature of truth in lending as far as the real estate sales industry is concerned is the regulation of advertising of real estate for sale. Simply stated, the law requires a full disclosure of the credit terms being offered. While some relaxation in the rules relating to advertising has occurred since the inception of this legislation, it is still quite important that credit terms, when advertised in connection with the sale of residential property, be clearly stated in compliance with the act. Advice of an attorney should be sought in determining the form and content of the advertising program to be pursued. The penalties for violation of truth in lending can be severe and under certain circumstances can even include imprisonment. It is therefore important to be aware of its impact on the real estate business.

## Real Estate Settlement Procedures Act (RESPA)

RESPA[24] differs from the earlier truth-in-lending legislation in terms of its purpose. While truth in lending had, as its primary goal, the *disclosure* of credit terms to borrowers, RESPA has as one of its goals the reduction in cost of obtaining credit in connection with real estate.[25] To a great extent, however, the terms of the act amplify upon the truth-in-lending concept of disclosure. The key to interpreting and understanding RESPA is the fact that the law relates to and governs every *federally related mortgage* loan transaction. Once this concept is accepted and applied to all residential mortgage loans, it is apparent that it means, effectively, *all* mortgage loans on residential real estate, since it is almost impossible to structure a residential sale today that does not involve a federally insured or guaranteed loan, or one that is not being made by a federally regulated lender.

RESPA provides, among other things, that it applies to:

(1) any loan secured by a first lien on 1- to 4-family residential property, including condominiums and cooperatives, which is made by any lender regulated by an agency of the federal government or whose deposits or accounts are insured by any agency of the federal government;

(2) any loan made, insured or assisted by any officer or agency of the federal government or under a housing or urban development or related program administered by the officer or agency;

---

[24] Public Law 93–533 (Dec. 22, 1974) as amended by Public Law 94–205 (Jan. 2, 1976).

[25] Public Laws 93–533 and 94–205, sec. 2.

(3) any loan which is intended to be sold by the originating lender to the Federal National Mortgage Association, the Government National Mortgage Association, the Federal Home Loan Mortgage Corporation, or any institution from which it is to be purchased by the Federal Home Loan Mortgage Corporation[26]

The above sweeping language leaves out very few residential mortgage transactions. While it is true that there are exceptions to the coverage of the act, they are either commercial in nature or of such a magnitude that the parties are presumed to be sophisticated enough not to require protection by federal regulation.

Other requirements are as follows:

(1) the use of a specified "Uniform Settlement Statement," which requires detailed itemization of charges and which must be used even if the person conducting the settlement is *not* the lender;

(2) the settlement statement must be made available to the borrower at least one day in advance of the settlement or closing;

(3) a special booklet entitled "Settlement Costs" is provided to all lenders who are then obligated by RESPA to make it available to the borrower not less than three days after the loan application is received; the contents of the booklet are specified by the act and regulations;

(4) the lender must provide at the time of the loan application good faith estimates of the closing costs to be anticipated by the borrower;

(5) the lender is limited in the amounts which may be required to be placed in escrow by the borrower to meet anticipated taxes, insurance premiums, and other charges;

(6) kickbacks, referral fees, and the like in connection with the placement of "real estate settlement business," such as title insurance, are prohibited and severe penalties are imposed for any violation of this portion of the act; lenders may not dictate the title insurance company to be utilized;

(7) the true identity of the borrower must be made available to regulatory officials, with certain exceptions.

In addition, RESPA requires that the Secretary of Housing and Urban Development (HUD) establish, on a limited basis, model recordation systems with the goal of simplification and reduction of costs of existing systems. HUD must also report on any recommendations it may have for further legislation. It is obvious from the above digest of the provisions of RESPA that continued federal involvement in and regulation of residential financing (and, therefore, sales) must be expected. More important, perhaps, is the fact that authority is granted to HUD to prescribe rules, regulations, and interpretations as needed. The result of this sort of provision in sweeping legislation of this nature is the creation of uncertainty

---

[26] Public Laws 93–533 and 94–205, sec. 102.

on a day-to-day basis that requires of the person active in the real estate business constant vigilance to change.

## FHA and VA Influences on Financing

### Introduction

In the daily conduct of the real estate brokerage business, as it is affected by governmental regulation in the area of finance, there is no greater or more significant influence than that of the Federal Housing Administration and the Veterans Administration. From an administrative viewpoint, and in terms of effect on marketing of residential housing, most active brokers think of the two as one aspect of federal control or effect. From a legal standpoint the two programs are quite different, however, and it is important to recognize the legal distinction because of the difference in practice. The fundamental difference is simply that FHA *insures* qualified mortgage loans and that the VA *guarantees* the repayment of qualified loans up to a given amount, which changes from time to time. In the FHA insured loan at least some down payment is required, and an insurance premium is included in the interest rate to subsidize the program. In the VA guaranteed loan, *no* down payment will be required (within limits) and the percentage of the loan guaranteed versus the entire amount of the loan provides the motivation to the lender to make the loan.

### Effect on Quality of Housing

While both FHA- and VA-supported mortgages may be used for new and relatively new housing, the two programs have had their greatest effect in the area of sales of older housing in the lower price range. Traditional mortgages—the "conventional" mortgages—are difficult to obtain on older properties unless the borrower is able to make a very substantial down payment at the time of purchase. The reason for this, of course, is that the lender's security is less valuable and less marketable in the event of a default. With the dramatic increase in the cost of housing in recent years, it has become far more difficult for buyers to accumulate enough money to make a large down payment, and the low or no down payment programs offered by FHA and VA backing have become very popular. It must be clearly understood, however, that FHA and VA are not lenders; they are insurers and guarantors. The loans are still made by mortgage-lending sources: banks, savings and loan associations, and mortgage companies. Nevertheless, because the loans are insured or guaranteed by FHA and VA, both of them exercise a great deal of control over the lending process. Initially, the proposed borrower must be "qualified" by FHA or VA in terms of ability to repay the loan and must have an acceptable credit history. This analysis is made by the lender in accordance with guidelines and forms dictated by FHA and VA. Final approval is the province of FHA or VA, however, rather than by the lender. Second, the property itself is subjected to an inspection and appraisal by appraisers who are designated by FHA and VA. The report of the inspector/appraiser will note all defects that need to be repaired before the property will qualify for a loan based on the appraised value. It is in this area that the programs have significantly influenced the upgrading of older housing. While the emphasis in the inspection may change from time to time, the report will usually stress such things as electrical wiring, insulation, roofs and guttering, septic systems, and exterior painting or repair. The objective, of course, is to make the property livable at the time of sale, so that the new owner will not have the financial burden of making such repairs in addition to the burden of making the mortgage payments. Without this requirement the loan would be questionable at the outset. The cost of the repairs must, as a general rule, be paid for by the seller. The program has resulted in the upgrading of a substantial stock of older homes.

**Interest Rates and Discount Points**

In order to make suitable housing more generally available at reasonable costs, both FHA and VA dictate the maximum rate of interest that may be charged to the borrower. This rate is changed from time to time, depending upon prevailing money market conditions, but it is generally lower than rates being charged for conventional mortgages. Since the FHA and VA supported loan is being made by a lender who is in the business for a profit, some adjustment must be made in order to induce the lender to make the loan at a lower rate than could otherwise be obtained. The solution has been the very often misunderstood "discount point." In understanding discount points, it is helpful to consider them as simply a rate-equalizing factor. That is, if the lender could obtain 9.75 percent on a conventional mortgage loan but is limited to an 8.75 percent rate on an FHA or VA mortgage loan it is apparent that there is no motivation to make the lower rate loan. In order to provide this motivation the lender is paid the difference in yield at the time of closing. This is accomplished by determining the difference in yield over the life of the loan in terms of a percentage of the loan and converting it into a number of "discount points." While the determination of the amount the lender will require at the time of closing may vary, a common rule of thumb is that for each ⅛ of a percent given up in the interest rate being charged, the lender will require one "point" in cash at the time of closing. A point is then converted to a percentage of the loan being made, with each point being equal to one percent. To illustrate, assuming that there is a full 1 percent difference between conventional rates and FHA or VA rates, and the amount of the *loan* (not the purchase price) is $20,000, the lender will require at the closing 8 points, or 8 percent of the loan, which in this case equals $1,600. This is interest that is being paid in advance. From a practical standpoint the borrower must repay the full amount of the loan, $20,000, with interest at, say, 8.75 percent. The lender, however, has actually advanced only $18,400 (the $20,000 loan less the $1,600 in points), which clearly increases the yield back up to that which could be obtained from a conventional loan of $20,000 at 9.75 percent.

### Regulation of Discounts

The FHA and VA regulations do not permit the borrower to pay the discount points, but they do permit the charging to the buyer of a 1 percent "origination fee." (To what extent this fee also constitutes interest in advance is debatable.) As a result there is only one source for the payment of the discount points: the seller. In effect the seller must accept a discounted price for the property. In our example, above, if the gross selling price was $22,000, it is obvious that, after paying the $1,600 worth of discount points, the true sales price is reduced to $20,400. There is, of course, no legal requirement that the seller agree to sell to a buyer who will obtain FHA or VA financing—and unless the sales contract obligates the seller to pay this expense, he cannot be compelled to do so. As a practical matter, however, his older house may not be marketable any other way. Therefore, the subject matter of discount points should always be covered in the purchase agreement. Usually, the seller will want to limit his exposure to this expense and will insert in the contract the maximum number of points he will pay. If at the time of closing a higher charge is made, the seller need not pay more than he has agreed to pay, and the deal may fall through. It is therefore customary to obtain a commitment in advance from the lender as to the amount of discount that will be charged. Lenders who specialize in FHA and VA supported lending usually have available free literature on the subject. Because of the frequent changes that occur in this field, they should be consulted for current information.

# Chapter 13

# Recent Mortgage Practice Developments

In this chapter the fundamental mortgage law principles discussed in Chapter 12 are amplified. Included are discussions of various mortgage forms that have developed to meet the needs of specific applications. Separate mortgage types for construction and development projects are covered, along with various types of junior mortgages. In recent years, changing conditions in credit markets have forced many changes in practice. One of the most striking changes has been the growth of seller-assisted financing, frequently referred to as "creative financing." In these arrangements the seller assumes the role of the supplier of credit, usually because of the limits on financing available from traditional sources. Not all of this activity has been defensive in nature. In many cases seller-assisted financing represents an aggressive approach aimed at maximizing profits. All of the forms of mortgage discussed here can be utilized by individuals who, because of their unfamiliarity with the lending function, need to be made aware of the consequences of such activity.

Seller-assisted financing may include several schemes that are intended to preserve existing financing at favorable rates. Sales arrangements that utilize the "assumption" or "wraparound" of existing mortgages are therefore covered in some detail. At the same time, lenders have taken steps to limit the use of these techniques by inserting in mortgages the "due-on-sale" clause. This clause accelerates the mortgage debt so that it is payable in full in the event of a sale of the mortgaged property. This clause effectively eliminates the assumption of existing financing in most cases. Various alternative mortgage plans have also been devised by lenders to share the risk of interest rate changes or to transfer that risk to the borrower. These devices are also included in this chapter.

A major development in mortgage financing over the years has been the organization of a well-defined market for the sale of mortgages by lenders to investors. While not new, this practice has been intensively developed in order to insure a constant source of funds for the residential mortgage market. Therefore, the mechanics of this process are discussed in some detail in this chapter. Even here, salability of the mortgage is an important consideration for the seller who provides financing. Often, seller-assisted financing is a matter of necessity; there is no intent on the part of the seller to invest in the mortgage. It is often an accommodation that must be offered in order to complete the sale. The ability to exchange the mortgage for cash is an important consideration. Organized markets are developing that ease the sale of such mortgages, but the mortgages must be carefully structured in order to be salable.

## Specific Forms of Mortgages

### Package Mortgages

The so-called package mortgage is one that not only includes the real estate but also expressly includes all fixtures and appliances on the premises. The package mortgage has been used extensively in recent years in the financing of houses. Such mortgages usually expressly include, as a part of the real estate, the heating and air-conditioning equipment, kitchen range, refrigerator, dishwasher, garbage disposal unit, washer and dryer, food freezer, and other such appliances.

The rights of persons having or acquiring a security interest in personal property that is to be attached to real estate so that it becomes a fixture and the rights of a person who acquires a security interest in fixtures are defined in the Uniform Commercial Code.[1]

The code does not define fixtures, but it does provide: "(1) The rules of this section do not apply to goods incorporated into a structure in the manner of lumber, bricks, tile, cement, glass, metalwork, and the like and no security interest in them exists under this Article unless the structure remains personal property."

Under this provision of the code, if the security interest attaches to the goods before they become fixtures, and is perfected as required by the code, it takes priority as to the goods over all persons who have an interest in the real estate. If the security interest attaches to the goods after they become fixtures, it has

[1] Uniform Commercial Code, Art. 9, Sec. 9–313.

priority over subsequently acquired interests in the real estate but is invalid against any person with an interest in the real estate at the time the security interest attaches if such person has not in writing consented to the security interest or has disclaimed an interest in the goods as fixtures. The above-described security interest in fixtures does not take priority over subsequent purchasers, lienees, or creditors who do not have knowledge of the security interest and who acquire their interest in the real estate before the security interest in the fixture is perfected. Also, an advancement under a prior encumbrance, if such advancement is made without notice or knowledge of the security interest in the fixture and before the security interest is perfected, has priority over the unperfected security interest.

Under the provisions of the code, the party having a security interest in a fixture may, in the event of default of the debtor, remove the fixture from the real estate, "but he must reimburse any encumbrancer or owner of the real estate who is not the debtor and who has not otherwise agreed for the cost of repair of any physical injury, but not for any diminution of the value of the real estate caused by the absence of the goods removed or by any necessity for replacing them."[2]

If an item of property is not attached to or used with the real estate so that it becomes a fixture, a mortgage on the real estate would not create a lien on such property. If the real estate mortgage is so drafted that it purports to create a lien on personal property on the mortgaged premises when such property is not a fixture, the effect of the filing of such a mortgage, as a real estate mortgage, on the described personal property will depend on the laws of the state. In general, to create a lien on personal property valid against bona fide purchasers or mortgagees for value or judgment lien creditors, the mortgage would have to be filed or recorded as a chattel mortgage; or in code states, it would have to be perfected as required by the code.

Intermountain Food Equipment Company (hereinafter referred to as Equipment Company) sold to Waller on a conditional sales contract certain kitchen equipment for use in the Hotel Washington. At the time of the sale and the installation of the equipment in the hotel, Connecticut Mutual Life Insurance Company had a real estate mortgage on the hotel real estate and a chattel mortgage on the equipment and personal property. Equipment Company filed its conditional sales contract as required by the statutes of the state. Default was made in the payments on the real estate and chattel mortgages, and also on Equipment Company's conditional sales contract. The real estate mortgage was foreclosed, and the mortgagee claimed that it had priority over Equipment Company's conditional sales contract. Equipment Company brought an action to recover possession of the kitchen equipment

---

[2] Uniform Commercial Code, Sec. 9–313(5).

covered by its conditional sales contract. The court granted Equipment Company's request.

Justice McFadden said: "In the instant action we are dealing with specific chattels sold under a duly recorded conditional sales agreement. The cause of action here is in regard to the specific items of personal property, the validity of the conditional sales agreement, and whether or not such agreement was breached as to entitle respondent to possession of such articles of personal property. In the mortgage foreclosure action the cause of action was based on the note, and the real and chattel mortgages given to secure that note. If it was to be contended in the mortgage foreclosure action that the specific articles of personal property covered by the conditional sales contract were subject to the lien of either the real estate or chattel mortgages there involved, it was incumbent upon the plaintiff in that action to make such allegation in specific terms and fully advise respondent herein. The law is generally well settled that where the removal of a fixture will not materially injure the premises, a seller retaining title to such property may assert his right against any prior mortgagee or vendor of the reality. And this is true regardless of notice to the prior mortgagee or vendor." *Intermountain Food Equipment Company* v. *Waller*, Idaho, 383 P.2d 612 (1963).

## Construction Mortgage

A construction mortgage is one given on real estate to secure a loan made for the purpose of enabling the borrower to erect a building on the real estate or to remodel or repair an existing building. Since the amount loaned will, as a general rule, be more than the value of the mortgaged real estate, either the lender will obligate himself to advance the money as it is needed to pay labor or material bills as they mature, or he will pay the entire amount to a trustee, who will be authorized to pay it out as required under the terms of the construction contract. The relation between the lender-mortgagee, the borrower-mortgagor, and the contractor will be defined either by the terms of the mortgage or by the terms of a supplemental contract entered into by the parties.

The courts in all the states have consistently held that a mortgage given to secure future advances that the mortgagee is obligated to make is valid, if properly executed and recorded, against all subsequent purchasers, mortgagees, or lien claimants, even though they acquired their interest in the real estate before the advances were actually made.[3] Under the usual terms of a construction mortgage the lender-mortgagee binds himself to make future advances, the total amount of which is a sum certain. Since the lender-mortgagee is obligated to disburse the money, each payment would relate back to the date of the mortgage and would have priority over claims against or interests acquired in the mortgaged property subsequent to that date but before the money is paid out.

---

[3] *Taulbee et al.* v. *First National Bank of Jackson et al.*, 279 Ky. 153, 130 S.W.2d 48.

Frequently, the sum loaned will be paid into a special bank account in the lender-mortgagee's name as trustee, or some third person may act as trustee of the fund. The trustee will sign all checks issued in payment for the work and materials. Under this arrangement, the mortgage or contract may provide that checks shall be signed by the trustee and countersigned by the borrower-mortgagor. Payments are usually made only on the production of an architect's or engineer's certificate.

If the money is held in trust, the trustee will be bound by any oral promise that he makes to laborers, materials handlers, subcontractors, or contractors to pay their claims out of the fund.[4] The trustee should keep accurate records of all amounts expended and all amounts promised; otherwise, he may obligate himself to make payments in excess of the amount of the trust fund or the sum covered by the mortgage.

### Blanket Mortgage

A blanket mortgage is one that creates a lien on several tracts of land or properties and includes a provision obligating the mortgagee to release individual tracts or properties from the mortgage when certain stipulated payments are made on the mortgage debt. For example, suppose that Archer has purchased a 20-acre tract of land, which he plans to subdivide into 20 lots. In order to obtain the funds necessary to develop the subdivision, he borrows money from the bank and gives the bank a mortgage on the 20-acre tract to secure the loan. Archer plans to obtain the money to pay the loan by selling lots. To facilitate carrying out the plan, a provision will be included in the mortgage whereby the bank will agree to release from the mortgage the lots sold, provided stipulated payments have been made in reduction of the mortgage debt. Such a mortgage is known as a *blanket mortgage*. Payments against the debt secured by such a mortgage are generally, however, not simply a pro rata portion of the debt; usually a somewhat higher repayment for each sale is required. If we assume, for example, that Archer in this case borrowed $20,000, the repayment from the sales might be required at $1,500 per lot rather than $1,000. In this way the lender is assured of repayment before the entire subdivision is sold. The risk that a few lots will remain unsold is therefore cast upon the developer rather than the lender.

The concept of the blanket mortgage has been expanded to include other situations than the development of vacant land for which it was first adapted. It is now frequently used to facilitate the purchase of a new residence by an individual who has not yet sold his existing residence, so as to have the proceeds of that

[4] *City National Bank & Trust Co. of Salem* v. *Hassler,* 9 N.J. Super. 153, 75 A. 2d 546.

sale available to apply against the purchase price of the new residence. In such a case, assuming that the borrower owns the existing residence free and clear or has a substantial equity in it, the lender will take a mortgage upon both properties until such time as the first one is sold. At that time the proceeds of sale are applied against the total debt, and the mortgage is released only as to the sold property while remaining in effect as to the newly purchased property. The use of this device permits the purchaser of new housing to buy under favorable terms and at his convenience, rather than awaiting the sale of his existing residence to generate the cash needed to make the purchase possible. The adaptation of the blanket mortgage for this use has been fostered by the savings and loan industry. It resulted from their historical limitation to the field of secured mortgage lending. Commercial banks frequently will use a simpler device: the swing loan. This loan is made for a short term and is unsecured; it is made on the strength of the borrower's promise to repay it from the proceeds of sale of the first property. In view of legislation enacted in 1980 and 1982, which greatly broadened the powers of savings and loan associations, the swing loan can now be utilized by them as well. While the blanket mortgage for this purpose appears cumbersome, it does provide continuous security for the lender.

### Leasehold Mortgages

As noted earlier in Chapter 12, any interest in land may be utilized as security for the repayment of a debt. This rule is subject only to the practical limitations of just what interest in land will be acceptable to the lender. Theoretically, a valid mortgage could be taken on a life estate or a future interest; however, in practice these are hardly ever defined clearly enough so that a lender will accept them. One interest that has become important in recent years is the long-term lease of real estate. In commercial applications particularly, leasehold financing has become quite popular because of the advantages it provides to both the owner of real estate and the user of real estate. For the owner of real estate, a long-term lease to a financially responsible tenant provides him with an income from the real estate while he is essentially passive, and the property will revert to him at the end of the lease. For the user of real estate assets, the long-term lease provides, in effect, ownership rights for an extended period of time without the investment of capital in ground. The essential ingredient that remains to be added is the construction of the necessary improvements with borrowed money. Lenders recognize that their primary source of repayment is the success of the user, and that the underlying real estate is only a secondary source in the event of default. They have also recognized that "ownership" as a tenant for a period of 30 to 50 years is the equivalent of absolute ownership because of the anticipated obsolescence of the improvements. Since the typical term of a commercial loan to construct business improvements will be shorter than the term of the lease, the loan is made without really anticipating a default and foreclosure. Even should they occur, however, the lender will still have an asset of considerable value against which to proceed. Loans for the construction of improvements are therefore frequently made upon the security of the leasehold estate and the improvements themselves.

In some cases, the land will be of such great value because of its location that the lender will require more security than just the leasehold and improvements. In such cases the lender may require that the owner of the ground, in effect, mortgage it to secure the repayment of his tenant's debt. This device is known as "subordinated leasehold financing." Under this approach the owner agrees to subordinate his lease to the lender's mortgage. For all practical purposes he is mortgaging the ground while the tenant is mortgaging the improvements. The lender, in the event of default, may proceed against both assets. The owner of the underlying real estate is generally compensated for this additional risk by a higher rental, as well as the retention of the right to cure any default by the tenant in order that he can protect his ownership rights from the possibility of foreclosure.

### The Open-End Mortgage

A type of mortgage known as an *open-end mortgage* is being used with increasing frequency, especially in the field of home financing. The open-end mortgage in general use includes a package provision (discussed under the heading "Package Mortgage," above). It further provides that the mortgage secures (1) a note executed by the mortgagor to the mortgagee and (2) any advances made by the mortgagee to the mortgagor, or his successor in title, for any purpose at any time. This provision is usually followed by a statement of a maximum amount to be secured by the mortgage, exclusive of any sums the mortgagee may pay in taxes, assessments, insurance premiums, and so forth, to protect his security.

The purpose of such a mortgage is to permit the mortgagee to make advances for the purchase of appliances, repairs, and remodeling; thus the mortgagor is enabled to cover all these indebtednesses by one mortgage, thereby saving the expense of making several loans and usually enabling him to finance his borrowing at a rate of interest lower than that charged on second-mortgage loans.

The open-end mortgage is valid and enforceable between the parties to the mortgage. However, the courts are not in accord as to the rights of subsequent purchasers, mortgagees, or lien claimants who have obtained rights in the mortgaged real estate after the execution and recording of the mortgage, but before advances are made under the terms of the mortgage.

Under the laws of those states that have adopted the Uniform Commercial Code, a security interest in goods that were to become fixtures, or a security interest in fixtures perfected before any advance is made, would have priority over the lien of the open-end mortgagee's advance. The Uniform Commercial Code does not affect the rights of subsequent real estate mortgagees and lien claimants other than those having a security interest in fixtures. In regard to such claimants, a majority of the states in which the question has been litigated have held that the optional advance has priority over intervening claims, unless the open-end mortgagee has actual notice or knowledge of the intervening claims at the time he makes the optional advance.

For example, suppose that the mortgagor has executed an open-end mortgage and thereafter borrows money from a lender other than the mortgagee, giving such lender a second mortgage on the real estate. If the first mortgagee, after the second mortgage is executed and recorded, makes advances under the open-end mortgage without actual notice or knowledge of the existence of the second mortgage, such advances will have priority over the recorded second mortgage. Under this rule the mortgagee in an open-end mortgage is not required to examine the records each time he makes an advance under the mortgage.[5]

However, if the second mortgagee or someone acting in his behalf gives the open-end mortgagee notice of the second mortgage, or if he has knowledge of it at the time he makes the advance, the lien of the second mortgage would have priority.

The minority view[6] holds that an intervening claim has priority over a subsequent advance. In the above example, under the minority rule the recorded second mortgage would have priority over subsequent advances made under the open-end mortgage, even though the first mortgagee had no actual notice or knowledge of the existence of the second mortgage. Under the minority rule the recording of the second mortgage or other claim is constructive notice to the first mortgagee. Under this rule the holder of an open-end mortgage, in order to protect himself, must examine the records before each advancement.[7]

---

[5] *Oaks.* v. *Weingartner et al.,* 105 Cal. App.2d 598, 234 P.2d 194.

[6] Held in Illinois, Michigan, Ohio, and Pennsylvania.

[7] *Ginsberg et al.* v. *Capitol City Wrecking Co.,* 300 Mich. 712, 2 N.W.2d 892.

## Second Mortgages

As noted earlier in Chapter 12, the owner of an interest in real estate may mortgage or encumber that interest as security for the repayment of a debt. In many cases the initial or first mortgage may secure a debt that is far less than the market value of the real estate. The mortgagor has the "equity" of the difference between the amount of the secured debt and the price the property would bring if sold. This difference is an interest of value that may be used as security for additional borrowing. The security device most often used in such additional borrowing is simply another mortgage on the same real estate. The mortgagor cannot pledge or mortgage more than he owns. The second mortgagee then must take a junior position to that of the first mortgagee, whose claim against the property has already been established. If the mortgagor fails to pay both debts, the first mortgagee is in a preferred position. Its debt must be completely paid first. Any excess funds that result from the foreclosure sale are then applied to the payment of the second debt. It is possible that there may even be third and fourth mortgages on the same property. In such a case each mortgagee must await the payment of those debts that are prior to and superior to its claim.

It would appear that the second mortgagee is in a poor position to enforce payment of the second debt. This is not the case. The second mortgagee has all of the same rights to bring a foreclosure action as the first mortgagee. These rights are limited only by the fact that the first mortgagee can insist upon full payment before the second mortgagee may receive any payment. In practice, the second mortgagee sues both the mortgagor and the first mortgagee. The first mortgagee must then participate in the foreclosure action or risk losing its preferred position. Therefore, *both* mortgages are foreclosed in the same lawsuit. The proceeds of sale are then paid in order of priority of the mortgages. Even the threat of foreclosure by the second mortgagee is therefore a strong enforcement weapon.

Second mortgages have found several uses in seller-assisted financing plans. For example, the seller may take back from the purchaser a second mortgage for all or a part of the down payment. The seller then becomes a second mortgagee. The first mortgagee, providing the basic financing, will be in a superior position. The rules already discussed will apply. Since the second mortgagee can look only to the owner's equity for security, his risk will be greater. Normally, this would justify a higher interest rate. This has not always been the case when traditional mortgage money has been scarce or expensive. In fact, it has often been necessary for sellers to offer a preferential interest rate on such mortgages.

The second mortgage may also be used to support a sale by assumption of an existing mortgage. If the balance due on the existing mortgage is low, the second mortgage may be used to supplement it. The rate on the second mortgage can be adjusted to "blend" with that of the existing mortgage. An example is set out below:

| | |
|---|---|
| Sales price | $100,000 |
| Down payment | 20,000 |
| Balance due | 80,000 |
| Existing mortgage | 40,000 |
| Second mortgage | 40,000 |

If the existing mortgage has a low rate of interest its assumption may be attractive. The balance of the financing needed can be provided by the second mortgage. Whether the seller must be the second mortgagee or not depends upon market conditions. The rate of interest on the second mortgage may be relatively high. The combination of the existing low-rate mortgage and the high-rate second mortgage may be blended to make the financing package attractive.

It is also possible to use the second mortgage at a below-market rate in combination with a first mortgage at the market rate. This represents a discount by the seller as well as the acceptance of a relatively high-risk debt. Such a combination may be the only practical way to market the property when long-term interest rates are very high. In any such case the seller must recognize the high risk that exists in the second mortgage because of the priority of the first mortgage. Whether or not a higher price can be charged for the property to compensate for this higher risk will depend upon market conditions.

### Wraparound Mortgages

From the concept of the second mortgage there has developed the "wraparound" mortgage used in commercial financing. It is utilized to secure additional financing when the existing first mortgage has been paid down to the point at which the borrower has a substantial equity in the property and the terms of the first mortgage are more favorable than those upon which additional credit is currently available. In such a case the mortgagor and second mortgagee may execute a new mortgage, which is designed to preserve the benefits of the first mortgage while making added funds available at more favorable rates than could be obtained by a completely new borrowing of the total amount needed. This second mortgage provides that the second mortgagee will take over the mortgagor's obligations under the first mortgage. In this sense the second mortgage is "wrapped around" the first mortgage. Its benefits may be best illustrated by the following example:

> The ABC Corp. owns real estate and improvements conservatively valued at $200,000, against which there is an outstanding first mortgage of $50,000 at 6 percent with 10 years remaining on the repayment schedule. The corporation needs an additional $100,000 for expansion and working capital, and could easily borrow $150,000 by a new first mortgage borrowing, of which $50,000 would retire the existing debt. Because of current money market conditions, however, the rate of interest for the new $150,000 borrowing would be 9 percent, thereby increasing the cost of debt service. Instead, a wraparound mortgage in the amount of $150,000 is negotiated with a lender at a rate of 7.5 percent. The reason for this favorable treatment is that the new lender actually lays out only $100,000 in cash and assumes the $50,000 obligation, which will be paid as due from the payments received from ABC. In effect, the second lender is earning 1.5 percent on funds not laid out and can therefore accept 7.5 percent on the $100,000 actually loaned. The effect to the lender is a net interest rate in excess of 9 percent that his money could otherwise earn, while the borrower realizes a substantial savings in interest expense. The first mortgage must, of course, be free of any prohibition against such a second mortgage.

The wraparound mortgage is a good illustration of the flexibility that exists in the mortgage, even though such flexibility is not immediately apparent when studying fundamental mortgage law. It has found application in seller-assisted financing of residential properties during the recent years of generally increasing interest rates. In such sales the seller will sell the property without paying off the existing mortgage but, as part of the sales transaction, agree to pay it off on schedule. The sale will include a down payment by the buyer plus a mortgage back to the seller for the entire difference between the sales price and the down payment. For example:

| | |
|---|---|
| Sales price | $50,000 |
| Down payment | 10,000 |
| Mortgage to seller | 40,000 |
| (Existing mortgage | 20,000) |

Upon receipt of payments from the buyer the seller will make the necessary payments against the existing first mortgage and will retain the difference. The rate charged on the wraparound mortgage will normally be higher than that on the existing mortgage. This is not, however, essential to the use of the wraparound. Whether the seller is profiting from the use of the wraparound or is really discounting on an installment basis will be determined by the market conditions that motivate the parties to use the wraparound. It must be recognized that the existing first mortgage remains superior to the wraparound mortgage and that the existing first mortgage must not prohibit a sale without accelerating the first mortgage debt. When these conditions are met, the seller holding the wraparound mortgage has tighter control than would a second mortgagee and will at least be aware of any default by the buyer at an early date. The seller could, of course, continue to make the payments on the first mortgage in order to avoid its foreclosure. This would permit time for the seller and buyer to work out an alternative payment program, a deed in lieu of foreclosure, or whatever other settlement appears necessary, without the pressure of an impending foreclosure by the first mortgage holder.

## Purchase Money Mortgages

Conditions in credit markets have from time to time severely hampered the marketability of both residential and commercial real estate. Often the seller of either type of property has found it necessary to become the sole supplier of credit in order to market the property at a desired price. In still other cases the seller has desired to participate in the financing as a form of long-term investment. To accomplish either of these goals the seller may take back, as a part of the purchase price, a mortgage on the property sold. Such a mortgage has come to be called a purchase money mortgage. It clearly represents the most direct fashion in which seller-assisted financing can be structured. Except for a slightly greater degree of protection, the seller in this situation occupies the same position as would be occupied by a commercial lender. The additional protection afforded such a seller is a priority over judgments against the buyer that existed before the purchase. This purchase money mortgage will also have priority over any other mortgage on the property that may have been executed by the buyer before he took title to the property. It will also prevail over mechanics' liens and dower or curtesy interests that attach upon acquisition of title.[8]

The acceptance by the seller of a purchase money mortgage as part of the sale price puts him in the position of lender as well as seller. In assuming such an unusual role he should be made aware of the limitations upon his rights to enforce the underlying obligation of the buyer. At a later point in this chapter are discussed some lender's considerations that should also be taken into account by such a seller. Primary among these are the due-on-sale clause and the marketability of the mortgage. In addition to the standard security considerations, the seller in this situation needs to be attentive to the warranties made by him during the sales transaction. The purchase money mortgage creates a continuing and personal relationship between seller and buyer. Under these circumstances any

[8] *Melrose* v. *Industrial Associates,* 136 Conn. 518, 72 A. 2d 469.

alleged or real breach of warranty made during the sales process can present difficult problems. Should the buyer withhold payments to enforce a claim for damages, the seller may be put to substantial expense to enforce his claim for payment of the mortgage debt.

## Recent Mortgage Developments

As suggested in the introduction to this chapter, recent years have seen considerable change in the residential mortgage area. Much of this change has resulted from frequent shifts in interest rates for the long-term loans traditionally used to finance residential purchases. The trend in interest rates has been generally upward; this has suggested to sellers that existing financing has an advantage if it can be preserved for a new owner. In some recent periods the ability to transfer this financing was almost essential in order to market properties at all. This was particularly true if the seller was not in a position to provide the financing himself by taking back a purchase money mortgage at a favorable rate of interest. This set of circumstances focused attention on procedures that had long been available but largely unused: the sale "subject to" the existing mortgage and the "assumption" of the existing mortgage. Both approaches had one important common feature: the existing mortgage with its favorable rate of interest fixed for some years into the future was not paid off at the time of sale. Instead it was kept in place for the benefit of the purchaser who made the future payments to the lender.

The essential ingredient to this approach to real estate financing was the long-term (often 30 years) amortized, fixed-interest mortgage, which was almost universally used in this country for residential financing for almost 50 years. Initially, as interest rates for new loans began to move upward, the preservation of the existing financing was a distinct advantage to the seller that often permitted him to charge a premium for his property because of his ability to transfer the existing financing to the buyer. At a later time, when mortgage rates reached historic highs (in excess of 16 percent), it became almost essential for the seller to transfer the existing financing. Otherwise he would find no buyers willing to borrow at such high rates, even if they were qualified to do so. Whether a seller wanted to participate in such a sale was no longer an issue. Without his cooperation on this point there would either be a sale at a greatly discounted price or no sale at all. The legal rules surrounding such sales are discussed in detail in this section. Included is the all-important question of the continuing liability of the seller for his original debt even after the sale.

During this period of time, mortgage lenders were under severe pressures resulting from their increasing cost of funds as compared to their low-yielding portfolios of mortgages with their remaining long terms and fixed interest rates. Sales subject to or by assumption of existing mortgages aggravated what was already a difficult position. In self defense, the mortgage industry changed its policies to attempt to limit such sales. Substantially all mortgage forms were amended to include a clause that accelerated the entire remaining balance of the debt in the event the mortgaged property was sold. This clause became known as the "due-on-sale" clause, and its application generated a great deal of litigation between borrowers and lenders over the validity of such a clause. Generally, the clause has been upheld, and this has drastically curtailed the transfer of existing financing from seller to buyer. This clause is discussed in detail in this section.

Largely as a result of the generally higher cost of mortgage money and the uncertainty of the future, new mortgage forms have been devised. In most cases the new mortgages have been redesigned to transfer the risk of future cost increases to the borrower. This is accomplished in some cases by simply shortening the term of the loan to compel periodic renegotiation of the interest rate. In others the rate is designed to adjust itself periodically on the basis of some economic indicator. The net effect of these mortgages is to shift the interest rate risk from the lender to the borrower. The legal characteristics of these devices are discussed in this section. Variations of the standard mortgage have appeared to serve other purposes. The *shared appreciation mortgage* creates a sort of partnership between owner and lender. The basic exchange is a lower interest rate in return for a share of capital appreciation. Some mortgages will permit the owner to borrow against the equity interest established over a period of years, the *reverse annuity* mortgage. These arrangements are also included in this section.

## Fully Amortized Mortgages

For a great many years the standard mortgage payment plan used in this country has been the fully amortized mortgage with a level monthly payment that includes

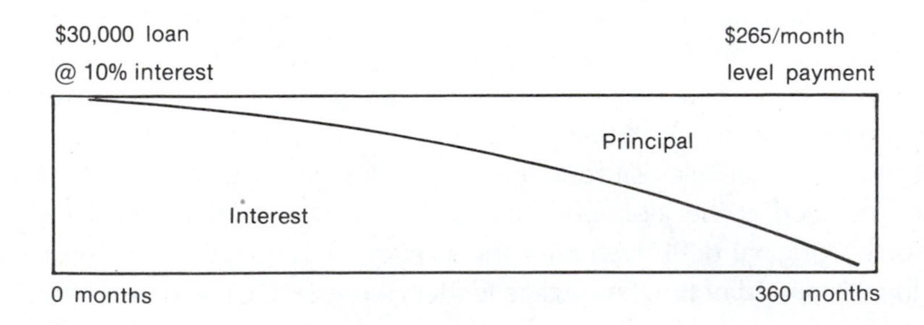

partial payment of principal plus accrued interest. A simple diagram of this payment plan is set out below:
At the outset of this schedule each monthly payment is mostly interest with only a small portion applied to reduce the loan balance. In this illustration the interest on $30,000 at 10 percent for 1 month equals $250, leaving only $15 to apply against principal debt reduction. In the ensuing month the interest on the reduced balance of $29,985 is $249.87, leaving $15.13 to apply to the debt. In the later stages of the repayment schedule this situation is reversed and the debt is ultimately retired. There are no significant legal lessons to be learned from this diagram, but it is helpful in understanding the modifications made by newer mortgage forms.

## Devices That Shorten the Term of the Loan

One approach to the interest rate risk problem has been simply to shorten the time for repayment of the loan. This approach presumes that the lender can forecast the cost of funds for some time into the future, at which time there will occur either a payoff of the existing balance or a renegotiation of the terms to reflect the rates that prevail at that time.

### The Balloon Payment

Simply shortening the term of a fully amortized mortgage would be an unacceptable answer to most borrowers. If the length of time for which the lender will accept a fixed interest rate is, for example, five years, the monthly payments to amortize are prohibitively high for the borrower. For a $30,000 loan at 10 percent for five years, they would be approximately $640 per month. A compromise is represented by the insertion into the mortgage of a call date upon which the remaining balance comes due but retaining the long-term amortization schedule. In our original example the diagram would appear as follows:

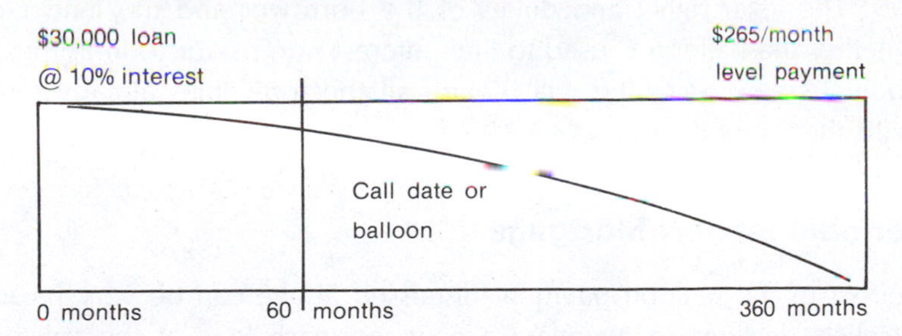


In this arrangement the monthly payments for the first five years are $265.00, as in our original example. On the call date, the "balloon payment" of the entire principal balance becomes due and payable. In this case it would be approximately $28,900.

When the balloon payment comes due it is the obligation of the borrower to pay it in its entirety. Failure to do so will be a default, which could lead to foreclosure and sale. This device compels the borrower to negotiate a new loan with the lender (or some other source) at then-prevailing rates. The obvious advantage to the lender is the opportunity to adjust the rate to a profitable level. Not quite so obvious is the fact that the borrower may have to requalify, and the lender might decline to make a new mortgage. In the absence of a commitment to do so the lender has no obligation to renew the loan. As with other private contracts, the timing of the balloon is negotiable. It may be very short in times when credit markets are unstable, but it can also be reasonably long when lenders are confident of interest rate trends and their ability to predict them.

The balloon payment originally appeared in commercial mortgages some years before it was adapted to residential mortgages. Its attraction persisted into the era of seller-assisted financing of residences. In times when interest rates are so high that buyers decline to borrow and leave the market the sellers have had to offer below-market financing to sell properties. The balloon payment is quite useful in the private purchase money mortgage. In these circumstances it serves as a discount-limiting device for the seller. If, for example, the purchase money mortgage is made at 12 percent when the prevailing rate is 16 percent, the seller is clearly discounting the price. That is, if he received all cash we presume he could invest it at 16 percent. Instead he is receiving 12 percent, thereby giving up the difference in earnings. The longer this arrangement continues, the greater the amount of discount. Therefore, in order to limit this discount, the balloon payment is incorporated into the mortgage. It operates in the same manner already described: when the balloon is due the buyer must pay off the balance of the loan. This may require that the buyer obtain new financing or renegotiate with the seller. The legal rights and duties of the borrower and the lender are the same whether the balloon is used to limit interest rate risk or to limit the amount of discount. A new financing will require all the formalities already discussed, along with their attendant costs.

## The Periodic Review Mortgage

The effect of the balloon payment discussed above can be very harsh if the lender (seller) declines to negotiate a new mortgage loan at the call date. As noted above, additional expense is involved in placing a new mortgage on the property. For these reasons the renegotiable rate mortgage was developed to permit the convenient continuation of the relationship with a simple adjustment in the interest rate. Usually such a commitment on the part of the lender will be conditioned upon such things as continued satisfactory financial condition of the borrower and the physical condition of the property. This mortgage recognizes with precision the problem that is at issue: the interest rate risk. Care must be taken, however, to protect the lender's security interest so that the expense of a new mortgage loan can be avoided. The problem is similar to that discussed earlier in connection with the open-end mortgage. That is, is it legally a new mortgage so that its priority does not date back to the date of the original mortgage? How much is revealed by the recorded instruments has an important bearing on this issue. If the record can be interpreted to classify this device as an open-end arrangement, the same questions of priority can arise. The ultimate solution to the rate review problem, from the lender's standpoint at least, may be the *demand mortgage loan.* In such a loan the note is a demand promissory note that can be called for payment at any time by the lender or noteholder. This approach has proven to be very undesirable from the borrower's standpoint because of the element of uncertainty that it introduces into the transaction.

## Devices That Transfer Interest Rate Risk

In certain credit market conditions it may be quite impossible to forecast interest rates with any degree of certainty even for short periods of time. At the same time, major periodic renegotiation is often unacceptable to borrowers. Lenders may then decide to make long-term commitments, provided they are completely insulated from interest rate risk. This can be accomplished by the use of a variable-rate provision in the mortgage, so that it will adjust itself as credit conditions change. Up to this point only *upside* interest rate risk has been considered. That is, we have concerned ourselves only with the possibility that rates may go up, resulting in losses to the lender if the interest rate in the mortgage is fixed. It is also possible that rates (and the lender's cost of funds) may decline during the period of a fixed-rate mortgage. When this happens the lender experiences something known as downside opportunity, while the loser is the borrower. It is true, of course, that the borrower might choose such a time to refinance, although the standard prepayment penalty clause might effectively prevent this. In any event the inclusion of a true variable-rate provision forces the lender to sacrifice the downside opportunity in order to avoid the upside risk. Typical mortgages of this type are discussed below.

## The Variable-Rate Mortgage

In the true variable-rate mortgage the interest rate charged is adjusted periodically on the basis of the movements of some economic indicator that is mutually acceptable to both the borrower and the lender. Using our earlier illustration of the fully amortized mortgage on a fixed rate, it will be apparent that adjustments in the interest rate from time to time will also require adjustments in the amortization schedule. If rates rise and if the term of the mortgage is fixed, then the monthly payments must increase in order to amortize the debt over the same period of time. In most cases, given the budget characteristics of such an amortization schedule, this increase will be unacceptable to the borrower. An alternative approach to this problem is to permit the payment level to stay constant while lengthening the term over which such payments will be made. The recorded documentation must clearly reveal such a possibility in order to protect the lender's security interest beyond the original term of the loan.

Questions related to the frequency of changes in the interest rate and the selection of the indicator that will dictate these changes are negotiable by the borrower and lender. The most important requirement for the indicator selected would seem to be that it should be beyond the control of either party. Even so, the parties have the power to agree upon any indicator, even the lender's cost of funds. Such a selection would appear to open the door to disputes over the matter of the lender's accounting practices, but it is still an indicator on which the parties might agree. Frequency of change in the interest rate would seem today to be limited only by the frequency with which the indicator changes. The practice is to limit these changes to no more than once a month even though the technology exists for making more frequent changes.

## Adjustable-Rate Mortgages

No significant distinction can be drawn between the variable-rate mortgage and the adjustable-rate mortgage. The adjustable-rate mortgage differs from the true variable-rate mortgage only in that the frequency of redetermining the interest rate and the amount by which it may be changed are limited. That is, the rate may be changed semiannually or annually, with some limit placed upon the extent of any one adjustment. This combination tends to require fewer and less drastic adjustments during the life of the mortgage. The same legal principles apply as would to the true variable-rate mortgage.

## Shared-Appreciation Mortgages

The shared-appreciation mortgage takes a different approach to the interest rate risk problem. Typically, such a mortgage will be negotiated at a fixed rate that is below prevailing market rates. The inducement to the lender to make such a loan is twofold: *(a)* the life of the mortgage is relatively short (seven or eight years), which limits the exposure to loss from the discounted interest rate being charged; and *(b)* at the expiration of the mortgage agreement the borrower must sell the property and share the appreciation in value with the lender. The lender is in a very real sense investing in the borrower's real estate. Presumably, the same lender who cannot predict interest rates for this period of time is comfortable in his ability to predict market appreciation. The amortization schedule used will normally be based upon a long-term payment schedule, with the termination point being structured much the same as the balloon payment already discussed. The major problem presented by this scheme is the requirement that the property be sold at some predetermined point in time. The arrangement presumes there will be an increase in market value of the property during this period. One obvious potential problem is the possibility that the borrower will not want to sell the property but would rather retain it. If this option is to be preserved some mechanism must be provided by which value can be ascertained and the lender paid its fair share of the appreciation. Also, the borrower must contemplate obtaining new financing, not just for the balance due on the original loan but also for the added burden of paying the lender its share of the appreciation. The entire concept depends upon continued appreciation of real estate values generally plus ease of marketing at the time the sale is triggered by the agreement. Elaborate care is necessary to clearly establish the rights of the parties and their duties at the termination point. Whether a court would order specific performance of the agreement to sell and, if so, under what circumstances, remains to be seen. Whether foreclosure is available to a lender who has an equity interest in the property is yet another unanswered question.

## Sales of Mortgaged Real Estate

### Right of Mortgagor to Sell

The mortgagor has the right to sell and convey, or to mortgage the mortgaged real estate or any part thereof to third persons. Any sale or mortgage of the mortgaged real estate does not affect the mortgagee's rights in the property. Ordinarily, the sale or mortgage of the mortgaged real estate may be made without the consent of the mortgagee.[9] The grantee of the mortgagor acquires all the rights of the mortgagor—that is, he has the right to the possession and use of the property, and the right to the rents and profits; but all the rights that he acquires are in subordination to the rights of the mortgagee under the mortgage.

The purchaser of the mortgaged property is not liable for the mortgage debt unless he contracts to pay it. The sale may be (1) free and clear; (2) subject to the mortgage; or (3) subject to the mortgage, the purchaser agreeing to pay the mortgage debt.

### Sale Free and Clear

If the mortgaged property is sold free and clear of the mortgage, the seller-mortgagor contracts to obtain from the mortgagee a discharge of the mortgage either before or at the time of the closing of the sale and the execution of the deed. A substantial portion of the sales of mortgaged real estate are sales free and clear of the mortgage.

Some mortgages contain acceleration clauses maturing the mortgage debt and making it due and payable on the sale of the mortgaged real estate by the mortgagor. In other transactions the purchaser may wish to refinance the mortgage, in which case, he will arrange to pay the existing mortgage and obtain a new loan and a new mortgage. It is not uncommon for the mortgagee to discharge the existing mortgage and take a new mortgage with the purchaser of the property as mortgagor.

In any sale of mortgaged real estate free and clear of the mortgage, the mortgagor is liable to the purchaser for any damage he may suffer as the result of the mortgagor's failure to obtain a discharge of the mortgage. As a general rule, the purchaser has the right to rescind the contract of sale if the seller-mortgagor fails to obtain a discharge of the mortgage.

The simplicity of the term *free and clear* belies the true complexity of such a transaction, even though it is quite common. Set out below are the documents used in such a sale. They are listed in the order in which they will appear in the public records after the sale has taken place:

1. Mortgagee No. 1 releases seller's mortgage.
2. Seller deeds property to buyer free and clear.
3. Buyer mortgages property to mortgagee No. 2.

The simplicity of the record does not indicate that this did not actually happen. The first mortgagee is quite unlikely to release its mortgage until the debt has

---

[9] *Vernon* v. *Lincoln National Life Insurance Co.,* 200 Ark. 47, 138 S.W.2d 61.

been paid. The money with which to do so comes from the buyer, who has obtained it from the second mortgagee. The second mortgage lender is not likely to make the loan without knowing that it is the first mortgagee on property owned free and clear by the buyer. In a very real sense, the transaction as it appears in the records could not have taken place. The reason that it appears to have taken place is that the closing process contemplates that all parties will be physically present at the same time and place under controlled conditions. The closing of the sale is a very formal affair at which all of the documents are executed and acknowledged *before* the second mortgage lender releases any funds at all. It is then the self-appointed duty of the second lender to take possession of all the documents. It will see that they are recorded promptly and, more importantly, in the proper order. This is essential to assure the second lender that it does in fact have a valid first lien on the property.

**Sale Subject to the Mortgage**

When the grantee of the mortgagor of mortgaged real estate takes the property subject to the mortgage, the conveyance amounts to a transfer to the grantee of whatever estate the mortgagor-grantor has in the mortgaged real estate after the mortgage debt is satisfied out of the real estate.[10] If the purchase price of the mortgaged real estate is a sum equal to the value of the property less the amount of the mortgage debt, the presumption is that the grantee purchased the land subject to the mortgage.

When mortgaged real estate is sold subject to the mortgage, the mortgagee's lien continues; and as between the mortgagor, the mortgagee, and the grantee, the mortgaged real estate is the primary source of the funds for the payment of the mortgage debt. If the grantee wishes to release the mortgaged real estate from the mortgage lien, he must pay the mortgage debt.[11] However, the grantee is not personally liable for the mortgage debt; and if the mortgage debt is not paid and the mortgage is foreclosed, the mortgagee is not entitled to a deficiency judgment against the grantee.

As between the mortgagor and the mortgagee, the mortgagor, after the sale of the mortgaged real estate subject to the mortgage, is surety for the payment of the mortgage debt up to the value of the mortgaged real estate and is individually liable to the extent the mortgage debt exceeds the value of the mortgaged real estate. Consequently, if the mortgagee, knowing that the mortgagor has conveyed the mortgaged real estate subject to the mortgage, releases the mortgage to the

---

[10] *Wolfert* v. *Guadagno et al.,* 130 Cal. App. 661, 20 P.2d 360.

[11] *Barkhausen* v. *Continental Illinois National Bank & Trust Company,* c Ill.2d 354, 120 N.E.2d 649.

grantee without the knowledge or consent of the mortgagor, the mortgagor will be released from his personal liability for the mortgage debt up to the value of the mortgaged real estate.[12]

If the grantee pays the mortgage debt and the mortgage is discharged and a release given, the grantee is not entitled to reimbursement. However, if the mortgagor-grantor has conveyed the mortgaged real estate subject to the mortgage and has paid the mortgage debt, he has recourse to the mortgaged real estate for reimbursement; but he cannot hold the grantee personally liable.[13]

This action was brought to recover a refund for gross income tax paid on the sale of real estate. Shirmeyer sold Prang a house on which there was a mortgage. Prang paid $800 down and later paid $2,760. The deed recited that the property was sold subject to the unpaid balance on a mortgage to Wayne Mortgage Company, Inc. Prang paid Wayne Mortgage Company, Inc., $4,200 and satisfied the mortgage on the property. Under the tax laws of the state, if Prang was not legally obligated to pay the mortgage debt, Shirmeyer was not obligated to pay the gross income tax on the mortgage debt paid by Prang, since such payment would not be classed as income to Shirmeyer. The court held that since the property was purchased "subject to the mortgage," Prang was not legally liable for the mortgage debt.

Judge Bobbitt said: "While it may be in the interest of the purchasers in this case to pay off the mortgage to Wayne Mortgage Company, Inc., yet, when they purchased the real estate here in question subject to the existing mortgage, they [the grantee-purchasers] assumed no personal liability for the payment of the mortgage . . . ; but took said real estate charged with the payment of the debt and such property became the primary fund out of which said mortgage must be paid.

"In securing the fund out of which said mortgage was to be paid the purchasers [Prangs] assumed only an equitable obligation to pay the debt secured by the mortgage, and the legal obligation for the payment of the debt secured by said mortgage remained that of the mortgagor [Shirmeyer]." *Ralph L. Shirmeyer Inc.* v. *Indiana Revenue Board,* 229 Ind. 586, 99 N.E.2d 847 (1951).

### Sale Subject to the Mortgage with Assumption of Mortgage Debt

The grantee of mortgaged real estate may take the property subject to the mortgage and may assume and agree to pay the mortgage debt. Whether or not the grantee has assumed and agreed to pay the mortgage debt will depend on the terms of the sales contract and on the circumstances surrounding the transaction. The courts have held that the agreement to assume the mortgage

---

[12] *First National Bank & Trust Co.* v. *Strong,* 112 Conn. 412, 152 A. 575.

[13] *Seaman's Bank for Savings in City of New York* v. *Samdbeck* 293 N.Y. 91, 56 N.E.2d 46.

debt need not be included as a provision of the deed, but may be included in the contract to sell; or it may be in a separate agreement, either written or oral; or it may be implied from the surrounding circumstances.[14]

The best practice, however, is that of including in the deed a provision stating that the conveyance is subject to a mortgage, describing the mortgage (date of mortgage, names of mortgagor and mortgagee, amount of mortgage and unpaid balance, and book and page of recordation), and further providing that the grantee "hereby assumes and personally agrees to pay the mortgage debt as part of the consideration for this conveyance." The important words are "assumes and agrees to pay the mortgage debt." If the grantee accepts a deed containing such a provision, with knowledge that the provision is in the deed, his intent to assume the mortgage debt will be clearly established.

In some instances in which the deed has stated the conveyance was subject to the mortgage but the parties, in negotiating the transaction, have agreed upon the full value of the real estate as the purchase price and have deducted from the purchase price the unpaid balance of the mortgage debt, the courts have held that the grantee was personally liable for the payment of the mortgage debt. The courts so holding have reasoned that it would be unfair to permit the grantee to withhold the grantor's money and not be liable for the payment of the mortgage debt.[15]

***Liability of Grantee.*** In assuming the mortgage debt, the grantee of the mortgaged real estate makes himself personally liable to the mortagagor-grantor for the payment of the mortgage debt, and he also makes himself personally liable for the mortgage debt to the mortgagee.[16] Although the courts are in substantial accord in holding that the grantee who has assumed a mortgage debt is personally liable to the mortgagee on the mortgage debt, there is considerable diversity of opinion as to the basis for holding the grantee liable.

In practice, the mortgagee will, on the mortgagor's default, bring action to foreclose the mortgage and will join in such action the mortgagor and all grantees who have assumed the mortgage debt. If, on foreclosure and sale, there is a deficiency, the mortgagee will be granted a deficiency judgment against the mortgagor and all the grantees who have assumed the mortgage debt. Since the mortgagee is entitled to only one satisfaction, he no longer has a claim against any

[14] California, New York, and Pennsylvania require the agreement to assume the mortgage debt to be included in the deed or in a separate written agreement.

[15] *Dimmitt et al.* v. *Johnson et al.,* 199 Iowa 996, 203 N.W. 261.

[16] *Stinert* v. *Galasso,* 363 Pa. 393, 69 A.2d 841.

of the parties defendant when he has collected his deficiency judgment. As between the mortgagor and the assuming grantees, the last assuming grantee is liable to all prior grantors.

For example, suppose that Alberts owns real estate, which he mortgages to Bates. Thereafter, Alberts sells the property to Call, who assumes the mortgage debt. Then Call sells to Deal, who assumes the mortgage debt; and Deal sells to Evans, who assumes the mortgage debt. The mortgage debt is not paid when due; Bates brings a foreclosure action joining Alberts, Call, Deal, and Evans as parties defendant. The mortgaged property, on the foreclosure sale, does not bring enough to satisfy the mortgage debt, and a deficiency judgment is entered against all the parties defendant. If Call pays the deficiency judgment, he will have a right to collect from Deal or Evans the amount paid; and if Deal pays, he can collect from Evans. Since Evans is the last assuming grantee, he is the one who is ultimately legally liable for the deficiency.

The mortgagee may expressly or by implication agree to release the mortgagor from his liability for the mortgage debt and accept the grantee in his place. This is known as a *novation,* which is, in effect, a new contract.[17]

Hafford and Smith entered into an agreement whereby Hafford exchanged a trailer for real estate, which was owned by Smith and which was subject to two mortgages. The deed executed by Smith conveying the real estate to Hafford included a clause following the description of the real estate indicating that the deed was executed subject to a mortgage to Savings and Loan Association; and the deed further recited: ". . . subject also to a deed of trust to Dave R. Ashmore and Lillian R. Ashmore, which buyer assumes and agrees to pay." Savings and Loan Association foreclosed its mortgage. Hafford contended that the assumption-of-mortgage clause was inserted by fraud and brought this action to be relieved from liability for the Ashmore debt. The court found that Hafford had agreed to assume the mortgage debt.

The court said: "It may be generally stated that a purchaser who accepts and holds land under a deed reciting that he has assumed and agreed to pay an outstanding mortgage, subjects himself to personal liability on the mortgage. This is one way in which the contract of assumption may arise.

"Admittedly, this rule is somewhat artificial—the contract of assumption is sometimes said to be 'implied' in such cases—and if the assumption clause is inserted through fraud or mistake of the grantor or scrivener, or the deed is accepted by the grantee without knowledge of the assumption clause, then the grantee incurs no personal liability to the mortgagee. Accepting the assumption clause without more, does not bind the grantee, though the deed may yet be effective as a conveyance of the land. In other words, the

[17] *Lynn Five Cents Savings Bank* v. *Portnoy,* 306 Mass. 436, 28 N.E.2d 418.

principle that a party must be presumed to know the content and meaning of a written instrument which he takes as evidence of title, does not extend so far as to conclusively impose on the grantee of mortgaged land a collateral personal liability for the mortgage debt formed upon a clause inserted in the deed without his knowledge and expressing an agreement which he has not made.

"It is true, as the appellants complain, that where the deed expressly provides for the grantee's assumption of an outstanding mortgage, the application of the principle is rather narrowly limited by the parol evidence rule. It appears that if a grantee who wishes to controvert the provisions of a conveyance containing an express assumption clause, after accepting it, must resort to equity to do so, he has the burden of proving non-assumption by clear and convincing proof." *Hafford* v. *Smith,* Mo. App., 369 S.W.2d 290 (1963).

### Subsequent Sales

Each subsequent purchaser who, as part of the transaction, assumes the mortgage debt thereby becomes primarily liable; all prior purchasers who have, as part of their purchase agreements, assumed the mortgage debt will become sureties along with the mortgagor. Since the assumption of the mortgage debt creates a principal-surety relationship, the law of suretyship is applied in determining the liabilities of the parties in regard to subsequent dealings.

Under the law of suretyship, if the creditor and the debtor enter into an enforceable contract that alters the terms of the original contract without the surety's knowledge or consent, and the surety does not ratify the contract or waive his rights as surety, the surety will be discharged from his obligation on the contract. Under this rule, any valid extension of time for the payment of the mortgage, or any agreement materially altering the terms of the mortgage given to the grantee who is primarily liable without the consent of the prior assuming grantees or of the mortgagor, will discharge such persons from their personal liability on the mortgage debt.[18] This rule is not followed in a majority of the states in an action against the mortgagor if the mortgage debt is evidenced by a negotiable instrument. The exception is based on the negotiable-instruments rule of law that an extension of time granted to an endorsee of the instrument does not discharge the party primarily liable on the instrument.[19]

### Due-on-Sale Clauses

During periods of rising interest rates, the assumption of an existing mortgage loan at an interest rate lower than that prevailing at the time of sale may be

[18] *Lynn Five Cents Savings Bank* v. *Portnoy,* 306 Mass. 436,28 N.E.2d 418.

[19] *Mortgage Guaranty Co.* v. *Chotiner,* 8 Cal.2d 110, 64 P.2d 138.

attractive to both purchaser and seller. To the purchaser, the lower rate on the existing loan will be of obvious attraction since a significant saving can be realized over the life of the mortgage. The seller may also benefit from the sale by assumption by obtaining a higher price for the property. The only party who will not benefit is the lender who has made a long-term loan at what appeared to be a profitable rate at the time of making the loan. If the loan were paid off at the time of sale, rather than being assumed, the lender could presumably lend that amount out again at the higher existing rates. As a result of the generally rising trend in interest rates in recent years, lenders have devised a means to compel the payoff of the loan balance at the time the property is sold during the term of the mortgage. This is accomplished by the addition of a clause that accelerates and makes immediately due and payable the entire remaining balance of the loan upon sale of the mortgaged property. The use of such *due-on-sale* clauses has come under heavy attack, but the courts have generally upheld their validity.[20] Such clauses are, however, prohibited in all mortgages insured by the Federal Housing Administration or guaranteed by the Veterans Administration.

As a practical matter, of course, the lender is primarily concerned with increasing the rate of return on the amount of the loan outstanding while retaining the quality of the security for the loan. In view of the fact that both the original mortgagor and the assuming buyer will be liable for the debt, and that the property remains the same, it would appear that in the sale by assumption the mortgagee is *more* secure than prior to such a sale. In some cases the courts have questioned the propriety of enforcing such clauses where the lender's security was clearly enhanced.[21] By and large, however, even if it is clear that the sole purpose of such a clause is to permit the lender to adjust the interest rate in return for waiving his right to invoke the due-on-sale clause, they have been generally found to be valid and enforceable.[22] Where instead of an assumption sale there is a sale by the mortgagor on a conditional sales contract, there is a conflict in recent decisions. In some cases there is recognized that no title is transferred at the time of such a sale and therefore the due-on-sale clause cannot be invoked,[23]

---

[20] *Miller* v. *Pacific First Federal Savings and Loan Association,* 86 Wash.2d 401 (1976); *Mutual Federal Savings & Loan Association* v. *Wisconsin Wire Works,* 71 Wis.2d 531, 239 N.W.2d 20 (1976).

[21] *Mutual Federal Savings and Loan Association* v. *American Medical Services, Inc.,* 66 Wis.2d 210, 223 N.W.2d 921 (1974).

[22] *Crockett* v. *First Federal Savings and Loan Association of Charlotte,* 289 N.C. 620, 224 S.E.2d 580 (1976).

[23] *Tucker* v. *Lassen Savings and Loan Association,* 12 Cal.3d 629, 526 P.2d 1169, 116 Cal. Rpts. 633 (1974).

while in others it has been found that the "equitable" title passes to the contract vendee and that this transfer is enough to invoke the clause.[24] Because the enforcement of such a clause is an equitable remedy the facts in each case will dictate the result at least where there has been no clear-cut sale by assumption.

Regardless of state law on the subject of the due-on-sale clause, it now appears that such clauses are valid when the mortgage is made by a federally chartered savings and loan association. This decision was ultimately rendered by the U.S. Supreme Court. The history of litigation in California is relevant. In the now famous case of *Wellenkamp* v. *Bank of America,*[25] the California court held that the due-on-sale clause was unenforceable because it violated state policy favoring the free alienability of real estate. The court was impressed by the fact that without mortgage assumptions there was no viable market. Subsequently the U.S. Supreme Court, in the case of *Fidelity Federal Savings & Loan Association* v. *de la Cuesta,*[26] decided in June 1982, held that state law was preempted by the regulations of the Federal Home Loan Bank Board, which regulates federal savings and loan associations. As a result of this decision the clause is enforceable by federally chartered savings and loan associations, regardless of the law of the state in which they operate.

## The Prepayment Penalty Clause

The subject of upside interest rate risk has already been discussed. It has also been suggested that in the fixed-rate mortgage there exists for the lender a certain amount of downside opportunity. That is, should interest rates (and the lender's cost of funds) fall during the term of the mortgage, its profit will be enhanced by the fixed interest rate in the note. To take advantage of this opportunity the lender must effectively discourage the borrower from refinancing the debt when interest rates fall. The method commonly employed is the inclusion in the note of the prepayment clause. It should be noted that the inclusion of such a clause does not *limit* the borrower's common-law contract rights; it effectively *expands* them. That is, there is no common-law right to pay a debt early. Therefore, the inclusion of a prepayment privilege in the note is a concession on the part of the lender. It can therefore be surrounded with whatever limitations the lender chooses to include. Since the inclusion of such a clause in the first place implies

---

[24] *Century Fed. Savings & Loan Association* v. *Van Glahn,* 144 N.J. Super. 48, 364 A.2d 558 (Chan Div. 1976).

[25] 21 Cal.3d 043, 582 P.2d 970, 148 Cal. Rptr. 379 (1978).

[26] 50 U.S.L.W.4916 (1982).

some forecast or anticipation by the lender, it is frequently the subject of true negotiation. The important point to bear in mind is that the borrower who desires the privilege of prepayment is already asking for a significant accomodation from the lender. He should expect that something will be required in return. That consideration will be the payment of a financial penalty to reimburse the lender for loss of anticipated profits. The inclusion of both the due-on-sale clause and the prepayment penalty clause in the same mortgage loan might appear to be unjustified, but the nature of long-term fixed interest rate financing seems to compel this degree of protection to induce lenders to engage in it.

### Sales of Mortgages

It is a popular misconception on the part of the borrowing public that mortgages are universally retained by their lenders. It is assumed by many that the bank, savings and loan association, or mortgage company places these loans in its portfolio of investments. This has not been the case for a long period of time. Quite the contrary is usually the case: these mortgages are usually sold to an investor looking for long-term, secured investments. Historically, life insurance companies were the ideal investors for mortgages. In recent years, largely through the establishment of the Federal National Mortgage Association (FNMA), such investments have been marketed to a broad range of investors, such as pension funds and even individuals. The reason the borrower is unaware of this practice is that the original lender continues to "service" his mortgage. That is, the original lender acts as an agent for the investor and all contact with the borrower is usually made through the lender. This mortgage servicing business is important fee-producing income for mortgage lenders, and a brief explanation of its workings is in order.

Mortgage servicing businesses are truly financial intermediaries. Often their business is financed with short-term loans of working capital from the commercial banking system. This capital is used to solicit and make mortgage loans, usually to residential home buyers. These mortgages are then sold to investors who frequently have neither the facilities nor the desire to accomplish the collection process and administration work required for such an investment. The investor will, therefore, usually appoint the mortgage servicing business (the originator of the loan) as its agent in return for a small percentage of gross collections. The mortgage servicing company has its capital restored from the sale of the mortgages so that it can make still more mortgages, and it has added to its servicing activity income. By continuing to recycle its capital in this fashion it is able to build up a substantial servicing business that generates significant fee income. More importantly, if the mortgages can all be sold at par or better and the interest expense on its line of credit minimized, the mortgage servicing company has acquired the service business without investing any funds of its own. Such a business obviously requires considerable skill in order to avoid heavy losses while acquiring the servicing business. Erratic and generally increasing interest rates in recent years have proved to be a most challenging obstacle to success in this field.

Fundamental to the mortgage servicing business (and the flow of funds it provides) is the sale of mortgages. Making the mortgages salable or negotiable at the outset is of paramount importance. Therefore, the technical rules that apply are discussed in this section. It should be borne in mind, however, that each individual seller who provides mortgage financing to his buyer has the same problems of marketability. As suggested earlier, very often the seller becomes a lender only through necessity and would prefer cash. To obtain it, that seller must contemplate the same problems of marketability that are faced by the mortgage servicing industry. The mechanics of marketing individual mortgages are beyond the scope of this book, but legal marketability of these mortgages is an essential requirement to the solution of the marketing problem.

## Assignment by the Mortgagee

### Nature of Assignment of Mortgage

In discussing the assignment of the mortgage by the mortgagee, it is important to keep in mind the fact that the mortgagee has two things: ownership of the debt and an interest in the real estate that secures the debt. At common law the title to the real estate was vested in the mortgagee; if he wished to transfer his interests, he was required to deed the real estate and assign the debt. This situation does not exist today. The mortgage cannot be transferred separately from the debt, and all the courts hold that since the mortgage is given for the sole purpose of securing the debt, any transfer of the debt carries with it the right to the security of the mortgage.

### Mortgage Accompanies Debt

Suppose that a mortgagee assigns the mortgage to Arthur and the mortgage debt to Bert. In such a case the benefits of the mortgage security would go with the debt to Bert. In all but a few states the courts would hold that the attempted assignment of the mortgage to Arthur was a nullity and that Arthur would take nothing by the assignment. In a minority of states the courts would decide that Arthur holds the mortgage as trustee for the benefit of Bert. In all states the practical result is the same—that is, Bert, as assignee of the debt, gets the benefit of the security.

## Nonnegotiable and Negotiable Debt

In determining the rights and duties of the parties involved in the assignment of a mortgage and the mortgage debt, we must first determine the nature of the mortgage debt. If it is nonnegotiable in form, the rules of general contract law relating to the assignment of contracts apply in determining the rights and duties of the parties. However, if the debt is negotiable in form—that is, if the debt is evidenced by a negotiable instrument, such as a negotiable promissory note—the law relative to the negotiation of negotiable instruments applies.

It is beyond the scope of this work to discuss in detail the law of assignment of contracts and the law of negotiable instruments; however, we shall state the general rules on which the rights of the parties are based.

## Assignment if Debt Is Nonnegotiable

The assignment of a contract is, in legal effect, the sale of intangible personal property, and the basic rules of the sale of property are applied in working out the rights of the parties. Since it is fundamental in the law of property that a person cannot transfer good title to property that he does not own, it is equally fundamental in the law of the assignment of contracts that the obligee (the creditor) cannot assign greater rights in the contract (the debt) than he has. Stated in other words, the assignee of a nonnegotiable debt takes the debt subject to all defenses that the debtor has against the creditor.

Under this rule the assignee of a mortgage securing a nonnegotiable debt will be able to enforce the mortgage only to the extent that he can enforce the debt. If the mortgagor has any defense to the debt—such as fraud, duress, lack of consideration, or payment—these defenses will be good against the assignee of the mortgage in an action to foreclose the mortgage.

To protect himself, the assignee of a nonnegotiable debt should give the mortgagor notice of the assignment. The rights of the assignee in the debt are fixed as of the time the debtor is given this notice. It must be direct notice to the debtor, but no special form is required. Good business practice requires the giving of written notice, and it should describe with certainty the debt assigned. The recording of the assignment of the mortgage is not notice to the mortgagor, since he owes no duty to check the records before making payment to the mortgagee. When notice of the assignment is given to the mortgagor, he owes a duty to pay the debt to the assignee. Payment to the mortgagee after such notice will not discharge the debt and mortgage. Also, all matters by way of setoff arising after notice of the assignment will be cut off, but defenses arising under the contract (counterclaims) will not be affected.

### Estoppel Certificate

Since the assignee of a nonnegotiable debt cannot know of outstanding defenses, he can protect himself, at least in part, by obtaining from the mortgagor-debtor what is commonly termed a *certificate of estoppel.* This is a statement by the mortgagor to the effect that he owes the debt, that the debt is of a certain amount, and that he has no defenses to or claims against the creditor.

If the mortgagor-debtor gives the prospective assignee such a statement before the debt is assigned, the mortgagor-debtor will not be permitted, as a means of defeating the rights of the assignee, to set up any defenses arising prior to the giving of the statement. The statement, if it is to be effective, must be obtained before the assignment is made. It will not protect the assignee against defenses arising out of a default in performance by the mortgagee-creditor after the giving of the statement.[27] For example, if Bert, in the hypothetical situation stated above, gives Clark an estoppel certificate at the time of the assignment, and thereafter Arthur defaults in the performance of the contract, Clark could not recover the full contract price. He could recover only the contract price less damages for defective performance.

An oral statement by the mortgagor-debtor is sufficient to prevent him from setting up defenses arising prior to the making of the statement. However, the prospective assignee, for full protection, should get the statement in writing, signed by the mortgagor-debtor. Oral statements are frequently difficult to prove in the event of a court action.

### Assignment of Negotiable Debt

If the debt is evidenced by a negotiable instrument, the law of negotiable instruments applies in determining the rights of the parties to the debt. In all but a small minority of states[28] the courts hold that since the mortgage follows the debt and its sole purpose is as security for the payment of the debt, the holder of the negotiable instrument evidencing the debt has the same rights in the mortgage as he has in the debt.[29]

Under the law of negotiable instruments a person to whom a negotiable instrument is property negotiated and who takes the instrument for value, before it is

[27] *Newtown Title & Trust Co.* v. *Admiral Farragut Academy,* 84 F. Supp. 527.

[28] Illinois, Minnesota, and Ohio.

[29] *Patrick* v. *Kilgore et al.,* 238 Ala. 604, 193 So. 112.

overdue and without notice or knowledge of defects in the title or of defenses to the instrument, takes the instrument free from defenses between the parties. If the instrument is a bearer instrument, it may be negotiated by delivery alone; but if it is an order instrument—payable to the order of a named payee—it must be endorsed and delivered to be properly negotiated.

Before a person can qualify as a holder in due course—one who takes free from personal defenses—the instrument must be complete and regular on its face. If any material provision of the instrument is omitted—such as the name of the payee, in case it is an order instrument—or if there are strike-outs or erasures on the instrument, it is not complete and regular on its face.

The taker of the instrument must give value for it. If he is a donee of the instrument or inherits it, he has not given value. He must take the instrument before it is past due, and he must take it in good faith—that is, without notice or knowledge that the party primarily liable has a good defense to the instrument.

If the holder of the instrument can qualify as a holder in due course, he takes it free from such defenses as fraud, duress, undue influence, lack or failure of consideration, and all other defenses personal to the parties to the instrument. However, he does not take free from real defenses, such as forgery, lack of capacity to contract, and other defenses that might be offered to prove that the instrument was invalid from its inception—that is, that it was never a valid instrument.

If the person taking the negotiable instrument evidencing the debt cannot qualify as a holder in due course or does not take from a holder in due course, his position is substantially the same as that of the assignee of a nonnegotiable debt, and the rules relating to the rights of the assignee of a nonnegotiable debt would apply in determining his rights.

Latney and wife executed to Dorne their negotiable promissory note secured by a deed of trust. Soldoro Corporation purchased the note, which was endorsed to it. The court held that Soldoro Corporation took the note as holder in due course. Latney refused to pay the note, and Soldoro Corporation assigned the note and deed of trust to Oshinsky for collection and foreclosure. The Latneys set up as a defense that they were induced to issue the note and execute the trust deed by fradulent representations as to the condition of the house they were purchasing, which was the mortgaged property. The trial court held that the defense was not available against the holder in due course. On appeal, the holding was affirmed.

Associate Judge Hood said: "The trial court properly ruled that the corporation was a holder in due course and that the defenses raised were not available against it." *Latney* v. *Oshinsky,* Munic. Ct. of App., D.C., 169 A.2d 687 (1961).

### Effect of Recording Assignment of Mortgage

There is considerable confusion as to the effect of the recording of an assignment of a mortgage on the rights of the parties. The recording statutes of some states require the recording of assignments of mortgages; those of other states permit, but do not require, the recording of such assignments; and those of a few states are so drafted that an assignment of a mortgage is not eligible for record.

In general, the recording of an assignment of a mortgage is not notice to the mortgagor of the assignment; and if the mortgagor, without having been given personal notice of the assignment, pays the mortgage debt to the mortgagee after the assignment and recording of the assignment, such payment will discharge the mortgage debt. Recording of the assignment of a mortgage is of little importance in regard to the rights of subsequent purchasers or mortgagees. The recorded mortgage is notice of its existence, and the subsequent purchaser or mortgagee has little or no interest in knowing who owns the mortgage debt. If the mortgage debt is evidenced by a negotiable instrument, the only way the debt can be discharged is by payment to the holder in due course of the negotiable instrument. Since the debt cannot be recorded, but can be assigned or negotiated without the assignment of the mortgage, the recording of the assignment has little effect on the rights of the owner of the debt. However, the recording of the assignment is important in one respect: It makes known the person who can discharge the mortgage of record.

### Partial Assignments

A single mortgage may be given as security for the payment of one debt or several debts, as, for instance, a series of notes or bonds. And even though the mortgage is given to secure a single debt, more than one person may eventually have an interest in it, since the mortgagee may assign interests in the debt to different assignees. In such cases the courts are not in accord as to the relative rights of the several assignees in the mortgage security.

One view, which is both logical and equitable and apparently the majority view, is that the several assignees share the mortgage security on a pro rata basis. Another view is that the assignees share in the order in which the assignments were made. A third view, which applies only to a series of notes or bonds, is that the assignees' rights attach in the order of the maturity of the notes or bonds which they hold.

# Chapter 14

# Deeds of Trust and Land Contracts

The significant differences between the mortgage and the deed of trust are first discussed in this chapter. Included is a sample form to illustrate the similarity between the two devices. The basic difference is the introduction of a third party, the trustee, to act as stakeholder to protect title to the security and to facilitate the foreclosure process.

Next considered is the land contract (contract for a deed), which is a well developed vehicle for seller financing. In recent years the use of the land contract has become widespread because of the frequency with which sellers have found that private financing is essential to the sale of real estate. It will be seen that the land contract provides a considerable degree of flexibility. This same characteristic also tends to make each land contract unique. As a result, it is necessary to be familiar with the general rules that are applied to all land contracts in order to successfully negotiate a specific contract. Attention to detailed provisions is required in order to adapt this relatively simple device to solve a complex real estate sales problem.

## Deed of Trust

### Nature of Deed of Trust

A deed of trust is a deed absolute given to secure the payment of a debt. It is, basically, a real estate mortgage and is an arrangement whereby the expense and delay incident to the foreclosure of a real estate mortgage are avoided. It is a three-party instrument. The parties are the lender, the borrower, and the trustee.[1] The borrower deeds the real estate to the trustee, who holds title for the benefit of the lender. In addition, the parties enter into a trust agreement whereby the trustee, on the default of the borrower, and at the request of the lender, is empowered to sell the real estate and pay the debt, the accrued interest, and the costs. Any surplus then is paid over to the borrower or to the parties who have junior claims on the real estate held in trust. The trust agreement also includes such other provisions as the parties deem expedient. In the event of a deficiency, of course, the lender will be entitled to pursue his remedies under the promissory note.

The deed of trust may be used as a means of securing a bond issue of a corporation. The trust agreement portion of such a deed given to secure a corporate bond issue is usually an elaborate document that sets out in detail the powers and duties of the trustee and the rights of the bondholders in the security. In essence, the bondholders surrender their individual rights to sue in the event of a default. The trustee then acts for the benefit of all of them. This avoids the necessity of a multitude of lawsuits for the same default.

### Characteristics of Deed of Trust

Those courts that have followed the early rule that any conveyance of real estate given to secure a debt is a mortgage, without regard to the form of the conveyance, hold that a deed of trust is a mortgage. In these states, deeds of trust are used little, or not at all.[2]

Some states have recognized the deed of trust as a conveyance in trust that vests legal title in the trustee, and have held that the statutes requiring judicial foreclosure of mortgages do not apply to deeds of trust. Deeds of trust with power of sale are used extensively in such states.[3] Most of these states have enacted statutes defining the rights and duties of the parties to a deed-of-trust transaction. Although a statute of the state may set up some requirements as to the sale of the property held by the trustee in the event of default, in none of these states is foreclosure by judicial sale required, nor is the borrower permitted a statutory period of redemption after the sale.

In the other states and territories the laws are such that deeds of trust and

---

[1] The trust concept was introduced in Chapter 8.

[2] Connecticut, Florida, Hawaii, Indiana, Kansas, Louisiana, Maine, Massachusetts, Michigan, Minnesota, Nevada, New Jersey, Ohio, Oregon, Rhode Island, Utah, Vermont, and Washington.

[3] California, Colorado (power of sale valid if public trustee is used), District of Columbia, Delaware, Mississippi, Missouri, Tennessee, Texas, Virginia, and West Virginia.

mortgages are used without discrimination. In several of the states, whether a deed of trust or a mortgage is used is more a matter of local usage than of the legal status of the deed of trust or mortgage.

In all states in which deeds of trust are used, the courts have not, in determining the rights and duties of the parties, followed the law of trusts through to a logical conclusion. In many, if not in most, of the deed-of-trust transactions, the courts have applied the law of mortgages in determining the rights and duties of the parties. The statutes of the states in which deeds of trust are used extensively play an important part in determining the rights and liabilities of the parties. There is no uniformity in these statutes; consequently, if a person wishes to use a deed of trust, he should consult a local attorney who is familiar with the law of the state in which the real estate involved is located.

### Rights under Deed of Trust

The rights of the borrower and the lender under the deed of trust are substantially the same as are the rights of a mortgagor and mortgagee under a real estate mortgage. Any interest in real estate that may be sold or mortgaged may be the subject matter of a deed-of-trust transaction. As a general rule, the borrower is left in possession of the property until default and sale by the trustee. If a borrower executes a deed of trust to real estate to which he does not at that time have title, the deed of trust, like a mortgage, will create a valid lien on the real estate conveyed if the borrower acquires title to the real estate conveyed during the life of the trust.[4]

### Deed-of-Trust Debt

There is no material difference between the mortgage debt and a debt secured by a deed of trust. The debt may be evidenced by a nonnegotiable or a negotiable instrument. The form of the debt—that is, whether it is nonnegotiable or negotiable—is important in determining the rights of a purchaser of the debt from the lender.

A deed of trust may be given to secure future advances in the same manner and to the same extent that a mortgage may be given to secure future advances. In the preceding chapter, a wide variety of mortgages was discussed. In each of these situations a deed of trust, in those states that recognize the deed of trust as a separate type of security instrument, could be substituted for the mortgage without changing the rights and duties of the parties in any material respect.

---

[4] *California Bank* v. *Bell et al.,* 38 Cal. App.2d 533, 101 P.2d 724.

## Insurance

The courts have recognized that the borrower and the lender each have an insurable interest in the real estate conveyed to the trustee. In solving problems involving the rights of the parties in interest to insure the real estate and their rights to the insurance money in the event of a loss covered by insurance, the law developed in regard to the insurable rights of the mortgagor and mortgagee has been applied without material alteration to the deed-of-trust relation.[5]

## Recording

The recording laws of the state in which the real estate is located apply to deeds of trust just as they apply to any other instrument that conveys an interest in real estate. If a deed of trust is executed in compliance with the recording statutes of the state in which the real estate is located, it is eligible for recordation. However, a deed of trust, like a conventional deed or mortgage, is valid between the parties to the instrument without being recorded, and it is also binding on parties taking the real estate with notice or knowledge of the outstanding interests created by the deed of trust.

There is one material difference between a deed of trust and a mortgage in regard to discharge on the payment of the mortgage debt. A mortgage is discharged either by an entry on the margin of the record or by the execution and recording of a certificate of discharge by the mortgagee. The only person who can clear the record of a deed of trust is the trustee, and this is accomplished by the trustee's reconveying the real estate to the borrower or his successor in interest on the payment of the debt secured by the deed of trust.

## Conveyance of Real Estate Held under Deed of Trust

The granting of real estate under a deed of trust does not deprive the borrower of all his interest in the property. His rights are, in substantially all respects, the same as are the rights of a mortgagor. He has the right to redeem the real estate by the payment of the debt, and from a practical standpoint the value of this right is the difference between the market value of the real estate and the amount of the debt. The borrower may sell this interest, or he may borrow money, using this interest as security, and give to the lender a second deed of trust or a real estate mortgage. Technically, the trustee under a deed of trust holds only a determinable or base fee in the real estate; and the borrower has a reversionary interest in the property. That is, the title to the property revests in the borrower on the payment of the debt.

If the borrower sells the real estate that is the subject matter of a deed of

---

[5] *Le Doux et al.* v. *Dettmering et al.,* 316 Ill. App. 98, 43 N.E.2d 862.

trust, the purchaser may buy free and clear, he may buy subject to the deed of trust, or he may buy subject to the deed of trust and assume and agree to pay the debt. In determining the rights and duties of a purchaser of real estate which is subject to a deed of trust, the law of mortgages applies.

Sipe sold the real estate in question to Baker, who executed a negotiable promissory note payable to Sipe in the amount of $4,500, which was secured by a deed of trust to Linus Harding, trustee. Baker sold the real estate to Ellen Criswell, who assumed and agreed to pay "the unpaid balance owing . . ." on the $4,500 note secured by the deed of trust to Linus Harding, trustee. Sipe negotiated the note together with the lien to Southwestern Fidelity Life Insurance Company. The deed of trust included the following provision: ". . . in the event of foreclosure under the power granted hereby, the owner in possession of said property shall thereby become a tenant at will of the purchaser at foreclosure sale. . . ."

The note was not paid when due, and the real estate was sold by the trustee to Southwestern Fidelity Life Insurance Company. Criswell refused to surrender possession of the property, and this action was brought to recover possession of the real estate and to obtain a judgment for damages. Judgment was given Southeastern Fidelity Life Insurance Company, and Criswell appealed, denying the existence of a landlord-tenant relationship The judgment was affirmed.

Justice Coleman said: "It is well settled that one agreeing to pay a note secured by a deed of trust lien, as part of the purchase price of the land so encumbered, cannot question the validity of such note or the lien securing it.

"The rights of the payee of a note secured by a mortgage, or a deed of trust, cannot be abridged or diminished by subsequent acts of the mortgagor, or grantor in such deed of trust. Mrs. Criswell, therefore, could occupy a no more favorable position than F. E. Baker. The agreement made by Baker as contained in the note assumed by Mrs. Criswell, and the deed of trust securing the same, is binding on Mrs. Criswell.

"By her acceptance of the deed from Baker, Mrs. Criswell agreed to pay the note described therein, and, from the recitation that the note was secured by a deed of trust, had constructive notice of the provisions of the deed of trust and impliedly agreed to all of them." *Criswell* v. *Southwestern Fidelity Life Insurance Company,* Tex. Civ. App., 373 S.W.2d 893 (1963).

### Assignment of Rights of Lender

The rights of a lender under a deed of trust do not differ in any material respects from the rights of a mortgagee. He is the beneficiary under the terms of the deed of trust and acquires, through the trustee, a lien on the real estate as security for the debt. He is the owner of the debt and may transfer it, together with his rights as beneficiary. The transfer of the debt carries with it the rights under the deed of trust. The debt and the lien securing the debt cannot be transferred as separate rights.

If the debt is nonnegotiable, the law of assignment of contracts applies in determining the rights of the parties. If the debt is evidenced by a negotiable instrument, the law of negotiable instruments applies in determining the rights acquired by one to whom the instrument is negotiated or transferred.

The assignment of mortgages differs materially from the assignment of the rights of the lender in a deed of trust in regard to the requirements for recording. Under the recording laws of most states, assignments of mortgages may be recorded and, in some states, must be recorded. When the lender in a deed of trust assigns his rights, the assignment need not be recorded; and under the recording statutes of some states it is not eligible for recordation. The assignment by the lender in no way affects the title or the duties of the trustee. Who owns the debt is of no concern to third persons dealing with real estate conveyed under a deed of trust. The recording of the deed of trust gives them notice of the lien on the real estate, and only the trustee or his duly appointed successor has the power to clear the record by executing a reconveyance of the real estate.

## Discharge of Deed of Trust

The payment of the debt secured by a deed of trust entitles the borrower to a discharge, but it does not discharge the deed of trust from the record. If the trustee has died, the borrower or his successor must have a successor appointed who can execute the required reconveyance. If the trustee arbitrarily refuses to act, the borrower or his successor must bring a court action and obtain a court order forcing the trustee to act.

There is considerable confusion as to the effect of a tender. Logically, it should discharge the deed of trust, since the deed of trust is basically a lien, and tender of performance, under the general rule, discharges a lien. However, whether or not a tender discharges the lien of the deed of trust depends on the statutes and decisions of the several states. It is fairly certain that the borrower or his successor is not entitled to a court order requiring the trustee to reconvey the real estate unless the borrower or his successor pays the debt.

Under the statutes and court decisions of some of the states the running of the statute of limitations on the debt bars any action on the mortgage. In some of the states so holding, the courts have held that the running of the statute of limitations on the debt does not deprive the trustee of his power to sell the property and apply the proceeds to the payment of the debt.[6] The courts base

[6] *Grant* v. *Burr.*, 54 Cal. 298.

their decisions on the ground that the trustee under the deed of trust has title to the real estate and that the statutes of limitations relating to title to real estate apply.

On May 7, 1956, MacClain executed his promissory note secured by a deed of trust on real estate owned by him to Northwestern Loan and Investment Company (hereinafter referred to as Northwestern), subject to a prior deed of trust to Federal Savings and Loan Association (hereinafter referred to as Federal). On August 30, 1956, Alcone's, Inc., obtained a judgment against MacClain and levied on the real estate. Thereafter the United States filed a tax lien on the property for unpaid income taxes, and the state of Colorado filed a second tax lien for unpaid state income tax.

MacClain became employed by Universal Securities, Inc. As part of MacClain's contract, Universal Securities, Inc., paid Northwestern the amount due on the MacClain note; Northwestern marked the note paid and returned it, together with a discharge of the deed of trust, to Universal Securities, Inc., and it delivered the note and discharge to MacClain. At the request of Chisen, MacClain's attorney, MacClain delivered the note and discharge to Chisen as security for the payment of attorney's fees owed to Chisen by MacClain. Chisen contended that his claim under the Northwestern note and deed of trust had priority over the claims of Alcone's, Inc., the United States, and the state of Colorado. The trial court held that Chisen's lien had priority; and on appeal, the judgment was reversed.

Chief Justice McWilliams said: "*Jones* v. *Sturgis* . . . holds that when a note secured by a deed of trust on real property is fully paid and satisfied the deed of trust ceases to be a lien on the property.

"In the instant case Universal prompted by reasons of its own and acting on behalf of its employee fully paid and satisfied the note; it received no purported assignment of the deed of trust but on the contrary accepted a release of the same. Under these circumstances the deed of trust ceased to be a lien and the fact that MacClain later came into possession of the note, deed of trust and release of deed of trust did not revive the lien interest." *Robinson* v. *Chisen,* Colo., 388 P.2d 759 (1964).

## Foreclosure of Deed of Trust

Although a deed of trust vests title in the trustee, and the trustee, under the typical trust agreement, owes a duty to sell the property on default by the borrower and on request by the lender, the sale of the property by the trustee is not the only remedy available to the lender. In some states the courts have held or the statutes provide that the power of sale in a deed of trust is cumulative and that the lender is entitled to foreclose by court action if he wishes to do so.[7] In

[7] *Bank of Italy* v. *Bentley,* 217 Cal. 644, 20 P.2d 940.

other states the lender may resort to court action and foreclose the deed of trust as a mortgage only if he can show that a sale by the trustee under the terms of the trust agreement would not be fair and just.[8]

The trustee under a deed of trust is a fiduciary and must not have an interest either in the debt or in the real estate. If he has such an interest, he is disqualified and cannot conduct the sale.[9] Also, the power of sale given to the trustee is personal to him and cannot be delegated to someone else. However, he may engage some other person to perform some of the ministerial duties pertaining to the sale. In some recent cases in which the trustee was a corporation, the courts have been more liberal in permitting delegation of the duties of the trustee.[10]

The rules discussed in the preceding chapter relating to the conduct of a sale under a power of sale in a mortgage apply generally to the conduct of a sale under a power of sale in a deed of trust. The statutes of the state in which the land is located and the provisions in the deed of trust must be complied with; and if they are not complied with, the sale, on proper action brought in a court having jurisdiction, will be set aside.

As a general rule, the trustee is not permitted to buy the real estate at such a sale. The lender, however, does have the right to bid and buy.

The Tomiyasus executed a second deed of trust to a trustee to secure the payment of $13,564 to the First National Bank. This was subject and subordinate to a first deed of trust in the sum of $38,968.29. The Tomiyasus were in default on both debts, and the First National Bank made the payments to the holders of the first deed of trust to prevent foreclosure. The First National Bank started foreclosure, and the sale was conducted as required by the state statutes. The sale was postponed seven times to give the Tomiyasus an opportunity to refinance, but their efforts in this respect were unsuccessful. The property was sold, subject to the first deed of trust, for $18,025.73, which was $1.00 more than the unpaid balance of the First National Bank's claim. The real estate sold was of the value of $200,000. Action was brought by the Tomiyasus to have the sale set aside on the ground of irregularities, fraud, misrepresentation, and inadequacy of the sale price. The trial court found there were no irregularities, fraud, misrepresentation, or collusion but, in spite of this finding, set the sale aside. On appeal, the holding was reversed.

Chief Justice Badt said: "The effect of this rule is that where such inadequacy stands alone, unaccompanied by any unfairness or other inequitable incident, it will not authorize the vacating of the sale. But it is universally recognized that inadequacy of price is a

---

[8] *George* v. *Zinn,* 57 W.Va. 15, 49 S.E. 904.

[9] *Morgan* v. *Glendy,* 92 Va. 86, 22 S.E. 854.

[10] *Randolph et al.* v. *Citizens National Bank of Lubbock et al.,* Tex. Civ. App., 141 S.W.2d 1030.

circumstance of greater or less weight to be considered in connection with other circumstances impeaching the fairness of the transaction as a cause of vacating it, and that, where the inadequacy is palpable and great, very slight additional evidence of unfairness or irregularity is sufficient to authorize the granting of the relief sought. . . . We think there can be no doubt under the authorities that where, *in addition to gross inadequacy of price,* the purchaser has, in the language of the United States Supreme Court, 'been guilty of any unfairness or has taken any undue advantage,'' resulting in such gross inadequacy and consequent injury to the owner of the property, he will be deemed guilty of fraud warranting the interposition of a court of equity in favor of the owner who is himself without fault.'' *Golden* v. *Tomiyasu,* Nev. 387 P.2d. 989 (1963).

## Sample Note and Deed of Trust

Set out below are a typical note and deed of trust. It will be immediately apparent that there is no fundamental difference between the sample note used here and that used in Chapter 13 in illustrating the transaction in which the mortgage is used as the security device. The only difference worthy of comment is that this form of note penalizes the borrower for prepayment of the debt. Such notes are not at all uncommon when the interest rate being charged is relatively high. Under such circumstances, lenders frequently desire to ''lock up'' the high rate being charged in order to avoid early repayment at a time when the money cannot be loaned again at such a favorable rate.

### Comments on Deed of Trust

A careful comparison of the sample deed of trust and the mortgage discussed in Chapter 12 will show that the only basic difference between the two devices is the method by which the creditor enforces its rights against the security, the real estate, in the event of default by the borrower. While it is true that the trustee sells the property for the purpose of generating funds to liquidate the balance of the debt, the lender in this form specifically reserves the right to bid at the sale. This feature gives the lender an added measure of protection since the lender is bidding not in cash but in terms of the balance due. As a result, if the sale will obviously bring a grossly inadequate price, the lender may ''buy'' it at the balance of the debt. There still exists the danger, as with the mortgage, that the liens of later creditors will be advanced in priority and will have to be paid before the property can be made marketable at a higher net price.

**Sample Note (secured by deed of trust and with penalty for prepayment)**

_______________, _______________
(City) (State)
_______________, 19_______
(Date)

For Value Received, the undersigned (Borrower) promises to pay to _______________, or order, the principal sum of _______________ Dollars ($_________), with interest on the unpaid principal balance from the date of this Note, until completely paid, at the rate of _______________ percent per annum. Principal and interest shall be payable at _______________ _______________, or such other place as the holder of the Note may designate, in consecutive monthly installments of _______________ Dollars ($_________), on the _________ day of each month beginning _________, 19_____. Such monthly installments shall continue until the entire debt evidence by this Note is fully paid except that any remaining indebtedness, unless sooner paid shall be due and payable on the _________ day of _________, 19_____.

If any installment under this Note is not paid when due and remains unpaid for thirty (30) days then the entire principal amount then outstanding together with accrued interest shall become immediately due and payable at the option of the holder of the Note and this option to accelerate during any default by Borrower may be exercised regardless of any prior forbearance by Lender. If suit is brought to collect this Note, the holder of the Note shall be entitled to also collect all reasonable costs of such suit including, but not limited to, reasonable attorney's fees.

If, within _________ years from the date of this Note, Borrower makes any prepayments in any twelve-month period beginning with the date of this Note or anniversary dates of this Note then Borrower shall pay the holder of the Note _________ percent of the amount by which the sum of such prepayments made in any such year exceeds _________ percent of the original principal amount of this Note.

Presentment, notice of dishonor, and protest are hereby waived by all makers, sureties, guarantors, and endorsers of this Note and it shall be the joint and several obligation of all of them and shall be binding upon them and their successors and assigns. All applicable exemption rights, whether by homestead or otherwise are hereby waived.

**Sample Note *(continued)***

The indebtedness evidence by this Note is secured by a deed of trust dated __________ and reference is hereby made to the deed of trust for rights as to the acceleration of the indebtedness evidenced by this Note.

________________________________ (SEAL)
________________________________ (SEAL)

**Sample Deed of Trust**

This deed of trust is made this _______ day of __________, 19_____, by and between the Grantor _________________________ (Borrower) of the County of ___________________, State of ____________________________________ and ______________________ as trustee, of the County of ____________, State of _________________ (Trustee), and _____________________, the Beneficiary, of the County of ____________, State of _____________________________ ______________(Lender).

Borrower, in consideration of the debt to Lender described below and the trust hereby created, does hereby sell, grant, and convey to Trustee, with power of sale, the real estate located in the County of ______________, State of _________________, and more particularly described as follows: _________
__________________________________________________________________
__________________________________________________________________
__________________________________________________________________
__________________________________________________________________
__________________________________________________________________
__________________________________________________________________

together with all the improvements, presently on the property and any which may be erected upon it in the future, and all easements, rights, and all fixtures now or later attached to the property including all replacements and additions, all of which are referred to in this deed of trust as the "Property";

To secure to Lender the repayment of the debt evidenced by Borrower's promissory note dated the _______ day of ______________, 19_____, (Note) in the principal amount of ________________________ Dollars ($__________) together with interest and providing for monthly installments of both principal and interest and due and payable on the _______ day of __________, 19_____;

## Sample Deed of Trust *(continued)*

Borrower hereby represents and covenants that Borrower is the lawful owner of the Property and has the right and power to convey the Property, that there are no liens or encumbrances on the Property and that Borrower generally warrants and will defend the title to the Property subject only to any limitations set out in this deed of trust or the title insurance policy which insures Lender's interest in the Property.

Borrower, Lender and Trustee hereby agree as follows:

1. *Payment of the Note.* Borrower will pay when and as due all payments on the debt evidence by the Note; all payments made shall be applied first against interest and then to principal on the Note.
2. *Taxes, Assessments, and Charges.* Borrower will pay all taxes, assessments, and other charges against the Property which would otherwise constitute a lien against the Property which would have priority over this deed of trust except that Borrower shall not be obligated to discharge any such lien when contesting its imposition by a legal proceeding which operates to prevent the attachment of the lien or any forfeiture of the Property.
3. *Insurance.* Borrower shall keep the Property and the improvements upon it insured against loss by fire or other hazards included within the term "extended coverage" in amounts as required by Lender except that Lender shall not require coverage in excess of the amount needed to pay the sums secured by this deed of trust. All insurance policies shall include the standard clause in favor of Lender and any insurance proceeds shall be paid first to Lender to be applied to the balance of the debt secured by this deed of trust with the excess, if any, paid to Borrower.
4. *Maintenance and Inspection.* Borrower agrees to keep the Property in good repair and shall not commit or permit waste of the Property. Lender shall have the right to inspect the Property at reasonable times and upon reasonable notice to Borrower of intent to do so.
5. *Condemnation.* All proceeds of any award for a condemnation or other taking of all or part of the Property are hereby assigned by Borrower to Lender; such proceeds shall be retained by Lender and applied to the balance of the debt secured by this deed of trust with any excess to be paid by Lender to Borrower.
6. *Forbearance Not a Waiver.* Any forbearance on the part of Lender to exercise any right or remedy available under this deed of trust shall not constitute a waiver of the right to do so at a later time. Neither shall the payment of taxes, assessments, insurance, and other charges against the property by Lender on Borrower's behalf constitute such a waiver.

**Sample Deed of Trust *(continued)***

7. *Successors and Assigns; Joint and Several Liability.* All obligations, duties, and benefits under this deed of trust shall be binding upon and inure to the benefit of the successors and assigns of both Lender and Borrower. All undertakings, covenants, or promises of borrower are hereby made joint and several obligations.

8. *Sale or Transfer of Property.* In the event of the sale or transfer of ownership of all or any part of the Property which is the subject of this deed of trust by Borrower without Lender's written consent, then Lender shall have the option to declare all sums secured by this deed of trust to be immediately due and payable without notice to Borrower.

9. *Default.* Upon the default by Borrower in the payment of any sums due Lender secured by this deed of trust or the breach of any covenant, promise, or undertaking included in this deed of trust, Lender shall have the right to declare all sums secured hereby to be immediately due and payable in full and may, without further notice to Borrower, invoke the power of sale provided for under applicable law. In pursuing such remedies as are available, Lender shall be entitled to recover all reasonable costs and expenses incurred including, but not limited to, reasonable attorney's fees.

10. *Sale by Trustee.* Immediately upon notice of default and intent to invoke the power of sale from Lender, Trustee shall proceed with the sale at public sale of the property. Notice of time and place of such sale shall be given to Borrower by Trustee and public notice shall be given as required by law. Trustee shall sell the Property at public auction to the highest bidder; Lender may purchase the property at such sale. Upon sale Trustee shall convey the Property to the highest bidder by special warranty deed.

11. *Application of Proceeds of Sale.* Upon the sale of the Property, Trustee shall apply the proceeds of sale; first, to all reasonable expenses of the sale, including Trustee's fees of _____ % of the gross sales price, reasonable attorney's fees, and costs of evidence of title; second, the payment of all taxes, assessments, and charges which are superior to the obligation secured by this deed of trust; third, to the discharge of all sums secured by this deed of trust. The excess, if any, shall be paid to the person or persons legally entitled to such excess.

12. *Release.* Immediately upon payment of all sums secured by this deed of trust Lender shall direct Trustee to release this deed of trust and Lender shall surrender the note or notes secured by this deed of trust to Trustee.

**Sample Deed of Trust *(concluded)***

In witness whereof, Borrower has executed and sealed this deed of trust.

__________________________(SEAL)
__________________________(SEAL)

State of ________________)
County of ________________) SS:

The foregoing instrument was acknowledged before me this ______ day of ________, 19____, by __________________________

________________________
Notary Public

My commission expires: ____________________

## Land Contracts

### Current Applications

The land contract has become a significant part of seller-assisted financing. It is not a new device but has been in common use for many years. When financing is readily available at reasonable rates through normal commercial sources the land contract has been limited to properties or borrowers that did not qualify for standard financing. In times of very expensive or scarce mortgage money the land contract has filled the void. Its flexibility makes it useful in the solution of a wide variety of financing problems. Because the land contract is a private agreement between the buyer and seller, a great deal of latitude exists in the terms that can be included.

The land contract should be distinguished from the standard agreement to purchase real estate for cash. The agreement to purchase is typically a very short-term contract. In it the seller agrees to transfer good title by deed and is usually given a brief time to furnish evidence that he has good title. The buyer agrees to pay a specified amount of cash when the deed is delivered and is generally given a short time in which to obtain mortgage financing. When these two tasks are completed, the contract is executed by the payment to the seller and the delivery of the deed to the buyer. Except for any lingering warranties as to the title or the quality of any buildings included in the sale, the contract is at an end. In the land contract, the seller is providing long-term financing, much the same as a mortgage lender. The security device used by the seller in the land contract sale is the retention of the legal title until the entire purchase price has been paid. The payment is usually amortized over a relatively long period of time. It is therefore frequently referred to as an installment sale. The buyer is normally given the right to possession immediately. The buyer retains possession so long as no default in the payment schedule occurs. In most cases the buyer also assumes the burdens of ownership: payment of taxes, insurance, and maintenance. All of these matters are subject to negotiation between the parties and need not all be present to have a sale by land contract.

During the life of the land contract the buyer has an ownership interest called the equitable title. The legal title, however, is retained by the seller. The buyer's interest is enforceable in an equitable proceeding to compel the seller to deed him the legal title when all payment has been made. This fact has led to the notion that the buyer is acquiring more ownership as time goes on and more payments are made. It is said that the buyer is building or establishing an equity in the property. This is an interest of value that can be sold, leased, or even mortgaged. The implication, however, that the buyer is acquiring some share of the legal title is incorrect. No portion of the legal title is transferred until final payment has been made. In the interim the buyer is strengthening his equitable claim to the legal title. In some states for certain purposes, such as inheritence taxation, the buyer is treated as the owner of a legal real estate interest. The general conclusion of our courts, however, has been that the buyer has a contract right that is personal property. The protection generally afforded the contract buyer has not equalled that given to the owner of mortgaged property. The consequences of such a rule, especially in hardship cases, has led some courts to abandon this position and to treat the land contract as a mortgage. It is then necessary to follow local foreclosure statutes, which may provide a substantial equity of redemption to the buyer. The reasoning of the cases is not very helpful, since there is no logical basis for finding that an installment sales contract is a mortgage. The result is generally justified on the basis of concepts of fairness to the buyer. Many privately negotiated default provisions are quite harsh, usually including some forfeiture concept, which has never been favored by our legal system. Imposing mortgage foreclosure rules upon the land contract default proceeding compels the seller to provide some grace period to permit the defaulting buyer to cure the default.

It is of course quite common for the parties to a land contract to include a negotiated grace period within which late payments can be made up and the contract returned to current status. If such a clause is used its terms are negotiable, but in practice many are seen that are more favorable to the buyer than the foreclosure statutes would be. That is, in the typical foreclosure statute the borrower is required to pay off the entire debt in order to redeem the property. Considerable difficulty can be encountered in obtaining new financing when in default. Many grace provisions in land contracts permit the defaulting buyer simply to bring the payments to current status. This may be far easier to accomplish.

### Land Contracts and the Due-on-Sale Clause

Whether or not the land contract is a completed sale that will trigger the due-on-sale clause in an existing mortgage on the property is an important question. In some jurisdictions the conclusion of the courts has been that the land contract is simply a security device and that there is no completed sale until the contract is completely performed. The distinction is quite significant. If the land contract is not a sale for the purpose of the due-on-sale clause, then the land contract is an ideal device for seller-assisted financing if existing mortgage terms are favorable. By retaining the legal title to the property the seller also retains tight control over the buyer's performance of the payment obligation. When there is a sale by assumption, on the other hand, the seller transfers legal title to the buyer and, along with it, leverage to compel the buyer to keep his assumption promise to pay the seller's debt. In many recent mortgage forms, the due-on-sale clause has been more specifically worded so that a sale by land contract will be a sale by agreement of the parties. If this is the case, of course, the question is settled by the agreement. If the mortgage fails to include a due-on-sale clause or if the clause is not triggered by a land contract sale by virtue of local law, then the land contract may still be an effective method of seller-assisted financing for preserving the benefits of an existing mortgage.

### Nature of Land Contract

Three types of real estate transactions that are closely related but that differ in some of their technical aspects are (1) the land contract, (2) a bond for title, and (3) a long-term escrow. They are all essentially security devices. In each of these the vendor of the real estate retains the technical title to the property, and the vendee takes possession and assumes the risks of ownership.

Under the terms of the land contract the buyer agrees to pay the purchase price, and the seller agrees to execute and deliver to the buyer a deed to the property when the payment of the purchase price is made. In a bond-for-title transaction the agreement between the purchaser and the seller is substantially the same as in a land contract. However, in addition to agreeing to deliver the deed, the seller executes a bond with sureties that provides for the payment to the purchaser of damages in the event the seller refuses or fails to execute and deliver the deed to the property as provided in the contract of purchase and sale. Under the terms of a long-term escrow the seller executes and delivers the deed to the escrow holder to be delivered to the purchaser when his part of the transaction has been performed. In all of these transactions the buyer is the equitable owner of the property.

This discussion will be based on the land contract; and any important difference between the land contract, bond for title, or long-term escrow will be noted.

Heinrich contracted to sell to Barlow and Beus, for the sum of $65,000, real and personal property consisting of a ranch and the farming machinery and equipment situated thereon.

Under the terms of the agreement the purchasers were to deposit with Idaho National Bank, as escrow holder, certain notes valued at $15,000, payable to the order of the purchaser, and were to pay the $50,000 balance in yearly installments of $5,000. The seller was to deposit with the escrow holder a warranty deed to the real property and title insurance policies, together with a bill of sale to the personal property and certain fire insurance policies. The contract and escrow agreement expressly provided that failure to make any payment when due or the failure of the maker of any of the notes to pay a note when due would be a default on the part of the purchaser, in which event the seller would be entitled to the possession of all the property and the escrow holder would return all instruments deposited by the seller. Default was made in the payment of certain notes, and the seller brought an action of attachment whereby he attached certain of the personal property sold under the contract of sale. Under the statutes of the state a person has no right to an attachment if his claim is secured. The trial court held that Heinrich's claim was secured and dismissed the attachment. On appeal, the dismissal of the attachment was affirmed.

Chief Justice Knudson said: "In *Fraser* v. *Clark,* the court was considering a contract which, like in this case, did not contain an express provision reserving title, but provided that sufficient deed and abstract should be deposited in escrow, for delivery upon purchasers' complete compliance, and that in case of purchasers' noncompliance, deed and abstract should be returned for cancellation and contract, at vendors' option, should become null and void and vendor entitled to possession of property. The court held that: 'Such provisions of the contract clearly provided a remedy for and security to the vendors for a breach thereof and under the provisions of R.C.M., 1947, p. 93–4301, precluded a rightful attachment and seizure of defendants' personal property in an action upon the contract upon which this suit was brought.'

"We therefore conclude that the contract here involved was an executory contract of sale under the terms of which appellants retained title as security for the payment of the purchase price. This being so, the contract was one expressly providing for security within the meaning of I.C. pp. 8–501, 8–502, and the attachment was properly discharged." *Heinrich* v. *Barlow,* Idaho, 390 P.2d 831 (1964).

## Form

There are no formal requirements for a valid land contract. Basically, it is a simple contract by the terms of which one party agrees to sell and another party agrees to buy a described piece of real estate. The buyer agrees to pay the stipulated purchase price over a certain period of time, and the seller agrees to execute and deliver to the buyer a deed to the real estate when the purchase price is paid. The rules of contract law are applied in determining whether or not the parties have entered into a valid, enforceable contract. These rules are discussed in Chapter 1.

A land contract, in order to be valid, does not have to be acknowledged, sealed, or witnessed. However, if the parties wish to record the land contract, it must be executed in compliance with the recording statutes of the state in which the land is located.

## After-Acquired Property

When a person contracts to sell real estate under a land contract, such contract will, in the absence of a special provision in the contract to the contrary, be construed as implying that the seller has a merchantable title to the property that he is contracting to sell. If the seller does not have a merchantable title, the buyer may, at his election, rescind the contract and recover any sum he has paid on the agreed purchase price. He may also have any note that he has given as evidence of the unpaid balance of the purchase price canceled, provided the note, if negotiable in form, has not been negotiated to a holder in due course.[11] If the seller does not have, at the time the contract is executed, a merchantable title to the real estate, but later clears his title and can convey, at the time for the execution and delivery of the deed, a merchantable title, the buyer cannot refuse to make payment and rescind the contract on the ground that the seller's title was not merchantable at the time the contract was executed.

## The Debt Secured by Land Contract

The only debt that can be secured by a land contract is the unpaid balance of the purchase price of the real estate that the seller has contracted to sell to the buyer. The land contract can be used to secure no other debt; it cannot be used as security for future advances. However, the standard land contract provides that the buyer shall pay all taxes, assessments, and insurance premiums; on his failure to do so, the seller may elect to pay such taxes, assessment, and insurance premiums, and add the amount disbursed to the unpaid balance due on the land contract.

---

[11] *Sutton* v. *Ford et al.,* 215 Ark. 269, 220 S.W.2d 125.

As a general rule, the purchase price that the buyer has contracted to pay for the real estate, the amount of the down payment, the amount and time of each subsequent payment, and the interest to be paid and how computed are set out in detail in the land contract. Although the debt may, in addition to the provision in the land contract, be evidenced by a separate instrument—either a negotiable or a nonnegotiable note—as a general rule, no separate instrument evidencing the debt need be executed.

### Recording

Recording is not essential to the validity of a land contract. Whether or not a land contract is eligible for recordation will depend on the recording statutes of the state in which the real estate is located. In any event, if the land contract is to be recorded, it must be executed in compliance with the recording statutes of the state in which the real estate is located.

If the buyer takes possession of the real estate and occupies it in such a way that possession and occupation are evident to any person inspecting the property, the buyer's interests would be protected without recording the land contract, since anyone buying from the seller, who is the owner of record, would take with notice of the rights of the party in possession. If the real estate is undeveloped land and the buyer cannot occupy the land in such a manner that his occupation would be obvious to others, the buyer's interests would not be protected unless the land contract was recorded, since, without recordation, a good-faith purchaser might have no notice or knowledge of the existence of the land contract and would take free of the interests of the land contract buyer.[12]

### Assignment by the Buyer

The buyer under a land contract has a property interest in the real estate that is the subject matter of the contract and may transfer such interest by assigning the land contract to a third person. The assignee acquires all the rights of his assignor (the buyer) and takes subject to all the obligations the assignor owes to the seller under the land contract. The buyer, by assigning the contract, cannot release himself from his obligations to the seller, unless the seller expressly agrees that he shall be released.[13] If the land contract includes a provision denying the buyer the right to assign the land contract without the written consent of the seller, an assignment in violation of the provision would give the seller the right to declare a forfeiture. The forfeiture, however, would not be enforced if the

---

[12] *Jarrett* v. *Arnerich et al.,* 44 Wash.2d 55, 265 P.2d 282.

[13] *Krueger et al.* v. *Campbell et al.,* 264 Mich. 449, 250 N.W. 285.

buyer or his assignee tendered full performance to the seller on his declaration of forfeiture.[14]

If the land contract has been recorded, each assignment of the contract should be recorded. If the land contract has been recorded and subsequent assignments are not recorded, and the seller, on final payment, deeds the property to an assignee who is not an assignee of record, the failure to record the assignments would create a defect in the record.

## Transfer of Real Estate by Seller

The seller is the owner of record of the real estate sold under a land contract; that is, he has legal title to the real estate. He also is the owner of the debt that the land contract secures. He may assign his interest in the land contract—that is, sell the debt—or he may sell the real estate subject to the outstanding rights of the land contract buyer.

If the land contract is not recorded and the buyer or his assignee or representative is not in possession, and the seller conveys the real estate to a good-faith purchaser for value, such purchaser will take free from the outstanding claims of the land contract buyer or his assignee. However, the seller would, in such a case, be guilty of breach of the land contract; and the buyer could hold the seller liable in damages, could rescind the contract and recover all payments made, or could require the seller to account to the buyer for the full consideration of the second sale.[15] The purchaser of real estate subject to an outstanding land contract is entitled to the payments due under the contract and owes a duty to convey the real estate to the buyer or his assignee as provided in the land contract.

## Rights of Seller on Buyer's Default

Since the courts have not recognized the land contract as a security transaction but have held it to be a contract to sell, the basis for the determination of the rights of the seller on the buyer's default is the provisions of the contract. The provisions normally included in land contracts are illustrated in the sample form later in this chapter.

As a general rule, if the buyer is guilty of a material breach of the contract, such as his failure to make payment when due, or if he repudiates the contract, the seller will be entitled to repossess the real estate, particularly when the land contract so provides.[16] However, if, after default but before the seller repossesses the property, or, having repossessed, before he changes his position in relation

[14] *Handzel et al.* v. *Bassi et al.*, 343 Ill. App. 281 99 N.E.2d 23.

[15] *Niles* v. *Groover,* 98 Ga. 461, 3 S.E. 899.

[16] *Murphy* v. *Yeast,* 59 Ariz. 281, 126 P.2d 313.

thereto and within a reasonable time, the buyer tenders the full amount of the unpaid balance of the purchase price, interest, and legitimate costs, the seller will be required to accept the tender and deed the real estate to the buyer as required by the terms of the land contract.[17]

If the buyer, after default, refuses to surrender the property, the seller may bring an action to recover possession. The procedure to be followed in such an action will depend on the statutes of the state in which the real estate is located.

In some states the seller, as a prerequisite to the bringing of a possessory action, must give the buyer either notice to quit or notice of forfeiture. The form of such notice, the time of the notice, how and on whom served, and so forth, will be set out in the statutes of the state in which the real estate is located. In some states the giving of notice to quit or notice of forfeiture may be waived by including an express waiver in the land contract. In other states, if the land contract includes a provision making time of the essence, no notice to quit or notice of forfeiture is required.[18] As a general rule, demand for possession, unless waived by the terms of the land contract, must be made as a prerequisite to the bringing of a possessory action.[19]

The standard form of land contract in common use includes a provision permitting the seller, on default by the buyer and repossession by the seller, to retain all payments made and all improvements of the property as rent and liquidated damages for breach of the contract. Unless the circumstances are such that the enforcement of such provision would amount to a penalty, it will be enforced, and the buyer will be held not to be entitled to the return of any of the purchase price he has paid[20] or to payment for improvements made.[21] As noted earlier, however, the courts in some states will not enforce such a provision if the buyer has established a substantial equity in the property.

If the seller wishes, he may, under the procedure statutes of some states, bring an action in the nature of a strict foreclosure if the buyer defaults. A decree of strict foreclosure, since it is an equitable remedy, will not be granted if the value of the land is substantially greater than the unpaid balance due under the land contract.[22]

If, on the buyer's failure to make the payments when due, the seller does not wish to repossess the real estate, he may resort to his remedies at law. He

---

[17] *Onekama Realty Co.* v. *Carothers,* 59 Ariz. 416, 129 P.2d 918.

[18] *Whitehurst* v. *Ratliff,* 198 Okla. 639, 181 P.2d 545.

[19] *Muirhead* v. *McCullough,* 234 Mich. 52, 207 N.W. 886.

[20] *J. F. Cantwell Co.* v. *Harrison et al.,* 95 Ind. App. 180, 180 N.E. 482.

[21] *Continental Oil Co.* v. *Bean et al.,* 171 Okla. 66, 41 P.2d 678.

[22] *Swanson* v. *Madsen et al.,* 145 Neb. 815, 18 N.W.2d 217.

may bring suit and recover a judgment for past-due installments; or he may, if the contract contains a provision giving him the right, declare the entire balance of the purchase price immediately due and payable, and bring an action to recover a judgment for this amount. If the seller brings suit to recover a judgment for the last installment due under the terms of the land contract or for the unpaid balance, he must tender into the court a deed that complies with the terms of the land contract.[23] Whether or not the buyer, in the event of suit for the unpaid balance of the purchase price, will be entitled to credit for installments paid or for improvements made to the property will depend on the terms of the contract and the circumstances of the particular case.

Boyd, by written contract, agreed to buy certain real estate for $17,500, of which $8,000 was represented by Boyd's promissory note payable on or before two years from its date, and the remainder was payable at $100 per month, including interest. The $8,000 note was secured by other property belonging to Boyd. Boyd defaulted in his monthly payments, and the Davies (the sellers) gave written notice of their election to terminate and cancel the contract and retake possession. Possession of the property was redelivered to the Davies. They then brought this suit upon the $8,000 note, to foreclose the mortgage. The trial court gave judgment to the Davies, and on appeal, the court reversed the judgment.

Justice Noble said: "The parties to a contract may provide for its rescission upon any terms agreeable to them, and this court has indicated that a provision for forfeiture of installment payments made prior to default, which approximate rent, will be approved, at least where reasonable notice of default is required by the contract. The sellers had the option to consider the contract still in force, sue for breach of its terms or the enforcement thereof, or, on the other hand, to disaffirm the contract and retain the payments made by purchasers as liquidated damages. Under the doctrine of election of remedies, they could not disaffirm it and sue for any part of its performance. It seems to be the general holding of the courts that a vendor may not maintain an action to recover any part of an unpaid purchase money where he has rescinded or forfeited a contract. Where a contract for sale of real estate is accompanied by the purchaser's note or other separate obligation for a part of the purchase price, termination or cancellation of the contract or claim of forfeiture under its terms, because of default by the purchaser, is generally held to destroy the consideration for the separate obligation of the purchaser and it is no longer enforceable against him.

"The trial court found as a fact that defendants only made five monthly payments, and that after written notice plaintiffs did elect to and did rescind the contract, and took possession of the real estate. Having declared a forfeiture, and elected to rescind the contract, it follows as a matter of law that there can be no recovery on the note representing an unpaid part of the purchase price. The rescission of the contract destroyed the consider-

[23] *Fairlawn Heights Co., Inc.* v. *Theis,* 133 Ohio St. 387, 14 N.E.2d 1; *Bridge Land Improvement Co.* v. *Meyers et al.,* 129 N.J.L. 164, 28 A.2d 601.

ation for the note which was given, not as payment, but as evidence of a payment to be made under the terms of the contract." *Davies* v. *Boyd,* 73 N.M. 85, 385 P.2d 950 (1963).

### Damages for Breach of Contract

As a general rule, the seller, on the buyer's default, may bring an action to recover damages for breach of contract. In such a case the general rules of the law of damages would apply in determining the amount of damages to which the seller is entitled. In general, the seller is entitled to recover judgment for the amount he can prove with reasonable certainty he has lost as the direct result of the buyer's breach of the contract.

### Buyer's Remedies on Seller's Default

If the seller refuses or fails to execute and deliver a deed to the property in compliance with the terms of the land contract, the buyer is entitled to the remedy of specific performance on the tender or payment of the purchase price and on the performance of his other obligations under the contract.[24] The buyer, on the seller's default or inability to perform, may elect to rescind the contract and recover all payments made, less a reasonable amount as rent for the use of the real estate.[25] When the buyer has, in good faith, made substantial improvements that enhance the value of the real estate, he may recover the value of such improvements.[26]

If the seller breaches the land contract in any material respect, or is unable or unwilling to convey title to the real estate to the buyer as required by the contract, the buyer, at his election, may bring an action to recover damages for the breach of the contract. The measure of damages usually applied in such cases is the amount of loss that the buyer can prove with reasonable certainty he has suffered as the direct result of the seller's breach of the contract.

Walter L. Talley, Inc., sold certain real estate to Council on land contract. After the execution of the contract and without the knowledge or consent of Council, Walter L. Talley, Inc., conveyed an easement of right of way across the property to De Kalb County to be used for the installation of a sewer trunk line through the property. Council gave notice of rescission of the contract and brought suit to recover the money paid. The trial court granted Council a judgment; and on appeal, the judgment was affirmed.

Judge Jordan said: "Where the vendor breaches an executory contract for the sale of

---

[24] *Sexton* v. *Waggoner,* La. App., 66 So.2d 634.

[25] *Passent et al.* v. *Peter Vredenburgh Lumber Co., Inc., et al.,* 325 Ill. App. 260, 60 N.E.2d 39.

[26] *Huggins et al.* v. *Green Top Dairy Farms, Inc., et al.,* 75 Idaho 436, 273 P.2d 399.

land, the vendee, if not himself in default, may elect to rescind the contract and recover the amount he has paid on the purchase price.

"The defendant vendor under the terms of the contract of sale was obligated to convey said property by warranty deed to the purchaser at the time the sale was consummated, subject to any incumbrances as specified in the contract. Since there were no incumbrances specified in the contract of sale, it was the vendor's duty under said contract to convey the subject property to the plaintiff vendee free and clear of any incumbrances. This is true for the reason that a general warranty in a warranty deed includes the covenant that the land being conveyed is free from incumbrances.

"Accordingly, where as here the evidence authorized the finding that the defendant vendor had placed an incumbrance upon the subject property by conveying an easement in it to De Kalb County for the purpose of installing and maintaining a sewer line through that property (which according to the testimony of the plaintiff rendered the property less valuable for the use intended) and had thus rendered the performance of its contract impossible, the plaintiff vendee who was not himself in default was entitled to rescind the contract and recover the amount he had paid on the purchase price." *Walter L. Tally, Inc.* v. *Council,* Ga. App., 135 S.E.2d 515 (1964).

## Typical Land Contract Provisions

While, as noted earlier, no particular form is required for a land contract sale, their widespread use has resulted in some degree of uniformity as to content. There follows a sample land contract, which is presented here to illustrate a typical transaction that would involve residential property. The comments that follow the form discuss only the more significant elements of the contract.

In the consideration of this form it should be kept in mind that it is very similar to forms in use today for relatively simple transactions, such as the sale of a single-family residence. In practice very sophisticated land contracts may be used for the sale of commercial properties such as an apartment complex. A complex land contract also may be utilized to obtain installment treatment of a capital gain for income tax purposes. Insulating the seller from early receipt of payment then becomes a crucial provision of the contract.

**Land Contract**

This agreement is made and entered into this _____ day of __________, 19_____, by and between __________________________, of __________ County, State of __________________ (hereinafter referred to as "Seller"), and __________________________, of ______________ County, State of ______________________ (hereinafter referred to as "Purchaser"), and witnesses that:

**Land Contract *(continued)***

For and in consideration of the performance of the acts and the payments required by this agreement by Purchaser, Seller agrees to sell and convey the real estate located in ______________________ County, State of ____________, commonly known as ________________, the legal description of which is as follows:

______________________________________________________________

______________________________________________________________

____________________hereinafter referred to as "the property").

The total sales price shall be ________________________________

__________________($__________) dollars, of which Seller hereby acknowledges receipt of ___________________________________________

($__________) dollars, as the initial payment from Purchaser.

*If Purchaser shall* pay to Seller at ______________________________

(or at such other place as Seller shall from time to time direct in writing) not less than ________________________ ($__________) dollars on the ______ day of __________, 19____, and on the ______ day of each succeeding month until the sales price, plus interest thereon at the rate of ______ percent per annum, computed ____________ on the then unpaid balance, is fully paid;

*and if until full and complete payment* is made in accordance with this contract, Purchaser shall:

(1) pay when due and payable the real estate taxes starting with the payment due on the ______ day of __________, 19____, and all taxes coming due and payable thereafter; the existing special assessments on said land described below: ____________________________________________________

______________________________________________________________

______________________________________________________________

______________________________________________________________

and all special assessments levied thereon after the date of this contract; any and all other charges of any kind hereafter levied or assessed against the property and which are not created or caused by Seller; and shall provide to Seller evidence of payment of all such taxes, levies or assessments on or before the next installment payment date after such payments become due and payable;

(2) insure the buildings and improvements presently on the property, if any, and deposit with Seller a paid-up policy or policies of insurance issued by companies satisfactory to Seller to cover the improvements against loss or damage

**Land Contract *(continued)***

through fire or hazards covered by the commonly used Extended Coverage Endorsement in the amounts determined by Seller; or, in the event Purchaser fails to pay premiums upon such insurance when due Seller may pay them and add the amount of the premiums to the unpaid balance then due under this land contract; such policies shall provide by endorsement that any loss shall be payable to Seller or Purchaser as their respective interests may appear;

(3) maintain the property, both land and buildings, in good condition and shall permit Seller to have access to the property during reasonable hours for the purpose of inspecting the property;

(4) refrain from using or permitting the property to be used for any unlawful purpose or purposes which will depreciate the value of the property;

(5) neither remove nor alter any existing buildings nor build new structures of any kind without first obtaining the written consent of seller;

(6) not violate any restrictions, conditions or covenants to be included in Seller's deed, said restrictions, conditions, and covenants being hereby made effective as of the date of this contract and are as follows:

______________________________________________

______________________________________________

______________________________________________

(7) neither assign this contract nor lease the property or any part thereof without first obtaining the written consent of Seller; should Seller consent to any assignment of this land contract Purchaser shall be obligated to pay Seller only for the costs of obtaining necessary credit information on the assignee; *then and in that event and at the time of final payment,* Seller shall execute and deliver to Purchaser a good and sufficient general warranty deed conveying the property to Purchaser in fee simple, subject to:

*(a)* all taxes, assessments, and charges described in clause (1), above, and those coming due and payable thereafter;

*(b)* all liens, encumbrances or other defects of title to the property created or caused by Purchaser;

*(c)* applicable zoning regulations in effect on the date of this contract or imposed during the life of this land contract;

*(d)* existing restrictions, conditions, and covenants now of record which affect the use of the property;

*(e)* all restrictions, conditions, and covenants specified in clause (6), above.

Seller further agrees to provide Purchaser (or his assignee) at the time of the delivery of the deed, at Seller's option, either: an abstract of title certified to the date of delivery of the deed, showing merchantable title in Seller subject

**Land Contract *(continued)***

only to such limitations upon Seller's deed as are specified in this land contract; or, an Owner's Policy of Title Insurance in the full amount of the purchase price specified above, said policy to be subject only to limitations, liens, or encumbrances as are assumed by Purchaser pursuant to this contract.

Interest shall, at the end of each __________ period, be computed upon the principal balance due and owing at the commencement of such period and added to the unpaid principal balance due and owing at the commencement of such period. From the balance thus obtained shall be deducted all payments made by Purchaser during said period, applying those payments first to the interest and the excess to reduction of the principal balance. The amount remaining after so applying Purchaser's payments shall stand as the unpaid principal balance for the next succeeding __________ period.

Seller may place or maintain a mortgage or deed of trust on the property for an amount not in excess of the then unpaid balance of the purchase price under this contract. Purchaser agrees that any lien created by such action of Seller shall be senior and prior to any claim of Purchaser under this contract, *provided,* however, that in the event Seller shall hereafter create such a lien upon the property Purchaser is entitled to written notice of such proposed action which notice shall diclose the name of the lender, the principal amount of the debt, the rate of interest, and the terms of payment, including the final payment date. In the event that the Seller's lender requires documentation to the effect that its lien shall be superior to any claim of Purchaser pursuant to this contract Purchaser agrees to execute any documents reasonably required to accomplish that end, however, Purchaser shall not be required to execute any document which would make Purchaser personally liable for the repayment of such debt incurred by Seller. After the execution and recording of any such mortgage or deed of trust Purchaser shall have the continuing right to pay down the balance due on the purchase price under this contract to an amount equal to the then unpaid balance of Seller's debt and to demand the general warranty deed provided for herein. In such event Seller shall promptly deliver such deed to Purchaser which deed shall, however, specifically provide that it is subject to the indebtedness and that Purchaser personally assumes and agrees to pay that indebtedness. This assumption of Seller's obligation by Purchaser shall be exercised in accordance with the terms and conditions of the mortgage or deed of trust, but when so exercised shall constitute full and final payment of Purchaser's obligations under this contract.

Time is of the essence of this contract. Should Purchaser fail to perform any act or acts, or fail to make any payment required by this contract, timely in accordance with the terms of this contract, then all payments made prior to

**Land Contract *(concluded)***

such default shall be retained by Seller as liquidated damages and compensation for the use of the property prior to the time of default and Seller shall thereafter have no liability or obligation to Purchaser under this contract. Immediately upon default, and without further demand or notice by Seller, Purchaser agrees to surrender to Seller peaceably immediate possession of the property together with all buildings and improvements thereon. Should Purchaser, upon default, fail to surrender possession as provided above, then Seller may proceed in any action at law or in equity for possession of the property and for damages suffered as the result of Purchaser's default.

Purchaser may make payments in excess or in advance of the amounts or times due under this contract and may pay the entire amount of the unpaid balance of the purchase price at any time without penalty for prepayment and with interest computed to the date of such payment.

Possession of the property shall be given by Seller to Purchaser on the ________ day of ______________, 19_____.

Further conditions to this contract are as follows: ____________________
____________________________________________________________
____________________________________________________________
____________________________________________________________
____________________________________________________________
____________________________________________________________

Both Purchaser and Seller expressly agree that this contract shall be binding upon, apply to, and inure to the benefit of their respective heirs, successors, and assignees in the same manner and to the same extent as it binds or benefits the parties themselves.

*In Witness Whereof,* the parties have signed, sealed, and delivered this contract in duplicate, each of which shall be an original, the day and year first written above.

Seller ____________________ Purchaser ____________________
Seller ____________________ Purchaser ____________________

(Assignment by purchaser, acceptance by assignee, and acceptance of the assignment by seller could be included in the land contract form at the outset. The same is true of the formal acknowledgment, which is required if the contract is to be recorded. They are omited here for brevity.)

## Comments on the Sample Land Contract

1. *The Real Estate Tax and Assessment Clause.* The shifting of the burden of payment of real estate taxes to the purchaser has become standard in sales by land contract. This transfer has some basis in pure logic—it is, after all, the purchaser who is occupying and using the property, so that it is hardly unconscionable to expect him to pay the taxes the property generates. As with the burden of casualty insurance, it is not uncommon for the seller to reserve the ministerial function of paying these taxes (in order to protect his security, the legal title) and to add this cost to the remaining balance due under the contract. The imposition of the ultimate liability for real estate taxes on the contract buyer has become so commonplace that it is seldom a matter of discussion, let alone negotiation, in the true sense of that term. Not only is the burden of payment shifted to the buyer but also the risks of increased rates of tax and increased valuations for tax purposes are transferred. Nevertheless, the inclusion of a well-drafted real estate tax clause is important to both the seller and the buyer *because these taxes affect the true total cost of the property.*

It also seems both appropriate and fair to shift the burden of payment of assessments for municipal improvements (such as streets, sewers, water, and the like) to the contract buyer. Again, the rationale would be that these improvements increase the value of the property being purchased and should be paid for by the ultimate owner of the property. It is important that the transfer of this burden to the contract buyer be clearly spelled out in the contract, since the general rule would otherwise impose this burden upon the holder of record title, the seller.

2. *The Insurance Clause.* During the term of the land contract, it is apparent that both the seller and the buyer have an interest in the property and its improvements and that each may insure that interest. That is, each has an "insurable interest" to be protected. What is not clear, however, is the question of who has the *duty* to insure. Actually, neither party has a duty to insure his own interest, let alone the other's interest. This is a matter that must be covered by the contract, and the typical resolution is a clause requiring the buyer to obtain and keep in force adequate insurance for the benefit of both parties. This is yet another burden of ownership transferred to the buyer during the term of the contract.

3. *Maintenance and Inspection Clauses.* It is quite common under the sale by land contract to impose upon the buyer the obligation to properly maintain the property and the improvements on it. This is but one of the burdens of ownership generally cast upon the buyer during the term of the contract. It is, of course, in the best interests of the buyer to properly maintain the property because he or she will ultimately own it; but the real purpose of the maintenance clause is to require the buyer to protect and preserve the seller's security. By making this a positive requirement, a failure of the buyer to comply will constitute a breach of the contract so that it can be terminated by the seller and the property retaken. At the same time such a clause is difficult to monitor, unless there is reserved in the contract the right to enter and inspect periodically to verify that necessary

maintenance is in fact being performed. In view of the nature of the buyer's interest in the property under a sale by land contract, it is doubtful that the right of inspection would exist without such a clause.

4. *The Improvements Clause.* In connection with a sale by land contract, the matter of existing and contemplated improvements should be given consideration by both parties. With regard to the existing improvements, the seller will want to restrict the rights of the buyer to physically remove them from the property, assuming that the use of the improvements is the primary motivation for the contract in the first place. This is typically the case when residential property is the subject matter of the property. In some other instances, however, the improvements may be of no value and be a hindrance to the proposed use of the property by the buyer. This can easily occur when dilapidated outbuildings are occupying tillable acreage, and the parties may contemplate their demolition and removal at the time of negotiation of the contract. Whichever is the case, their contract should clearly spell out their intentions in order to avoid later disputes.

5. *The Use Clause.* Whether and to what extent the buyer's use of the property will be restricted (other than by local ordinances, including zoning) must be established in the contract itself. The seller will frequently require more protection than just a prohibition against illegal use. Indeed, he or she must require that the buyer refrain from breaching any existing private or restrictive covenant since such violation might jeopardize his or her legal title. At the same time any additional restrictions upon the use of the property, which the seller intends to include in the ultimate deed, must be established in the contract so that the buyer will be legally obligated to accept them. Such protection is also necessary to protect the value of any property retained by the seller, whether he intends to keep it or sell it to others. For example, if the property being sold is a parcel that will be included in a planned subdivision that will be subject to protective covenants in all deeds, it will be essential that these same covenants be spelled out in the land contract.

6. *Assignment and Lease Clause.* Many land contracts contain an absolute prohibition against assignment. In the absence of any provision at all, the land contract would be freely assignable by the buyer just as almost all other contracts may be assigned. This particular form of contract contemplates the possibility of assignment, but permits the seller to retain a strong element of control by requiring his approval prior to assignment. Under general contract rules, the fact that the purchaser assigns his rights under the contract in no way relieves him of primary liability for the performance of his duties under the contract. It is also quite common to include in the land contract a prohibition against the leasing of the property during the term of the contract by the buyer to a third party. Typically, the reasoning behind such a prohibition is the concern that the tenant may be less responsible in caring for the property than the contract buyer

7. *The Mortgage Clause.* If there is already an existing mortgage or deed of trust against the property at the time of the execution of the land contract, whether or not this fact is made known to the buyer, the lien thereby created will not be affected by the sale and the contract buyer's rights will be subservient to those of the lienholder. Even if there is no such preexisting secured debt upon the property, however, the seller

may find it necessary or desirable to create it even after entering into the land contract. Because this action adversely affects the seller's ability to perform his side of the bargain, it seems that the contract buyer is entitled to be notified of such intended action by the seller. The lender, if aware of the land contract, will insist upon the contract buyer's acquiescence and recognition of the superiority of the lien of the mortgage or deed of trust.

8. *Liquidated Damages Clause.* Under the basic doctrine of freedom of contract, courts have traditionally upheld a good-faith effort by the parties to determine in advance what damages will result from a breach of their contract. This is particularly true in cases when the *actual* damages would be difficult or impossible to accurately determine at the time the contract is breached. The inclusion of such a clause eliminates the need for time-consuming and expensive litigation. Therefore, it is quite appropriate for the parties themselves to establish this amount in their agreement, and such clauses are enforceable. There is, however, the possibility that one party or the other may be in a commanding bargaining position and force upon the other a "liquidated damages" clause, which is so onerous that it will be interpreted by a court to be a "penalty" clause, an economic club that the court will find unenforceable.

The point to be made is that the wording of the clause itself is not the determining factor in characterizing the clause as a "liquidated damages" clause or as a "penalty" clause. One must apply the clause to the factual situation in order to see its economic effect upon the parties. The recent trend in the courts has been to follow this procedure and to characterize such provisions as penalties only if the buyer has built up a "substantial" equity. If the equity is insignificant, such clauses are still being upheld. The important change that has occurred is that our courts will now *entertain* such suits in the first place. In the negotiation and drafting of the liquidated damages clause, it is clear that more care is now necessary to insure that the clause will meet the test of essential fairness.

9. *The Prepayment Clause.* By the very nature of general contract law, if terms of payment and delivery are specified with reasonable certainty, there is generally no right on the part of one party to tender performance ahead of schedule and to demand immediate performance by the other party. It is therefore important that a prepayment clause be included if the parties desire to clearly establish this right.

# Section 5

# Sales of Real Estate

The marketing of real estate is a technical and challenging business. Considerable knowledge of a broad range of legal rules is essential if one is to be successful in this field. We have already given attention to many detailed aspects of real estate law. In this section we will explore still others that are directly related to the sales process and that involve the application of contract law to real estate marketing. We will see that the number of details that must be considered in such a sale results in a complex contract between the seller and buyer. The negotiation of these details into a contract of sale is but the first step in the transaction. The manner in which this contract is performed is yet another area to be explored.

At the outset the specialized business of real estate brokerage is discussed in detail. It will be seen that the real estate broker functions as a professional agent, usually on behalf of the seller. This principal-and-agent relationship is created by a special form of contract called a *listing.* Because the broker is an agent, the law of principal and agent, as it has developed in connection with real estate sales, must be understood. We will see that varying degrees of commitment to this relationship are available to the owner. The broker may be retained on a basis in which he competes with other brokers retained by the seller. The broker may, on the other hand, be the exclusive agent, with no others having the authority to represent the owner. His competition then will be limited to the owner himself who may retain the right to sell the property directly to prospects of his own. Finally, the seller may grant the broker an exclusive right to sell, so that the broker is assured of a commission even if the owner himself finds a buyer. It will be apparent that the broker will be motivated in proportion to the degree of assurance that he will be compensated for his efforts.

The market for real estate is inefficient and localized. In an attempt to improve its effectiveness, the brokerage industry has developed certain innovations, such as the multiple or shared listing association. In such an arrangement a number of brokers share the authority to represent the owner in the sale of his property. The way in which this is accomplished is an agreement between the cooperating brokers that permits each of them to exercise the authority given by the owner to the listing broker. Of course, such an arrangement violates a fundamental rule of the law of principal and agent: the agent may not delegate his responsibilities to others. Therefore, in order for such a system to be established the owner must clearly authorize such delegation. Still greater efficiencies are perceived by the participants in the national franchise systems that exist today. Associations of cooperating brokers across the country seek to expand the localized character of the real estate market by the sharing of information and facilities.

Regardless of the attempts to modernize real estate brokerage, the ultimate sale almost universally comes down to one-on-one negotiations between the seller and the buyer, with one or two brokers assisting the parties in reaching their agreement. It is this negotiating process that makes real estate brokerage unique. Values, to be sure, may be estimated by appraisals, but they are finally established by the buyers and sellers through the negotiation process. Lawyers say that real estate is a "horse": it is worth what the parties think it is worth. The rules for the negotiation of contracts are therefore fundamental to the real estate marketing process.

Because the real estate broker is a *professional* agent, certain standards of competence are expected of him in the conduct of his business. The broker may incur financial liability to his principal for any failure to meet these standards that results in a loss to the principal. This is an area in which significant development has taken place in recent years. The broker is expected to be an expert in matters directly related to the real estate itself, such as the quality of the building. To compete effectively the broker must also be knowledgeable in real estate finance, for without finance the sale will not take place and no commission can be earned. It is also apparent that the broker must have substantial legal knowledge in many areas. To the extent that the broker's efforts go beyond pure selling activity, the law requires him to have and use the knowledge and skill he claims to have or risk being liable to his principal. The mere possession of a real estate license is enough to constitute a warranty of competence and the practicing broker must, to a great extent, guarantee the quality of his services.

The unauthorized practice of law by brokers is considered in this section. Because of the technical nature of the real estate sale, the large sums involved, and the long-term nature of real estate decisions, important agreements about property rights are entered into by the parties to the sale. It is the broker's function to assist them in making these decisions. There is no real question as to whether or not the real estate broker practices law as part of the brokerage business. It is obvious that he does so. The real question is to what extent is that practice of law *unauthorized?* This important limitation on brokerage activities is considered here along with the related activities of property management and appraisal.

In Chapter 16 the purchase agreement between the seller and buyer is considered in detail. While it is certainly true that all documents involved in the real estate sale—from the listing on through to the deed and mortgage—are important, it is the purchase agreement that dominates. It is the purchase agreement that spells out in precise detail the obligations and rights of the parties. The purchase agreement for real estate seems to be in conflict with any trend toward simplification of legal documents. There is a great variety of matters to be included in such an agreement: the quality of the type of deed and the extent of the seller's warranties; the terms of payment, including any form of seller-assisted financing; the allocation of property tax liabilities; the division of rentals and transfer of deposits; the point at which insurable interest will pass; the definition of the subject matter through a survey or other technique; the quality of the buildings and any included systems and appliances; and a great deal more in some transactions.

The purchase agreement can become a quite elaborate document that requires the agreement of the parties on a wide variety of issues. It is not usually a contract that is expected to be immediately performed. Indeed, very often the entire contract will be contingent upon the ability of the parties to accomplish certain steps successfully. For example, the entire sale may be dependent upon the buyer's ability to obtain financing upon certain terms. His ability to do so will be a condition that must be met before he will be obligated to go through with the transaction. How long a time will be granted to obtain the financing needed? What financing must he accept, whether it is desirable or not? Does the seller have the right to obtain financing for the buyer who procrastinates? These issues must be settled for a very practical reason: while they remain open, the property will be off the market and the seller will be unable to negotiate with other buyers. This possible loss of a market is an important financial consideration, and the seller is likely to insist upon some sort of penalty in the purchase agreement to cover this possible loss.

The settlement of and agreement upon all of the issues included in the typical purchase agreement can be a lengthy process. It may include offers and counteroffers between the parties that will modify and adjust the ultimate agreement in stages. The most important question to be settled between the parties is of course the price to be paid. The desire of the seller to obtain the maximum price may best be served by the negotiation process involving the services of a knowledgeable real estate broker. Many times, however, the maximum selling price can be best achieved by the use of a completely different process: the auction sale. In recent years the auction sale of real estate has become much more widely used in the real estate business. The advantages of the auction method are seen at the extremes. It may bring top dollar when the property is in great demand by providing a forum for direct and open competition between interested buyers. At the other extreme is the mandatory sale of property that is less than desirable, the distress sale. The advantages of the auction sale are not limited to these two extremes. When conducted by a professional auctioneer using advanced marketing techniques, the auction today is proving to be an attractive alternative to the negotiated sale technique. A discussion of the auction sale and the rules under which such sales are conducted is therefore included in Chapter 16.

Finally considered in this section is the important step of completing the purchase agreement. Ordinarily the real estate sale is not immediately performed upon reaching agreement to do so. It may take a month or more for the parties to complete all the preliminary steps to prepare for the ultimate performance of their purchase agreement: the closing. It is at the closing that the deed is finally delivered and the money for it is paid. Prior to this ritual all of the details will have been completed by others: the mortgage lender, the abstractor, the surveyor, the attorney, and others. It is at the closing that the work of all these participants is finally inspected and determined to be in accordance with the commitments made in the purchase agreement. The documents are all executed at the closing and made ready for the recording that will memorialize the event. All of the details that must be attended to in preparation for the closing, as well as the records that must be made of what happens at the closing, are considered in Chapter 17.

In view of the number of activities required before the closing, it is not uncommon to find that one or more details cannot be successfully resolved in time. When this happens there are two alternatives. One possibility is that the closing will simply be postponed until the detail can be completed. This is frequently unsatisfactory because other tasks may have to be redone because of the lapse of time. For example, all prorations might have to be recalculated. The loan documents might all have to be regenerated. The title work might have to be updated. Indeed, the price might even have to be adjusted. When the detail is one that will be resolved within a short time it is often decided to have the closing without regard to the unresolved issue. To protect the parties and to be sure that the detail will in fact be attended to, an escrow may be established. In the escrow arrangement an independent third party will be appointed to act as a stakeholder for the parties to the sale. The escrow agent will undertake the protection of both parties in accordance with their agreement and the instructions furnished to the escrow agent. This important function is also discussed in Chapter 17 in connection with the closing.

# Chapter 15
# Real Estate Brokerage

## Introduction

Real estate brokerage is perhaps the most visible aspect of the real estate business. This is the result of the highly competitive nature of real estate brokerage, which creates a need for extensive advertising to attract business. The creation of a principal-and-agent relationship through the use of a specialized contract, the listing, is the important first step in conducting a successful brokerage business. Therefore, this chapter explores the variations of this relationship that have become common. A sample of such a contract, along with a discussion of it, is also included. The listing contract creates more than just opportunity for the broker. It also obligates him to perform the function of finding a buyer for the seller's property. In the course of this effort there is exposure to liability for failure to adequately perform his obligations. This is an important aspect of brokerage management because the broker employs salespeople, subagents, for whom he is also responsible, even though his control is slight because of the nature of the work.

Performance by the broker, finding a buyer, is of course essential to his claim for the agreed commission. When and under what terms the seller is obligated to pay the broker for his services are questions of obvious importance to both of them. The major reason for this importance is that selling expense, as a function of total sales price, has become significantly higher in recent years. Coupled with the effect of inflation on real estate prices, which has also become great, this means that commissions are now big-money considerations. The dollar value of real estate commissions paid in a given year is very sizable. Partly as a result of this fact the industry has been singled out for direct regulation through licensing laws. Other activities that are closely related to brokerage include property management and appraisal of real estate for a wide variety of purposes. These subjects are also included in this chapter.

## The Broker

Although the real estate business is not confined to brokerage, it is an important activity of substantially all persons engaged in such business. The real estate broker is an agent employed by a seller or buyer to negotiate the sale, purchase, or exchange of real estate on a commission contingent on success. He acts as a special agent for multiple principals. His primary function is to act as an intermediary between the buyer and the seller, aiding in the negotiations leading up to the sale, purchase, or exchange of real estate. He may, however, perform other services connected with the completion of the transaction, such as, for example, the procuring of financing.

The services performed by the real estate broker differ in many important respects from those performed by other common types of brokers—the stockbroker and commodity broker, for instance. The real estate broker's relation to the public is such that in a majority of the states, he must, before acting as a broker, obtain a license by establishing his integrity, character, and ability to serve his customers efficiently. The brokerage business is one of long standing and is very specialized. As a result, there has evolved in connection with this business a well-developed body of law, which reflects for the most part the established customs and usages of the business. Generally, the applicant, in order to obtain a real estate broker's license, must show through an examination reasonable knowledge of such laws, customs, and usages.

## Nature of Real Estate Brokerage

A person operating a real estate brokerage business acts as an independent businessman and also as an agent in the sale, purchase, or exchange of real estate. As an independent businessman, he determines the policies of his office. He hires and compensates his employees and directs their activities in connection with the business and in general is responsible for the operation of the business. As an agent, he represents the persons who engage his services, and he owes a duty to them to exercise care and skill in carrying out their instructions.

His duties are generally confined to the advertising of the property and to the finding of a person ready, willing, and able to deal on the terms stipulated by the broker's principal or acceptable to him. In the accomplishing of the objective of the agency, the broker may, and in many instances will, perform many connected services. Usually, the broker does not have the authority to bind his principal to a contract to sell or to make a conveyance of the listed property; such authority may, however, be conferred on him.[1]

Mrs. Todd owned real estate which she listed with Horton, a licensed real estate broker. A standard-form listing contract was executed by Mrs. Todd. Horton signed in the name of Mrs. Todd, as her agent, a contract to sell the real property. Mrs. Todd refused to perform the contract and, when sued, set up Horton's lack of authority to execute a contract to sell as her agent. The court held that Horton had no authority to execute a contract to sell as agent for Mrs. Todd.

Justice Oxner said: "It is well settled that a real estate broker, under the ordinary contract of employment, has no implied authority to execute a contract of sale in behalf of his principal. He is generally a special agent, with limited powers, whose usual duty is simply to find a purchaser ready, able and willing to enter into a contract upon the terms and conditions fixed by the owner." *Gallant* v. *Todd,* 235 S.C. 428, 111 S.E.2d 779 (1960).

## The Real Estate Salesman

The real estate salesman occupies a unique place in the operation of a real estate brokerage business. In a majority of the states, he must, like the real estate broker, prove his character, integrity, and ability and obtain a salesman's license. The duties he is licensed to perform are more limited than those granted the real estate broker, and the salesman generally must work out of the office of a licensed real estate broker.

The salesman may be an independent contractor, or he may be an employee of the broker. If the arrangement with the broker permits the salesman to work when and if he wishes, if he is permitted to find his own prospects and is not obligated to contact prospects referred to him by the broker, and if he is in general permitted to "work on his own," his relation to the broker will be that of an independent contractor. If the salesman works regular hours under the direct supervision and control of the broker and owes a duty to follow the reasonable instructions of the broker in regard to the work to be performed, he is an employee of the broker.

In either case the primary duty of the real estate salesman is to contact persons interested in purchasing property. It is his job to learn all he can about the prospect, either from personal interviews or from outside sources; to determine which listed properties the prospect is in a position to buy and in which he may be interested;

---

[1] *Queen City Lumber Company* v. *Fisher,* N.D., 111 N.W.2d 714.

and to induce the prospect to sign a proposition to purchase a certain property. The salesman is the contact man. He makes the representations and sales talks that induce the prospect to contract to purchase the property. Many people engaged in the real estate business operate both as brokers and as salesmen. This is usually true of persons operating small real estate brokerage businesses.

## Creation of the Real Estate Broker-Owner Relation

### Relation of Broker

The broker-owner relationship is created by the agreement of the parties, and from a legal standpoint the relationship is that of principal (the owner) and agent (the broker). Although such a relationship is created by agreement, a contract of employment is not necessary for its creation. All that is necessary is that the owner expressly or impliedly indicate his willingness to be represented in a transaction by another person, the broker, who, either expressly or impliedly, indicates his willingness to act under the direction and control of the owner.

The broker may act gratuitously, and the authority to act may be either oral or in writing. The creation of the relationship and the authority to act should not be confused with the statutory requirement of a writing as the basis of a broker's right to collect a commission earned. In the real estate brokerage business the relationship of owner and broker will, with few exceptions, be created by a contract that will authorize the broker to represent the owner in a transaction involving the owner's property.

### Listing Contracts

The contract between an owner and a broker whereby the broker is authorized to find a buyer or a renter for the owner's real property is known as a *listing*. A person wishing to purchase real property having certain characteristics may engage a broker to act in his behalf. An agreement of this nature is not, as a general rule, referred to as a listing; it is a contract of agency.

Some states[2] have enacted statutes, somewhat in the nature of statutes of frauds, which provide that any contract for the payment of a commission for the procuring by one person of a purchaser for the real estate of another shall not be valid unless the same shall be in writing, signed by the owner of such real estate.

---

[2] Arizona, California, Idaho, Indiana, Iowa, Kentucky, Michigan, Montana, Nebraska, Utah, Washington, and Wisconsin.

The statutes of some states are so worded that only contracts to pay a commission on the sale of real estate are included, whereas others stipulate that not only sales but also rentals and other transactions involving real estate are included.[3] These statutes differ in another important respect, in that some of them make the oral agreement to pay a commission null and void, and of no effect. Under this type of statute the broker can recover nothing if the contract to pay a commission is oral.[4] Other types of statutes provide that no action shall be brought to enforce an oral contract to pay a commission. The courts of some states having this type of statute have permitted the broker to recover a commission based on the benefits conferred on the owner as the result of the services rendered.[5] The suit is not on the contract, but is in quasi contract. In those states that require listing contracts to be in writing, the writing, as a general rule, need not be a complete contract but only a note or memorandum; however, such note or memorandum, if it is to be sufficient, must show the broker's authority to act.

The standard listing contract form is merely an authorization for the broker to act for the owner and is not a guarantee by the broker of the sale or rental of the listed property. The broker is, as agent of the owner, obligated to use his best efforts to accomplish the objectives of the agency.

## Listing Contract Forms

The nature of a real estate broker's business is such that it makes the use of a well-drafted listing contract form very desirable. By the use of such a form the broker minimizes the risk of loss of commissions as the result of an inadequate writing or of misunderstandings.

All of the above-discussed risks may be avoided by the use of a carefully drafted and well-rounded listing contract. Listing contract forms are prepared and made available by local real estate associations. The broker may use these forms, or he may prefer to use a listing contract drafted by his attorney. If a form contract is used, extreme care should be exercised in filling in the blanks. The broker should obtain the signature of both husband and wife, if the owner is married; and the terms of the contract should be explained to the owner before he signs.

---

[3] *Wooley* v. *Wycoff,* 2 Utah, 2d 329, 273 P.2d 181.

[4] *Krause* v. *Boraks,* 341 Mich. 149, 67 N.W.2d 202.

[5] *Clinkinbeard* v. *Poole, Ky.,* 266 S.W.2d 796.

## Kinds of Listing Contracts

Listing contracts in common use are classified under four general headings: (1) open listings, (2) exclusive agency, (3) exclusive right to sell, and (4) multiple listings.

***Open Listing.*** Under the terms of an open listing contract, no restrictions are placed on the owner's right to sell, either through his own efforts or through other brokers. The owner has the right to list with as many brokers as he chooses and is liable for a commission only to the first procuring broker, that is, the first broker to procure a buyer ready, willing, and able to purchase the property on the terms of the listing or other terms acceptable to the owner.[6] When a buyer is procured by any broker with whom the property is listed or by the owners, the agencies of all other brokers are automatically terminated—that is, no notice of the sale or of procurement of a buyer or of the termination of the agency is required.[7]

Unless the listing contract clearly states the restrictions placed on the owner's right to sell through his own efforts or through other brokers, the courts will hold it to be an open listing. Any restrictions on the owner's right to deal with his property as he wishes must be voluntarily assumed and clearly stated. From the standpoint of the broker an open listing is not desirable. When such a listing is used and the property is listed with several brokers, a controversy may arise as to who is entitled to the commission in a situation where one broker has discussed the sale of the property with a prospect and perhaps shown it to him and then at a later date another broker or the owner concludes a sale with the prospect.

Roberts listed property with Gardner. The listing was for a reasonable time, at a specified price, and "subject to prior sale." Gardner found a buyer; but before he could present the buyer to Roberts, another broker produced a purchaser acceptable to him. The court held that the listing was a nonexclusive (open) listing.

Justice Williams said: "Since the plaintiffs were not given an exclusive right to sell, they assumed the risk of knowing that the land might be sold by the owner or another agent before they could find a purchaser, ready, able and willing to buy on the terms specified, and that such a sale would *ipso facto* revoke their agency." *Roberts* v. *Gardner et al.,* Okla., 275 P.2d 245 (1954).

***Exclusive Agency.*** Under the terms of an exclusive agency contract the owner appoints the broker with whom he has listed the property his exclusive agent

---

[6] *Brinkman* v. *Peel,* 222 Ark. 345, 260 S.W.2d 448.

[7] *Roberts* v. *Gardner et al.,* Okla., 275 P.2d 245.

for the procuring of a purchaser for the property during the term of the listing. Under the exclusive agency contract the owner obligates himself to pay a commission to the listing broker if the property is sold during the term of the listing by the listing broker "or by any other person." An exclusive agency listing contract does not deprive the owner of his right to sell the property to a buyer procured by his own efforts; and if the owner does sell to such a buyer, the agency is terminated, and the listing broker is not entitled to a commission. In the event the listing contract is prepared for or by the broker and the terms are ambiguous, the court will hold that it is an open listing or an exclusive agency, not an exclusive right to sell.

Bursley listed a trailer court for sale with Nicholas. The listing contract provided that Nicholas was to have "for a period of six months from this date the exclusive right to sell the property at the price and terms acceptable to me: $97,000.00. Cash down payment $35,000." The contract further provided: "3. The commissions are to be paid whether the purchaser be secured by you or any other broker." Bursley sold the trailer court to Shark, a purchaser procured solely by the efforts of Bursley. The court held that the listing created an exclusive agency and that Nicholas was not entitled to a commission.

Chief Judge Allen said: ". . . the absence of an unequivocal provision in the contract that the owner has given up his inherent right to sell his property, . . . leads us to the conclusion that the lower court must be affirmed that the amended complaint failed to show an exclusive right and authority to sell sufficient to preclude the owner from selling the property without obligation to Nicholas." *Nicholas* v. *Bursley,* Fla., 119 So.2d 722 (1960).

***Exclusive Right to Sell.*** Under the terms of an exclusive right-to-sell contract, the owner obligates himself to pay the broker the agreed commission if the property is sold during the term of the listing, regardless of who procures the buyer.[8] The owner has the right to sell the property through his own efforts, but the fact that the owner has procured the buyer and made the sale does not relieve him from paying the broker his commission.[9]

If the broker wishes to obtain the advantages of an exclusive right to sell, he must draft his contract with exceptional care.[10] Some courts have held that a listing contract that merely states that the broker has the "exclusive right to sell" creates an exclusive agency, not an exclusive right to sell,[11] whereas other courts have held that it gives the broker an exclusive right to sell.[12] A carefully drafted

---

[8] *Bell* v. *Dimmerling et al.,* 140 Ohio St. 153, 78 N.E.2d 49.

[9] *Herrell* v. *Piner,* 78 N.M. 664, 437 P.2d 125 (1968).

[10] *Dorman Realty & Ins. Co.* v. *Stalvey,* 212 S.E.2d. 591 (S.C. 1975).

[11] *Roberts* v. *Harrington,* 168 Wis. 217, 169 N.W. 603.

[12] *Torrey & Dean, Inc.* v. *Coyle,* 138 Ore. 509, 7 P.2d 561.

listing contract will protect the broker and should prevent controversy if it states in unequivocal language that the broker has the exclusive right to sell and that the broker will be paid his full commission if the property is sold during the term of the listing, no matter who procures the buyer.

Barnes listed property for sale with West. The listing contract included the following provision: "Should I, or anyone acting for me, including my heirs, sell, lease, transfer or otherwise dispose of said property within the time herein fixed for the continuance of the agency, you shall be entitled nevertheless to your commission as herein set out." Barnes, while the listing was in force, sold the property to a buyer procured by his own efforts and refused to pay West the stipulated commission. West sued Barnes, and the court granted West a judgment.

Justice Richards said: "Assuming that the listing agreement complied in all respects with the provisions of Sec. 28, Art. 6573a, V.C.S. [statute of frauds] there being no question of fraud in its execution, appellant [West] would be entitled to recover the compensation due him under the terms of the exclusive listing contract which had been breached by appellee [Barnes] by the sale to Ben Newman." *West* v. *Barnes,* Tex. Civ. App., 351 S.W.2d 615 (1961).

***Multiple Listing.*** Multiple listing is not recognized as a distinct kind of listing contract. It is an agreement among a number of the brokers in a city or area whereby any broker who is a party thereto may sell property for which another broker, who is also a party to the agreement, has an exclusive right-to-sell contract. A multiple listing starts with an exclusive right-to-sell listing. The member brokers set up a multiple listing exchange, and all listings are registered with the exchange. The usual multiple listing agreement gives each member broker the right to sell any property registered with the exchange. When a property is sold, the selling broker and the listing broker divide the commission. The basis for the division of commission is set out in the multiple listing agreement. If the listing broker sells the property, he receives all the commission.

Since an agent cannot delegate his authority to any other person without the consent, either express or implied, of the principal, a listing contract should be so worded that the owner consents to the arrangement.

Fay listed her property for sale under a multiple listing contract. Mercner, a member of the board of realtors, procured a purchaser for the property, but Fay refused to pay the stipulated commission. Fay, when sued, set up as a defense that Mercner was not named as broker in the listing contract. The court held that Mercner was entitled to the commission.

Judge Molineux said: "The multiple listing agreement herein contained an express authorization, to wit, 'the undersigned as owner hereby gives to said active broker members of the Westfield Board of Realtors the exclusive right to sell . . . the property described on the reverse side hereof. . . .' Furthermore, the multiple listing agreement was directed to all active broker members of the Westfield Board of Realtors of which plaintiff [Mercner] was one. The recent case of *Looman Realty Corporation* v. *Broad Street National Bank of Trenton* is ample authority for the proposition that an alleged party to a contract who is indicated, although not specifically named therein, may sue on the contract after proving that he was in fact an intended party." *Mercner* v. *Fay,* 71 N.J. Super. 519,177 A.2d 481 (1962).

## Franchising and Referral Systems

In its efforts to create a more efficient market for real estate, the industry has developed networks of cooperating brokers on a nationwide basis. Since the motivation for many sellers on the one hand and buyers on the other is a transfer or change of location from one part of the country to another, referral systems have existed for many years. Under the typical referral system a broker who has a local client moving to another area will put his client in contact with a cooperating broker in the area into which the client is moving. Should the broker in the new area be successful in selling that client a home, he will be obligated to share his commission with the broker who referred that client to him in accordance with the arrangement between the brokers. Early systems met with mixed success, usually because of the lack of an effective method of policing them and to assure the "forwarding broker" that he would in fact be paid a portion of the commission. Present systems have attempted to resolve this problem.

Franchise systems normally include a referral system, but go much further. They usually include common advertising programs, both national and local, and a common marketing approach and training program. While the concept of franchising is not new in American business generally, its entry into the real estate brokerage business is of relatively recent origin. The growth of real estate brokerage franchising has been explosive during recent years. As with any device that has the effect of giving one broker or group of brokers a competitive advantage over others to whom it is not available, franchising has stirred considerable controversy and has attracted the attention of both state and federal regulatory agencies. There is a well-developed body of law in both areas covering the relationship between the franchisor and franchisee. The regulation of the sales of franchises is generally patterned along the lines of SEC controls over the corporate securities sales industry. That is, disclosure of relevant information regarding the integrity and financial responsibility of the franchisor is of great importance. The relationship between the franchisor and franchisee does not have an important influence upon the general public and the purchasers and sellers of housing, and it has not therefore been an area into which state real estate commissions have yet entered. Because of the interstate character of such operations, there appears to be a very real possibility that direct federal regulation of real estate brokerage practices may result. (An exhaustive review of the subject of governmental regulation of real estate franchising appears in volume 12 of *Real Estate, Probate and Trust Journal,* published by the American Bar Association, at page 580, Fall 1977).

## Sample Listing Contract

Set out below is a sample exclusive right-to-sell listing contract that illustrates the clauses typically found in such an agreement. The exclusive right-to-sell listing is most commonly used, particularly in the residential real estate brokerage business. Because of the variations in local law and practice from one state to another, and even within a particular state from locality to locality, the listing contract actually used should be prepared by a local attorney who is familiar not only with the applicable state law but also any local practice that may be unique to the area in which the form will be used. The form presented here is somewhat simpler than those normally encountered in practice in order that attention may be focused upon the key elements of such a contract.

### Sample Exclusive Right-to-Sell Listing Contract

This contract is made and entered into at ______________________________, State of ______________, on this ______ day of ____________, 19______, by and between ____________________________________________________________ as the owner or owners (herein "Owner") of the real estate described below (herein "the Property") and ____________________________________________ as licensed real estate broker (herein "Broker") and witnesses that Owner and Broker hereby agree as follows:

1. Broker hereby agrees to use his best efforts to find a purchaser for the Property upon the terms set out in this contract or upon such other terms as may be acceptable to Owner. Owner agrees that Broker shall have the exclusive right to sell the Property during the time specified by this contract upon the terms specified below or any other terms accepted by Owner.[A]

2. In consideration for Broker's acceptance of this contract and in return for Broker's undertaking to find a purchaser for the Property, Owner hereby agrees that:

*(a)* if Broker, Owner, or any other person finds a purchaser ready, willing, and able to purchase the Property upon the terms of this contract or any other terms accepted by Owner, then Broker shall have completed the performance

**Sample Exclusive Right-to-Sell Listing Contract *(continued)***

of this contract and Owner shall pay Broker a commission for services in an amount equal to ______________ (_____%) percent of the gross sales price, but not less than $__________;[B]

*(b)* if negotiations with a potential purchaser are begun by Broker, Owner, or any other person during the period of this contract and the Property is sold to that purchaser within __________ days after the expiration of this contract on the same terms as specified above or other terms accepted by Owner, then Owner shall pay Broker a commission on the same basis as set out above.[C]

It is further agreed by Owner and Broker that:

1. Broker is hereby authorized to retain, as Owner's agent, any earnest money deposit which may be made by a potential purchaser until the sale is completed. In the event the purchaser defaults, the earnest money deposit is to be first applied to Broker's out-of-pocket expenses in connection with the anticipated sale and the balance shall be divided equally between Owner and Broker. Both Owner and Broker, however, agree to take all necessary action to enforce any contract entered into with a purchaser to collect all money due under such contract.[D]

2. Broker or Broker's representatives (including other brokers and their representatives under any multiple or shared listing arrangement to which Broker is a party) shall have access to the Property at reasonable times for the purpose of presenting it to prospective purchasers. Broker is authorized to advertise the property for sale and to place a "For Sale" sign upn it.[E]

3. The price set out in this contract includes any and all indebtedness owed by Owner on the Property including mortgages, assessments for municipal improvements, real estate taxes, and balances owed on personal property or fixtures to be sold with the Property. Any balances presently due shall be paid by Owner prior to or at the time of sale of the Property unless the contract of sale shall provide otherwise.

4. Owner represents that no other party has an ownership interest in the Property and that upon sale Owner will execute a general warranty deed and will provide evidence of a marketable or insurable title to the Property.[F]

5. Owner and Broker agree that the Property is to be offered for sale without regard to race, creed, color, sex, or place of national origin in accordance with all applicable State and Federal laws.

This listing contract shall be effective from ____________________ A.M./P.M. of ________________________, 19________, up to _______________ A.M./P.M. of _________________, 19_____. The agreed upon listing price is $_______

**Sample Exclusive Right-to-Sell Listing Contract** ***(concluded)***

cash, or upon other terms acceptable to Owner. The Property which is the subject of this contract is located at ______________________________, the legal description of which is: ______________________________
______________________________
______________________________
______________________________

Owner and Broker agree that this contract is freely entered into and is binding upon the heirs, personal representatives, and assigns of each of them and is to be interpreted in accordance with the laws of the State of ______________.

______________________________
(OWNER)

______________________________
(OWNER)

______________________________
(BROKER)

## Explanations of Clauses in Sample Listing Contract

A. The initial paragraph of this form is designed to satisfy the technical requirement of consideration, particularly on the part of the broker. In return for the commitment made by the owner to grant the exclusive right to sell to the broker, there must be some positive undertaking by the broker. Here it is the broker's promise to use her or his "best efforts" to locate a purchaser. While the specific steps that will be taken by the broker to attract a buyer might be spelled out in detail, this can be quite cumbersome and is seldom seen in practice. The term "best efforts" is broad enough to impose upon the broker the duty to take such steps to market the property as are customary in the community for similar properties.

B. Section 2 (a) of the form illustrates several very important points. Initially, it clearly spells out the right of the broker to the agreed-upon commission, no matter who sells the property during the term of the listing contract. It is also important to emphasize the obligation to pay the commission, even if the property is sold at a different price or upon terms other than cash. Typically, the listing price is intended to be an "asking" price, rather than the very lowest price that the owner will accept. In order to avoid disputes on that point, this clause obligates the owner to pay a commission at the agreed-upon rate even though the property may be sold at a price lower than the listing price. Provision is also made for a minimum commission amount, expressed in dollars. The reason for the inclusion of this provision is to assure the broker that the commission paid will cover expenses as well as provide a minimum profit. In practice it is found that the sales effort for even very low-priced property will cost a specified amount of money, which might not be recaptured by the rate of commission agreed upon.

C. This clause is intended to protect the broker from collusion between the owner and a potential purchaser who might otherwise agree privately to a sale after the listing contract has expired. Such a sale, by eliminating the broker's commission, could result in a sale at a lower price to the buyer with a higher net to the seller. How long the period of time after the expiration date this protection is available is a matter for negotiation between the parties; however, local practice will also frequently have an effect. Some forms presently in use impose a period of one year. There is a real danger that a modern court might refuse to enforce a clause of that duration on the grounds that it is not reasonable to presume that the buyer purchased a year after the term of listing as a result of the broker's efforts. The shorter this period is, the more likely it is to be found enforceable. Clearly, it is important that the clause be fully explained to the owner by the broker, and also that the broker advise the owner of each and every prospective purchaser with whom discussions or negotiations are held during the term of the listing.

D. The true function of the earnest money deposit is discussed in detail in the next chapter; however, it is essentially a good-faith deposit made by the purchaser and retained until the sale is completed, at which time it is applied to the total purchase price. In the event that the sale is not completed through no fault of the purchaser, the earnest money must be returned. Under this form the broker is authorized to retain this deposit, even though it technically belongs to the owner. The reason for this procedure is greater assurance to the broker that it will be available to be returned if the sale is not consummated. Many state licensing laws require that the broker maintain a separate escrow account for such funds that belong to others and provide heavy penalties for commingling such funds with the broker's own monies. In the event the purchaser defaults, then the earnest money is usually forfeited as liquidated damages and the owner and broker can divide this money on whatever basis they have established in the listing contract. The provision included in this form is commonly seen. Of course, both the owner and the broker are more interested in seeing that the contract with the purchaser is concluded, and under this form each is obligated to attempt to compel performance by the purchaser.

E. This clause clearly authorizes the broker to take effective action to promote the sale of the property and grants the right to share the listing with other brokers. As noted in the text discussion, this authority must clearly appear in the listing contract.

F. Clauses 3 and 4 of this form attempt to make clear to the owner the obligations undertaken in the sale of the property so that there will be no misunderstanding as to what will be the net proceeds paid at the sale. They also emphasize the quality of title that is being offered to purchasers, and make it the owner's obligation to be prepared to perform when the sale is closed. Whatever expense this may involve is the owner's burden, and under the doctrine of specific performance, the owner may be compelled so to perform, even at great expense. Of course, this obligation is spelled out in the purchase agreement itself, but it is included in the listing contract to forewarn the owner of this potential expense. At the same time, a failure of the owner to perform, under these clauses, will not affect the obligation to pay the broker's commission.

A wide variety of additional information will typically be included in the listing contract that will facilitate the sale of the property. Usually included will be a detailed description of the property and its improvements, including the number of rooms, their size, type of construction, unusual features of the house, and the like. While this information is not essential to the basic contract between the parties, it is not uncommon for the listing contract to include a provision to the effect that the owner warrants that the information provided is accurate. The reason for the inclusion of such a provision is the protection of the broker and owner in the event that a charge of misrepresentation is made by the buyer of the property. In this event it will be important to determine the source of the misinformation, so that liability can be clearly established if there has in fact been a material misrepresentation of the quality of the property.

## Liability of Real Estate Broker

### Relation of Broker to Owner

The real estate broker is the agent of the owner and, as such, owes the duties of a fiduciary to his principal, the owner. In his fiduciary relation to the owner, the broker owes a duty of undivided loyalty. He must never put himself in a position where his personal interests conflict with the interests of the owner.[13] As a professional agent, he owes a duty to advise the owner as to the various aspects of the transaction that he is negotiating on the owner's behalf. The broker will not be permitted to buy for or sell to himself property listed unless he makes a complete disclosure of all aspects of the transaction, including an honest appraisal of the value and including also any prospective increase in value of which the broker may have knowledge.

The broker is a professional agent; and by offering his services as a broker, he represents that he possesses certain special skills. He will therefore be required to possess the skill and exercise the care usually possessed and exercised by brokers engaged in similar activities in the community. This includes a knowledge of the characteristics of the area in which he is carrying on his business. He will be expected to know real estate values in his area, and will owe a duty to advise the owner as to the value of his property and as to any other matters connected with the transaction if such matters come within the scope of the services usually rendered by brokers doing business in the community. A broker cannot escape liability by pleading ignorance.

---

[13] *Lerk* v. *McCabe et al.*, 349 Ill. 348, 182 N.E. 388.

Harper, a farmer who had had little business experience, listed his 700-acre farm with Reese. The listed price was $45,000. There was a $15,000 mortgage on the farm. Reese presented to Harper a purchase agreement in which the purchase price was stated as $30,000; encumbrances—none. Reese did not explain the terms to Harper, and he executed the agreement, expecting to get $30,000 for his equity in the farm. The agreement was canceled, but Reese sued Harper to recover a commission. The court held that Reese had failed to fulfill the duties he owed to Harper and the Reese had not earned a commission.

Justice Crockett said: ". . ., persons who trust their business to such agents [brokers] are entitled to repose some degree of confidence that they will be loyal to such trust and that they will, with reasonable diligence and in good faith, represent the interests of their clients. Unless the law demands this standard, instead of being the badge of competence and integrity it is supposed to be, the license would serve only as a foil to lure the unsuspecting public in to be duped by people more skilled and experienced in such affairs than are they, when they would be better off taking care of such business for themselves." *Reese* v. *Harper,* 8 Utah 2d 119, 329 P.2d410 (1958).

***Broker Representing Both Parties.*** In an exchange of property the broker may represent both parties to the exchange. In such a situation the broker owes a duty to make a full disclosure to all parties involved, and all the parties must consent to the dual representation.[14] A failure to make a full disclosure and obtain the consent of all interested parties is a fraud on those who do not know of, and consent to, the dual representation; and on the discovery of the fraud, they may rescind the transaction. The broker cannot collect a commission from either party, since the entire transaction is tainted with fraud. If the broker has permission to act for both parties, he must act with the utmost good faith, honesty, and impartiality. If the broker favors one party or colludes to defraud one of the parties, he will be liable to the injured party for the loss suffered.

Mathews brought an action to foreclose a mortgage, and Tabrosky asked that the transaction which gave rise to the mortgage be set aside on the ground that the broker who represented Tabrosky also represented Mathews without his (Tabrosky's) knowledge or consent. The court held the transaction was voidable at the election of Tabrosky.

Judge Shannon said: "No principle is better settled than that a man cannot be the agent of both the seller and buyer in the same transaction, without the intelligent consent of both. Loyalty to his trust is the most important duty which the agent owes to his principal. Reliance upon his integrity, fidelity, and ability is the main consideration in the selection of agents; and so careful is the law in guarding this fiduciary relation that it will not allow an agent to act for himself and his principal, nor to act for two principals on opposite sides of the same transaction. In such cases the amount of consideration, the absence of undue advantage, and other like features are wholly immaterial. Nothing will defeat the principal's right of remedy, except his own confirmation, after full knowledge

---

[14] *Ledirk Amusement Co., Inc., et al.* v. *Schechner et al.,* 133 N.J. Eq. 602, 33 A.2d 894.

of all the facts. Actual injury is not the principle upon which the law holds such transactions voidable." *Tabrosky* v. *Mathews,* Fla., 121 So.2d 61 (1960).

***Broker Purchasing Property.*** The strictness with which the interests of the owner of property are guarded from fraudulent or unethical conduct of a broker is reflected in the cases in which the broker, either directly or indirectly, purchases the listed property without making a full disclosure to the owner of the broker's interest in the transaction. Any such transaction is a breach of the fiduciary duty owed by the broker to the owner. If the broker purchases the property directly, or sells it to a relative or confederate who will at a later date convey the property to the broker, or convey it as directed by the broker and pay the broker the resulting profit or a portion thereof, or if the broker sells the property to a partnership of which he is a member or to a corporation in which he has substantial stock ownership, the courts will hold that such transactions are voidable unless a full disclosure of all the facts is made to the owner and after such disclosure the owner voluntarily consents to the transactions.[15]

Schepers listed a 160-acre farm for sale with Marvin Lautenschlager to be sold at the best available price but not less than $150 per acre. Marvin Lautenschlager learned that Yost would pay $200 per acre for the farm but did not disclose to Schepers this information and other information he had relative to the value of the farm. Marvin Lautenschlager induced Schepers to sell the farm to William Lautenschlager, Marvin's uncle, for $150 an acre, which Marvin represented as the best price obtainable. Later, William Lautenschlager sold the farm to Yost for $200 an acre. Schepers sued Marvin and William Lautenschlager for $9,200—$8,000 profit on the farm and $1,200 commission paid Marvin. The court granted Schepers a judgment of $1,200 against Marvin and of $8,000 against William.

Justice Messmore said: "An agent is required to disclose to his principal all the information he has touching the subject-matter of the agency and his relation to his principal forbids his becoming a purchaser thereof for his own benefit, in any way without the full knowledge by the principal of this fact, and the principal's acquiesence therein, with such knowledge. . . . A commission cannot be collected by the agent for his services as such, if he has wilfully disregarded, in a material respect, an obligation which the law devolves upon him by reason of his agency." *Schepers* v. *Lautenschlager,* 173 Neb. 107, 112 N.W.2d 767 (1962).

## Relation of Broker to Buyer

In general, the relation of the broker to the buyer of a listed property is no different from that of any agent to a third person with whom the agent is dealing

---

[15] *Utlaut* v. *Glick Real Estate Co., Inc.,* Mo., 246 S.W.2d 760; *Anderson* v. *Griffith,* 501 S.W.2d 695 (Tex. Civ. App. 1973).

in behalf of his principal. The broker is not a party to any contract to sell negotiated for, and in the name of, the owner. If the owner fails or refuses to perform the contract to sell, the broker is not liable to the buyer for damages for breach of contract. If a down payment has been made by the buyer and the money has been turned over to the owner by the broker and the owner defaults in his performance, thus entitling the buyer to the return of the down payment, the broker is not liable to the buyer for the down payment. If the buyer has signed a proposition the terms of which differ from those stated in the listing, and the buyer makes a payment to the broker as evidence of good faith, the broker is liable to the buyer for the amount of this payment if the owner refuses to accept the offer.

An agent is liable for his wrongful acts (torts). If a broker, in selling property, knowingly misrepresents the property for the purpose of inducing the prospect to buy and the prospect does buy, justifiably relying on the broker's misrepresentations, the broker will be liable to the buyer in a tort action for deceit. In the event of such a misrepresentation, the buyer may elect to rescind the purchase, tender the property back to the owner, and recover the purchase money or any part of it that has been paid. The guilty broker would be liable to the owner for any commissions paid, unless the owner was a party to or had knowledge of the deceit.

Jeanette Clark, a saleswoman for Lelah T. Pierson, Inc., a licensed real estate broker, in showing to Beth Merrill a house which was listed for rent, neglected to warn Merrill of the dangerous stairway to the basement. Merrill, due to the dangerous stairway, fell down the stairs and suffered serious injuries. Merrill sued Buck, the owner of the house, Lelah T. Pierson, Inc., and Clark in tort, and the court granted Merrill a judgment for $65,700 against all defendants. On appeal, the judgment was affirmed.

Justice Dooling said: ". . . We are satisfied that, having affirmatively undertaken to show the house to plaintiff [Merrill] in the regular course of their [Lelah T. Pierson, Inc., and Clark] business with the purpose of earning a commission if she decided to rent it, the defendants [Pierson, Inc., and Clark] were under a duty of care to warn her of a concealed danger in the premises of which they were aware and from which her injury might be reasonably foreseen if she did become a tenant. . . .

"These defendants [Pierson, Inc., and Clark] claim that the furthest extent of their possible duty was to take care that plaintiff [Merrill] was not injured while she was examining the house in the company of defendant Clark, but this argument overlooks the fact that the tour of inspection was for the very purpose of persuading plaintiff [Merrill] to become a tenant and that the possibility of her injury from the concealed hazard if she did become a tenant was reasonably forseeable unless she was advised of the latent danger." *Merrill* v. *Buck,* 25 Cal. Rptr. 456, 375 P.2d 304 (1962).

The liability of brokers for misrepresentation is today an area in which there is considerable development. More and more frequently our courts are reaching the conclusion that a broker will be held liable not only for what he actually knew but also for such facts as he should have known. For example, misrepresentation as to the number of square feet in a residence by a broker has been found to be actionable.[16] This increased exposure to liability has led to the use of exculpatory clauses that are added to the purchase agreement. These clauses provide, in effect, that the buyer will not hold the broker liable for any defect in the property purchased. Such clauses have been found ineffective as a defense against a charge of misrepresentation.[17]

### Broker's Liability to Salesperson

When a broker employs a salesperson, they enter into a contract of employment. The primary obligation of the broker is to fulfill the contractual promises made to the salesperson. Even though it is not expressly stated in the contract, if the salesperson is compensated on a commission basis, the broker is obligated to provide reasonable aid in the negotiation of a deal. The broker owes a duty not to "steal" a sale from his or her salesperson nor to collude to deprive that person of a commission.

## Liability of Real Estate Salesperson

### Relation of Salesperson to Owner

In most respects, the salesperson's liability to the owner who has listed property with the broker is the same as that of the broker. The salesperson owes a duty of undivided loyalty to the owner. He or she owes the same fiduciary duty to the owner as that owed by the listing broker. In showing the property and making a sales talk, the salesperson has a duty, both to the owner and to the prospective buyer, not to make false and fraudulent representations; if the salesperson does make such representations, he or she will be individually liable in tort for resulting injuries. If a salesperson has taken a listing in behalf of the broker and, as a means of inducing the owner to list the property, has made promises he or she is not authorized to make, the salesperson will be individually liable to the owner for breach of such promises.

---

[16] *Gaston* v. *Hartzell,* 89 N.M. 217, 549 P. 2d 632 (1976).

[17] *Wise* v. *Dawson,* 353 A.2d 207 (Del. Super. 1975).

### Salesperson's Liability to Buyer

The salesperson is not liable on the contract of sale that he or she has negotiated in behalf of the owner unless he or she is expressly made a party thereto. The salesperson may by express agreement make himself or herself a guarantor or surety on the contract. If the salesperson, in negotiating a contract of sale, exceeds his or her authority and makes promises that do not bind the owner, the salesperson will be individually liable to the buyer for breach of his or her implied warranty of authority. However, since a salesperson's authority is usually limited to the finding of a buyer, this rule would apply only in rare instances.

### Salesperson's Liability for Wrongful Acts

The salesperson is individually liable for his or her wrongful acts. If, in order to induce a sale, he or she knowingly makes false representations as to material facts to the buyer, and the buyer contracts in justifiable reliance on the false representations, the salesperson is individually liable in a tort action of deceit for the resulting injury. Likewise, if a salesperson, in transporting a prospective buyer to a property for the purpose of showing it, drives negligently and injures the buyer by such negligence, the salesperson is individually liable for the resulting injury. The same rule would apply if the prospective buyer is injured while on the property if the injury is the result of the salesperson's negligence. Failure on the part of the salesperson to warn the buyer of known dangerous conditions of the premises is generally held to be negligent conduct.

### Salesperson's Liability to Broker

The salesperson—whether an employee, agent, or independent contractor—owes a duty to perform his or her services in such a manner that the legitimate business objectives of the broker are furthered. If the salesperson is an independent contractor, he or she will not be under the direct control and supervision of the broker; however, the salesperson will be liable to the broker if he or she is guilty of a breach of contractual obligations.

The salesperson who is an employee or agent of the broker owes the duties of a fiduciary to the broker. The salesperson owes a duty to follow the instructions of the broker, unless the broker instructs him or her to perform an illegal or wrongful act or to follow a course of action that is detrimental to his or her health. The salesperson must account to the broker for all money received by him or her in the course of employment. If the salesperson commingles money belonging to the broker or the owner with his or her own money, he or she becomes individually liable to the broker for the full amount. Depositing money belonging to the broker in the personal checking account of the salesperson is a commingling of monies. If a salesperson uses money or property of the broker for his or her individual purposes—for example, buys groceries or makes payments on a car—he or she is guilty of the crime of embezzlement.

## When Commission Is Earned

### Terms of Contract

A worker is entitled to be paid when the work is done. This familiar rule applies to the broker, but it does not aid in deciding when the work is completed. In order to determine when the work is finished, one must read the listing contract, in case such a contract has been drafted and signed. If the listing contract provides that the commission is payable "on the completion of the transfer of the property," no commission is earned until the transfer has been made.[18] The courts have interpreted the provision "commission is payable from the proceeds of the sale" as making the completion of the transaction a prerequisite to the owner's duty to pay a commission. Other stages in the transaction may be designated as the point at which the commission is earned.[19] The listing contract may stipulate that the commission will be paid out of cash actually paid to the owner and will be payable only as the cash is received. In any such case the broker is entitled to his commission if the owner arbitrarily and without reasonable cause or in bad faith refuses to complete the sale.

Clark, a broker, and Hovey, an owner, executed a listing contract which included the following provision: ". . . Clark agrees to accept $500 in full payment of commissions. . . . It is further agreed by both parties that this $500 shall not be paid from the first $5,000 paid Hovey . . . but shall be paid by Hovey to Clark from the first $500 received by Hovey from Green after the $5,000 has been paid." Hovey could not give good title, and the contract of sale was never carried out. Clark sued Hovey to recover a judgment for $500 commission. The court held that Clark was not entitled to a commission.

Chief Justice Rugg said: "The rights of the parties depend upon the terms of their agreement, which is in writing and not ambiguous. It fixes the price which the plaintiff [Clark] is to receive. It stipulates in unequivocal words that the compensation shall not be paid by the defendant [Hovey] until after he has received $5,000 on account of the sale. The written agreement between the parties supersedes the ordinary rule that a broker has earned his commission when he has procured the execution of a valid agreement for sale." *Clark* v. *Hovey,* 217 Mass. 485, 105 N.E. 222 (1914).

---

[18] *Fowler* v. *Davidson et al.,* 44 Minn. 46, 46 N.W. 308.

[19] For example, passage of title; *Hayman Management Co.* v. *Dura Corp.,* 45 Mich. App. 522, 206 N.W.2d 754 (1973).

## Lack of Specific Agreement

If there is no specific agreement, either written or oral, as to when the commission is payable, the generally accepted rule is that the commission is earned and payable when the broker has produced a buyer ready, willing, and able to buy on the terms stated in the listing or agreed upon at the time the broker was engaged. *Ready and willing* means that the buyer will, at the present time, sign a contract to purchase the property on the terms set by the owner when the property was listed with the broker. *Able* means that the buyer either has or can obtain the funds necessary to make the payments stipulated in the listing.[20]

Whether or not, in addition to procuring a buyer ready, willing, and able to purchase, the broker owes a duty to aid in closing the sale will depend upon local custom, in the absence of a listing contract stating the broker's duties. If the broker does follow through and aid in the closing of the sale, the courts are unanimous in holding that he has earned the commission.

## Necessity for a Binding Contract

In order that the broker may be entitled to his or her commission, the buyer procured by the broker must be ready and willing to enter into a binding, enforceable contract to buy. If the buyer is ready and willing to make an oral promise to buy but will not sign a written contract, the broker has not earned his or her commission. An oral contract to purchase land is not enforceable. If the buyer reserves the right to cancel the contract on the happening of a contingency, such as not being able to borrow money to make the down payment, the commission is not earned until the contingency has occurred and the buyer has become absolutely liable on the contract.[21] Also, if the broker induces the owner to give the buyer an option on the listed property, the broker has not earned his or her commission unless and until the buyer exercises the option.[22]

Gresser listed property for sale with Martineau. Martineau procured a buyer, Lotton, who signed a purchase contract which provided that Martineau would, within 30 days, arrange financing. Also, special provisions were written into the purchase contract form. Financing was not arranged within the 30-day period; and thereafter, Gresser listed the property with another broker, who sold it to Lotton. Martineau sued Gresser to recover his commission, and the court held (1) that failure to fulfill the condition for the obtaining of financing rendered the contract unenforceable and (2) that the adding of the provisions

---

[20] *Reynor* v. *Mackrill,* 181 Iowa 210, 164 N.W. 335.

[21] *Cooper* v. *Liberty National Bank,* 332 Ill. App. 459, 75 N.E.2d 769.

[22] *MacNeill Real Estate* v. *Rines,* 144 Me. 27, 64 A.2d 179.

to the purchase contract amounted to the illegal practice of law and that the contract was an illegal contract.

Judge Swaim said: "A broker in pursuance of his employment, may have the parties execute a contract, after he has procured a purchaser, ready, and willing to enter into written contract on the employer's or seller's terms, and when the written contract is entered into, there can be no issue, as to whether the person procured was 'ready and willing and able to perform.' However, it is the broker's duty, in such a case to see that the parties enter into an 'enforceable contract' and a 'binding contract of sale and purchase.' Here, a contract of purchase and sale was signed. Was it enforcible? Was it binding?" (NOTE: The court answered both of these questions in the negative.) *Martineau* v. *Gresser,* 190 Ohio Op.2d 374, 182 N.E.2d 46 (1962).

## Closing of Sale by Person Other Than Broker

Controversy frequently arises as to who is entitled to the commission when a broker has contacted or interested a prospect but actual sale has been made by another broker or by the owner, or when the closing of the deal has been delayed until the term of the listing has expired. The general rule is that the procuring broker is entitled to the commission. Who the procuring broker is depends on the facts of the particular case.

Under an open listing the broker who first finds the prospect who purchases the property has earned the commission. If several brokers have prospects for property listed on an open listing, the broker whose prospect first signs a contract to purchase the property is entitled to the commission. When a buyer has signed a contract to purchase property listed on an open listing, the agency of all other brokers is automatically canceled without the giving of notice. The courts have held that the broker is the procuring cause and is entitled to the commission in the following situations: (1) if the broker has contacted a prospect who later contracts to buy the property; (2) if a prospect, in answer to a broker's advertisement, contacts the owner and contracts to buy the property; and (3) if a broker contacts a prospect and this prospect brings the property to the attention of some third person who contracts to buy the property.

Strodtbeck listed his ranch with Wood on an open listing. Wood contacted Fulton, who agreed to purchase the ranch but did not have money to make a down payment. Arrangements were made with Strodtbeck's attorney to make the down payment on November 26 and sign a purchase contract, but Fulton did not obtain money for the down payment. On December 1, Strodtbeck sold the ranch to a purchaser obtained by another broker and paid that broker his commission. On December 2, Wood and Fulton called at the office of Strodtbeck's attorney ready to make the down payment and execute a contract for the purchase of the ranch and were told that the ranch had been sold. Wood sued Strodtbeck to recover a judgment for claimed commission. The court held that Wood was not entitled to a commission.

Chief Justice James T. Harrison said: "Under a non-exclusive listing contract defendants, [Strodtbecks] must be permitted to choose, when two buyers are under consideration, with which one to deal. The listing contract in question here provided authority to the broker to execute a preliminary contract in accordance with its terms. Plaintiff [Wood] did not see fit to do so. Too, Fulton could always have refused to go through with his proposed purchase, . . ." *Wood* v. *Strodtbeck,* Mont. 382 P.2d 170 (1963).

## Sale Following Exclusive Agency Listing

Under an exclusive agency listing the broker is entitled to his commission if the property is sold to a buyer obtained by the listing broker or any other broker; but if the owner finds a buyer through his own efforts, the listing broker is not entitled to a commission. If the listing is either an open listing or an exclusive agency listing, the broker should give the owner notice as soon as he procures a buyer ready, willing, and able to buy. If a broker does not give notice and the owner, before he has knowledge of the broker's having procured a buyer, contracts to sell to a buyer procured by the owner's own efforts, the broker will not be entitled to a commission.

Kabel listed all the lots in a new subdivision with McKinney. The listing contract appointed McKinney Kabel's "exclusive selling agent." Kabel canceled the contract with McKinney, and McKinney sued Kabel to recover a commission on all the lots in the subdivision. McKinney was paid his commission on all lots sold by him prior to the termination of the listing. The court held that McKinney was not entitled to a commission on the unsold lots.

Judge Samuel said: "A real estate broker who has only an exclusive agency to sell is not entitled to a commission on sales made by the owner himself. Such a contract does not give the broker the exclusive right to sell the property; it simply precludes the owner from appointing any other agent during the life of the contract. The jurisprudence clearly distinguishes the appointment as an *exclusive agent* from the contract of employment conferring upon a real estate broker the *exclusive right to sell,* which latter entitles the broker to commissions on all sales during the life of the contract including those made by the owner." *McKinney Realty Company* v. *Kabel,* La. App., 131 So.2d 567 (1961).

## Sale Following an Exclusive-Right-to-Sell Listing

Under an exclusive-right-to-sell listing, the broker is entitled to her commission if the property is sold before the listing expires. Frequently, a controversy arises when the listing is for a specified time and the property is sold to a buyer who was contacted by the broker during the term of the listing, but who did not enter into the contract of sale until after the term expired. If negotiations are in progress at the time the listing expires, the courts have held that the term of the listing is, by implication, extended until the transaction is closed. In such a case the broker is entitled to her commission.[23] If, after the listing has expired, negotiations are renewed with a prospect contacted by the broker and such negotiations culminate in a sale, the broker is not entitled to a commission unless she can prove that the owner and the buyer delayed negotiations for the purpose of depriving her of her commission, in which event the courts have allowed the broker to recover her commission. If the listing contract provides that a commission will be paid to the broker if the property is sold within a stipulated time after the listing expires to a prospect contacted by the broker during the term of the listing, the courts have enforced the provision and allowed the broker to recover her commission. Some—but not all—courts have held that if the owner and buyer have delayed closing the transaction until after the expiration of the extended period, the broker would not be entitled to a commission, even though she could show that the delay was for the purpose of depriving her of her commission.[24]

### Broker's Right to Commission if Seller Defaults

Under the general rule that a broker has earned his commission when he has produced a buyer ready, willing, and able to purchase the property on the stipulated terms or on terms acceptable to the owner, the courts have held that default on the part of the owner to consummate the sale will not relieve him from paying the broker his commission. If the broker knows, or under the circumstances should know, that the owner's title is defective, the court will, as a general rule, hold that the broker impliedly contracts to produce a buyer who will take the property subject to the defective title or that it is the duty of the broker to work out a deal whereby provision is made for the removal of the defect.[25] If an owner, after he has executed a purchase-and-sale agreement, refuses, without good cause, to complete the transaction, the broker is entitled to his commission.[26]

Gaither listed his property with Williams. Williams found a buyer ready, willing, and able to purchase the property on terms acceptable to Gaither, but the transaction was never consummated. Gaither never submitted a title in accordance with the purchase

---

[23] *Covino* v. *Pfeffer,* 160 Conn. 212 (1970).

[24] See *West* v. *Barnes,* Tex. Civ. App., 351 S.W.2d 615 (1961).

[25] *Pasley* v. *Barber,* Alaska, 368 P.2d 548.

[26] *Blunt* v. *Wentland,* 250 Iowa 607, 93 N.W.2d 735.

agreement and refused to pay Williams a commission. Gaither, when sued, set up as a defense that the sale was never consummated. The court granted a judgment to Williams.

Presiding Justice Peek said: "Under the uncontradicted facts, since the defendants [Gaithers] accepted the offer made by persons procured by plaintiff [Williams] who were ready, willing and able to purchase the property, plaintiff [Williams] had then performed all acts incumbent upon him and he was entitled to the agreed commission. . . .

"Whether the sale was prevented by the failure of perfect title or by mere will of the vendor makes no difference. In either case the compensation had been earned by the agent." *Williams* v. *Gaither,* 20 Cal. Rptr. 779 (1962).

In a recent case the rules regarding the right of the broker to a commission were summarized as follows: "When a broker is engaged by an owner of property to find a purchaser for it, the broker earns his commission when: *(a)* he produces a purchaser ready, willing, and able to buy on the terms fixed by the owner, *(b)* the purchaser enters into a binding contract with the owner to do so; and *(c)* the purchaser completes the transaction by closing the title in accordance with the provisions of the contract. If the contract is not consummated because of lack of financial ability of the buyer to perform, or because of any other default of his, there is no right to commission against the seller. On the other hand, if the failure of completion of the contract results from the wrongful act or interference of the seller, the broker's claim is valid and must be paid."[27]

Also, if the property is arbitrarily withdrawn by the owner, the broker will be entitled to the full commission—provided the contract clearly provides for this possibility.[28]

## Termination of Relationship

The relation of principal and agent may be terminated by either party at any time, with the exception of an agency coupled with an interest. The broker-owner relation is not an agency coupled with an interest. However, if the contract of employment is breached by the termination of the relation, the injured party is entitled to recover damages for breach of contract. If the owner notifies the broker that he terminates the relation and withdraws the property before the expiration of the term, the damages recoverable by the broker will depend on the circumstances of the case. If the broker is negotiating with a prospect and can prove that the prospect would have contracted to purchase the property,

---

[27] *Tristram's Landing, Inc.* v. *Wait,* 327 N.E.2d 727 (Mass. 1975).

[28] *Hunt* v. *Smallridge,* 321 N.Y. S.2d 825 (Sup. Ct. 1971); *Blank* v. *Borden,* 11 Ca. 3rd 963, 115 Cal. Rptr. 31 (1974).

or if the broker can prove that the owner terminated the listing arbitrarily and without reason or in bad faith, the broker will, as a general rule, be awarded a judgment for the full amount of his commission.[29]

Under other circumstances, the amount of the judgment may be smaller. If no time for expiration of the listing is stated in the listing contract, the courts have generally held that the listing is for a reasonable time. Reasonable time is always determined on the basis of the facts and circumstances of each case.[30]

## Licensing Laws

### State Statutes

A majority of the states have enacted statutes making it unlawful for a person to act as a real estate broker or a real estate salesman without first obtaining a license. The purpose of these statutes is to protect the public from being defrauded by dishonest and unethical real estate brokers or salesmen. The statutes are not uniform in their provisions; yet they have many provisions that are similar as to the basic requirements. All the statutes require both brokers and salesmen to establish their honesty, truthfulness, and good reputation. The methods of establishing good character vary widely. Most statutes require the applicant for a license to establish his competence to act as a broker or salesman by taking an examination, and most states require a written examination. The license fee for a broker is more than the fee for a salesman. The license must be renewed periodically. Although the penalties for transacting business as a real estate broker or real estate salesman without a license vary widely, in no state can an unlicensed broker or salesman recover a judgment for the agreed commission in a court action, since the contract to pay the commission is an unlawful one. The effect of the licensing statute is to make illegal the contract to pay a commission.[31] The fact that the broker or salesman negotiating a contract to sell land is unlicensed does not in any way affect the legality of the contract negotiated. The only contract affected by the licensing statute is the contract of employment—the contract to pay a commission.

### Scope of Licensing Statutes

The scope of the licensing statutes varies. Some are broad and include all contracts affecting an interest in real estate, such as the negotiation of leases

---

[29] *Bartlett* v. *Keith,* 325 Mass. 265, 90 N.E.2d 308.

[30] *Harris* v. *McPherson,* 97 Conn. 164, 115 A. 723.

[31] *Firpo* v. *Murphy et al.,* 71 Cal. App. 249, 236 P. 968.

and real estate mortgages.[32] Other statutes are narrower in their scope and include only contracts to sell land.

## Illegal Practice of Law by Brokers

### Questionable Activities of Brokers

In the selling or managing of real estate, a wide variety of documents must be prepared for execution by the parties involved in the transaction. In this connection, questions may arise from time to time as to the legal rights of the parties or as to the legal significance of some phase of the matter. For example, to what extent may a broker go, without engaging in the practice of law, in preparing the documents to be executed in connection with a transaction he is handling? Also, is a broker engaging in the practice of law when he advises the parties to a transaction as to the legal phases of the transaction?

These questions have not been litigated in all of the states; even in those states in which they have been the subject of lawsuits, there is some difference of opinion. However, the courts in such states are in accord in holding that if the broker accepts a fee for preparing documents or gives advice as to the legal rights of the parties to a sale which he is handling as broker for the parties, he is engaging in the unauthorized practice of law.

### Limits of Activity

The extent to which a broker may go in preparing documents used in connection with a transaction he is negotiating presents a question that is difficult to answer. One view is that the broker is employed to find a buyer for the property, and that when he has found a buyer, he has fulfilled the duty he owes to his employer. Under this view the broker would be permitted to prepare only those instruments that are "preliminary" in nature—that is, instruments such as a memorandum of the transaction or deposit receipts. A licensed attorney should be employed to draft the documents necessary for the closing of the sale—as, for instance, the deed, the mortgage, the deed of trust, assignments of leases, or releases of mortgages.[33] If the broker, in addition to collecting his commission, makes an extra charge for preparing the documents executed in connection with the closing of the sale, he has been held to be practicing law illegally.[34]

---

[32] *Cohen* v. *Scola,* 13 N.J. Super. 472, 80 A.2d 643.

[33] *Keyes Co.* v. *Dade County Bar Association et al.,* Fla., 46 So.2d 605.

[34] *Commonwealth* v. *Jones & Robbins, Inc., et al.,* 186 Va. 30, 41 S.E.2d 720.

The more liberal view, held in the majority of the states in which the question has been litigated, is that a broker is not engaged in the unauthorized practice of law when he fills in the blanks in standardized forms that have been approved by a licensed attorney, provided that such instruments are prepared and used as an incident to a transaction the broker is handling, and provided further that no extra charge is made for such service.[35] Wisconsin has set up a commission that is authorized to approve standardized forms that a broker is permitted to use in the negotiating and closing of a sale of real estate.[36]

The holdings in other states place varying degrees of restrictions on the extent to which a broker may prepare the various documents used in the course of the negotiation and in the closing of a sale of real estate.[37] Giving advice as to the legal significance of the documents prepared in connection with the closing of a transaction, and advising persons as to their legal rights and duties or as to the course of action that they should follow in a real estate transaction, have been held to be engaging in the practice of law.[38] In some states the courts have held that the selection of the forms to be used and the filling-in of the blanks amount to the giving of legal advice, and that a broker who performs such services for his employer is engaged in the unauthorized practice of law.

The examination of an abstract of title and the giving of an opinion as to the state of the title to the real estate covered by the abstract are clearly outside the province of the broker. A broker or property manager may serve notice of default in payment of rent or of default in the payment of installments on a land contract or mortgage; but he cannot bring a court action in behalf of his employer to recover a judgment for rents, or for installment payments, or for the recovery of the possession of the real estate.[39]

## Expanding Obligations of Brokers

With the increase in mandatory education for brokers and salespersons in recent years there has also come a pronounced trend by our courts to require a greater

---

[35] *Conway-Bogue Realty Investment Company et al.* v. *Denver Bar Association et al.*, 135 Colo. 398, 312 P.2d 998. Apparently, this view is held in Colorado, Idaho, Illinois, Massachusetts, Michigan, Minnesota, Missouri, Nebraska, New York, North Dakota, Ohio, and Pennsylvania.

[36] *Reynolds* v. *Dinger*, 14 Wis.2d 193, 109 N.W.2d 685.

[37] *Creekmire* v. *Izard, Ark.*, 367 S.W.2d 419; *Indiana State Bar Association* v. *Indiana Real Estate Association*, Ind., 191 N.E.2d 711; *State Bar of Arizona* v. *Arizona Land Title and Trust Company*, 91 Ariz. 293, 371 P.2d 1020; *Arkansas Bar Association* v. *Block*, 230 Ark. 430, 323 S.W.2d 912.

[38] *People* v. *Sipper*, 61 Cal. App.2d 844, 142 P.2d 960; *People ex rel. Illinois State Bar Association et al.* v. *Schaefer*, 404 Ill. 45, 87 N.E.2d 773.

[39] *Ingham County Bar Association et al.* v. *Walter Neller Co. et al.*, 342 Mich. 214, 69 N.W.2d 713; *In re Wenger*, 61 N.Y.S.2d 686.

degree of knowledge and skill on the part of all persons engaged in real estate brokerage. In certain instances they are not only permitted but even *required* to take certain actions that would usually constitute the practice of law. Consider the following:

A licensed broker representing a seller as agent for the sale of real estate permitted the sale to be completed partly for cash, with the balance of the price to be paid over a period of years under a promissory note from the buyer to the seller. No mortgage or deed of trust was used to secure the payment of the note, and the seller deeded the property outright to the buyer. Later the buyer defaulted and also filed for bankruptcy. Since the seller was unsecured, he became a general creditor only and entitled to share pro rata in the proceeds of the sale of the property with the other general creditors. In a later suit by the seller against the broker to recover the loss suffered, the broker's defense was that the giving of advice regarding securing the debt by mortgage or deed of trust would have constituted the unauthorized practice of law and he could not be liable for failing to do so. The court held that the broker was obligated to provide such advice and a failure to do so rendered him liable to the seller for the seller's loss. *Morley* v. *J. Pagel Realty & Insurance,* 27 Ariz. App. 62, 550 P.2d 1104 (1976).

How far our courts might go in such situations is a conjecture. It does seem clear, however, that those active in real estate brokerage do have an obligation to provide sound advice to those who reasonably rely upon them and pay them. The above example, taken from an actual case, provides a difficult dilemma for the broker. Whether recommending security for a long-term substantial debt is legal advice or just good business advice is arguable. Where the need for legal advice is evident, clearly the broker should urge the seller or buyer to consult an attorney. In fact, in view of the significance of the typical real estate transaction, the broker should recommend this action as a matter of course.

## Civil Rights Legislation

While civil rights legislation affects everyone, including the individual seller of real estate, it has a direct and important effect upon brokerage operations and management. Civil rights legislation, as it applies to the real estate business, is designed to assure that all persons will have an equal opportunity to acquire the ownership or use of suitable housing, and that they are not subjected to discrimination in the process. The controls imposed on the real estate industry result from both federal and state legislation, much of which is overlapping. That is, federal policy has been to encourage the states to take the initiative in this area. As a general rule, therefore, if there is an adequate remedy under state law and that state law is being adequately enforced, then relief under the federal law is not available. Nevertheless, the federal laws and administrative rulings and procedures must be looked to as the yardstick by which the adequacy of state protection of civil rights will be measured. While federal legislation has been in effect for over 100 years (the Civil Rights Act of 1866), the Federal Fair Housing Law (Title VIII of the Civil Rights Act of 1968) provides the definitive rules that apply today and this discussion is therefore based on the modern legislation.

## The Federal Fair Housing Law

Fundamentally the law makes it illegal for anyone to practice discrimination based upon race, color, religion, sex, or national origin in connection with the sale or rental of housing. The primary intent of the law is to make sure that minority groups have equal access to suitable housing, but the law goes further than this. It also prohibits practices that damage nonminority groups through the threatened intrusion of minority groups into nonminority neighborhoods when such threats, either express or implied, are made with profit as their motivation.

The key provision of the Federal Fair Housing Law is expressed in Title VIII, Section 804, as follows:

*(a)* ". . . it shall be unlawful—to refuse to sell or rent after the making of a bonafide offer, or to refuse to negotiate for the sale or rental of, or otherwise make unavailable or deny, a dwelling to any person because of race, color, religion, sex, or national origin.
*(b)* to discriminate against any person in the terms, conditions, or privileges of sale or rental of a dwelling, or in the provision of services or facilities in connection therewith, because of race, color, religion, sex, or national origin.
*(c)* to make, print, or publish, or cause to be made, printed or published any notice, statement, or advertisement, with respect to the sale or rental of a dwelling that indicates any preference, limitation, or discrimination based on race, color, religion, sex, or national origin, or an intention to make any such preference, limitation, or discrimination.
*(d)* to represent to any person because of race, color, religion, sex, or national origin that any dwelling is not available for inspection, sale, or rental when such dwelling is in fact so available.
*(e)* for profit, to induce or attempt to induce any person to sell or rent any dwelling by representations regarding the entry or prospective entry into the neighborhood of a person or persons of a particular race, color, religion, sex, or national origin."[40]

---

[40] 42 U.S.C.A. 3604.

Several new terms have been created to describe the prohibited discriminatory practices, the definitions of which are continuously being refined by our courts and regulatory bodies. These are discussed below.

**Steering**

The general term *steering* has come to include all of the practices spelled out in Subsections *(a)* through *(d)* above. The basic definitions of the prohibited activities are not difficult to comprehend, but recognition of them in practice can be troublesome. Overt and obvious discrimination is seldom seen, but subtle and less obvious forms are difficult to detect and eliminate. As a result, the authorities charged with enforcement of the law (the departments of Justice and of Housing and Urban Development) are directing their efforts toward these less obvious forms of discrimination. These efforts include the testing of practices of sales and rental agents. The definition of steering is, therefore, gradually expanding to include every procedure, technique, or device that has the effect of limiting the availability of housing to a prospective purchaser or tenant for discriminatory reasons. Our courts, in interpreting the law, have found that the *intent* to discriminate need not be shown if discrimination *in fact* exists,[41] and that a pattern of discrimination may be found even when there is no evidence of overt acts of discrimination.[42] They have also found that the law applies to individuals dealing with their own properties.[43] Steering is obviously a concept that is a significant for any real estate brokerage operation, and whatever controls are necessary to assure compliance with the law by salespersons must be imposed by the managing broker because our courts have found brokers liable for the discriminatory acts of their employees.[44] In addition, a very strong argument can be made that steering violates the basic principles of successful salesmanship.[45]

**Blockbusting and Panic Peddling**

The two terms *blockbusting* and *panic peddling* have come into being to describe the practices prohibited by Subsection *(e),* above. The two terms are frequently used interchangeably; however, each has a separate meaning, even though the two practices often go hand in hand. Blockbusting is the sale to a minority member of property located in a nonminority neighborhood with the

---

[41] *U.S.* v. *L & H Land Corp., Inc.,* D.C. Fla. 1976, 407 F. Supp 576.

[42] *U.S.* v. *Reddock,* C.A. Ala. 1972, 467 F.2d 897.

[43] *Lucas* v. *Hooper, D.C. Tnn. 1974, 381 F. Supp. 1222.*

[44] *Marr* v. *Rife,* C.A. Ohio 1974, 503 F.2d 735.

[45] William D. North, "Unravelling the Steering Riddle," *Realtors® Review,* November 1977, pp. 4–9.

intent to create a change that will motivate others in the neighborhood to sell their properties. The intent to achieve this end is frequently demonstrated by an exorbitant purchase price paid by the minority purchaser. Panic peddling is the next step in the process; it consists of using the results of blockbusting to persuade other owners to sell in order to avoid the purported loss in value that is to be anticipated. Panic peddling may also occur without blockbusting by merely representing to property owners that blockbusting is imminent.[46] As with steering, the subtle practice of panic peddling may be difficult to detect and eliminate.

### Enforcement of the Law

There are several methods by which the Federal Fair Housing Law may be enforced. Initially, the law requires that conciliation methods be attempted; however, if such action is not effective provisions for formal legal action are included. The law provides that a civil suit may be brought for damages and that in addition to the actual damages that may be proved punitive damages up to $1,000 may also be awarded.[47] The injured plaintiff may also recover his attorney's fees if he can demonstrate an inability to pay them. In such civil suits the courts have held that damages need not be limited to provable cash losses but may also include payment for the plaintiff's "emotional distress and humiliation" that result from the discrimination.[48] When a pattern of discriminatory practice is evident, the Attorney General may bring suit for an injunction against it.[49] In addition to these sanctions *the loss of the sales agent's license* is common under state law.

## Management

### Relation of Owner and Manager

The real estate manager is the agent of the owner. His legal position is similar to that of the manager of a branch office or branch store. He is a general agent—that is, an agent vested with general power involving the exercise of judgment and discretion. He is usually empowered to transact all business connected with the property entrusted to him. The property manager is generally authorized to negotiate leases, collect rents, make ordinary repairs, keep the premises in a

---

[46] *Sanborn* v. *Wagner,* D.C. Md. 1973, 354 F. Supp. 291.

[47] 42 U.S.C.A. 3612.

[48] *Steele* v. *Title Realty Co.,* C.A. Utah 1973, 478 F.2d 380.

[49] 42 U.S.C.A. 3613.

rentable condition, pay taxes, and perform many other additional services. He is a fiduciary and must use his best efforts to further the legitimate interests of his principal. The principal is liable for the acts of his manager done within the scope of the venture.[50]

### Authority and Duties of Manager

The manager may be authorized to keep the property insured and take care of tax matters, such as attending hearings on tax assessments. However, in all his activities, he must comply with the instructions of the owner. The manager cannot lawfully substitute his judgment for the judgment of the principal (owner).[51]

The manager owes a duty to keep accurate accounts and to make an accounting to the owner at such periods as have been agreed upon, and also at any time the principal requests one. The manager owes a duty not to commingle the money of the owner with his own money. He should keep a separate account for money handled for each owner. If he does not keep separate accounts, he makes himself personally liable to the owner for all money of the owner coming into his hands.[52]

Development Company engaged a rental agent to manage an apartment building. The agent had exclusive management and supervision of the building. The rents were collected by the agent, whose duty it was to pay all bills, render a monthly accounting, and remit any remainder to Development Company. The president of Development Company made periodic inspections of the premises.

The rental agent purchased coal for the heating of the building from Fadeley. The coal was billed to Development Company. The president of Development Company had purchased coal for the building on a few occasions. Development Company refused to pay for the coal, claiming that it was the obligation of the rental agent and that he had no authority to pledge the credit of Development Company. The court held Development Company liable.

Associate Justice Quinn said: "Appellee's [Fadeley's] evidence indicated that they apparently intended to contract with appellant [Development Company] through its agent, and they did offer testimony that Mr. Hamburger [Development Company's president] himself placed several orders. The fact that Mr. Hamburger ordered coal on a few occasions and also made inspections of the premises tends to show that he retained some measure of control over the rental agent's activities, the usual test in determining whether one is an agent or an independent contractor." *National City Development Company* v. *Fadeley,* Munic. Ct. of App., D.C., 148 A.2d 306 (1959).

---

[50] *Medley* v. *Trenton Investment Co.,* 205 Wis. 30, 236 N.W. 713.

[51] *Granite State Fire Insurance Co.* v. *Mitton et al.,* 98 F. Supp. 706.

[52] *Wangsness* v. *Berdahl,* 69 S.D. 586, 13 N.W.2d 293.

## Appraisal

### Nature of Appraisal

An appraisal is a valuation or an estimation of the value of property. There are many situations in which an appraisal of property is required by law; but as a general rule, no standards of experience, education, or ability have been set up for the person or persons who make the appraisal. Some such qualification as "freeholder of lawful age" may be required, but little else. Almost all that is asked for is that the person appointed as appraiser act honestly and give his unbiased opinion of the value of the property he is appointed to appraise.

Since about 1930, in the business world, and especially in connection with the appraising of real estate, an effort has been made to develop standards for appraisals and to train persons for the work. As a result, the appraising of real estate has come to be recognized as professional in character; and although it has not as yet reached the status of a profession, there has been much progress in that direction.

### Legal Liability of Appraiser

There is no developed body of law that defines the legal liability of appraisers who hold themselves out as skilled in the art of appraising and who demand a fee for the performance of their services. Such persons would, by analogy, be classed as persons performing professional services, and their liabilities would be analogous to the liabilities of such persons. Since there is a dearth of cases in which the liability of appraisers has been litigated,[53] we shall base our discussion on cases that involve the liability of certified public accountants and others performing similar services.

The person who holds himself out as possessing special skills and who contracts to perform duties requiring the exercise of such skills must possess and exercise that degree of proficiency that is usually possessed and exercised by persons in the community performing such services. Applying this rule to the appraiser, if A, who holds himself out to be an expert appraiser, is employed to make an appraisal, he must possess and exercise the same degree of care and skill in making the appraisal as is possessed and exercised by other appraisers practicing in that locality. If he fails to come up to this standard and, as a result of his lack of care and skill, his appraisal is materially in error and the person employing

[53] *Baxter* v. *Gapp & Co.,* 159 Times Reports N.S. 586.

him acts on the appraisal to his injury, the appraiser will be liable for the resulting injury.[54]

## Rules That May Apply

As a general rule, an agent owes the duty of care and skill, and can be held liable for breach of such duty only by his principal. However, if the agent is engaged to perform professional services, if he knows that third persons will deal with his principal in reliance on opinions rendered by him, and if he intentionally renders a false opinion, planning thereby to mislead the third person to his injury, the injured third person can recover a judgment against the agent in an action of deceit for the damage he has suffered. The courts have extended the liability of the professional agent to third persons who have relied on the agent's report to the principal in situations where the agent has been guilty of gross negligence, in that he has failed to follow even the most elemental rules of his profession in the performance of his duties. The courts have held the agent liable to the injured third person on a theory of constructive fraud.[55]

An FHA appraiser reported that property which Neustadt was contemplating buying was eligible for a mortgage at the appraised value of $22,750; and in reliance on this appraisal, Neustadt purchased the property. The appraisal had been negligently made. The house was not properly constructed, and it cost Neustadt $8,000 to remedy the defects. Neustadt sued the United States to recover a judgment for damages suffered as the result of the negligent appraisal made by its agent. The court of appeals granted Neustadt a judgment.

Circuit Judge Soper said: "It is abundantly clear that the government owed a specific duty to the plaintiff [Neustadt] in this case even though there was no contractual relationship between them. The situation is similar to that considered by Judge Cardozo in *Glanzer* v. *Sheppard,* where it was held that a public weigher, who was employed by the seller of goods and who overstated the weight of the merchandise, was liable in damages to the buyer who bought them on the faith of the weigher's certificate. It was pointed out in the opinion that the defendant was not held merely for careless words but for careless performance of the act of weighing.

"So in the pending case, the wrongful conduct complained of does not consist merely or chiefly in the communication to plaintiffs [Neustadt] whereby they were notified that the Housing Commission had appraised the property for mortgage purposes at $22,750,

---

[54] *City of East Grand Forks* v. *Steele et al.,* 121 Minn. 296, 141 N.W. 181.

[55] *Ultramares Corporation* v. *Touche,* 225 N.Y. 170, 174 N.E. 441.

but primarily in the negligent appraisal itself whereby they were led to pay more for the property than it was worth. *United States* v. *Neustadt,* 281 F.2d 596 (1960).

(NOTE: The judgment in this case was reversed. The Supreme Court, Mr. Justice Whittaker, held that the claim of the home purchaser [Neustadt] arose out of the misrepresentation and hence was not actionable against the United States under the Federal Tort Claims Act). *United States* v. *Neustadt,* 366 U.S. 696, 81 S. Ct. 1294.

# Chapter 16
# The Purchase Agreement

## Introduction

As indicated earlier, the purchase agreement is a real contender for the title of the most important document in the real estate business. The reason for this is the fact that it includes all of the many details that must be considered in the sale of real estate and commits both the buyer and the seller to the final terms of the sale. While the fact that real estate is often considered a necessity makes it desirable that real estate sales agreements be simplified, this has not been the trend. In fact, the expanding concepts of consumer protection and product liability have led to greater complexity in such agreements. The continuing growth in the number of ways in which real estate sales may be financed has also increased the complexity of this contract. In this chapter checklists and a sample agreement are used as vehicles to illustrate the number of subjects that must be considered.

The auction sale of real estate is considered in this chapter because of the unique usage of the purchase agreement in such a sale. The purchase agreement is inherently complex. The auction sale is just as inherently simple. To have the benefit of the simplicity of the auction and the protection of the detailed purchase agreement requires skillful use of both devices. The popularity of such sales has increased enormously in recent years, and the auction sale has become quite significant in the area of real estate sales.

### Function of Purchase Agreement

A purchase agreement in writing is not a prerequisite for a valid sale of real estate; it is, however, good insurance against misunderstandings and controversies that could lead to expensive legal action. If the parties reach what they believe to be a mutual understanding but do not draft and sign a purchase agreement, either party could withdraw from the deal at will without incurring legal liability. This is the result of the statute of frauds, which requires that agreements relating to real estate must be in writing in order to be enforceable in a court of law. The purchase agreement should be in writing; should set out in clear, concise language the terms of the agreement, and the rights and liabilities of the parties; and should satisfy the essential requirements for a valid, enforceable contract.

### The Broker

The broker who has negotiated the sale or purchase of real estate will not, in the normal real estate transaction, be a party to the purchase agreement and, under the laws of several states, will not be permitted to draft and have executed the purchase agreement. The drafting or the giving of advice to the parties to a purchase agreement has been held to be the practice of law.

A broker could become a party to such a contract by signing it as a guarantor of the performance of either the buyer or the seller. If a broker should sign such a contract as guarantor, he would be assuming an obligation entirely outside the normal scope of services performed by real estate brokers.

### Broker as Third-Party Beneficiary

A broker might be named in the contract of sale as a third-party beneficiary, but this would not make him a party to the contract, nor would it make him liable for the performance of the contract. It would only give him certain rights under the contract. Suppose, for example, that the contract of purchase and sale expressly provides that one of the parties to the contract will pay to the broker (naming him) a stipulated sum as compensation for services rendered in the negotiation of the sale. In such a case the broker could, if he is not paid, bring a suit on the contract and recover a judgment for the amount of the promised compensation.[1]

## Drafting the Purchase Agreement

### Planning the Draft

The drafting of a purchase agreement, if the transaction involved is relatively complex, should be referred to a competent attorney. The broker, however, should

---

[1] *Hartmann* v. *Windsor Hotel Co. et al.*, 132 W. Va. 307, 52 S.E.2d 48.

be familiar with the matters that will be included in a well-drafted agreement, since he will have directed the negotiations leading up to the sale. If matters that should be included in the agreement are not discussed and settled prior to the actual drafting of the agreement, disagreements may arise that could result in the loss of the sale. A competent attorney will draft a document that states in clear, well-chosen language the terms of the agreement, so that it will be free from ambiguities and can be readily understood.

It is important that the drafted purchase agreement be complete and that it cover all phases of the transaction. If the writing is incomplete, it will not serve as a note or memorandum, and the agreement will be unenforceable under the statute of frauds. If the writing is complete on its face but omits items that should have been included, neither party, in the event of a lawsuit, will be permitted, over the objection of the other party, to offer oral evidence to establish the omitted terms. If the parties so agree, omitted terms may be inserted, and in a proper action the court has the power to re-form the writing and order such terms inserted, provided the party bringing the action can prove by clear and unequivocal evidence that the omitted terms were left out by mistake or oversight. The attorney drafting the agreement has to depend, for the most part, on the broker to furnish him the information necessary to enable him to draft a complete agreement.

### Matters to Be Considered

No two transactions are alike. Each transaction should be carefully checked and every possible point considered, so that the writing will be complete. The following are the principal items that should be considered and, if pertinent, included. This is not an exhaustive list of points that could arise in real estate transactions.

**1. *Name of Seller.*** The seller must be named in the agreement and should be designated as *seller* or *vendor.* If the property is owned by co-owners and all are joining in the sale, all the co-owners must be named as sellers. If the seller is a partnership or corporation, the contract should so indicate. Also, if the seller or sellers are natural persons, the contract should state the marital status of each.

**2. *Name of Spouse.*** The spouse should be named in the agreement as seller and should join in the execution of the agreement if the real estate is located in a state whose laws require that a spouse must join in the execution of the deed in order to convey clear title to the real estate.

**3. *Name of Buyer.*** The buyer must be named in the agreement and designated as *buyer, purchaser,* or *vendee.* If there are two or more buyers, they should be named; and the agreement should state whether they are buying as tenants in common or as joint tenants, or, if husband and wife, as tenants by the entirety. If the buyer is a corporation or partnership, the agreement should so state. Also, if the buyer is purchasing the property in his capacity as trustee, the agreement should so state. In all instances the buyer's name should be spelled in the agreement as it is to be spelled in the deed of conveyance.

**4. *Sale Price.*** The agreement must state the sale price; otherwise, it will be incomplete.

**5. *Extension of Credit.*** If there is no provision in the agreement for the extension of credit to the buyers, it will be held that the terms of payment are cash. If credit is to be extended, the agreement should state the terms in detail. The amount and time of payment of the down payment, the amount of subsequent payments, when each payment is to be made, where payable, rate of interest to be paid, whether the unpaid balance is to be evidenced by a negotiable promissory note or a series of promissory notes, and how the unpaid balance is to be secured should all be stated.

**6. *Security to be Given.*** If credit is extended, the nature of the security to be given should be stated in detail. If the unpaid balance is to be secured by a purchase-money mortgage, trust deed, installment sales contract, pledge of securities, or guarantee of payment by third persons, the terms of the security agreement should be set out in detail.

**7. *Description of Real Estate.*** The description of the real estate sold must be such that it can be identified from the description. However, in the drafting of the agreement the description should be as complete as the circumstances permit.

**8. *Type of Deed.*** The agreement should state the type of deed that is to be executed by the seller—that is, whether general warranty, special warranty, bargain and sale, or quitclaim. If the type of deed is not stated, the court will, in the event of a lawsuit, presume that the type of deed customarily used in the community was intended, usually a general warranty deed.

**9. *Title to be Conveyed.*** The agreement should clearly state the quality of the title to be conveyed. While it has become almost the universal custom in form contracts to require a marketable title and a strong argument might be made that custom has become law, there is serious doubt that this is the case. Many courts have held that the risk as to the quality of the title is the buyer's risk, unless the contract clearly specifies that a marketable title is to be furnished by the seller.[2] The contract may provide that the seller will furnish an insurable title, a title satisfactory to the attorney of the buyer, or a title free from all defects and encumbrances.

*a. Marketable title.* A marketable title is one free of defects, such as mortgages, tax liens, and other liens and encumbrances. It is a title under which the buyer may have quiet and peaceful enjoyment of the property, and one that could be sold to a reasonable and prudent purchaser familiar with all the facts relative to the title to the property.[3] If the buyer wishes to refuse to close the deal on the ground that the title is not marketable, he must discover the defects in the title and point them out before he pays his money and accepts the deed.[4] After he has accepted the deed, he cannot rescind the transaction and recover his money. However, if the seller has given a warranty deed, the buyer could recover damages if the defect was a breach of the warranty.

A provision in the agreement to the effect that the seller would convey a marketable title would justify the buyer in refusing to accept title subject to an easement, unless the easement was visible and beneficial, such as the easements of the utility companies that service the property.[5]

As a general rule restrictions on the property, if not provided for in the agreement, are deemed to be defects in the title, which would justify the buyer in rejecting it; but restrictions imposed by zoning ordinances or state statutes on the use of the property are not defects in the title to real estate. If the buyer wishes to make a particular use of the property, he should include in the agreement a provision that would give him the right to refuse the property if it could not be used for a stated purpose.[6]

*b. Title insurance.* The buyer may wish to protect himself by either insuring the title or providing that the seller shall deliver with the deed a policy of title

---

[2] *Patton on Titles,* 2d. ed., sect. 41, West Publishing Co., St. Paul, Minn., 1957.

[3] *Myrick* v. *Austin,* 141 Kan. 778, 44 P.2d 266.

[4] *Stack* v. *Commercial Towel & Uniform Service,* 120 Ind. App. 473, 91 N.E.2d 790.

[5] *Wheeler* v. *Beem,* 111 Kan. 700, 208 P. 626.

[6] *Campbell* v. *Heller,* 36 N.J. Super. 361, 115 A.2d 644.

insurance insuring the title against all defects except those specifically listed in the agreement. A policy of title insurance does not guarantee a title free from defects, but it does obligate the insurance company that writes the insurance to pay for any loss suffered as the result of covered defects. The buyer may wish to provide that the seller will convey a title that will be insured by an insurance company named by the buyer.

*c. Attorney's approval of title.* The buyer may wish to stipulate in the agreement that the title shall be satisfactory to an attorney to be selected by the buyer. If the agreement includes such a provision, the buyer will not have to accept title until it is approved by the attorney selected. However, the attorney must act honestly. If the attorney acts collusively or capriciously in refusing to approve the title, or if he refuses to act or delays for an unreasonable length of time, the buyer will not be permitted to refuse to accept title, if title is proved to be marketable, on the ground of the attorney's failure to approve the title.

*d. Title free from all defects and encumbrances.* If the agreement provides that the seller will convey a title free from all defects and encumbrances, the purchaser will have the right to reject the title if it is subject to any type of defect or encumbrance. The buyer could not reject the title if it was free from all except technical defects that could be corrected by affidavits or quitclaim deeds.

**10. *Surveys.*** If the boundaries of the real estate are not clearly marked, the buyer may wish to have a survey made, in order to determine and correct boundaries. In such a case the agreement should stipulate who is to pay for the survey and should set out the obligations of the parties in the event the survey reveals that the true boundaries differ from those represented to be the boundaries at the time the property was examined. As a general rule, minor differences would not justify rejection of the title, unless there was an express stipulation in the agreement to that effect.

**11. *Encroachments.*** As a general rule, if there are encroachments on the property being purchased, or if the structures on the property being purchased encroach on adjoining property or streets or alleys, such encroachments create in the title to the property a defect that would justify the buyer in rejecting the title. Some courts have held that if the encroachment is minor in nature—for example, not more than one or two inches—it is not material and will not justify rejection of the title. If there are, on the real estate sold or on the adjoining property, structures that are set close to the boundary line, there should be inserted in the agreement a clause that defines the rights of the parties in the event the structures encroach either on the property sold or on the adjoining property.

**12. *Time of Existence of Stipulated Title.*** A person may agree to sell property and not be guilty of a breach of the agreement even though he does not have title to the property at the time he negotiates the sale. The seller will not need to have title to the property until the time for the delivery of the deed. If the agreement sets a time for the closing of the deal—that is, for the delivery of the deed and the payment or the securing of the purchase price—and at that time the seller cannot convey to the buyer the title provided for in the agreement, the courts will, as a general rule, give the seller some additional time in which to free the title of defect. However, if the circumstances are such that the buyer would suffer substantial injury if the time of performance were delayed, he may, if he so elects, rescind the sale if the seller does not tender performance on time. If the agreement expressly stipulates that "time is of the essence," the buyer has the right to rescind the contract if the seller does not tender performance within the stipulated time.

**13. *Abstract of Title or Torrens Certificate.*** The agreement should provide for the furnishing of an abstract of title or, if the property is registered under the Torrens system of land titles, for the furnishing of a Torrens certificate of title. As a general rule, the seller will have an abstract of title. The abstract should be brought down to date and certified as of that date. The agreement may also stipulate that at the time the deal is closed and the deed is recorded, the abstract be again brought down to that time and certified as of that date. This will show whether any liens were acquired against the property during the time between the first certification of the abstract and the closing of the deal. If a Torrens certificate is to be furnished, the time of certification should be stated. Title insurance may be specified.

It should be made clear in the agreement which of the parties is to pay the costs of obtaining the abstract or of bringing it down to date, or of obtaining the Torrens certificate, or issuance of title insurance.

The time allowed the seller to obtain the abstract or have it brought down to date should be stated. Likewise, the time allowed the buyer to have the abstract examined and defects pointed out should be indicated.

Provision should be made for the removal of discovered defects and a time set within which the seller would be permitted to remove existing defects.

**14. *Earnest Money.*** In many real estate transactions the buyer will make a deposit as a guarantee of his performance of the agreement. The agreement will provide that if the seller cannot perform or fails to perform, the payment made by the buyer will be returned. The agreement will usually provide that if the buyer refuses or fails to perform, he will forfeit his deposit as liquidated damages. Such a provision is enforced by the courts, unless the amount of the deposit is greatly in excess of any possible loss suffered by the seller as the result of the buyer's breach.

The amount of the deposit is a matter to be determined by the parties. The seller, for his protection, should request a deposit large enough to cover any expenses he might incur in having the abstract brought down to date; costs of surveys, if any; brokers' commissions; and any other foreseeable expenses.

**15. *Known Defects in Title.*** As a general rule, the agreement will provide that the purchaser will accept title subject to known defects, such as easements for utilities, or restrictions. For the buyer's protection, this clause should set out specifically the defects that are excluded from the seller's obligation to convey a marketable title or are to be excluded from the coverage of a policy of title insurance. If the excluded defects are stated in broad, general language, the buyer may find that he is, in effect, contracting to accept title "as is" and will have to take whatever title the seller has, without regard to existing defects in it.

**16. *Mortgage on Property.*** If there is a mortgage on the real estate sold, the seller may convey the property free and clear; the purchaser may buy subject to the mortgage, or he may buy subject to the mortgage and assume and agree to pay the mortgage debt.

*a. Discharge of mortgage.* If the real estate is sold free and clear, the seller is obligated to obtain a discharge of the mortgage. Allowing the buyer to withhold from the purchase price the amount of the unpaid balance of the mortgage debt plus accrued interest is not sufficient. A mortgagee is under no obligation to accept payment of a mortgage debt until the due date and may demand a premium if he accepts earlier payment. If the seller has sold free and clear, he must negotiate for and obtain the discharge, paying all premiums, costs, and so forth, incident to obtaining and recording the discharge.

*b. Sale subject to mortgage.* If the sale is subject to the mortgage but the buyer is not assuming the mortgage debt, care must be exercised in drafting the agreement. The courts have held that if the agreement states an agreed purchase price and provides that the purchaser will pay the stated price less the unpaid balance of the mortgage debt and buys subject to the mortgage, the buyer will hold the amount of the mortgage debt as agent or trustee for the mortgagor and will be obligated to pay the mortgage debt when it falls due.[7]

If the buyer does not assume the mortgage debt, the agreement should not state a purchase price other than the amount the buyer is to pay the seller for his equity in the property. For example, suppose that the agreed value of the property sold is $15,000, and the unpaid balance of the mortgage debt and accrued interest is $8,000. The contract should state that the buyer agrees to pay $7,000 for the property "subject to the mortgage," and should describe the mortgage in detail, specifying the book and page where it is recorded.

c. *Sale subject to mortgage, buyer to pay mortgage debt.* If the purchaser buys subject to the mortgage, and assumes and agrees to pay the mortgage debt, the agreement should set out the terms of the mortgage in detail, specify the amount of the unpaid balance of the mortgage debt and accrued interest, and state clearly that the buyer takes "subject to said mortgage, and assumes and agrees to pay the mortgage debt and accrued interest according to the terms of the mortgage and note secured thereby."

**17. *Conditions.*** The buyer may be willing to agree to purchase the real estate but may be unable to meet the seller's terms unless he can borrow money to make the down payment or can sell property he already owns or can obtain certain employment. The seller may be willing to agree to sell subject to the buyer's negotiating the loan, selling the property, or obtaining the position.

In such a situation an agreement of purchase and sale containing all of the terms of the sale will be drafted, and a clause will be inserted providing that the buyer will not be bound to perform the agreement unless or until the stipulated event occurs. Such a provision must be carefully worded and must describe with clarity the event that must happen before the buyer is bound. If the event is the obtaining of a loan or the selling of property, the time within which the loan must be obtained or the property sold should be stated.

In addition, the seller may wish to stipulate that he will have the right to negotiate a loan on the buyer's behalf, stating the terms of the loan or the right to find a lender for the property to be sold. In such situations the buyer owes a duty to act honestly and use his best efforts to bring about the event; if he refuses to act, or if he follows a course that will delay or prevent the occurrence of the event, the court may hold that he is guilty of breach of the agreement.[8]

---

[7] *Flynn et al.* v. *Kenrick et al.,* 285 Mass. 446, 189 N.E. 207.

[8] *Lach* v. *Cahill et al.,* 138 Conn. 418, 85 A.2d 481.

**18. *Possession.*** The agreement should state the time at which the seller is to surrender possession to the buyer. If the property is in the possession of someone other than the seller, the agreement should specifically provide that the seller will take whatever action is necessary to obtain possession of the property and will surrender possession to the buyer on or before a stipulated date.

**19. *Assignment of Leases and Adjustment of Rents.*** If the property is rental property and is sold subject to outstanding leases, the agreement should provide for the examination of the leases by the buyer or his attorney, for the assignment of the leases to the buyer, and for the adjustment of rents. If leases are assigned, notice of the assignment should be given to the tenants; and they should be instructed to pay all rents due and payable after a stated date, to be agreed upon by the seller and buyer, to the buyer or to his order.

**20. *Taxes and Assessments.*** The agreement should provide for the payment of taxes and assessments that are unpaid at the time of the sale. In most communities, established custom regarding the payment of taxes and assessments will apply if no provision is included in the agreement of sale covering this point. However, misunderstanding can be avoided by including in the agreement a provision setting out specifically the arrangement regarding the payment of taxes and assessments.

**21. *Destruction of Buildings.*** The courts are not in accord as to which of the contracting parties must stand the loss if the buildings on the real estate are damaged by fire, flood, or wind after the agreement to sell is executed but before the sale is closed and the deed delivered to the buyer. The agreement should cover this contingency.

The agreement may provide that in the event the buildings are materially damaged by fire, flood, or wind, the buyer will be discharged from his obligation to buy and will have refunded to him any down payment that he has made. Or it may provide that the buyer will assume the risks of the destruction of buildings by fire, flood, or wind and will, in all events, perform the agreement and pay the full purchase price. Such a clause will specifically define the risk, and the party who assumes such risk will be in a position to insure it.

**22. *Insurance.*** The agreement should provide for the adjustment of the policies of insurance on the improvements on the real estate and should provide for insurance after the execution of the agreement but before the conveyance.

A policy of insurance does not go with the property insured. Insurable interest in property is determined at the time of loss. A policy of property insurance is not assignable without the consent of the insurer. If property is conveyed to the buyer and the seller no longer has any interest in the property, the buyer has no right to collect on insurance obtained by the seller, unless the seller has assigned the policies to the buyer with the consent of the insurer. In a sale of improved real estate the agreement should provide either for the assignment of existing policies and the adjustment of the premium or for the cancelation of the policies, leaving the purchaser to obtain such insurance as he wishes.

If property insured by the seller is destroyed or damaged after the execution of the agreement but before conveyance, and the seller collects the insurance, the majority of courts hold that the seller is entitled to the insurance money if the buyer has the right to rescind the agreement or if the seller must stand the loss. However, if the buyer is obligated to accept a conveyance of the property and pay the full purchase price, he is entitled to the insurance money.[9] A safe course to follow would be for both the seller and the buyer to insure their respective interests in the property, or for the buyer to insure and include a provision in the policy covering the seller's interest as it may appear.

**23. *Sale of Land and Contract to Construct Building.*** If a person agrees to sell a tract of land and to build a house or other structure on the land, the resulting contract is a combination of a contract to sell real estate and a contract to build, and should contain all the provisions essential to both types. Building contracts are discussed in Chapter 18. As a general rule, the courts will grant specific performance of a contract to sell real estate—that is, they will force the seller to convey the real estate—but will not grant specific performance of a building contract. Some courts have granted specific performance of a combined sale of land and building contract,[10] whereas other courts have refused to do so.

**24. *Violation of Ordinances.*** For the buyer's protection the agreement should provide that in the event any structure on the premises is so constructed that it violates a city ordinance—lacks fire escapes, proper sanitary facilities, and so forth—the seller will correct any defect, unless the buyer is purchasing subject to the defects, in which case the agreement should so state. If the seller is to correct the defects, the closing of the deal can be expedited by getting an estimate of the cost and having the seller leave in the hands of the buyer or in escrow sufficient funds to cover the cost of the work to be done.

---

[9] *Vogel* v. *Northern Assurance Company,* 219 F.2d 409.

[10] *Edison Realty Co. et al.* v. *Bauernschaub et al.,* 191 Md. 451, 62 A.2d 354.

**25. *Utility Bills, etc.*** If the real estate is being serviced by utilities, some provision should be made for the prorating of utility bills or for having meters read and the account transferred to the new occupant at the time he takes possession.

**26. *Fixtures and Crops.*** The agreement should clearly state which of the articles that are in the nature of fixtures are to go with the real estate. If the seller wishes to remove any plantings from the premises, the agreement should clearly state what plantings are to be removed and within what time they are to be removed.

If the real estate sold is farm land, the agreement should state which crops are to go with the land and which are to remain the property of the seller. It should also define the seller's right to remove reserved crops.

**27. *Miscellaneous.*** During the negotiation of the sale of real estate, the parties may raise special questions regarding the property and the rights in the property that are to be retained or transferred. Careful note should be made of all matters, and a clause setting out the agreement of the parties relative to such special items should be included.

## Sample Purchase Agreement

There follows a sample form of purchase agreement that is similar to many forms in common use today. The foregoing discussion of the various matters to be considered in completing such a form should be kept in mind.

### Sample Agreement to Purchase Real Estate

The undersigned (herein "Purchaser") hereby offers to purchase from the owner (herein "Seller") the real estate located at ______________________________ ______________________________ in the city of ______________________, County of ______________, State of ________________, the legal description of which is: ______________________________________________________
______________________________________________________
______________________________________________________
______________________________________________________
upon the following terms and conditions:

1. Purchase Price and Conditions of Payment

The purchase price shall be ________________________________ Dollars ($__________) to be paid in accordance with subparagraph __________, below:

**Sample Agreement to Purchase Real Estate *(continued)***

A. *Cash.* The purchase price shall be paid in its entirety in cash at the time of closing the sale.

B. *Cash Subject to New Mortgage.* The purchase price shall be paid in cash at the time of closing the sale subject, however, to Purchaser's ability to obtain a first mortgage loan within __________ days after the acceptance of this offer by Seller in the amount of $______________________, payable in not less than _______ monthly installments, including interest at a rate not to exceed _______ % per annum. Purchaser agrees to immediately apply for and seek such financing. If such financing cannot be obtained within the time specified above then either Purchaser or Seller may terminate this agreement and any earnest money deposited by Purchaser will be promptly refunded.

C. *Cash Subject to Existing Mortgage.* The purchase price shall be paid in cash at the time of closing the sale after deducting from the purchase price the then outstanding balance due and owing under that existing mortgage in favor of ______________________________________________________________, dated __________, 19_____, in the original amount of $_____________; Seller, by accepting this offer, represents that the present unpaid balance of such mortgage debt is approximately $______________________ as of ____________, 19_____.

D. *Cash With Assumption of Existing Mortgage.* The purchase price shall be paid in cash at the time of the closing of the sale after deducting from the purchase price the then outstanding balance due and owing under that existing mortgage in favor of _____________________________________________________, dated __________, 19_____, having a present balance of approximately $__________________, as of _________, 19_____, which the purchaser hereby assumes and agrees to pay in accordance with its terms and to perform all of its provisions; purchaser shall pay any and all payments coming due after the closing of the sale. Any transfer fees required by the mortgage shall be paid by _______________________.

E. *Sale by Land Contract.* The purchase price shall be paid in accordance with that certain land contract attached hereto and incorporated into this contract by this reference. The down payment to be made at the time of closing this sale shall be $_______________ and the balance of $_______________ shall be paid at the rate of $_______________ per month including principal and interest at the rate of _____ % per annum.

**Sample Agreement to Purchase Real Estate *(continued)***

2. Earnest Money Deposit

As earnest money Purchaser deposits $_______________ with the broker which shall be applied to the purchase price at the time of closing the sale. In the event that this offer is not accepted by Seller this earnest money deposit shall be promptly refunded to Purchaser by the broker. In the event that this offer is accepted by Seller and Purchaser shall fail to perform the terms of this agreement the earnest money deposit shall be forfeited as and for liquidated damages suffered by Seller. Seller is not, however, precluded from asserting any other legal or equitable remedy which may be available to enforce this agreement.

3. Real Estate Taxes, Assessments, and Adjustments

Real Estate Taxes accrued against the property shall be prorated through the date of closing the sale and Seller shall pay all taxes allocated to the property through that date and Purchaser shall pay all taxes thereafter. Seller shall pay at or prior to the closing of the sale all assessments and charges upon the property for municipal improvements through the date of acceptance of this offer to purchase. Rents, if any, shall be prorated through the date of closing and all rents deposits shall be transferred to Purchaser. Existing casualty insurance shall be cancelled/prorated through the date of closing.

4. Title to the Property

Seller shall provide Purchaser prior to the closing and promptly after the acceptance of this offer, at Seller's expense and at Seller's option an abstract of title to the property brought down to date or an owner's policy of title insurance in an amount equal to the purchase price, said abstract of policy to show marketable or insurable title to the real estate in the name of Seller subject only to easements, zoning, and restrictions of record and free and clear of all other liens and encumbrances except as stated in this offer. If the abstract or title policy fail to show marketable or insurable title in Seller a reasonable time shall be permitted to cure or correct defects. Seller shall convey title to Purchaser at the time of closing by a good and sufficient general warranty deed free and clear of all liens and encumbrances except as otherwise provided in this offer and subject to easements, zoning, and restrictions of record.

5. Possession of the Property

Purchaser shall be given possession of the property on _______________, 19_____. A failure on the part of Seller to transfer possession as specified will not make Seller a tenant of Purchaser, but in such event Seller shall pay to Purchaser $__________ per day as damages for breach of contract and not as

**Sample Agreement to Purchase Real Estate *(continued)***

rent. All other remedies which Purchaser may have under law are reserved to Purchaser.

6. Risk of Loss

The risk of loss by destruction or damage to the property by fire or otherwise prior to the closing of the sale is that of Seller. If all or a substantial portion of the improvements on the property are destroyed or damaged prior to the closing and transfer of title this agreement shall be voidable at Purchaser's option and in the event Purchaser elects to avoid this agreement the earnest money deposited shall be promptly refunded.

7. Improvements and Fixtures Included

This offer to purchase includes all improvements, buildings, and fixtures presently on the real estate including but not limited to electrical, gas, heating, air conditioning, and plumbing equipment, built-in appliances, hot water heaters, screens and storm windows and doors, venetian blinds, drapery hardware, awnings, attached carpeting, radio and television antennas, trees, shrubs, flowers, fences and

______________________________________________

______________________________________________

______________________________________________

presently installed and in use on the real estate. Seller warrants that all improvements, fixtures, and appliances are or will be fully paid for at the time of closing and will be in their present condition excepting only normal wear and tear up to the time of closing.

8. General Conditions

It is expressly agreed that this agreement to purchase real estate includes the entire agreement of Purchaser and Seller. This agreement shall be binding upon the heirs, personal representatives, successors and assigns of both Purchaser and Seller. This agreement shall be interpreted and enforced in accordance with the laws of the State of ________________.

9. Special Conditions

______________________________________________

______________________________________________

______________________________________________

______________________________________________

______________________________________________

**Sample Agreement to Purchase Real Estate *(concluded)***

10. Time for Acceptance and Closing

This offer is void if not accepted by Seller in writing on or before ________ A.M./P.M. of the ________ day of ________, 19____. Closing of the sale shall take place ________ days after Purchaser's receipt of an abstract showing marketable title in Seller or a title insurance binder showing insurable title in Seller.

This offer is made at ____________, State of ____________, this ________ day of __________, 19____.

______________________
(PURCHASER)

______________________
(PURCHASER)

*Acceptance by Seller*

The foregoing offer to purchase real estate is hereby accepted in accordance with the terms and conditions specified above. The undersigned hereby agrees to pay a brokerage fee of $________ to ____________, broker, in accordance with the existing listing contract.

Dated this ________ day of ________, 19____.

______________________
(SELLER)

______________________
(SELLER)

## Execution of Purchase Agreement

### Signing the Purchase Agreement

The purchase agreement should be signed by both the buyer and the seller; and if either or both are married, the spouse or spouses also should sign. However, in those states in which either the husband or the wife may deal with his or her individual real estate without the spouse's joining, only the signature of the title owner of the real estate is necessary. If the real estate is owned or is being purchased by two or more persons holding or purchasing as co-owners, all interested persons and their spouses (with the exception noted above) should sign.

If the real estate is owned or is being purchased by a corporation, the purchase agreement will be signed in the name of the corporation by an officer or agent thereof. A careful check should be made to ascertain (1) whether the purchase or sale of the real estate has been duly authorized by action of the board of directors of the corporation and (2) whether the officer or agent signing the agreement on behalf of the corporation is authorized to do so.

As a general rule, a partner has authority to bind the partnership, provided the purchase or sale of the real estate involved is within the scope of the partnership business.

### Signature by Agent

The agreement may be signed by a duly authorized agent on behalf of either the buyer or the seller, or both. Oral authorization to sign is sufficient to bind the principal. However, it is customary to employ a written authorization; if the agreement is to be recorded, the recording laws require a written authorization. The written authorization must be executed with the same formality as is required for the execution of the agreement.

Good business practice requires a written authorization. A person dealing with an agent must determine the scope of the agent's authority. If the agent exceeds his authority, the principal is not bound. The agent should be required to produce his written authority; and the person dealing with the agent should read it carefully to determine the extent of the agent's authority. Authority of an agent to "sell" does not give him the authority to execute a contract to sell or a deed. Authority of an agent to execute a contract or deed does not, as a general rule, give him the authority to sell on credit.

A person may act as the agent of his undisclosed principal, in which event the agent will contract in his own name and will be bound by the contract. On the discovery of the existence of the agency, the person dealing with the agent can elect to hold either the agent or the undisclosed principal on the contract.[11] (In Pennsylvania, both are liable.)

If an owner has refused to sell to a particular individual and that particular individual employs an agent to purchase the property for him, the agent to conceal the identity of his principal, the seller may, on discovering the true principal of the agent, refuse to perform the contract.[12]

### Sealing, Acknowledgment, Witnessing, and Delivery

A purchase agreement is, in legal effect, a contract; and a contract to sell real estate does not have to be sealed to be valid. Likewise, an acknowledgment

---

[11] *Hollywood Holding & Development Corporation* v. *Oswald,* 119 Cal. App. 21, 5 P.2d 963.

[12] *Wloczewski* v. *Kozlowski,* 395 Ill. 402, 70 N.E.2d 560.

is not essential to the validity of the agreement. However, under the recording statutes of most states, such an agreement would have to be acknowledged if it is to be eligible to record. As a general rule, purchase agreements are not recorded and are therefore not acknowledged.

The same rule applies to the witnessing of the purchase agreement. Witnesses are not essential to the validity of the agreement, and there is no reason for having the agreement witnessed unless the parties wish to record it and the statutes of the state require that a contract must be witnessed if it is to be eligible to record.

An agreement to sell real estate is not effective until it is delivered. The same rules of law apply to the delivery of a contract as to the delivery of a deed (see "Delivery of Deed" in Chapter 9).

It is recommended that the agreement be prepared in duplicate, and that both the buyer and the seller sign it at the same time, each signing both copies and each keeping a copy.

If the buyer submits a prepared agreement as an offer to buy, he should submit two copies; he should include a clause in the agreement (offer) to the effect that if the seller wishes to accept the offer, he must sign and return to the buyer a copy of the agreement within a stated period of time—for example, five days. If the seller does not act within the stipulated time, the offer will terminate.

### Recording

As a general rule, agreements to sell real estate—except the installment land contract, which is discussed in detail in Chapter 14—are short-term contracts and are not recorded. Under the recording statutes of some states, such agreements are not eligible to be recorded. There is some risk involved in not recording the agreement to sell. For instance, if the seller, after executing an agreement to sell, conveys the real estate to an innocent purchaser for value who has no notice or knowledge of the agreement to sell at the time the property is conveyed to him, the innocent purchaser acquires a title that is good against the contract buyer. The contract buyer's only remedy is a suit against the seller for damages for breach of contract.

## Effect of Purchase Agreement

### Rights Acquired by Buyer

When an agreement to sell real estate is fully executed, the buyer acquires property rights in the real estate, although he does not acquire title until a deed to the property is executed and delivered to him. The buyer's rights in the property are called the *equitable title* to the property. This, in effect, indicates that in a proper action the court will force the seller to deed the property to the buyer if the buyer has performed or tendered performance of his obligations under the agreement.

### Buyer's Right to Assign

Unless the contract of sale contains a clause prohibiting the transfer of the buyer's interest in the real estate, the buyer can sell his property right—transfer his equitable title. This is known as an *assignment* of the agreement. The assignee—buyer of the equitable title—acquires all the rights of the buyer and, on the performance of the buyer's obligations, is entitled to a deed from the seller. The buyer continues to be liable to the seller for the performance of his obligations under the agreement; he cannot relieve himself of his obligations by assigning the agreement. The buyer of the equitable title (the assignee) is not liable to the seller unless, as a part of the assignment, he assumes and agrees to perform the obligations of the buyer. The seller, the buyer, and the assignee may enter into an agreement whereby the assignee promises the seller that he (the assignee) will perform the obligations of the buyer, and the seller accepts the assignee's promise of performance in the place of the obligations of the buyer and agrees to release the buyer from his obligations. This is known as a *novation.*

### Buyer's Remedies

If the seller is unable to fulfill his obligations under the agreement or refuses to do so, the buyer has an election of remedies. He may (1) rescind the agreement, (2) bring an action to recover damages, or (3) bring an action asking specific performance of the agreement.

If the buyer rescinds the agreement, he thereby puts an end to it. He will be entitled to the return of any payments made or anything given in part performance and will be required to return anything that he has received from the seller in part performance. In a court action in which the remedy granted is rescission of the agreement, the court endeavors to put the parties as nearly as possible in the same positions they would have held if they had never entered into the contract.

In a suit for damages the buyer is entitled to be compensated for any financial loss that he can prove he has suffered as the direct result of the seller's breach of the agreement. The usual elements of damages would be the down payment made by the buyer or the value of any property conveyed to the seller as part payment, any actual out-of-pocket expenses paid by the buyer, and loss of profits on the transaction. To recover for loss of profits, the purchaser will have to prove beyond a reasonable doubt that the market value of the property at the time the seller was to convey it to him was greater than the agreed price. The buyer must prove the amount of this difference with reasonable certainty.

When the court grants the remedy of specific performance, it forces the seller, on receiving payment of the purchase price, to give the buyer a deed to the real estate. Whether or not a court will grant the remedy of specific performance rests in the sound discretion of the courts. If the buyer has induced the seller to enter into an unfair and inequitable agreement to sell, and its specific enforcement would impose an unjust hardship on the seller, the court may refuse to grant the remedy of specific performance.[13] As a general rule, the court will decree specific performance of an agreement to sell real estate.

### Defective Title

If the seller's title is defective, the buyer may, if he wishes, ask for specific performance of the agreement. If the defect in the seller's title is of such a nature that it can be compensated for by a reduction of the purchase price, and the buyer did not know of the defect at the time the agreement was executed, the court, as a part of its decree of specific performance, will abate part of the purchase price. For example, if the seller is only a part owner of the property, or if the land area is less than the area called for in the agreement, the court may grant a proportional reduction in the purchase price; or if there is a mortgage, mechanic's lien, or judgment lien on the property, the court will reduce the purchase price by the amount of the mortgage or lien. However, if the buyer knew of the mortgage or lien at the time he entered into the agreement, he would not be entitled to a reduction in the purchase price.

If there is a provision in the agreement that it shall be void in the event the seller's title proves defective, the buyer would not be entitled to a remedy if the seller's title is defective, but he would be entitled to the return of his down payment.

### Misrepresentation and the Like

If the buyer is induced to enter into the agreement by misrepresentation or undue influence, he may rescind it. If he is induced to enter into the agreement by fraudulent representations or duress, he may rescind the agreement, or he may retain the property and bring suit in tort and recover tort damages. In a

---

[13] *Saunders* v. *Davis et ux.,* 31 Tenn. App. 674, 220 S.W.2d 883.

fraud case, tort damages are, as a general rule, the difference between the value of the real estate conveyed and its value if it had been as represented.

### Remedies of the Seller

The remedies of the seller correspond in most respects to the remedies of the buyer. The seller may (1) rescind the agreement, (2) declare a forfeiture, (3) recover damages, (4) tender a deed and recover a judgment for the purchase price, or (5) ask for specific performance.

If the seller rescinds the agreement, he returns what he has received and recovers possession of the real estate. If the buyer has been in possession, the seller is entitled to reasonable rent for the time the buyer was in possession.

The seller is not entitled to declare a forfeiture unless this right is expressly reserved in the agreement. When the seller declares a forfeiture, he retains all payments made by the buyer and recovers possession of the real estate.

In a suit for damages the seller must prove the amount of the financial loss he has suffered as a direct result of the buyer's breach.

Typically, the amount of the loss is demonstrated by a resale of the property at a lower price. In a recent case, a sale took place at $60,000. After a breach of this contract, the seller resold the property at a price of $54,000. The court held that the difference between the two prices was the correct measure of the seller's damages.[14]

In some states the seller may tender a deed and recover a judgment for the purchase price of the property. This remedy is practically the same as the remedy of specific performance. If the remedy of specific performance is granted, the court will decree the performance of the agreement on the part of the buyer. The seller, in turn, must perform his obligations under the agreement.

## Auction Sales of Real Estate

### Introduction

Sales by use of the auction process have, in recent years, become a very important method of marketing real estate. For many years the auction sale of real estate was thought to be simply a way of assuring the completion of forced sales, such as foreclosure and tax sales. It is true today that such sales use the auction process and it remains true that such sales seldom bring full market value.

---

[14] *Harris* v. *Dawson,* 360 A.2d 706 (Pa. Superior Court 1976).

The two, the auction sale and low prices, do not necessarily go hand in hand. Upon careful analysis of such distress sales it will usually be found that statutory procedures place severe limitations upon the conduct of the auction. At the same time, most such sales are conducted by the sheriff or other elected official rather than by a professional auctioneer using effective marketing techniques to enhance the sale. When sales of real estate are conducted at *private* auctions the results are far different.

At this point some clarification of terms is necessary so that meaningful comparisons between auction sales and sales by private treaty (negotiated contract) can be made. The term *public auction* has two meanings, one of them technical and the other one of popular usage. A true public auction is one that is in strict accordance with some statutory provision that dictates the conditions under which the sale *must* take place. For example, sales of real estate for the nonpayment of real estate taxes are always dictated in all details by statute. The reason for the formality of the procedure is, of course, that a citizen is being deprived of his property by his government. One would expect such a sale to be very carefully controlled by statute. When the term public auction is used by a professional auctioneer conducting a sale as agent for a private owner, the term means something substantially different: it is public only in the sense that the general public is invited and welcomed to participate in the sale. The rules under which such sales are conducted are, however, essentially private in nature. They are established by the auctioneer and the seller and made known to the bidders. They are definitely not controlled or strictly limited by statutory rules and can be so structured as to employ whatever marketing techniques are appropriate. As a result, there is no arbitrary "damper" put on the sale, no statutorily mandated price. Market forces alone will determine the price.

When the real estate to be sold is of such value and attraction that more than one interested buyer is in evidence, the auction process provides a unique opportunity to arrive at the highest price obtainable by creating a forum in which serious buyers can compete with each other. Very often such property is difficult to value or appraise. It may be impossible to predict the maximum selling price that it will bring. Such properties as prime farmland that may also have development potential because of its location have provided striking illustrations of the value of the auction process. Such a property may have two distinct values, one the maximum that can be economically paid for farming purposes; the other the maximum that can be feasibly paid for development purposes. Each of these values may be impossible to determine by normal appraisal techniques. If a property is sold on a negotiated basis, the establishment of the price by negotiation with a limited number of buyers may be far lower than that which might have been obtained. The auction provides a way to permit competing uses and buyers to arrive at the true maximum price.

There is also present at all auction sales at which true competition develops between two or more buyers a sense of urgency that requires those buyers to act. In negotiated sales it is one thing to tell a potential buyer that someone else is also interested in an attempt to prompt him to make an offer. At an auction the fact of competition is quite obvious. Buyer procrastination is held to a minimum. The delays frequently encountered in negotiated sales are eliminated. To achieve this it is necessary that the auction be conducted in a professional manner and that it be carefully prepared for, including effective advertising. Such conditions simply do not exist in the statutory public sale. They can be made to exist in the privately conducted public auction sale. In this material we will consider some of the fundamental legal rules that apply to all auctions that are not statutory public auctions, with emphasis, of course, on the sale of real estate.

**Auctions Distinguished from Negotiations**

As we have seen in our consideration of contract law the negotiation process permits each party to change position in response to communication from the other. The offeree need not simply accept or reject an unsatisfactory offer. He may instead make a counteroffer in which the offeree becomes the offeror on new terms. The roles of the parties may change several times during a negotiation before agreement is reached or the attempts to do so are abandoned. In the auction process the seller does not make an offer to sell. He publicly declares the conditions upon which he will consider offers. (This is not essentially different from the seller who signs a listing contract with a broker.) The offer is made by the bidder and it is the function of the auctioneer, as agent for the seller, to respond to that offer. There are three possible responses: (1) acceptance, in which case a contract of sale will result; (2) a rejection of the bid if the seller has reserved this right; and (3) continued solicitation of bids without either accepting or rejecting the first bid. The bidder's offer will remain viable unless the bidder withdraws it before it is accepted. There is one other obvious possibility: another higher bid. When a higher bid is made the existing bid is rejected by legal implication. Perhaps one way of describing what is happening at the auction sale is to visualize the sale as one in which the auctioneer is negotiating with *all* the bidders simultaneously.

The foregoing discussion is based upon the procedure most commonly used in this country: the English auction, in which the bids are made in increasing amounts until there are no higher bids made. At that point, unless the seller has reserved the right to decline all bids, the auctioneer must accept the highest bid if made by a responsible bidder and a contract of sale will result. On occasion a different type of auction sale may be conducted: the Dutch auction. This type of auction was designed for sales of perishable goods and is therefore rarely seen in this country in connection with real estate sales. In the Dutch auction the *seller* offers to sell at a specified price. The bidders can accept the offer to sell, which will result in a completed sale. If they make no response there can of course be no contract. The sale progresses at a Dutch auction in decreasing prices offered by the seller. That is, if there is no acceptance within a specified period of time the offering price is reduced. It continues to be reduced until there is an acceptance or until the goods are withdrawn by the seller, if the seller has reserved the right to do so.

The auction sale represents a distortion of the negotiation process since it is impractical to continuously change the *terms* of the sale. Changes in terms as well as in price are easy to introduce into the negotiated sale. For example, assume an offer to purchase real estate for $40,000 on a land contract with a $5,000 down payment. It is simple to respond with a counteroffer to sell at $37,500 cash. Both the price and the terms have been easily altered. Because of the structure of the auction sale, however, and in order to put all bidders on the same footing, the terms must be uniform for all of them. To this extent the seller at the auction sale has surrendered some of his negotiating flexibility. It therefore becomes critical to the success of the auction sale that terms that are likely to be attractive to all bidders be established at the outset.

**Sales with and without Reserve**

The basic approach to the auction sale in this country requires that a decision be made by the seller either to accept the highest bid that will be made, regardless of amount, or to establish a minimum price below which he is not obligated to accept bids. He may go further and refuse to be committed to accept *any* bid, but this position militates against a successful auction. The two basic choices are sales *with reserve* or *without reserve*. The conditions of the sale are advertised before the sale and almost universally repeated to the bidders at the beginning of the sale. If the sale is being conducted *without* reserve then the seller must accept the highest bid, no matter how unsatisfactory that bid may be. If, on the other hand, the sale is *with* reserve then the reserve price established by the seller will determine whether or not the highest bid must be accepted. If the highest bid is below the reserve price the seller does not have to accept it, but if it is above the reserve price it must be accepted. There is a presumption established by the Uniform Commercial Code that all auction sales are *with* reserve unless they are advertised or represented to be without reserve.

Whether an auction sale should be conducted with or without reserve is more a question of strategy than one of law. The sale without reserve exposes the seller to the risk that the sale will bring substantially less than the desired price. On the other hand the very existence of a reserve price has a tendency to do one of two things: (1) it may reduce the competition to a point where the reserve price is not reached, or (2) it may effectively establish the *maximum* price the property will bring. In the one case, the expense of the sale, which may be substantial, will have been wasted. In the other, the full benefit of the auction process will have been lost. Because of the complexity of the real estate sale generally, the difficulty in establishing the precise terms that will motivate bidders, or an unreasonably high reserve price, such sales frequently abort. From a marketing standpoint the public nature of the auction sale tends to confirm the market value of the property in the minds of other potential buyers. That is, reports of the prices bid will be common knowledge in the community, and it will be more difficult to negotiate a substantially higher price even with other buyers who did not bid at the auction.

It frequently happens that a sale of real estate with reserve will elicit bids within negotiating range even if they do not reach the reserve price. In such cases it is often quite practical to continue the sales effort on a negotiated basis between the seller and the highest bidder. That is, the auction process may flush out the best prospect and identify him for continued pursuit on the basis of a negotiated sale in which both price and terms can be adjusted more easily. It is suggested that the auctioneer who handles such a transaction has changed his role from that of auctioneer (which may not require a real estate license) to that of real estate broker (which almost universally does require a real estate license).

### The Law of the Auction

The auction sale is hardly a new device. There is evidence of its use as far back as 500 B.C. Nevertheless, down to the present day there has not developed any extensive body of law that relates specifically to auction sales. Very little attention is devoted to the auction, even in the Uniform Commercial Code. There has been surprisingly little litigation reported over the auction process itself. The conclusion, which seems to compel acceptance, is that the law of the auction is established by the auctioneer. The advertising of the auction and the terms under which it will be conducted are peculiarly within the control of the auctioneer.

Bidders are not obligated to attend the auction nor to participate even if they do attend. It must be presumed that if they do participate they impliedly accept the conditions of the sale as established by the auctioneer. So long as the auctioneer's conduct of the sale is consistent with the advertised and announced terms of the sale, the bidder cannot complain because he is, after all, a volunteer. If such an assumption can be accepted it clearly follows that understanding the terms and conditions under which the auction is being conducted is the responsibility of the bidder. At a well-attended auction there will, to be sure, be many witnesses capable of testifying as to the events that occurred at the auction. What happened at the auction, however, is seldom the issue. The nature of the agreed-upon rules is the crucial question; if the bidder, by attending and participating, has accepted the rules established by the auctioneer then that issue may be foreclosed.

**The Real Estate Auction**

The inclusion of the subject of auction sales immediately following the discussion of the offer to purchase is not accidental. It has already been noted that at the auction sale the seller is handicapped by his inability to continually adjust the terms of payment in response to the bidders. By now it must be apparent that the typical offer to purchase is a lengthy and involved legal document that settles a wide variety of issues between the seller and the buyer. How is it practical to conduct an auction sale in which the only issue that is unresolved is the price? In the final analysis, to successfully conduct an auction sale of real estate this goal must somehow be achieved.

In the negotiated sale of real estate, the offer to purchase is filled out in its entirety by the buyer. It is the buyer who dictates the way in which real estate taxes will be apportioned, rents will be divided, the quality of title that must be delivered, and so on. It is then up to the seller to accept this elaborate offer in its entirety if he wishes to sell at the price offered. Many of the detailed terms and conditions will have a definite influence upon the true proceeds of sale. Terms of payment alone may dramatically change the true amount of the offer. For example: a land contract offer of $50,000 with payments to be made in equal installments for 20 years at 4 percent interest is not the same as $50,000 cash at the time of closing. The offer to purchase must, therefore, spell out what the buyer will do clearly enough to be understood.

The same thing must happen at the auction sale if it is to be successful; however, the seller rather than the buyer will spell out all of the terms of the sale except for the purchase price. By doing so the seller at the auction sale has, acting through the auctioneer, established with precision and in detail the basis upon which he will consider or accept offers. In a sense the offer to purchase, complete with all information except the price, becomes the law of the auction. In this way all bidders are on an equal footing, and their offers or bids can be easily evaluated against each other. The auction process demands this degree of regimentation. To permit bidders to bid on various terms would create chaos and make immediate comparison impossible.

From a practical standpoint the statement of terms and conditions upon which bids will be considered is crucial to the success of the auction sale. Depending upon economic and market conditions, it may be unrealistic to expect true competitive bidding if the seller insists on receiving the entire purchase price in cash at the time of the sale. In the recent period of very high interest costs for mortgage money, sellers frequently found that no sale was practical without some form of seller participation in the financing. Such a fact must be considered in the auction sale as well as the negotiated sale. In order to secure active competition for the property the seller may have to offer attractive financing. Failure to take this into account could result in an aborted sale.

# Chapter 17
# Closings and Escrows

## Introduction

No matter how the sales agreement between the buyer and seller of real estate has been established, its performance is usually a time-consuming process. Many steps in this process will require the use of specialists and experts representing each of the parties. This has led to recognition of the *closing* or completion of the sale as a separate area of activity. In a great many cases the closing will be conducted by the mortgage lender who is financing the sale, on the theory that its interest in the successful completion of the work is the same as that of the two parties to it. In certain areas of the country, separate service organizations, called escrow companies, have emerged to meet this need. The parties themselves can perform this function and, at least in some states, so can their brokers. In other states, however, the closing of the real estate transaction is the exclusive province of the attorney. No matter who supervises the closing, the process is both time-consuming and technical, requiring careful attention to many important details. The closing is the performance by the parties of their purchase agreement. Once it is completed and performance by each has been accepted by the other, it may be impossible to reopen the matter and change or correct some important detail.

Occasionally some detail cannot be resolved quickly enough to permit the closing to take place as scheduled. The detail may be of great significance, great enough that the purchase price should not be paid until the matter is settled.

At the same time, postponing the closing may have undesirable consequences. The solution is the use of an escrow agreement that will permit the closing to take place on a conditional basis. This procedure is discussed in this chapter after the discussion of the closing itself.

## Closing the Sale

### Precautions Buyer Should Take

Before a buyer enters into an agreement to buy real estate, he should examine the property and satisfy himself that the property is what he wants. If it is residential property, he should check the community in which it is located, the schools, churches, transportation facilities, sanitary facilities, zoning ordinances, restrictions, whether or not it is in a flood area, and anything else that might affect the value of the property.

If the property is commercial property, he should check zoning ordinances, character of surrounding property, transportation facilities, traffic flow, and similar matters. After the buyer has entered into an agreement to buy, it is too late to rescind the transaction. The seller should check the buyer's credit and satisfy himself that the buyer is able to fulfill his part of the contract.

Before the buyer accepts a deed to the property and pays or secures the purchase price, he should check each point of the agreement and be certain that the property satisfies every condition in it. When the purchaser accepts the deed and pays his money, the agreement is merged in the deed; it is then too late to object to the performance rendered by the seller. The only provisions of the agreement that are not merged into the deed are those that clearly state or unquestionably imply that they are to be performed after the transaction is closed.

One of the principal reasons for the buyer and seller of real estate to enter into an agreement to buy and sell, preliminary to the closing of the transaction, is to afford the buyer an opportunity to have the title to the property investigated. If the evidence of title is based on an abstract of title, the buyer should check to be certain that the abstract has been prepared by a competent, reliable abstractor. He should have the abstract examined by an experienced real estate attorney.

The certificate of the abstractor should be checked to ascertain what records have been examined and abstracted. Any records—such as notices of mechanics' liens, federal tax liens, old-age assistance liens, probate court records, *lis pendes* records, recognizance or bail bonds, circuit court records, superior court records, criminal court records, transcript of judgment records of all federal courts in the state, and tax records—should be carefully checked, if the certificate of the abstractor does not include them.

If the evidence of title is to be a certificate of title, the buyer should demand or obtain a certificate of title prepared by a competent attorney experienced in making title examinations. If the property is registered under the Torrens system, the register should be checked to ascertain whether there are liens and encumbrances against the property that are not mentioned in the agreement. If the title is to be an insured title, the buyer should have a commitment from the insurer who is to write the policy of insurance.

### Adjustment if Title Is Defective

If the seller is unable to convey a marketable title or a title that satisfies the requirements set out in the agreement, the buyer is not obligated to accept the title and may rescind the agreement. If no specific time is set for the closing of the sale, or if a specific time is set but time is not made of the essence, the seller will have a reasonable time to cure the defects in his title. However, if the defects are such that they cannot be cured within a relatively short period of time, and especially if they are such that a suit to quiet title would be required to cure them, the seller would be in default, and the buyer would have the right to elect to rescind the agreement or to grant the seller time in which to cure the defects in his title. If an extension of time is to be granted, an agreement as to the adjustment of interest, rents, and so forth, should be drafted and signed by the parties.

### Matters to Be Checked by Buyer

After the agreement has been executed, and before the sale is closed, the buyer should perform the following:

1. Check the boundaries of the property. Have a survey made, if needed.
2. If a survey is made, have the surveyor indicate whether or not there are encroachments.
3. Ascertain the terms of any mortgage on the property, and obtain from the mortgagee a statement of the unpaid balance of the mortgage debt plus interest and any other charges up to date for the closing. Does the mortgage contain a clause providing that on the sale of the property the mortgage debt becomes due and payable?
4. If payments made by the mortgagee include expenditures for taxes, insurance

premiums, and so on, obtain from the mortgagee a statement of the accruals in such accounts as of the closing date.

5. Check with persons in possession, and ascertain the rights that they claim in the property. Also, check with the parties in possession as to what items attached to the premises they claim as their property.
6. If the property is rental property under lease, obtain the leases, and have them examined by an attorney. Have the attorney prepare a schedule showing the principal provisions of the leases, such as options either to renew the lease or to purchase the property, unexpired term of the lease, rent received, services to be rendered by the landlord, and all other related matters.
7. Have the attorney prepare assignments of the leases, notices to the tenants of the sale of the property, and notices to make future payments of rent to the buyer; have these assignments and notices signed by the seller on the closing date.
8. If the property is an apartment house or office building or similar building that is supervised by a manager, or if the landlord-seller employs the staff that services the building, notice should be given to the manager and other building employees terminating their service. If the buyer wishes to continue their service, new contracts of employment must be negotiated. A contract for personal services is not assignable.
9. Rent adjustments should be computed as of the closing date.
10. Taxes and assessments should be investigated, and any adjustment of taxes and assessments should be computed as of the closing date.
11. All insurance policies should be checked; and if they are to be assigned, the consent of the insurer should be obtained. The adjustment of the premiums should be computed.
12. The building should be inspected to ascertain whether or not any zoning or other ordinances are being violated.
13. The premises should be checked to ascertain whether any restrictions on the property are being violated.
14. Arrangements should be made to have all utility meters read (if the seller has furnished the utilities) and the account transferred to the name of the buyer. If utilities are on a tax basis and charged against the property, the meters should be read on the closing date and the utility bills adjusted.
15. The premises should be inspected immediately prior to closing the sale to make certain that no fixtures, shrubs, or chattels that are to go with the property have been removed.
16. If the seller is a corporation, the corporate records should be investigated

to ascertain whether or not proper corporation action has been taken to authorize the sale, and to determine which officer or officers are authorized to execute the deed in the name of the corporation.

### The Deed from Seller to Buyer

The deed should be prepared prior to the closing date, and the attorneys of both the buyer and the seller should examine the deed and check the following:

1. The names of the grantor and grantees should be spelled correctly. Is the grantor's name spelled the same in the prepared deed as it was in the deed granting the property to him?
2. The description of the property should be checked against the description in the deed granting the property to the seller. This description should not be copied slavishly; if there are errors, they should be corrected.
3. If either the grantor or the grantee is a corporation, the corporate name must be exactly as written in the charter; the state of incorporation and the location of its principal place of business should be shown.
4. The corporate deed should show the authority under which the conveyance is made.
5. Restrictive covenants should be properly drafted.
6. Exceptions and reservations in the deed should correspond to the provisions in the contract.
7. If the property is mortgaged or a purchase-money mortgage is to be given, the mortgage should be correctly described. Does the buyer take subject to the mortgage, or does he take subject to the mortgage and assume and agree to pay the mortgage debt?
8. Any liens or encumbrances excepted in the deed should correspond to those provided for in the contract to sell.
9. Necessary waivers of homestead and dower rights should be included in the deed.
10. Obligations that are to be fulfilled after closing should be stated in the deed.
11. The type of deed should be that stipulated in the contract of sale.

### Mortgage or Deed of Trust and Note

If the seller is taking a purchase-money mortgage or a deed of trust and a note to secure the unpaid balance of the purchase price of the real estate, these instruments should be prepared in advance; the names of the parties, description of the real estate, terms of payment, rate of interest, provisions for insurance, and so forth, should be checked to be certain that they are correct and that they comply with the provisions of the contract to sell.

The buyer may borrow money and secure the loan by giving a mortgage or deed of trust on the real estate, and thus obtain the money to pay the seller in full. In such a situation the mortgage or deed of trust will be executed, as a general rule, as a part of the closing of the sale. The loan and the terms of the mortgage or deed of trust will have been negotiated as a separate transaction, but both the sale and the loan will be closed at the same time, since the lender will not wish to pay out his money until the mortgage or deed of trust and deed are executed, and the seller will not wish to deliver a deed until he is paid the agreed purchase price.

In regard to the loan, if the money is borrowed from an institution, the institution will use a standard form of mortgage or deed of trust. In Federal Housing Administration loans, government forms are used. The Veterans Administration furnishes forms to be used in its loans, but the employment of these forms is not compulsory. The loaning institution may use its own forms if they comply with Veterans Administration regulations.

Mortgages and deeds of trust are discussed in Chapters 13 and 14, respectively.

### Documents to Be Delivered to Buyer

The documents to be delivered to the buyer on the closing of a transaction will depend on the type of property that has been sold and the terms of the sale. The following is a list of the documents commonly delivered to the buyer at the closing:

1. The deed to the real estate.
2. The surveyor's plat, if the sale is a sale of a part of a large tract owned by the seller and a survey has been made. This plat is either delivered with the deed or attached to the abstract.
3. Abstract, certificate of title, or title insurance policy. If the buyer has borrowed money and given a mortgage or deed of trust on the property as security, these documents will, as a general rule, be delivered to the lending institution.
4. Receipt for purchase money.
5. If an existing mortgage has been paid and discharged, a discharge of the mortgage together with the mortgage and cancelled notes.
6. If an existing mortgage is assumed, a statement of the amount of the unpaid balance of the mortgage debt and accrued interest.
7. Leases and assignment of leases on the property or any portion thereof.
8. Money deposited by tenants as security for payment of rent.
9. Letters to tenants notifying them of the sale and advising them to pay future rent to the buyer.

10. Service contracts that are not terminated at the time of the sale, such as exterminator contracts.
11. Last receipts for taxes, special assessments, water tax, and other charges.
12. In some localities, an affidavit of title covering all possible liens that would not be shown by the abstract or that may have been obtained after the certification of the abstract but before the buyer has had an opportunity to record his deed.
13. A copy of the closing statement.

### Documents to Be Delivered to Seller

If the buyer is paying the seller cash for the property, as a general rule, all that will be given to the seller is a check—usually certified—for the amount due him, together with a copy of the closing statement.

If the seller is taking a purchase-money mortgage or a deed of trust and a note for the unpaid balance, the following will be delivered to the seller on the closing of the sale:

1. Check or cash for the down payment.
2. Mortgage or deed of trust.
3. Note or series of notes for the unpaid balance. As a general rule, a simple note providing for amortized payments of principal and interest in monthly installments will be used.
4. Insurance policies naming seller as an insured party.

## Closing Statements

### Content of Statement

A closing statement, which summarizes the transaction, should be prepared and signed by both the buyer and the seller. Such a statement should show:

1. Date.
2. Names and addresses of the seller and buyer.
3. Address of the real estate sold, or short description, if farm land.

Following this should be an itemized statement of credits due the seller and credits due the buyer. These items should be listed in separate columns.

The items credited to the seller would usually include the following:

1. Purchase price.
2. Unearned insurance premiums.

3. Escrow deposits, taxes, and insurance.

The items credited to the buyer would usually include the following:

1. Earnest money deposit.
2. Additional down payment (if any).
3. Balance on mortgage (held by _________).
4. Interest on mortgage.
5. If there is a second mortgage on the property, the balance on the second mortgage and interest should be placed in this column. (If payments made on the mortgage include prepayment of taxes, insurance premiums, and so forth, the amount of the prepayment on these items would be placed in the seller's column.)
6. Real estate taxes.
7. Prorated rents.

Any additional items for which the buyer is entitled to credit should be itemized. The total in the buyer's column should be subtracted from the total in the seller's column to show the total payment due the seller from the buyer.

The statement should also include an itemization of the seller's expenses if a broker has represented the seller in the negotiation of the sale. This enumeration would include all sums paid out by the broker and the commission due the broker in one column, and all payments made to the broker in another column. The difference between the totals in these two columns would be the amount to be paid to the seller or the broker, as the case may be. The following would usually appear in such an itemization: In one column would be a record of cash received by the broker; in the other column would be a listing of all cash disbursements made by the broker, such as expenditures for continuation of abstract and the broker's commission.

A short summary of the agreement of the parties relative to the transaction is recommended. Such a summary would include:

1. Date possession is to be given to the buyer.
2. Name of the person to whom the abstract was delivered.
3. Receipt for keys delivered to the buyer.
4. Receipt for copies of the survey delivered to the buyer.
5. Notation as to the assignment of insurance policies.
6. Name of the person to whom the assignment of the escrow deposit was sent.
7. Time at which the next payment on the mortgage is due, and the amount of the payment.

8. Time at which the next payments on taxes and assessments are due.
9. Time at which the notices to tenants were sent.
10. Time at which the rents are due, and amount of the rents.

Other items may be added; those to be included will depend on the nature of the particular transaction.

### Checking Statement

The statement should be carefully checked with the buyer and the seller, in the presence of each other, and should be signed by both as an indication of its correctness. A copy of the statement should be delivered to both the buyer and the seller.

### Importance of Statement

Such a statement is important in two respects: (1) any questions or misunderstandings will be cleared up at the time the transaction is closed, thus minimizing the possibility of future disputes; (2) the parties will be bound by the statement in the event of a dispute. The statement can be set aside if one of the parties has been induced to sign by misrepresentation, fraud, or duress. Also, if a mistake has been made in computing the amounts due each person and the party benefiting from the mistake refuses voluntarily to correct the mistake, the court, in a proper action, will grant a decree ordering correction.

## Nature of Escrow

### The Objective of an Escrow

An escrow has been created when a deed or other instrument, the terms of which import a legal obligation, is delivered to a third person, other than the grantee in the deed or the obligee in another instrument, and such third person is to deliver the deed or instrument to the grantee or obligee on the performance of some designated act by the grantee or obligee or on the occurrence of a certain event. The third person to whom the deed or instrument is delivered is known as the *depository* or *escrow holder.*[1]

The principal objective of an escrow is to minimize the risks incident to the sale of real estate. If the transaction involves property of substantial value, there will be, as a general rule, several matters that must be coordinated before the

---

[1] *Home-Stake Royalty Corporation et al.* v. *McClish et al.,* 187 Okla. 352, 103 P.2d 72.

deal is completed. This will necessarily cause a time lapse between the execution of the purchase agreement and the final payment and delivery of the deed. If the escrow is used and during this time any difficulty is encountered that would prevent the concluding of the sale, each party can have returned to him that which he has deposited with the escrow holder and can be put in the position he occupied before he entered into the transaction.

**Example of Escrow Transaction**

The following situation will serve to illustrate the use of an escrow:

Allen has contracted to sell a house to Ball. Under the contract of sale, Allen is obligated to execute and deliver a warranty deed and an abstract of title certified to a stated date; to deliver receipted water, real estate, and personal property tax bills; and to execute an affidavit that no work has been performed on the house during the last 60 days for which a mechanic's lien could be filed. At the time Ball signed the proposition to buy, he paid $1,000 as evidence of good faith. He has contracted to pay $4,000 on the examination of the abstract, provided the abstract shows merchantable title in Allen, and to execute a purchase-money mortgage on the house securing a negotiable promissory note for $20,000 drawing 5 percent interest and payable $200 the first of each and every month, including interest computed monthly, until the note is paid in full. In this transaction, Allen and Ball enter into an escrow agreement, and First Bank is selected as depositary (escrow holder) and agrees to act as such. Instructions to First Bank will be drafted and signed by Allen and Ball.

In working out the transaction, the following steps will usually be taken: The $1,000 paid by Ball will be turned over to First Bank. Allen will execute a warranty deed and deliver it to First Bank, and will also have the abstract brought down to the stated date and certified by the abstractor. He will file the receipted water, real estate, and property tax bills, and will execute the affidavit; all of these will be delivered to First Bank and made available to Ball or his attorney for examination.

Ball will execute the mortgage and note, and deliver them to First Bank, where they will be made available to Allen or his attorney for examination. If Ball, on examination of the abstract and documents delivered to First Bank by Allen, finds them free from defects, he will pay $4,000 to First Bank.

Allen or his attorney will examine the mortgage and note; if he finds them satisfactory, he will so indicate to First Bank. When Allen and Ball have certified to First Bank that all is in order, and when all required documents have been delivered and all required payments have been made to First Bank, the documents and money in its possession will be delivered and paid to whichever of the parties is entitled thereto, thus completing the transaction.

**Requirement for a Valid Escrow**

An escrow is a contract. Therefore, in order to have an instrument operate as an escrow, there must be parties having sufficient capacity to contract, a proper subject matter, and a consideration; and the parties must have actually and validly contracted in respect to the subject matter. The essentials of the escrow used in a real estate transaction are as follows:

1. There must be a valid, enforceable contract of purchase and sale of real estate. An oral contract to sell real estate cannot be the basis of an escrow, since such a contract is unenforceable under the statute of frauds.[2]
2. The deposit of the deed or other instruments with the depositary must be absolute and beyond the control of the grantor or obligor.[3]
3. The escrow agreement must contain a condition. By the very nature of an escrow, the delivery of the deed or instrument held by the depositary must be conditioned on the performance of some act or on the happening of some event.[4]
4. The depositary must be some disinterested person. The grantee or his agent cannot act as depositary.[5]
5. The deed or instrument delivered in escrow must be duly and validly executed.[6]

Young and Bishop negotiated for the purchase and sale of described real estate. Young as buyer and Bishop as seller negotiated an escrow agreement which set out in detail the terms of the sale. The following clause was typed on the face of the escrow agreement: "NOTE: The Escrow is subject to and conditioned upon Supplemental Trust Escrow Instructions which are to be submitted to Escrow Agent, which supplemental instructions will be made part of this Escrow." The parties did not succeed in reaching an agreement on the terms of the supplemental instructions. Young brought suit asking specific performance, and Bishop defended on the ground that no enforceable contract of sale was entered into, since no separate contract in writing for the sale of the real estate was executed, and that no supplemental instructions to the escrow were agreed upon. The trial court

---

[2] *Jozefowicz et ux.* v. *Leickem,* 174 Wis. 475, 182 N.W. 729.

[3] *Lindsey et al.* v. *Hornady,* 215 Ark. 797, 223 S.W.2d 768.

[4] *Lechner* v. *Halling et al.,* 35 Wash.2d 903, 216 P.2d 179.

[5] *Wells* v. *Wells,* 249 Ala. 649, 32 So.2d 697.

[6] *Collins* v. *Kares,* 52 S.D. 143, 216, N.W. 880.

granted judgment on the pleadings to Bishop, and Young appealed. The judgment was reversed, and a trial was ordered.

Justice Johnson said: "Briefly stated, a contract of sale of real estate and an escrow arrangement are not interchangeable entities. A binding contract of sale must exist with respect to the subject-matter of the escrow instrument to support an enforceable escrow. A good definition of the generic term 'escrow' is this: an escrow is a written instrument which by its terms imports a legal obligation, and which is deposited with a third party, to be kept by the depository until the performance of the prescribed condition or the happening of a certain event, and then to be delivered over to the grantee, promisee or obligee. In short, an escrow is a conveyancing device designed to carry out the terms of a binding contract of sale previously entered into by the parties.

"It is the general rule that the conditions upon which the instrument is to be deposited in escrow may rest in, and be proved by, parol, and an instrument placed in escrow may be enforced although the escrow agreement is not in writing. This rule, however, does not permit enforcement of a contract for the sale of real estate unless there is a binding obligation for such sale under the statute of frauds.

". . . Suffice to say, the pleadings before us present material fact issues which preclude the granting of a judgment on the pleadings." *Young* v. *Bishop,* 88 Ariz. 140, 353 P.2d 1017 (1960).

## Who May Act as Depositary

In determining who may act as depositary of an escrow, the courts have applied basic legal principles. An escrow holder (depositary) represents both the buyer and the seller; in doing so, he acts in a fiduciary capacity. He must not, therefore, put himself in a position where his personal interests conflict with the performance of his fiduciary duties. Furthermore, since he acts for both parties to the transaction, he must act with absolute impartiality. Consequently, a person who is the agent or attorney of one of the parties, and thereby owes a duty to further his principal's or client's interests, is disqualified and will not be permitted to act as depositary unless it is clear that his acting as such is not hostile to his principal's interests.[7]

Another basic legal principle applied in determining who may act as a depositary is that the delivery of a deed to the grantee, if the deed contains no conditional clause, passes title to the grantee on delivery. And the courts have held that even though an agreement has been entered into between the grantor and grantee whereby the grantee would hold the deed in escrow until the fulfillment of a condition or the happening of some event, such an agreement would not prevent the passing of the title of the real estate involved to the grantee.[8] Consequently,

---

[7] *Levin* v. *Nedelman,* 141 N.J. Eq. 23, 55 A.2d 826.

[8] *Logue et al.* v. *Von Almen et al.,* 379 Ill. 208, 40 N.E.2d 73.

the grantee cannot act as the depositary, since the objective of the escrow is to prevent the vesting of the title in the grantee until the terms of the escrow are fulfilled. Some recent decisions, however, have not followed this rule rigidly.[9]

The mere entrusting of a deed or other instrument to the grantee or obligee is not a delivery of the instrument; if a deed or instrument is entrusted to a grantee or obligee to be transported and given to the depositary, title will not pass at the time of the entrustment. However, if the grantee or obligee, in breach of duty, retains possession of the instrument, title will pass, and oral evidence is inadmissible to prove that the delivery was conditioned.[10]

The leaving of the deed in the possession of the grantor defeats the objective of escrow.

### The Escrow Agreement

The parties to the escrow agreement are the grantor, the grantee, and the depositary. Although the escrow agreement need not be in writing in order to be enforceable, it should be in writing for the protection of the parties. The agreement will set out the delivery of the deed or instrument to the depositary, and will state that the depositary is to hold the deed or instrument and is to deliver it to the grantee or obligee on the fulfillment of stated conditions or on the happening of certain events. As a general rule, instructions to the depositary, stating the conditions on which the deed or instrument is to be delivered to the grantee or obligee and the disposition of the deed or instrument on default, and so forth, will be set out in detail.

### Instructions to Depositary

The instructions to the depositary may be oral; but for the protection of all interested parties the instructions should be in writing, carefully drafted, and specific in their provisions. As a general rule, the instructions will include the following:

1. Name of the depositary.
2. Names of the buyer and seller.
3. Statement of documents to be deposited by the seller—such as deed, abstract of title or certificate of title showing marketable title in seller or policy of title insurance, insurance policies and assignments of insurance policies, leases properly assigned, notices to tenants to pay future rent to the grantee, tax receipts, receipts for payment of assessments, canceled mortgage notes, discharge of mortgage, and so forth. The documents to be deposited by

[9] *Chillemi* v. *Chillemi,* 197 Md. 257, 78 A.2d 750.

[10] *Carlisle et al.* v. *MacDonald et al.,* Tex. Civ. App., 200 S.W.2d 436.

the seller will depend on the nature of the property sold and the terms of the contract of purchase and sale.

4. The conditions to be performed by the buyer or the event on which delivery is to be made to the buyer—usually, payment of the purchase price, or part payment and execution of note and mortgage securing the note.
5. Disposition of the money paid to the depositary by the buyer—taxes, liens, and charges to be paid out of such money, and conditions under which the balance is to be paid over to the seller.
6. Direction for delivery of the deed, leases, assignments of leases, insurance policies and assignments of policies, and so on, when conditions are satisfied.
7. Directions for recording the deed, whether it is to be recorded immediately or on fulfillment of conditions or merely delivered to buyer without being recorded. For the protection of the buyer the deed should be recorded immediately, and the buyer should execute a quitclaim deed to the seller to be recorded in the event the seller cannot convey clear title to the buyer.
8. Time within which the seller must cure defects in his title, if any are discovered.
9. Disposition of money and documents deposited if the seller cannot convey title as provided in the contract of purchase and sale.
10. Payment of charges of the depositary, recording fees, broker's commission, attorneys' fees, and any other fees connected with the transaction.

The instructions should be signed by the buyer and the seller, and should have endorsed on them a statement to the effect that the depositary has read, understood, and approved the instructions; this statement should be signed by the depositary.

**Relation of Depositary to the Parties**

The depositary is frequently referred to as the *agent* of both parties; but he is not an agent, since he is not subject to the control of either party. He is also referred to in some instances as a *trustee;* but he is not a trustee, since he has title to none of the deeds or instruments in his possession. He is merely a conduit used in the transaction for convenience and safety. He is a third party to whom the grantor and the grantee have entrusted certain authority by the escrow agreement. When the depositary knows the terms of the agreement, he acts by virtue of his own powers and is responsible for his actions. He does not act as agent of anybody.[11]

---

[11] *Nickell et ux.* v. *Reser et al.,* 143 Kan. 831, 57 P.2d 101.

In the event the parties to the escrow are in discord as to their rights to the instruments or to the funds held in escrow, the depositary should refuse to accede to the requests of either party. He is a mere stakeholder and should, by following the proper course of action, force the dispute into the court where his responsibility could be determined.

Foreman contracted to purchase a farm owned by Todd and Fisher. Bonner Ferry Bank acted as escrow holder, and it complied with the terms of the escrow. The title to the farm was defective, and Foreman brought suit against Todd and Fisher and Bonner Ferry Bank, contending that Bonner Ferry Bank acted as the agent of Todd and Fisher. The trial court dismissed the action against Bonner Ferry Bank, and Foreman appealed. The holding of the trial court was affirmed.

Justice McQuade said: "The authorities are divided as to whether an escrow holder is the agent of both parties to the transaction, or is a third party to whom the principals have entrusted certain duties. This is succinctly set out in *Nickell* v. *Reser:*

"'. . . the deposit of an instrument in escrow cannot be made with one who is the agent of either of the parties to the instrument . . . for if the depositary is the agent of the grantor, the instrument is retained by him; if the agent of the grantee, there is a delivery of the instrument. To the extent the term agent is applicable, it is a limited agency, with duties and powers limited to the terms of the escrow agreement.'

"Duties of an escrow holder are those set out in the escrow agreement. The holder acts as a depositary, and is not concerned with nor responsible for defects in the title to the property. Plaintiffs [Foremans] must look to their grantors, not to the depositary, nor its officer, for title." *Forman* v. *Todd,* 83 Idaho 482, 364 P.2d 365 (1961).

## Duties and Liabilities of Depositary

The depositary is bound by the terms and conditions of the escrow agreement, and he owes a duty to follow the instructions in the escrow contract without deviating in any respect. He is obligated to withhold delivery until the conditions upon which delivery is conditioned have been fulfilled or until the event upon which delivery is conditioned has happened. He owes an equal duty to make delivery when the conditions are fulfilled or when the event has occurred.

The delivery by the depositary to the party entitled to possession of the instrument on the fulfillment of the condition or on the happening of the event is known as the *second delivery.*

If the terms and conditions of the escrow agreement are not fulfilled, the depositary owes a duty to redeliver the deed, instrument, money, or whatever has been deposited with him to the parties who deposited it.

If the depositary fails to fulfill the duties imposed on him by the escrow agreement, he will be liable in damages to the injured party for any loss resulting directly from the depositary's breach of duty. For example, suppose that the depositary, under the terms of the escrow agreement, owes a duty to hold a deed and not to deliver it until the purchase price is paid in full. And then, in breach of his duty, he delivers the deed to the grantee without being paid the purchase price. The depositary would be liable to the grantor for the full purchase price.[12]

If the seller is unable to convey a title that complies with the provisions of the contract of purchase and sale, the depositary owes a duty to return to the grantee the earnest money the depositary holds; and if the depositary fails to make such payment, he will be liable to the grantee for the full amount of the earnest money.

If written instructions are given to the depositary and at the same time, or at some later time, oral instructions are given, the depositary will not be liable if he follows the written instructions and fails to carry out the oral instructions.[13]

The courts have consistently held that if the depositary delivers the deed to the grantee without the conditions for delivery having been fulfilled or without the event on which delivery was conditioned having happened, the delivery of the deed is unauthorized, and no title passes to the grantee. However, if, after the wrongful delivery, the grantor ratifies the acts of the depositary, title will vest in the grantee.[14]

Amen entered into a contract for the purchase of a tavern. The purchase price was $74,300, payable $10,000 in cash, $54,300 by a note and deed of trust, and $10,000 by the buyer's (Amen's) assumption of certain debts. Title Company acted as escrow holder. The escrow agreement was in writing and was signed by the parties and by Title Company as escrow. The agreement provided: "Any debts over $10,000 will be paid by Merced County Title Company out of the proceeds of the sale." Title Company and the sellers were given notice of a tax claim in the amount of $4,749.84, but Amen was not given notice of the claim, either by the state or by Title Company. Title Company paid $10,000 of debts exclusive of the tax claim and paid the proceeds of the sale to the seller. As a result, Amen was forced to pay the $4,749.84 tax claim. Amen sued Title Company for breach of contract and in tort for negligence. The court held Title Company was liable.

Justice Traynor said: "An escrow holder must comply strictly with the instruction of the parties. Upon the escrow holder's breach of an instruction that it has contracted to perform or an implied promise arising out of the agreement with the buyer or seller, the

---

[12] *Keith* v. *First National Bank of New England, North Dakota,* 36 N.D. 315, 162 N.W. 691; *Kirby* v. *Woolbert,* 48 Wash.2d 141, 291 P.2d 666.

[13] *Colorado Title and Trust Co.* v. *Roberts,* 80 Colo. 258, 250 P. 641.

[14] *Bradshaw* v. *Superior Oil Co.,* 164 F.2d 165.

injured party acquires a cause of action for breach of contract. Similarly if the escrow holder acts negligently, 'it would ordinarily be liable for any loss occasioned by its breach of duty.'" *Amen* v. *Merced County Title Company,* 25 Cal. Rptr. 65, 375 P.2d 33 (1962).

## Embezzlement of Funds

Frequently, the receipt of money is involved in the duties of a depositary. If the escrow agreement so provides, the depositary may deposit the money received in his own bank account; but if he does deposit it in his own account, he must keep a balance in the account equal to the amount of escrow money deposited. Failure to do so is an embezzlement of the escrow funds.

If the depositary uses for his own purposes money deposited in escrow, he is guilty of embezzlement. The deposit of money with the depositary does not create a debtor-creditor relation between the depositary and the party depositing the money.

If the depositary embezzles the money deposited with him before the fulfillment of the condition or the happening of the event, the loss falls on the party who deposited the money. The courts have held that the depositary holds such money as agent of the party who deposited it. However, if the embezzlement occurs after the fulfillment of the condition or the occurrence of the event, the party entitled to the money must bear the loss.[15]

Cradock purchased certain land from Cooper. The Internal Revenue Service had a claim against Cooper which Cradock's attorney, one Boland, claimed was a lien against the land. Cradock and Cooper agreed to allow Boland to hold $15,000 of the purchase money, out of which he was to discharge the claim of the Internal Revenue Service. The parties entered into a written escrow agreement, by the terms of which the $15,000 held by Boland, as escrow holder, would be paid to Cooper if the claim was settled; and if the claim was not settled, Boland was to pay the claim out of the $15,000 and give any balance to Cooper.

The agreement was signed by Boland, attorney at law, escrow agent, Cradock, and Cooper, and the $15,000 was paid to Boland "to be held for and on behalf of W. R. Cooper, subject to the following conditions." The terms and conditions were as set out above.

Boland used $4,100 of the money to settle the claims and misappropriated the balance, $10,900. Cooper claimed that Cradock must stand the loss, since Boland was his attorney. The trial court held that each party should stand one half of the loss. Cradock appealed. The judgment was reversed, and the court held that Cooper must stand the loss.

---

[15] *Angell* v. *Ingram et us.,* 35 Wash.2d 582, 213 P.2d 944.

Associate Judge Vassar B. Carlton said: "According to the law as set forth in 30 C. J. S. Escrows, paragraph 7 d, p. 1202; and in 19 Am. Jur., Escrow, Section 15, p. 432, the attorney of the grantor of the subject matter of the escrow agreement may act as escrow agent so long as his duties do not involve a conflict of interest with, or a violation of, duty to his client as principal, and so long as the condition of the escrow is not made dependent upon the client's volition.

"The primary purpose of the escrow was to remove a cloud from the title of the property. This is consistent with the interest of the defendant. The defendant retained absolutely no control of the money deposited. It was placed beyond his reach for all purposes and all times.

"Under the normal escrow situation where the escrow agent defaults prior to performance of the escrow condition, the loss falls upon the depositor, for he is deemed to have retained legal title to the subject matter of the escrow, and is deemed to be entitled to the return of such subject matter, should the other parties fail to perform.

"There is a clear exception to this rule whether under the circumstances of the escrow agreement the depositor would not be entitled to the return of the subject matter under any circumstances, irrespective of performance of the terms of the agreement.

"In the instant case, the escrow money was held by Charles E. Boland under the terms of the agreement, to be paid either to satisfy a United States tax lien or to the sellers, as the remaining portion of the purchase price. It is clear that the purchaser, Cradock, retained no legal title to these funds, for he was not entitled to their return under any circumstances.

"We, therefore, conclude that as a matter of law Charles E. Boland became the agent of the sellers, the plaintiffs herein; and, accordingly, the unfortunate loss must fall upon the plaintiffs under the legal principles enunciated above." *Cradock* v. *Cooper,* Fla., 123 So.2d 256 (1960).

## When Title Passes

The modern view, and the one most widely held today, is that the deed held in escrow becomes the deed of the grantee on the fulfillment of the conditions or on the happening of the event set out in the escrow agreement. The passing of the title to the grantee does not depend on the second delivery by the depositary.[16]

Although a deed deposited in escrow does not convey title until the conditions set out in the escrow agreement have been fulfilled or the event has happened, the courts have held that the deed will be treated as relating back to and taking effect at the time it was originally delivered to the depositary. This doctrine has been adopted by the courts to effectuate the intentions of the parties to the escrow. If, after the deed to the real estate is delivered to the depositary, but before the fulfillment of the condition or the happening of the event and the

---

[16] *Osborn* v. *Osborn,* 42 Cal.2d 358, 267, P.2d 333.

passing of title to the grantee, the grantor should die, become insane, marry, or change his legal status in any other manner, his change in status would in no way affect the validity of the deed deposited in escrow. Under the doctrine of relating back, the validity of the deed and the rights of the parties are determined as of the date of the first delivery of the deed to the depositary.[17]

The doctrine of relating back will not be applied if, by its application, the title taken by the grantee will be limited or defeated. For example, suppose that the grantor, at the time he executes the deed to the real estate and deposits it with the depositary, does not have title to the property or has defective title, but before the second delivery—the delivery by the depositary to the grantee—he acquires title or clears his title of the defects. The grantee would acquire the title that the grantor has the power to convey at the time of the second delivery—a good title free from defects.

### Right to Rents and Profits

The courts have held that in the absence of a provision in the contract of purchase and sale defining the rights to the rents and profits from the real estate, the grantee is entitled to the rents and profits from the date the deed to the real estate is deposited with the depositary.[18]

### Intervening Rights of Third Persons

Between the time of the first delivery of the deed and the second delivery by the depositary to the grantee, third persons may acquire rights in the real estate. If, at the time the deed is delivered to the depositary, it is recorded and there is nothing in the deed or on the records to show that the deed is held in escrow, the grantee would be the owner of record. If the grantee should sell or mortgage the property and thereafter fail to fulfill the conditions set out in the escrow agreement, no title would vest in the grantee, and the purchaser or mortgagee would take nothing. However, if, in addition to permitting the recording of the deed, the grantor permitted the grantee to take possession of the property, and the purchaser or mortgagee of the property made the purchase or loan in good faith, for value, and without notice or knowledge of the existence of the escrow, such purchaser or mortgagee would be protected. The grantor would be estopped from setting up his title to defeat the rights of the purchaser or mortgagee.[19]

---

[17] *Cowden* v. *Broderick & Calvert, Inc., et al.,* 131 Tex. 434, 114 S.W.2d 1166.

[18] *Scott* v. *Sloan et al.,* 72 Kan. 545, 84 P. 117.

[19] *Quick* v. *Milligan,* 108 Ind. 419, 9 N.E. 392.

## Recording of Deed

If the deed delivered in escrow is not recorded and the grantee is not in possession of the real estate, any person, as a general rule, to whom the grantor conveys, mortgages, or leases the real estate, if such person takes in good faith, for value, and without notice or knowledge of the escrow, will acquire rights in the property.[20] However, some courts have applied the doctrine of relating back to this situation and have held that if the grantee fulfills the conditions set out in the escrow agreement, his title relates back to the first delivery, and he takes free of claims of third persons arising as the result of acts of the grantor subsequent to the delivery of the deed to the depositary.

## Effects of Escrow on Insurance

Since title to the real estate does not pass to the grantee until the fulfillment of the condition or the happening of the event set out in the escrow agreement, the grantor has an insurable interest in the property, and any damage to the property before the fulfillment of the condition falls on the grantor.[21]

---

[20] *Meade et al.* v. *Robinson et al.*, 234 Mich. 322, 208 N.W. 41.

[21] *Dow* v. *Fireman's Ins. Co. of Newark, N.J.*, 115 Kan. 190, 221 P. 1112.

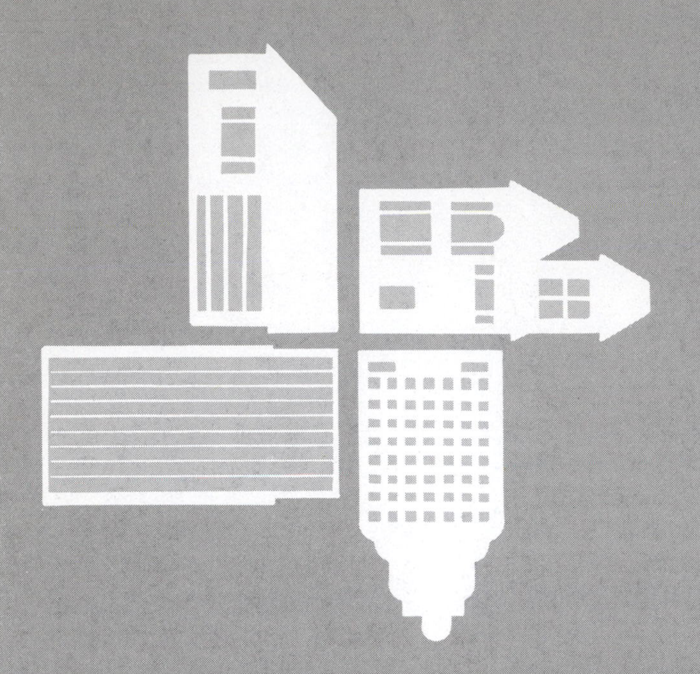

# Section 6

# Using Real Estate

In order to obtain the maximum return upon capital invested in the purchase of real estate, a wide variety of options must be considered. If one is the owner of real estate and has substantial sums invested in it, development of the property may increase that value dramatically so that the property can then be sold at a substantial profit. There is expense involved in performing this development and there is risk involved that the hoped-for profit may not be realized. *Development* here is used to denote that function of dividing real estate (whether it be just the land, buildings, or both) into their most desirable and marketable portions and adding to that property the most desired and needed services to make it more valuable. The most obvious application of this concept is seen in residential subdivision development.

Development of a residential subdivision may begin with the acquisition of a large parcel of ground presently being used for some other purpose. Ordinarily it is agricultural ground that is located on the edge of a growing city or town. At the time of purchase it may have little value other than its proximity to the growing community. In order to profit from this investment it is necessary that the property be divided into many smaller parcels of a size suitable for the construction of a home. This will broaden the market by making each parcel affordable. More than simply dividing it up, however, is necessary to make it marketable at a profit. We must add those facilities normally associated with residences: streets for access; electricity and gas service; telephone service; water and sewage disposal systems. We must, in order to profit, make the parcels usable to the people who will buy them for residential purposes.

Depending upon our analysis of the market and the strength of the demand that we forecast for these parcels, we may go much further in our development. We may include a wide variety of additional improvements that make a residential environment more attractive and, therefore, more valuable. We may further increase the value of each lot in the subdivision by imposing limitations upon the uses to which each lot may be put; the size, type, and cost of each building to be erected; the amount of ground that each lot owner must leave vacant in order to provide light and air space for all buildings. We might also increase the size of each lot so as to insure more privacy for each lot owner. Each of these steps, particularly the last one mentioned, may increase the price that must be charged in order to make a profit. There is a serious risk that the resulting price will be more than the market will bear. In this section we will explore the legal aspects of this area of activity.

Once the ground is developed, the next step is the construction of buildings to make it useful to people. Very often the construction activity will be the building of a house to be used as a residence with no thought of monetary profit. The "income" from such buildings is in the form of the amenities that it provides, those characteristics that make it a desirable home. In other cases the hope of profit will be much more direct. It will be based upon the expectation that it will be rented to a user in order to generate rental income from the investment. The topic of construction in this section will cover both types of building. Contractual arrangements and rules of interpretation of them have been developed for this area of real estate activity. The role of the architect as interpreter, designer, and, sometimes, referee in the construction process will be considered in some detail.

The leasing of real estate is an area of great significance in the real estate business. By the use of the lease we can transfer from the landlord to the tenant almost all of the benefits of ownership in return for the obligation to pay rent on a continuing basis. On the one hand the lease permits the tenant to have as much ownership as is needed or desired without the investment of a large sum of capital to have it. On the other hand the lease permits the landlord to convert the ownership of a valuable real estate asset into a stream of income that may last for a very long time and provide profits far in excess of what would be realized from an outright sale. Negotiating the arrangement between these two parties requires skill and knowledge of a great number of technical rules. An almost infinite variety of landlord-tenant relationships can exist because of the flexibility of the lease concept. The general rules that have developed and that are considered in depth in this section must be adapted to this wide range of relationships. New applications are always evolving as the continually increasing cost of real estate motivates more aggressive use of the available supply.

Private restrictions on the use of real estate have already been mentioned in connection with the development process. The subject is of significance because restrictions imposed upon real estate may limit its use for a great many years. These restrictions directly affect the value of the real estate to which they apply. When initial development occurs, these restrictions usually enhance the value of the real estate. That is, it is made more valuable by virtue of the limitations placed upon it and its neighboring properties. At some point in time, however, these same restrictions may seriously depress property values. This is seen in areas where redevelopment from residential to commercial usage appears most desirable. Private restrictions may prevent desirable changes in use and therefore limit value.

In a great number of areas in this country it has been concluded that private developers are not the only persons who have an interest in limiting the use of privately owned real estate. So does the general public have an interest to protect. The protection of the public's interest is accomplished by zoning ordinances, which limit the uses to which private property may be put. Such ordinances usually forbid the intrusion of industrial or commercial uses into residential neighborhoods. Various zones are carved out, in which activities or uses are segregated. Industrial uses will be provided a zone. Residential uses will be provided a different zone. Between them, as a buffer, may be provided zones for light industrial, commercial, and multifamily uses. The zoning system is superimposed upon the existing system of private restrictions. A specific property may be subject to two sources of restriction that may be in conflict with each other. Both may either enhance or limit the value of the property. The conflict between the two frequently has an unhappy result for the property owner: compliance with whichever of the two is the more restrictive. These related subjects are also considered in this section.

# Chapter 18
# Real Estate Development and Construction

## Introduction

Discussed in this chapter are some of the creative activities in the real estate business. One is the development of ground for more intensive and more profitable use. Another is the design and construction of improvements (buildings) to generate still more income from the land. In each case the intent of the developer or the builder is to increase the value of the real estate. This may be done to enhance its sales price, to make it income-producing, or both.

In development, raw ground (or, sometimes, reclaimed areas subject to redevelopment) that may have a relatively low value is improved by the addition of streets, water and sewage facilities, power and heating sources, as well as other essential services. The property then becomes more valuable simply because it may then be used for more purposes. Subdivision development usually proceeds along these lines. More ambitious developments may be very elaborate and may include such amenities as golf, tennis, or swimming facilities, and even a private club for property owners. In either case real estate development today is no longer a simple business. Governmental regulations over land use must be complied with. Complex legal arrangements are necessary to define the work to be done and the liabilities if it is improperly done or not completed. Unusual forms of financing will often be required. Finally, market forces will dictate the services that the property must offer in order to be salable at a profit. The developer will require the services of the surveyor, the engineer, the architect, various contractors, public utilities, and local government officials. All of these people (plus attorneys, accountants, bankers, and brokers) play a role in the developer's success or failure. In the final analysis, however, it is the developer who takes the risks, and they are substantial. There is competition between properties as well as between developers. The developer is a risk-taking investor as opposed to a commission merchant.

The development of ground in such a way that it will be suitable and desirable for building is the first step. This will be true whether the ground is destined for residential, commercial, or industrial use. Next comes the process of construction of improvements that will maximize profits from the use of the ground. In central city office districts it is easy to see that the more usable floor space that can be put on the property, the greater is its profit potential. In residential areas the "income" that the resulting building will generate takes the form of amenities. The greater the desirability of the building to the user, the greater will be its value. Generally, buildings are built by property owners who desire to maximize profits either in the form of rental income or personal satisfaction. The building itself is carried out by the contractor, who may in turn use as subcontractors a wide variety of specialists. Between the owner and the contractor must come still another specialist to define the work to be done and, quite often, to supervise the actual construction: the architect. The architect's role in the building and construction process is quite significant. Initially, of course, the architect translates the owner's ideas and goals into a design that is practical and cost-efficient. That is, it must be possible to execute the design at a cost that permits a profit to be earned from the resulting building. The architect will also usually be responsible for policing the project to see that the building is in fact built according to his drawings and specifications. The architect's judgment and knowledge are indispensable in making many decisions associated with construction: substitution of lower-cost materials or techniques without sacrifice of quality being just one example. Frequently the architect will also serve as judge in determining when the building contractor is to be paid. Construction lenders, as we have seen, are not likely to advance funds until recognizable progress has been made. They will often require an architect's certification that a stage of construction has been completed before they will release the funds to pay for it.

The contract to build is an important document, since it spells out what the owner must accept and what the building contractor must do to be paid. A wide range of difficulties may be encountered in a building project of any magnitude. They range from delays caused by weather, strikes, and acts of God to extreme difficulty of the work or even impossibility. The contractual relationship between the owner and the contractor is therefore discussed in some detail.

The quality of performance is a separate issue; the subjects of warranties of quality made by express agreement or legal implication are also covered. Finally, the concept of some form of guarantee or insurance that the work will be completed, the performance bond, is also discussed in some detail.

## Real Estate Development

### Subdividing

The first step in land development is the subdividing of the raw land into smaller tracts preparatory to further development. The subdividing may consist of measuring the lots and placing stakes to indicate the boundaries of the lots, or it may involve the improvement of the tract by laying water and sewer mains, bringing in utilities, paving streets, and building sidewalks. The acquisition of the land involves no special legal problems. The conveying and financing of the purchase of land are discussed in other chapters. There are certain legal requirements and safeguards that the subdivider should consider before he undertakes his project.

### Governmental Regulations

If the tract to be subdivided lies within the boundaries of an incorporated city, or if the township or county has adopted a regional plan, the subdivider should carefully check the zoning ordinances of the city, or the regional plan of the township or county, in order to be certain that his proposed use of the land and his planned layout of streets and alleys in no way conflict with established regulations. If he cannot carry out his plan under existing regulations, he may attempt to have the zoning ordinance or regional plan amended, or try to get a waiver of the particular restriction that conflicts with his plan, or alter his plan so that there is no conflict. Usually, a planning board is given the power to waive designated restrictions included in a zoning ordinance or in an adopted land plan.

### Restrictive Covenants

If the subdivision is located in an unrestricted area, the subdivider may wish to place restrictions on the use of the land; if the land is in a restricted area, the subdivider may wish to place restrictions on the use of the land in excess of the restrictions under the zoning ordinance or land plan. This can be accomplished by placing appropriate restrictive provisions in the recorded plat and in the deeds of the lots. Zoning ordinances and restrictive covenants are discussed in Chapter 20.

## Plats and Dedication

In establishing a subdivision, a plat is prepared and recorded. This plat should show the boundaries of each tract or lot; the roads, streets, and alleys therein; and the easements for utilities and public parks or any other rights in the land dedicated to the public. In addition, all restrictions on the use of the land should be clearly stated on this recorded plat. Since this plat will be the basis for future conveyances, the subdivision should be carefully surveyed, and all measurements and notations made by the surveyor should be accurately entered thereon.

In laying out the subdivision, it is a wise plan to establish monuments and make all measurements from these monuments. In the event of controversy as to boundaries, fixed monuments control over measurements.[1] Stone or concrete markers may be used to designate the corners of lots or tracts; and if used, such markers would control over measurements stated on the plat. The use of such markers gives a builder greater assurance that a structure erected on the lot does not encroach on the adjoining lot. When a plat has been recorded and accepted as required by law, the streets, alleys, and other portions of the land that are shown on the plat as being set aside are thereby dedicated to the public and become public property. Under the statutes of some states, such dedicated land is owned by city or other governmental unit in fee simple. Under the statutes or laws of other states, the city or governmental unit acquires an easement or a determinable fee. A common-law dedication confers only an easement on the governmental unit. If land is once dedicated to a public use, the public right over such land continues until the plat is vacated or the dedicated property is abandoned. Generally, the statutes of the state set out the procedure that must be followed to effect the vacation of property dedicated to public use. Abandonment occurs when the use for which the property is dedicated becomes impossible of execution or when the objective of the use wholly fails.[2] The public right in dedicated lands is not lost by mere nonuse, and rights in land dedicated to public use cannot be acquired by adverse possession or prescription.[3]

The owners of a tract of land platted it and recorded the plat, which showed a street, Ocean View Drive, abutting the waters of New River Sound. Burkart, who purchased a

---

[1] *Village of Davidson* v. *Cartwright,* 236 Mich. 249, 210 N.W. 226.

[2] *Adams et al.* v. *Rowles,* 149 Tex. 52, 228 S.W.2d 849.

[3] *City of Billings* v. *Pierce Packing Co. et al.,* 117 Mont. 225, 161 P.2d 636.

block of lots abutting Ocean View Drive, claimed that since the plat showed the boundary of his lots to be the center of New River Sound, he had exclusive riparian rights to all lands between Ocean View Drive and the center of New River Sound. The city of Fort Lauderdale claimed the riparian rights for the public. The court held that the city acquired, by virtue of the dedication, an easement in the riparian rights and that Burkart had only the rights of a member of the public.

The court said: "A deed which describes property by reference to a plat makes the plat as much a part of the deed as if it were actually copied in the deed.

"A dedication of lands for public street purposes, absent a clear intent to the contrary, does not divest owner of title, but only subjects the land and title to easement, and if easement is lawfully terminated, title of land remains in dedicator or his successors in interest, free and clear of easement.

"Where a street was laid out so that it was bounded on one side by navigable waters, dedication of street to public operated to relinquish to public, and to merge in the public right, dedicator's individual right of access to open navigable waters in front of dedicator's uplands, and owners of upland were not vested with riparian rights to exclusion of riparian rights accruing to the easement for the dedicated street even though they owned the underlying fee in street." *Burkart* v. *City of Fort Lauderdale,* Fla., 156 So.2d 752 (1963).

## Federal Regulation

Certain broad areas of federal regulation may have a strong bearing upon the development and marketing program that will be pursued. While the legislation discussed below may be of little significance in some developments, the cost of compliance needs to be taken into account by the developer.

## Interstate Land Sales Full Disclosure Act

Title XIV of the Housing and Urban Development Act of 1968[4] is designed to curb abuses in the interstate promotion and sale of unimproved land. There are two basic requirements of the act that are designed to protect the buying public. The first of these is the requirement that the seller file a "statement of record" with the Office of Interstate Land Sales Registration. This statement is required to spell out, in considerable detail, basic information about the property and the sales transaction itself, all as specified in the act. Second, there must be furnished to each purchaser a "Property Report," which represents a full disclosure of information about the property offered for sale. The basic purpose

[4] 15 U.S.C.A. 1701.

of the legislation is therefore that of requiring disclosure. It also includes, however, a "cooling off" period, which permits the purchaser a 48-hour period within which to rescind the transaction unless the property report was furnished to him 48 hours prior to signing the contract of sale.

### When the Act Applies

Whenever a seller proposes to sell or offer for sale in interstate commerce 50 or more unimproved lots, then the act applies and such offering may not be made until the seller has filed and received approval of the statement of record. This statement must include a great deal of information, including the identity of the sellers; the legal description of the property to be sold; the condition of the title to the property, with emphasis on any restrictions; the terms and conditions of proposed sales; a statement regarding access to the property and availability of utilities; a sample of the deed that will be used; financial statements for the developer; and other documents as may be required for the protection of purchasers.[5] There are several exceptions to the requirement of filing the statement spelled out in the act that are beyond the scope of this discussion; however, the regulations issued do create an important exception for *intrastate* developments of subdivisions having fewer than 300 lots, all within one state, that will be offered in only that state. In addition, not more than 5 percent of these lots may be sold to nonresidents, and the advertising and promotion of sales must be limited to that state. This last requirement may be difficult to meet when the subdivision is near the border of another state; the regulations recognize this fact, and an advance opinion may be secured to the effect that a particular offering is exempt.

### Protection Afforded the Purchaser

As noted earlier, in addition to the Statement of Record that must be filed and approved, the seller must provide a Property Report to the purchaser either prior to or at the time of signing the contract. If not provided with this report at least 48 hours prior to the signing, the purchaser has 48 hours after that time within which to rescind the contract. If there is no property report furnished at all, then the purchaser may rescind at any time.[6] If neither a Statement of Record has been filed nor a Property Report presented to the purchaser, the act gives the purchaser a civil remedy for damages. The mere filing of the statement and

---

[5] 15 U.S.C.A. 1705.

[6] U.S.C.A. 1703.

furnishing of the report, however, do not foreclose an action by the purchaser against the seller if fraud or deceit have been practiced, or if the Property Report is deliberately untrue, misleading, or incomplete.[7] There are also criminal sanctions for fraud, including fines or imprisonment, or both.[8]

### State Law Protection

In addition to the requirements of the federal legislation, many states have recently amended their laws to greatly restrict and monitor the activities of out-of-state developers or sellers of unimproved land. Some legislation goes so far as to require the deposit, with a local financial institution, of the deed that will be given to the purchaser at the time the total price has been paid. This requirement recognizes the fact that many such sales are by land contract or contract for deed.

## Environmental Controls

While most of the forms of environmental legislation are not aimed directly at control of the real estate business, it is clear that they have a significant effect on the uses to which private property may be put and that they must therefore be given consideration in making real estate decisions. Great emphasis has been placed upon environmental control during the past 10 years, and the cause of antipollution is receiving wide support from many sources. The problem is not new and neither is legislative control a new idea. As far back as 1899 the United States had on its books water pollution control legislation (Refuse Act of 1899) that included provisions for fines and prison sentences; however, its enforcement left a great deal to be desired. Today we have on the books a wide variety of air, noise, water, and pesticide pollution statutes, and it is clearly beyond the scope of this book to consider them all even in limited fashion. Nevertheless, the reader should bear in mind that any of them might have a substantial influence on a particular real estate project.

### Regulation against Misuse of Land

At the same time there is a more direct body of controls that cannot be ignored: regulation against the misuse of land. Today it is not at all unusual for the developer of real estate to find himself burdened by many restrictions that only a few short years ago would have been considered necessary only for aesthetic purposes.

---

[7] U.S.C.A. 1709.

[8] U.S.C.A. 1717.

That is, the requirements of dedication of a portion of a subdivision for common use by all residents, the preservation of open space between structures, and so forth, are frequently imposed today as conditions for the granting of approval to proceed with development. The basic tool for controlling the development of real estate is the police power manifested by the exercise of zoning controls. In addition to this, of course, the power of eminent domain may be utilized to take property for environmental purposes. It is also important to recognize that private legal action in the form of lawsuits against nuisance and trespass is becoming a more and more widely accepted method of forcing environmental control.

**National Environmental Policy Act of 1969**

The basis for the present-day impetus behind environmental control is the National Environmental Policy Act of 1969 (Public Law 91–190) of January 1, 1970, which clearly established a national policy to "encourage productive and enjoyable harmony between man and his environment" and, among other things, "to establish a Council on Environmental Quality." This was followed shortly by the Environmental Quality Improvement Act of 1970 (Public Law 91–274) of April 3, 1970, which established the Office of Environmental Quality. A series of Executive Orders following these two pieces of legislation were designed to implement the policy established by the congressional action. The motivation of federal action in this area has been to impose the requirement that *all* federal agencies control activities under their jurisdictions in such a way that they will "protect and enhance the quality of the environment."

**Civil Suits**

At the same time there has been a corresponding movement by the courts to recognize that the protection of the environment is a legitimate basis upon which individuals should be entitled to bring suits (usually for injunctive relief) whether or not they can demonstrate clearly that the action complained of will result in substantial economic loss. That is, the courts have recognized what Congress has recognized: that protection of man's environment is a fundamental right that is entitled to be protected by legal action. Also, the courts appear to have relaxed their traditional reluctance to grant injunctive relief, which has always been considered an extraordinary remedy. In large part this shift stems from the fact that an injunction that halts a development is the only effective way to prevent irreparable harm that may not even be measurable in terms of money damages.

**Anticipated Developments**

Besides the federal actions noted above, many states have enacted legislation in the area of environmental protection and control. Real estate business people need to be familiar with these requirements because they affect the purely business aspects of real estate. More importantly it must be noted that this body of law and regulation is still developing and is in an almost constant state of change. At the same time it must be recognized that certain other national policies may be in conflict with the cause of environmental control and improvement, either in a specific area or at a specific time. It cannot be expected that there will be an orderly, logical development. It appears clear, for example, that the "energy crisis" will create serious conflicts in governmental policy, and that these conflicts will influence the development of the law of environmental control.

## Building

### Permits

If the area in which a builder plans to operate is regulated, the builder will be required, as a general rule, to obtain a building permit from some designated official or board. The procedure for obtaining a permit will be set out in the state statutes or municipal ordinances. There is no uniformity as to the procedure to be followed in obtaining a permit or in the standards established for the granting of a permit. As a general rule, the builder must submit the plans for the proposed building or improvement to the designated officials, who check the plans; if the proposed building or improvement complies with established zoning ordinances and safety regulations, the permit will be granted. In many localities a building inspector checks the work as it progresses. If any phase of the construction does not comply with established building standards, the building inspector has the power to halt the work and order the defective work corrected or defective materials replaced.

If a builder is operating in an unregulated and unrestricted area, he is free to build as he wishes, being restrained only by the common-law requirement that a person will not be permitted to use his land in such a manner as to create a nuisance.

### Surveys

Before a builder starts construction, a survey should be made of the tract on which the building is to be erected. An encroachment on adjoining land or the violation of a restriction may result in serious trouble and expense for the builder. A builder is obligated to keep the structure wholly within the boundaries of his own land. If any portion of the building—such as, for example, a bay window, the eaves, or gutters—extends over the boundaries, the builder is guilty of encroaching on the adjoining land and the owner of the adjoining land may remove the overhanging portion of the building or, by court action, force the builder to remove it. If a part of the building is on the adjoining land, the owner of that land has the right to force the removal, unless the cost would be excessive in relation to the injury caused by the encroachment, in which case the person guilty of the encroachment will, in effect, be forced to purchase the land or an easement of right to build on the land on which the encroachment stands. All doubts as to the value of the land are resolved in favor of the innocent party.

### Violation of Restrictions

If the building violates existing restrictions, such as extending over the setback line or over the side yard line, any interested person may, upon discovering the violation, obtain an injunction, which will enjoin the builder from continuing the work, and may obtain a court order, that will require the builder to alter the structure so that it will comply with the restrictions.

### Lateral Support

An adjoining landowner is entitled to have his land supported in its natural condition, but a person excavating on his land is not obligated to provide support for a structure erected on adjoining land.[9] If one is excavating on his land and the excavation is such that it will cause no damage to adjoining land in its natural state, but there are structures on the adjoining land the weight of which causes the land to sink, the injured property owner cannot recover damages for injury to his land and buildings resulting from the excavation, unless he can prove that the excavating was done negligently and that if it had been done with reasonable care, his property would not have been damaged.

One contemplating an excavation that he has reasonable ground to believe will cause damage to the land and buildings on the adjoining property owes a duty to give the adjoining property owner notice of the intent to excavate and the general nature of the proposed excavation in time to afford him an opportunity to protect his property.[10] Some state statutes and municipal ordinances have been enacted that define the duty of a person excavating on his land to protect the land and buildings of adjoining landowners.

---

[9] *Prete* v. *Cray,* 49 R.I. 209, 141 A. 609, 59 A.L.R. 1241.

[10] *S.H. Kress & Co., Inc.,* v. *Reaves,* 85 F.2d 915.

Michelsen owned a lot 22 feet wide and 132 feet long on which there was a building 22 feet wide and 50 feet long. On the rear of the lot was a cesspool. A sewer line ran through the cesspool out to the city main. Upton, who owned the adjoining lot, excavated on his lot to a depth of eight feet below the base of the foundation of Michelsen's building. The excavation was two feet from the Michelsen lot line. Upton did not give Michelsen formal notice of his excavation activities, but Michelsen was present every day and had full knowledge of what was being done. As the result of rain, the cesspool overflowed and caused the soil under Michelsen's building to crumble and the building to collapse. Michelsen sued Upton to recover a judgment for the damage to his building. The court held that Upton was not liable.

Justice Messmore said: "Knowledge or reason to know, of the danger arising from an excavation is necessary to contributory negligence. . . . But when he knows or has reason to know of the danger he is guilty of contributory negligence if he fails to take such precautions as an ordinarily prudent man would take under like circumstances to guard his premises against harm.

"The rule in regard to contributory negligence of the adjoining owner appears to be that where such negligence is the proximate cause of the injury, or where it has materially contributed to the injury, there can be no recovery." *Michelsen* v. *Upton,* 175 Neb. 743, 123 N.W.2d 850 (1963).

## Types of Building Contracts

Although building contracts do not differ basically from other types of contracts, they may be classified as to the risks assumed by the parties. The builder may enter into a *general* contract. Under such a contract the contractor obligates himself to construct a building according to certain plans and specifications. He assumes all the risks incident to the fulfillment of the contract. He personally contracts for all labor and materials, and furnishes all tools and equipment necessary for the completion of the work. He is not an agent of the builder. Under a *unit type of operation* the builder acts as his own general contractor and contracts for certain units of the work. He is responsible for the coordination of the work but is not liable as principal for the debts incurred by his contractors for labor and materials.

In some instances the builder may do the work himself or hire the necessary labor. He may purchase the materials and supervise the work, either directly or through an employee, thereby assuming all the risks of the venture.[11]

[11] If labor and material bills are not paid, the laborer or materialman may be entitled to a mechanic's lien on the building. Mechanics' liens on real estate are discussed in Chapter 6. The more detailed aspects of contracts to build are discussed in this chapter.

## The Contract to Build

A contract to build does not differ in its basic requirements from any other type of contract. That is, the parties to such a contract, if it is to be valid, must reach a mutual agreement that is supported by consideration; they must have capacity to contract; and the objective of the contract must be legal. However, the nature of the relationship created and the scope of the rights and duties of the parties to a contract to build give rise to many special legal problems, a knowledge of which is important to anyone who engages in such activity.

A person who wishes to erect a building need not necessarily enter into a contract to build. He may proceed in several different ways. He may, for instance, prepare his plans and buy the materials needed and do the work himself, or he may engage the services of laborers and direct their work; in either case, no contract to build will be involved. Ordinarily, however, the person who wishes to build will contract with a builder to construct a building according to plans that have been agreed upon by the owner and the builder. Usually, in such a situation a simple contract to build is drafted and executed by the parties. In major building operations, however, an architect will, as a general rule, be employed to draft plans and specifications; and the person who wishes to build will contract with a builder to erect such a structure according to the prepared plans and specifications. The contract will, in most instances, define and set out in some detail all the items connected with such work. A person who wishes to build may use other procedures; but such procedures will, as a matter of course, be combinations of those mentioned above.

### Scope of Discussion

The scope of this work does not permit a detailed study of all combinations of building contracts. Consequently, we shall use—as a basis for our discussion of contracts to build—the situation in which an architect is employed to prepare the plans and specifications and to supervise the work, and in which the contract to build is let to a contractor, who furnishes a performance bond protecting the owner, laborers, and materialmen. During the discussion, brief references will be made to some of the more important variations from this procedure.

## The Architect

### Nature of Services Rendered by Architect

The first step to be taken in a major building project is the preparation of the plans and specifications by an architect. Usually, he will make preliminary sketches, followed later on by a draft of more detailed plans. He will be expected to determine the types and strength of materials to be used in the building and to answer the many technical questions that arise during the course of the planning of the building. Generally, the architect, or a fellow architect working under his supervision, will supervise the actual construction of the building. As a matter of fact, the architect performs the professional services connected with the building operation.[12]

**Authority of Architect**

An architect acts primarily as an employee or as an agent of the owner. He may, however, be called upon in some instances to decide a dispute, in which event he will act as an impartial judge. Since the architect is to act as employee and agent of the owner, the duties, authority, and power of the architect should be carefully defined in the contract of employment. The capacity in which the architect acts will depend on the services he is to perform. If he is employed only to prepare preliminary sketches or plans and specifications, the relationship between him and the owner will be that of employee and employer, and he will owe a duty to follow the general instructions of the owner. He would not, however, be obligated to follow instructions that would result in the planning of a building that would be unsafe or in violation of regulatory statutes.

The architect may be employed to superintend the construction of the building and, in some instances, to serve as clerk of the work. In performing such services, he will be acting as agent of the owner. It will be his duty, as superintendent, to check the work as it progresses and make certain that the contractor is complying with the terms of the contract and erecting a building in accordance with the plans and specifications. If he is acting as clerk of the work, he will be on the job at all times during the construction of the building. He will inspect all materials that go into the building and keep a constant check on the work as it progresses.

As agent of the owner, the architect does not have general authority to bind his principal, but he does have authority to do whatever is reasonably necessary to carry the work to completion.[13] Unless the contract of employment confers on the architect such authority, the architect does not have the authority to change or alter the plans or specifications in any material respect.[14] He does have the authority to order minor changes that may be necessary to correct minor errors in the plans or specifications.

---

[12] *Payne* v. *De Vaughn,* 77 Cal. App. 399, 246 P. 1069.

[13] *Davis* v. *Bush & Lane Piano Co.,* 124 Ore. 585, 265 P. 417.

[14] *Nick Warisse Baking Co.* v. *National Concrete Construction Co.,* 218 Ky. 422, 291 S.W. 356.

When the architect is employed to superintend the work, he has implied authority to inspect the materials brought onto the premises by the contractor for incorporation into the building and to reject unfit materials.[15] He also has implied authority to direct the work, and to order the contractor to correct work that is not performed in a proper manner and in accordance with the plans and specifications.

As a general rule, the architect is given authority to decide disputes arising during the course of the work. If the architect is employed to superintend the construction, authority to settle controversies would be implied, even though such authority is not expressly conferred on him by the contract of employment. The architect, in settling disputes, must act as an impartial judge, favoring neither the owner nor the contractor.

### Ownership of Plans and Specifications

In the absence of any provision in the employment contract to the contrary, the courts have held that the plans and specifications are the property of the owner, and that he—not the architect—is entitled to them.[16] If the architect refuses to deliver the plans and specifications to the owner, the architect is not entitled to his fee. The contractor has the right to possession and use of the plans and specifications during the execution of the work, but he acquires no ownership rights in them.

### Architect's Duties and Liabilities

Although the architect is employed by the owner and in many respects acts as agent of the owner, he also, in some situations, acts as an independent judge. Since the architect is employed to perform professional services, he is obligated to bring to the work the degree of care and skill possessed by architects who practice the profession in that locality. He must possess and exercise a degree of skill that is equal to the average skill possessed and exercised by those engaged in the profession. He owes a duty to apply his skill, ability, judgment, and taste reasonably and without delay or neglect. If the architect is negligent, either in the preparation of plans and specifications or in the supervision of the work, and the owner or contractor is injured as the direct result of the architect's negligence, he will be held liable for the resulting harm.[17]

If the architect fails to perform his work up to the standards of the profession

---

[15] *Stimson Mill Co.* v. *Feigenson Engineering Co. et al.,* 100 Wash. 172, 170 P. 573.

[16] *Hutton v. School City of Hammond,* 194 Ind. 212, 142 N.E. 427.

[17] *Palmer et al.* v. *Brown,* 127 Cal. App.2d 44, 273 P.2d 306.

and, as the result of his directions, the owner suffers a loss, the architect will be liable to the owner for the loss suffered. He is not an insurer of his own work; he does not guarantee that the plans and specifications that he prepares will be perfect; nor does he, if he supervises the work, assure the owner that he will detect every defect in the construction of the building.[18] He does, however, obligate himself to fulfill his duty of loyalty and good faith, and to exercise care and skill in the preparation of the plans and specifications and in the supervision of the work.

Smith, wishing to build a house, employed Goff, a licensed architect, to furnish "complete architectural services, including preliminary plans, working drawings and specifications, and periodic supervision." Goff prepared the plans and specifications, but the lowest bid for the erection of the house was $16,000, which Smith felt was more than he could afford. After considerable negotiation and revision of the plans and specifications, the contractor agreed to furnish all materials and perform all work for $10,500. The contract provided that the work was to be performed in a good and workmanlike manner.

When the house was completed, the Smiths moved in, but they soon began to discover defects in the work and brought this suit against Goff, as architect, and the contractor to recover damages. The jury found for Goff, and judgment was rendered accordingly. Smith appealed, and the court of appeals affirmed the judgment.

The court said: "The issue so far as the architects are concerned was whether they used that degree of professional care required of them in the origination of the plans and specifications and in the supervision of the construction. The court instructed the jury on this issue. The use of various materials in the building which were not the same as those in the original specifications presented the question of the architects' professional judgment as to the suitability of the material for the purpose. The same is true concerning the methods employed 'to maintain the initial effect of the building.' So also, concerning the architects' supervision of construction. Architects are only required to exercise ordinary professional skill and diligence and to conform to accepted architectural standards; their contracts do not guarantee perfect plans or satisfactory results. Architects are only liable for failure to exercise reasonable care and professional skill in the preparation and execution of their plans according to their contract. Here the contract did not call for the use of any certain materials in the preparation of the plans by the architects. They were required to use their professional judgment. This issue was properly submitted to the jury by the court's instruction which stated that the law required that the architects perform their contractual duties with 'ordinary care and diligence.' This was the only issue made by the evidence as to them, for it was undisputed that architects furnish 'complete architectural services including preliminary plans, working drawings and specifications . . .' as well as '. . . revisions in his plans made necessary by excessive costs. . . .' The jury verdict is conclusive on the controverted issue." *Smith* v. *Goff,* Okla., 325 P.2d 1061 (1958).

---

[18] *Surf Realty Corp.* v. *Standing et al.,* 195 Va. 431, 78 S.E.2d 901.

## The Contractor

### Letting the Contract to Build

If a person wishes to let a contract to build, he will need to select a contractor. He may contact one he knows or one who has been recommended to him and negotiate the contract with him, or he may contact several contractors and request each to submit a bid for the job. If a governmental unit wishes to build, it will advertise for bids and let the contract to the "lowest and best" bidder. A similar practice is frequently followed by private owners—corporations, partnerships, or individuals—if the work to be done involves a substantial outlay of money. Large developers may employ, on a full-time basis, architects, engineers, managers, and the necessary skilled and semiskilled workers whom they need for their construction, and purchase in wholesale quantities the materials needed and proceed to erect the buildings (usually homes) and sell the finished product. This type of operation is not based on a building contract.

If the job is to be let on bids, such bids will, as a general rule, be based on the plans and specifications prepared by the architect. The owner may also include with the plans and specifications a copy of the contract that the successful bidder will be required to sign, or he may state in the invitation that some standard form of contract will be used. Unless the owner advertises or states that the contract will be let to the low bidder without reservation, the bid is an offer; there is no contract until the owner notifies the bidder that his bid is accepted. If the owner, in attempting to accept a bid, alters in any material respect the terms of the bid, the bid is thereby rejected, and no contract ensues.[19] However, if the bidder consents to the change, a contract will result.

### Legality of Contract

A building contract is void if its execution requires the performance of an illegal act. For example, a contract to build a structure that would be in violation of a valid regulatory statute or city ordinance would be illegal and void.[20] However, a contract to construct a building that would not be in violation of any statute or ordinance, but that the owner intends to use in the operation of an illegal business, would not be illegal.[21] If the contract is illegal, the contractor, as a general rule, can recover nothing.

---

[19] *R. J. Daum Construction Co.* v. *Child et al.,* 122 Utah 194, 247 P.2d 817.

[20] *Eastern Expanded Metal Co.* v. *Webb Granite & Construction Co.,* 195 Mass. 356, 81 N.E. 251.

[21] *Thomas v. Owens et al.,* 206 Okla. 50, 241 P.2d 1114.

## Mistake

When the contractor submits a bid and it is accepted, a contract results, and the contractor is obligated to perform. He should therefore use great care in preparing his bid, as he cannot, as a general rule, escape liability on the ground that he made a mistake in his computation. Under some circumstances, a bidder may be granted relief from a unilateral mistake.

If the mistake is not the result of negligence but is clerical, and the bidder did not have a reasonable opportunity to check the figures because of the circumstance under which the bid was made, relief will generally be granted, unless rights of third parties have intervened and the parties cannot be restored to their original positions.[22] In granting such relief, the bidder who has made the mistake may be required to stand any costs incident thereto.[23] Furthermore, an owner will not be permitted to take advantage of a mistake that he knows, or should know, has been made. For instance, if several bids are submitted and one of them is materially less than the others, the courts have held that the inadequacy of the bid is sufficient to put the owner on notice that an error has been made in preparing the bid.

Mistakes made by an architect or engineer in computing the amount due the contractor at the various stages of the work will be corrected.

The city of Portland advertised for bids on a sewage disposal project. Rushlite Auto Sprinkler Co. (hereinafter referred to as Rushlite) submitted a bid of $429,444.20 accompanied by its certified check for $21,472.21, which was to be retained by the city if Rushlite failed or refused to enter into a contract for the work. When the bids were opened, it was discovered that the next high bid was $671,600, or $242,155.80 more than Rushlite's bid. Rushlite immediately notified the city that it had omitted an item for steel of $99,225.68. Rushlite requested that its bid be withdrawn and its certified check be returned. The city refused the request and cashed the check. Rushlite brought suit to recover the amount of the check. Rushlite's bid was compiled by an adequate staff of estimators. The trial court granted Rushlite a judgment, and the city appealed. The judgment was affirmed.

Judge Rossman said: "We believe that it is manifest from the evidence that the difference between the plaintiff's bid and the next high was so large that all of those concerned with the undertaking were rendered uneasy. The plaintiff's officers at once returned to their work sheets, fearing that they must have committed a mistake. The City Engineer, according to his own words, found the variation so great that it 'scared us to death.' . . . The bid aroused suspicion in all minds. We think that the difference appraised the City that a mistake had probably been made.

---

[22] *Graham et al.,* v. *Clyde,* Fla., 61 So.2d 656.

[23] *School District of Scottsbluff* v. *Olson Construction Co. et al.,* 153 Neb. 451, 45 N.W.2d 164.

"We believe that in this State an offer and acceptance are deemed to effect a meeting of the minds, even though the offeror made a material mistake in computing his offer, provided the acceptor was not aware of the mistake and had no reason to suspect it. But if the offeree knew of the mistake, and if it was basic, or if the circumstances were such that he, as a reasonable man, should have inferred that a basic mistake was made, a meeting of the minds does not occur. . . .

"It is unnecessary to state once more that the proof in cases of this kind must possess a high degree of cogency. The bidder must prove, not only that he made a material mistake, but also that the offeree was aware of it. In this case, the facts which we have mentioned are unchallenged.

"It is our belief that although the plaintiff alone made the mistake, the City was aware of it. Where it accepted the plaintiff's bid, with knowledge of the mistake, it sought to take an unconscionable advantage of an inadvertent error. Equity is always prepared to grant relief from such situations." *Rushlite Auto Sprinkler Co.* v. *City of Portland,* 189, Ore. 194, 219.P.2d 732 (1952).

## Interpretation of Contract

The contract to build should be prepared with care. Both parties are bound by the contract as drafted. Although the terms of the contract may be modified or canceled by the mutual agreement of the parties, neither party, in the event of a dispute and lawsuit, will be permitted to offer parol (oral) evidence to show that the terms of the contract were intended to be different than those expressed in the writing; nor will either party be permitted to offer parol evidence to add terms to the contract, unless it is clear from a reading of the contract that it is incomplete.

It is the duty of the judge to interpret a written instrument. The judge, in interpreting a contract, will read the contract in its entirety and give the language its ordinary meaning. Technical words will be given their technical meaning, unless it is clear that such was not intended.

In the building trade, certain words have acquired a special meaning; when such words are used in a contract to build, they will be interpreted according to their accepted meaning in the trade.

As a general rule, when the contract to build refers to the plans and specifications, the court will hold that they become a part of the contract. A well-drafted contract to build will state expressly that the plans and specifications are incorporated into and become a part of the contract.

## Stipulations for Alterations and Extras

The terms of a contract will be enforced by the courts unless they have been induced by misrepresentation or fraud, or unless they are illegal. If the owner and contractor include in the building contract a provision stipulating that the owner will not be held liable for any additional costs resulting from alterations or extra work ordered unless the alteration or extra work is authorized by a written order signed by the owner, such provision will be held to be valid and will be enforced by the courts.[24]

As a general rule, such a provision in a building contract cannot be canceled or waived by the acts of the supervising architect or engineer, or by the clerk of the work.[25] The parties to the contract may, however, by mutual agreement change or cancel any of the terms of the contract, including stipulations regarding alterations or extra work. A party to a contract may, expressly or by his conduct, waive rights granted him by the contract. If an owner orally orders alterations or extra work and permits the contractor to carry out the order and then refuses to pay for the extra costs, the courts will hold that the owner has waived his right to set up the lack of an order in writing and will hold him liable for the reasonable value of the alteration or extras in case there is no agreement as to the amount to be paid.[26]

Broderick entered into a contract with Moorehead under which Moorehead agreed to erect a warehouse for Broderick. During the course of the construction the plans were changed, and the structure actually erected was an automobile paint shop. The contract provided that any extras must be authorized in writing. Many changes were made in the plans and many extras added without written authorization.

Broderick failed to pay for the extras, and this suit was brought to impose a mechanic's lien on the property. Broderick set up as a defense that the extras were not authorized in writing. The court held that the requirement for written authority had been waived, and Broderick appealed. The judgment was affirmed.

Judge Kanner said: "The contract we are here considering specified that any extras must have been authorized in writing by the owners. This we recognize as valid. We also recognize, however, that such a provision may be waived; and a waiver of the provision may be established by the subsequent course of dealing between the parties. Ordinarily, a written agreement cannot be abrogated nor modified by executory or parol agreement; but if the parol agreement has been accepted and acted upon by the parties, this rule does not apply. 'Extras,' by statutory definition, consist of labor or services performed or materials furnished for the improvement of real property authorized by the owner in addition to labor, services, or materials covered by a previous contract between the same

---

[24] *Brandolini v. Grand Lodge of Pennsylvania Order of Sons of Italy in America,* 358 Pa. 303, 56 A.2d 662.

[25] *Van Buskirk et al.* v. *Board of Education of Passaic Twp., Morris County,* 78 N.J.L. 650, 75 A.909.

[26] *Frank T. Hickey, Inc.* v. *Los Angeles Jewish Community Council,* 128 Cal. App.2d 676, 276 P.2d 52.

parties. In the case here considered, the testimony, supported in part by the exhibits, amply establishes that during construction of the building there were many changes in the plans authorized by the owners for extras incorporated in the construction, although these authorizations were not made in writing by the owners." *Broderick* v. *Overhead Door Company of Fort Lauderdale, Inc.,* Fla., 117 So.2d 240 (1959).

**Liability of Parties**

If either party to a building contract fails to perform his obligations under the contract, he will be liable to the injured party for any loss suffered as the direct result of the breach. Also, if the architect fails to perform his obligations, or is negligent or dishonest in the performance of his duties, with the result that either the owner or the contractor suffers a loss, the architect will be liable to the aggrieved party.

If a principal contractor subcontracts units of the work, he owes a duty to coordinate the different units so that the subcontractor will not be caused unnecessary delay in the performance of his work. If the principal contractor fails to make such a coordination or fails to perform his part of the work, and the subcontractor is delayed in his work and thereby suffers a loss, the general contractor may be held liable to such subcontractor for the loss suffered.[27]

If the owner acts as his own general contractor and lets units of the work to different contractors, he can protect himself from the liability for failure to coordinate the work of the unit contractors by including in each unit contract a provision to the effect that each unit contractor shall be responsible to the other unit contractors for damage to work or persons, or for loss caused by neglect or by failure to finish the work at the proper time. Such a provision is a third-party beneficiary provision, and an injured unit contractor would have a right to bring suit against the unit contractor whose conduct or failure to perform was the direct cause of the loss.

The contractor is not liable for damage to or destruction of the building by fire, flood, and so forth, after the building is completed. Nor is he liable for damage to the building if such damage results from some weakness in the structure, from fault in the soil, or from similar causes.[28] The contractor is not a judge of the sufficiency of the specifications and is not liable if the completed structure is defective because of inadequacies in the plans and specifications.

The contractor does owe a duty to inspect materials delivered on the job and to reject faulty materials, but he is not liable if the defects are such that

---

[27] *Guerini Stone Company* v. *P. J. Carlin Construction Company,* 248 U.S. 334, 39 S. Ct. 102.

[28] *Puget Sound National Bank of Tacoma* v. *C. B. Lauch Const. Co.,* 73 Idaho 68, 245 P.2d 800.

they would not be discovered by an ordinary inspection. Unless the contractor expressly warrants the work or specifically undertakes to produce a building of specified quality, he is not liable if he performs the job in a workmanlike manner in accordance with good usage and accepted practices in the community, and if he follows the plans and specifications.[29] The contractor is liable if he fails to follow plans and specifications and the deviation results in defective work, or if he is negligent in the performance of the work.

The owner is liable for his failure to make payments for the work when due, and unreasonable delay in making payments will justify the contractor in abandoning the work. The owner does not guarantee the sufficiency of the plans and specifications. If the owner is to furnish materials, he is not liable for defects in the materials furnished.

If the work is let to several contractors and a provision is inserted in each contract to the effect that each contractor shall be responsible to the others for damage to work or persons, or for loss caused by neglect or by failure to finish the work at the proper time, the owner will not be liable for damages resulting from the negligence of the several contractors.

As a general rule, the architect is not a party to the contract to build; ordinarily, he is not liable if either the contractor or the owner breaches the contract. However, if the architect is superintendent of the work and is given the authority to decide certain matters arising during the course of the work or to issue architect's certificates authorizing payment for work done, he will be held liable if, through collusion or fraud, he favors one party over the other or issues a certificate when it should not be issued. The architect is not liable for honest errors in judgment.

### Performance of Contract to Build

If there are no specific provisions in the contract to build setting up standards of performance, the contractor must perform the work up to the general standards for such work in the community.

The contract may provide that the work shall be done to the satisfaction of the owner. If the contract does so provide and the work is such that it involves fancy, taste, or judgment—as, for example, the painting of murals—the owner will not have to accept the work if he is honestly dissatisfied. If the work is such that it involves only operative fitness or mechanical utility, the owner will have to accept the work if it would be satisfactory to a reasonable person.[30]

---

[29] *Mann v. Clowser et al.,* 190 Va. 887, 59 S.E.2d 78.

[30] *Erikson* v. *Ward,* 266 Ill. 259, 107 N.E. 593.

Contracts to build provide frequently that payment of the installments due on the contract shall be made only on the production of an architect's or engineer's certificate that would state the amount due, and that the work performed was satisfactory. The contract may also contain a provision requiring, before the final payment is made, the production of a certificate by the architect or engineer that would certify that the work has been completed according to plans and specifications. If the contract to build contains such a provision, the contractor must obtain the required certificate before he is entitled to payment. If the contract sets out the form or content of the certificate, the certificate presented must fulfill these requirements.

The certificate of the architect or engineer is conclusive as to the rights of the parties, if the contract so provides, unless the architect or engineer has exceeded his authority in issuing the certificate.

In all cases in which payment is to be made on the production of an architect's or engineer's certificate, the architect or engineer must act honestly and must exercise his honest judgment concerning the matters to which he certifies. If the owner prevents the issuing of the certificate, or if the certificate is collusively, fraudulently, arbitrarily, or capriciously withheld, the contractor will be allowed to recover without the production of such a certificate.[31] Likewise, if a certificate is collusively or fradulently issued when the contractor is not entitled to a certificate, the owner is not required to make payment on the production of the certificate.

James I. Barnes Construction Company (hereinafter referred to as Barnes) contracted to build a school building for Washington Township of Stark County (hereinafter referred to as School) for the contract price of $143,878, payment to be made on the production of an engineer's certificate issued by Zechiel. When the work was completed, the county commissioners inspected it; at that time, they discussed defects in the building and said that they would not accept the floors because they were composed of poured concrete and were very uneven. Work was done on the floors to improve them; and subsequently, Zechiel issued to Barnes a final engineer's certificate. During the course of the work, Zechiel had failed to make required tests; the walls had cracks about every 20 lineal feet, the roof leaked, the glazed tile wall was improperly finished, and the work had not been done in a workmanlike manner. School refused to make the final payment, and Barnes sued. On the trial, Barnes introduced the contract and the engineer's certificate as proof that he was entitled to the final payment. The trial court held that Barnes was not entitled to the final payment, and he appealed. The judgment was affirmed.

---

[31] *Haugen et al.* v. *Raupach et al.,* 43 Wash.2d147, 260 P.2d 340.

Judge Myers said: "It is a rule of law in Indiana that when a contract provides that work shall be done to the satisfaction, approval or acceptance of an architect or engineer, he is thereby constituted a sole arbitrator by the parties, who are bound by his decision in the absence of fraud or such gross mistakes as to imply bad faith or a failure to exercise honest judgment. His decision is not conclusive to the extent that it cannot be reviewed by a court. It is only *prima facie* correct, and the burden is upon the other parties to show fraud or mistake.

"In our opinion there was sufficient evidence, together with all reasonable inferences deducible therefrom for the jury to have found that the engineer's certificate was not issued after the exercise of honest judgment by the engineer, or was issued as the result of gross mistake of fact on the part of the engineer." *James I. Barnes Construction Company* v. *Washington Township,* Ind. App., 184 N.E.2d 763 (1962).

## Stages of Performance

The courts recognize three stages of performance of a contract:

**1. *Satisfactory Performance.*** A contract to build according to plans and specifications can hardly be performed without some slight deviation from the plans and specifications. If the contractor has performed the work up to the accepted standards for that type of building in that community, he has rendered satisfactory performance and is entitled to recover the contract price.

**2. *Substantial Performance.*** If the contractor has made an honest effort to perform the work according to the terms of the contract but the result is not up to accepted standards, yet the defects are such that they do not weaken the structure, and the building will serve, in a reasonable manner, the needs of the owner, the owner will be required to accept the building. However, he will be entitled to a reduction in the contract price to compensate for the defective performance.[32]

If the faults can be corrected without unreasonable cost, the measure of damages will be the cost of remedying the defects. If the building would have to be reconstructed, or substantially reconstructed, the measure of damages would be the difference between the value of the building as constructed and its value had it been constructed according to the terms of the contract.

**3. *Partial Performance.*** If the contractor abandons the work before completion, or if he completes the work but his performance is materially defective,

---

[32] *Nees et al.* v. *Weaver,* 222 Wis. 492, 269 N.W. 266.

he will have partially performed the contract. The nature of a contract to build is such that the owner, as a general rule, will derive some benefit from partial performance. The work cannot be returned to the contractor. If the contractor has only partially performed the contract, he cannot recover in a suit on the contract. However, he will be entitled to some payment for the benefits conferred on the owner by his partial performance. As a general rule, the amount to which the contractor is entitled is the contract price less the cost of completing the work in compliance with the terms of the contract.

### Death or Incapacitating Illness of Contractor

If the contractor is prevented by sickness or death from completing the performance, recovery may be had, as a general rule, for the value of the services rendered. Likewise, if the contract calls for the remodeling or repair of a building and, during the course of the work, the building is destroyed without the fault of either party, the contractor can recover for the value of the work done and for materials furnished up to the time of the destruction of the building.[33]

### Owner's Prevention of Performance

If the owner, without justification, prevents the contractor from completing the contract, the contractor may recover the contract price less the cost to the contractor of completing the building according to the provisions of the contract.

Reid and Kelly entered into a contract whereby Reid contracted to make designated repairs on Kelly's dwelling house and to erect a stairway adjoining it. When the work was completed, Kelly claimed that certain items were not properly done, and he refused to pay Reid the balance due. Reid offered to correct any defects in his work and set a day when he would be present to do so; but before the day arrived, Kelly notified Reid "not to come back or do anything more on the job." On the trial of the case the jury found that the defects in the work were not material and that Kelly prevented Reid from completing the work. The court entered judgment for Reid, and Kelly appealed. The judgment was affirmed.

Judge Cave said: "Thus the pleadings and the evidence clearly established that Kelly would not permit Reid to correct any deficiencies in the work, if there were any.

"The law is well established that, 'where a party to the contract forbids its performance by the other, or interferes with its performance by the other to an extent which amounts to a refusal of performance, the party thus interfered with may recover as if he had performed his contract.' There are many cases announcing this doctrine." *Reid* v. *Kelly,* Mo. App., 300 S.W.2d 542 (1957).

---

[33] *Matthews Construction Company* v. *Brady,* 104 N.J.L. 438, 140 A. 433.

## Delays in Performance

If there is a provision in the contract stating that the building must be completed within a certain time, failure to complete the building within that time will not justify rejection of the building, since time is not of the essence of a contract to build. However, the contractor will be liable for damages for late performance. If there is no stipulation in the contract as to the time for the completion of the building, the contractor will owe a duty to pursue the work with reasonable diligence. Many contracts to build provide that the building shall be completed within a specified time, and that the contractor, on his failure to complete the building within the time specified, will pay a designated sum as liquidated damages for each day he is late.

Delays are excused if the contractor is prevented from completing the building by the acts of the owner. Delays resulting from strikes, inclement weather, or inability to obtain necessary materials are not excused, unless the contract to build so provides.

## Waiver

A waiver is a voluntary relinquishment of a known right, or such conduct as warrants an inference of the relinquishment of such right. The owner may accept defective performance of a contract to build and waive his right to demand strict performance. A waiver may be expressed either orally or in writing, or the waiver may be implied from the conduct of the parties.[34] If the conduct of the owner clearly indicates his intent to accept the work without making a claim for imperfections, he will have waived the defects. Acceptance of the work implies a waiver of known defects; but it does not imply a waiver of unknown latent defects—that is, defects which could not be discovered by reasonable inspection.[35]

The mere occupancy and use of the building do not constitute a waiver of defects. However, if the owner takes possession of and uses the building without in any way indicating his intent to hold the contractor responsible for deficiencies, such action is strong evidence of his intent to waive defects. This is particularly true if the defects are minor in nature.

Payment of the contract price with the knowledge of defective performance does not, as a matter of law, constitute a waiver; but such payment is strong evidence of an intent to waive known imperfections and will be held to be a waiver unless there are other facts to negate such intent. Payment is not a waiver of unknown or latent defects.

---

[34] *Standard Construction Co., Inc.* v. *National Tea Co. et al.,* 240 Minn. 422, 62 N.W.2d 201.

[35] *Michel* v. *Efferson et al.,* 223 La. 136, 65 So.2d 115.

## Damage to or Destruction of Building

When a person contracts to produce a result, he assumes the risks incident to the production of the promised result. A promisor may, by inserting appropriate provisions in his contract, relieve himself from defined risks. Also, incapacitating illness or death, intervening illegality, or destruction of the subject matter essential to the performance of the contract will, under the rule of impossibility, relieve the promisor from his duty of performance. This rule is of major importance in determining whether the owner or the contractor will bear a loss resulting from damage to or destruction of a building being erected, remodeled, or repaired.

If the contractor has contracted absolutely and unconditionally to erect a new building for a stipulated amount, he must bear any loss or damage to the building before its completion.[36] This would be true even though the building was being paid for in installments. However, if payments are to be made at various stages of the work, the courts have generally held that the owner will bear the loss resulting from damage to or destruction of the work completed and paid for, but the contractor will bear the loss of that stage of the work under construction but not completed.

The courts have usually held also that if payments are made periodically for the work completed during a stated period—for example, if payment is to be made on the 10th of each month for all materials delivered on the job and all labor done on the building up to the 1st of each month—the owner will bear the loss for materials paid for, and the contractor will bear the loss for that part of the period for which payment is not due.[37]

When the contract is for the remodeling or repair of or an addition to an existing building, and the building is damaged or destroyed and it is impossible to complete the work, the owner must bear the loss as to the work completed at the time of the damage to or destruction of the building, and the contractor will bear the loss resulting from his having made preparation—such as, for instance, having bought materials—for the performance of the job.

If various units of the work are let to separate contractors, the destruction of the building without the fault of either party will discharge the contractor from his obligation, and he will be entitled to payment for the part of the work that he has completed. If the contract is entire and indivisible, the general contractor will bear the loss; otherwise, the loss falls on the owner.[38]

---

[36] *Goin* v. *Board of Education of the City of Frankfort,* 289 Ky. 645, 183 S.W.2d 819.

[37] *Keel* v. *Eastern Carolina Stone & Construction Company,* 143 N.C. 429, 55 S.E. 826.

[38] *American Surety Co. of New York et al.* v. *San Antonio Loan & Trust Co.,* Tex. Civ. App., 98 S.W. 387.

This was an action by the Board of Education, Township of Woodbridge, against Kane Acoustical Company to recover for damage by fire to a partially completed school building, claimed to have been caused by the negligence of Kane Acoustical Company. As a part of the case, the judge had to determine the liability of the parties to a building contract when the building was damaged during the course of the construction.

Judge Gaulkin said: "In the absence of contractual arrangements to the contrary, the risk of loss by fire to a new building in course of construction is presumed to fall upon the builder. If it burns, it must be rebuilt by the builder, without additional compensation. Since we do not have the Woodbridge-Lyons contract, we have no means of telling whether that was the situation here.

"If these policies were builder's risk policies, in the form commonly used in New Jersey today, and if the owner had not yet paid anything for the building when the fire happened, and had no pecuniary interest therein covered by the policy, the builder ordinarily would be entitled to all of the insurance money and the owner to none. The same would be true if the builder rebuilt after the fire, before the insurance monies were paid over by the insurance companies. On the other hand, other circumstances (or the policies or contracts) may give the owner the right to some or even all of the proceeds. Again, without the data mentioned above, we cannot tell what the rights of the parties are." *Board of Education, Township of Woodbridge* v. *Kane Acoustical Company,* 51 N.J. Super. 319, 143 A.2d 853 (1958).

### Agreement to Modify Contract

The parties to a contract have the right, by mutual agreement, to cancel or alter the terms of the contract. However, any promise by an owner to pay the contractor additional compensation if he will complete the work according to the terms of the contract, or any promise by the owner to permit the contractor to substitute different or cheaper material in the performance of the contract is, as a general rule, unenforceable for lack of consideration.[39]

The courts have held that if unforeseen and unforeseeable difficulties are encountered in the course of the work and the owner promises to pay the additional cost resulting from such difficulty, the promise will be enforced.[40]

### Right to Rescind Contract

Rescission of a contract is the repudiation or the unmaking of the contract and the placing of the parties in the same position that they held before entering into the contract. The parties may enter into a mutual agreement to rescind the contract, or if one of the parties is guilty of a material breach, the injured party

---

[39] *Dahl* v. *Edwin Moss and Son, Inc.,* 136 Conn. 147, 69 A.2d 562.

[40] *Linz* v. *Shuck,* 106 Md. 220, 67 A. 286.

may have the right, and may elect, to rescind the contract. If a person wishes to rescind on the ground of material breach, he must act within a reasonable time after the breach. Permitting the other party to proceed with the performance of the contract is a bar to the remedy of rescission.

A contract may be rescinded for failure of the owner to make payment when due, provided the contractor is not in default in the performance of the work. Unreasonable delay in the execution of the work is ground for rescission. The inability of either party to perform his duties under the contract is ground for rescission. If one party repudiates the contract, the other party has the right to rescind the contract.

On the rescission of the contract, no recovery can be had for damages.[41] After rescission, the parties may enter into a new contract for the work, or they may agree to changes in the terms of the contract and proceed with the work. If the parties cannot agree and the case reaches the court, the judge will decree an equitable adjustment of the matter, placing the parties as nearly as possible in the same position that they occupied before entering into the contract.

## Residential Builders' Warranties

Major developments in the law of builders' warranties have occurred in recent years, and concepts of warranty are continuing to be developed both by our courts and legislative bodies. At the same time, the demand by the buyers of housing for express warranties of quality have given great impetus to private insurance programs. Each of these developments is discussed below.

### Court-Imposed Implied Warranties

Express warranties as to the quality of materials and workmanship are not new to the residential construction field; however, implied warranties have been greatly expanded by recent court decisions. Courts are now finding as a matter of course that there exists an implied warranty of habitability in the sale of new residences, and that this warranty exists quite apart from any express warranties made in the contract to build.[42] This development parallels the earlier development of warranty law in the area of consumer products. At the time of construction and sale of a new house, the existence of the implied warranty of habitability is easily established by virtue of the contract between the builder and the purchaser

[41] *Miller-Piehl Equipment Co. et al.* v. *Gibson Commission Co. et al.,* 244 Iowa 103, 56 N.W.2d 25.

[42] *Hartley* v. *Ballou,* 286 N.C. 51, 209 S.E.2d 776 (1974).

because of the existence of *privity of contract* between the parties. Recent cases have, however, extended this implied warranty of habitability to subsequent purchasers of the house. In these cases there is no privity of contract, no direct contractual relationship between the builder and the subsequent purchaser. The conclusions reached by these cases make it clear that the builder's warranty, at least against latent defects that would not be found during a reasonable inspection by the buyer, extends to both original purchasers and subsequent purchasers.

The existence of certain types of defects may not become apparent for a rather extended period of time after construction is completed. Typical of this type of defect is faulty site preparation, which may result in a gradual settling of the house and severe damage to foundations and basement walls. From the builder's standpoint, the fact that the extended period of time for which the implied warranty of habitability may run poses serious problems in determining his exposure to liability. The cases that have been decided in this area tend to find that the warranty exists, that it extends to subsequent purchasers at least so long as the defect is not apparent, but they do not establish specific time limits for the warranty and the exposure to liability. In some states it has been found desirable to establish such a definite period by statute. The uncertainty has also led to the establishment of such insurance programs as the HOW program.

### The HOW Program

In response to the need created by case law development of the implied warranty of habitability and the need for builders to limit their exposure to liability, the HOW program (Home Owners Warranty Corporation) was developed by the National Association of Home Builders. Essentially, the HOW program provides insurance to the homeowners against major structural defects for a 10-year period. During the first two years the builder is expected to cover major defects, but should the builder fail or refuse to do so, the insurance program covers the homeowner against this possibility. While the HOW program is not the only warranty or insurance program that has emerged, it has achieved great prominence by virtue of the support of the National Association of Home Builders. The wide publicity given to its feature of 10-year coverage against major structural defects will undoubtedly influence future court decisions on the question of how long the implied warranty of habitability should run. That is, the general acceptance of the 10-year period by builders and purchasers would seem to indicate that extension of the implied warranty for a longer time is not reasonable. There is, of course, no way to accurately predict the future course of case law in this area; however, a strong argument can be made that the buying public feels that 10 years of protection is adequate. In an aggravated case, however, particularly if personal injury results from defective construction, courts may very well ignore the standard set by warranty or insurance programs.[43]

**Federal Warranty Legislation**

The Magnuson-Moss Warranty/Federal Trade Commission Act,[44] while originally conceived as a vehicle to curb abuses in the automobile and appliance industries, has been extended to cover warranties given by builders of new homes. The act does not require that any warranties be made at all by the builder; however, the buying public has come to expect at least some form of warranty with the purchase of any product and particularly with costly products. The purchase of a new home clearly falls in the "costly" category. In addition, the trend in recent years has been to build in a wide variety of appliances and to make them an integral part of the home. The willingness of mortgage lenders to cover the cost of many appliances under the package mortgage has tended to foster and encourage this trend. As a result of these factors, at least some limited warranty on personal property incorporated into new homes must be given in order to promote their sales. As noted above, the federal warranty act does not require that a warranty be given by the new home builder; but when any warranty is given, it must meet the requirements of the federal act. The federal act does permit the builder to limit the extent of the warranties that are made; however, to be effective, these limitations must be clearly stated and must meet the highly technical requirements of the act as implemented by regulations issued by the Fair Trade Commission, which became effective December 31, 1976. The intent of the law and the regulations is to require that the builder—before the purchase—make the buyer aware of the extent or limitations of the warranties being made. Until the act and regulations have been tested in the courts, it is not clear to what extent federal regulation of warranties of housing and its components will be effective. It is clear from the act itself, however, that it is not intended to preempt existing state laws covering implied warranties, discussed earlier.[45]

## Checklist

No two contracts to build would, as a general rule, contain the same provisions. However, in drafting a contract to build, there are certain matters that should

---

[43] Further information on this subject can be found in "The Home Protection Program," published by the National Association of Realtors, 1975.

[44] 15 U.S. Code, Sections 2301 *et seq.*

[45] For an excellent discussion of the act see: Kenneth G. Peters, "How the Magnuson-Moss Warranty Act Affects the Builder/Seller of New Housing," *Real Estate Law Journal,* vol. 5, no. 4, 1977.

be considered and covered by the contract if they are applicable to the particular undertaking. The following should be considered in drafting most contracts to build. The list is not intended to be an exhaustive one.

1. Date of the contract.
2. Name of the contractor and his address.
3. Name of the owner and his address. It is customary to name the contractor and designate him as *contractor,* and thereafter refer to him in the contract as *contractor.* Likewise, it is customary to name the owner and designate him as *owner,* and thereafter refer to him in the contract as *owner.*
4. Description, in general terms, of the building to be constructed.
5. A statement of the duties to be assumed by the contractor, such as the duty to furnish all materials and labor, and to do all other things necessary to the construction of the building.
6. A statement that the building is to be constructed according to plans and specifications prepared by the architect, naming the architect and identifying the plans and specifications by the architect's identification numbers or symbols.
7. A statement that the plans and specifications are a part of the contract.
8. A statement of the time for the completion of the work. This provision should not only state a time for the completion of the work, but should include provisions for adjustment of the time of completion in the event of changes in the work, or in the event of strikes, fire, flood, or other causes of delay that are beyond the control of the contractor.
9. A statement as to the payment of the contractor. This provision will set out the method of payment of the contractor—whether a lump sum, a unit price, the cost of the work plus a percentage of the cost, the cost of the work plus a fee, or some combination of these.

   As a general rule, payments will be made as the work progresses. The contract should define specifically when such progress payments are to be made—whether they are to be made as units of the work are completed or at stated periods; and if at stated periods, whether they are to be a portion of the total sum to be paid or are to be computed on the basis of the labor performed and materials delivered on the job.

   If the work is let on cost plus a percentage of the cost, or cost plus fee, the method of determining the cost and the reimbursement of the contractor should be stated in detail. Also, the method of determining the fee and the time of paying it should be stated.
10. A statement as to acceptance of the work and as to final payment. The

contract should provide for the final inspection and acceptance of the work and the making of the final payment. A provision should be included to the effect that the acceptance of the building and the making of the final payment will not constitute a waiver by the owner of his right to claim damages for latent defects in the work.

11. A statement as to the issuing of an architect's certificate for payment for the work. The contract should provide for payment only on the presentation of an architect's certificate stating the amount due. The general form of the certificate should be set out, and a provision should be included to the effect that the certificate does not bar the owner from making claim for defective work discovered at a later date.
12. A statement of the powers and duties of the architect. The contract should set out the general powers of the architect to supervise the work, and the contractor's obligation to follow the instructions of the architect. It should also set out the detail drawings to be prepared by the architect and the rights of the contractor if the architect delays unreasonably in preparing necessary detail drawings.

    The duty of the architect to instruct the contractor in the performance of the work should be defined, together with a statement as to the person to whom instructions are to be given—contractor, contractor's superintendent, foreman, or subcontractor—and the method of giving instructions (orally or in writing).

    The preparation of shop drawings and their approval should be covered.
13. A statement as to who shall be the owner of the drawings, plans, specifications, models, and so forth, prepared by the architect.
14. A statement as to materials, appliances, employees, and the like. The contract should set out in detail which of the parties is to pay utility and material bills, pay for appliances used in the course of the work, and pay and discipline employees, and so on.
15. A statement as to the making of surveys, obtaining of permits, and so forth. It should be stated in the contract which of the parties is to provide surveys, make tests, obtain permits and easements, and so on.
16. A statement of the contractor's liability for failure to protect the work, the adjoining property, the public, and the employees of the owner, subcontractors, and contractor.
17. A statement as to the supervision of the work. The duty of the contractor to have the work properly supervised at all times should be defined in the contract.
18. A statement as to changes in the work, extras, and so on. The contract

should set out in detail the owner's right to order changes in the work and to order extras. Orders for changes or extras should be in writing. Cost of such changes and extras should be determined before the work is done; all changes and extras, and the cost thereof, should be approved in writing by the architect.

19. Provision for correction of defective work, or deductions therefor.
20. A statement as to delays and extensions of time. The rights of the parties in the event of delays or extensions of time should be carefully defined.
21. A statement as to the right to rescind. The circumstances under which the owner may rescind the contract and complete the work, and the contractors' liability, should be carefully set out. Also, the circumstances under which the contractor may rescind the contract, and his rights on rescission, should be set out with equal care.
22. A statement as to insurance and bonds. The contract should state the insurance coverage each party should obtain—contractor's liability insurance; owner's liability insurance; fire, wind, and flood insurance; and so forth—together with a statement as to which party is to be protected by such insurance. Also, if bonds are to be furnished, the nature of the bonds and the beneficiary of the bonds should be set out in detail.
23. A statement as to assignment of the contract. It is customary to include a provision denying the contractor the right to assign the contract.
24. Arbitration. A clause providing for the arbitration of all disputes of every kind and nature that the parties and the architect cannot settle by mutual agreement is recommended. Such clause should set out the procedure to be followed in the arbitration.

## Bonds

### Purpose of Bond

Whenever a person contracts to do public works, he is usually required to execute a bond with sufficient sureties to protect the governmental unit against liability and loss resulting from his defaults. The nature of the bond, the amount of the penalty, the persons protected, and all other material features of the bond will, as a general rule, be set out in the statutes or ordinances of the governmental unit having jurisdiction over the work. We shall not attempt to discuss the features of such bonds.

In private building, the contractor may give a bond to protect the owner from liability and to protect him also against loss resulting from the contractor's failure to perform the contract. Sometimes the owner gives a bond to protect the contractor and others against liability or loss.

### Nature and Scope of Surety's Liability

The extent of the liability of a surety on a contractor's bond or on an owner's bond will not exceed the liability of the contractor or the owner. If the contract is invalid, no action can be maintained against the surety.[46] The scope of the liability of the surety is determined by the provisions of the bond.

Under the common-law rule the provisions of a bond were strictly construed; all ambiguities and doubts were resolved in favor of the surety. Some courts follow this rule if sureties are individuals who are acting without compensation. However, most contractors' bonds are surety bonds, and the majority of courts construe such bonds most strongly against the compensated surety and in favor of the beneficiary under the bond.[47] As a general rule, the provisions of the contract between the owner and the contractor will be taken into consideration in construing the bond.

### Persons Entitled to Benefits of Bond

A carefully drafted bond will state specifically the persons who are the beneficiaries of the bond. The courts have generally held that persons furnishing materials or labor may recover on a building contractor's bond to the owner, when the bond is intended for the owner's protection against the claims of materialmen and laborers, even though they are not named as beneficiaries in the bond.[48]

The intention of the parties is of outstanding importance in determining who is entitled to the benefits of the bond. The intent of the parties to the bond will be determined by reading the bond and the contract between the contractor and owner, and taking into consideration the conduct of the parties and all other surrounding facts and circumstances.

In all cases, if the conditions of the bond are clearly stated and are unequivocal, such conditions will prevail. For example, if the bond is clearly conditioned to indemnify the owner for any pecuniary loss resulting from the breach of any of

---

[46] *Smith Engineering Co.* v. *Rice,* 102 F.2d 492.

[47] *Maryland Casualty Co.* v. *Cunningham,* 234 Ala. 80, 173 So. 506.

[48] *Knight & Jillson Co.* v. *Castle et al.,* 172 Ind. 97, 87 N.E. 976.

the terms of the contract between the contractor and the owner, materialmen and laborers would have no right of action on the bond.

Phoenix Indemnity Company (hereinafter referred to as Phoenix) executed a performance bond as surety in connection with a contractor's public construction contract, by the terms of which Phoenix guaranteed the payment by the contractor for materials, supplies, or labor used directly or indirectly by the contractor or subcontractors and, in addition, provided for the payment of all bills for "*services* furnished to the principal in connection with the contract." The contractor failed to pay the premiums on liability insurance which, under the terms of the contract, he was obligated to carry. Suit was brought against the contractor and Phoenix to recover a judgment for the amount of the premiums. Phoenix contended that its bond did not guarantee payment of such items as insurance premiums. The trial court entered a judgment against Phoenix, and it appealed. The judgment was affirmed.

Judge Sturgis said: "While this is a case of first impression in Florida, it is the general rule that whether a surety for compensation will be held liable for unpaid insurance premiums depends strictly upon the terms of the bond as construed in the light of applicable statutes.

"Contracts of suretyship for compensation are to be construed most strongly against the surety and in favor of the indemnity which the obligee has reasonable grounds to expect. They are regarded in the nature of an insurance contract and are governed by rules applicable to such contracts. The maxim that 'sureties are favored in the law' has no application to contracts of suretyship by one engaged in the business for hire. The provisions of the bond should be considered as a whole and given that effect which was logically intended by the parties as shown by the entire instrument. Applying those principles to the admitted facts in this case, it is apparent that the contractor and surety knew that no work could be done under the contract until the insurance was provided, that premiums would be charged therefor, that the insurer would become obligated to perform services on behalf of the contractor, and that such services would be consumed in the course of the work in the same sense that other materials were consumed, such as electricity, steam, transportation, and the like, which are not physical and visible materials.

"We recognize the word 'services' as having a connotation distinct from 'labor, material and supplies,' although the latter may to some extent be connected with the former. By the Mechanics' Lien Law the lien is imposed for the services of certain persons who usually are employed by the owner rather than the contractor, namely, architects, landscape architects, and engineers. The Mechanics' Lien Law also recognizes 'services' of persons other than materialmen and laborers. Thus persons who enter into contracts with the contractor for performance of part of the contractor's work are defined as subcontractors and are provided with a lien for their 'services.' Under its terms, the contract in suit could not have been fulfilled without the 'services' rendered by the appellee or some other insurer rendering a like service." *Phoenix Indemnity Company* v. *Board of Public Instruction of Alachua County,* Fla., App., 114 So.2d 478 (1959).

## Discharge of Surety

Usually, any alteration in the contract to build, any extension of time for performance, or any other change in the contract, if such change would affect the risk of the surety, will discharge the surety, unless he consents thereto.[49]

Any breach of a duty imposed on the owner will discharge the surety, if such breach will result in an increase of the risks of the surety. For example, if the contract requires the owner to keep the work insured against damage by fire and the owner fails to insure, thus resulting in a loss that injures the surety, the surety will be discharged.

As a general rule, a contract to build will include a provision permitting alterations as the work progresses. Although there is some diversity in the cases, the courts have usually held that if alterations are permitted by the contract, the making of alterations without the consent of the surety will not discharge the surety.[50] In all cases, if the bond expressly provides that alterations may be made, the making of alterations will not discharge the surety.

Usually, a contract to build will provide that all alterations must be authorized in writing by the architect and that the cost thereof shall be agreed upon by the parties before the alterations are made. The courts are not in accord as to the effect of making alterations without complying with the formalities set out in the contract. In some jurisdictions the courts have held that failure to observe such formalities will discharge the surety; in others the courts have decided that such formalities are for the benefit of the owner and the contractor, and that they can be waived by them without affecting the liability of the surety.

There are three views as to the effect on the liability of the surety when the owner makes premature payments to the contractor. (1) A few courts hold that premature payments have no effect on the liability of the surety; (2) some courts have held that a prepayment reduces the liability of the surety by the amount of the prepayment; and (3) the majority of the courts hold that premature payment discharges the surety.[51]

---

[49] *Woodruff* v. *Schultz et al.,* 155 Mich. 11, 118 N.W. 579.

[50] *Massachusetts Bonding & Ins. Co.* v. *John R. Thompson Co.,* 88 F.2d 825.

[51] *Anthony P. Miller, Inc.* v. *Needham,* 35 F. Supp. 332.

## Materialmen and Laborers

If a bond expressly makes materialmen and laborers the beneficiaries, a breach of the contract to build will not defeat the rights of the materialmen or laborers to recover in an action against the surety on the bond.[52]

If the surety, with knowledge of facts operating to discharge him from liability, either expressly or impliedly indicates his intention to continue to be bound as surety, he will thereby waive his right to claim he is discharged.[53]

---

[52] *Hochevar* v. *Maryland Casualty Co.,* 114 F.2d 948.

[53] *Spring Garden Building & Loan Assn.* v. *Rhodes,* 126 Pa. Super. 102, 190 A. 530.

# Chapter 19

# Leasing Real Estate

Leases may not be everything in real estate investing or in commercial real estate finance, but they are way ahead of whatever is in second place. The lease is the vehicle by which the owner extracts income from investment real estate. The lease is the vehicle by which the tenant obtains substantially all of the benefits of ownership without having to invest the capital to buy it. The lease is the real collateral to which the banker looks when financing investment building. The lease may convert a capital investment into an ordinary income tax deduction. The lease is also the way in which the residential tenant obtains exclusive possession of desirable living space without the burdens and long-term commitment of home ownership. The lease is of profound importance in the real estate business. Unfortunately, the law of leasehold estates is as archaic as any we will encounter. Many rules governing the landlord-tenant relationship are unchanged over the past 100 years or more. Much of the law must still be found in very old judicial decisions that are difficult to relate to modern business reality.

The negotiation of a commercial lease is an art that requires extensive knowledge of the law of landlord and tenant. Even the preparation of a short-term residential lease is a challenging task that is the province of the real estate lawyer. While many form leases appear to leave a great deal to be desired in terms of clarity and precision, they are far better than reliance upon the common-law rules that would otherwise apply. Throughout this chapter it should be kept in mind that the formal lease contract represents an opportunity to clearly define the relationship between the parties with regard to all details. Failure to take advantage of this opportunity places the parties at the mercy of outmoded common-law rules that may serve neither one of them well.

Despite all of its technicalities the lease provides us with an arrangement that is quite versatile and flexible. It may be short-term (a month is quite common) or it may be long-term (99 years is not unheard of). It may transfer some or all of the burdens of ownership to the tenant, such as the duties to insure, pay taxes, and perform maintenance and repairs. It may transfer to the tenant most of the benefits of ownership, such as the right to erect buildings and to borrow on the strength of the leasehold estate. In short, the lease can be used to tailor-make the interest desired or required by the tenant. This great degree of flexibility does not happen by accident. The lease must be carefully and precisely structured in order that both the landlord and the tenant will receive maximum benefit without undue exposure to loss.

The basic leasehold estates recognized at common law were discussed earlier, in Chapter 3. It is important to recognize that the strict rules relating to these interests have led to the widespread use of specific lease agreements that are intended to avoid these rules. Modern leases are designed to avoid the problems generated by the strict application of the common-law rules. It is rare today to encounter in practice any common-law lease form that has not been modified in some way by the parties. It is nevertheless necessary to explore the common-law rules that would otherwise apply. It is only by doing so that we can understand the significance of the clauses commonly used in the modern lease.

## The Lease

### Essentials of a Valid Lease

In determining whether or not an agreement results in a valid lease, the courts have applied contract law. The parties must reach a mutual agreement (offer and acceptance), their promises must be supported by consideration,[1] the parties must have the capacity to contract, and the objective of the lease must be legal. No particular words are necessary to create the relation of landlord and tenant. The lease may be written, oral, or implied, depending on the circumstances,[2] and the provisions of any applicable statute of the state in which the leased real estate is located will become a part of the lease.

---

[1] *In re Wilson's Estate,* 349 Pa. 646, 37 A.2d 709.

[2] *Cooperative Building Materials, Inc.* v. *Robbins & Larkey et al.,* 80 Cal. App.2d 832, 183 P.2d 81.

A lease will be declared to be void for illegality if it is made with the knowledge and intention of the landlord that the leased premises are to be used for immoral or illegal purposes.[3] There is some diversity of opinion as to what facts would be sufficient to establish "knowledge and intention" on the part of the landlord. Some courts have held that mere knowledge of the illegal use without collusion or participation in the illegal act on the part of the landlord is not sufficient to invalidate the lease. However, the courts have held the lease to be invalid if the landlord, after discovery of the illegal use, sanctions such illegal use.

## Requirement of Writing

The provisions of the statute of frauds generally apply to leases; therefore a lease that will not be performed within one year from the making thereof must be evidenced by a note or memorandum in writing signed by the party to be bound or his duly authorized agent. However, in a few states an oral lease for a period in excess of one year is valid. For example, in Indiana an oral lease for a period not to exceed three years is valid.[4]

If the provisions of the statute of frauds are not complied with, the lease is unenforceable. The courts are not in agreement as to the character of the tenancy arising when a person enters into the occupancy of the real estate under an unenforceable lease. Some courts hold that the tenancy is a tenancy at will.[5] Other courts have held that the term of the tenancy is for the same period of time as that provided for the payment of rent in the unenforceable lease. For example, if rent is payable in monthly installments, the tenancy will be a tenancy from month to month; whereas if the rent is payable in yearly installments, the tenancy will be a tenancy from year to year. A few states have held that the tenancy will be for the period of time that can be lawfully created by a parol (oral) agreement.[6]

Minnie Newsom had a life estate in premises known as the Cox survey. Her stepson, C. W. Newsom, had inherited a one-half interest in the land. He was in possession of the land, and Mrs. Newsom brought suit to recover possession and to obtain $1,400 rent. She based her claim to rent on an oral four-year lease. The court granted Mrs. Newsom possession of the land but denied her a judgment for the rent on the ground that the oral four-year lease was unenforceable. On appeal, the denial of the judgment for rent was affirmed.

---

[3] *Weizman et al.* v. *Chapin,* 51 Ohio Abs. 26, 79 N.E.2d 668.

[4] *Burns Indiana Statutes (Annotated),* 1949 Replacement, Title 33, Sec. 101.

[5] *Greenway Wood Heel Co., Inc.* v. *John Shea Co.,* 313 Mass. 177, 46 N.E.2d 746.

[6] *Lyle* v. *Munson,* 213 Mich. 250, 181 N.W. 1002.

Chief Justice Grissom said: "Mrs. Minnie Newsom contends the judgment should be reversed insofar as it denies her recovery of rent on the Cox survey. The court found that Mrs. Newsom orally leased the Cox survey to C. W. Newsom for a term longer than one year. We agree with the court's holding that this parol agreement was unenforceable under the statute of frauds. The court correctly denied Mrs. Newsom a judgment for rent on the Cox survey." *C. W. Newsom* v. *Mrs. Minnie L. Newsom,* Tex. Civ. App., 371 S.W.2d 894 (1963)

## Execution of the Lease

As a general rule, the lease must be signed by the landlord. Since it is, in effect, a conveyance of an interest in real estate, the signature of the landlord is necessary to give effect to the lease. Although the signature of the landlord's spouse is not essential to the validity of a lease, the spouse should sign if it is a long-term lease, thereby conveying or releasing any claim to a dower interest in the leased real estate that would be adverse to the rights of the tenant.

If the tenant enters into possession under the lease, his signature is generally not essential to the validity of the lease; however, the absence of the tenant's signature may, under some circumstances, render the lease invalid. Good business practice requires the signing of the lease by both the landlord and the tenant.

Whether a lease will be valid without attestation or acknowledgment will depend on the statutes of the state in which the real estate is located. As a general rule, neither attestation nor acknowledgment is essential to the validity of the lease. However, if the lease is to be recorded, it must be executed in compliance with the recording statutes of the state in which the real estate is located. The statutes of some states expressly provide for the recording of leases for a term of five years or longer.

As is true of written instruments generally, the lease, in order to be operative, must be delivered and accepted.

## Parties to a Lease

The correct names and addresses of the parties to a lease should be set out with the same degree of care as is exercised in naming the parties to a deed. If the landlord is married, the spouse should be joined, so that any interest that the spouse may have in the property will be bound by the lease.

If the leased real estate is owned by joint tenants or tenants by the entirety, all the tenants should join in the execution of the lease. If the landlord or tenant is a corporation, its authority to execute the lease should be checked. Likewise, if the landlord or tenant is a fiduciary, the power of such fiduciary to execute the lease should be carefully investigated.

If a lease is signed by an agent of the landlord, it should be signed in the name of the landlord, with the name of the agent added, together with appropriate words designating that the agent is signing in a representative capacity. If the lease is a long-term lease that should be recorded, the agent's authority should be in writing and executed with such formality as will make the lease eligible for recordation.

### Description of Premises

The premises leased should be so described that their extent is clearly stated. A description by street number should never be used, since such a description does not identify the land intended to be included in the lease. If a lease of an entire building describes the premises by street number, the courts usually hold, in the absence of facts showing a contrary intent, that the lease includes the land generally used in connection with the building.

If the lease is for a part of a building—such as a floor of a building, office space, or an apartment—the extent of the premises should be carefully set out. If the tenant is to have the privilege of using storage space in the basement or other part of the building, such fact should be stated in the lease, since the terms of a written lease cannot be added to or altered by parol evidence.[7] In describing the leased premises, it is wise to follow the practice used in a description of real estate being conveyed by a deed and, in addition, to include a statement of the tenant's right to light and air, and use of driveways, alleys, stairways, elevators, halls, and so forth, especially if the entire premises are not leased to a single tenant.[8] If the lease is for a part of a building, the attachment of blueprints of the leased premises will make more certain the area leased.

### Examination of Title

As a general rule, the tenant does not demand that the landlord furnish an abstract certified to date for examination. Such a practice would be wholly unwarranted if the lease were for a relatively short term. However, if the lease is for a long term, such as 50 or 99 years, and the tenant is to construct a building on the leased real estate, he should exercise the same precautions as he would if he were purchasing the property.

### Statement of Term

The term of a lease is the time the lease will run and should be set forth with precise dates. Good business practice requires that the date of the beginning

---

[7] *Harmony Cafeteria* v. *International Supply Co.,* 249 Ill. App. 532.

[8] *Richard Paul, Inc.* v. *Union Improvement Co.,* 33 Del. Ch. 113, 91 A.2d 49.

of the term and the date of its ending be stated, together with a statement of the total period of the lease. The following would be an acceptable statement for the term of a lease: "for a term of 10 years beginning July 1, 1965, and ending June 30, 1975." If a lease states that the term is for "10 years from July 1, 1965," there is a diversity in the decisions as to whether the term commences on July 1 or on July 2. If the statement of the term is ambiguous and the court cannot determine with reasonable certainty the period for which the lease is to run, it will hold that the lease creates a tenancy at will.[9]

The courts have held that a lease is valid if it may be renewed at the option of the tenant as often as the tenant may elect to do so. However, the courts do not favor such terms in a lease, and will hold that a perpetual lease has not been created unless the language of the lease and the surroundings clearly indicate that such was the intention of the parties.

In some states, there is a statutory limitation on the terms of agricultural leases; and in some states, leases for 100 years or more are prohibited by statute.

On October 3, 1958, Kalicki's predecessor in title, as landlord, entered into an "advertising lease" with Bell as tenant. The lease was "for a term of one or more years at a yearly rental of $15 payable in equal annual installments, and the Landlord grants the Tenant an option to renew this lease for like period or periods at the same rental." The lease provided that it "shall enure to the benefit of and be binding upon the personal representatives, heirs, successors and assigns of the parties hereto." Kalicki gave Bell notice of termination of the lease as of October 3, 1962. Bell refused to recognize the legality of the termination notice, and Kalicki brought an action for unlawful detainer. Judgment for Kalicki, and Bell appealed. Judgment was affirmed.

J. A. D. Sullivan said: "The ruling by the trial court was correct. The law does not favor perpetual leases or covenants for continued renewals of a lease which tend to create a perpetuity. An option for renewal of a lease will not be construed as granting to the tenant the right of perpetual renewals unless the intention to create such right is clearly and unequivocally expressed in the instrument.

" '. . . It is the rule that a provision in a lease in general terms for a renewal or continuance of the lease will be construed as providing for only one renewal. This rule is based on the principle that the courts do not favor perpetuities, and unless the lease expressly or by clear implication provides that the second lease shall contain a covenant for future or perpetual renewals, it will be construed as providing for only a single renewal. . . .' 32 Am. Jur., Landlord and Tenant, p. 968, p. 813 (1941).

"Thus, it has been held that a provision in a lease (with privilege of renewals for similar

---

[9] *Farris* v. *Hershfield,* 325 Mass. 176, 89 N.E.2d 636.

periods) did not entitle the tenant to more than one renewal." *Kalicki* v. *Bell,* 83 N.J. Super. 139, 199 A.2d 158 (1964).

### Possession of Leased Premises

In many, but not all, states the landlord is bound to give the tenant actual possession of the leased premises. If the premises are occupied by a holdover tenant or adverse claimant at the date for the beginning of the term, the landlord would owe a duty to bring whatever action was necessary to recover possession and would have to bear the expense of putting the tenant in possession.[10] In some states the landlord is bound to give the tenant only the right of possession; in case the premises are occupied, the tenant himself must bring action to recover possession.[11] The tenant, for his own protection, should insist that the lease provide that the landlord would put the tenant in actual possession of the leased premises at the beginning of the term.

### Rent

Rent is the consideration paid for the use and occupation of property. Parliament, by statute in 1738, gave a landlord the right to recover, as rent, the reasonable value of the use and occupation of land, even though there was no provision in the lease whereby the tenant expressly promised to pay rent. Many states have enacted similar statutes, and in other states the landlord has been allowed to recover reasonable rent on the theory that such right is a part of the common law. The payment of rent is not essential, however, for the creation of the landlord-tenant relation, and such relation can be created by express agreement without a duty to pay for the use and occupation of the property.[12]

Rent is usually payable in money but may be paid in service or in property other than money. It may also be paid by the surrendering of some right or by the assumption of some burden on the part of the tenant, which right or burden he is not legally bound to surrender or assume. The lease should clearly define the rent to be paid and the medium to be used; and if no rent is to be paid, the lease should so state.

If there is in the lease no provision that stipulates when, where, and how the reserved rent is to be paid, and if, at the same time, there is no statute or established custom that controls, the rent will be payable at the end of the term of the

---

[10] *Adrian* v. *Rabinowitz,* 116 N.J.L. 586, 186 A. 29.

[11] *Ward et al.* v. *Hudson et al.,* 199 Miss. 171, 24 So.2d 329.

[12] *Enslein* v. *Enslein,* 84 Ohio App. 532, 82 N.E.2d 555.

lease, at the location of the leased premises, and in one payment. It is therefore customary to include in the lease an express provision defining when, where, and how the rent shall be paid.

For example, if the term of the lease is five years, the yearly rental $2,400, and the place of payment the office of the manager of the real estate, the following provisions would define the payment of rent adequately: "The lessee agrees to pay the lessor as rent for said premises, at the rate of $2,400 per annum, from January 1, 1965, to December 31, 1969, payable in equal monthly payments, in advance, on the first day of every month at the office of Bryan Realty Co., 163 Main Street, Odon, Indiana, or at such other place as the lessor may designate."

After a lease is in force, a promise by the landlord to reduce the rent or a promise by the tenant to pay additional rent is of doubtful validity. The courts have, in most instances, considered a lease to be a contract and have held a promise to reduce or to increase the rent to be void for lack of consideration. Some states have, however, enacted statutes that provide that a promise by a landlord to reduce rent is valid, even though not supported by consideration, if such promise is in writing.

A carefully drafted lease should clearly define rent concessions, such as, for instance, free rent for a period as a bonus for prompt payment of rent, or credit on rent for repairs made or for services rendered by the tenant, if any such concessions are to be made; and in the event the lease grants the tenant renewal rights, it should clearly state whether or not the rent concessions are to apply to the renewal or holdover term of the lease.

The lease, especially a long-term lease, may, in addition to the payment of stipulated installments of rent, provide that the tenant will pay all real estate taxes and special assessments, will pay all water and sewer taxes, will keep the buildings insured and pay the premiums on such insurance, and will pay all other similar expenses. If such a provision is included in the lease, arrangement should be made for adjustment if the tax period or insurance period and the lease period do not coincide.

If the tenant is to pay water, sewer, and like charges, a provision should be made for the separate metering of such services, and they should be clearly defined. A provision in a lease that the tenant is to pay charges for water will not impose on him an obligation to pay charges for sewer service.[13]

If the lease provides that as part of the rent the tenant is to assume the burden

---

[13] *Black* v. *General Wiper Supply Co.,* 305 N.Y. 386, 113 N.E.2d 528.

of keeping the premises insured and is to pay the premium, the lease should set out in detail the risks to be covered by the insurance. In addition, the lease should provide that the property be insured with insurance companies that are reasonably satisfactory to the landlord and that the insurance policies, together with evidence of the payment of the premiums, be delivered to the landlord. Failure of the tenant to obtain the required insurance within a reasonable time after notice by the landlord is a default on the part of the tenant, and the landlord should be granted the right to obtain the required insurance and charge the premiums to the tenant.

The courts have held that failure to pay extra rent in the form of taxes, special assessments, insurance, electricity, water, and so forth, where the lease expressly provides that the tenant shall make such payments, is a default that gives the landlord the right to bring dispossession proceedings for nonpayment of rent.[14]

### Stabilizing Rent Return

The purchasing power of the dollar fluctuates from time to time; and over long periods, it has consistently decreased. In drafting long-term leases, therefore, it is desirable to provide for increases or decreases in rent to compensate for this fluctuation. So-called escalator clauses similar to those included in labor contracts have been used; these are based on the consumer price index or on some similar index for determining price fluctuations. In some instances the value of the leased property is used as the basis for determining rent, and provision is made in the lease for periodic reappraisal of the leased property. The most common basis used in commercial leases is the amount of the business transacted on the premises by the tenant. Such leases are termed *percentage leases.*

### Percentage Leases

Percentage leases are used in the mercantile business. The rent to be paid is based, at least in part, on a percentage of the business transacted on the premises by the tenant. The lease may provide for the payment of a minimum monthly rental plus a percentage of gross sales over and above a stated amount; it may provide for the payment of a monthly rental plus a percentage of gross sales; or it may provide for the payment of a monthly rental plus a percentage of gross sales, with a maximum rental. In some instances the percentage may be based on net income or gross profits; but such provisions are not recommended, because of the difficulty of determining net income or gross profits.

A percentage lease should carefully define the basis on which the rent is to

[14] *Chicago Housing Authority* v. *Bild,* 346 Ill. App. 272, 104 N.E.2d 666.

be computed. It should state the period for determing sales—that is, monthly, annually, or some other period—and whether there is to be a "carry-over" from one period to another. It should also carefully define gross sales and should state definitely whether merchandise returns, unpaid charge accounts, discounts allowed for prompt payment or payment of cash, and so forth, are included.

The type of report to be submitted by the tenant and the landlord's right to inspect the books of the tenant should be definitely set out in the lease. Generally, if the lease provides for the payment of a maximum rent and the tenant pays the maximum, the lease should provide that the landlord is not entitled to an accounting or the right to inspect the tenant's books.

The lease should provide that the tenant shall conduct the business continually throughout the year; or if the business is seasonal and is not operated during a part of the year, the lease should include a clause providing for the adjustment of rent and defining the basis for the adjustment. There are cases that hold that the court will not imply in a percentage lease a covenant that requires the tenant to continue the business for which the premises are leased.[15]

Stern leased premises at 108 North Front Street to Richard Stark. The lease provided that it could be assigned, the assignee assuming all the obligations under the lease, and that the premises were to be used for the purpose of operating a retail store for the sale of general wearing apparel and for no other purpose without the written consent of the lessor. The term was for five years, from August 15, 1956, to August 14, 1961. The rent received was 5½ percent of the annual gross sales, "provided that in no event shall the annual rental agreed to be paid by the lessee during said period be less than $4,800." The $4,800 fixed minimum was payable $400 on the fifteenth of each and every month, beginning August 15, 1958. Stark leased the adjoining building, 110 North Front Street, and requested permission to break through the wall and connect the two buildings, but Stern refused to give such permission.

During the last two years of the lease period, Stark made no sales from 108 North Front Street but used it for office space and display purposes and paid the minimum rent each month. Stern sued to recover a judgment based on 5½ percent of the gross sales made from 110 North Front Street. The court denied Stern a judgment; and on appeal, the decision was affirmed.

Judge Gabel said: "Where a lease provides for rental based on a percentage of sales with a *fixed substantial adequate minimum,* and there is no express covenant or agreement to occupy and use the premises, no implied covenant or agreement will be inferred that the lessee is bound to occupy and use the premises for the purpose expressed in the lease. Under such a lease, lessee has no obligation to occupy and use the premises for any stated definite period of time and his obligation under such a lease is limited to the

---

[15] *Dickey* v. *Philadelphia Minit-Man Corp.,* 377 Pa. 549, 105 A.2d 580.

payment of the basic minimum rental to the end of the term when he no longer occupies and uses the premises for the purpose expressed in the lease.

"It is therefore the judgment of the Court that first, the defendants cannot be charged with any fraud, deceit, scheme or plan to divert business from the leased premises. Second, the express conditions of said lease have not been breached by the defendants. Third, there is no express or implied covenant in said lease requiring defendants to occupy and use the premises for the sale of general wearing apparel. Fourth, the lessee in paying the minimum rental of $4,800.00 per annum paid a substantial adequate rental and the plaintiffs are not entitled to any percentage of sales made in the adjoining premises." *Kretch* v. *Stark,* 92 Ohio Abs. 47, 193 N.E.2d 307 (1962).

### Security for Payment of Rent

The landlord may secure the payment of the rent provided in the lease (1) by contracting for a lien on the tenant's property, (2) by requiring the tenant to pay a portion of the rent in advance, (3) by requiring the tenant to post security, or (4) by requiring the tenant to have some third person guarantee the payment of the rent. In some states the landlord is given a statutory lien on the crops and on the tenant's personal property that is on the leased premises.

The nature of the lien acquired by the landlord by inserting in the lease a clause giving him a lien on the property of the tenant as security will depend on the language of the lease. A lease clause giving a landlord a lien on the tenant's property as security for the payment of rent has been held in different cases to be a chattel mortgage, an equitable lien, and/or a declaration of trust. Such a lien has generally been held to be valid, but it will not attach to the property of a third person that has been brought onto the premises by the tenant.

As a general rule, the landlord's lien is enforceable against the tenant and all persons claiming through him with notice of the lien, but it is not enforceable without notice against good-faith purchasers for value. Whether or not the landlord can protect his interests by recording or filing the lease or a notice of the lien will depend on the statutes of the state in which the real estate is located.

The landlord may require the tenant to pay a substantial portion of the rent in advance. If the provision in the lease is properly worded and the payment is held to be a payment of rent in advance, the landlord may, on default by the tenant, retain the rent paid. However, if the provision in the lease is not carefully worded, the court may hold the advance payment to be a deposit of money as security, and require the landlord, on breach of the lease by the tenant, to refund to the tenant any amount of the deposit over and above proven damages.[16]

---

[16] *Brooks et al.* v. *Coppedge,* 71 Idaho 166, 228 P.2d 248, 27 A.L.R.2d 645.

The tenant may post security for the payment of rent. The security posted usually takes the form of cash or securities, such as stocks and bonds, or it may be both cash and securities. If cash is deposited with the landlord as security, some courts have held that a debtor-creditor relation is created and that the landlord may use such money as he wishes. Other courts have decided that the landlord holds the deposit as pledgee and that his use of the deposit in his business is not authorized.[17]

If securities are deposited, the landlord will hold such securities as pledgee. In the absence of a provision in the lease to the contrary, the tenant will be entitled to the income from the securities so long as he is not in default. Generally, the provision for the deposits of securities will permit the tenant to substitute securities, provided the market value of the securities deposited does not fall below a stated amount.

Instead of depositing money or securities with the landlord, the tenant may have some person, either as guarantor or as surety, guarantee the payment of the rent. A guarantee must be in writing and signed by the guarantor or surety.

The person acting as guarantor or surety may sign, with the tenant, the lease in which the guarantee provision is included; or he may sign a separate guarantee agreement. In the event payment of rent is guaranteed by a guarantor or surety, the landlord should not enter into any agreement with the tenant that alters in any way the material provisions of the lease, unless the guarantor or surety consents to the alteration. Any alteration of the terms of the lease without the consent of the guarantor or surety will release the guarantor or surety from his liability on the lease, unless he later ratifies the alteration.

Several states have enacted statutes giving the landlord a lien on the tenant's crops and personal property on the leased premises for unpaid rent. Such statutes are not uniform in their provisions, and the statutes of the state in which the real estate is located apply.

In October 1952, Gordon Motors, Inc., leased certain premises from Martin for a term of five years. In February 1954, Gordon Motors, Inc., was placed in receivership, and the lease was abandoned. Martin then released the premises at the same rental but for a five-year period from May 1, 1954. At the time Gordon Motors, Inc., executed the lease, it paid five months' rent in advance. The rent provision in the lease relative to the advance payment was as follows:

> The Tenant further covenants and agrees at the time of the signing of this lease to pay the Landlord the sum of Three Thousand One Hundred and Eighty-Seven Dollars and Fifty Cents ($3,187.50), representing rental for the months of June, July, August,

---

[17] *Colantuoni* v. *Balene,* 95 N.J. Eq. 748, 123 A. 541.

September and October, 1957, less the sum of Seven Hundred Seventeen Dollars and Twenty Cents ($717.20), representing interest at 4½% for the term of five (5) years, or a net sum of Two Thousand and Four Hundred Seventy Dollars and Thirty Cents ($2,470.30). This payment is for the rent of such months exclusively and does not relieve the Tenant from his obligation to pay the sum of $637.50 on the first day of each and every month during the continuance except the months of June, July, August, September and October, 1957.

After the expiration of the term, Lochner, receiver for Gordon Motors, Inc., demanded that Martin refund the advance payment made by Gordon Motors, Inc. The new lessee had paid the rent in full. Martin refused, and Lochner brought suit to recover a judgment for the advance rent. The trial court held that Martin was entitled to retain the advance rent, and Lochner appealed. The judgment was affirmed.

Judge Prescot said: "The chancellor thought that the recent case of *Tatelbaum* v. *Chertkof* was controlling, and we agree. In cases of this nature, where a lease requires payment of rent in advance as distinguished from a security deposit, it is well-established law that the lessor may retain the payment upon default of the leasee in paying rent for a previous period, constituting a breach of the lease, in the absence of a provision for its refund, for the right and title thereto passes upon the execution of the lease or the payment required, and prevention of its application to the part of the term for which it was paid arises from the lessee's own misconduct.

"The reasons for the above principle are apparent. Rent does not accrue from day to day, but accrues on the day it is payable. Accordingly, the rent herein involved, although paid for a portion of the term four and one-half years in the future, was accrued, and became the property of the landlord, on the day it was paid.

"Ordinarily in determining whether money paid as in the case at bar be a payment of rent or a deposit for security, we must arrive at the intention of the parties as manifested in the terms of the lease construed in the light of surrounding circumstances. It is, of course, significant that the parties in the lease specifically termed the payment as 'rent.'

"We hold that as the money was received by the appellees for the payment of rent in advance, title thereto passed unto the appellees at the time of payment; and, under the circumstances of this case, they are not unjustly enriched by its retention." *Lochner* v. *Martin,* 218 Md. 519, 147 A.2d 749 (1959).

## Use of Leased Real Estate

In determining the tenant's right to use the leased real estate, the courts treat his interest as property and apply the rules of law relative to the alienation of property. The tenant's right to the use and occupation of the property gives him complete control, and anyone, including the landlord, who comes onto the property, without the tenant's consent, express or implied, is liable to him in an action of trespass. The tenant may use the leased real estate for any lawful purpose unless the purpose for which it may be used is expressly set out in the lease.[18] He may not commit waste; that is, he may not do anything that would damage the reversion, such as, for instance, tear down buildings or cut ornamental trees.

The tenant's use of the leased real estate may be limited by provisions in the lease that specify that the property shall be used only for certain purposes or that prohibit certain designated uses. Any provision in a lease limiting the use of the premises will be strictly construed; if the provision is ambiguous, it will be construed most strongly against the landlord and in favor of the tenant; consequently, restrictive covenants in a lease should be drafted with great care.

A provision limiting the use of the premises to stated purposes *only* will be upheld; but if the stated purpose becomes illegal or is prohibited by governmental regulations, the lease may be terminated on the ground of commercial frustration. If the use provision is so drafted, however, that the restriction is general rather than specific and the circumstances are such that the tenant's use of the property is not totally or almost totally defeated by the regulation, the courts have generally held that the lease is not terminated.[19]

The tenant may wish to have a provision included in the lease whereby the landlord promises not to lease other parts of the building for competing uses. If such a provision does not expressly provide that the landlord himself shall not operate a competing business in the building, he will not be prohibited from doing so. Such restrictive provisions are valid; they are not contracts in restraint of trade. If restrictive provisions are not carefully worded, they may become the source of considerable ligitation.[20]

If a tenant leases an entire building for business purposes, he will have, in the absence of a restrictive provision in the lease, the right to maintain signs on the outer walls and to erect signs on the roof.[21] As a general rule, signs cannot be maintained on residential property; consequently, if anyone, such as a doctor or dentist, leases residential property and wishes to put up a sign on the property, he should see that the lease defines his right to maintain a sign.

If the tenant leases only a part of a building, he may maintain signs on the part of the premises that he leases, provided there is no clause in the lease restricting his right. If he wishes to erect a protruding sign, a license may be required, in which case the tenant would have to acquire the license. In all leases, provisions defining the tenant's right to maintain signs should be included.

---

[18] *Bovin* v. *Galitzka,* 250 N.Y. 228, 165 N.E. 273.

[19] *Lloyd et al.* v. *Murphy,* Cal.2d 48, 153 P.2d 47.

[20] *Peoples Trust Co.* v. *Schultz Novelty & Sporting Goods Co., Inc.,* 244 N.Y. 14, 154 N.E. 649.

[21] *400 North Rush, Inc.* v. *D. J. Bielzoff Products Co.,* 347 Ill. App. 123, 106 N.E.2d 208.

On October 6, 1958, Weiss leased a storeroom to Speedi. The purpose clause of the lease read as follows:

"7. Lessee covenants that during the term of this lease or any renewal thereof: *(a)* It will use the leased premises for the conduct of a self-service laundry and the sale and display of such items as are normally sold by self-service laundries."

On October 14, 1958, Weiss leased to Bevy the adjoining storeroom to be used to "conduct and carry on a general laundry business in all its branches; to conduct and carry on the business of cleaning, pressing. . . ." The lease further provided that during the term of the lease the lessors "will not suffer occupancy of any storeroom building owned by them . . . by another dry cleaning or shirt laundry or combination of the two within a radius of three miles from the premises herein described excepting a coin-operated automatic laundry situated in the adjacent storeroom."

On November 19, 1962, Speedi started installation of two coin-operated dry cleaning machines, and Bevy brought an action asking that Speedi be enjoined "from installing and/or operating any dry cleaning equipment in the premises. . . ." The trial court refused to grant the injunction; and on appeal, the injunction was granted.

Presiding Judge Kovachy said: "Accordingly, we hold that the purpose clause of the Speedi lease was couched in plain, ordinary and unambiguous language; that in the light of the surrounding circumstances and the situation of the parties, the unmistakable import of the expression 'for the conduct of self-service laundry' was that the lessee be permitted to conduct a business for the washing of clothes with coin-operated washing machines; that the parties clearly understood and intended that only such business be conducted on the premises; that the use of coin-operated dry cleaning machines did not come within the purview of the purpose clause incorporated in the Speedi lease and that as a consequence the judgment of the Court of Common Pleas was contrary to law.

"It follows, therefore, that Speedi, by installing the two coin-operated dry cleaning machines, was competing with the dry cleaning business of Bevy's in direct violation of the lease granted it by lessors to the irreparable injury of Bevy's. Furthermore, Bevy's had a binding written promise from the lessors to protect it from competition in its business insofar as the rental of property owned by the lessors was concerned and since the lessors had failed to take steps to protect Bevy's in the matter, Bevy's had the right to invoke a court of equity to enjoin Speedi from installing and continuing the use of coin-operated dry cleaning machines in competition with it in its dry cleaning business." *Bevy's Dry Cleaning and Shirt Laundry, Inc.* v. *Streble,* Ohio App., 194 N.E.2d 595 (1963).

Davis leased certain premises to Wickline. The lease included the following paragraph:

"Fourth: It is covenanted and agreed between the contracting parties that during the term of this lease the premises hereby leased shall be used for the purpose of a drug store and for no other purpose—and that during the term of this lease or any renewal thereof the lessee shall operate the premises as a drug store."

Wickline ceased to operate the drugstore and did not use the premises for any other purpose but continued to pay the reserved rent. Davis contends that Wickline is obligated to operate a drugstore on the premises during the entire term of the lease. The trial court held that Wickline was not obligated to operate a drugstore on the premises; and on appeal, the judgment was affirmed.

Justice Wittle said: "In addition to what has been said two well defined rules of construction mitigate against the position urged by Davis in this case: (1) a contract of lease is to be construed favorably to the lessee and against the lessor; and (2) breach of covenant to sustain forfeiture is construed strictly against forfeiture. The instrument must give the right of forfeiture in terms so clear and explicit as to leave no room for any other construction.

"Keeping these principles in mind an examination of paragraph 'Fourth' of the lease is in order. The pertinent clauses are: . . . the premises hereby leased shall be used for the purpose of a drugstore and for no other purpose.'

"This clause is clearly restrictive in nature, simply requiring the building to be used for no other purpose than a drug store. The remaining clause: 'and that during the term of this lease or any renewal thereof the Lessee shall operate said premises as a drug store.'

"This latter clause simply makes the restriction of the first clause applicable to the option to renew for a ten year term which was granted to Wickline under the lease.

"If it had been intended by Davis that Wickline operate, at all costs, a drug store for ten years, such a burdensome obligation should have been spelled out in clear and explicit terms and should have included some standard of measurement by which the conduct of Wickline could have been measured.

"We have been cited to no authority, nor have we found any, supporting Davis' contention in this case." *Davis* v. *Wickline,* Va., 135 S.E.2d 812 (1964).

## Repairs

At common law the tenant had an implied duty to make those minor repairs necessary to preserve the property in substantially the same condition as that at the commencement of the term, ordinary wear excepted. Conditions have changed radically, especially as applied to residential tenancies, and such tenants seldom make or are expected to make even minor repairs. Several states have enacted statutes either expressly imposing on the lessor a duty to keep the leased premises in reasonable repair or making his failure to repair punishable by fine or imprisonment.

In multiple-unit residential property and in office buildings the landlord usually contracts to provide such services as heat, air conditioning, hot water, elevators, and janitor. The landlord, as a general rule, retains control over the common elements—for instance, stairways, halls, lobbies, and entrances; and he therefore owes a duty to keep them in reasonable repair, and if he fails to do so, and, as a result of his breach of duty, a tenant, a guest of a tenant, or an invitee is injured, the landlord may be held liable in tort.

The lease may set out the duties of the landlord and tenant to make repairs. Repair provisions in a lease should state clearly the scope of the duties of the party who has agreed to make repairs. For example, a provision granting the landlord the right to enter the premises and make repairs imposes on the landlord no duty to make repairs.[22]

The extent of the obligation of the party who has agreed to make repairs will depend primarily on the language of the provision in the lease. A general provision to make repairs will not impose on the promisor an obligation to make structural changes in the building or to make improvements. An agreement to repair will not, as a general rule, require the promisor to restore the building to a sound or good state and to maintain it in a condition suitable for the purposes for which it is leased. In general, if a tenant agrees to keep the leased premises in repair, he is obligated to place and keep the buildings in reasonable repair.[23] An agreement to keep the leased premises in repair does not impose an obligation to rebuild a structure destroyed without the fault of the promisor.

A promise to repair made by a tenant of only part of a building imposes on him no obligation to repair parts of the building that he does not occupy. Likewise, a promise by the landlord to make specific repairs imposes on him no obligation to make repairs not specified.

A provision for repairs should clearly state whether or not the party assuming the obligation to make repairs is to repair the inside or the outside of the building, or both, and whether or not repairs to the roof are included.

If the landlord is to make repairs, he has implied assent to enter and make repairs. As a general rule, if the landlord is obligated to make repairs, he is not in default unless he has actual or constructive notice of the need for repairs, or has actual knowledge that repairs are needed and has had a reasonable opportunity to make them.[24]

In November, 1954, National Biscuit Company (NBC) leased three warehouses from Baehr. The lease provided that the lessor would keep the building painted, make all outside repairs and all repairs of a permanent nature, and all alterations and additions required by fire underwriters, public utility companies, or municipal or state authority. Paragraph 10 of the lease provided as follows:

> 10. The Lessee covenants and agrees during the continuance of this lease to maintain landscape planting and to make all ordinary interior repairs and it is hereby agreed that any single repair job, the reasonable cost of which is $100.00 or over and which

[22] *Stone* v. *Sullivan,* 360 Mass. 450, 15 N.E.2d 476.

[23] *Ingalls et al.* v. *Roger Smith Hotels Corporation,* 143 Conn. 1, 118 A.2d 463.

[24] *Harris* v. *Edge et al.,* 92 Ga. App. 827, 90 S.E.2d 47.

> is not clearly an ordinary interior repair as distinguished from a structural repair or a repair of a permanent character, shall be considered a repair of a permanent character under the terms of this lease. Lessee agrees to make all repairs whatsoever on the demised premises made necessary by the negligence, carelessness, misconduct, or fault of the Lessee or its agents, licensees or invitees.

Incinerators in the warehouses needed extensive repairs and the parties agreed that new ones should be installed. The cost of the new incinerators installed was $1,188 each, or a total of $3,564. NBC installed the three incinerators and sued Baehr for the recovery of the cost of making the three installations. The court granted NBC a judgment; and on appeal, the judgment was affirmed.

Judge Ervin said: "It is a hornbook law that where the terms of a lease are not ambiguous, interpretation and construction of the contract are questions for the court. The court's function is to determine the intention of the parties from the language used.

"We agree with the interpretation placed upon these leases by the court below. We think it is clear that the repair here involved was one of a permanent character and that if there was any doubt about this question, the $100.00 provision of paragraph 10 requires that it be treated as a repair of a permanent character, the responsibility for which rested upon the lessor." *National Biscuit Company* v. *Baehr Brothers,* Pa. Super., 199 A.2d 494 (1964).

### Landlord's Rights to Enter and Inspect

The landlord has no right to enter the leased premises or those parts of the leased premises that are in the exclusive occupation of the tenant, unless such privilege is provided for by the terms of the lease. Generally, a lease will grant to the landlord the right to inspect the premises during the term of the lease. Such a provision should clearly define the landlord's right to inspect, stating the frequency of his inspections and the time of day when he is to make his inspections.

If the landlord is to be permitted to show the premises to prospective purchasers or lessees, his rights in this respect should be defined with a reasonable degree of certainty.

### Tenant's Tort Liability

The tenant has the exclusive right to the occupation and control of the premises during the term of the lease; consequently, he is primarily liable for the conditions and use of the premises. If the tenant creates a nuisance on the premises, he will be answerable to those suffering therefrom. He will also be liable in tort for damages to persons who are injured while on the premises, provided such injury results from a breach of duty owed to the injured person by the tenant. The fact that the use of the premises by the tenant is not a violation of the provisions of the lease does not relieve him from liability to third persons.

Any use of property that results in an unreasonable interference with another's use and enjoyment of his property is a nuisance. No one has absolute freedom in the use of his property, since he must be restrained in his use by the existence of equal rights in his neighbor to the use of the neighbor's property. Such a rule does not prohibit all use that annoys or disturbs his neighbor in the enjoyment of his property, but rather prohibits the use that constitutes injury to a legal right of the neighbor.

Whether the particular use constitutes a private nuisance generally turns on whether the use is reasonable under the circumstances. The test to be applied is the effect of the condition on ordinary persons with reasonable dispositions and ordinary health, and possessing average and normal sensibilities.[25] As a general rule, when a lawful business is properly operated and the location is proper, the operation of the business will not be enjoined as a nuisance, even though the operation of the business may interfere to some extent with the enjoyment of property in the vicinity.[26]

A tenant's tort liability to persons coming onto the premises or to those using the highway adjacent to the premises will be determined by the application of the law of negligence. If the tenant is in sole and exclusive occupation of the premises, he will be responsible to third persons for the condition of such premises. He will also owe a duty to persons using the highway upon which the leased real estate abuts to keep the premises free from conditions dangerous to such persons. For example, the courts have held that such a tenant would be liable to persons injured as the result of the tenant's having left unguarded an excavation adjacent to the highway, or of his or her having neglected to repair a loose sign, a defective fire escape, or a weakened structure that foreseeably might fall and injure a person using the highway.[27]

The tenant's liability to a person coming onto the leased real estate will depend on the relation of the tenant to the person and the surrounding circumstances. If the person is a trespasser, the tenant owes him no affirmative duty—that is, the trespasser takes the premises as he finds them. The tenant does, however, owe a duty not to injure such person willfully; and if he knows that a trespasser is on the premises, he owes a duty to use reasonable care not to cause him injury.

A licensee is a person who is on the premises with the express or implied consent of the tenant. For example, a person is a licensee if he is on the premises

---

[25] *Beckman et al.* v. *Marshall et ux.*, Fla., 85 So.2d 552.

[26] *Antonik et al.* v. *Chamberlain et al.*, 81 Ohio App. 465, 78 N.E.2d 752.

[27] *Smith et al.* v. *Claude Neon Lights*, 110 N.J.L. 326, 164 A. 423.

with the consent of the tenant for the purpose of hunting or fishing, or if he is a guest, or if he has come onto the premises to transact business with an employee of the tenant.[28] The tenant owes a duty to warn a licensee of known dangerous conditions on the premises and to refrain from conduct that it is foreseeable might injure him.

An invitee is a person who is on the premises, with the express or implied consent of the tenant, for the purpose of conducting business with the tenant. The tenant owes a duty to an invitee to keep the premises in a reasonably safe condition. The customers of a tenant who operates a retail store on the premises are invitees, and the tenant owes a duty to such persons to keep those parts of the premises in which they would ordinarily be present in a reasonably safe condition and to warn them of any condition that it is foreseeable might cause injury.

For many years courts drew a distinction between the so-called business invitee, who was on the premises for the purpose of doing business with the tenant, and the social invitee. Different standards of care were developed; however, the trend in the cases today is to ignore this distinction and to consider the circumstances of each case on an individual basis in the determination of the standard of care to be required.[29]

## Landlord's Liability

In recent years there has been a dramatic change in the law relating to the landlord's liability to the tenant for defects that are not obvious but that are potentially dangerous. There is now a clearly recognized duty on the landlord to provide "habitable" premises at least for residential purposes.[30] While this duty is generally referred to as an implied warranty of habitability, the theory upon which liability is imposed upon the landlord varies from one jurisdiction to another. In some states the basis of liability is, in fact, a warranty implied from the lease contract between the parties. That is, it is a contract theory. In

---

[28] *Gotch* v. *K. & B. Packing & Provision Co.,* 93 Colo. 276, 25 P.2d 719.

[29] *Autonieivicz* v. *Reszcynski,* 70 Wis.2d 836, 236 N.W.2d 1 (1976); and *Webb* v. *City and Borough of Sitka,* Supr. Ct. Alaska, March 21, 1977, 561 P.2d 731.

[30] *Lemle* v. *Breeden,* 51 Hawaii 426, 462 P.2d 470 (1969); *Javins* v. *First National Realty Corp.,* 428 F.2d 1071 (D.C. Cir., cert. denied, 400 U.S. 925 (1970); *Green* v. *Superior Court,* 111 Cal. Rptr. 704 (Super. Ct. 1974); *Steele* v. *Latimer,* 214 Kan. 329, 521 P.2d 304 (1974); *Old Towne Development Company* v. *Langford,* 349 N.E.2d 743 (Ind. App.). The doctrine has not generally been extended to commercial leases: *E. P. Hinkel & Company* v. *Manhattan Co.,* 506 F.2d 201 (D.C. Cir. 1974); *Service Oil* v. *White,* 542 P.2d 652 (Kan.).

others, the liability is based on a negligence theory: that the leased property was under the control of the landlord and that the landlord has a duty of care toward those to whom the property is leased, regardless of the provisions of the lease contract.

If the landlord has promised to keep the premises in repair, he will not be liable in tort for his failure to perform his contract, but he may be held liable in tort if he makes the repairs in a negligent manner and, as a result of his negligence, the tenant is injured. The courts have, under some circumstances, held that the landlord's failure to make repairs when he has notice or knowledge of the defective condition of the premises is negligence and have imposed tort liability on him.[31]

The landlord's tort liability to third persons will depend on the relation between the landlord and such third persons, and on the circumstances of the particular case. The landlord will be liable to persons using the highways on which the leased premises abut and to neighboring landholders, if such persons are injured as the result of the landlord's having negligently permitted dangerous conditions to develop on the leased real estate. This liability will continue for such period of time after the tenant takes possession as will give him a reasonable opportunity to correct the condition.

The courts have generally held the landlord liable to third persons who are injured as the result of the dangerous or defective condition of real estate leased to a tenant if the leased real estate is to be used for public purposes. Such real estate as entertainment halls, amusement parks, athletic arenas, wharves, and so forth, would fall in this class. However, the landlord's liability does not extend to all real estate leased for purposes that require that the premises be open to the public. Such real estate as retail stores, restaurants, offices, and so on, would be included in ths class. [32]

***Property Leased to Several Tenants.*** Although the courts are not in complete accord as to the extent of the landlord's liability when the real estate is leased to several tenants and the landlord retains control of those portions of the premises used in common by the tenants, they uniformly hold that if, as the result of the landlord's negligence, such portions of the premises are permitted to become unsafe, the landlord will be liable to persons who are injured as the result of his negligence.[33] The landlord is liable not only to such injured tenants but also

---

[31] *Florence Looger* v. *James R. Reynolds,* 324 N.E.2d. (Ill. 1975).

[32] *Warner* v. *Fry,* 360 Mo. 496, 228 S.W.2d 729.

[33] *Durkin* v. *Lewitz,* 3 Ill. App.2d 481, N.E.2d 151.

to third persons, such as guests of tenants or persons making business calls on tenants, if such third persons are injured while lawfully using the passageways, elevators, or other commonly used portions of the premises.

Some states have enacted statutes expressly imposing on landlords the responsibility for keeping multiple-unit dwellings in repair and holding the landlord liable to persons who are injured as the result of the landlord's failure to fulfill his duty.

Strickland leased a residence to Zuroski and agreed to take care of the premises. The guttering and downspout near the back door of the house became defective and allowed water to fall from the roof and collect on the concrete walk immediately outside the rear door of the house. Zuroski notified Strickland that the downspout was defective and needed repair, but no repairs were made. On February 11, 1961, water from melting snow and ice on the roof of the house had collected on this walk, and ice had formed. Zuroski was injured when she slipped and fell on this ice. Zuroski sued Strickland in tort to recover damages for her injuries. The trial court granted Zuroski a judgment; and on appeal, the judgment was affirmed, Justice Bower dissenting.

Justice Boslaugh said: "As was pointed out in the Van Avery case, the American Law Institute adopted the view that the landlord is liable. Restatement Torts, s. 357, p. 967, provides as follows:

" 'A lessor of land is subject to liability for bodily harm caused to his lessee and others upon the land with the consent of the lessee or his sublessee by a condition of disrepair existing before or arising after the lessee has taken possession, if *(a)* the lessor, as such, has agreed by a covenant in the lease or otherwise, to keep the land in repair, and *(b)* the disrepair creates an unreasonable risk to persons upon the land which the performance of the lessor's agreement would have prevented.' The rule as stated is qualified under the heading of 'Comment: . . . Nature of lessor's duty': in part as follows: 'Since the duty arises out of the existence of the contract to repair, the contract defines the extent of the duty. Unless the contract stipulates that the lessor shall inspect the premises to ascertain the need of repairs, a contract to keep the interior in safe condition subjects the lessor to liability if, but only if, reasonable care is not exercised after the lessee has given him notice of the need of repairs.'

"It is our opinion that the rule as stated in the Restatement is the better view and it is the rule which we adopt as the law of this state. The reasoning which supported the decision in the Fried case supports the decision which we have reached in this case." *Zuroski* v. *Strickland's Estate,* 176 Neb. 633, 126 N.W.2d 888 (1964).

Asher Coal Mining Company (hereinafter referred to as Asher) leased some land to be mined for coal, and the lessee adopted the method of strip mining. Asher was fully aware of the nature of the mining operation thus conducted. The mining operation resulted in the displacement of topsoil, rock, shale, and other types of strata. After the cessation of the strip-mining operation, Asher did not restore the land to prevent soil erosion or excessive drainage along natural watercourses. As a result of the condition created, following a heavy rainfall, vast quantities of loose rock, dirt, and coal were washed down the mountainside, obstructing natural watercourses, causing the flooding of Green's premises, and depositing debris thereon, thereby injuring his land.

Green sued Asher in tort to recover a judgment for the damage to his land. The trial court dismissed the complaint, and Green appealed. The judgment was reversed.

Commissioner Clay said: "The authorities heretofore discussed recognize that the owner of land may be held liable for the acts of his lessee under the following conditions: the particular use or exploitation of land must be such that harm to others is likely to ensue unless precautions are taken; the owner must consent to, authorize or be cognizant of this use; and the injury must be such as can reasonably be anticipated from such use.

"In a sense the leasing of land for exploitation is a method of use of it by the owner. He may not utilize it so as to cause injury to others. Therefore, if the expected operations under the lease result in such injury as may be reasonably anticipated, the owner has been a party to the wrong and cannot disclaim liability because he did not personally create the condition or commit the wrongful act. The significant considerations are the cognizable potentialities of danger and the reasonable predictability of injury.

"Applying the law to the facts stated in the complaint, we find a sustainable legal theory of liability. Asher was in the mining business. The leasing of this land was for the purpose of carrying out mining operations through a third party. Strip mining by the lessee was authorized. The topography of the land involved was such that debris from this operation would likely be cast or eroded into mountain streams, as a result of which damage to lower riparian owners could be reasonably anticipated." *Green* v. *Asher Coal Mining Company,* Ky., 377 S.W.2d 68 (1964).

## Landlord's Exculpatory Clause

The standard exculpatory clause found in most leases relieves the landlord from liability to the tenant for the landlord's negligent acts. Such clauses are usually written in very broad terms. (A typical clause is included in the form lease later in this chapter.) Along with the development of the implied warranty of habitability, discussed earlier, there has also developed a strong tendency on the part of our courts to severely limit the effectiveness of such clauses or even to ignore them altogether on the grounds that they violate public policy.[34] At the present time this development in the law is restricted to leases of residential property, and has not been extended to leases of commercial or industrial property; however, mobile homes have been covered.[35]

---

[34] *Papakalos* v. *Shaka,* 91 N.H. 265, 18 A.2d 377 (1941); *Weaver* v. *American Oil Co.* 257 Ind. 458, 276 N.E.2d 144 (1971).

[35] *College Mobile Home Park & Sales* v. *Hoffman,* 72 Wis.2d 514, 241 N.W.2d 175 (1976).

### Alterations

A tenant has no implied authority to make alterations or improvements to the leased premises.[36] If the lease is a long-term lease, it should, in order to protect the tenant, make provision for the improvement, alteration, or removal and replacement of existing improvements. If the lease does not contain an express provision providing that improvements made by the tenant shall remain his property and that he shall have the right to remove the improvements at the termination of the lease, any permanent improvement made by the tenant immediately becomes the property of the landlord.[37]

If the lease contains a provision for alterations or improvements or for the erection of a building on leased real estate, blueprints and specifications for the work should be approved by the parties and attached to the lease. If this is not practical, then the parties to the lease should set out in detail the nature of the work to be done. Unless the work to be done is set out with reasonable certainty, the agreement may be held to be void for uncertainty of terms.[38]

If the work is to be done by the tenant, provision should be made protecting the landlord's interest against the filing of the mechanics' liens against the property. Under the mechanic's lien laws of most states a provision in the lease against mechanics' liens will not deprive mechanics and laborers of their right to liens. In order to protect the landlord, the lease should require the tenant to obtain waivers of liens or to post security; or it should require the tenant to pay to the landlord, his agent, or appointee the cost of the improvement, out of which payment the landlord would then pay for the improvement.

If personal property is to be attached to the leased real estate, the lease should state whether the tenant is to be permitted to remove such property on the termination of the lease or whether it is to become the property of the landlord. Such a provision should include a clause protecting the landlord from chattel mortgages on or conditional sales of such property.

## Damage to or Destruction of Improvements

At common law, when leases of real estate were predominantly leases of agricultural land, the courts held that damage to or destruction of the improvements did not relieve the tenant from his obligation to pay the rent to the end of the term.[39] The major benefit accruing to the tenant in such leases was the use of

---

[36] *Kavanaugh et al.* v. *Donovan,* 185 Va. 85, 41 S.E.2d 489.

[37] *County of Prince William, Virginia* v. *Thomason Park, Inc.,* 197 Va. 861, 91 S.E.2d 441.

[38] *Brooks* v. *Smith,* Ky. 269 S.W.2d 259.

[39] *Lewis et al.* v. *Real Estate Corporation,* 6 Ill. App.2d 240, 127 N.E.2d 272.

the land. In commercial and residential leases of today, however, the principal value accruing to the tenant is the use of the improvement; consequently, the application of the common-law rule to such leases results in injustice to the tenant. Some states, by statute, have relieved the tenant from the payment of rent if the improvements on the leased premises are destroyed or are damaged to such an extent that they become unfit for occupancy.

The lease should make provision for the adjustment of the rent, for the repair or rebuilding of damaged or destroyed structures, for the time allowed for the restoration of the premises, and for the right of the tenant to terminate the lease if the improvements are destroyed or damaged extensively. If insurance has been provided, the lease should make provision for the application of insurance collected. The provisions in a lease covering the destruction of or damage to the leased premises are difficult to draft. If not carefully drafted, they may be the source of expensive litigation.[40]

### Condemnation

If the leased real estate is taken by condemnation, the lease is terminated, and the tenant is entitled to compensation for the value of the unexpired period of his term. The value of a lease is determined by computing the difference between the rental value of the premises at the time they were condemned and the rent reserved for the unexpired term.

The tenant's claim to the award is paramount to the claim of the landlord; under some circumstances, the tenant's claim could exhaust the award and thus leave nothing for the landlord. In order to avoid this result, the parties may include in the lease a provision terminating the lease in the event of condemnation or private sale. If the lease provides that title to the tenant's fixtures or title to improvements made by the tenant shall vest in the landlord on the termination of the lease, provision should be made whereby the tenant is compensated if the lease is terminated by condemnation.

Two situations may present some problems difficult to solve: (1) the condemnation may be only partial; and (2) the condemnation may be of only a part of the term—for example, two years of a ten-year term may be condemned.[41] In order to protect both the landlord and the tenant against these disadvantages, the lease should include a provision terminating the lease in the event of such a condemnation.

If only a part of the premises is condemned, the rent, as a general rule, is

---

[40] *Siegel* v. *Goldstein,* 148 N.Y.S.2d 266.

[41] *United States of America* v. *Petty Motor Co.,* 327 U.S. 372.

not abated; but the tenant has a claim against the award for the present value of the excess rent he is required to pay over and above the value of the use of the part of the premises not condemned.[42]

The rights of the parties in the event of a partial condemnation should be set out in the lease. Since it would be exceedingly difficult to work out, before condemnation, a satisfactory formula for the division of the award, the lease should provide for the right of the tenant, under defined circumstances, to terminate the lease. If the parties do not wish to provide for termination of the lease, they should provide either for the determination of the rights of the landlord and tenant by appraisal or for the arbitration of their rights.

## Right of Tenant to Assign, Sublet, or Mortgage

A lease vests in the tenant a property interest in the leased real estate, and the courts have held this interest to be his personal property. They have therefore applied basic principles of property law in determining the tenant's right to assign, sublet, or mortgage his interest in the leased property. Since free alienation is a basic property right, the tenant may, in the absence of statutory limitations or contractual restrictions in the lease, dispose of or encumber his interest as he wishes.[43]

When a tenant assigns his lease, such an assignment conveys his entire interest in the leased real estate. He does not, however, relieve himself from his obligation to pay rent or from his liability for damages if the lease is breached. The assignor of a lease is surety for the performance of the lease by the assignee.

As a general rule, the courts have held that a change in membership of a partnership or in the participation of a corporation in a corporate merger is not an assignment of a lease held by the partnership or the corporation. However, if a partnership or corporation enters into a lease that contains a clause restricting the assignment of the lease, express provision should be included that would define the rights of the parties in the event of a change in membership of the partnership or a merger of the corporate tenant.

When a tenant sublets all or any part of the leased premises, he then becomes a landlord in relation to the sublessee, but he remains a tenant to the owner and is primarily liable to him.

When a tenant mortgages his leasehold rights, he encumbers whatever property rights the lease vests in him; and on default and foreclosure, his rights may be

---

[42] *City of Pasadena* v. *Porter,* 201 Cal. 381, 257 P. 526.

[43] *Hyman* v. *230 So. Franklin Corporation,* 7 Ill. App.2d 15, 128 N.E.2d 629.

sold. In no event can he grant greater rights in the leased real estate than he has under the lease.

An absolute restriction on the tenant's right to assign, sublet, or mortgage would be against public policy and void, but reasonable restrictions are enforced. A restriction frequently included in a lease denies the tenant the right to assign the lease or sublet the premises or any part thereof without the written consent of the landlord. If the lease contains such a provision, it should also provide that the landlord cannot withhold his consent unless he has a valid reason for doing so. In some cases the courts have held that the landlord must act in good faith in withholding his consent.

If the landlord grants the tenant the right to assign the lease, this will not be restricted, unless the landlord, in granting such right, expressly provides that it shall be restricted.[44]

### Conveyance of Leased Real Estate and Assignment of Lease by Landlord

If the landlord conveys the leased real estate, his grantee will take the property subject to the rights of the tenant. The landlord will remain liable on all the covenants in the lease, unless the lease includes a provision relieving the landlord from all liability on the lease in the event of the conveyance of the leased real estate.

The landlord may assign his rights in the lease without conveying the leased real estate. Such an assignment is substantially equivalent to the assignment of a contract. The assignee acquires all the rights of the landlord under the lease, but the landlord is not released from his liability on the lease.

### Landlord's Right to Terminate Lease for Tenant's Default

The lease usually gives the landlord the right to take possession of the leased premises on the default of the tenant. In some states the landlord's right to re-enter on the default of the tenant is defined by statute. If the lease contains a clause granting the landlord the right to re-enter on the default of the tenant, it should also contain a clause, for the protection of the tenant, requiring the landlord to give notice of default to the tenant and giving the tenant a reasonable time to cure the default.

For the protection of the landlord the lease should provide that in the event of default on the part of the tenant and re-entry by the landlord, the lease will not be terminated, and the tenant shall remain liable for all damages resulting

[44] *Bauer et al.* v. *White et al.*, 225 Mo. App. 270, 29 S.W.2d 176.

from his default. The lease should also provide that if the landlord takes possession of the leased real estate, he does so as agent of the tenant and has the right to relet the leased real estate as agent of the tenant and hold the tenant liable for the rent reserved, crediting the rent received from the reletting of the premises to the amount owed by the tenant.

### Eviction of Tenant

An eviction is the depriving of the tenant of the beneficial use or enjoyment of the leased real estate, or a material part thereof, by some intentional and permanent act on the part of the landlord or at his instigation. The essentials of an eviction are that it be effected by some affirmative act or default of the landlord, or through his procurement, or by paramount title. An eviction is not necessarily limited to a situation in which the landlord actually dispossesses the tenant. If the landlord deprives the tenant of the beneficial use of the premises, such act amounts to an eviction.[45]

The landlord's failure to perform the covenants in the lease may amount to a constructive eviction. For example, if the landlord has covenanted to keep the premises in repair or to provide certain services, his failure to perform may amount to an eviction, provided his default is material. Failure to repair the premises, allowing the premises to become untenantable, failure to supply heat or elevator service, or permitting the premises to become overrun by insects and vermin have been held to amount to a constructive eviction.

The landlord is not responsible for the acts of third persons or of cotenants, unless such acts are done with the authority or consent of the landlord. Also, acts of public authorities that deprive the tenant of the use and enjoyment of part or all of the leased real estate are not an eviction.[46]

### Notice to Terminate Lease

If a lease is for a definite term, no notice to quit is required; but if the lease is from period to period, such notice is required. The time for giving notice is set by statute in most states. At common law, if the period was from year to year, the time for giving notice was six months. In many states the time for giving notice to terminate a year-to-year lease has been shortened by statutory enactment. If the period is for less than a year—for example, from month to month—the time for giving notice is the period of the lease. A month's notice

---

[45] *Lindenberg* v. *MacDonald et al.,* 34 Cal.2d 678, 214 P.2d 5.

[46] *McNally et al.* v. *Moser et al.,* 210 Md. 127, 122 A.2d 555.

is usually required to terminate a month-to-month lease, and a week's notice is required to terminate a week-to-week lease.

There are some differences in the rules followed in the several states in the computing of time. In some states the first day of the period is counted, and the last day is not; in other states the first day is not counted, but the last day is. In a few states both the first and the last days are excluded in counting time. Sundays and holidays are counted, unless the last day falls on a Sunday or a holiday, in which case it is not counted.

If the notice given for termination of a lease is in excess of the minimum time required by the statute or by the provision in the lease, the notice is effective;[47] but if it is given for a shorter period, it is ineffective. For example, if the statute requires that 30 days' notice must be given to terminate a lease, a notice of 31 or more days would be effective, but a notice of 29 days would be ineffective. Whether or not the 29 days' notice would serve to terminate the tenancy at the end of the succeeding period would depend on the wording of the notice.

The notice should be specific and unequivocal, and in writing. Oral notice may be sufficient in the absence of a statute requiring the notice to be in writing. The notice may be given by the landlord or his duly authorized agent, and should be given to the tenant or his duly authorized agent. In giving notice to an agent of the tenant, the landlord should make certain that the agent of the tenant has authority to act in the matter.

### Renewal Privileges

A clause in the lease may give the tenant the right to renew the lease. Such a clause may give the tenant the right to renew on the giving of notice at a designated time before the expiration of the term, or it may provide for automatic renewal, unless the tenant or the landlord gives notice at a designated time before expiration of the term that he does not elect to renew the lease.

### Provision for Adjustment of Rents

A provision in the lease for adjustment of the rent must be reasonably specific if it is to be valid.[48] A statement of the rent to be paid or a provision for the determination of the rent by an appraisal has been held to be sufficient. As a rule, a provision for renewal implies the renewal shall be on the same terms as the existing lease. However, the renewal clause should state whether the renewal

[47] *Hastings* v. *Nash,* 215 Ark. 38, 219 S.W.2d 225.
[48] *Slayter* v. *Pasley,* 199 Ore. 616, 264 P.2d 444.

lease shall include a renewal clause. It should also define the rights of the tenant to fixtures attached or the improvements made to the leased real estate.

## Holding Over

A situation involving a holding-over arises only if the lease is for a specified term. Under such a lease the tenant owes a duty to surrender possession of the leased real estate at the expiration of the term; and if he fails to do so, he will be holding possession wrongfully and will then become a tenant at sufferance. When a tenant holds over, the landlord may elect to bring an action of ejectment and have the tenant evicted, or he may waive the wrong and treat such holding over as a renewal of the lease.[49] The tenant, since he is the wrongdoer, has no election in the matter; he cannot force himself on the landlord as a tenant. If the landlord consents to the holding-over, or the landlord and tenant enter into an agreement whereby the tenant will be given a period beyond the termination date of the lease, then he will not be held to be a tenant holding over.

There is some diversity in cases as to the nature of the tenancy created by the tenant's holding over and the landlord's acceptance of him as a tenant. Some courts have held that a tenancy at will is created. However, it is generally held that if the original term is for a year or more, the lease created by the holding-over and acceptance by the landlord will be for a year. If the term is for less than a year, the holdover term will be for the same period as the original term.[50] A few courts have held the rent period to be the basis for the term of the lease after the holding-over. For example, these courts have held that if the rent reserved is payable quarterly, the term will be for a quarter; and if the rent is payable monthly, the term will be for one month.

As a general rule, failure by the tenant to surrender the premises at the expiration of the term is a holding-over, and the reasons for the tenant's failure to surrender the premises are immaterial. Some courts have held that if the tenant is prevented from surrendering the premises at the expiration of the term because of his sickness or by an act of God, his failure to surrender will be excused, and no new term will be created. If the tenant is prevented from surrendering the leased real estate because he is suffering from a contagious disease and is quarantined, there is no holding-over that will entitle the landlord to hold the tenant for another term.

There is some diversity in decisions of cases in regard to the effect of a notice given to the tenant before the expiration of the term that if the tenant holds

---

[49] *Sinclair Refining Company* v. *Shakespear et al.*, 115 Colo. 520, 175 P.2d 389.

[50] *Mahoney* v. *Lester et al.*, 118 Mont. 551, 168 P.2d 339.

over, the rental will be at a higher rate. Some courts have held that if the tenant holds over, he is liable for the increased rental.[51] Other courts have held that if the tenant objects to the increased rent, he will not be bound to pay the increase.

Several states have enacted statutes defining the rights of the landlord and the tenant in the event the tenant holds over.[52] Under the provisions of some such statutes the landlord may recover double or triple damages. In the absence of a statute the landlord may recover, as damages for holding over, only the reasonable rental value of the leased real estate for the period of time the tenant has held over, unless the landlord can prove that he has suffered special damages.

There may be included in the lease a provision defining the rights of the parties in the event the tenant holds over. Such provisions are enforced by the courts, unless they are of such a nature that the court would declare them void as against public policy.

Selk sold a 320-acre tract of land with a shack thereon to David Properties, Inc. (hereinafter referred to as David), and took a purchase-money mortgage on the real estate to secure an unpaid balance of $45,000. Selk was permitted to live in the shack rent-free until October 20, 1959, when the parties executed a written lease in which David leased "the house and premises heretofore occupied by him" to Selk for a term ending at midnight, December 31, 1959. Selk did not surrender possession; and on February 17, 1960, David wrote Selk, demanding possession of the premises and stating: "You are hereby instructed to vacate these premises immediately. Your continual occupation shall be at your own risk, and I shall charge rent for the use of these premises at the rate of $300 per month." Selk did not vacate the premises, and he paid no rent.

On February 16, 1961, David wrote Selk a second letter in which he demanded possession of the property and the payment of $3,600 rent for twelve months, and again stated that the rent would be $300 per month. David did not pay the $9,000 installment on the mortgage when due, and Selk filed suit to foreclose the mortgage. David filed a counterclaim for $7,200 past-due rent. The trial court dismissed the counterclaim, and David appealed. The dismissal of the counterclaim was reversed.

Associate Judge Roger J. Waybright said: "In answer to the contention that Selk did not occupy the entire 230 acres but only the shack, a tenant who without the consent of his landlord retains possession of part of the premises must be considered as holding over as to all. As to the counterclaim, in this case, the defendant, as the landlord, had at least several courses of action available when the plaintiff, as the tenant, continued to live on the leased property after expiration of the term of the lease. The defendant could

---

[51] *State ex rel. Needham* v. *Justice Court in and for Township and County of Silver Bow et al.,* 119 Mont. 89, 171 P.2d 351.

[52] *Corthouts* v. *Connecticut Fire Safety Service Corporation,* 2 Conn. Civ. 34, 193 A.2d 909.

probably have chosen to demand the double the monthly rent' provided for by the statute; it elected not to do so, and the plaintiff could not force the defendant to do so. The defendant undoubtedly could have treated the plaintiff as a trespasser, and sued or counterclaimed against the plaintiff for damages for depriving it of reasonable rental value and any special damages; it elected not to do so, and neither the plaintiff nor the chancellor could force it to do so. The defendant also could waive the wrong occasioned by the holding over and treat the plaintiff as a tenant, demanding an increased rent of the plaintiff if the plaintiff chose to remain on the property; this the defendant elected to do, and neither the plaintiff nor the chancellor could force it to claim damages instead of rent.

"When a landlord demands a different rent for continued possession of property it owns, and a tenant receives the demand and thereafter continues on in possession without protest, the tenant impliedly agrees to pay the rent demanded. Those were the facts shown by the evidence in the case, and that rule must be applied to the facts." *David Properties, Inc.* v. *Selk,* Fla., 151 So.2d 334 (1963).

## Option to Purchase

The lease may include a provision giving the tenant an option to purchase the property either during or at the expiration of the term. If the lease is a long-term lease and the included option is to run for a long time, there are many things that must be considered. Some definite formula for determining the price should be set up. The valuation of the real estate may be left to appraisers, provided a formula for determining the price is set up by the parties. If the price is to be agreed upon by the parties, the option is void for uncertainty of terms. If the price is specified in the lease, it may become a bargain price before the expiration of the option.

Provision for the mortgaging of the property during the term should be made. If the tenant is to erect buildings or make improvements to the property, the option—if the price is to be fixed by an appraisal—should state whether or not the value of the buildings erected or the improvements made by the tenant should be included or excluded in making the appraisal.

When the option is exercised, it immediately becomes a contract of sale. Consequently, the option should set out all the material provisions of a contract to sell—such as price, terms of payment, time and place of closing, type of deed to be given, nature of title to be conveyed, adjustments to be made, who is to furnish abstract, and so forth.[53] A contract of sale may be prepared and attached to the lease, and included in the option by reference to the contract.

The provision should also state whether or not the option is assignable. The courts have generally held that if the lease is assignable and is assigned, the op-

---

[53] *Rich* v. *Rosenthal,* 223 Ark. 971, 268 S.W.2d 884.

tion is assigned as part of the lease; and if the lease is not assignable, the option is not assignable.

The lease may provide for the termination of the option on the default of the tenant. If the landlord re-enters on the default of the tenant, the option generally terminates; but if the default on the part of the tenant is not material and the landlord does not re-enter, the option is not terminated, unless it is expressly provided that the tenant cannot exercise the option until he has fully and punctually performed all of the covenants in the lease.[54]

As a general rule, the tenant is required to give notice of his election to purchase under the option. If his notice of election to purchase changes or adds to the terms stated in the option, it is not an acceptance of the option but is, in legal effect, a rejection of the option and a counteroffer.

Instead of giving the tenant an option, the lease may give the tenant the first right to buy. Such a provision requires the landlord, in the event he decides to sell the property, to give the tenant the right to purchase the property at the price and on the terms of a good faith offer that the landlord is willing to accept.

Kahn leased a store building to Schoonover for the term beginning on November 1, 1956, and ending on October 31, 1959. The lease included the following provision: The lessee "shall have the option to purchase the premises leased herein for the sum of $15,000 at any time during the term of this lease by giving written notice of the same to lessor 30 days in advance of the exercise of this option." Kahn sold the premises to Dloogoff before the expiration of the term of the lease. Schoonover had made extensive improvements to the building during the term of the lease. Kahn contended that Schoonovers' only remedy was an action against Dloogoff for specific performance. The trial court granted Schoonover a judgment against Kahn for damages; and on appeal, the judgment was affirmed.

Commissioner Maughmer said: "Appellants assert that Schoonover never tried to exercise the option by giving the prescribed 30 days' notice and say he could have enforced the option against the purchasers, the Dloogoffs. Defendants by their sale of the property had made it impossible for them to perform under the option. They had breached the covenant conferring an option to purchase. As stated in 51 C.J.S. Landlord and Tenant 88, p. 648: 'In case of a breach of a covenant conferring on the lessee an option to purchase, the lessee is entitled to recover damages sustained by him.' See *Barling* v. *Horn et al.*, where, under a different situation, specific performance was decreed. It is possible that plaintiff might produce evidence under which he might secure specific performance from the Dloogoffs but we shall not pursue or speculate upon this possibility. Defendants by their act in conveying the property made it impossible for them to honor the option. Plaintiff is not required to seek recompense for defendants' breach of the

---

[54] *Cook* v. *Young*, Tex. Civ. App., 269 S.W.2d 457.

option covenant from the Dloogoffs. He may seek damages from the defendants directly." *Schoonover* v. *Kahn,* Mo. App., 377 S.W.2d 535 (1964).

## Share-Crop Leases

The relation created by an agreement to raise crops on shares will depend on the intention of the parties, as evidenced by the terms of the agreement, the conduct of the parties, and all the surrounding circumstances. The relationship may be that of employer and employee (cropper), or landlord and tenant, or the parties may be partners or joint adventurers. Although the relationship cannot be conclusively determined from any one thing, if the owner of the land retains possession, furnishes the seed, tools, and so forth, for planting and harvesting the crop, and the person who plants, cultivates, and harvests the crop is to receive a share of the crop for his work, the relationship, as a general rule, is that of employer and employee.[55]

If the exclusive possession of the land is given to the person who cultivates it, and particularly if such person furnishes the tools, part of the seed, and so forth, necessary for the raising and harvesting of the crop, the relation which arises is, as a general rule, that of landlord and tenant.[56] An agreement to raise a crop on shares does not usually constitute the parties partners or joint adventurers, unless the agreement clearly manifests an intention to create such a relationship.[57]

In some states the relation and rights of the parties to a sharecrop agreement are determined to some extent by statutes. In the absence of a statute the rights of the parties will be determined by the terms of the share-crop agreement. If the relation of the parties is that of employer and employee, the employer is the owner of the crop until it is divided. If the relation is that of landlord and tenant, the tenant is the owner of the crop until it is divided. In some states the owner of the land and the person raising the crop own the crop as tenants in common or joint tenants.

## Residential Leases

Residential leases, especially leases of apartments, are frequently prepared in advance by the landlord or his property manager, and the tenant accepts the lease as drawn if he wishes to rent the apartment. Also, in smaller communities, residential property is frequently rented on a month-to-month basis without the

[55] *Hampton* v. *Struve,* 160 Neb. 305, 70 N.W.2d 74.

[56] *California Employment Commission* v. *Kovacevich,* 27 Cal.2d 546, 165 P.2d 917.

[57] *Koch* v. *Murphy et al.,* 151 Kan. 988, 101 P.2d 878.

parties having any clear agreement as to their rights and duties. In such a situation, there is usually a fairly well-defined usage that will determine the rights of the parties in the event of a dispute.

If a tenant has a television set or contemplates the acquisition of one, he should be certain that his lease gives him the right to erect and maintain an outside television aerial.

## Sample Lease Form

Here follows a simplified form of lease for residential space. It will be apparent that it does not fall into any of the standard types of lease discussed in the text. This is generally the case in actual practice because of the unsuitability of the classic lease for many modern lease arrangements. Efficient property management demands that the same form be consistently used so that administrative procedures can be standardized. Without this standardization, the risk that an important notice date may be overlooked, with adverse consequence to one or both of the parties, is greatly increased.

**Sample Residential Lease**

This lease is made and entered into this _____ day of ________, 19_____, by and between ______________________________________________
(herein "tenant") and ______________________________________________
(herein "Landlord") and witnesses that:

1. Landlord hereby leases to Tenant, for the sole purpose and use as a residence for Tenant and Tenant's immediate family, the residential space known as Apartment No. _____, in the building located at ___________, City of ____________, State of ___________, (herein "the property") upon the terms and conditions set out in this lease.

2. The term of this lease commences on the _____ day of _________, 19_____, and terminates on the _____ day of _________, 19_____. The agreed upon rent is $__________ per annum and is payable in equal monthly installments of $__________ in advance on the first day of each and every month during the term of this lease. Rental payments are to be made to Landlord at ______________________________________________
____________________________or at such other place as Landlord may direct by written notice to Tenant.[A]

**Sample Residential Lease *(continued)***

3. Landlord hereby acknowledges receipt from Tenant of the sum of $__________ as and for a deposit to secure Tenant's performance of the terms of this lease. At the termination of this lease either by its terms or by the mutual agreement of the parties this deposit shall be returned to Tenant within ________ days less any amount necessary to cover the cost of repairs made necessary by Tenant's occupation and use of the property. Landlord shall not be liable for the payment of interest on this deposit nor be required to keep the deposit segregated in any way.[B]

4. Tenant agrees that during the term of this lease Tenant will neither assign nor sublet the property without the written approval of Landlord and that in the event of such approval Tenant will remain liable for the performance of all the terms and conditions of this lease.

5. Tenant promises that no waste will be committed to the property; that the property will be used for the purposes stated above only and for no other; that the property will not be used for any unlawful purpose and that no violations of existing zoning ordinances will be committed or permitted by Tenant; that no use will be made of the property which will increase the hazard of fire or to cause the rates for casualty insurance to be increased; that no alterations or additions to the property will be made without the written consent of Landlord; that any additions or improvements made to the property during the term of this lease whether made by Tenant or Landlord, except for the movable personal property of Tenant, shall become the property of Landlord.

6. Landlord reserves the right to enter the property at reasonable times and during normal business hours for the purposes of inspecting the property and Tenant promises that this right of access will not be denied or restricted. During the last ________ days of the term of this lease Landlord may enter the property and show it to others and may advertise the property for rent by affixing signs to the property or in any other manner customarily used in the community.[C]

7. Tenant promises to pay the rent as specified above and to surrender the property to Landlord at the end of the term of the lease in as good condition and repair as it is in at the commencement of this lease, ordinary wear and tear excepted.

8. In the event of default by the Tenant in the performance of any of the terms and conditions of this lease, including but not limited to the timely

**Sample Residential Lease** ***(continued)***

payment of the agreed upon rent, and such default shall continue for _______ days after the due date for rent or notice by Landlord to cure any other default, then Landlord shall have the right to retake possession of the property without further notice to Tenant. If Tenant has abandoned the property, Landlord may rent the property to another without such action constituting an acceptance of a surrender of Landlord's rights under this lease and Tenant shall continue to be liable for the agreed-upon rent less the net amount of rent which Landlord receives from any new tenant after the deduction of Landlord's expenses of repossessing and re-renting the property. Landlord shall have the right to take possession of any personal property of Tenant found on the property and may sell such property in any manner Landlord selects and apply the proceeds of sale to Tenant's obligations to Landlord.[D]

9. Tenant hereby agrees that Landlord shall not be liable to Tenant or any person invited onto the property by Tenant for any injury or damage to either person or property which may result from the condition of the property or due to any act of Landlord or Landlord's employees whether negligent or not; nor will Landlord be liable for any such injury or damage resulting from the act of any other tenant in the building or any other person in the building or which results from any casualty or accident in or around the building in which the property is located. Tenant further agrees to hold Landlord harmless for any liability to any other person which results from any act of Tenant or any person invited onto the property by Tenant.[E]

10. In the event of the complete or substantially complete destruction of the property by fire or other casualty, and Landlord shall decide to neither rebuild nor repair the property, then this lease shall terminate without further obligation on the part of either Tenant or Landlord. In the event, however, that Landlord decides to rebuild or repair, then the rent specified above shall not be payable for so long as the property remains untenantable. Landlord shall have no liability to Tenant for any loss or inconvenience suffered as the result of such fire or other casualty.[F]

11. Landlord promises that Tenant shall have peaceful and quiet enjoyment of the property for the term of this lease so long as Tenant shall pay the agreed rental and perform all other terms and conditions of this lease.

12. Tenant has inspected the property before signing this lease and by signing it agrees that the property is in good condition and that all appliances being furnished with the property are in good working order. Any repairs which

**Sample Residential Lease *(concluded)***

are required to such appliances during the term of this lease shall be paid for by Tenant and such repairs shall be made only by persons approved by Landlord.

13. This lease shall be binding upon Landlord and Tenant and their respective heirs, personal representatives, successors, and assigns and shall be governed by the laws of the State of ______________________________ .

In witness whereof the parties have executed this lease on the date written above.

______________________________
Landlord

______________________________
Tenant

## Comments on Sample Residential Lease

A. This clause is intended to create an estate for years and therefore provides for a specific termination date. This tenancy has the advantage of having a clearly predictable term so that both the landlord and tenant can plan accordingly. Conversely, it requires some affirmative action by both of them prior to the end of the term if it is desired to continue the relationship. This, of course, requires negotiation of a new lease with possibly quite different terms, and this may be undesirable to whichever party has been able to negotiate favorable terms into the initial lease.

B. The handling of the security deposit can be a matter that generates controversy between the landlord and tenant. In some cases, additional forms are utilized that provide more specifically the condition of the leased property, with a written statement signed by the tenant to the effect that a detailed inspection has been made and that there are no defects at the outset of the term of the lease. Disagreements as to the cost of repairs also can arise. Local law should be consulted to determine if there is some requirement that security deposits be held in escrow for the tenant's protection. The accounting treatment of the deposit by the landlord may be important from an income tax standpoint, and an escrow arrangement may also be desirable for the landlord as well as the tenant.

C. All of the undertakings and concessions made by the tenant are normally included in modern form leases in order to avoid the operation of the concept that a lease grants to the tenant an estate in land with broad rights of ownership and freedom to deal with the property. This is generally not the intent of the parties to a lease of residential space.

D. The inclusion of broad powers by the landlord in the event of default is also quite typical in form leases; however, their validity is doubtful. The use of force in the dispossession of a tenant in particular can have disastrous consequences for the landlord in the form of damages payable to the tenant in an appropriate legal action. The clause does have value to the landlord since many defaulting tenants will surrender the property peaceably. Failing this, however, the only safe course for the landlord to pursue is an eviction proceeding under local law.

E. The broad exculpatory clause, or "escape hatch," is standard boilerplate in almost all leases of residential space; however, the developing law of the implied warranty of habitability casts considerable doubt on its effectiveness, particularly against acts of the landlord. In several states the lease will be interpreted by the courts as though the clause was not in the lease, and the general rules of warranty and negligence law will be applied.

F. Some form of destruction-and-damage clause is usually included to protect both the tenant and the landlord. Under the estate theory of leases, the tenant might be obligated to pay rent even if the building was destroyed. Under the contract theory of leases, the landlord might be obligated to immediately rebuild even at prohibitive expense.

# Chapter 20
# Restrictions and Zoning

It is a familiar concept that real estate is not movable. As a result it must generate value in the place where it is located. It would appear that any limitation that is placed upon the use to which it may be put would automatically reduce the value of the real estate. The market is, after all, a localized one by the very nature of real estate. A limitation upon its use would appear necessarily to reduce its value. This is not always the case. If the limitation being considered were applicable only to one piece of property, then its value would surely diminish. If, however, the limitation is one that applies to all properties within a given area, the value of each of them may increase. How does this result? Limitations that are general result in uniformity within a given area. Where all property owners are limited in the use of their properties for residential purposes only, a neighborhood is created that cannot be intruded upon by commercial users, which might make it a less desirable place to live. This in turn would decrease property values, at least for residential purposes.

There are two ways in which the segregation of uses of real estate may be accomplished. The first of these is the use of privately imposed restrictions upon future use. These might be imposed upon a tract of land by a subdivision developer for the purpose of enhancing the value of each individual building lot. The value of each lot would be increased because the owner would be assured that no undesirable use could occur on nearby lots. This approach is the very heart of subdivision development and without it high property values could not be created or maintained. The second way of restricting the use of real estate is through the public control known as zoning. Under the concept of zoning, local government attempts to achieve—in an entire city or county—what the developer of a subdivision achieves by private controls. In most zoning schemes, a pattern is established in an attempt to divide the governmental unit into areas, each limited to one class of use: heavy industrial uses will be isolated in a specific area; residential uses will be isolated in another. The goal of zoning is to enhance and preserve property values in all districts as well as to improve the quality of community life.

Conflicts occur between the two systems, and specific properties become battlegrounds when the limitations that apply diminish value. Social changes take place that make old restrictions and zoning plans obsolete. Modifying the old plans to accommodate new uses is frequently both difficult and expensive. In some areas zoning has never been adopted, on the theory that the market is the best determiner of "highest and best use" for a particular property. In other areas there is direct conflict between the private restrictions and the public zoning. It is important to recognize that there are two separate systems at work at the same time and that the limitations imposed by each of them must both be considered in establishing the value and usefulness of a particular property. Each of these two approaches is explored in depth in this chapter.

## Private Restrictions

### Introduction

The owner of real estate has the right to sell and convey such real estate and the right to use it, but neither is an absolute right. The courts have distinguished between restrictions on the owner's right to sell and his right to use. In general, a provision in a deed that grants a fee simple estate to the grantee and that provides that the grantee will not sell, mortgage, or convey in any other manner the estate or an interest therein is, under the law in the United States, void; it is a direct restraint on the free alienation of the property, and as such is against public policy.[1] The Kentucky Supreme Court has held that a restraint on alienation of real estate is valid, provided the restraint is for a reasonable period.[2] Reasonable restraints on the use of real estate are generally upheld.

---

[1] *Braun et ux.* v. *Klug et ux.*, 335 Mich. 691, 57 N.W.2d 299.

[2] *Hutchinson* v. *Loomis*, Ky., 244 S.W.2d 751.

## Creation of Restrictions

A restriction may be created by a reservation or condition in a deed, by a covenant included in or annexed to a deed, by a declaration in a trust imposing a restriction on the sale or use of the real estate held in trust, or by a zoning ordinance. We shall confine our discussion primarily to restrictions on the use of land created by covenants either in a deed or annexed thereto, and to restrictions under zoning laws.

## Nature of Covenants and Conditions

A covenant is a promise in writing, and, as we shall use the term, is a clause in a deed whereby the grantee, his heirs, and assigns are bound by the promise stated in the clause. A condition is a clause in a deed that provides that if a stated event or events happen, or if the vendee, his heirs, and assigns make a stated use of the granted real estate or fail to live up to the requirements of the condition, title to the real estate will revest in the grantor or his heirs. A deed containing a condition conveys a determinable or base fee.

There is some conflict in the decisions of the court as to whether a provision in a deed will be interpreted as a covenant or a condition if such provision is framed in the terms of a condition but does not include a clause stating that on the breach of the condition the title to the real estate will revert to the grantor and his heirs. The courts do not favor conditions; and in case of doubt, many courts have interpreted such clauses as covenants.[3] The intention of the parties, however, governs; and if it is clear from all of the circumstances that the parties intended the provision as a condition, it will be so held. If the restraint provision expressly provides that on breach of the condition, title will revert to the grantor, his heirs, or assigns, such provision will be upheld.[4]

## Validity of Restraint on Use

The validity and enforceability of a restraint on the use of real estate will depend on its scope, nature, and purpose. If it is so broad in its terms that it prevents the free alienation of the property, or if it is repugnant to the estate granted, it will not be enforced.[5] However, if the restraint is reasonable and its purpose is not against public policy, the courts will generally uphold such restriction. For example, covenants that, in order to assure the maintenance of an area as a

---

[3] *Barrett* v. *County of Washoe,* 86 Nev. 730, 476 P.2d 8 (1970).

[4] *Superior Oil Company* v. *Johnson et al.,* 161 Kan. 710, 171 P.2d 658.

[5] *Grossman et ux.* v. *Hill et al.,* 384 Pa., 590, 122 A.2d 69.

high-class residential district, restrict the size of the lots, the location of the buildings on the lot, their design, character, and cost, and restrict businesses, especially types of businesses that are offensive, are generally upheld.

Prior to 1948, the courts usually upheld covenants restricting the occupancy of real estate to a defined class of persons or precluding the occupancy of real estate by a defined class of persons when the classification was based on race.[6] However, in 1948, the U.S. Supreme Court held that a racial restrictive covenant was unenforceable by court action.[7] The Supreme Court held that the covenants standing alone do not violate any provision of the 14th Amendment to the Constitution and are not void, but that the enforcement of such a covenant by the courts would be a denial of the equal protection of the laws and therefore contrary to the 14th Amendment.

Since that time there has developed a line of cases that further determine the limits to which private restrictions can be imposed without violating civil rights. For example, restrictions upon a subdivision that clearly make it impossible for any but the wealthy to purchase lots have come under heavy attack in the courts.

### Effect of Invalidity of Restrictive Covenant or Condition

A restrictive covenant or condition that is void, inoperative, or illegal does not affect the validity of the grant or divest the grantee of the estate granted. In general, the void, inoperative, or illegal covenant or condition is, in legal effect, canceled; and the grant stands free from the covenant or condition.[8]

The Buckworths acquired lot No. 8 in block B in Sullivan Heights and shortly thereafter began to build a house thereon. Carrol County Development Corporation owned lots in Sullivan Heights and brought suit to enjoin the Buckworths from continuing to build on the ground of breach of restriction. The recorded plat of Sullivan Heights contained sixteen provisions restricting the use of the lots in that plat. Restriction No. 5 required that "before any building, or any addition or alteration thereto, shall be commenced, plans and specifications therefor, showing height, and location of building with respect to topography and ground elevation, shall first be submitted to and approved in writing by the Blooms, 'their heirs and assigns.' " The Buckworths did not comply with this requirement; and on the trial, they contended that this restriction was void.

Chief Judge Brune said: "We are unable to agree with the Chancellor's view that restriction No. 5 is void. Restrictions in similar terms requiring submission and approval of plans

---

[6] *Swain et al.* v. *Maxwell et al.,* 335 Mo. 448, 196 S.W.2d 780.

[7] *Shelly et ux.* v. *Kramer et ux.,* 334 U.S. 1, 68 S. Ct. 836; *Hurd et ux.* v. *Hodge et al.,* 334 U.S. 24, 68 S. Ct. 847.

[8] *Andrews* v. *Hall et al.,* 158 Neb. 817, 58 N.W.2d 201.

have been upheld in *Peabody Heights Co.* v. *Willson.* The latter cases show that approval or disapproval must be reasonable and that the power must be exercised in good faith. (Note: The court held that the development company acquired no right to enforce the restriction.) *Carrol County Development Corporation* v. *Buckworth,* Md., 200 A.2d 145 (1964).

A true dilemma may occur for a developer when lots have been purchased in reliance upon a restriction that is later found to be unenforceable. One court has held that in such a situation there is a breach of warranty by the seller.[9]

**Interpretation of Restrictions**

In no area of the law is there found a greater divergence of opinion among the courts of the several states than in the interpretation and construction of covenants restricting the use of real estate. There are basic principles of law that are generally followed, but there is little uniformity in the results. The courts recognize that since restrictions on the use of real estate are in derogation of its free and unhampered use, they are to be strictly construed and all doubts resolved against them, yet the intention of the parties governs. The intent of the parties in respect to a restrictive covenant is to be gathered from the entire context of the instrument.

In the event the language used is not clear in its meaning, it will be construed most strongly against the grantor, and the restriction will not be extended beyond the clear meaning of the language used.[10] Also, if there is any uncertainty as to whether the provision is intended as a covenant or a condition, the courts will hold that it is a covenant.[11]

**Restrictions on Subdivisions**

When the plat of a new subdivision is prepared and recorded, the plat will, as a general rule, state the restrictions placed on the use of the land. Each deed will refer to the plat and the restrictions placed thereon. In this manner the restrictive covenants will be included in the deed by reference and will be binding on all grantees. If the property conveyed is not a part of a recorded plat, the restrictive covenants will be included in each deed.

A wide variety of restrictive covenants is included in recorded plats and deeds. Unless such convenants are drafted with the utmost skill and care, the desired

---

[9] *Hinson* v. *Jefferson,* 287 N.C. 422, 215 S.E.2d 102 (1975).

[10] *Link* v. *Texas Pharmacal Company,* Tex. Civ. App., 276 S.W.2d 903.

[11] *Gallagher* v. *Lederer et al.,* 60 Ohio Abs. 323, 102 N.E.2d 272.

result will not be attained. In interpreting restrictive covenants, the court will read the entire instrument and give the language used its accepted meaning. However, since restrictive covenants limit the grantee's right to use the real estate for all lawful purposes, the courts will not extend the scope of the restriction by implication.[12]

Cleveland Realty Company developed a tract of land known as the Cleveland Springs Estate. The Realty Company developed a part of the property for residential and recreational purposes, and located thereon a nine-hole golf course. On May 25, 1926, it caused to be recorded a plat of the development, showing lots, streets, and the golf course. Certain provisions and restrictions were included in the plat. The provisions pertinent to the case were as follows: "Developers 'do hereby dedicate the streets and alleys as indicated on the plat to the public use forever. . . .' "

"We further dedicate the golf links and playgrounds, and the land occupied by the same indicated on the map, for such use and pleasure of the owners of the lots. . . .

"We restrict the use of all lots shown on this plat . . . in the following manner, to wit:

"1. The lots shown on this plat are to be used as the location of residences, with only one residence to the lot. . . ."

Lots in the development were sold, and homes were erected thereon. A right of way 22 feet wide across the golf course between the No. 7 green and the No. 8 tee connecting with Fairway Drive was granted to Hobbs, who began construction of the road. Residents of the development brought suit, asking that the construction of the road be enjoined and that the grant of the easement of the right of way be declared void. The trial court entered a judgment adverse to the plaintiffs; and on appeal, the holding was reversed.

Justice Moore said: "Where lots are sold and conveyed by reference to a map or plat which represents a division of a tract of land into streets, lots, parks and playgrounds, a purchaser of a lot or lots acquires the right to have the streets, parks and playgrounds kept open for his reasonable use, and this right is not subject to revocation except by agreement. It is said that such streets, parks and playgrounds are *dedicated* to the use of lot owners in the development. In a strict sense it is not a dedication, for a dedication must be made to the public and not to a part of the public. It is a right in the nature of an easement appurtenant. Whether it be called an easement or a dedication, the right of the lot owners to the use of the streets, parks and playgrounds may not be extinguished, altered or diminished except by agreement or estoppel. This is true because the existence of the right was an inducement to and a part of the consideration for the purchase of the lots. Thus, a street, park or playground may not be reduced in size or put to any use which conflicts with the purpose for which it was dedicated." *Cleveland Realty Company* v. *Hobbs,* N.C., 135 S.E.2d 30 (1964).

---

[12] *Premium Point Park Association, Inc., et al.* v. *Polar Bar, Inc., et al.,* 306 N.Y. 507, 119 N.E.2d 360.

### Interpretation of Special Terms

In drafting restrictive covenants to be included in a deed or plat, one should avoid negative terms, since it is difficult, if not impossible, to set out specifically all of the uses that the grantor might wish to prohibit. Instead, a statement of the permitted uses should be made, and this statement should be followed by a provision prohibiting all other uses. In stating the permitted uses, broad general language and abstract terms should be avoided.

For example, such terms as "for residence purposes," "for dwelling purposes," or "not to be used for commercial purposes" are so broad in their connotation that they invite litigation. The courts have generally held that a restriction "for residential purposes only" is violated by the erection of a church, school, parking lot, filling station, or rest home, or by the operation of a retail store or a similar business in a portion of a house in which the family lives; but at the same time, the courts have held that such a restriction is not violated by the erection of apartment buildings.

The courts of the several states are not in accord in their interpretation of a covenant that restricts the use of the real estate to "dwelling purposes." One line of decisions holds that the erection of an apartment building does not violate the covenant—that apartment buildings are dwellings. The other line of decisions holds that an apartment building is not a dwelling and that the erection of an apartment on the real estate is a violation of the covenant.

A restrictive covenant should make clear that the restriction is meant to apply to both the land and the buildings erected on the land. However, the courts have generally interpreted a restrictive covenant as applying to the use of both the land and the buildings thereon, unless the wording of the restriction is such that it is clear that the intent is that it apply only to the use of the buildings.[13]

Hunsinger owned a 35-acre tract of land. He conveyed 25 acres of the tract to Chester Villa Development Company by deed which permitted subdivision of the land into building lots. The land was subdivided, and 89 separate one-family residences were constructed on the lots.

Hunsinger conveyed the remaining 10 acres by a deed which contained the following restriction: "The property shall be used for residential purposes only and the houses to be erected thereon shall contain at least 950 square feet of floor space and shall be at least seventy percent (70%) brick or stone construction."

---

[13] *Hoover* v. *Waggoman,* 52 N.M. 371, 199 P.2d 991.

The grantee of the 10-acre tract planned to construct a multifamily building thereon which contained more than 950 square feet of floor space and was more than 70 percent of brick or stone construction. The residents of the 25-acre tract brought suit asking that the construction of the multifamily building be enjoined. The injunction was denied; and on appeal, the order denying the injunction was affirmed.

Commissioner Davis said: "The weight of authority is said to hold that a restriction to 'residence' or 'residential purposes,' of itself, does not prohibit multiple dwellings. See 14 A.L.R.2d 1403, p. 9. In the same annotation, 14 A.L.R.2d 1376 et seq., the diversity of decisions in various jurisdictions is recorded. It is observed that the courts are in substantial agreement that a restriction to 'residence' purposes, standing alone, does not prohibit multiple dwellings, but this unanimity disappears when the modifying term 'a,' 'one' or 'a single' is prefixed to the word 'residence.'

"We must seek the intention of the grantor from the language used, considered in light of such factors as the general scheme of the subdivision. We may not substitute what the grantor may have intended to say for the plain import of what he said. We believe it is proper to assume that draftsmen of restrictive covenants—including the covenant now before us—acquaint themselves with decisions of the court relating to their effect. Certainly, such draftsmen should be familiar with legal precedents touching upon the subject matter with which they deal; they should be entitled to place some reliance in past constructions by the courts. The McMurtry decision is old and well known; it was in full effect in 1955 when the instant restriction was drawn. We observed in McMurtry and in many other decisions that draftsmen of such covenants may readily use language expressly prohibiting the use of property. The failure to use such specific language warrants the view that it was a deliberate and intended omission.

"As noted, there is no general scheme applicable to the ten acre tract. We hold that the residents of the 25-acre tract cannot be cosidered beneficiaries of the subsequently written restriction of the ten acre tract. The scheme of the 25-acre tract subdivision affords no dispositive basis for construction of the restriction under consideration. Thus, we are left with language substantially identical with that used in McMurtry. We perceive no reason for departing from the rationale of McMurtry, as it applies to the facts of the case at bar." *McMahan v. Hunsinger,* Ky., 375 S.W.2d 820 (1964).

Other courts have broadly defined such terms as "dwelling house" to permit use as a children's home and declined to equate "dwelling house" with "single family residence."[14]

A modern development in housing, the mobile home, has created a conflict in the courts in the interpretation of subdivision restrictions that prohibit "tents, trailers, shacks, or other temporary structures." Different courts considering the matter have arrived at conflicting conclusions. That a mobile home is a trailer

---

[14] *Berger* v. *State,* 71 N.J. 206, 364 A.2d 993 (1976).

or temporary structure and violative of restrictive covenants in a residential subdivision has been one conclusion.[15] Another conclusion has been reached, however, particularly where the character of the attachment or placement of the home is of a more permanent nature.[16] This conflict in the cases emphasizes the importance of clarity in the drafting of restrictive covenants.

### Who May Enforce a Condition or a Restriction

If the restriction is in the form of a condition in a deed and includes a reversion clause, the grantor or his heirs, on breach of the condition, have the right of re-entry; however, a stranger to the conveyance or a creditor of the party having the right of re-entry cannot avail himself of the right.[17] At common law, such right of re-entry could not be assigned or transferred; and in some states, either by statutory enactment or by court action, the common-law rule has been established. In some states, however, the right of re-entry for a condition broken is assignable or transferable after the condition is broken but not before; and in a few states, by statutory enactment, the right of re-entry has been made assignable generally.[18]

A restrictive covenant may be enforced by the parties to the agreement, and it may also be enforced by persons who are not parties to the agreement if the restriction is imposed for their benefit. If a restrictive covenant is personal to, and for the sole benefit of, the grantor, it is enforceable only by the grantor.[19]

Whether or not a restriction on the use of real estate is imposed for the benefit of others will depend on the intent of the parties to the agreement. In general, restrictions imposed pursuant to a general plan of development are imposed for the benefit of all owners of the real estate that is included in the general plan and may be enforced by any owner against any other owner who purchased with notice of the restriction.[20]

A general building scheme is one under which a tract of land is divided into building lots, the deeds to such lots to contain uniform restrictions. All the deeds, or substantially all of them, must contain restrictive covenants that are uniform or reciprocal.

A general building scheme may also be set up by recording a plat or map of

---

[15] *Mouille* v. *Henry,* 321 So.2d 77 (La. App. 1975); *McBride* v. *Bekrman,* 28 Ohio Misc. 47, 272 N.E.2d 181 (1971).

[16] *Hussey* v. *Ray,* 462 S.W.2d 45 (Tex. 1970).

[17] *Federal Land Bank of Louisville* v. *Luckenbill et al.,* 213 Ind. 616, 13 N.E.2d 531.

[18] *Fitch et al.* v. *State,* 139 Conn. 456, 95 A.2d 255.

[19] *Levy et al.* v. *Dundalk Co.,* 177 Md. 636, 11A.2d 476.

[20] *Condos et ux. v. Home Development Company, Inc., et al.,* 77 Ariz. 129, 267 P.2d 1069.

the subdivided tract that contains the restrictions. Under this latter plan the deeds should include a clause that incorporates the restrictions in the recorded plat by reference—for example, "as per plat thereof, recorded in Plat Book 27, page 62, in the office of the Recorder of Marion County, Indiana." The mere conveyance of individual lots to various grantees by deeds containing building restrictions is not of itself sufficient to create a general building scheme.

Whether or not a restrictive covenant is for the benefit of common grantees or only for the benefit of the grantor will be determined from the language of the restriction, interpreted in the light of the surrounding circumstances.[21]

A grantee is not bound by a restrictive covenant unless he has either actual or constructive notice of the restriction. A grantee has constructive notice of a restriction if such restriction is contained in a recorded instrument, such as a plat or map, and is referred to in his deed.[22] Also, a grantee is charged with notice of a building restriction if such restriction is contained in the recorded deed to his grantor or in a recorded deed in the grantee's chain of title.

The owner of real estate adjoining a restricted plat cannot enforce the restrictions, even though he would benefit by such enforcement, since it was not imposed on the tract for his benefit.[23]

Beeler Development Company (hereinafter referred to as Beeler) brought this action to enjoin the enforcement of a restrictive covenant providing: "No residential lot shall be re-subdivided." Dickens and other lot owners in their cross petition asked that Beeler and those holding under it be enjoined from present and future violations. Beeler contended that Dickens and the other lot owners had no right to enforce the restrictive covenant. The trial court enjoined Beeler and those holding under it from violating the restriction, and Beeler appealed. The appellate court affirmed the injunction.

Justice Thornton said: "If the language of the restriction is given its plain and ordinary meaning, it means that a lot may not be subdivided. This restriction, along with others, was used as an inducement to purchasers. When a purchaser buys and builds in reliance on the restrictions, he acquires some rights and his land is also burdened. These restrictions run with the land for the period of their existence. Every owner in the addition has a dominant estate over that of his neighbors, and the neighbors are dominant over his. Each owner has the right to enforce the covenant as written. This is true so long as the circumstances remain the same. It is also true without regard to the action of the other owners; they may waive their own rights but not those of others." *Beeler Development Company v. Dickens,* 254 Iowa 1029, N.W.2d 414 (1963).

---

[21] *Copelin v. Morris et al.,* Ohio Com. Pl., 101 N.E.2d 18.

[22] *McDonald et al.* v. *Welborn et al.,* 220 S.C. 10, 66 S.E.2d 327.

[23] *Townsend et al.* v. *Allen et al.,* 114 Cal. App. 2d 291, 250 P.2d 292.

## Restrictions by Mutual Agreement

Restrictions may be imposed on the use of real estate by the mutual agreement of the owners of neighboring or adjoining land. For example, if the owners of all the lots in a described block mutually agree that the buildings shall be a certain distance from the street and that only one single-family dwelling shall be erected on each lot, such an agreement is enforceable by and against the parties to the agreement and their assigns having notice of the restriction.

## Waiver or Abandonment of Restrictions

A restriction on real estate may be waived or abandoned by the party or parties for whose benefit the restriction was imposed. Whether or not a restriction has been waived or abandoned must be determined from the facts of each individual case.

Mere acquiescence in a violation of a restriction is not a waiver of the right to enforce the same restriction against another violation of the restriction, nor is it an abandonment of the restriction.[24] As a general rule, if a grantee has violated a restriction, he will not be permitted to hold another lot owner for a similar violation of the restriction. However, if his violation is minor in nature, he will be permitted to enforce the restriction against a more extensive violation by others.[25]

If the violations of the restrictions have been numerous and of such a nature that they destroy the general building scheme originally intended to be established, the restrictions will have been abandoned.

If an owner knows that a restriction is being violated, but makes no objection, and permits the violator to spend substantial sums on the property, he will not be permitted to complain of the violation. However, if the owner does not know of the violation and, in the ordinary course of events, would not learn of the violation, he has the right to bring an action against the violator when the learns of it.

Restrictions may be modified or terminated by the consent of all who are affected by it. A restriction placed on real estate by the grantor for the benefit of grantees of lots cannot be modified or terminated by the consent of the grantor alone.

Bartlett subdivided a tract of land into 107 lots of varied sizes, most of which were 165 feet in width and from 250 to more than 1,100 feet in length. The deeds to the

[24] *Hogue et al.* v. *Dresszen et al.*, 161 Neb. 268, 73 N.W.2d 159.

[25] *Moore et ux. v. Adams et al.*, 200 Ark. 810, 141 S.W.2d 46.

original lots contained numerous restrictions, none of which prohibited the subdividing of the lots, but they prohibited the construction of more than one house or dwelling place on a lot as originally platted. A number of lots, at the time of this suit, had been subdivided and two houses built on the lots as originally platted.

Fritz owned lot 74, which he subdivided, the south part thereof being 275 feet in length. Fritz contracted to sell this south 275 feet of the lot to Berry, who planned to build a dwelling thereon. Watts, who owned lot 24 in the subdivision, brought an action asking that Fritz be enjoined from subdividing his lot and from building two dwellings on lot 74. The trial court granted the injunction, and the injunction was dissolved on appeal.

Justice Hershey said: "Defendants make the further contention that while it is their position that there are no restrictions in the deed which prohibit subdividing the lots and placing more than one dwelling on a lot as originally platted, yet even if there were such a restriction, plaintiff has waived any right to enforce it by previous acquiescence in prior violations. The parties do not agree as to the facts concerning this matter. However, the evidence showed that there had been several subdividings of lots in the subdivision with the building of more than one dwelling on a lot as originally platted. Plaintiff, himself, acknowledged that one such subdividing and building took place across the street from him after he purchased his property. The developer's man in charge of his salesmen himself subdivided at least three lots and these subdivided lots had homes built on them. There is no showing that plaintiff took any action to prevent the subdividing of the lot across the street from him or the building of a dwelling on it other than to talk to the developer and possibly an attorney. No positive preventative action was taken.

"Minor violations of a restriction will not prohibit the subsequent enforcement of it. However, where there has been acquiescence of prior violations of the very substance of a general plan or particular restriction, the plaintiff will be held to have waived any right he may have had to enforce it. Thus, in Wallace v. Hoffman, the court said: 'The law is well settled that even where a general plan is shown the restrictions under the plan will not be enforced where violations have been acquiesced in.' It appears to us that even if the restrictions here were construed to prohibit the subdividing and the building thereon, yet plaintiff has so acquiesced in prior violations as to be unable to enforce any such restriction." *Watts* v. *Fritz,* 29 Ill.2d. 517, 194 N.E.2d 276 (1963).

### Termination of Restriction

A building restriction may be terminated by a lapse of time stated in the restrictive covenant, by merger, by material change in the neighborhood, or by the mutual agreement of the parties in interest. In some instances the restrictions are imposed on the real estate for a definite time, as, for instance, 30 years. Such a restriction is terminated by the expiration of the time limit. If a person acquires an entire plat after it has been filed along with its restrictive covenants, the restrictions on the plat are terminated, and such purchaser is not bound by them.

The courts have refused to enforce restrictions when they no longer serve their desired purpose because of material changes in the neighborhood, and instead tend to depreciate the value of the restricted property.[26] Such a situation arises when the business and industrial area of a city, through growth, gradually encroaches on the residential area until such area is no longer suitable for residential purposes.

If all of the owners of the property in a general building scheme or all common grantees mutually agree to terminate or alter existing restrictions on their property, such agreement will be enforced unless its provisions are against public policy.

The subdivision involved was platted, and the restrictions were placed on record on May 16, 1957. Baker purchased lots 1 through 4 on February 9, 1960. At that time the tract adjacent to these lots was reserved for commercial use. Across the street was a shopping center which was constructed in 1960, and in an adjoining block was the State Tuberculosis Hospital. After Baker bought his lots, the only structure erected in the subdivision which tended to change the character of the neighborhood was a Baptist church. Baker brought this action seeking the removal of the restrictions on his lot, basing his request on the ground of changes in the neighborhood. The relief requested was denied; and on appeal, the decision was affirmed.

Acting Chief Judge Allen said: "Equity is permitted to relieve against restrictions where there has been a radical change in the character of a new neighborhood, or an entire change in the circumstances. Generally, in such controversies, the facts of each case must be considered and the case must stand or fall on these facts.

"In the present case before the Court, it does not appear that in the approximately two years and seven months, since the purchase by Plaintiffs, the neighborhood has changed so radically in character, in a manner which could not be anticipated by Plaintiffs, so as to require action by the Court. The Court finds that the only change, which has taken place, of which the Plaintiffs might not have been aware at the time of their purchase, is the construction of a Baptist Church, in another block of the subdivision. The Court finds that this, in itself, is not enough to sustain the Plaintiffs' Complaint, and under all of the circumstances, the same should be dismissed." *Baker* v. *Field,* Fla., 163 So.2d 42 (1964).

## Zoning

### Nature and Purpose of Zoning

Zoning is the division of a city or other governmental unit, such as a township or county, by legislative regulation into districts, and the prescription and applica-

---

[26] *Wolff v. Fallon et al.,* 44 Cal.2d 695, 284 P.2d 802.

tion in each district of regulations having to do with structural and architectural designs of buildings and of regulations prescribing the use to which the buildings and land within the designated districts may be put. Zoning regulations are, in effect, restrictions placed on real estate by governmental action. The objective of zoning is the promotion of the health, safety, morals, and general welfare of the public. Through zoning, the character of the building erected, the use of the buildings, and the use of the land within the zoned district are regulated for the purpose of assuring the residents of the zoned area a suitable location in which to live, or in which to carry on their businesses or manufacturing.

Zoning differs from municipal planning in that the principal objective of municipal planning is to bring about a systematic development of the municipality or area, with particular reference to the location of streets, alleys, squares, parks, and playgrounds;[27] whereas the objective of zoning is to regulate the use to which the buildings and land within a district might be put. A municipal plan may be implemented through the enactment of zoning legislation.

## Source of Power to Zone

Each nation has sovereign power necessary to accomplish the legitimate ends and purposes of its government. In the United States, both the federal and the state governments have the right to restrict the individual use of real estate, provided such restriction is for the purpose of protecting the health, safety, morals, and public welfare of the people.[28] This power is generally referred to as the police power of the state. It is not an unlimited and unrestricted power; its exercise is subject to the limitations imposed on it by the federal and state constitutions. The power to enact zoning regulations is usually delegated to the municipality, and its power is subject to the limitations placed on it by the state legislature.[29] In some states the townships and counties have been given the power to enact zoning regulations.[30]

Anderson owned 3.4 acres of land which had been placed in a single residence A district (a residential district in which the minimum lot area for permitted use was 22,500 square feet). Much of Anderson's tract was swampy, as was more than 25 percent of the town. It would have cost Anderson approximately $102,500 to render the land suitable for residential development, so he brought suit asking that the zoning law be declared

---

[27] *Seligman et al.* v. *Belknap et al.,* 228 Ky. 133, 155 S.W.2d 735.

[28] *Kessler et al.* v. *Smith et al.,* 104 Ohio App. 213, 142 N.E.2d 231.

[29] *Attorney General* v. *Inhabitants of the Town of Dover et al.,* 327 Mass. 601, 100 N.E.2d 1.

[30] *Shick et al.* v. *Ghent Road Inn, Inc.,* Ohio App., 132 N.E.2d 479.

to be void. The court held that the zoning law was valid, and the decision was affirmed on appeal.

Justice Spiegel said: "The standard by which the validity of a zoning by-law is to be determined has been stated frequently in the opinions of this court. 'Every presumption is to be afforded in favor of the validity of an ordinance and if its reasonableness is fairly debatable the judgment of the local authorities who gave it its being will prevail. . . . It will be sustained unless there exists no substantial relation between it and the expressed purposes of the statute. Conversely, it will be held invalid if it be arbitrary or unreasonable, or substantially unrelated to the public health, safety, convenience, morals or welfare.'

"There is nothing in the record to indicate that if the petitioners' land were developed for home sites, a market for this land or for the homes that could be built thereon would be lacking, nor is there any reason for us to conclude that the land is substantially better suited for nonresidential uses. The zoning by-law before us does not appear to have been adopted only because of aesthetic considerations; on the contrary, the judge of the Land Court stated that the 1955 zoning ordinance, as applied to the petitioners' land, 'has a substantial and reasonable relation to the public welfare of the town.' Finally, the judge in substance asserted that, in view of the prevalence of marshland in Wilmington, to invalidate the zoning by-law as applied to the petitioners' tract would be to 'deny the town an opportunity to adopt any zoning.' It may well be that the zoning by-law does not permit the petitioners to realize maximum profits from the use of their land, but this is not sufficient cause to invalidate it." *Anderson* v. *Town of Wilmington,* Mass., 197 N.E.2d 682 (1964).

### Exercise and Limits of Power

A zoning ordinance must not violate the 14th Amendment of the Constitution nor the provisions of the constitution of the state in which the real estate is located, or it will not be valid. Zoning legislation is void where the means used to regulate the use of property are destructive, confiscatory, or so unreasonable that they are arbitrary.[31] The tests generally applied in determining the validity of zoning legislation are:

1. Is the zoning made by districts?
2. Is the zoning for the general welfare of the people?
3. Does the zoning promote the public health, safety, or morals?
4. Are the provisions of the zoning ordinance clear and specific?
5. Is the zoning free from discrimination?
6. Has the power to enact zoning ordinances been exercised in a reasonable manner?

---

[31] *Dooley* v. *Town Plan and Zoning Commission of the Town of Fairfield,* Conn., 197 A.2d 770.

As a general rule, the zoning, in order to be valid, must be made by districts and not by individual pieces of property. Although the establishment of the boundary lines of a district must be more or less arbitrary since the property on one side of the line will not differ greatly from the property on the other side of the line, there must nevertheless be some rational basis for the establishment of the boundary line of the district.[32]

A municipality, in establishing zoning districts, must set up classifications as the basis for their establishment. The municipality has broad discretionary powers in establishing zoning classifications; but the classifications must be reasonable, uniform, and nondiscriminatory.[33]

The answers to questions 2 through 6 will depend on the circumstances of each case. The courts have developed general standards that serve as a guide, but they are not conclusive. Building heights, setback lines, side yards, type of building materials, and similar regulations, when applied to a residential zone, have been upheld on the ground that they protect the public health and safety through the assurance of fresh air and the reduction of fire hazards. Similarly, the courts have generally upheld the regulation of lot sizes, minimum floor areas of residences, and the minimum cubic contents of buildings on lots, on the ground that the control of population density in an area reduces the amount of traffic, reduces the fire hazard, prevents overcrowding with an accompanying lowering of moral standards, and in general provides a healthier, safer area and a better moral environment in which to live and rear children.

Those opposing such ordinances argue that since there is no limit placed on the number of occupants of a house, such ordinances cannot be upheld on the basis of health. They admit that the ordinances may be justified on the ground of aesthetic considerations but contend that aesthetic considerations alone are not sufficient to support the ordinances. The final outcome of the controversy is in doubt. However, the trend is toward the upholding of such ordinances.[34]

In the earlier decisions the courts held that a zoning regulation could not be supported on the basis of aesthetic considerations alone. They are now, however, in accord in holding that zoning regulations may extend beyond strict considerations of health, safety, and morals, and that aesthetics should not be ignored,[35] and even that aesthetic considerations alone will support the validity of a zoning ordinance.[36]

---

[32] *Mundelein States, Inc., et al.* v. *Village of Mundelein,* 409 Ill. 291, 99 N.E.2d 144.

[33] *Katobimar Realty Company et al.* v. *Webster,* 20 N.J. 114, 118 A.2d 824.

[34] *Hitchman et al.* v. *Oakland Township et al.,* 329 Mich. 331, 45 N.W.2d 306.

[35] *John Donnelly & Sons, Inc.* v. *Outdoor Advertising Board,* 339 N.E.2d 709 (Mass. 1975).

[36] *Westfield Motor Sales Co.* v. *Westfield,* 129 N.J. Super 528 (1974).

The validity of a zoning ordinance prohibiting outdoor advertising signs other than those related to a business conducted on the premises was involved in an action brought by United Advertising Corporation, which wished to erect in the business and industrial area of the city outdoor billboards not related to the business conducted on the premises. The court held that the regulation was valid.

The Court said: "Much is said about zoning for aesthetics. If what is meant thereby is zoning for aesthetics as an end in itself, the issue may be said to be unexplored in our State, but if the question is whether aesthetics may play a part in a zoning judgment, the subject is hardly new. There are areas in which aesthetics and economics coalesce, areas in which a discordant sight is as hard an economic fact as an annoying odor or sound. We refer not to some sensitive or exquisite preference but to concepts of congruity held so widely that they are inseparable from the enjoyment and hence the value of property. Even the basic separation of industrial and commercial from residential, although obviously related to so much of the quoted statute as speaks of health and hazard, rests also on the aesthetic impact of uses upon the value of properties. Surely no one would say today that an industrial structure must be permitted in a residential district upon a showing that the operation to be conducted therein involves no significant congestion in the streets, or danger of fire or panic, or impediment of light and air, or over-crowding of land, or undue concentration of population. So also the recognition of different residential districts, with varying lot sizes, setbacks, and the like, rests upon the proposition that aesthetics should not be ignored when one seeks to promote 'the general welfare' as the statute says, 'with a view of conserving the value of property and encouraging the most appropriate use of land throughout such municipality.' Our cases deem aesthetics to be relevant when they bear in a substantial way upon land utilization." *United Advertising Corporation* v. *Metuchen,* 42 N.J. 1, 198 A.2d 447 (1964).

## Basis for Zoning

When a municipality or area is zoned, the basis for zoning is the nature of the use of the land and buildings permitted within the area. The municipality or area will first be zoned for such general uses as residential, commercial, and industrial. These areas will then be further zoned for more special purposes that fall within the scope of the general use. For example, an area zoned as residential may be further zoned for single-family, duplex, four-family, or multiunit residences. An area zoned for commercial use may be further zoned on the basis of the type of businesses carried on within the area—as, for example, retail outlets, garages and filling stations, cleaning and laundering establishments, or wholesale outlets. Likewise, an area zoned as industrial may be further zoned for specialty manufacturing, light manufacturing, or heavy manufacturing.

Also, the courts have upheld reasonable zoning regulations that restrict the use of land, apart from the use of the buildings or other structures thereon. An ordinance restricting a zone as residential may exclude such uses of the land as the excavation of clay beds, the removal of loam, the drilling of wells, or the use of the land as a private or public dump.[37]

## Regulations Must Be Reasonable

Since to be valid a zoning regulation must be reasonable, uniform, and nondiscriminatory, no dogmatic statement in regard to the basis for zoning will be accurate. However, the courts have generally upheld zoning ordinances based on certain general classifications. For example, they have usually supported ordinances restricting the use of real estate as to the architectural and structural design of the buildings, the setback line, the height of buildings, and the area of lot covered by the buildings.[38] Such restrictions can be justified on the basis of safety, health, and general welfare. For example, reduction of fire hazards and control of traffic contribute to safety; assurance of fresh air and sunlight contributes to the health; and maintenance of a desirable residential area contributes to the general welfare.

## Modification or Amendment and Repeal of Zoning Ordinance

A zoning ordinance may be modified or amended, provided the action taken is within the powers conferred on the legislative body by the state. A modification or amendment of a zoning ordinance, in order to be valid, must be justified on the ground that because of changing conditions, justice requires the modification or amendment enacted.[39]

Amendments to zoning ordinances should be made with caution and only when changing conditions require a modification of the regulation. A zoning ordinance can be changed only when the change is not arbitrary and not unreasonable.

An amendment of a zoning ordinance that involves only one piece of property or a small area may be declared invalid, since such zoning would be considered spot zoning. Such an amendment should be made only when changing conditions or new or additional facts have intervened, and when a refusal to make the change would result in grave injustice to the owners of the property. Any change

[37] *Garron* v. *Teaneck Tryon Company et al.,* 11 N.J. 294, 94 A.2d 332.

[38] *Davis et al.* v. *City of Omaha et al.,* 153 Neb. 460, 45 N.W.2d 172.

[39] *Moerder* v. *City of Moscow et al.,* 74 Idaho 410, 263 P.2d 993.

must be justified on the ground that it is beneficial to the health, safety, morals, or general welfare of the public.[40]

## Nonconforming Use

When an area is zoned for a particular use, there may be property within the area which, at the time of the enactment of the zoning ordinance, is being used for purposes other than those permitted under the ordinance. Such property is known as *nonconforming property*. For example, if, at the time an area is zoned for single-family dwellings, there are in the area an apartment building and a retail store, these would be classed as nonconforming property.

As a general rule, the zoning ordinance will provide that a then existing nonconforming use may be continued;[41] to do otherwise could be, in many instances, unjust and inequitable, and it might be illegal on the ground of taking property without due compensation. To what extent a change in the nonconforming use of a building will be permitted will depend on the provisions of the zoning ordinance and the nature and scope of the change in the use of the property. As a general rule, a change to another nonconforming use of the same general character but more restrictive in its nature is allowed, but a change to a less restrictive use is prohibited.[42]

An increase in the amount or intensity of the use of nonconforming property is permitted, provided there is no material change in the character of the use made of the property. However, unless it is permitted by the zoning ordinance, an extension of the nonconforming use to areas of the property not so used at the time the ordinance was enacted is not allowed.[43]

A building devoted to a nonconforming use at the time of the adoption of a zoning ordinance may be repaired from time to time. It may not, however, be enlarged by alteration or addition; nor will the owner be permitted to make alterations or additions which will extend the nonconforming use or prolong the life of the building, unless provisions in the ordinance give him such right.[44]

Whether or not a building devoted to a nonconforming use may be repaired or reconstructed if it has been damaged, destroyed, or demolished will depend on the provisions of the zoning ordinance. Under the provisions of some zoning

---

[40] *Partain et al.* v. *City of Brooklyn et al.,* 101 Ohio App. 279, 133 N.E.2d 616.

[41] *Application of O'Neal,* 243 N.C. 714, 92 S.E.2d 189.

[42] *Steudel et al.* v. *Troberg et al.,* 76 Ohio App. 136, 63 N.E.2d 241.

[43] *De Felice et al. v. Zoning Board of Appeals of Town of East Haven et al.,* 130 Conn. 156, 32 A.2d 635.

[44] *Selligman et al.* v. *Von Allmen Bros., Inc.,* 297 Ky. 121, 179 S.W.2d 207.

ordinances the repair or reconstruction of a nonconforming building is prohibited if the damage to the building exceeds a stated part of the building or a stated percentage of the financial value of the building.

If a nonconforming use of a building that existed at the time of the adoption of the zoning ordinance is discontinued or abandoned, the right to reestablish the nonconforming use is lost. Whether or not a nonconforming use has been discontinued or abandoned is a matter of fact to be determined in each case.

A temporary or seasonal cessation of the nonconforming use is not a discontinuance or abandonment of it. Also, permitting a building to stand vacant because of inability to lease the building, because of financial inability to continue the business, or for other similar reasons is not, as a general rule, a discontinuance of the nonconforming use.[45]

The nonconforming uses of property may be (1) nonconforming buildings, (2) nonconforming use of buildings, (3) nonconforming use of land, and (4) nonconforming lot sizes. In several states, various plans to eliminate nonconforming uses have been adopted. The nature of the nonconforming use to be eliminated has played an important part in the working-out of the plans. One plan adopted to eliminate nonconforming buildings and nonconforming use of both buildings and land is the compulsory amortization of the nonconforming property. This is accomplished by compelling the discontinuance of the nonconforming use within a stated time. However, the time allowed for the discontinuance of such use must be reasonable.[46] The constitutionality of a zoning ordinance prohibiting the continuance of a nonconforming use of property within a restricted area, provided the prohibition is reasonable and not arbitrary, has been upheld.[47] In a few instances, nonconforming property has been condemned under the power of eminent domain.

If the area is undeveloped and the lots do not conform in size, no serious problem is presented, since permits to build on the nonconforming lots could be denied, thereby forcing the owner into making the lots conform.

McKinney brought suit to enjoin Riley from operating an automobile junk yard and to compel enforcement of a zoning ordinance. McKinney's land abutted the Riley property, and the junk yard was 1,000 feet from his dwelling house. The zoning ordinance provided: "No junk yard may continue as a nonconforming use for more than one year after the effective date of this ordinance without special permit from the Board of Adjustment

[45] *Appeal of Langol,* 175 Pa. Super. 320, 104 A.2d 343.

[46] *City of Los Angeles* v. *Gage et al.,* 129 Cal. App. 558, 274 P.2d 34.

[47] *Hadacheck* v. *City of Los Angeles,* 239 U.S. 394.

The Board of Adjustment shall prescribe the conditions under which special permit shall be granted." The zoning ordinance became effective in March, 1956. Riley had started his junk yard in a small way in 1955, operating it as a part-time occupation; but by 1960, he was devoting full time to the junk business. He was burning cars on an average of three times a week. The injunction was granted, and Riley was ordered to discontinue the operation of the junk yard within forty-five days. On appeal, the holding of the trial court was affirmed.

Justice Wheeler said: "Zoning by its very nature is restrictive and regulatory as to the use of land and buildings and provisions which permit expansion and extension of existing uses are generally strictly construed. The finding that the business had been greatly extended and that its conduct was harmful and improper to a segment of the public was warranted. 'Pre-existing nonconforming uses may be "allowed to continue but not to multiply when they are harmful or improper." '

"We next consider whether enforcement of the ordinance by requiring termination of use of the land for a junk yard was a proper exercise of the police power. The validity of provisions requiring the termination of nonconforming uses within a specified period of time has been upheld as a proper exercise of the police power, provided at least that on balance, the public benefit outweighs the private injury, and the time allowed is reasonable.

"While the authorities upholding such amortization ordinances are by no means unanimous, we think that prima facie they are not unconstitutional. The defendant here had ample warning in 1957, when his application was denied, that his conduct of the business was considered a violation of the ordinance. Yet he continued to conduct a greatly expanded nonconforming use until the operations were held to be a public and private nuisance.

"In view of the finding that the defendant's use was a public and private nuisance, the order allowing a year in which to terminate the use was a reasonable and valid application of the ordinance and within the police power." *McKinney* v. *Riley,* N.H., 197 A.2d 218 (1963).

## Recent Developments in Zoning

The trend in recent years has been to permit greater flexibility in zoning ordinances. So called "Euclidian zoning"—named after the U.S. Supreme Court's decision in the classic case of *Euclid* v. *Ambler Realty Co.,*[48] which provided for static patterns of controls—has been modified by the development of such concepts as the "floating zone" and the "planned unit development." Under the concept of the floating zone, there is no territorial restriction on the map as to the placement of, say, an apartment building in an area zoned for single-

---

[48] 272 U.S. 365 (1926).

family residential use only. What is required is that the proposed high-density use meet the requirement of the enabling legislation that permits its inclusion in the single-family residential area. When the statutory requirements are met (showing that there will be no harmful effect upon the neighborhood), the particular location is rezoned to permit the insertion of the high-density use. Considerable resistance to this approach has been met because it appears contradictory to well-established zoning concepts. The most troublesome aspect of the floating zone is that the location of the new "zone" cannot be predicted. The accompanying argument against the floating zone is that it endorses "spot zoning," which benefits one property owner only; however, if such a zoning scheme is part of a comprehensive plan designed to benefit the entire area it would appear to be consistent with the general concept of zoning.

The planned unit development (PUD) has met with less resistance, partly because it generally involves a relatively large area within an existing general zoning area, as opposed to utilizing only one specific parcel. In the planned unit development, there are clusters of townhouses and other compatible single and multiple family units within the development, which is not restricted to only single-family residences of the traditional type. Greater effective utilization of the land is achieved without sacrificing open space and other amenities normally associated with the single-family residential neighborhood. Another reason for the more widespread acceptance of the PUD is that no commercial or industrial usage is contemplated, as is often the case in the floating zone. It is this difference between the two concepts which led the Pennsylvania courts to reject the floating zone on the one hand and to accept the planned unit development on the other.[49]

In still another important area the law relating to zoning is being subjected to attack and resulting in change: civil rights. Zoning ordinances that are inherently discriminatory, such as an ordinance limiting the size of residential lots to not less than five acres, have been struck down by the courts. Other ordinances—and even the refusal of zoning boards to modify them to permit higher density housing—have also been attacked as discriminatory and as violating the 14th Amendment. One major area of difficulty in these cases has been the determination of just what makes a local zoning ordinance (or the refusal to change it) discriminatory. There are two possible avenues to follow: the *effect* of the ordinance, resulting in discrimination; and the *intent* of the ordinance to achieve that discrimination. While such cases will undoubtedly be considered on an individual basis

---

[49] *Eres v. Zoning Board of Adjustment,* 401 Pa. 211, 164 A.2d 7 (1960); and *Chevey v. Village 2 at New Hope, Inc.,* 429 Pa. 626, 241 A.2d 81 (1968).

by the courts, the U.S. Supreme Court has ruled that the *intent* of the ordinance to achieve discrimination, as opposed to the factual effect of discrimination, is the deciding test.[50] Because of the importance of the question, the burden of showing whether or not intent to discriminate motivated the zoning action complained of may be crucial in a given case. That is, where the *effect* of discrimination exists, at least in an aggravated case, the burden of proving *intent not to discriminate* may be cast upon the defendant. As a practical matter, proving the lack of intent to do what has actually occurred may be an even greater burden than the duty to prove positive intent.[51]

The perpetuation of economic and social segregation in an expanding community by the use of exclusionary zoning ordinances has also been struck down by the courts where the ordinance effectively prohibited low- and moderate-income families from the community.[52]

## Historical Landmark Preservation

The extent to which the power to zone may be exercised without constituting it a "taking" under eminent domain is being severely tested today in communities' efforts to preserve historic buildings. Recent legislation throughout the country may require the owner to retain it, as opposed to taking it from him. This is the practical effect of legislation that prohibits demolition or further development of the property. Litigation in this area has proceeded on the theory that such regulation is an unwarranted exercise of the zoning power. There is a strong argument to be made that an enforced *retention* of property that does not yield an economic return consistent with its market value is a form of taking. An important recent case in this area involved the Grand Central terminal building in New York City. The owners desired to develop the air rights over the terminal by constructing a high-rise office building but were prohibited from doing so by local landmark preservation laws. In dealing with an attack upon the constitutionality of the law, the New York Court of Appeals declined to conclude that there had been a taking of private property for a public use because the development rights could be transferred to other nearby properties also owned by Penn Central.[53] This case was subsequently appealed to the United States Supreme Court and,

---

[50] *Village of Arlington Heights* v. *Metropolitan Housing Development Corporation,* 97 S. Ct. 555 (1977).

[51] Tamila C. Jensen, "A Supreme Court Zoning Decision," *Business Horizons,* August, 1977.

[52] *Southern Burlington County N.A.A.C.P.* v. *Township of Mount Laurel,* 67 N.J. 151, 336 A.2d. 713 (1975).

[53] *Penn Central Transportation Company* v. *City of New York,* 366 N.E.2d 1271 (1977).

in June 1978, the decision of the New York Court was affirmed. It is worthy of note, however, that this was not a unanimous decision: three of the justices dissented on the ground that there had clearly been a taking of private property. (The transfer of development rights to air space in connection with landmark preservation is treated exhaustively by John J. Costonis in *Space Adrift: Landmark Preservation and the Marketplace* [Champaign: University of Illinois Press, 1974.]

The future direction of the courts in this area is, to a great extent, dependent upon the claim of the property owner and the issue presented by that claim. For example, there are many situations in which the property owner will not *want* the action taken considered to be a taking under eminent domain. To do so might result in a forced sale of valuable property rights at a price far below the potential value of the property without being encumbered by "landmark" status. In such a case the property owner has no desire at all to "sell" the property but, rather, wishes only to use it free of restriction based on its historical significance.

### Administration of Zoning Regulations

As a general rule, zoning regulations are administered by a named official, by a board, or by a commission. The powers of an official, board, or commission are only such as are conferred on them, expressly or by implication, by statute or ordinance. Such administrative officers, boards, or commissions may not abuse the discretion vested in them.

The procedure to be followed will be set out in the zoning ordinance, and it must be substantially complied with. Usually, provision is made to take an appeal from the original decision to a board of appeals. The decision of this board is subject to judicial review.

In substantially all jurisdictions a board of appeals or a similar body is given the power, within prescribed limits, to grant to property owners variances or exceptions allowing nonconforming uses of property. Variances and exceptions are granted only when the denial of the variance and exception would result in unnecessary hardship or practical difficulties.[54]

### Enforcement of Zoning Restrictions

The penalties that may be imposed for violation of the zoning ordinances depend primarily on the enabling statutes granting powers to the municipality or zoning

---

[54] *Ernest* v. *Board of Appeals on Zoning of City of New Rochelle,* 79 N.Y.S.2d 798; affirmed 298 N.Y. 831, 84 N.E.2d 144.

area. Under the provisions of some ordinances, violation of the ordinance is made a criminal act; and the penalty for violation of the ordinance may be a fine or imprisonment, or both.

In addition to its power to impose a criminal penalty for violation of a zoning ordinance, the municipality may also seek the civil remedy of injunction against further violation of the ordinance. And even though municipal officials have permitted the zoning ordinance to be violated for a number of years, such fact will not prevent the city from bringing an action and obtaining an injunction against further violation of the zoning ordinance.[55] If the violation of the zoning ordinance is of such a nature that it creates a nuisance, the city, under some circumstances, may order a building demolished.

### Effect of Zoning Ordinances on Restrictive Covenants

As a general rule, a zoning ordinance will not be held to abrogate the restrictive covenants in a deed or plat;[56] if the ordinance imposes more stringent restrictions on the use of the land or buildings in the district than those imposed by the restrictive covenants in the deeds or plats, the zoning ordinance will control. A state, under its police power, may enact legislation or confer on a municipality or other governmental unit the power to adopt ordinances that will abrogate existing covenants in deeds or plats, or which will render void certain classes of restrictions. Also, in some cases the courts have held that a zoning ordinance that classifies the land and buildings in a less restrictive category than that imposed by the restrictive covenants in the deed or plats is evidence of a change in the neighborhood, which change justifies the court in refusing to enforce the restrictive covenants.

Nevertheless, that the more restrictive covenant will be enforced even in the face of a less restrictive zoning ordinance remains the basic rule.[57]

## Building Permits

### Nature of Building Permit

As a general rule, if a municipality or other governmental unit has adopted zoning ordinances, it will also adopt ordinances requiring any person who wishes to build, alter, or repair a building within the jurisdiction of the municipality or

[55] *Leigh et al.* v. *City of Wichita et al.,* 148 Kan. 607, 83 P.2d 644.

[56] *Finn et al.* v. *Emmaus Evangelical Luthern Church et al.,* 329 Ill. App. 343, 68 N.E.2d 541.

[57] *Blackstead v. Peva,* 88 N.M. 563, 544 P.2d 278 (1975).

unit first to obtain a building permit. Such ordinances are constitutional and valid, provided the regulations are reasonable.

### Application for Permit

In order to obtain a building permit, it is necessary, as a general rule, to file an application that complies with the provisions of the ordinance. Under the provisions of some ordinances, plans and specifications for the proposed building must accompany the application.[58]

### Checking Application

After the application is filed, it will be checked by a designated official. If it is in proper form and the proposed building, alteration, or repair is in conformity with the zoning and building regulations, a permit will be issued. If a permit is denied, the applicant will be notified and will be given an opportunity for a hearing on the permit; and if the permit, on the hearing, is still denied, he may then resort to the courts.

### Rights Conferred by Permit

A building permit is not a contract with the municipality or governmental unit; it is merely evidence of the applicant's compliance with regulations. The municipality may limit the time of starting construction under the permit; but if the permit fixes no time for starting construction, it must be started within a reasonable period.[59] The rights conferred by a building permit are not assignable, but they do pass with the land as an incident of the conveyance thereof.

---

[58] *Opinion of the Justices of the Senate,* 333 Mass. 783, 128 N.E.2d 563.

[59] *Village of Sand Point* v. *Sand Point County Day School,* 148 N.Y.S.2d 312.

# Index

**N–O**



**P**

*This book has been set VideoComp, in 10 and 9 point Optima, leaded 3 points. Section numbers and titles are 24 point Helvetica Bold. Chapter numbers and titles are 20 point Helvetica Bold. The size of the type page is 29 by 44 picas.*